EXPLORATIONS IN AEROSPACE LAW

EXPLORATIONS

IN AEROSPACE LAW

selected essays

by John Cobb Cooper

1946-1966

edited by Ivan A. Vlasic

Montreal
McGill University Press
1968

JOHN COBB COOPER
1887–1967

A Tribute

*W*HILE it is often difficult to write of a colleague who has just left us, so strong was John Cobb Cooper's spirit and influence in the Institute of Air and Space Law and in the Faculty of Law as a whole that although his recent passing was deeply mourned, his memory and his works combine to have his "presence" remain, vibrantly, at McGill.

This volume of selected works, edited by Professor Ivan A. Vlasic, was the natural result of Professor Cooper's long association with the Institute of Air and Space Law as Founding Director and teacher, and later as benefactor through the gift of his Collected Papers and his library to the extensive Air and Space Law collection of the Faculty.

John Cooper and I talked often about publishing his papers. In due course an outline of the project commended itself to him, and the burden of editorship was then carried by Professor Vlasic, who now brings this valuable project to successful completion.

Professor Vlasic's introduction swiftly traces the story of John Cooper's development as the dean of air and space lawyers in North America, perhaps in the Anglo-American world. What is remarkable about his growth as a scholar and as a significant influence in governmental decisions is the fact that he came to this career with little scholarly equipment in the traditional sense, for he had practised law, after being admitted to the Bar of Florida, under the older clerkship rules without having had the benefit of a modern formal education in a law school. He was a highly imaginative man able to apply a variety of skills and a taste for technical matters to the new field of air law and later to space law. The papers which follow tell the story of the growth of his ideas, but they say nothing about the personal charm, the delightful companionship and the always comforting counsel that he offered to colleagues at McGill and elsewhere, I am sure, while pursuing a busy professional life. Nor do the papers tell of his

vii

influence over such important organizations as the International Air Transport Association, whose principal Legal Adviser he was for almost all of the first two decades of its existence.

But above all, as these papers disclose, John Cooper will be remembered for having provided an analytical framework within which to see the evolving rules of air law and space law, and for relating that framework to the older, traditional legal notions of private and public law. It is a long road from the Roman maxim *cujus est solum, ejus est usque ad coelum* to speculations about boundaries in space and liability for damage by space vehicles. But that highway was traversed by John Cooper in a series of often brilliant and original exercises in legal imagination to the point where he was able to provide, before he passed on, his own unified field theory of air and space law, viewing it as a continuum, and forever after making it impossible for others to separate them into artificial, doctrinal, or institutional categories. The Faculty of Law and the Institute of Air and Space Law have much pride in being able to publish his principal contributions to the law of this "aerospace" age.

Maxwell Cohen
Dean, Faculty of Law
McGill University

September 1967

Foreword

*T*HE PURPOSE of this volume is to satisfy a long-felt need—to make available under one cover a representative selection of aerospace essays by Professor John Cobb Cooper, the first Director of the Institute of Air and Space Law in Montreal, and widely regarded as one of the outstanding contributors to the study of the legal problems of aeronautics and astronautics. His death at the age of 80, on July 22, 1967, as this publication was nearing completion, ended a remarkable career and left a gap in the international legal community which will be difficult to fill.

John Cobb Cooper's interest in aeronautics dated back to his student days at Princeton University. However, his full time association with the aviation industry materialized only after twenty years of a distinguished law practice in his native Florida, climaxed by his election as the President of the Florida Bar Association. In 1934 he joined civil aviation, an industry at that time still very much in its infancy and struggling to assert its role as a safe and useful mode of rapid transportation. Since then, over a span of several decades devoted to the problems of flight, he has acted as adviser both to the government of the United States and to international organizations, and has occupied positions of eminence in the business and academic communities.

Professor Cooper's career as a representative of the United States at international conferences began in 1932, when he was appointed a member of the International Technical Committee of Aerial Legal Experts (CITEJA). The following year he was already Chairman of the U.S. delegation to a diplomatic conference on air law, held in Rome, where he signed the Convention on Liability for Damages to Third Parties on the Surface (Rome Convention, 1933) on behalf of the United States. In 1944 Professor Cooper attended the historic Chicago Conference as adviser to the U.S. delegation and Chairman of one of the conference's drafting committees. There he participated very actively in the preparation of the Convention on International Civil Aviation, the basic charter for the world's air navigation. When the International Air Traffic Association resumed its activities, now under the name of International Air Transport Association, shortly after the Second World War, Professor Cooper was appointed as its first Legal Adviser. In this position, which he held uninterruptedly from 1946 to 1964, he participated in the many meetings of the Legal Committee of the International Civil Aviation Organization and in several diplomatic conferences at which important air law conventions were drafted.

John Cobb Cooper's career in the business world has been equally distinguished. For more than a decade, from 1934 to 1945, he was Vice-President of the largest international air carrier—Pan American World Airways. In this role he negotiated many important route agreements, including those which made possible the inauguration of the first trans-Atlantic and the first trans-Pacific scheduled air services. During his tenure of office civil aviation made tremendous strides, and by the time he retired from Pan American the airplane was firmly established as an indispensable mode of transportation and as an integral part of the transportation system of every mature nation.

As Professor Cooper was fond of saying, he fulfilled an old ambition when, upon leaving the world of business in 1945, at the age of 58, he joined the academic community. Elected member of the prestigious Institute for Advanced Study at Princeton in 1946, he was at last afforded an opportunity to devote all his time and energy to research and study of the problems of aviation. To this new field of endeavour he brought all those virtues which had characterized his career as legal counsel and businessman—vision, industry, honesty, and an analytical mind. After only a little more than a year at Princeton, Cooper published his first major work—*The Right to Fly*—a masterful analysis of the many interdependent factors—historical, political, economic, military and geographic—which determine the aviation policies of nation-states and, ultimately, the international law of the air. While not essentially a legal treatise, *The Right to Fly* nevertheless soon came to be recognized as a valuable manual for the understanding of the legal regime of airspace and the law of international air navigation. Shortly after the original publication in English, the book appeared in French and Spanish translations. This work not only won international acclaim but also marked the auspicious beginning of a new career that was to last two decades. In this time John Cobb Cooper enriched the literature of air and space law in terms both of breadth and of quality to an extent that may easily remain unequalled.

McGill University was probably the principal beneficiary of the scholarly phase in Cooper's life. It was primarily through his efforts that in 1951 the Institute of International Air Law (now Institute of Air and Space Law) was established. As its first Director, Cooper was instrumental in shaping the Institute into an academic center of world-wide reputation which today provides unique facilities for advanced study, research, and graduate work in air and space law. Even after his retirement as Director in 1955, he continued to lecture in the Institute on an occasional basis until a short time before his death.

The contribution of Professor Cooper to the study of aerospace law, as the appended bibliography illustrates, covers almost every aspect of aeronautical and space activities that can be subject to legal regulation. There is scarcely a major area of interest to those concerned with the law of air and space which he has not, at one time or another, explored. It is a matter of profound regret that, as a consequence of budgetary limitations, no more than one third of his aerospace articles could be accommodated in this volume. For that reason it was thought desirable to concentrate upon the areas in which his contribution was most significant. These areas, in the editor's opinion, are: the history of air law, the fundamental principles of air law (notably airspace sovereignty and nationality of aircraft), and space law. While Professor Cooper generously cooperated with the editor in the preparation of this publication, he was not, however, responsible for the choice of particular essays or for their arrangement in the book. In making his selections, the editor was guided by the over-all quality and originality of each essay, its present availability to the general public, the degree to which the essay adds to the completeness of coverage attempted in the book, and the extent to which it reflects the development of the author's ideas. To place articles thus selected in perspective, the editor requested the author to prepare for each item a brief introductory note. Professor Cooper kindly obliged by submitting an "author's note" which appears in italics before every essay in the collection. To remain as faithful to the original version as possible, the citations in all essays have remained essentially the same as when first published. Only the discovered typographical errors have been eliminated and, when necessary, the citations have been completed. This policy of faithful reproduction of the original accounts for the lack of uniformity in citations.

The twenty-eight essays included in this book are organized in six parts: I—Aerospace Law and Power: Some Basic Thoughts; II—Rights in Airspace: From Antiquity to the Advent of Aircraft; III—The Evolution of the Modern Principle of State Sovereignty in Airspace; IV—The Legal Status of Flight Vehicles; V—The Emerging Principles of Law for Outer Space; and VI—Selected Problems in International Regulation of Aerospace Activities.

The essays presented in Part One deal primarily with problems relating to the scope and terminology of air and space law and with the economic and political bases of air power. The phrase "aerospace law," which appears in the title of this part and in the title of the book as well, was coined by Professor Cooper some time ago to indicate his belief that a single branch of law should govern all "man-made flight." The selections here assembled are designed to introduce the more specific problems analyzed in the subsequent parts. The article entitled "Air Law—A Field for International Thinking" originally appeared in the [*U.N.*] *Transport and Communication Review*, and the article "Notes on Air Power in Time of Peace" in *Air Affairs*, both since defunct and therefore difficult to obtain. Apart from that reason, their reprinting in this collection seemed justified because it provides, in the former, an insight into Cooper's early attitude towards the legal problems of the coming space age and, in the latter, the indispensable background for the study of aerospace law.

Part Two consists of a single item, Cooper's classic dissertation on the origin of the oft-invoked maxim *cujus est solum* and its relevance to the contemporary law of the air. The painstaking research involving perusal of a vast number of relevant sources led him to conclude, *inter alia*, that in Roman Law *coelum* (airspace) was subject to private and exclusive rights, whereas *aër* (air), being an element used for breathing, was incapable of appropriation; that the maxim itself was not of a Roman law origin; and, perhaps most importantly, that the tridimensional character of the territory pertaining to the organized bodies politic had been recognized as early as Roman times. Whether or not one agrees with Cooper's central conclusion that "States [have since Roman times] claimed, held, and in fact exercised sovereignty in the airspace above their national territories" is less important in the evaluation of this work than the fact that it is the most comprehensive study of the subject available and is a magisterial example of disciplined scholarship.

In Part Three the evolution of the modern concept of state sovereignty in airspace is traced from the first diplomatic conference dedicated exclusively to the problems of air navigation (Paris 1910), through the Peace Conference of 1919, to the Chicago Conference of 1944. Professor Cooper was too young to partake in the scholarly debates or diplomatic negotiations about the regime of airspace which began in earnest early in this century. His meticulous research, however, brilliantly illuminates the salient features of the era during which the modern principle of state sovereignty in airspace was being formulated. As a result of his systematic and comprehensive analysis, the formative period of the law of the air is no longer enshrouded in obscurity and speculation. It is worth noting in this connection that for certain historic events, for example the Paris Conference of 1910 and the United States' participation in the preparation of the Paris Convention of 1919, Cooper's writings are in effect the sole available source of information, apart from official documentation, which is increasingly difficult to obtain. Part Three also includes articles dealing with the status of airspace over the Arctic (Chapter 10), above the high seas (Chapter 11), and with the conflict between federal and state rights in navigable airspace over the United States (Chapter 9).

Part Four contains what may well be not only the finest piece of legal scholarship to originate from Cooper's pen but also the best historical and comparative study of the concept of nationality as applied to aircraft undertaken to date. Originally prepared in 1949 for the Air Law Committee of the International Law Association, the study was, because of its length, reproduced only in a briefest summary in the Association's Report of the Copenhagen Conference, 1950. In the present volume the full English text of this excellent study on the legal status of aircraft appears for the first time in print. The study begins with an analysis of the legal status of the older forms of transport vehicles (vessels, railway trains, and automobiles), and then follows the evolution of the concept of nationality of flight instrumentalities from the nineteenth century balloons to the modern aircraft The sheer wealth of pertinent historical information found in this essay and the scope of analysis undertaken by Cooper recommend "A Study of the Legal Status of Aircraft" as indispensable reading to anyone interested in air law. The original essay, of course, did not deal with spacecraft, though it acknowledged the existence of "such flight instrumentalities as guided missiles." On the urging of the editor, Professor Cooper kindly agreed to prepare for this volume a special supplemental note in which he addressed himself to the more recent problem of space vehicles and their legal status. His conclusion that "Nationality has become a necessary, not merely an advisable spacecraft characteristic" is bound in this formative period of space law to affect the thinking both of academics and of decision-makers.

The essays presented in Part Five of this volume explore in detail various problems created by the penetration of man-made instrumentalities into outer space. The opening essay contains Cooper's celebrated address on "High Altitude Flight and National Sovereignty," delivered in January 1951 at the Escuela Libre de Derecho in Mexico City. In this much reprinted and debated essay he drew attention to recent developments in rocketry, and first among his contemporaries, posed the question of the legal regime of space above and beyond the "airspace." He had raised the same question three years earlier in a little-known lecture delivered before the restricted audience of the U.S. Naval War College in Newport, Rhode Island. Thus, almost a decade before the launching of the first artificial satellite, John Cobb Cooper saw the need for international law to "determine what parts of flight-space can become or are parts of the territory of sovereign States and what parts of such space must be free for the use of all peoples." (The relevant parts of this lecture are reproduced in this volume as an addendum to Chapter 13.)

The focal point of interest to Professor Cooper in these pioneering explorations was the problem of drawing a line of demarcation between the sovereign "airspace" and the space beyond, as the latter was becoming increasingly accessible to man-made vehicles. Concern for the establishment of such a jurisdictional boundary permeates most of his contributions included in Part Five and there is hardly an aspect of this much discussed question which has not been examined by Cooper. In his continuing search for a solution of what he believed to be the principal problem of space law, namely, the uncertainty in regard to the upper limit of states' sovereignty, he suggested a variety of bases upon which the problem of the accommodation between the inclusive and exclusive competences of states in navigable space might be solved. Having established himself not only as the originator of the concept of boundaries but also as its most eloquent and influential advocate, not surprisingly he was often criticized, particularly for the occasional revisions of his proposals. It is to Cooper's credit that once the technological basis of his proposals changed, he did not hesitate to adapt his concepts to new conditions. A man less sensitive to the requirements of responsible scholarship might have been tempted to ignore the change rather than to admit the possibility of error on his part. He remained adamant, nonetheless, in persisting to urge that a boundary must be found. The vindication of Cooper's concern for the establishment of such a boundary may be closer than he himself dared anticipate. At its sixth session, held in Geneva from June 19 to July 14, 1967, the Legal Subcommittee of the U.N. Committee on the Peaceful Uses of Outer Space commenced a study of questions "relative to the definition of outer space" and requested its sister Scientific and Technical Subcommittee to examine urgently this problem and prepare a list of scientific criteria that could be helpful in the legal regulation of the matter. (U.N. Doc. A/AC.105/37, p. 8, 14 July 1967.)

In addition to this and other basic issues relating to the emerging law of outer space, this part of the book also incorporates an essay on U.N. participation in the development of principles and rules for the new domain and an essay on the legal questions raised by the imminence of man's landing on the moon.

Part Six of this collection consists essentially of two distinct groups of studies—one devoted to problems of air law and the other to the problems of space law. Both groups are placed under the same general heading because the basic design of the book appears to preclude their inclusion in the preceding parts. Articles in the air law group were written not too long after the end of World War II and reflect the influence of a period which has been both the most destructive in terms of human values and the most productive in terms of technological progress and innovation. The first article in this group—"Air Transport and World Organization"—reviews the prospects and problems of postwar civil aviation from the perspectives of the United Nations Charter and the Chicago Convention; the second article—"The Bermuda Plan: World Pattern for Air Transport"—analyzes the landmark air services agreement concluded between the United States and Great Britain in February 1946, and assays its significance in the context of national and international civil aviation policies; and the third article—"Internationalization of Air Transport"—explores in some detail various schemes, advanced prior to and during the Chicago Conference, which were designed to regulate (or even to eliminate) competition in international air commerce on a global basis. These studies retain their usefulness despite the passage of time, not merely for the information they provide about an important phase in the development of the present regime of international air transport, but also, and perhaps more importantly, for ideas relevant to many of the problems which still face us.

These essays are followed by three more recent articles dealing with certain aspects of space law which are of great current interest. Two of the articles—"Self-Defense in Outer Space and the United Nations" (Chapter 25) and "The Manned Orbiting Laboratory: A Major Legal and Political Decision" (Chapter 26)—focus upon the legality of military uses of outer space in the framework of general international law and relevant resolutions passed by the U.N. General Assembly. The third article analyzes the general principles of liability for damage caused by space activities as set forth in the U.N. Declaration of Legal Principles and relates these principles to the regime established in 1952 under the Rome Convention on Damage Caused by Foreign Aircraft to Third Parties on the Surface. The article expresses the author's concern with the existing arrangements involving the uncoordinated regulation of flight vehicles by two different agencies (United Nations and ICAO) in the absence of a satisfactory definition of either aircraft or spacecraft. The solution suggested by Cooper can be found in the essay, concluding both Part Six and the book, entitled "The Chicago Convention—After Twenty Years." In his judgment "a single set of future rules must govern all international flight, at whatever altitude." This may well be the most important message emanating from Cooper's explorations in aerospace law, and is quite possibly a solution that will ultimately be adopted by international law.

I. A. V.

September 1967.

Acknowledgments

*A*s IN ALL comparable publishing endeavors, the completion of this undertaking would not have been possible without the support and assistance of many persons.

I owe a special debt of gratitude to Maxwell Cohen, Dean of the McGill Faculty of Law, who was not only the principal sponsor of this project while Director of the Institute of Air and Space Law, but remained its firm intellectual and moral supporter throughout. Mr. Peter Sand, a former colleague in the Institute and now Visiting Professor at the Faculty of Law of the Haile Sellassie University in Addis Ababa, was an enthusiastic collaborator in the early phases of the enterprise. Mr. Howard Culver, a student in the Institute during the 1966–67 session, has ably cooperated in the compilation of the bibliography of Cooper's aerospace contributions and has had a lion's share in the preparation of indexes.

The officers of McGill University Press, Miss Margery Simpson and Mrs. Margot M. Smith in particular, were invariably helpful and patient. Miss Marianne Scott, Law Librarian, selflessly provided the necessary assistance even during the difficult period of transfer of the library holdings into the new law building.

This volume could not have appeared without the kind permission of a number of publishers to reproduce materials originally published under their auspices. Each is identified on the title page of the appropriate chapters.

Last, but not least, it is a pleasant duty to express profound appreciation for the support provided by the Canada Council, which generously offered financial assistance when it became obvious that the Institute's funds alone were insufficient to cover the cost of the publication.

I. A. V.

Contents

Part Four

THE LEGAL STATUS OF FLIGHT VEHICLES

Part Five

THE EMERGING PRINCIPLES OF LAW FOR OUTER SPACE

Part Six

SELECTED PROBLEMS IN INTERNATIONAL REGULATION OF AEROSPACE ACTIVITIES

Appendices

PART ONE
Aerospace
Law and Power:
Some Basic Thoughts

1
Air Law—
A Field for
International Thinking

Reprinted from 4 [U.N.] Transport
and Communications Review *1*
(*1951*).

Author's Note. This study was originally entitled, "Air Law: Subject Matter: Terminology, Definition." With that title, it was distributed in September, 1951 to the members of the first class which entered the Institute of International Air Law, now the Institute of Air and Space Law, at McGill University. The article illustrates the fact that the author has always felt that a single branch of the law should include all rules applicable to man-made and man-controlled movement of any flight instrumentality in all space above and beyond the surface of the earth.

AIR LAW, like Maritime Law, can be satisfactorily defined only by a statement of its subject matter. Both Air Law and Maritime Law are concerned with particular types of geographic and physical areas. Both deal with certain characteristic and limited forms of human activity in those areas, also with the instrumentalities employed to carry on such activities.

The subject matter of Maritime Law has been developed through many centuries. In general it may be defined as the branch of the law concerned with those areas on the earth's surface covered by navigable waters and their use by man for commerce, fishing, or similar activities, also the instrumentalities employed, such as vessels and other marine craft.

Air Law is largely a development of the twentieth century. Its subject matter has not been clarified by the long series of decisions of courts and arbitral tribunals, by negotiations between governments, treaties and other international agreements, or by the customary practices of war and peace available as recognized sources of Maritime Law. Even now scientific progress is already forcing reconsideration of certain basic Air Law rules. The ever-increasing speed of aircraft, the continued extension of the height above the earth's surface at which they can be operated, the rapid development of rockets and guided missiles—all are creating new problems which cannot be settled on a purely national basis. International thinking is demanded.

In general it may be said that Air Law is concerned with certain areas in space above the earth's surface, with certain human activities in those areas, and with the instrumentalities used in connexion therewith, such as aircraft. But it must be understood that this is not a definitive statement. Although too general and incomplete, it does illustrate many of the problems presented.

To state with any accuracy the present subject matter of Air Law, no matter what may have been the situation even in the recent past, requires a new and accurate determination as to the three funda-mental elements involved: (1) the nature and extent of the areas in space where "Air Law" is applicable; (2) the forms of human activity to be regulated in those areas; and (3) the instrumentalities involved.

THE NATURE AND EXTENT OF THE AREAS IN SPACE WHERE "AIR LAW" IS APPLICABLE

For many years prior to the twentieth century man had studied the possibility of human flight and whether such flight could be practically controlled. Development proceeded along two divergent paths toward a single hoped-for objective.

One group sought success through the use of various devices which might be called "airships" (including what we now term balloons, both free and dirigible). They hoped that such devices would rise by reason of buoyancy, being lighter than the air through which they operated. The other group were attracted by the mechanics of the flight of birds and believed that a machine could be developed which, though heavier than the air it displaced, would fly through the reactions of the machine to the gaseous air in which it moved. Both approaches to the problem assumed the necessity of "air" to make flight possible. Both assumed that the only area in which flight could take place was an area in which was found atmosphere composed largely of this gaseous air.

As early as the seventeenth century Francesco de Lana proposed the construction of an airship which he thought might rise through the air supported by four large thin copper spheres. He argued that if the air were exhausted from these spheres, or copper balloons, the machine would fly. Of course his proposed airship was never constructed. But a century later, in 1783, balloons were built and successfully flown—the first made buoyant by smoke-laden hot air, and others, a little later, through the use of hydrogen. From then on the development of balloons made rapid progress. Blanchard and Jeffries crossed the English Channel in a balloon in 1785. Observation balloons were used in the wars following the French Revolution. In the nineteenth century balloons were repeatedly employed during the Franco-Prussian war to carry messages and officials across the German lines and into and out of Paris, then under siege.

In 1852, before the Franco-Prussian war, a crude dirigible had been flown in France powered with a steam engine driving a rotating propeller. Improved dirigibles were flown in 1883 by the Tissandier brothers and in 1884 by Renard and Krebs. Finally in 1899, as the nineteenth century was coming to a close, von Zeppelin began the construction of the first of the great rigid dirigibles which were to bear his name. One was successfully flown over Lake Constance in 1900. The following year Santos-Dumont began his series of remarkable dirigible experimental flights in and near Paris.

From de Lana in 1670 to von Zeppelin and Santos-Dumont in the early twentieth century, the principle of buoyancy applied to aircraft lighter-than-air gradually progressed to ultimate success.

Long before de Lana designed his theoretical airship, Leonardo da Vinci, in the late years of the fifteenth century, had devoted one phase of his cosmopolitan genius to a series of remarkable studies of mechanical flight. Some of his original drawings are in existence and models have been made of certain of the machines which he designed, particularly a helicopter-like structure intended to rise by means of a rotating mechanical screw. Other experimenters in the late eighteenth century carried forward the study of mechanical flight. In the early nineteenth century Sir George Cayley finally produced the scientific designs which led directly to the present airplane. When Cayley was working no engines were in existence sufficiently powerful and light to drive an aircraft heavier than air. Most of the progress of the nineteenth century was necessarily limited to the construction and actual use of gliders.

As lighter and better motive power became gradually available, many men, such as Stringfellow and Maxim in England, Ader in France, and Langley in the United States, experimented with the adaptation to self-powered flight of glider-designed aircraft. But it remained for the Wright brothers, after the nineteenth century had come to a close, to demonstrate the first real success in the long efforts of man to fly in a machine self-powered and heavier than the air which supported it. When the Wrights finally succeeded at Kitty Hawk in 1903, mechanical flight, as envisioned by Leonardo da Vinci and his long line of successors, had become a fact.

By the early years of the twentieth century, successful controlled flight had thus been achieved using aircraft both heavier and lighter than air. Flight in both types of aircraft involved motion through the "airspace" and required the presence of gaseous air to make flight successful. Flight outside the airspace was deemed physically impossible.

Until human flight had become subject to some degree of control, little need existed for legal regulation. But when this long-sought goal of control of flight had been achieved, legal regulation began to emerge. As one of the early writers, Lycklama à Nijeholt, said in 1910: "Whilst the technical expert from one century to another was engaged in investigating the problem of the navigation of the air, the jurist could afford to look on calm and unmoved as one experiment after another failed. . . . So long as there were available only undirigible balloons, dangerous and expensive, absolutely unfit for regular traffic, aerial navigation was therefore necessarily confined to some very infrequent ascents, such as attractions at exhibitions, for pleasure trips or scientific excursions and most occasionally for military purposes; it did not create situations and relationships demanding the immediate attention of the legislator." The same author adds: "Recent years have proved such a splendid success for aeronautics that really it seems justifiable for law to begin to take its share in the aerial labour."[1]

Technical development had gradually produced airships and airplanes which required the presence of gaseous air to sustain flight. These could be used only in areas of space next the earth's surface where such air was present in sufficient quantities to provide "lift". This technical development tended to limit the scope and terminology of Air Law, for the jurist does not normally concern himself with situations where human activity is deemed impossible.

In 1902 Professor Ernest Nys, of the University of Brussels, first gave a definite name, "droit aérien", to the new and expanding branch of the law. This term was used by Nys in a report to the Institute of International Law at its 1902 session and in an almost identical article appearing the same year.[2] Nys argued that the real legal problem to be met by jurists involved the status of the space occupied by the air and not the legal status of the gaseous air itself; that the law is in general the regulation of human relationships; that the relationships which he was discussing were formed in a gaseous envelope around the earth; that these relationships came into being when air navigation occurred. He said: "The theatre of action is the atmosphere—that is to say, the gaseous layer which is composed principally of air . . ." While Nys thus fixed the "atmosphere" as the "theatre of action" or area under discussion it is certain that his thinking was necessarily limited by the theory that flight could not occur beyond the atmosphere.

A careful analysis of the writings of the other principal early jurists indicates that the new term "Air Law" was intended to include all human flight deemed physically possible in the areas of space deemed usable, although this was then assumed to comprise only the space above the earth's surface in which flight of aircraft lighter-than-air was already possible and in which the flight of aircraft heavier-than-air could then be considered possible. As this usable space around the earth was identified by the presence of the gaseous sub-

---

[1] *Air Sovereignty*, The Hague, M. Nijhoff, 1910.

[2] "Droit et aérostats," *Revue de droit international et de législation comparée*, vol. 34, 1902.

stance called "air" and was thus separated from all universal space beyond, the body of legal rules to be applied to flight was quite logically termed "*droit aérien*" or "Air Law".

But nothing in the development of this branch of the law indicates that some other branch of the law should include the regulation of flight in other areas of space beyond the areas where gaseous air is present. To contend that the rules of Air Law are applicable only within the "airspace" would assume that this term "airspace" is now capable of legal and practical definition. Such, however, is not the case. Any attempt to put a definitive limit on the height of the "airspace" is impractical. The average distance, for example, between the molecular collisions is considered indicative generally of the density of the air. At a height of approximately 65,000 feet (a region in which the atmosphere is so rarefied as to make normal airplane flight most difficult) this has been calculated as so minutely small as three one-billionths of a foot. But at a height of 393,700 feet, an area far below that of the range of several existing rockets, the distance between such molecular collisions is considered greater than five-sixths of a foot. Scientific comparisons of this kind show the almost total absence of what we would normally call "air" in those areas far below the regions where rockets are now known to operate. These calculations also demonstrate the practical impossibility of saying at what exact height above the earth's surface the "airspace" ends. Nor does it appear helpful to define the airspace for legal purposes as the maximum flight altitude for balloons or conventional type aircraft employing "air" both for lift and engine operation. Improved designs of new flight instrumentalities would constantly elevate the altitude at any given time and make such a definition meaningless as an exact legal term.

Admittedly "airspace" has been used in treaties and other documents of great international significance to state the most important single rule of international air law. The first article of the Convention relating to the Regulation of Aerial Navigation adopted at Paris in 1919 said: "The High Contracting Parties recognise that every Power has complete and exclusive sovereignty over the air space above its territory. For the purpose of the present Convention the territory of a State shall be understood as including the national territory, both that of the mother country and of the colonies, and the territorial waters adjacent thereto." When that convention was adopted, flight in areas of space above those regions where the gaseous air was sufficient to provide lift for flight instrumentalities was not yet possible and the statement had some meaning.

But the same terminology unfortunately, appears in the Convention on International Civil Aviation, adopted at Chicago in 1944 and now in effect. The first article of this convention is as follows: "The contracting States recognize that every State has complete and exclusive sovereignty over the airspace above its territory." This is nothing more than an international determination that the legal status of *part* of usable space has been settled. Each State has, under this rule, exclusive sovereignty over whatever area above the surface of the State may, under any given circumstances, be included in the term "airspace". But no international decision has yet been made as to the legal status of those areas of space above this "airspace" even though such areas are today usable for such flight instrumentalities as rockets or guided missiles. International legal thinking must solve the resulting difficulties.

The writer of this article must accept some degree of responsibility for the present confusion. As chairman of one of the drafting committees at the Chicago Conference in 1944, he reported out the present article 1 which had been adapted from the Paris Convention. In behalf of the drafting committee, he recommended its adoption. It is proper to record, however, that this was done in the absence of any suggestion by technical authorities present that flight would soon become possible in areas of space where gaseous air was not present in sufficient quantities to consider these areas as "airspace".

It has been argued that the problem could be solved if the term "airspace" in the Chicago Convention were construed to include any area of space in which man-made or man-controlled flight *might* exist. But the acceptance of such a theory would lead to an impossible international legal position. It seems obvious that we must agree that there is an upper boundary in space to the territory of the subjacent States. In the first place, under no possible theory can it be said that a State can exercise sovereign rights in outer space beyond the region of the earth's attraction, calculated to be about 161,000 miles (256,000 kilometers) above the earth's surface. All of the classic arguments to sustain the theory of state sovereignty in space have gone back to the proposal that it is the right and duty of a State to protect itself and that this protection can be considered adequate only when the subjacent State has the right to control, as part of its territory, those regions above it which if used by other States might bring damage and loss to persons and property on the State below. Even under this old rule, the outer boundary of the State cannot be further than the point where the earth's attraction will govern the movement of an object in space so that such objects will "fall" to the earth. But, in the second place, it is doubtful whether any legal theory can be sustained which could place the upper limit of the territory of a State even as high as the outer limit of the earth's attraction. It has been calculated that a rocket with a theoretical initial speed of about 25,000 miles per hour might be driven up to this enormous height to attempt the control of the area concerned for the State below. It would take a rocket travelling even at this tremendous velocity well over six hours to reach the theoretical distance of 161,000 miles beyond the earth's surface where the sun's attraction begins to predominate. By the time the rocket reaches this far-distant region, it might itself have passed through the theoretical territory of several States. The earth is rotating. If the rocket is driven directly upward it will not be for a very long period directly above the surface territory of the State which fired it. Any theoretical possibility of a State controlling regions of space up to the limit of the earth's attraction seems practically out of the question. It would seem untenable, therefore, to insist that a State has the right to claim territory even out into space as far as the earth's attraction extends, much less into space beyond. Perhaps the territory of each State should be considered as extending upward into space as far as then scientific progress enables the strongest State in the international community to control space above it. This might give some reasonable construction to the Chicago Convention. Agreement might be reached that the technical term "airspace" in the convention should be thus construed. Again international thinking is demanded.

The entire question as to the proper construction of article 1 of the convention is still open. If and when agreement is reached, the rules to be applied in both areas where gaseous air is present and in the areas beyond should be included in a single branch of the law. This, for convenience, we can still designate as "Air Law". Its rules will include provisions as to the right of each State to control space up to the agreed altitude as well as the rights of all States in the outer space beyond. For this broader view of "Air Law", new terminology may be needed, to be discussed hereafter.

THE FORMS OF HUMAN ACTIVITY TO BE REGULATED BY AIR LAW

The scope of Air Law as a rule of human and international conduct has at times been confused by the inclusion within its régime of the legal rules applicable to wireless (radio) telegraphy and telephony. The background of this confusion is historical. In 1900 the distinguished French jurist, Fauchille, suggested to the Institute of International Law the study of a new subject, "The Legal Régime of Aerostats". The Institute agreed, naming Fauchille as first reporter and Nys (whose resulting report was mentioned earlier in this article) as second reporter. The following year Fauchille published his celebrated treatise on "Air Territory and the Legal Régime of Aerostats".[3] In 1902 he

---

[3] Paul Fauchille, *Le Domaine aérien et le régime juridique des aérostats*. Paris, 1901.

presented to the Institute a detailed report and a proposed code of law governing the use of the "air" by all types of balloons. His major thesis was that "the air is free" and that subjacent States have in the air only such rights as are necessary for their self-preservation. Neither his report nor that of Nys, filed at the same time, were then discussed by the Institute.

Wireless telegraphy had been developed in the last decade of the nineteenth century and in the early years of the twentieth, at about the time that the control of flight became a factor in national and international life. In 1896 Marconi had taken out his first wireless patent. In 1903 the use of wireless telegraphy had already increased to such a point that an international conference was held in Berlin to consider its regulation. In 1906 some of the legal questions appeared to the Institute of International Law to be similar to those involved in the regulation of air navigation, covered by the still unconsidered reports of Fauchille and Nys. The Institute added the study of "International Regulation of Wireless Telegraphy" to its programme and directed Fauchille to prepare and present a report, this report to be discussed with the basic articles of Fauchille's earlier balloon code. As Fauchille stated, these articles related to the "nature of the air and the rights of states over the atmosphere". Fauchille presented his report and proposed international wireless telegraph code at the 1906 Institute session where it was discussed with the basic articles of the balloon code. The joint discussion resulted from Fauchille's continued insistence on the erroneous theory that "the fundamental difficulty which is at the base of both subjects is that of the nature of the air and the rights of states over the atmosphere."

Fauchille's basic fallacy appears both in his 1906 report to the Institute and in his verbal presentation of the matter during the subsequent discussions. He argued that the legal status of the air was the fundamental question, rather than that of the status of the areas in space in which flight or wireless telegraphy occurred. He had accepted the erroneous scientific theory that wireless telegraph messages were transmitted by some kind of wave motion in the gaseous air, and, therefore, thought that the legal status of the air was the point of contact between the regulation of flight and the regulation of wireless telegraphy. He stated that wireless telegraphy consisted of vibrations produced by electric impulses displacing in the air concentric layers or waves. His language was based on a statement contained in an article published in 1906 by Louis Rolland[4] in which Rolland had relied on Branly, a contemporary French physicist and an early

---

[4] "La Télégraphie sans fil et le droit des gens," *Revue générale de droit international public*, vol. 13, 1906, pp. 58–92.

experimenter in wireless telegraphy, for this explanation of the physical phenomena involved in wireless telegraphy.

Such a theory is now considered unsound. Modern science indicates that electro-magnetic wave propagation, or radiation, does not require the presence of air. While it may be admitted that the refractive characteristics of certain layers of the ionosphere (an area in the upper atmosphere beginning about sixty miles above the earth) appear to make possible some phases of long distance high-frequency wireless communication, this area of upper space bears little physical resemblance to the air mass close to the earth used by aircraft in ordinary flight. But the erroneous scientific theory presented by Fauchille was accepted by some jurists studying Air Law and the mere fact that the Institute of International Law in 1906 had discussed at the same time the regulation of human flight and the regulation of wireless telegraphy was accepted as a decision that both forms of regulation dealt with identical problems as to legal rights of States in the airspace.

Fortunately, within a few years after the 1906 meeting of the Institute, the matter was clarified in French language terminology. The term *"droit aérien"* was repeatedly used as applicable only to air navigation. This trend culminated in the authoritative 1934 definition of *"droit aérien"* by Fernand de Visscher, describing the subject matter of *"droit aérien"* as including the body of rules regulating the air milieu and its use from the point of view of air navigation, and excluding the regulation of wireless telegraphy.[5] The same position was followed in 1947 by Lemoine in his currently accepted textbook.[6]

The term "Air Law" as now used by authoritative British writers also excludes from its scope the regulation of wireless telegraphy and other forms of man-made radiation in space and limits its field to the regulation of those forms of human activity relating to flight. But this distinction was not always followed. Professor Hazeltine in his book *The Law of the Air* published in 1911 included legal questions connected with both wireless communication and air navigation. However, McNair, in delivering the Tagore Law Lectures of 1931 at Calcutta on "Air Law", excluded wireless telegraphy from his subject matter. These lectures were afterwards published in 1932 in London under the title *The Law of the Air*. In the recently published second edition of *Shawcross and Beaumont on Air Law*, the authors have noted that Air Law has been used by some writers to include the law relating to radio transmission, but have stated in a note that "this is an unjustifiable extension of its proper meaning".

---

[5] "Les Conflits de lois en matière de droit aérien," Hague, *Académie de droit international, Recueil des cours*, vol. 48, 1934–II.

[6] Maurice Lemoine, *Traité de droit aérien*, Paris, Sirey, 1947.

It is perhaps in the United States that the scope of the term "Air Law" has been most confused. The earlier studies limited its application to problems affecting flight. But in 1922 Professor Garner, lecturing and writing on "The Development of International Aerial Law"[7] included questions of wireless transmission. He was followed by other authorities. However, since the Second World War most writers in the United States have accepted the English and the French practice of dealing with radio law as a special branch of law applicable to electro-magnetic or other forms of radiation in space, entirely separate from the body of rules governing the flight of aircraft.

International uniformity would seem to require that the well-considered majority opinion be followed, and that the term "Air Law" be limited to the subject matter here under consideration. Rules applicable to the transmission of wireless (radio) messages or other forms of radiation should be excluded. Air Law should be concerned with questions involving flight, and related subjects. Other forms of human activity in space should be excluded.

INSTRUMENTALITIES REGULATED BY AIR LAW

The regulatory parts of Air Law ought not to be limited to the narrow category of flight instrumentalities usually termed "aircraft". This fallacy arises primarily from the historic importance of the 1919 Paris Convention and its annexes. As already stated, that convention dealt with state sovereignty over the "airspace". It also dealt with "aircraft" as the instrumentalities used by States in the airspace. Annex A to the convention included "Classification of Aircraft and Definitions". While the term "airspace" was not explained, the term "aircraft" was defined as comprising "all machines which can derive support in the atmosphere from reaction to the air". Aerostats, balloons, airships, aerodynes, aeroplanes and gliders were by other definitions included in the term "aircraft". The Paris Convention dealt, therefore, only with such flight instrumentalities.

This terminology, widely and correctly used so long as flight instrumentalities could not be operated beyond the areas where gaseous air was present to provide lift, has tended in more recent years to limit unnecessarily and improperly the scope of Air Law.

The language of the Chicago Convention of 1944 and certain of the "Standards" since adopted by the International Civil Aviation Organization has furthered this trend. The Chicago Convention, like the Paris Convention which preceded it, deals solely with airspace and with aircraft. Annex 7 to the convention, entitled "Aircraft Nationality

---

[7] *Recent Developments in International Law*, Calcutta, 1925, p. 141.

and Registration Marks", which became effective 1 July 1949 as an ICAO Standard, defines aircraft as "any machine that can derive support in the atmosphere from the reactions of the air". This definition is further amplified by the following:

"Aeroplane"—a power-driven heavier-than-air aircraft, deriving its lift in flight chiefly from aerodynamic reactions on surfaces which remain fixed under given conditions of flight. "Airship"—a power-driven lighter-than-air aircraft. "Balloon"—a non-power-driven lighter-than-air aircraft.

None of these definitions is believed properly applicable to such presently used devices and instrumentalities as rockets and guided missiles which are self-propelled and can be and are being used in various forms of man-made and man-controlled flight beyond the atmosphere. They do not require support "in the atmosphere from reactions of the air".

It is not necessary to decide here whether the provisions of the Chicago Convention are or are not applicable to such instrumentalities as rockets and guided missiles while passing through the "airspace". Nor is it necessary to discuss the cognate question as to whether the International Civil Aviation Organization has any jurisdiction as to the regulation of flight outside the "airspace", nor whether it has, itself, denied such jurisdiction by its carefully adopted definition of "aircraft". The important problem to be noted here is that neither the language of the Chicago Convention nor the definitions included in its annexes can be considered as a limitation on the scope of Air Law as a juridical field for international thinking.

The law cannot ignore any form of human activity, particularly if such activity affects the relations between nation-states as well as between individuals. If Air Law is to present an adequate, complete and well-rounded body of rules for the government of all forms of human activity relating to what may properly be termed "flight", then the rules of Air Law should include regulatory provisions applicable to every form of instrumentality which produces man-made or man-controlled flight through space above and beyond the surface of the earth. If this broad view of the scope of Air Law be not accepted, arbitrary and illogical distinctions must be made between various types of flight instrumentalities with resulting practical and legal confusion.

TERMINOLOGY SUGGESTED

The scope of Air Law will thus be seen to include man-made and man-controlled movement of any flight instrumentality in all space above and beyond the surface of the earth. Electro-magnetic or other radiation through space is excluded. Under this view of Air Law, the much-used terms "air navigation", "airspace", and "aircraft"—the basis of most present definitions—are either too limited or are unintelligible. Each of the old definitions implied that the body of rules under consideration should be limited to activity in the gaseous air with machines requiring support from such air. This terminology must be broadened. The approach to new problems created by scientific progress might even seem to require an abandonment of the term "Air Law". It could readily be suggested that we should refer to the "Law of Space and Flight". But the term "Air Law" in English, and its equivalents in other languages, has gained such wide use that it seems advisable not to abandon it. But the subject matter must be well understood. To keep the old and new problems within the same branch of the law would seem to require nothing more than to restate and revise the technical terminology to be used. The objective would be to retain "Air Law" in the status in which it was first conceived—namely, as the branch of the law regulating man-made flight in usable space.

Air Law, as here presented, is primarily concerned with *flight* and the areas in which such flight may occur. Its scope is not limited to such activities as are now carefully and technically described in annex 2 to the Chicago Convention adopted by the International Civil Aviation Organization and effective 15 August 1948, entitled "Rules of the Air". This annex states that the rules of the air "shall apply to aircraft operating within the territory of a contracting state and aircraft bearing the nationality marks of a contracting state wherever they may be . . .." Air Law is concerned with a much broader field of human activity.

To meet this situation the terms "flight", "flight-space", and "flight instrumentality", should be used where "air navigation", "airspace", and "aircraft" are now customarily used. The two basic definitions are "flight" and "flight-space". They may be restated as follows:

Flight includes any movement through space of man-operated or man-controlled devices or instrumentalities (to be known as "flight instrumentalities") such as balloons, dirigibles, airplanes, rockets, guided missiles, or space ships.

Flight-space means so much of universal space above and beyond the surface of the earth as is now used or may hereafter be used as the area in which flight takes place.

A DEFINITION OF AIR LAW SUGGESTED FOR INTERNATIONAL CONSIDERATION

As stated at the opening of this article, Air Law can be satisfactorily defined only by a statement of its subject matter. With this in mind

14

and using the terminology suggested above, the following definition is now proposed:

Air Law comprises the body of legal principles and rules, from time to time effective, which govern and regulate:

First:

a) Flight-space;

b) Its relationship to land and water areas on the surface of the earth;

c) The extent and character of the rights of individuals and States to use or control such space for flight or other purposes;

Second:

a) Flight;

b) The instrumentalities with which flight is effected, including their nationality, ownership, use or control;

c) The surface facilities used in connexion with flight, such as airports and airways;

Third:

a) The relationships of every kind affecting or between individuals, communities or States arising from the existence or use of the area of flight (flight-space), or the instrumentalities or facilities used in connexion therewith or to make flight effective.

Careful consideration will demonstrate that this definition includes within its terms those parts of Air Law which might fall within such arbitrary classifications as public or private law, also municipal, state or international law. A single definition is deemed preferable. That here proposed is submitted for study by those concerned with the practical and theoretical aspects of flight and the relationships which flow therefrom. It is not put forward as being entirely original. It reflects a view which has gradually appeared as jurists dealing with the international phases of the subject have sought to analyse the entire problem. Wide acceptance of this broad view of Air Law is deemed necessary to avoid future misunderstanding and to further unified world-wide thinking.

2

Notes on
Air Power
in Time of Peace

Reprinted from 1 Air Affairs *80*
(*1946*)

Author's Note. This 1946 study covers part of the research which preceded publication of "The Right to Fly" a year later. Air power is here defined as "the ability of a nation to act through the airspace, in other words, to use controlled flight—such, for instance, as the flight of aircraft." The national characteristics stated as supporting air power were later restated in "The Right to Fly" as factors contributing to a nation's *capacity* to fly, and the basic necessary elements of air power were there shown to be the total of a nation's capacity to fly plus its politico-legal rights. Aerospace law is and was directly involved. Even in this "space age" and after twenty years, the author would change little of this article's early analysis. The definition might be amended by substituting "aerospace" for "air space" and by adding the words "spacecraft and rockets" at the end. But air power today, as it was at the end of World War II, is still indivisible, including both the civil and military capacity of a nation to fly at any height limited only by the extent of its politico-legal rights.

T HESE NOTES are directed toward the following questions:

a) What is the basic nature of air power?

b) What are the principal conditions and elements which, during peace, contribute to or limit the air power available to the nation concerned for its national objectives, civil or military?

These notes do not deal with the use of air power in time of war— a matter involving questions of military strategy and national policy which the author is quite unqualified to discuss. Nor do they deal with the vital changes which the outbreak of any future war will immediately cause in certain of the political, economic, and geographic conditions which support or limit national air power in time of peace.

Nothing but a most tentative answer can now be given to either of the stated questions. Any final and definitive analysis of the basic and essential nature of air power—its elements or its ultimate effect on our civilization—will for some years be extremely difficult, if not impossible.

The impact of air power on world affairs is so recent that our generation can hardly appraise it properly. It must be remembered that air power has come into existence, has reached its present position of enormous importance, within the adult lives of men still active. The Wright brothers in 1903 first demonstrated man's ability to control flight. This was the real beginning of air power. Orville Wright is still alive.

17

The dramatic public appeal that has attended the amazing expansion of air power through and in the years between two World Wars makes particularly difficult any logical, disinterested approach. Books—some good, some bad—and magazine and newspaper articles without number, have fought over and greatly publicized the question of whether military air power has made obsolete all other phases of military and naval power, and whether air power did or did not determine the final course of World War II. The sudden emergence of the atom bomb at the end of World War II as an instrument of mass destruction has further complicated any clear thinking. Years from now, the historian, the sociologist, the economist, and the political scientist will each have had a more reasonable opportunity to determine how much of the drama and publicity of the early years of air power meant anything, and what were the vital and permanently important factors in its development.

Any definition of air power involves consideration of the word "power" itself. It is unfortunately true that in the thinking of the present generation the word "power" has taken on a rather sinister connotation. When we speak of "power" in connexion with international problems, almost unconsciously we think of force (improperly used) and of aggression.

The difficulty with the use of the word "power" has been especially felt in the case of air power. Repeatedly "air power" has been used as being entirely synonymous and co-extensive with "military air power", whereas military air power is only one phase of national air power. For example, a well-known English writer, author of many aviation books, writing in 1933, said:

> Air power is simply the power of a nation possessing an air force adequate to the calls of its national policy to support that policy in the last resort by forcible methods which, being new, are not regulated by any traditional law and custom of war.[1]

and again in 1938:

> Air power is indeed simply the ability to come and go in the air on warlike errands.[2]

Thinking such as this, linking air power solely with the preparation for or the prosecution of war, and ignoring its civil functions, has clouded the whole problem. Today, if you ask the man in the street for a definition of air power, you will find nine times out of ten that he thinks of air power only in connexion with armed force.

---

[1] J. M. Spaight, *Air Power and War Rights*. London, Longmans Green, 1933. p. 1.

[2] *Air Power in the Next War*. London, Geoffrey Bles, 1938. p. 4.

This popular fallacy does not, fortunately, extend to the majority of the thinking men in the air forces.

II

Much has been written about the late Brigadier General William Mitchell and his accurate predictions of the importance of military air power. In 1921 he insisted:

We must remember that, as we develop our commercial power in the air, just so much more do we develop our means of national defense.[3]

Later he brought forward one of the earliest and still one of the most exact definitions of air power:

Air Power may be defined as the ability to do something in the air. It consists of transporting all sorts of things by aircraft from one place to another, and as air covers the whole world there is no place that is immune from influence by aircraft.[4]

The same thinking is evidenced in the third and last report of General H. H. Arnold as Commanding General of the U. S. Army Air Forces:

Air Power includes a nation's ability to deliver cargo, people, destructive missiles and war-making potential through the air to a desired destination to accomplish a desired purpose.

Air Power is not composed alone of the war-making components of aviation. It is the total aviation activity—civilian and military, commercial and private, potential as well as existing.

Military Air Power—or Air Force—is dependent upon the air potential provided by industry . . . .[5]

In England, Brigadier General P. R. C. Groves (who had been the British air representative at the Paris Peace Conference in 1918–19, and later British air representative at Geneva), writing in 1934 pointed out that "in the long run, the only safe and reliable foundation of national air power lies in commercial air development"; also that air transport had the dual significance of being "a means to strengthen air defence" as well as "to establish closer commercial and political contact

---

[3] *Our Air Force*. New York, E. P. Dutton, 1921. p. 158.

[4] *Winged Defense*. New York, G. P. Putnam, 1925. p. xii of Preface.

[5] U. S. War Department. *Third Report of the Commanding General of the Army Air Forces to the Secretary of War*, November 12, 1945. Washington, U. S. Govt. Print. Off., 1945. p. 61.

between the several parts of the Empire and to help to open up some of its vast undeveloped territories."[6]

Both General Mitchell and General Groves clearly understood that air power (especially in time of peace) and military air force were not synonymous, and that military air force was simply one manifestation or use of national air power.

In a more recent English book, *The Use of Air Power*, by Flight Lieutenant V. E. R. Blunt, the same line of thought is thus stated:

> Air Power is not, as a great many people suppose, the ability to put bombers and fighters into the air in large numbers, any more than sea power represents the ability to put large numbers of warships on the sea.
>
> Sea power is built up of ship building capacity, of strategically placed ports and naval bases, and of ships, all enabling vast quantities of material to be transported to places and positions where it will serve its purpose best. It does not matter whether that cargo is a peaceful cargo of wool, or a fifteen inch shell fired from a battleship and exploding on a target. It is sea power which has got it there.
>
> Air power is exactly the same. It consists of the capacity of aircraft factories, the number of strategically placed aerodromes and bases, and of planes, all enabling vast quantities of material, both warlike and peaceful, to be transported and placed in positions where they will serve their purpose best. It does not matter whether the material transported is mail, parachutists, infantry, guns, shells or bombs. It is air power which gets it there.[7]

As indicated earlier in these notes, much of the popular confusion as to the nature of air power is due to an improper significance given the word "power" itself. Its primary definition is simple and is fundamental to clear thinking. Webster says that: "Power is the ability to act." The Oxford English Dictionary, somewhat more elaborately but with exactly the same result, defines "power" as: "Ability to do or effect something or anything, or to act upon a person or thing." Bertrand Russell philosophically suggests this definition: "Power may be defined as the production of intended effects."[8]

Proceeding from the definition of Webster that "Power is the ability to act," the author of these notes suggested in an earlier article the following definition of air power:

---

[6] *Behind the Smoke Screen.* London, Faber & Faber, 1934, p. 230–231.

[7] *The Use of Air Power.* 1st Amer. ed. Harrisburg, Pa., Military Service Publ. Co., 1943. p. 1.

[8] *Power—A New Social Analysis.* New York, W. W. Norton, 1938. p. 35.

20

Air power is the ability of a nation to act through the airspace, in other words, to use controlled flight—such, for instance, as the flight of aircraft. It is part of national power, to be used at home or abroad, in peace or in war. Though its uses are various, both military and civil, it is basically indivisible. The armed air forces represent but one use of the nation's air power. Civil and commercial aviation are supported by and spring from the same basic national elements.[9]

This last quoted statement seems consistent with the views expressed both by General Mitchell and General Arnold, although it was actually drafted prior to reading either of their above-quoted definitions.

III

Assuming, then, that the basic nature of air power is the ability of the nation to "do something in the air," "to act through the airspace" by the use of "controlled flight", or this concept stated in other words, it is next necessary to distinguish between the principal uses of air power and the conditions or elements which contribute to or limit the available national air power, then to determine what are such conditions and elements. In no practical way other than through the evaluation of its elements can air power be measured in time of peace, or can the air power of one nation be compared with that of another. The writer of these notes is strongly of the opinion that the air power of any nation, as is true of national power in general, is still incapable of direct and absolute measurement. Its tangible elements, however, when determined, are, to some extent, capable of direct measurement, or at least of useful comparison with those of another nation.

If international control of national air power be found necessary for world peace, such control must undoubtedly be exercised either (a) by directly limiting particular uses of air power, or (b) by controlling ascertained elements. It is obvious that even in time of peace, air power may be a means of international commercial aggression or infiltration, if not an actual military threat, becoming, thereby, in either case a possible cause of future war. To determine whether control of air power is possible, practical, or advisable, an accurate analysis is needed of its uses and its elements.

As to the uses of air power, it is submitted that "The basic idea of air power is transport."[10] Its primary use, whether in peace or in war, is to provide the world with many kinds of transport through the air. The strength or weakness of air power in any given nation at any

---

[9] "Air Power and the Coming Peace Treaties." *Foreign Affairs*, April, 1945. v. 24, no. 3, p. 441–452.

[10] Blunt. *Op. cit.* p. 1.

given time is evidenced by its relative ability to furnish such air transport as may be then required by the national aims and objectives, whether civil or military.

The elements of air power, on the other hand, are those national conditions, resources, factors, characteristics and efforts, which, when combined, are responsible for the existence of national air power.

The situation is something like that in a small town with a single water tank to supply its needs. The springs, which are the sources of the water to be stored, the pumping machinery to carry the water to the tank, the ability of the inhabitants and the material resources of the town required to build the water system, all of these, and others, are the elements bringing into existence the stored power within the reservoir and determining to what extent it is available. From this reservoir, in turn, flows the water needed for the town's daily normal use. From the same reservoir flows the water required in an emergency to put out a fire which might destroy the community. This is a homely metaphor, but, to the author, it illustrates the difference between the elements of national air power on the one hand and its civil and military uses on the other.

In any determination of the basic elements of air power, an examination of those conditions which affect national power generally would be most useful. Unfortunately space does not permit this to be done here. Anyone wishing to pursue the matter further will find very helpful the recently published *Fo   dations of National Power* edited by Harold and Margaret Sprout.[11]

Admiral Mahan's discussion of sea power is, of course, the classic example of an analysis of the elements of a particular phase of national power. After outlining his general basis of historic sea power (production—merchant shipping to move the products of industry—overseas colonies and other markets for this produce—and a navy to guard the trade routes), he turned to long range factors, stating:

> The principal conditions affecting the sea power of nations may be enumerated as follows: I. Geographical Position. II. Physical Conformation, including as connected therewith, natural productions and climate. III. Extent of Territory. IV. Number of Population. V. Character of the People. VI. Character of the Government, including therein the national institutions.[12]

Every subsequent analysis of the various phases of national power has certainly been influenced by Mahan. One of the earliest, and by far

---

[11] *Foundations of National Power.* Princeton, N. J., Princeton University Press, 1945.

[12] A. T. Mahan, *The Influence of Sea Power upon History.* Boston, Little, Brown, 1939. p 28.

the best analysis of the elements of air power yet published, although almost twenty-five years old, is still fresh and accurate. It omits certain conditions, particularly political, which subsequent developments have made important. It fails to distinguish between long range inherent natural characteristics and temporary conditions. But, notwithstanding this, the analysis is surprisingly good. It is found in the Report of the Sub-Committee on Aircraft to the Conference on the Limitation of Armament held in Washington, D. C. in 1921–22. This Sub-Committee, which included representatives of the United States, Great Britain, France, Italy and Japan, was charged with the duty of determining whether or not it was practical to limit the number, character and use of aircraft, as part of military disarmament. The Sub-Committee answered in the negative. As part of its work, this Sub-Committee had, however, come to an agreement as to the elements of air power, realizing, apparently, that the determination of such elements was necessary prior to any decision as to whether limitation was practical. The Sub-Committee included in its report the following analysis:

Summary of conclusions arrived at by the Committee on number, character and use of aircraft. The Committee are agreed that among the more important elements which influence the power that a nation may exert by means of aircraft are the following:

1. The adaptability of its people to aeronautics.
2. Geographical location and characteristics of the territory occupied by the nation and its dependencies.
3. The ability to produce and maintain aircraft and accessories.
4. The amount and character of aeronautical activity outside the military establishment, such as commercial and civil aeronautical activities, and sport and pleasure flying.
5. The size and efficiency of its air establishment for military purposes consisting of (*a*) the active establishment, including permanent headquarters, bureaus, squadrons, schools, technical establishments, depots of material and personnel, etc.; (*b*) the reserve establishment, including organized and unorganized reserve personnel and war reserve of material.[13]

This report includes a short discussion of each of the listed subjects. Its full text is available as an appendix to Mr. J. Parker Van Zandt's recent book, *Civil Aviation and Peace.*[14]

---

[13] Conference on the Limitation of Armament. WASHINGTON, D. C., November, 1921-February, 1922. Washington, U. S. Govt. Print. Off., 1922. p. 262.
[14] *Civil Aviation and Peace.* Washington, D. C., Brookings Institution, 1944. p. 101.

It is interesting to note that General Mitchell was one of the original members of this Sub-Committee on Aircraft, and, at its second meeting, suggested "that the only practicable limitation as to the numbers of aircraft that could be used for military purposes would be to abolish the use of aircraft for any purpose." France was represented on the Sub-Committee by Captain Albert Roper, the same able and efficient officer now serving as Secretary-General of the Provisional International Civil Aviation Organization in Montreal. He also raised the question as to whether "it was really practicable to impose a limitation even if so desired."[15] The Sub-Committee certainly approached the analysis of air power from the correct basis, namely, that its civil and military functions spring from the same elements.

In two recent publications discussing certain phases of air power, its elements are stated to be air commerce, the air forces, and the aircraft industry. An analogy to sea power is drawn on the apparent basis that Mahan defined sea power as made up of seaborne commerce, the navy, and the shipbuilders. This interpretation of Mahan very obviously omits his detailed consideration of such long range factors as the geographical position, conformation and extent of national territory, number and character of population, and character of the national government and institutions.[16] The result is that both of these ably written publications emphasize certain factors (the aircraft manufacturing industry and the civil and military aviation establishments) without detailed analysis of the national conditions and characteristics from which spring these short range factors.[17]

IV

As indicated above, the basic elements of air power fall into two general classes. The first of these determines roughly the usable national air power at any given time and for a short time thereafter. The second class measures the potential air power of a nation, an area, or group of nations, over a longer period.

In the first class, as to any one nation, are the following:

1. *Aeronautical Industry*, including existing aircraft and associated manufacturing plants, with the necessary engineering and research organizations.

2. *Aeronautical Facilities*, including airports, aeronautical repair

---

[15] Conference on the Limitation of Armament. . . . *Op. cit.* p. 196.

[16] Mahan. *Op. cit.* p. 28.

[17] Eugene E. Wilson, *Air Power for Peace.* New York, McGraw-Hill, 1945. p. 8.

National Planning Association. *National Policy for Aviation.* Washington, The Association, 1946. (Pamphlet nos. 51–52, March, 1946.)

24

and maintenance shops, radio, meteorological, and other air navigation facilities.

3. *Civil Air Establishment*, including all transport, private or other non-military flying, with its aircraft and other flight equipment, personnel and supplies in use or in reserve and quickly available.

4. *Military Air Establishment*, including all military flying, with its aircraft and other flight equipment, personnel and supplies in use or in reserve and quickly available.

The elements of national air power in this group have several things in common. They are visible and acquired national assets, each depending on the conscious acts of peoples or their governments. Together they will provide national air transport in its widest sense, in peace or war. Being capable of fairly accurate measurement at any given time, they can furnish a comparison of the apparent and immediately usable air power of two or more nations.

But, conversely, the disappearance of one or even all of these elements, while affecting national air power, does not destroy its potentials. This is most important in any realistic study of the historic and political significance of air power. For example, consider France at the date of its liberation during World War II. These visible elements of air power were practically non-existent. But to assume that France was without air power potential and must no longer be considered as a factor in world air power would have been most shortsighted. And of even more importance, consider the present status of Germany and Japan. Each is without usable air power as measured by these short range factors. But their air power potential, particularly that of Germany, is an ever present danger to future world peace unless the real fundamentals are recognized, and, if possible, controlled, so that potential as well as usable air power is carefully limited to the extent deemed necessary.

Aeronautical Industry, in being, furnishes the air fleet and its necessary replacements and *Aeronautical Facilities* the maintenance and physical aids for the *Civil* and *Military Air Establishments*. But neither one nor all of these are the fundamental elements of national air power. They are mere evidences of its present status. Potential air power, which the statesman, as well as the strategist and the common citizen, must study if he wishes to guard the nation's future well-being, goes much deeper and depends on more basic considerations.

Notwithstanding the difficulties of any present estimate of these long range air power factors, it is apparent that some are now emerging and can be considered as reasonably fixed. For the purpose of this limited discussion, the following are suggested as the principal conditions and elements which, *over a long period*, will contribute to or limit the air power available for national objectives, either the normal civil objectives of peace or the military objectives of emergency or war:

1. *Geographic Conditions*, including the location, extent, physical conformation, climate and weather, of the national territory and its dependencies.

2. *Resources*, including economic and material resources in national territory and available elsewhere.

3. *Population*, including the size, temperament, general educational level, and adaptability for aeronautics (flying, aircraft manufacturing, and allied industries).

4. *Industrial Development*, including the general national technological level, as well as manufacturing, engineering and research available or adaptable for aeronautics.

5. *Political Conditions*, including national incentives, government policies, and national aeronautic rights.

Some explanation is necessary to show the direct effect of each of these elements on national air power.

1. GEOGRAPHIC CONDITIONS

a) LOCATION

Of any two nations, that nation has the greatest air power potential, other things being equal, which is so located that it can normally reach the larger number of its air objectives with less flying and by more direct routes, particularly if such routes need not cross intermediate foreign territory. The following examples are of interest: *Soviet Russia* (including Siberia)—one enormous single national land mass with direct air routes: north across the Arctic Ocean to Canada and thence to the United States; east across Bering Sea and the Pacific Ocean to Alaska and Canada; south and east to China, Afghanistan, and India; south and west to Iran, Turkey, and the Middle East; west and northwest to Continental Europe and Scandinavia. *United States*— land mass in center of North America with direct air routes north to Canada; northeast across the Atlantic Ocean to Europe (temporarily by way of British-controlled Newfoundland); south to Mexico, Central America, Canal Zone, and northerly countries of South America including Brazil; west and south across the Pacific Ocean via American-controlled Hawaii, Midway, and Wake Islands, and Canton Island (jointly controlled with Great Britain) to the Philippines, southern China, the Dutch East Indies, Australia and New Zealand; *Brazil*— land mass (larger than United States) in center of South America, with direct air routes to every country in South America, except Chile, as well as most practical route across South Atlantic to Africa and Europe. *Germany* (prewar including Austria)—direct air routes to practically every continental European country of importance, including Great Britain, via North Sea, also to Scandinavia and Soviet Russia via the Baltic Sea. *Great Britain*—direct overwater air routes to Scandinavia, continental Europe, Africa, and North America.

b) EXTENT OF NATIONAL TERRITORY

Comparatively few countries have single territorial blocks large enough for favorable internal development of aviation. These include the United States, Canada, Brazil, Argentina, Soviet Russia (with Siberia), China, and Australia (also India if it becomes an independent sovereignty). Modern range of aircraft is such that the full advantage of aviation (both for civil air transport and for military services) and hence the development of air power, cannot be realized within such small territorial units as France, the British Isles, Italy, the Scandinavian countries, the South American countries except Brazil and Argentina. Prewar Germany was in an intermediate class. Its internal area, including Austria, was sufficient for reasonably satisfactory aviation development.*

c) PHYSICAL CONFORMATION, WEATHER AND CLIMATE OF NATIONAL TERRITORY

Favorable terrain, weather and climate definitely affect air power by making national flying easier, safer and more economical. Of countries of large area, the United States has very definite advantages, with European Russia probably second. In the United States a combination of favorable terrain for safe flying and easy construction of airports, with weather and climatic conditions permitting practical all year flying, lack of long heavy fog periods or torrential rainy seasons —all contribute to the comparatively easy development and use of air transport and hence air power. Large desert areas in Australia and North Africa—semi-Arctic regions in northern Canada, Soviet Russia,

---

* No national asset is more important to air power than the size of a nation's territory. This is particularly true if national territory is included in a single land mass. Every nation has the right under the doctrine of airspace sovereignty to reserve for itself air traffic in its own territory. The larger the national land mass, the more the internal air traffic of the nation is developed, thus building a reserve supply of aircraft usable elsewhere in an emergency, as well as the aircraft maintenance and manufacturing industries needed to support its internal aviation, together with the trained airmen and ground crews, navigation facilities, and airports. Air power builds and rebuilds itself. As a nation increases its national flying, the greater becomes its actual air power as well as its potential air power, and the more easily can it expand its air establishments, industry, and facilities in time of emergency. "The Fundamentals of Air Power," An Address delivered in the Library of Congress on January 7, 1948, p. 14.

and Siberia—water and jungle conditions in the upper Amazon regions of Brazil—these are handicaps which the continental United States does not suffer, in comparison with other nations of larger or similar area.

d) DEPENDENCIES

No argument is needed other than an examination of a world map to prove the importance to U.S. air power, civil and military, of its Pacific Ocean dependencies—Alaska, the Aleutian, Hawaiian, Midway, Wake, Guam, and Canton Islands. Every practical trans-Pacific air route must use one of these intermediate bases. Through their control the U.S. developed the first trans-Pacific commercial air service and its pre-eminent Pacific position.

The British air position in the Atlantic Ocean was for years and is today almost as important. Possession of Newfoundland and Bermuda gave to Great Britain early control of the Atlantic air routes. While Bermuda has no longer its early position as an Atlantic stepping-stone Newfoundland will still be used on most trans-Atlantic flights until the rapidly increasing useful range of large transport aircraft permits non-stop flights between continental United States and continental Europe. When this occurs, the importance of Newfoundland, as well as Bermuda, in any calculation of air power potentials, will rapidly decrease.

Dependencies have an additional geographic importance in the development of national air power. Certain countries, as pointed out above, such as Great Britain, France, and the Netherlands are handicapped due to the small size of their respective homelands and consequent physical inability to develop the volume of flying needed for the normal growth of national air power. Air routes developed by such countries to their far-flung colonial dependencies provide the national flying denied to them in domestic air operations.

2. RESOURCES

In the national resources which affect air power must be included those resources, economic and material, necessary for the construction, maintenance and operation of civil and military air fleets, with all necessary accessories and facilities. It is obvious that a nation's entire economic position is involved in this complicated process. Although space does not here permit detailed discussion, it should be noted that financing an adequate air manufacturing industry is now such a major national economic problem that the industry exists on a large scale only in the United States and Great Britain, to a limited extent in certain other countries including France, Canada, and Australia, and to an unknown extent in Soviet Russia.

Material resources, including raw materials, are also of major importance. The presence in national territories of steel, aluminium, copper, rubber, petroleum products—to name only a few—may make or break national air power. The presence or absence of stockpiles of such materials as against emergency expansion must also be considered in evaluating this element of air power in any given nation.

Of equal importance is the geographic and political ability of a nation to obtain access to such vital raw materials not found within its homeland. Consider the position of the United States before synthetic rubber was available and after Japan had cut off most of the normal import supply. Consider also the future air power position of Great Britain with no homeland production of petroleum products and forced to rely on tanker seaborne imports. If cut off from adequate aviation fuel and lubricating overseas supplies, its air power would cease to exist.*.

---

* Almost as important, is the status of the raw materials needed to construct aircraft, aircraft engines, and parts, as well as the fuel required for their operation. This is one of Great Britain's real air power handicaps. Practically any kind of material that goes into the construction of its aircraft and all the petroleum products needed for fuel and lubrication in its aircraft engines must be imported from far overseas. In this respect both the Soviet Union and the United States have certain advantages. The petroleum industry of the Soviet Union has certainly expanded, and I am personally inclined to think that it can now rely on its internal sources of supply for aircraft fuel and lubrication without importation. The Soviet Union is, of course, handicapped by very difficult inland transportation conditions in northern and north-eastern Siberia. It must be recalled, however, that the great Siberian rivers which flow from south to north are open during part of each year and that the Trans-Siberian Railway crosses each of these rivers in southern Siberia, thus providing combined rail and water transportation for supplies to the Siberian Arctic coast. Also, with the use of efficient icebreakers the Soviet Union has developed summer seaborne traffic as another source of supply for its Arctic territory.

The metallurgical resources of the Soviet Union are very little known. Within the last few years they have certainly been tremendously developed, and the Soviet Union is probably approaching self-sufficiency in the matter of materials needed for the construction as well as the operation of its aircraft.

The raw material position of the United States has been a matter of serious debate. It is quite impossible to review it at this time. Suffice it to say that in the construction of modern aircraft certain light metals are necessary and also certain scarce metals for the required alloy steels. Last year I made a study of this problem with the result that I found that the plans for the construction of one type of modern high-speed transport aircraft indicated that the materials to be used would be approximately 58 percent aluminum and 34 percent alloy steel. It is my information that the United States is deficient in and must import certain of the metals needed for these alloys. As to our supply of aluminum, without which I do not believe we could maintain an adequate air fleet, I call your attention to the language of a report as to the

3. POPULATION

The numbers of the nation's population must, of course, be taken into consideration in connexion with its air power. As between two nations, if the population of one greatly exceeds the population of the other, some advantage will accrue to the former. However, the temperament, general educational level, and adaptability for aeronautics, and other psychological qualities of the population, are of very much more importance.

It will be recalled that the Committee on Aircraft, in reporting to the 1921–22 Washington Disarmament Conference, listed this as one of the "more important elements which influence the power that a nation may exert by means of aircraft," stating:

> Interest of the general public in aeronautics seems to be inherent in some nations; in others it is dormant or almost lacking. The confidence of a people in aeronautics in general is undoubtedly a factor worthy of serious consideration when estimating the air power of that country.[18]

After twenty-five years little can be added to this statement, except to emphasize that the ever-increasing technical qualifications required

---

wartime use of strategic raw materials made by a special Senate committee in 1946. Aluminum is a refined product of what is known as bauxite. The Senate committee said that "the United States never had large resources of bauxite, except in the State of Arkansas. These fields were large enough only for a year or two of production at our maximum rate. We are, therefore, dependent for our supply of bauxite on South America in particular, and to some extent on the Pacific areas. Unless we can develop new industrial methods . . . the United States will always be dependent in this very basic industry on its ability to import from abroad."

Petroleum products are needed for aircraft fuel and lubrication. Raw rubber is needed for aircraft tires. If the air power of the United States is to be maintained, adequate supplies of these basic materials are absolutely necessary. The United States has been in the past the greatest producer of petroleum. Whether we have already arrived at the time, or whether we are approaching the time when we must depend on importation of petroleum products, is a subject of wide debate. As to rubber, we certainly must rely on the imported raw product unless we maintain our capacity for synthetic production developed during the war.

Maintenance of air power for the future requires the most careful consideration as to the sources from which the United States will obtain the needed raw materials, metals, fuel, rubber, and all of the other products required for the construction and operation of aircraft. To the extent that stockpiling may be necessary, it must not be neglected. To the extent that the manufacture of synthetic products will be required, we will forget it at our peril. "The Fundamentals of Air Power," An Address delivered in the Library of Congress on January 7, 1948, pp. 16–18.

[18] Conference on the Limitation of Armament. . . . *Op. cit.* p. 264.

of personnel engaged in flying, in aircraft manufacturing, and in the maintenance and operation of aeronautical facilities, including such devices as radar and blind landing equipment, have yearly made the general educational level of the population more important. Particularly under emergency conditions, when the personnel of the civil and military air establishments and the aircraft industry must be rapidly increased, the adaptability of the nation's population and its general educational level may well determine the success or failure of the vitally needed expansion. This was never better evidenced than in the crisis which faced the United States after Pearl Harbor. Had the American people not been possessed of the undefined psychological qualities which indicate an adaptability for aeronautics, as well as the general educational level which made possible training over a very short period resulting in efficient technical personnel, the results of World War II would have been quite different.

4. INDUSTRIAL DEVELOPMENT

Akin to the effect on national air power of the general educational level of a nation is the effect of the general national technological level. As has already been stated, the construction, maintenance, and operation of the modern civil and military air fleets, which are the vehicles transforming potential into usable air power, is a complicated process involving the nation's whole economic structure. It also involves its technological ability and adaptability. The aircraft industry is necessarily dynamic. It must continually move forward. Its technical advance does not depend only on its own engineers, comparatively few in number, but rather on the mass training, thinking and accomplishments of men in many allied industries. The high technological levels existing in Great Britain and in the United States have made possible the development of radar equipment, jet propulsion, and the many other engineering advances which are revolutionizing air transport and directly affecting potential national air power. This high technological level is the backbone of the manufacturing, engineering, and research resources of the nation.

The presence or absence of a national manufacturing industry is vital to air power. The nation which relies on the import of all of its aircraft is in a position to have its air power completely cut off in an emergency. But even more important is the long-range factor of the national ability to reconstruct or expand its aircraft manufacturing industry to meet changing conditions or emergencies. After World War I, Germany, through its national high technological level and the energy and training of its engineers and craftsmen, rebuilt its aircraft manufacturing industry, without which Hitler would never have fought World War II. Any country without a definite plan, as well as ability, to maintain the high standards of its aircraft manufacturing and allied industries is greatly handicapped. The Sub-Committee on Aircraft in its report emphasized this point.[19]

So far as the future position of the United States is concerned, the entire problem was adequately and forcefully presented in the 1945 "Report to the Air Coordinating Committee of the Sub-committee on Demobilization of the Aircraft Industry,"[20] and in the National Planning Association's recently published "National Policy for Aviation."[21]

The aircraft manufacturing industry, in being at any particular time, is one of the short-range and visible factors of usable air power. The more important element of potential air power is the national ability to maintain that industry, to continue its technical advance, and to be able in an emergency to increase many times its output capacity.

5. POLITICAL CONDITIONS

a) NATIONAL INCENTIVES

The existence of national incentives must be recognized as one of the long-range background elements of air power. A few examples will illustrate their importance.

In all of the great powers with any pretension to air power, national defense has been, since World War I, a major incentive. World War II has proven beyond doubt that the nation without air defense is helpless in time of emergency. England will never forget the "Battle of Britain" nor will Germany forget the air attacks which destroyed its industries.

Many other national incentives quite outside the direct sphere of military air power can easily be identified. In the United States, the development of high speed interstate air transport and efficient foreign and international air trade routes were among the driving forces behind the development of national air power. In Germany, the desire for national economic and trade reconstruction, followed by the evident Nazi ambition to use the development of foreign air routes as vehicles of nationalist and ideological propaganda and commercial infiltration

---

[19] *Ibid.* p. 264.

[20] U. S. Air Coordinating Committee. *Report to the Air Coordinating Committee of the Sub-committee on Demobilization of the Aircraft Industry.* Washington, U. S. Govt. Print. Off., 1945. p. 28-65. (Hearing before the Surplus Property Subcommittee of the Committee on Military Affairs and Industrial Reorganization Subcommittee of the Special Committee on Economic Policy and Planning. U. S. Senate, 79th Congress, 1st Sess., pursuant to S. Res. 46 and S. Res. 33, Part 1, Oct. 29, 1945.)

[21] National Planning Association. *Op. cit.*

(with military infiltration always in the background), were characteristic incentives. In Great Britain, in France, and in the Netherlands, the dual desire was never overlooked to tie the distant dominions and colonies to their respective empires and to develop inter-dominion, inter-colonial, and foreign air trade routes. Great Britain's historic supremacy on the sea was openly acknowledged as an adequate reason for maintaining a similar position, if possible, on the trade routes of the air. In China, in parts of Soviet Russia, of Brazil, of Canada, and of Australia, air transport is the only existing practical means of reasonably rapid internal communication and transportation. Such a domestic economic situation is the strongest possible incentive to develop national air power. Soviet Russia is also involved in a period of maximum national economic expansion. For this air power is an acknowledged necessity.

These are but a few of the national incentives affecting air power. They must always be considered in any analysis, no matter how elementary.

b) GOVERNMENT POLICIES

Mahan pointed out the great importance of the attitude of government in the development and support of a nation's sea power. He found this to be true particularly in time of peace, stating:

> The government by its policy can favor the natural growth of a people's industries and its tendencies to seek adventure and gain by way of the sea; or it can try to develop such industries and such seagoing bent, when they do not naturally exist; or, on the other hand, the government may by mistaken action check and fetter the progress which the people left to themselves would make. In any one of these ways the influence of the government will be felt, making or marring the sea power of the country in the matter of peaceful commerce; upon which alone, it cannot be too often insisted, a thoroughly strong navy can be based.[22]

If this statement is paraphrased by substituting the word "air" for the word "sea" and "air power" for the words "sea power," little further discussion is needed.

c) AERONAUTIC RIGHTS

As was once said, "Obviously any discussion of air power has postulated the existence of flight."[23] A people without the political

---

[22] Mahan. *OP. cit.* p. 82.
[23] Edward Warner, "Douhet, Mitchell, Seversky: Theories of Air Warfare." (IN Earle, Edward M., ed. *Makers of Modern Strategy.* Princeton, N. J., Princeton University Press, 1944. p. 485.)

right to fly under its own flag and for its own purposes is without air power. Such is the normal status of colonies, protectorates and mandates, no matter how large may be the population or territory. The British Dominions, on the other hand, although part of the British Commonwealth, have each the fundamental elements of sovereignty and each have separate national power, including air power. But as to India, under its present undetermined status, the position is not so clear.

Assuming that the right of a people to fly exists, thus presuming the existence of national air power, the extent of such right, politically as well as geographically, is a primary condition affecting such national air power. Under international law each nation normally has sovereignty over its airspace. In the language of the new *Convention on International Civil Aviation* adopted at Chicago in 1944 and now awaiting ratification. "The contracting States recognize that every State has complete and exclusive sovereignty over the airspace above its territory."[24] Language to the same legal effect is in the Air Navigation Convention (Paris, 1919), and also in the *Pan American Convention on Commercial Aviation* (Havana, 1928), to which the United States is a party; and in separate statutory provisions of practically every nation. Under this theory of sovereignty, a nation uses its airspace as it may determine and can exclude all others therefrom except as and when permission may be granted.

Selfish as it may be, the exclusive national use for air transport of the airspace over a nation's own territory and outlying bases adds to the air power of the nation concerned. When a nation confers on another nation the right to use, for air transport purposes, the airspace, territory, or outlying bases of the former, this adds to the air power of the latter and may materially lessen the air power of the former. For example, the exchange of rights between the United States and Great Britain, under which the United States may land in Newfoundland for refueling on trans-Atlantic flights, and Great Britain may land in the United States and in Hawaii for refueling on trans-Pacific flights, directly affects the air power of both nations, to an extent and in a manner not yet determined. Similar examples might be cited from many other parts of the world.

V

These notes are admittedly fragmentary and incomplete. They are now brought forward in the hope that they may provoke interest and

---

[24] International Civil Aviation Conference. CHICAGO, ILL. Nov. 1 to Dec. 7, 1944. *Final Act and Related Documents*. Washington, U.S. Govt. Print. Off., 1945. (U.S. Department of State. Publication no. 2282.)

such resulting discussion and criticism as they may warrant. Air power is a dynamic subject. It holds a place of ever-growing importance in our national life, whether in peace or in war. It is absolutely necessary that we understand its nature and its background. These notes have suggested a definition as well as some of the elements that contribute to or limit national air power. It is hoped that they will fill a useful purpose.

3

Outer Space and the Law: An Engineering Problem

Reprinted by permission of the
American Institute of Aeronautics
and Astronautics
from 6 Astronautics *64 (October*
1961). © *American Institute of*
Aeronautics and Astronautics 1961.

Author's Note. This article appeared in *Astronautics*, one of the publications of the American Rocket Society. It was addressed to readers who were in most part professional engineers and scientists, and was designed in part to indicate the author's basic view that the law is a social, engineering science charged with the duty of formulating rules governing and sustaining society. The particular problem considered is the relationship of the law to human conduct in "outer space".

MAN IS INVOLVED today in one of the most revolutionary projects of recorded history: Seeking to expand our earthbound social structure into outer space.

The great "voyages of discovery" of our 15th and 16th centuries were courageous European efforts to find new routes to old civilizations in Asia, culminating by accident in expanding the European social structure to an already inhabited America. Phoenician voyages more than 2000 years earlier, into the Atlantic and thence south along Africa and north to Britain, were farsighted commercial ventures. Prehistoric migrations of unknown motivation were simply movements from one area to another in which man could still depend on earth, water, and breathable air.

Now we seek to determine whether an ordered society can be made to function in space beyond the air and on celestial bodies of unknown physical characteristics. In this project, the social engineering science known as "the law" must play its part, already too long delayed.

The term "law" may have a special significance to the scientist or the engineer. Roscoe Pound, for years Dean of the Harvard Law School, when discussing "Theories of Law" in his recent textbook on jurisprudence, noted that the word "law" is in use outside the field of the jurist. Thus, he points out, an old use is to mean the order of the universe, while a modern derivative use is to refer to "regular sequences of phenomena explained by a hypothesis of rules or principles underlying the sequences."

Dean Pound undoubtedly had in mind such rules as the "laws of motion," the "law of gravitation," and many others. The scientist and engineer know that these "laws" are ignored or violated at his peril. The sanction is real and may be disastrous: professional failure and physical collapse of his project.

To the jurist, however, "the law" is the aggregate of a set of rules governing human conduct in society, many carrying sanctions to

37

assure enforcement. Since early times, philosophers have disagreed as to exactly which rules are to be included. But, as Dean Pound also pointed out, a common use of the term "law" by jurists of all schools "is to refer to the regime of adjusting relations and ordering conduct by the systematic application of the force of a politically organized society." This is an engineering concept.

In 1947, Arthur L. Goodhart (now Master of University College, Oxford) contributed an essay to a volume in honour of Dean Pound, published under the title "Interpretations of Modern Legal Philosophies." Prof. Goodhart there defined law as a "rule of human conduct which is recognized as being obligatory." In referring to Dean Pound's development of the "engineering interpretation" of law, Prof. Goodhart said: "To describe law as a piece of social engineering is not to talk in terms of analogy; it is a statement of actual fact, for law is a framework without which a society cannot exist. If this framework collapses, then the whole society will collapse with it. In constructing our society . . . it is therefore necessary to plan the framework with care, because if it is too rigid or too limited or too weak, then our society will suffer from these defects."

The law now faces its own engineering problem in outer space. Prof. Goodhart's words are directly applicable. The basic and engineering sciences are already doing more than their part in providing needed vehicles and equipment, and in planning for the future. The medical, psychiatric, and biological sciences are going forward actively with the problem of adapting man to new conditions. Otherwise, human life, as we know it on our little speck of solid matter in the universe, cannot be maintained in outer space.

Only the social engineering science of the law has been slow in its task of providing adequate rules of human conduct. Further delay or eventual failure will lead to disastrous chaos. For, as Prof. Goodhart said, the law is the framework without which a society cannot exist, and, if the framework collapses, the whole society will collapse with it.

In my personal judgment, any sound and effective framework will require new international agreement, preferably on a worldwide basis. Time does not permit the gradual development of customary rules. The dynamism of high-altitude flight demands immediate consideration. It seems obvious that the legal social structure now applicable in the "airspace" adjacent to the earth cannot be adapted to outer space.

For many years, the legal principle has been accepted that each State is sovereign in the airspace over its national lands and waters, that its unilaterally determined laws and regulations apply there to the exclusion of all others and that it has the sole and exclusive right to permit, control, or deny flight in its airspace. On the other hand, over the high seas, the airspace is not part of the territory of any State and flight is open to all, as is navigation on the free seas. An aircraft in flight passing above one State and into the airspace over another State moves through an invisible boundary from one jurisdiction and legal regulation to another. Similarly, an aircraft moving from the airspace over a State to the airspace over the high seas faces the same situation.

Obviously such a system is impossible in outer space. If national sovereignty of any State extends indefinitely upward, chaos in outer space must follow. It will never be possible in practice to determine with accuracy when satellites and future spacecraft, traveling at tremendous speeds, pass from the operative area of one set of rules to that of another. The legal framework will collapse of its own inherent weaknesses. The first international task must therefore be to fix an upper limit to national sovereignty with its rights of unilateral regulation.

When this is done, an international decision must be reached as to how and by whom the rules of human conduct in outer space are to be fixed. This requires a decision as to the legal status of outer space. It is suggested that it should have the status of the high seas as accurately stated in 1826 by a great American jurist, Mr. Justice Storey of the Supreme Court in the case of *The Marianna Flora*.

> Upon the ocean, then, in time of peace, all possess an entire equality. It is the common highway of all, appropriated to the use of all; and no one can vindicate to himself a superior prerogative there. Every ship sails there with the unquestionable right of pursuing her own lawful business without interruption; but whatever may be that business, she is bound to pursue it in such a manner as not to violate the rights of others.

The world has used the high seas as a transport medium since prehistoric times. For at least two centuries, States have accepted the fact that its use is free to all. Likewise, we have accepted the legal doctrine that every ship has nationality and that the State of the flag is thereby responsible for its international good conduct when away from home. With this background, international law has built up the rights and responsibilities between States as to the use of the high seas and the rights and responsibilities between citizens of the same State, or between citizens of different States, when traveling on the high seas.

If outer space has the same status as the high seas, the remainder of the structure to be provided by the law must be determined by international agreement, a reasonably practical task if the world desires to live in peace. Necessary rules and regulations could be provided by an international convention or the nations of the world could by agreement delegate to an international organization the power to adopt rules thereafter to be enforced as law. But first the foundation must be established.

Many groups, especially since Sputnik I was launched, have studied these and other problems involved in the construction of a legal framework for the extension of human society into outer space. Such purely legal groups as the International Law Association, the American Bar Association, and the American Society of International Law are making most valuable contributions. Of equal importance is the fact that engineering groups have now realized that the law as a social engineering science must take its part in the future development and use of outer space. The American Rocket Society, for example, several years ago established a Technical Committee on Space Law and Sociology. More recently, the International Astronautical Federation, of which ARS is a member took somewhat similar action. At its 1960 conference in Stockholm, it approved the statutes of two affiliates, the International Academy of Astronautics and the International Institute of Space Law. Membership in the Academy is divided into three sections—basic sciences, engineering sciences, and life sciences. The latter includes "medical and other sciences dealing with life and survival in space," and jurists were included in the original founding membership of this section.

The purposes of the International Institute of Space Law include "carrying out tasks which may be considered desirable for fostering the social science aspects of astronautics, space travel, and exploration." In 1959, while the institute was in process of organization, the IAF at its London conference authorized Andrew G. Haley, its General Counsel, to name Working Groups to consider and report on questions of space law. These Groups are now part of the Institute. They are dealing with such questions as the legal status and boundaries of airspace and outer space, the legal status of rocket and space vehicles and of celestial bodies, radio regulation for space-flight activities, damage caused by space vehicles, and other cognate subjects. The conclusions will be made available to such international governmental organizations as may hereafter be charged with drafting an agreement to build a legal framework for outer space.

Theodore von Kármán, as director of the Academy, desiring to assure cooperation between the work of the Academy and of the Institute, appointed in 1960 a joint commission on "Technical Aspects of Space Law." L. R. Shepherd, past president of the British Interplanetary Society and a former president of the IAF, was named vicechairman, with this writer as chairman. This commission will seek first to analyze questions of sovereignty in space. As Dr. Shepherd has stated: "The scientific problem is that of defining meaningful physical criteria upon which legal rulings might be based. Obviously there can be no single phenomenon which gives a clean cut answer to this problem and final resolution of the matter could only come from a careful consideration of a number of relevant physical phenomena."

But the work of any nongovernmental group must in the last analysis be purely advisory. Certainly it must be the task of the United Nations to build the actual framework to support any future human society in outer space. The UN has in fact tacitly acknowledged the need for action. On Dec. 12, 1958, the General Assembly adopted a resolution which recognized "the common interest of mankind in outer space, and that it is the common aim that it should be used for peaceful purposes only." The same resolution created an Ad Hoc Committee of certain member States and directed it to report on various questions including "the nature of legal problems which may arise in the carrying out of programs to explore outer space." Unfortunately, certain of the States appointed to membership on the Committee refused to participate in its deliberations. However, the majority went forward and on July 14, 1959, filed a report concurred in by representatives of Argentina, Australia, Belgium, Brazil, Canada, France, Iran, Italy, Japan, Mexico, Sweden, United Kingdom, and the United States.

This report is a historic document. Perhaps its most important contribution is the finding that the principles of the United Nations Charter and of the Statute of the International Court of Justice are not limited in their operation to the confines of the earth. If this recommendation is finally accepted, it means that the rule of law in outer space or on any celestial body hereafter occupied by any member of the UN will be governed by the broad terms of the Charter.

On the basic question of whether outer space shall be free for the use of all nations, the report indicated that launchings during the IGY 1957–1958 and subsequently were "on the premise of the permissibility of the launching and the flight of the space vehicles which were launched regardless of what territory they passed 'over' during the course of their flight through outer space." The Committee then indicated that with this practice "there may have been initiated the recognition or establishment of a generally accepted rule to the effect that, in principle, outer space is, on condition of equality, freely available for exploration and use by all in accordance with existing or future international law or agreements." While this statement is somewhat cryptic in its terms, it may properly be taken as a clear indication that the national sovereignty of States carrying with it unilateral flight control should not be extended into outer space.

However, the Committee decided that the determination of "precise limits for airspace and outer space did not present a legal problem calling for priority consideration at this moment." With this latter conclusion I must disagree. The dividing line must be established, for

41

certainly the entire report is an acknowledgment that flight in the air-space and flight in outer space are not subject to the same regulations.

The Ad Hoc Committee report was not formally considered by the UN General Assembly, presumably because of non-participation in its preparation by certain important States. Instead in December 1959, a new "Committee on the Peaceful Uses of Outer Space" was established consisting of Albania, Argentina, Australia, Austria, Belgium, Brazil, Bulgaria, Canada, Czechoslovakia, France, Hungary, India, Iran, Italy, Japan, Lebanon, Mexico, Poland, Roumania, Sweden, USSR, United Arab Republic, United Kingdom and the United States.

The directives to the new Committee are quite similar to those given to the Ad Hoc Committee. Among other things, the new Committee is directed to study the nature of legal problems which may arise from exploration of outer space. Apparently this Committee has not yet acted. The construction of a legal framework for human society in outer space does not appear to have gone forward in the UN since the preparation and filing of the report of the Ad Hoc Committee discussed above. It is hoped that this situation will not continue too long.

In September 1960, in his address to the UN General Assembly, President Eisenhower warned the world, saying: "Another problem confronting us involves outer space. The emergence of this new world poses a vital issue: Will outer space be preserved for peaceful use and developed for the benefit of all mankind? Or will it become another focus for the arms race—and thus an area of dangerous and sterile competition? The choice is urgent."

If this solemn warning is not heeded, the world may fail in the great project of expanding successfully our earthbound social structure into outer space.

4

Aerospace Law—
Subject Matter and
Terminology

Reprinted by permission of the
Journal of Air Law and Commerce
from 29 Journal of Air Law and
Commerce *89 (1963).*
© Journal of Air Law and
Commerce *1963.*

Author's Note. This article was published twelve years after the article on "Air Law—A Field for International Thinking." During that period the term "air law" had come into use as the equivalent of "aeronautical law", and a new term "space law" to cover rules applicable to flight above the "airspace". The term "aerospace" had also come into use in certain technical and scientific fields when used as a designation for all areas above the surface of the earth used for flight, in substance, synonymous with the term "flight space" which the author had suggested in 1951. This article, published in 1963, indicates the author's continued conviction that a single branch of the law should include all rules applicable to flight no matter at what height. The term "aerospace law" was suggested so that legal as well as scientific thinking should be better coordinated.

A s THE TERMS *Air Law* and *Space Law* are now used, they represent nothing more than phases of the law directly and indirectly applicable to man-made flight. To avoid existing and future confusion both should be included in a single branch of the law. This might be termed *Aerospace Law.*

Aerospace was defined in a glossary published in 1959 by the Research Studies Institute as Maxwell Air Force Base as follows: "The earth's envelope of air and the space above it, the two considered as a single realm for activity in the flight of air vehicles and in the launching, guidance, and control of ballistic missiles, earth satellites, dirigible space vehicles, and the like." The terms *aerospace engineering* and *aerospace sciences* are now widely used to indicate the indivisible and inclusive character of engineering and scientific actions and functions related to flight at any altitude. The term *aerospace power* was also used in the same glossary as representing the "power of man, derived from his ability to fly vehicles in the air and in space." The official journal of the Air Force Association, *Air Force and Space Digest,* is designated by its publishers as *The Magazine of Aerospace Power.*

The proposal that a single branch of the law should include all rules and regulations applicable to flight, is not new. My own views were expressed in a memorandum prepared for the opening of The Institute of International Air Law at McGill University in 1951, several years prior to the launching of Sputnik 1. These views were repeated and expanded in an article entitled "Air Law—a Field for International

Thinking."[1] I then urged that the term *Air Law* be used in a broadened sense.

Discussing Article 1 of the Chicago Convention of 1944 and its recognition that "every State has complete and exclusive sovereignty over the airspace above its territory," I said:

> Each State has, under this rule, exclusive sovereignty over whatever area above the surface of the State may, under any given circumstances, be included in the term *airspace*. But no international decision has yet been made as to the legal status of those areas of space above this *airspace* even though such areas are today usable for such flight instrumentalities as rockets or guided missiles. International legal thinking must solve the resulting difficulties.

After asserting that "it seems obvious that we must agree that there is an upper boundary in space to the territory of subjacent States," the statement continued:

> The entire question as to the proper construction of Article 1 of the Convention is still open. If and when agreement is reached, the rules to be applied in both the areas where gaseous air is present and in the areas beyond should be included in a single branch of the law. This, for convenience, we can still designate as *Air Law*. Its rules will include provisions as to the right of each State to control space up to the agreed altitude as well as the rights of all States in the outer space beyond. The law cannot ignore any form of human activity, particularly if such activity affects the relations between nation-states as well as between individuals. If Air Law is to present an adequate, complete and well-rounded body of rules for the government of all forms of human activity relating to what may properly be termed *flight*, then the rules of Air Law should include regulatory provisions applicable to every form of instrumentality which produces man-made or man-controlled flight through space above and beyond the surface of the earth. If this broad view of the scope of Air Law be not accepted, arbitrary and illogical distinctions must be made between various types of flight instrumentalities with resulting practical and legal confusion.

I then urged that the terms *flight*, *flight-space* and *flight instrumentality* should be used where the terms *air navigation*, *airspace* and *aircraft* were customarily used, suggesting the following two basic definitions:

> Flight includes any movement through space of man-operated or man-controlled devices or instrumentalities (to be known as *flight*

---

[1] See Chapter 1.

instrumentalities) such as balloons, dirigibles, airplanes, rockets, guided missiles, or space ships.

Fight-space means so much of universal space above and beyond the surface of the earth as is now used or may hereafter be used as the area in which flight takes place.

It would appear that the present widely used term *aerospace* is practically identical in meaning with the term *flight-space* suggested in 1951. But the possible suggested broad use of the term *Air Law* to cover all flight and related activities was not widely accepted. Instead most writers still use the term *Air Law* in the narrow sense as the equivalent of aeronautical law. *Aeronautics* has been defined as the "art, science, or business of designing, manufacturing and operating vehicles that move through the air." In this sense McNair said in opening the first edition of his *Law of the Air* in 1932: "The aim of this book is to state the aeronautical law of England."

Since orbital flight became a fact, the new term *Space Law* has been widely used, but without exact analysis or definition. One thing is, however, very clear—if *Air Law* and *Space Law* are to be treated as separate branches of the law, overlapping will certainly result, even dangerous contradiction. Confusion already exists. In the mushrooming literature of official and academic statements, conferences, addresses, and learned papers, it is quite impossible to determine the exact extent of *Space Law* subject matter. At times it seems limited to those rules geographically applicable in areas of usable space beyond the airspace— admittedly an uncertain boundary. At other times the term *Space Law* seems to include any regulation of those flight instrumentalities capable of outer space flight, wherever they are, even while in the airspace or on the ground. This is not a healthy situation. The rules of law should be clear and their application unquestioned.

Some of the difficulties which must arise in treating space law as a subject apart from air law, are illustrated in the recently published *Draft Code of Rules on the Exploration and Uses of Outer Space*, prepared by a Study Group of the David Davies Memorial Institute of International Studies, London. The Chairman of the Study Group was Professor R. Y. Jennings, Whewell Professor of International Law at Cambridge, and the reporter was Mr. J. E. S. Fawcett, Fellow of All Souls College, Oxford. The Group included many other highly qualified experts. The publication is perhaps the best and most useful which has thus far appeared dealing with the assigned subject matter. The introduction states that the Study Group "concluded that this is a good time to publish a document bringing together what appear to be the basic principles of the developing space law." An examination of the resulting rules discloses, however, that the able authors found it necessary to include rules which are certainly within the historic and logical province of air law, even in its limited sense of aeronautical law. For example, the draft code includes a definition of *aircraft*. Also it proposes the following: "Air Space means the volume of space between the surface of the earth at sea level and an altitude of 80,000 meters above it." This definition is in substance an addition to or modification of Article 1 of the Chicago Convention of 1944. The altitude of the absolute and unilateral sovereign rights of the subjacent State in the airspace is an integral part of one of the primary rules of any complete statement of air law subject matter.

Also particularly noteworthy is paragraph 2.4 of the *David Davies Memorial Institute Proposed Rules*, reading as follows: "No State or international body shall put the airspace, outer space or the celestial bodies, to uses which cause, or are likely to cause, modifications of the environment of mankind unless the prior agreement of the appropriate international body has been obtained that such modifications are acceptable." Clearly this rule would be applicable to aircraft in the airspace if the use came within the prohibited categories. Paragraph 4.1 seems also designed, at least in part, to state new rules applicable to the use of airspace, perhaps requiring a modification of the Chicago Convention of 1944 to become effective. The suggested rule is as follows:

No spacecraft launched from the territory of any State may at any state of its flight enter the airspace of another State without the consent of that State: provided that

a) such consent shall not be withheld if prior notice has been given to that State of the intended flight, and it has been shown to its satisfaction that the flight is solely for scientific and peaceful purposes and shall be so controlled as to obviate danger to aircraft;

b) any craft capable of operating both as a spacecraft and as an aircraft shall for the purpose of its use of the airspace be deemed to be an aircraft;

c) a manned spacecraft may enter the airspace without prior consent for the purpose of making an emergency landing, but shall be subject to the provisions of Section *b*.

Paragraph 6.1 deals with liability, stating:

The State or States or international body responsible for the launching of a spacecraft shall be liable for any breach of this Draft Code in which it may be involved, for any injury or loss caused by the spacecraft, or any part of it

a) by physical impact, contamination, or otherwise, to any person or property whatsoever outside the territory of the State responsible for the flight of the spacecraft;

b) as a result of collision or navigational interference, to any aircraft,

    1. in the airspace of another State; or

    2. of a nationality other than that of the spacecraft, without proof of negligence in the operation of the spacecraft being required.

The rules thus proposed appear to be applicable in outer space, and also under certain circumstances, in the airspace and on the surface of the earth. These rules would require the modification of present aeronautical rules, or the adoption of new rules applicable on the earth and in the airspace, and would affect flight instrumentalities other than spacecraft.

Careful examination of the entire group of rules as proposed by the Study Group headed by Professor Jennings shows clearly that it is not possible to consider *Space Law* except as a part of a wide general branch of the law dealing with flight and flight instrumentalities of all kinds. Any more narrow approach must lead to incomplete and inaccurate results, or to contradiction with existing rules applicable to airspace flight.

Much more important than any academic or theoretical efforts are the separate and apparently uncoordinated programs of the International Civil Aviation Organization (ICAO) and the United Nations (through its Committee on the Peaceful Uses of Outer Space). A brief statement of the present situation would appear to be useful. ICAO was created by the Chicago Convention on International Civil Aviation of 1944, referred to above. The convention repeatedly uses the terms *airspace* and *aircraft*. ICAO has the power under the convention to adopt international standards and procedures dealing with matters concerned with the safety, regularity and efficiency of air navigation. Pursuant to this authority it has, in an annex to the convention, defined *aircraft* as "any machine which can derive support in the atmosphere from reactions of the air." This is substantially the same definition adopted over forty years ago in an annex to the Paris Convention of 1919. ICAO has also the power to adopt *rules of the air*. Article 12 of the convention specifically provides that each contracting State undertakes to keep its own regulation in these respects uniform to the greatest possible extent with those established under the convention, and that over the high seas the rules enforced shall be those established under the convention. Thus far ICAO does not appear to have taken any action recognizing the use of the airspace by flight instrumentalities other than *aircraft*. Nor has it directly or indirectly sought to determine or state the extent of the area above the surface of the earth in which its *rules of the air* may be deemed valid.

ICAO has, however, through its Legal Committee sponsored various international conventions including the Rome Convention on liability for damage caused by aircraft to third persons and property on the surface of the earth. It is also engaged in drafting a convention dealing with collisions between aircraft. Assuming the continued use of the forty-year-old definition of aircraft, it would appear that neither the ICAO rules of the air, nor the Rome Convention on liability for surface damage, nor the draft convention on collisions can be construed to cover activities related to flight instrumentalities designed primarily for flight above and beyond the airspace, even though such instrumentalities may pass through the airspace when ascending to or descending from outer space.

Man-made flight is a unique phenomenon, involving a very particular form of human activity. Types of flight instrumentalities may differ. Strata of space in use may vary. But the identity of the basic human effort remains constant. It is obvious that the aggregate of the legal rules applicable to flight should cover all of its phases, but, at the same time should represent, where practical, a single solution for each separable problem. This desirable result may not follow the present separate efforts of ICAO to develop *Air Law* and those of the United Nations as to *Space Law*. ICAO seems concerned solely with the regulation of the flight of *aircraft* and the United Nations with *spacecraft*. Grave danger exists that unrelated, or even contradictory, rules may result. The present situation is confused.

In December 1961 the General Assembly of the United Nations adopted the much discussed Resolution 1721 (XVI) in which it commended to States for their guidance in the exploration and use of outer space the principles that international law, including the U.N. Charter, applies to outer space and celestial bodies and that outer space and celestial bodies are free for exploration and use by all States in conformity with international law and are not subject to national appropriation. The resolution then invited the Committee on the Peaceful Uses of Outer Space, "to study and report on the legal problems which may arise from the exploration and use of outer space."

When the Legal Sub-Committee of the United Nations Committee met in 1962, regulatory proposals were put before it by the U.S.S.R. and by the U.S.A. dealing with the rescue and return of astronauts and spacecraft in case of accidental or emergency landings. Also the U.S.A. made a proposal on liability for damage or loss caused by spacecraft. No final recommendations were made by the Legal Sub-Committee, nor by the main committee. At the 1962 meeting of the General Assembly all of these proposals were referred back to the Committee on Peaceful Uses of Outer Space for further consideration.

It is noteworthy that both the U.S.S.R. and the U.S.A. proposals as to assistance to astronauts and the return of space vehicles and personnel in case of accidental or emergency landing dealt solely with occurrences taking place on the earth's surface and with actions which should follow. The U.S.A. proposal as to liability dealt with injury or damage caused by a space vehicle "on land, on the sea, or in the air." No proposal was made as to what rule of liability should be adopted in case of collisions between space vehicles in outer space. So far as the records disclose, ICAO took no part in the formation of these proposals nor was it represented by an observer at the United Nations Committee meetings. The apparent difficulty is that the U.S.S.R. is not a member of ICAO. Any views which ICAO might have as to space flight would not be binding upon the U.S.S.R. Obviously at this stage in the political-legal formulation of flight rules the agreement of the U.S.S.R. is necessary if they are to become effective, because only the U.S.S.R. and the U.S.A. are actively involved in flight in outer space. But it does seem unfortunate, that the proposals made in the United Nations Committee regarding accidental landing of space vehicles seem to have taken no direct account of Articles 25 and 26 of the Chicago Convention dealing with aircraft in distress and with the investigation of accidents. If the proposals before the United Nations should mature into an international agreement, then problems will arise as to whether such new agreement, or the Chicago Convention provisions, will apply, dependent only on the type of flight instrumentalities involved. These problems would be particularly difficult if such flight instrumentality could be used in the airspace and also in outer space.

The proposals as to liability placed before the United Nations Committee covered in part the same subject matter as the Rome Convention dealing with damage to third parties or property on the surface of the earth and in part the subject matter of collisions between flight instrumentalities. These proposals do not seem to have been correlated with the Rome Convention nor the ICAO Draft Convention on collisions. We are thus faced with the possibility of varying, or even contradictory sets of rules depending for their application on a factual determination of the type of flight instrumentalities in use. It is apparent that the United Nations approach to *Space Law* is that it should be the aggregate of the rules applicable to flight instrumentalities capable of outer space flight, wherever they are. But no definition of outer space has been offered.

As I have long argued, a single branch of the law must eventually be accepted to govern all man-made flight, and the rules finally adopted should be as uniform as can be found practical. This branch of the law, as suggested in the opening of this article, might be termed *Aerospace Law*. Its subject matter might be thus stated:

Aerospace Law comprises the body of legal principles and rules, from time to time effective, which govern and regulate:

First:

a) Aerospace, being the earth's envelope of air and the space above it, the two considered as a single realm for activity in the flight of air vehicles and in the launching, guidance, and control of ballistic missiles, earth satellites, dirigible space vehicles, and the like;

b) Its relationship to land and water areas on the surface of the earth;

c) The extent and character of the rights of individuals and States to use or control such space, or parts thereof, or celestial bodies therein, for flight or other purposes;

Second:

a) Flight;

b) The instrumentalities with which flight is effected, including their nationality, ownership, use or control;

c) The surface facilities used in connexion with flight, such as airports, other launching or landing areas, navigation facilities and airways;

Third:

a) The relationships of every kind affecting or between individuals, communities or States arising from the existence or use of the area of flight (aerospace), or the instrumentalities or facilities used in connexion therewith or to make flight effective.

Careful consideration will demonstrate that this definition includes within its terms those parts of *Aerospace Law* which might fall within such arbitrary classification as public or private law, also municipal, state or international law. A single definition is deemed preferable. But the major objective must never be lost sight of—the necessity of accepting a single branch of the law to cover all phases of man-made flight.

PART TWO
Rights in Airspace: From Antiquity to the Advent of Aircraft

5

Roman Law and the Maxim "Cujus est solum" in International Air Law

Reprinted from Institute of International Air Law, McGill University, Publication No. 1, 1952.

Author's Note. The Paris, Havana, and Chicago Conventions each recognized the prior existence of a general rule of international law that every State, whether or not a party to the Convention, is sovereign in the airspace above its national land and waters. While at the Institute for Advanced Study in Princeton, working with the benefit of a Rockefeller Foundation grant, this author's research convinced him that such a rule had long existed and that its beginnings went far back into history. The evidence became clear that even Rome, as a State, had created and regulated rights of the landowner in space above the earth's surface, thus asserting national sovereignty, for otherwise such private rights could not have existed. The research necessary to explore this problem occupied about one year and involved a study of the classical Roman law texts, which had never been part of the author's academic background, together with the early printed editions of the *Digest* in which are found the comments of the twelfth and thirteenth century glossators. The results were assembled at the Institute for Advanced Study and were printed later as Publication No. 1 of the Institute of International Air Law at McGill University. The major findings are today still believed to be sound: (*a*) that the "Cujus est solum" maxim itself was not a Roman law text; (*b*) that, however, Roman and successor legal systems did, in fact, create and regulate exclusive rights giving the landowner either use or ownership in usable space above his land. Thus the State asserted airspace sovereignty many centuries before the age of flight.

THE PRIMARY RULE of international air law[1] was first formally stated in Article 1 of the Convention Relating to the Regulation of Aerial Navigation, signed at Paris 1919: "The High Contracting Parties recognise that every Power has complete and exclusive sovereignty over the air space above its territory . . ."

---

[1] *International Air Law* may be defined as that body of legal principles and rules included within the scope of both international law and air law. To apply this definition it is necessary to state the scope of both.

"*International Law* governs relations between independent states. The rules of law binding upon states, therefore, emanate from their own free will as expressed in conventions or by usages generally accepted as expressing principles of law and established in order to regulate the relations between

The same rule was restated in Article I of the Convention on International Civil Aviation, signed at Chicago in 1944 and now in effect: "The contracting States recognize that every State has complete and exclusive sovereignty over the airspace above its territory."

Both of these articles constitute international recognition of a prior existing rule. Both assert in substance that sovereign states held territorial rights in the airspace above their surface territories irrespective of and prior to either of the conventions. For the student of legal history this raises an immediate problem: How long in fact had states exercised sovereign rights in space?

The answer is that such rights had been claimed and exercised as far back into history as proof may exist of the creation and protection by state law of exclusive private property rights in such space.

II

Protection and regulation of exclusive public or individual rights in areas used by the citizens of a state are functions of that state in the exercise of its territorial sovereignty. Such rights can continue to exist only by direct or implied act or consent of the state. The rule was well stated in the following language by one of the pioneers in the development of air law: "The State cannot give the landowner a right of property or of use over the airspace above his land, if that airspace is not submitted to its sovereignty. Consequently, by giving such a right to the landowner, the State says that it considers itself sovereign over the airspace."[2]

---

these co-existing independent communities or with a view to the achievement of common aims." *The S. S. Lotus* (France v. Turkey), Permanent Court of International Justice, Judgment 9, Sept. 7, 1927, Ser. A, No. 10, p. 18; Manley O. Hudson, *World Court Reports*, Washington, Carnegie Endowment for International Peace, 1934–43, Vol. 2, (1935), p. 35. For the author's definition of *Air Law* see AIR LAW—A FIELD FOR INTERNATIONAL THINKING, see *supra* at 15.

[2] Johanna F. Lycklama a Nijeholt, *Air Sovereignty*, The Hague, M. Nijhoff, 1910, p. 34.

See also: Ernest Zitelman, "Luftschiffahrtrecht," *Zeitschrift für internationales privat — und offentliches Recht*, Vol. 19, 1909, pp. 476–477; Dionisio Anzilotti, "La condizione giuridica dello spazio atmosferico nei rapporti internazionali e le sue consequenze in ordine alla navigazione aerea," Congresso gioridico internazionale per il regolamento dalla locomozione aerea, 31 maggio—1–2 giugno 1910, *Atti e relazioni*, Verona, Società tipografica cooperativa, 1910, p. 163; statement of Sir Erle Richards (then Chichele Professor of International Law and Diplomacy at Oxford) in his lecture, *Sovereignty over the Air*, Oxford, Clarendon Press, 1912, where he said (p. 12): ". . . of course, the recognition of the rights of individual proprietors 'usque ad coelum' involves the assertion of State sovereignty to the same extent.";

Much of the confused thinking in dealing with air law problems in the past has stemmed from failure to realize that land and usable space above are legally indivisible and necessarily constitute a single social unit. Usable space is not an appurtenance to the land below but with such land forms the basic integrated sphere of human activity and has been for that reason treated by states as part of their territory. A state may not impose sanctions within the territory of another state.[3] If a state is found to be protecting exclusive rights in a fixed area through its governmental processes, the area concerned must be within its own territory, for a state cannot legally impose its will in any area to the exclusion of all other states if such area is outside its accepted and recognized territory.[4] The only valid exceptions to this rule are found in acts committed in war time.

International Law Association, *Report of the Committee upon Aviation* to the 28th Conference, Madrid, 1913, p. 532, which took a similar position; Albert G. de La Pradelle. "De l'origine de la maxime *cujus solum, ejus coelum,*" *Revue générale de droit aérien*, Vol. 1, 1932, p. 294; Antonio Ambrosini, *Instituzioni di diritto aeronautico*, 2nd ed., Rome, Ufficio editoriale aeronautico, 1940, p. 67.

As to territorial sovereignty in Roman times, Fiore, discussing the "Right of Imperium" noted that "Roman jurists considered the right of imperium as so exclusively territorial that they defined territory as the whole of the lands over which command and coercive power could be exercised," citing Digest L. 16.239.8 as follows: "'Territorium' est universitas agrorum intra fines cuiusque civitatis: quod ab eo dictum quidam aiunt, quod magistratus eius loci intra eos fines terrendi, id est summovendi ius habent." [Pasquale Fiore, *International Law Codified and its Legal Sanction . . .*, translated from 5th Italian edition by Edwin M. Borchard, New York, Baker Voorhis, 1918, Bk I, Title X, Sec. 247 (p. 174 of translation)]. Modern research as to treaties indicates that national rights (external sovereignty) as against all the world had been developed in Roman times on a territorial basis to a much greater extent than usually realized. [Coleman Phillipson, *The International Law and Custom of Ancient Greece and Rome*. London, Macmillan, 1911, Vol. 1, pp. 295–298.]

[3] "Now the first and foremost restriction imposed by international law upon a State is that—failing the existence of a permissive rule to the contrary—it may not exercise its power in any form in the territory of another State." *The S. S. Lotus*, supra. (It is not believed that subsequent discussion in this opinion, applicable to the particular facts before the Court, in any way derogates from the basic rule as stated above.)

[4] It is no exception to this rule that certain kinds of national jurisdiction have been recognized on the high seas, particularly to suppress piracy and to provide for the more complete enforcement of certain national laws, such as smuggling and customs regulations. ". . . all governments, for the purpose of self-protection in time of war or for the prevention of frauds on its revenue, exercise an authority beyond [territorial waters]." *Manchester* v. *Massachusetts*, 139 U.S. 240, p. 258 (1891).

See also: *The Apollon, Edon. Claimant*, 9 Wheaton (22 U.S.) 362, p. 371 (1824); Philip G. Jessup, *The Law of Territorial Waters and Maritime*

For the purpose of this study it will be sufficient if the existence of public and private rights in space above lands on the surface is traced back to Roman times. A careful examination of the rules of property found in Roman law and of those later rules which are evidenced by the Latin, though non-Roman, maxim *Cujus est solum, ejus est usque ad coelum* will demonstrate that at least since Roman times states have continuously recognized, regulated, and protected rights in space held by the owner or occupant of lands on the surface below. These rules of property are rules of private law, but for the reason indicated above the existence of such private rights constitutes the major and, in fact, the conclusive proof that states have always claimed and exercised territorial sovereignty in space above their surface territory to the extent needed to make valid the public and private rights in space mentioned above.

III

As early as Roman times the law recognized exclusive rights, both public and private, in space in connection with the use and enjoyment of the land below. The existence of these rights with the remedies provided for their protection or regulation demonstrates that Roman law did not hesitate to provide the same degree of state control in areas above the surface as it did on the surface itself wherever and whenever deemed advisable or necessary.

Roman law was essentially practical. It dealt with conditions under which man lived, the social problems that arose from day to day, the extent to which the processes of law were required and were applicable to settle disputed points. It recognized and dealt primarily with property questions. It was particularly concerned with interests in land and its use. The writings of the great Roman jurists show the utter fallacy of attempting to deal with public or private rights in land as if such land were merely a flat surface entirely dissociated from space above.

Roman law recognized that space is the reservoir for the air which man breathes and is the access to the heavens from which comes the light and heat of the sun; that man uses parts of space when he walks on a public road or private path, or when he builds a house or grows

Jurisdiction, New York, G. A. Jennings, 1927, Chap. 5, pp. 241–276; Charles Cheney Hyde, *International Law*, 2d rev. ed., Boston, Little Brown, 1945, Vol. 1, Secs. 144–144a, pp. 460–462, Secs. 235–235a, pp. 777–785; Charles Evans Hughes, "Recent Questions and Negotiations," *American Journal of International Law*, Vol. 18, 1924, pp. 229–245 (address before the Council on Foreign Relations, New York, January 23, 1924.)

crops or trees. Space above the lands of the Roman state was recognized as an integral part of the habitable earth.

Modern writers are generally in accord that Roman law thus recognized and protected rights in space. Unanimity of opinion does not, however, exist as to whether such rights were rights of complete ownership or merely rights to so much of the airspace as needed for the enjoyment of the surface property below.

Roby, writing of the classical Roman law in the time of Cicero and the Antonines (three to six centuries prior to the Justinian Institutes and Digest), said of ownership ("dominium") that it was the full right of doing whatever one liked with a thing and that in substance the owner of land had the full and free use of all above and below his land.[5] Roby also held that ownership included control over lands or buildings and freedom from interference with the air above and the ground below.[6]

Buckland, writing of the Roman law of Justinian as well as of the classical period, was of the opinion that, had the Romans been forced to face modern problems, they would probably have held that there was no upper limit of ownership, and that rules for height of buildings and for overhanging trees were merely limitations of ownership in the general interest.[7]

Goudy felt that had the Roman jurist been compelled to deal with the flight of aircraft, rights of property in the "coelum" (airspace) would have been sufficient to prevent air transit over a man's ground and that interdicts would have been granted to prevent such transit if damages were caused or threatened.[8]

After an independent re-examination of the sources in the Corpus Juris Civilis to determine the rights in Roman law of the landowner in airspace above his property, Lardone said: "Has the landowner any rights in the air column above his property according to Roman law? The general conclusion reached is as follows: 1. According to the wording of the Sources, the landowner is given expressly by Roman law the control of the air column above his property at low altitudes, for instance, the height of buildings, of trees, etc. 2.

---

[5] Henry John Roby, *Roman Private Law in the Times of Cicero and of the Antonines*, Cambridge, Cambridge Univ. Press, 1902, Vol. 1, p. 414.

[6] *Ibid.* p. 498.

[7] William Warwick Buckland, *The Main Institutions of Roman Private Law*. Cambridge Univ. Press, 1931, pp. 103–104.

[8] Henry Goudy, "Two Ancient Brocards," in: *Essays in Legal History read before the International Congress of Historical Studies held in London in 1913*, edited by Paul Vinogradoff. London/New York, Oxford Univ. Press, 1913, p. 231.

According to the *spirit* of the Sources, such private control can be extended to *any altitude*."[9]

De Montmorency held that under Roman law the state enjoyed a right of eminent domain in space above Roman soil and that control of the airspace was retained by the Roman state insofar as the airspace was not essential to the enjoyment of the land beneath.[10] He hence disagreed with Roby as to the extent of the right of the individual in the airspace, but insisted even more strongly that the state claimed and controlled such airspace.

Von Jhering, in Germany upon a re-examination of the original sources, concluded that the owner of the soil was also owner of the airspace above, but only to the extent required to satisfy his practical needs, and that Roman jurists would not have accepted such an "abuse of logic" as property in space without limit.[11]

Both Guibé[12] and Sauze,[13] in France, denied that Roman law created rights of ownership in the airspace but admitted that the subjacent owner had a right exercisable at any time to build up to an indefinite height or otherwise enjoy the use of his land and have such use protected by law.

Pampaloni and Bonfante, in Italy, each made an independent re-examination of the original sources. Pampaloni was of the opinion that in Roman law the owner of the soil had the exclusive power over contiguous airspace, which at times appeared equivalent to ownership.[14]
Bonfante, in one of the ablest presentations of the entire question thus

---

[9] Francesco Lardone, "Airspace Rights in Roman Law," *Air Law Review*, Vol. 2, 1931, p. 455. Lardone was at that time Associate Professor of Roman Law at the Catholic University in Washington, D. C.

[10] James E. G. de Montmorency, "The Control of the Air Spaces," in: Grotius Society, *Problems of the War*, London, Sweet & Maxwell, 1917, Vol. 3, p. 67.

[11] Rudolf von Jhering, "Zur Lehre von den Beschränkungen des Grundeigenthümers in Interesse der Nachbarn," *Jhering Jarhbücher für die Dogmatik des Bürgerlichen Rechts*, Vol. 6, 1863. Translated by O. Meulenaere under title "Des restrictions imposées aux propriétaires fonciers dans l'intérêt des voisins," in Rudolf von Jhering, *Oeuvres choisies*, Paris, A. Marescq, 1893, Vol. 2, pp. 101–144.

[12] Henri Guibé, *Essai sur la navigation aérienne en droit interne et en droit international*, Caen, E. Lanier, 1912, pp. 35–42.

[13] Eugène Sauze, *Les Questions de responsabilité en matière d'aviation*, Paris, M. Giard & E. Brière, 1916, pp. 23–55. For general comment on this subject, see also: Clement L. Bouvé, "Private Ownership of Airspace," *Air Law Review*, Vol. I, 1930, pp. 232–257, 376–400.

[14] Muzio Pampaloni, "Sulla condizione giuridica dello spazio aereo e del sottosuolo nel diritto romano e odierno," *Archivo giuridico*, Vol. 48, 1892, p. 59.

far available, also concluded that Roman law gave limited rights of ownership in the airspace above.[15]

All of these authorities thus emphasized the territorial status of Roman airspace and the continuing sovereign control by the Roman state above the surface of the earth. The landowner was held to be protected by the state at least to the extent of the use of so much of the airspace as might from time to time be needed in connection with the enjoyment of the surface property below.

IV

An examination of the pertinent original texts of the Institutes, the Digest, and the Code of Justinian[16] may be useful as a background for the comments of the learned writers quoted in the previous section. Roman law dealt with interests in the airspace over public lands, over non-commercial lands, such as religious property and tombs, and over private lands.

Public lands included highways which were the property of the

---

[15] Pietro Bonfante, *Corso di diritto romano*, Rome, Attilio Sampaolasi, 1926–28, Vol. 2, Pts. 1 & 2, Chap. 12, pp. 218–229.

No serious present day analysis of the difference between sovereign state rights and private property rights in space is complete without the most careful consideration of Bonfante's arguments. He concludes in substance that sovereign state rights may extend upwards without limit so far as human dominion may be exercised, but that private property rights must have an economic basis and that the upper limit of private space ownership is at the point where such ownership ceases to have any economic interest or purpose for the landowner.

[16] Justinian ruled as emperor of the eastern Roman Empire with its capital at Constantinople, A.D. 527–565. In A.D. 528 he appointed ten commissioners to draft a new "Code" covering the "constitutions" or imperial enactments. This was completed the following year. In 530 a committee of sixteen compilers headed by Tribonian commenced the compilation of the great mass of Roman law, then contained in some two thousand books. The compilation was completed in 533 and thereafter known as the "Digest". It includes extracts based on the writings of thirty-nine jurists—those of Ulpian and Paul constituting about one-half of the work. Justinian also ordered the compilation of a more elementary work, particularly for the use of law students, now known as the "Institutes." Both the Digest and the Institutes became law December 30 A.D. 533. In 534 a new Code was prepared and the Code of 529 withdrawn. The subsequent enactments of Justinian, between 535 and 564, were afterwards collected and are known as the "Novellae." The Institutes, the Digest, the Code and the Novellae together constitute the "Corpus Juris Civilis," In this paper all references to the Corpus Juris Civilis, unless otherwise noted, refer to the Krueger-Mommsen edition, Berlin, Weidmannos, 1915–1928.

state though open to general use.[17] The original Roman texts admit of no doubt that the state retained control of the airspace over such public places to an indefinite height and prohibited all interference. The following quotation from Paul (Digest VIII.2.1) is conclusive:

> If public ground or a public road comes in the way, this does not hinder the servitude of a *via*, or an *actus* or a right to raise the height of a building, but it hinders a right to insert a beam, or to have an overhanging roof or other projecting structure, also one to the discharge of a flow or drip of rainwater, because the sky over the ground referred to ought to be unobscured.[18]

The word "sky" as translated by Monro is "coelum" in the original Latin of the Digest and the word "unobscured" is "liberum." The latter part of this quotation is better understood when translated "because the airspace over the land referred to ought to be free." Of this text, Goudy said: ". . . which means, I take it, that the airspace above the road should be free to all, like the road itself."[19] This is another way of saying that the airspace has the same legal status as the surface below.[20] The word "coelum" often appears as "caelum".

---

[17] William Warwick Buckland, *A Text-book of Roman Law from Augustus to Justinian*, Cambridge, Cambridge Univ. Press, 1921, p. 184.

[18] Charles Henry Monro, tr., *The Digest of Justinian*, Cambridge, Cambridge Univ. Press, 1904–09, Vol. 2, p. 68. A *via* was a general right of way, while an *actus* was usually a right of way for vehicles. See: Thomas Collett Sandars, ed., *The Institutes of Justinian*, London/New York/Bombay, Longmans Green, 1903, p. 118, translating Institutes II.3.Pr.

The Latin test of Digest VIII.2.1 reads: "PAULUS *libro vicensimo primo ad edictum* Si intercedat solum publicum vel via publica, neque itineris actusve neque altius tollendi servitutes impedit: sed immittendi protegendi prohibendi, item fluminum et stillicidiorum servitutem impedit, quia caelum, quod supra id solum intercedit, liberum esse debet."

For further discussion of this passage, see: Bonfante, *op. cit.* pp. 220, 221; Bouvé, *op. cit.* pp. 244, 246; Goudy, *op. cit.* pp. 230, 231; de La Pradelle, *op. cit.* pp. 295, 297, 300; Lardone, *op. cit.* p. 458; Arnold D. McNair, *The Law of the Air*, London, Butterworth, 1932, p. 14; de Montmorency, *op. cit.* p. 65; Richards, *op. cit.* p. 11; Edward C. Sweeney, "Adjusting the Conflicting Interests of Landowner and Aviator in Anglo-American Law," *Journal of Air Law and Commerce*, Vol. 3, 1932, pp. 365, 369. See also: Henri Guibé, *op. cit.* p. 36.

[19] Goudy, *op. cit.* pp. 230–231.

[20] Professor Dionisio Anzilotti, later a member and president of the World Court, prepared a paper for the Verona 1910 conference entitled "The Legal Status of Atmospheric Space in International Relations and its Consequences in Regard to Air Navigation" ["La condizione giuridica dello spazio atmosferico . . .," *op. cit.*]. In this paper [p. 162] discussing Digest VIII.3.1 and Digest XLIII.24.22.4, he noted the existence of a "simple and rational" principle affirmed by the Roman texts that atmospheric space follows the legal status of the land.

Lands which had been given a religious character, also tombs, could not be dealt with commercially as private property.[21] The air-space over such lands was (as in the case of public property) considered as having the legal status of the surface, and could be protected by legal process against private encroachment. For this purpose the interdict "quod vi aut clam" was used in pre-Justinian legal procedure. This interdict was a special order or decree of the praetor obtainable to stop work in progress, to undo what had been done, or to obtain compensation for injury when public lands, religious lands, tombs, or private lands of the plaintiff were affected.[22] This interdict was in use at least as early as the time of Cicero. Its initial beginning words "quod vi aut clam . . ." have been translated as "Anything that has been done by force or stealth in the matter now in question you are to restore, if it is not more than a year since there was the power of suing."[23] "Force" was the doing of a forbidden thing, and "stealth" was implied in keeping the action complained of from the knowledge of the party concerned.

Book XLIII of the Digest is devoted to the various interdicts, and Title 24 to the interdict "quod vi aut clam." As in many other parts of the Digest, statements of substantive law are included with statements of applicable procedure in case of a breach of recognized rights. So, in this case, Venuleius states both the rights to be protected and the remedy (Digest XLIII.24.22.4):

> If a person shall have built a projection, or allowed rain-water to fall from a roof, into a sepulcher, even though he may not have touched the grave monument itself, he can rightly be summoned for action against a sepulcher by violence or stealth, since not only is the actual place of interment part of the sepulcher, but also all the sky above it; and therefore he can be summoned on the charge of violation of a sepulcher.[24]

---

[21] Buckland, *Text-book of Roman Law, op, cit.* p. 185.

[22] For general description of this interdict and its application in classical Roman law, see: Roby, *op. cit.* Vol. 1, pp. 521–525. See also: Sandars, *op. cit.* pp. 488–489.

[23] Roby, *op. cit.* Vol. 1, p. 521.

[24] The Latin text reads: "Si quis proiectum aut stillicidium in sepulchrum immiserit, etiamsi ipsum monumentum non tangeret, recte cum eo agi, quod in sepulchro vi aut clam factum sit, quia sepulchri sit non solum is locus, qui recipiat humationem, sed omne etiam supra id caelum; eoque nomine etiam sepulchri violati agi posse."

For other translations, see: Lardone, *op. cit.* p. 459; Sweeney, *op. cit.* p. 366.

For further discussion of this passage, see: Anzilotti, *op. cit.* p. 162; Bonfante, *op. cit.* p. 220, 221; Bouvé, *op. cit.* pp. 234, 244; Goudy, *op. cit.* p. 230, de La Pradelle, *op. cit.* pp. 295, 297; Lardone, *op. cit.* pp. 459, 461; McNair, *op. cit.* p. 14; de Montmorency, *op. cit.* p. 65; Sweeney, *op. cit.* pp. 366, 369.

Again the Latin word "coelum" is used and is generally translated as "sky." If the word "airspace" is used in the translation instead of the word "sky", the passage has an even more accurate meaning. Of this use of the interdict, Roby says: "Any work *on or connected with land* comes within the interdict . . . ; turning the rainfall on to a tomb or making a projection over it, even though it be not touched, for *all above the tomb up to the sky belongs to it.*" (italics supplied)[25] Goudy notes tht the interdict is available in this case "just as much as if the *solum* itself had been encroached upon."[26] It is evident from this citation that airspace to an indefinite height above the tomb was considered as an integral part of the lands covered by the tomb and was so protected by Roman law.

V

Usable space over private lands was likewise protected from encroachment. The only matter not entirely clear is the height above the surface to which the landowner had the right to control the airspace in connection with his use of the surface. The power of the state to grant, limit, or protect private interests as rights in this airspace was not questioned and was exercised without limit as and when the state so determined.

Ulpian, writing on the special prohibitory interdict available with reference to the cutting of trees,[27] quotes the form of the interdict used when a tree from one property hangs over a *building* on a neighbor's property (Digest XLIII.27.1.Pr.):

> The Praetor says: If a tree hangs from your buildings over his, and it is your fault for not cutting it, then I forbid the use of force to prevent him from cutting that tree and keeping it for himself.[28]

Evidently a decree similar to a modern injunction would be issued to protect the property rights of the neighbor in space over his buildings at whatever height the trespassing tree might be. For such purpose the neighbor could enter on your property and cut down your tree and haul it away protected by the interdict.

---

[25] Roby, *op. cit.* Vol. 1, pp. 521–522.

[26] Goudy, *op. cit.* p. 230.

[27] Title 27 of Book XLIII of the Digest is entitled "De arboribus caedendis." For general discussion of this interdict, see: Roby, *op. cit.* Vol. 1, p. 508.

[28] The Latin text reads: "ULPIANUS *libro septuagensimo primo ad edictum* Ait praetor: 'Quae arbor ex aedibus tuis in aedes illius impendet, si per te stat, quo minus eam adimas, tunc, quo minus illi eam arborem adimere sibique habere liceat, vim fieri veto,'"

For discussion of various parts of Digest XLIII.27.1, see: Bouvé, *op. cit.* p. 246; de La Pradelle, *op. cit.* p. 296; Lardone, *op. cit.* pp. 459, 465; McNair, *op. cit.* p. 13; de Montmorency, *op. cit.* p. 63; Sweeney, *op. cit.* p. 369.

Ulpian continues, quoting the second form of the interdict applicable to *cultivated land* (Digest XLIII.27.1.7):

> Further the praetor says: If it is your fault for not trimming to within fifteen feet of the ground a tree which hangs from your field onto his, then I forbid the use of force to prevent him from trimming it and keeping the wood for himself.[29]

The difference between the two uses of the interdict is thus explained in the text (Digest XLIII.27.1.8 & 9):

> The praetor says also, and the Law of the Twelve Tables is to the same effect, that tree branches up to fifteen feet should be trimmed; this was done to prevent harm to the neighboring estate by the shade of a tree. This is the difference between the two heads of the interdict; if a tree hangs over buildings it should be cut down; but if it hangs over a field, it should be only trimmed up to fifteen feet of the ground.[30]

The latter text is particularly interesting as illustrating how ancient was the appreciation by Roman law of the need to protect the landowner's interest in the space over his fields, for the Twelve Tables came into force perhaps as early as 450 B.C.

These passages as to the cutting of trees have been variously construed.[31] But no matter what the proper construction may be, it is certain that the landowner was given control of airspace over his field up to fifteen feet along the boundaries of his field, and was not prohibited from otherwise using the space over his field. When a projection over a building was involved, the rights of the owners of the building in the space above were not limited. In whatever manner these passages be construed they are clear evidence of a continuing legislative control of the airspace by the state and an acknowledged power of the state to adjust airspace rights between various landowners.

An interesting and much discussed text from Ulpian (Digest VIII.5.8.5) indicates that the lessee of a cheese factory was prohibited from permitting smoke to go up and into higher adjoining houses.

---

[29] The Latin text reads: "Deinde ait praetor: 'Quae arbor ex agro tuo in agrum illius impendet, si per te stat, quo minus pedes quindecim a terra eam altius coerceas, tunc, quo minus illi ita coercere lignaque sibi habere liceat, vim fieri veto.'" See also Note 28 *supra*.

[30] The Latin text reads: "Quod ait praetor, et lex duodecim tabularum efficere voluit, ut quindecim pedes altius rami arboris circumcidantur: et hoc ideirco effectum est, ne umbra arboris vicino praedio noceret. Differentia duorum capitum interdicti haec est: si quidem arbor aedibus impendeat, succidi eam praecipitur, si vero agro impendeat, tantum usque ad quindecim pedes a terra coerceri." See also Note 28 *supra*.

[31] See Note 28 *supra*.

This was apparently considered a trespass on another's property by interfering with the airspace above it.[32]

A little discussed text, but one of great importance, is also from Ulpian (Digest IX.2.29.1). It holds that in case of a roof from one house extending over another house, the owner of the latter should not break off the offending projection, but should bring an action based on the fact that the owner of the projection had no right to have such a projection. This is another case of substantive law stated in connection with a discussion of remedies or procedure.[33]

Other passages of the Corpus Juris Civilis throw further light on the interests of individual landowners in space. Most of these additional texts have to do with servitudes held by the owner of one "praedium"[34] or "estate" on another estate. The servitudes affecting land were of two kinds, "urban" where buildings were involved (even though in the country), and "rustic" as to cultivated lands.

In Book VIII of the Digest, on Servitudes, Paul is quoted as follows (VIII.2.24):

> Whoever has a building which is, with good right, superposed on another may lawfully build on the top of his own structure as high as he pleases, so long as this does not (tend to) impose on the buildings underneath a more burdensome servitude than they ought to have to bear."[35]

---

[32] The Latin text reads: "Aristo Corellio Vitali respondit non putare se ex taberna casiaria fumum in superiora aedificia iure immitti posse, nisi ei rei servitutem talem admittit. idemqui ait: et ex superiore in inferiora non aquam, non quid aliud immitti licet: in suo enim ali hactenus facere licet, qua tenus nihil in alienun immittat, fumi autem sicut aquae esse immissionem: posse igitur superiorem cum inferiore agere ius illi non esse id ita facere."

For further discussion of this passage, see: de La Pradelle, *op. cit.* p. 2951; Lardone, *op. cit.* p. 458.

[33] The Latin text reads: "Si protectum meum, quod supra domum tuam nullo iure habebam, reccidisses, posse me tecum damni iniuria agere Proculus scribit: debuisti enim mecum ius mihi non esse protectum habere agere: nec esse aequum damnum me pati reccisis a te meis tignis."

See particularly: Bonfante, *op. cit.* pp. 221, 222, 223.

[34] For discussion as to translation of the word "praedium" and generally as to servitudes, see: Buckland, *Text-Book of Roman Law, op. cit.* pp. 258–264; Sandars, *op. cit.* pp. 118–119.

[35] Monro, *op. cit.* Vol. 2, p. 75. See also: Lardone, *op. cit.* p. 458, for a different translation.

The Latin text reads: "PAULUS *libro quinto decimo ad Sabinum* Cuius aedificium iure superius est, ei ius est in infinitio supra suum aedificium imponere, dum inferiora aedificia non graviore servitute oneret quam pati debent."

For further discussion of this passage, see: de La Pradelle, *op. cit.* p. 295; Lardone, *op. cit.* p. 458; McNair, *op. cit.* p. 14.

This text is particularly interesting in that the original Latin of the Digest uses the words "in infinito" (translated by Monro "as high as he pleases"). The same passage was translated by Lardone as "up to the skies." Obviously it is the clear meaning of the original Latin text that there is no legal limit to which the building can be built. This in turn must mean that the state was prepared to enforce its law and exercise its regulatory and territorial powers up to whatever height the owner of the building might be able to build.

The right of the landowner to build up as far as he wishes is even more succinctly stated in a text from the Justinian Code (Code III.34.8):

> One is in no wise prevented from constructing his building higher provided his building acknowledges no servitude.[36]

This is a most important text. As will be noted, certain quotations from the Digest to be cited hereafter might leave the impression, when considered alone, that building once constructed could never be raised except by permission of adjoining property owners. That this provision of the Code was in fact based on prior recognized Roman law, and was not merely a new legislative act by Justinian, is evidenced by the following citation from Ulpian (Digest VIII.2.9):

> Where a man, by raising the height of his own house, cuts off the flow of light to that of his neighbour, but is not subject to a servitude in respect of the latter, there is no right of action against him.[37]

Among the urban servitudes stated in both the Institutes (II.3.1) and the Digest (VIII.2.3) is that by which one building may be encumbered by a servitude preventing its being raised and thereby affect the light of a neighboring building. Some of the passages on this subject are ambiguous and have led to various conclusions by learned writers. In some cases it has been thought that general building restrictions may have been enforced by Roman law which denied the right of the landowner to raise a building above the height first used, even in the absence of a servitude.[38]

---

[36] The Latin text reads: "Altius quidem aedificia tollere, si domus servitutem non debeat, dominus eius minime prohibetur. in pariete vero tuo si fenestram Iulianus vi vel clam fecisse convincatur, sumptibus suis opus tollere et integrum parietem restituere compellitur."
For further discussion of this passage, see: de La Pradelle, *op. cit.* p. 301; Lardone, *op. cit.* p. 458; McNair, *op. cit.* p. 16; Sweeney, *op. cit.* p. 366.

[37] Monro, *op. cit.* Vol. 2, pp. 69–70. The Latin text reads: "ULPIANUS *libro quinquagensimo tertio ad edictum* Cum eo, qui tollendo obscurat vicini aedes, quibus non serviat, nulla competit actio." For further discussion of this passage, see: Sweeney, *op. cit.* p. 366.

[38] These are the passages that led de Montmorency [*op. cit.* p. 64] to the view that anything in the nature of airspace other than the airspace contained in the building originally erected remained the property of the state in Roman

As to building on vacant ground, the Digest was clear. For example, Papirius Justus is quoted to the following effect (Digest VIII.2.14):

> The Emperors Antoninus Augustus and Severus Augustus declared by rescript, with reference to vacant ground over which no one has a servitude, that the owner, or anyone else with his consent, is free to build on it, if he leaves clear the statutable space between the spot and the neighbouring block.[39]

Some difficulty has, however, been caused by certain texts regarding rebuilding, such as that in Digest XLIII.24.21.2 which directs that in case of new work (rebuilding) "measurement should be made both of the ground and of the airspace [coelum]."[40] Obviously this is a statement of a rule indicating that new work should not occupy airspace previously unoccupied. To the same effect is the following statement from Ulpian (Digest VIII.2.11):

> Where a man wishes to block out his neighbour's lights or to construct anything at all which interferes with their convenience, he must bear in mind that he is bound to observe the form and position of the original buildings. 1. If you have got no agreement with your neighbour as to how high a building which you have taken in hand to construct may be raised, you can have an arbiter appointed."[41]

---

law. Thereafter, according to him, the height of the building could be increased only with the consent of the state or the neighbors.

Sandars notes [*op. cit.* p. 121] certain provisions in Tacitus and Suetonius as to specific building restrictions and concludes that according to the provisions of the Digest neighbors could waive the restrictions.

Roby admits, [*op cit.* Vol. 1, p. 500, note 1] that it is "not easy to explain why the exercise of any owner's ordinary rights [to build up] should be regarded as special privilege, and as the result of a neighbour's being under a servitude."

[39] Moore, *op. cit.* Vol. 2, p. 71. The Latin text reads: "PAPIRUS IUSTUS *libro primo de constitutionibus* Imperatores Antoninus et Verus Augusti rescripserunt in area, quae nulli servitutem debet, posse dominum ve lalium voluntate eius aedificare intermisso legitimo spatio a vicina insula."

For further discussion of this passage, see: Lardone, *op. cit.* p. 461; Sweeney, *op. cit.* p. 369.

[40] The Latin text reads: "In opere novo tam soli quam caeli mensura facienda est."

For further discussion of this passage, see: Bonfante, *op. cit.* p. 220; Goudy, *op. cit.* p. 231; de La Pradelle, *op. cit.* p. 301; Lardone, *op. cit.* p. 461; McNair, *op. cit.* pp. 14, 15; Sweeney, *op. cit.* p. 369.

[41] Monro, *op. cit.* Vol. 2, p. 70. The Latin text reads: "ULPIANUS *libro primo de officio consulis* Qui luminibus vicinorum officere aliudve quid facere contra commodum eorum vellet, scient se forman ac statum antiquorum aedificiorum custodire debere. 1. Si inter te et vicinum tuum non convenit, ad quam altitudinem extelli aedificia, quae facere instituisti, oporteat, arbitrum accipere poteris."

It is the belief of the present author that the two texts last quoted were from passages that must have originally referred to certain building restrictions, not matters of general law. This is conjecture, based on the contradiction between these passages and others cited. If any general contradiction did exist, it was legislatively removed by the Code. The Justinian Code, as we now have it, was completed after the Digest and Institutes. It contained legislative matter of certain of the earlier emperors as well as those of Justinian. The clear and unequivocal provisions of the Code as cited above (Code III.23.8—for Latin text, see Note 36 *supra*.), permitting unlimited building in the absence of a servitude is a re-enactment of one of the constitutions of the Emperor Diocletian in the year A.D. 293.[42] This date is later than the writings of most of the jurists included in the Digest. The particular provision may have been re-enacted by Justinian to obviate any confusion.

In no event, however, does this ambiguity change the legal position so far as the authority and power of the state is concerned. Under one interpretation, the state is presumed to have fixed the height of buildings when they were first erected and to have retained control of any increase which the owner thereafter wished to make. Under the other interpretation the private landowner was given by the state either full ownership or control of usable space above his building, rights of occupancy and protection from interference—that is, rights protected by the state, which could be limited only by the landowner submitting his building to a servitude for the benefit of a building owned by someone else.

VI

The conclusion reached in the last section as to the existence under Roman law of public and individual rights in space over Roman lands are neither contradicted nor affected by other Roman texts as to the "air" being "common to all." The distinction between "air" and "airspace" was as clear in Roman law as it is today. The legal status of the air (or atmosphere) which men breathed was not the same as that of the space through which the air circulated.

The compilers of the Justinian Institutes divided "things" into two general classes—those capable of private ownership and those not capable of private ownership. Of the latter it was said that some things by the "law of nature" belonged to all men, some to the public, some to no one, and some to corporate bodies or associations (Institutes

---

[42] Lardone, *op. cit.* p. 458, note 6.

II.1.Pr.).[43] Then follows the famous passage in the Institutes which has been quoted in every modern discussion of the "freedom of the seas" or "freedom of the air" (Institutes II.1.1):

> By the law of nature these things are common to mankind—the air, running water, the sea, and consequently the shores of the sea. No one, therefore, is forbidden to approach the seashore, provided that he respects habitations, monuments, and buildings, which are not, like the sea, subject only to the law of nations."[44]

The general principle stated in this passage was adopted from earlier texts of the Roman jurists, particularly the following from Marcian (Digest 1.8.2):

> Some things are by natural law common to all, some belong to a community (universitas), some to nobody, most things belong to individuals; and they are acquired by various titles in the respective cases. 1. To begin with, by natural law, the following are common to all: air, flowing water, the sea, and consequently the seashore.[45]

Celsus, writing of the circumstances under which pilings might be driven into the shores and the sea, remarked that "the use of the sea is common to all men, like that of the air," (Digest XLIII.8.3)[46]

---

[43] See: Buckland, *Text-book of Roman Law*, pp. 182–188; Sandars, *op. cit.* pp. 88–90; Rudolf Sohm, *The Institutes: A Textbook of the History and System of Roman Private Law*, translated by James Crawford Ledlie, 3d ed., Oxford, Clarendon Press, London/New York, H. Frowde, 1907, pp. 301–305.

[44] Sandars, *op. cit.* p. 9. The Latin text [quoted from Sandars, p. 90] reads: "Et quidem naturali jure communia sunt omnium haec; aer et aqua profluens et mare et per hoc litora maris. Nemo igitur ad litus maris accedere prohibetur, dum tamen villis et monumentis et aedificiis abstineat, quia non sunt juris gentium, sicut et mare."

For further discussion of this passage, see: Bouvé, *op. cit.* pp. 232, 244; de La Pradelle, *op. cit.* p. 295; Lardone, *op. cit.* p. 461; McNair, *op. cit.* p. 13; de Montmorency, *op. cit.* pp. 61, 65; Sweeney, *op. cit.* p. 368.

[45] Monro, *op. cit.* Vol. 1, pp. 39–40. The Latin text reads: "MARCIANUS *libro tertio instituionum* Quaedam naturali iure communia sunt omnium, quaedam universitatis, quaedam nullius, pleraque singulorum quae variis ex causis quique adquirunter. 1. Et quidem naturali iure omnium communia sunt illa; aer, aqua profluens, et mare, et per hoc litora maris."

For further discussion of this passage, see: Bouvé, *op. cit.* p. 232; de La Pradelle, *op. cit.* p. 295; Lardone, *op. cit.* p. 461; Sweeney, *op. cit.* p. 368; G. D. Valentine, "The Air—A Realm of Law," *Juridical Review*, Vol. 22, 1910, p. 17.

[46] The Latin text reads: "CELSUS *libro trigensimo nono digestorum* Litora, in quae populus Romanus imperium habet, populi Romani esse arbitrer: 1. Maris communem usum omnibus hominibus, ut aeris, iactasque in id pilas eius esse qui iecerit; sed id concedendum non esse, si deterior litoris marisve usus eo modo futurus sit."

For further discussion of this passage, see: Bouvé, *op. cit.* p. 232; de La Pradelle, *op. cit.* p. 295; Lardone, *op. cit.* p. 461; Sweeney, *op. cit.* p. 368.

Ulpian, discussing the question as to whether a man could prevent fishing in the sea in front of his house, had said that "the sea is common to all as well as the shores, just as the air," (Digest XLVII. 10.13.7).[47]

In each of these passages the Latin word used is "aer." This word was adopted into the Latin without change in spelling or meaning from the Greek. It is continuously used to refer to the air we breathe—to distinguish the gaseous lower atmosphere from the pure "aether" above.[48] Classical Latin is replete with instances of the use of the word "aer" as one of the elements—the air needed to sustain life. Cicero for example said: "The earth is entirely surrounded by this life-giving and breathable element, of which the name is the air [aer], a Greek word, but accepted by us through use, common in Latin."[49]

The Roman jurists of the classical period, as well as the compilers of the Justinian Digest and Institutes, usually distinguished between the words "aer," as the atmosphere we breathe, and "coelum," as the area (sky or airspace) in which the air circulates. None of the Roman texts ever refer to the "coelum" as being "common to all," and therefore not capable of becoming private property. As will appear from the passages cited in the previous section, when space was to be measured for inclusion in a new building (so as to insure against infringement of a neighbor's rights) the word "coelum" was used, not "aer."[50] When the law required space over public ground or a highway to be kept free and unobstructed, the word "coelum" was again used;[51] also when referring to the space to be protected over a tomb as being part of the tomb itself.[52] "Coelum" (airspace) was subject to private and exclusive rights. "Aer" (air) was common to all men. There was no confusion. One represented an area and the other the element used for breathing.[53]

---

[47] The Latin text reads: ". . . et . . . mare commune omnium est et litora, sicuti aer . . ."

For further discussion of this passage, see: Bouvé, *op. cit.* p. 232; de La Pradelle, *op. cit.* p. 295, 299; Lardone, *op. cit.* p. 461; Sweeney, *op. cit.* p. 368.

[48] Harper's *Latin Dictionary:* Forcellini, *Totius latinitatis lexicon.*

[49] "Terra circumfusa undique est hac animali spirabilique natura, cui nomen est aër, Graecum illud quidem, sed perceptum jam tamen usu a nostris; tritum est enim pro Latino, Cic. N.D. 2, 36, 91." Harper's *Latin Dictionary*, see under "Aer."

[50] See Note 36 *supra.*   [51] See Note 18 *supra.*   [52] See Note 24 *supra.*

[53] "It was the *aër*—the omnipresent medium, never at rest and incapable of appropriation—that was *res communis*. It was so because necessary for the life and health of all. But in contrast with it the *coelum* was *res soli* and capable more or less of appropriation by the owner of the soil . . . The common use of *aer* is indeed asserted by many passages in the Digest, but private ownership of the *coelum* is also asserted. There is no inconsistency.": Goudy, *op. cit.* pp. 231–232.

Few apparent exceptions to the carefully distinguished use of these two words have been found. Only one is of any importance. It has been curiously overlooked by the commentators. In the passage from the Digest cited above (Digest XLVII.10.13.7), Ulpian says:

> If however I prohibit anyone from fishing in front of my buildings or mansion, what should be said? Am I liable for damages or not? For indeed the sea is common to all as well as the shores, just as the air [aer], and it has often been ruled that one cannot be prevented from fishing: nor from bird catching, except that one may be prevented from entering another's field.[54]

This passage is often cited as evidence that rights of private property cannot exist on the shore and in the sea and that therefore Roman law denied exclusive fishing rights in the sea. Its application to air law, though somewhat incidental, must also be noted. Ulpian seems to use the word "aer" as applicable both to the gaseous air supporting the bird in flight and to the airspace through which the bird flew. He apparently holds that the flight of an arrow or other missile used to kill wild birds over lands not owned by the hunter did not constitute a trespass although trespass would occur if the hunter entered the lands. This passage is support for the views that space ownership rights in Roman law were limited to areas close to the surface, or that incidental and transitory interference with airspace above the landowner's property was not actionable, provided no real damage was caused, even though such space was part of the property. It has a legal effect

---

Sandars [op. cit. p. 91], discussing Institutes II.1.1—that the air and the sea were common to mankind—has no doubt that Roman law meant the air we breathe when using the word "aer," for he notes that "a man may inhale the air or float his ship on any part of the sea."

Lardone [op. cit. pp. 461–462], notes that the glossators and commentators gave no particular explanation of the word "aer" except that Donnellus refers to "aer ad spiradum [air for breathing]."

Sohm [op. cit. p. 303] includes in "res omnium communes" "the open air" and in the same paragraph refers to it again as "the atmosphere of the earth."

[54] The Latin text reads: "Si quem tamen ante aedes meas vel ante praetorium meum piscari prohibeam, quid dicendum est? me iniuriarum iudicio teneri an non? et quidem mare commune omnium est et litora, sicuti aer, et est saepissimo rescriptum non posse quem piscari prohiberi: sed nec aucupari, nisi quod ingradi quis agrum alienum prohiberi potest."

See also Note 47 supra.

Lardone [op. cit. p. 461] notes a doubtful reading in the Latin text of Digest XVIII. 1.40.3. This is usually given as "Ex eo quod avibus ex aere cecidisset . . . [Something which had been dropped from the air by the birds]". He notes that certain manuscripts, however, read "ex ore [from the mouth of the bird.]" In no event could this passage from the Digest be considered an important exception to the general rule that "aer" was not used to express the airspace subject to appropriation by the landowner.

quite similar to that passage cited earlier in which it was held that branches projecting from a neighbor's field are prohibited over my field only up to a height of fifteen feet, because the higher branches do not cause real damage to the field. The rule is different if any branches are over my house which permanently obstruct my airspace.[55]

VII

Considering together all of the available passages from the Digest, the Institutes and the Code, no actual conflict exists. On the contrary, the applicable passages are quite consistent. As stated earlier, Roman law was very practical. It recognized conditions under which man lived.

The original texts show the following: (1) that the airspace over lands not subject to private ownership, such as public and religious lands, had the same legal status as the surface, and that the state exercised control in such airspace to prevent any encroachment; (2) that the airspace over private lands was either (a) the exclusive property of the landowner up to an indefinite height, subject to building restrictions or other state-imposed limitations, or (b) remained under the control of the state subject to a vested exclusive right of occupancy or user by the landowner to the extent from time to time permitted by the state; and (3) that the gaseous "aer" needed to sustain life was common to all men, but that this did not prevent the landowner having vested rights in the space (coelum) through which the "aer" circulated above his property.

So far as international air law is concerned, it is not important whether Roman law created rights of ownership, or of user, in the landowner. The authority of the Roman state as to airspace over Roman lands was exercised without limit whenever and to such height as was found necessary to protect public or private rights to occupy and use such space. Both lands on the surface and usable space above were under the continuing direct or indirect control of the state. Together such lands and space constituted a three-dimensional area in which Roman law was fully effective. This is the primary test of the extent of national territory. It would, therefore, appear that the concept of the inclusion of usable space and lands below within the territory of a state has existed since Roman times.

VIII

When Justinian became emperor in Constantinople, barbarians ruled Italy. In the previous century Rome had been captured by the Goths, had paid bribes to the Huns, had finally been looted and almost

---

[55] See Notes 28, 29, 30 *supra*.

destroyed by the Vandals. Roman law, though still vaguely recognized in Italy,[56] was certainly fast disappearing. That it finally survived must be credited to the military victories of Justinian. Less than twenty years after his legal compilers had finished their work in Constantinople, his armies had overrun Italy and a single Roman emperor again ruled in both east and west. Roman law was given its chance to come back into the land from which it had sprung.

In A.D. 554 Justinian formally ordered the Corpus Juris Civilis to be published and put into effect in Italy.[57] This return of Roman law in the purity of the Justinian compilations preserved it for the future of western Europe.[58] Even though the rule of the eastern empire collapsed in Italy within a few decades after the death of Justinian, and Germanic tribes took over most of the peninsula, the Corpus Juris Civilis never thereafter entirely disappeared from the Italian law courts. Roman law was secure for posterity.

Its second revival must be credited to the School of the Glossators at Bologna. In the period of its greatest activity (A.D. 1100–1250), the school devoted itself to a detailed re-examination of the Corpus Juris Civilis in the original texts. "The glossators," as Sohm says, "rediscovered the Digest in the sense that they brought home its meaning—and, with it, the meaning of Roman jurisprudence—to the minds of men once more."[59]

The glossators were annotators. In their notes, or "glosses," appended to various sections of the Corpus Juris Civilis they sought by cross-references to bring together various passages of the Digest which seemed interrelated. They also sought by such glosses to clarify what they considered to be the meaning of the text. Their views reflect both their interpretation of the Roman texts and a statement of the law as they believed it to exist in their own day. The works of the glossators show the existence of rights in space in the twelfth and thirteenth centuries, just as the original Roman law texts provided for rights in space protected by law in Roman times.

The last and perhaps the greatest of the glossators was Franciscus Accursius.[60] To him are accredited certain of the glosses directly

---

[56] Sohm, *op. cit.* p. 125.

[57] Joseph Louis Elzéar Ortolan, *Explication historique des Instituts de l'empereur Justinien . . .*, 11th ed., Paris, E. Plon, Nourrit, 1883–4, Vol. 1, p. 498.

[58] *Ibid.* p. 499; Sohm, *op. cit.* p. 133.   [59] Sohm, *op. cit.* p. 139.

[60] Franciscus Accursius—born Florence, Italy, 1182, died 1260. Under his direction the *Glossa ordinaria* (sometimes known as the "Great Gloss") was completed at Blogna about A.D. 1250, containing most of the comments and remarks made up to that time on the Code, the Institutes, and the Digest. According to the Encyc. Britannica [11th ed., Vol. 1, p. 134] the best edition of the *Glossa* is that of Godefroy published at Lyons 1589.

applicable to the texts of Roman law dealing with the legal relationship between land and the space above.[61] The most important gloss is that which appears as a note to the famous passage of the Digest (VIII.2.1) describing limitations on servitudes when a public highway intervened between two properties concerned. The original text of the Digest stated that the airspace over the highway ought to be free ("quia coelum, quod supra id solum intercedit, liberum esse debet").[62] The gloss to this passage, as attributed to Accursius, reads as follows: "Nota. Cujus est solum, ejus debet esse usque ad coelum, ut hic, & infra 'quod vi aut clam' i f. § pen." This may be translated "Whose is the soil, his it ought to be up to the heavens; as here and later in Digest XLIII.24.22.4."[63]

The cross-reference in the gloss is to the passage in the Digest which

---

The eldest son of Accursius (also named Franciscus)went to England on the invitation of King Edward I and lectured on the law for a time at Oxford. This may have been the connection between the work of the glossators at Bologna and English legal thinking.

For other data as to life and career of Accursius, see: Bouvé, *op. cit.* p. 248; McNair, *op. cit.* pp. 15, 17, note 1; Sohm, *op. cit.* pp. 136–137; Sweeney, *op cit.* p. 364.

Grotius [53, Prolegomena to *De jure belli ac pacis libri tres*, translation of 1646 edition by Francis W. Kelsey, Oxford, Clarendon Press, London, H. Milford, 1925 (*Classics of International Law* No. 3—publications of the Carnegie Endowment for International Peace, Division of International Law, Washington, D.C.), Vol. 2, p. 28 of translation] lists Accursius with Bartolus as among those "who long ruled the bar." This indicates the great influence of the work of Accursius as the head of the Bologna school.

[61] Bouvé, *op. cit.* pp. 247–248; de La Pradelle, *op. cit.* p. 300; McNair, *op. cit.* p. 15; Sauze, *op. cit.* pp. 25–26; Sweeney, *op. cit.* pp. 363–364.

Guibé [*op. cit.* p. 38] is generally credited with having done research work verifying Accursius as the author of the most important glosses affecting the problem.

[62] For full Latin text and citations as to this passage, see Note 18 *supra.*

[63] This text of the gloss has been verified as appearing in the following fifteenth and sixteenth century editions of the Digest: Venice, J. Le Rouge, 1477; Nuremberg, Koberger, 1482; Venice, Herbort, 1482; Venice, 1484; Venice, M. de Tortis, 1488; Venice, Raynaldus de Novimagio, 1489; Venice, B. de Tortis, 1490; Venice, Torresanus, 1491; Venice, B. de Tortis, 1494; Venice, B. de Tortis, 1498; Lyons, 1531; Lyons, 1537; Lyons, Hugonem, 1542; Paris, Guillard & Desboys, 1548; Lyons, 1552; Paris, Merlin, 1559; Paris, Merlin, 1566; Lyons, J. Uusultus, 1566; Lyons, Hugonem, 1572; Paris, 1576; Antwerp, Nutii, 1576; Lyons, 1580; Venice, 1584; Lyons, 1589.

The name of Accursius is appended to the gloss in the 1477 and 1491 Venice editions listed above. Guibé [*op. cit.* p. 38] notes the signature of Accursius ("Acc.") in a 1519 Paris edition. See also as to this gloss: Sweeney, *op. cit.* p. 365; de La Pradelle, *op. cit.* p. 300; McNair, *op. cit.* p. 15.

states that the airspace ("coelum") over a tomb is part of the tomb.[64] Both the passage to which the gloss is a note and the passage mentioned in the cross-reference dealt with airspace over lands not private property.

It is the present author's view that this gloss of Accursius to Digest VIII.2.1 was a statement by the glossator that the rule in the text of the Digest applicable to space over public property should also apply to space over private property. This would mean that the glossator construed the law to be that airspace over lands privately owned ought to be ("debet esse") free and unobstructed without limit—in other words, that the law was effective to protect from encroachment the airspace over private as well as public lands.

Available fifteenth and sixteenth century editions of the Code contain important glosses to the passage in Code III.34.8. This is the passage which provides that no right of action exists against one who raises his own house if there is no existing servitude.[65] The gloss is found in several different forms. One of the earliest, as expanded, reads as follows: "Videtur ergo quod quodlibet praedium praesumitur liberum nisi probetur contrarium est enim cuiuslibet usque ad celum . . ."[66] This may be translated as: "It was adjudged, therefore, that every property is presumed free unless the contrary be proved, for everyone's [right] extends up to the skies."

In several other fifteenth century editions the word "usus" is inserted between the words "cuiuslibet" and "usque" so that it might be translated as follows: "It was adjudged, therefore, that every property is presumed free unless the contrary be proved, for everyone's use extends up to the skies."[67]

In certain other fifteenth century editions, the words "unus usus" have been inserted instead of the word "usus" alone,[68] so that the

---

[64] See Note 24 *supra*. Guibé [*op. cit.* p. 39] quotes a gloss by Accursius to this passage in the following words "coelum, quod supra solum intercedit, liberum esse debet." He notes [p. 40] that Accursius never used at any time an expression equivalent to "property in space," but said only that "he who has the land, ought to have up to the heavens" ("celui qui a le sol doit l'avoir jusqu'aux cieux."). He apparently feels that the original glosses of Accursius have been construed by later authors into forms similar to the well-known maxim attributing the ownership of the landowner up to infinity.

[65] See Note 36 *supra*.

[66] Mainz, Schoeffer, 1475, folio [84] verso. See also: McNair, *op. cit.* p. 16; de La Pradelle, *op. cit.* p. 301; Sweeney, *op. cit.* p. 367, note 126.

[67] This text of the gloss has been verified as appearing in the following editions: Nuremberg, Sensenschmidt, 1475; Venice, J. Le Rouge, 1478; Basle, Wenssler, 1487; Nuremberg, Koberger, 1488; Venice, Georgius Arrivabenus, 1491.

[68] Venice, B. de Tortis, 1490, 1495, 1496 folio [56] verso.

gloss might be translated as follows: "It was adjudged, therefore, that every property is presumed free unless the contrary be proved, for everyone's use alone extends up to the skies."

In the sixteenth century the early forms of this gloss materially changed. In certain editions it has been found to read: "Videtur ergo quod quodlibet praedium praesumitur liberum nisi probetur contrarium est enim cuiuslibet solum usque ad coelum."[69] The gloss in this form might be translated as follows: "It is adjudged, therefore, that every property is presumed free unless the contrary be proved, for whosoever is the land, his it is up to the skies."

In other sixteenth century editions of the Code the last sentence of the gloss reads "est enim eius usque ad coelum, cuius est solum."[70] This late form of the gloss bears a strong resemblance to the English legal maxim "cujus est solum ejus est usque ad coelum" to be discussed later.

Two other glosses (quoted by de La Pradelle) are also of interest. To the passage in the Digest VIII.2.9, stating that no right of action exists where a man by raising the height of his house cuts off the flow of light to that of his neighbor, unless subject to a servitude, the following gloss has been found: "Quia coelum quod supra aedes meas est usque ad coelum, si non debeo alii servitutem."[71] This might be translated: "Because the airspace which is above my house extends to the skies if I owe no servitude to another." Again the gloss does not indicate space ownership but merely a right of the landowner to build upward without limit if no servitude prevents.

Also to the passage in the Digest XLIII.24.21.2, providing that in the case of new work both airspace and land must be measured, the following gloss has been found: "Quia coelum quod supra aedes meas est usque ad coelum liberum esse debet."[72] This gloss might be translated: "Because the airspace which is above my house ought to be free

---

[69] Lyons, Francoys Fradin, 1527, folio 117, verso; Lyons, 1537, folio 122 verso; Lyons, Johannes Ausultus, 1567, columns 487 & 488; Lyons, 1580 columns 487 & 488.

[70] Lyons, 1532 ,folio 122, verso; Lyons, Hugonem, 1542, folio 122, verso; Lyons, 1553, p. 286; Paris, Merlin, 1559, columns 575 & 576; Paris, Merlin, 1566, columns 575 & 576; Lyons, 1569, columns 575 & 576; Lyons, Hugonem, 1572, columns 575 & 576; Paris, 1576, columns 653 & 654; Antwerp, Nutii, 1576, columns 575 & 576; Venice, 1584, columns 653 & 654; Lyons, 1585, columns 487 & 488; Lyons, 1589, columns 653 & 654.
As to this and similar late forms of the gloss, see also: McNair, *op. cit.* p. 16; Sweeney, *op. cit.* p. 367, note 126; de La Pradelle, *op. cit.* p. 301.

[71] de La Pradelle, *op. cit.* p. 301. For Latin text of Digest VIII.2.9, see Note 37 *supra.*

[72] de La Pradelle, *op. cit.* p. 301; McNair, *op. cit.* p. 15, also notes this gloss.

up to the skies." In both this gloss and the one noted just previously, the word "coelum" as first used has the significance "airspace" as in the Digest itself. The second use of the word "coelum" in the phrase "usque ad coelum" appears in a sense not found in the Digest, but which seems to be similar to the phrase "in infinito" used in the Digest in the sense of "without limit" or "as high as one pleases."

A critical examination of the available glosses shows the following: (1) that in the earliest glosses (particularly in those which can be attributed to Accursius and his thirteenth century school) there is a clear indication that the landowner had *rights* in space protected by law. The original gloss to Digest VIII.2.1 continued in the form "cujus est solum ejus *debet esse* usque ad coelum" through the sixteenth century. This does not appear to be a statement claiming absolute ownership; (2) that in other forms of the gloss (particularly that to Code III.34.8) various editors amended the gloss so that in the sixteenth century it might be construed as a statement of ownership of space to an indefinite height by the owner of lands on the surface; (3) that these and other glosses show without question that from the twelfth through the sixteenth century the law of the subjacent state was always effective in space to the extent necessary to protect the legal rights to the use of such space given by the state to its citizens.[73]

---

[73] See also: a) the note "De aere" of Bartolomeo Cipollo [*Tractatus illustrium in utraque tum pontificii tum Caesarei, de contractibus licitis,* Venice, 1584, p. 243]. Cipolla died about 1477. In this note he says: that the use of the air like the sea and the seashores is common; that the air ought to be free above a house up to the skies ("aer supra domum nostrum debet esse liber usque ad coelum"), citing the gloss referred to in section VIII *supra;* that it is not lawful to build a bridge over a public way. He cites other cases indicating that the airspace above both public and private lands is protected by law from encroachment; also an amusing case of a clown banished from Ferrara who went to Padua, there placing some Paduan soil in a cart, returned to Ferrara in the cart contending without avail that he was on Paduan soil and not in the territory of Ferrara—but Ferrara evidently protected its territorial sovereignty, although the clown was not touching its land.

b) The statement of Cujacius in the sixteenth century that "Quo jure est coelum oedem jure esse debet solum et contra," which might be translated as "Whatever is the legal status of the airspace, the same ought to be the status of the land and vice versa." [Quoted by Goudy, *op. cit.* p. 230.]

c) The statement of Godefroy in the sixteenth century commenting on Digest VIII.2.1 (the same passage covered by the principal gloss of Accursius) and Digest XLIII.24.22.4, as follows: "Cujust solum, ejus coelum," probably meaning that the legal status of lands and airspace are the same. [Sauze, *op. cit.* p. 27. See also: Notes 18 and 24 *supra* for Latin text of passages referred to by Godefroy.]

IX

Grotius, writing in 1625, recognized the existence of the application of law in space above land. In his Book II, Chapter 2, Sec. 3 (1) of the *De jure belli ac pacis*, writing of the reasons why the sea could not become subject to private ownership, he said: "The cause which led to the abandonment of common ownership here ceases to be operative. The extent of the ocean is in fact so great that it suffices for any possible use on the part of all peoples, for drawing water, for fishing, for sailing. The same thing would need to be said, too, about the air, if it were capable of any use for which the use of the land also is not required, as it is for the catching of birds. Fowling, therefore, and similar pursuits, are subject to the law laid down by him who has control over the land."[74] Grotius added the following note: "And the right of habitation. 'It is necessary to measure the sky as well as the ground,' says Pomponius, *Digest*, XLIII.xxxiv.21 [§ 2]; add also *Digest* XVII. ii.83."[75]

---

[74] p. 190 of translation.

[75] An interesting discussion and commentary on the views of Grotius as to the sea, compared to the air and its uses, is found in the notes by Henricus de Cocceius [Hugonis Grotii *De jure belli ac pacis libri tres*, cum annotatis auctoris, nec non J. F. Gronovii Notis, & J. Barbeyracii Animadversionibus; Lausanne Marci-Michaelis Bousquet, 1751, Vol. 2, pp. 86–87].

Cocceius apparently felt that Grotius had held that the air as distinguished from the sea could come into private ownership—in which view Cocceius is referring to breatheable air and not to airspace, for he says (translated from the Latin): [words in italics are Grotius' statements; words not italicized are Cocceius' remarks]

"*The same should be said about the air if there could be any use of it.* The comparison made by the author [Grotius] between air and the sea is poor. For the sea is a thing where the substance can be separated from the use, and so in that instance there is one kind of right in respect of substance, and another in respect of use. The air however consists in being consumed, i.e., its very substance is consumed by use, and such things can only be said to be occupied in so far as we use them. Furthermore, the author is wrong in saying that there is no use of air *per se*, for B. Stryk (in *Disput. de jure principis aereo.*) has well set forth the important effects of the law of air. [Stryk's dissertation is discussed in Section X *infra*.]

"*That is for bird-catching.* The author's meaning, obscure though it be, seems to be this: like the *sea* so also the *air* can be occupied neither in whole not in part, even if there could be any use of the air apart from terrestrial aid—i.e., if men could live in the air without touching the earth. Since however there can hardly be use of the air without terrestrial aid, the author concludes from this that air follows the law of the earth, and so the air can be occupied not *per se*, but by the rights of the earth. This he illustrates by example of bird-catching: for birds which fly in the air are truly *res nullius*, and so far may be taken by anyone, for the air is common like the sea. But, he says, one who has occupied a field can prohibit another from entering the estate, and so prevent the right of using the air indirectly through land right.

Grotius, going back to the original Latin texts (not to the glosses), nevertheless recognized that the landowner had rights in airspace over

Here also the author in this notes adduces dwelling rights: for air is occupied by the position of a building, and this occupation too comes about through land law. This argument has more subtlety than truth. By its nature air can be occupied neither *per se* nor by land law, since it is not such a thing that it can be occupied, i.e., can be brought under our power. Since therefore air is in no-one's ownership, anyone may use it and no-one can be excluded from its use. The example of bird-catching clearly does not apply here: for bird-catching is use not of the air but of the earth, nor does use of the air consist in taking birds, but in breathing and inhaling air. See Diss. procem. XII, par. 217.

"*Whence these things derive their law from him who has sovereignty of the earth.* The effect of this is that bird-catching can be prohibited by civil law. And this is what Grotius says *passim*; dominion can be forestalled by civil law. (Dissert. Procem. VI, par. 18, n. 1) Indeed private individuals too who share dominions, can prevent others from entering their estates to hunt: not to the effect that the bird should not belong to its taker, for it is a *res nullius* and falls to the occupier, but so that an action for damages may apply to the one who enters another's estate against the will of the master."

As further evidence that Cocceius confused air with airspace and for that reason disagreed with the views expressed by Grotius, see the following additional comment from Cocceius' Dissertation Procem. XII. 217 [*op. cit.* Vol. 6, pp. 379–380] referred to in the above-quoted notes:

"Among things common or public by the law of nations are included;

"I. AIR, for the extent of the particles which form air is inexhaustible, indefinite, and indeterminate, and changes from moment to moment; and so by its own nature cannot be occupied, i.e., brought into our power and custody.

"Since therefore there is no-one who can say that the air is his, it necessarily follows that its use is common, and open to all peoples and individuals, because no-one has a legal right of prohibition. Any man therefore can hunt birds, and whatever is taken in the air becomes immediately the property of the taker, even in a place whose ownership has been occupied by another: for both the air and the bird itself belong to no-one.

"Note 1. Grotius decides that air can come into private ownership, and in this respect its nature is unlike that of the sea, since it has no use for which use of the earth is not necessary. Since therefore this land receives its law from the one who has sovereignty over the land, he concludes that the air too can receive its law from the sovereign, and says that on these grounds bird-catching can be forbidden.

"It should however be well understood that prohibition of the law does not prevent the air from remaining common, i.e., belonging to no-one, and does not prevent a bird taken in the air from becoming the property of the taker. The Roman laws show us that a wild beast, even though taken on the property of another, becomes the property of the taker, since what belongs to no-one falls to the occupier. He who takes it, however, if he has, against the prohibition of the law, entered the estate of another, may be liable for an action for damages from the owner of the estate. Even although then an estate may belong to a person by the right of *dominium*, it still does not follow from this that he is the owner also of the air, much less of the birds flying in the air, since neither the air nor a bird is ever in the physical possession of the owner."

his property and that the law applicable to the land would be applied in space over the land.

If Grotius did not directly discuss the possibility of sovereignty in space above lands, the same cannot be said of Pufendorf. The latter, in his *De jure naturae et gentium*,[76] Book IV, Chapter 5, Sec. 5, discussing the right which men had to maintain sovereignty over the sea and the possibility of it being done physically by the use of ships, said: "Now it is obvious that the gift of God, whereby man was given the right to assume sovereignty over the land included also the sea. A twofold command was given: Have dominion over the fish of the sea and over the beasts of the land. But sovereignty over animals is inconceivable without the right as well of controlling the element which they inhabit, so far as its nature allows. Mention is made of the fowls of the heaven as well, yet since man has been denied the ability to be in the air to the extent that he rest in it alone, and be separated from the earth, he has been unable to exercise sovereignty over the air, except in so far as men standing upon the earth can reach it. But it has been possible for sovereignty to be exercised more widely on the sea by means of ships, which are now brought to the highest degree of perfection, and not only serve for the transport of burdens but also carry on war over the domains of Neptune in a far more terrible form than it is waged upon land."[77]

Pufendorf's statement is a clear holding that so far as man had used the air (airspace) over the land, to that extent at least had the state already assumed and exercised rights of sovereignty in space.

X

The first treatise in which air law is separately considered, so far as is now known, is the dissertation *De jure principis aereo*, presented in October 1687 by an otherwise unknown scholar, Jean-Etienne Danck, a candidate for a law degree at the University of Frankfurt. This treatise was presented before Samuel Stryk, then a professor of law at Frankfurt (Germany), and was afterwards included in Stryk's collected works known as *Strykii opera* published in Florence in 1837–1841.[78] The dissertation evidences wide knowledge and research in

---

[76] Samuel Pufendorf, *De jure naturae et gentium libri octo*, translation of 1688 edition by C. H. Oldfather and W. A. Oldfather, Oxford, Clarendon Press, London, H. Milford, 1934, (*Classics of International Law* No. 17— publications of the Carnegie Endowment for International Peace, Division of International Law, Washington, D.C.).

[77] p. 560 of translation.

[78] Vol. 5 (1838), p. 1190. The existence of this dissertation was disclosed by Nys in 1911 ["Une dissertation du XVIIIe siècle sur le droit aérien,"

the Corpus Juris Civilis, classical writers, and contemporary law writers including the works of Grotius and others.

The purpose of the dissertation, as its title implies, was to present the law of the air as applied to the prince or ruler—in other words, to present legal questions on sovereignty in the airspace. It states in great detail the general position of space rights as of the latter part of the seventeenth century.

Air law, according to the treatise, is defined as the law concerning the air and those things which are in the air and which border upon it. The question is raised as to whether the ruler can sustain rights over the air in view of the provisions of Roman law that the air is common to all and is free. But it is held that this does not limit the power of the ruler because jurisdiction over everything connected with the earth is entrusted to the ruler by divine power. So the ruler should use his powers for various purposes such as prevention of pollution of the air which might bring disease. The rights of society must be conserved.

Discussing the building rights of the ruler, the treatise points out that under the law the ruler is not limited by building restrictions in constructing his castle, although such restrictions are applicable to his subjects. Citing the Digest of Justinian as to the airspace over tombs being kept free (XLIII.24.22.4), and the provision that the airspace over highways and other public lands should also be free (VIII.2.1), as well as the gloss on the latter provision, discussion in Section VIII *supra*, he states that the "coelum" which is above anyone's land ought to be free ("liberum esse debet"—paraphrasing this gloss of Accursius). He continued that while the air follows the land and so to him whose is the land should be the air even up to the skies, nevertheless and notwithstanding these private space rights, the ruler can control private building. Classical authority is cited as to the existence of building restrictions in Rome enacted by the Emperors Hadrian and Trajan. An ordinance of the German Empire of 1559 requiring the destruction of castles which menaced the security of travelers below is also cited. All of these provisions show the existence of sovereignty of the ruler in space, overriding private building rights.

The treatise also points out that in the German Empire the air rights were part of the "regalia" or source of personal income of the ruler. Accordingly the ruler levied a tax on windmills, and private interests were not allowed to construct windmills using the air belonging to the ruler except upon payment of the tax and receipt of a

---

Revue de droit international et de législation comparée, Vol. 43 (2nd series, Vol. 13), 1911, pp. 323–325]. Nys does not mention the book in which he found the dissertation, but it is assumed to be the same source referred to in the text.

license. Also under German law sovereignty over the air carried with it a monopoly held by the ruler of the privilege of engaging in the hunting of birds.

While much of the treatise deals with matters which now appear of little importance, its purport is very clear. As of the time in which it was prepared the law of the states of the German Empire recognized complete control by the ruler in space above the earth's surface for any purpose to which such space had then been put. Clearly space was as much a part of the territory in which the ruler exercised sovereign powers as were the lands below. In fact, in some ways the ruler seems to have had even greater powers in space than on territorial lands.

XI

No less clear was the English common law as to the recognition and protection by national law of rights in space.

In the sixteenth century the principles of Roman airspace law made their first presently determined appearance in English law, not however in the actual language of the Corpus Juris Civilis or even of the original glosses to the Digest, but rather in one of the more arbitrary forms of the maxim "Cujus est solum, ejus est usque ad coelum." ("Who owns the land owns even to the skies.") In the case of *Bury* v. *Pope* (1586, Cro. Eliz. 118), at the end of the report of the case, appears the following. "Nota.—Cujus est solum, ejus est summitas usque ad coelum. Temp. Ed. I."[79] The maxim as here stated might be translated as "Who owns the land, his is the highest place even to the skies." The word "summitas" is not found in classical Latin.

The maxim, in its more ordinary form, appears in the often-cited passage from *Coke on Littleton* (written about 1628): "And lastly, the earth hath in law a great extent upwards, not only of water, as hath been said, but of ayre and all other things, even up to heaven, for *cujus est solum ejus est usque ad coelum. . . .*"[80]

Selden in the *Mare clausum*, published about seven years after Coke,[81] being a much sounder scholar than Coke, returned to the original Roman texts to sustain his position on rights in space. Dis-

---

[79] Whether this means that the rule stated in the maxim had been in force in England since the time of Edward I has been much discussed. For general comments on the case, see: Harold D. Hazeltine, *The Law of the Air*. London, Univ. of London Press, 1911, p. 62; McNair, *op. cit.* p. 17; Sweeney, *op. cit.* p. 355.

[80] L. I. C. I. Sect. 1. 4 (a).
For the most complete available discussion of the various forms in which this maxim has appeared, see: Sweeney, *op. cit.* pp. 355–373.

[81] John Selden, Mare clausum: *The Right and Dominion of the Sea . . .*, translated by J. H. Gent, London, 1663.

cussing the possibility of possession and sovereignty over the seas and other bodies of water and arguing by analogy from the status of the air and the space in which it circulated, he insisted (in the language of the 17th century English translation from the original Latin) that the fluid nature of water and its continued shifting in a channel no more prejudiced "Dominion and Possession, than the fluid nature of the Aër doth the Dominion and Possession of that space which confines a Hous from the Foundation upward."[82] Citing Pomponius in Digest XLIII.24.21.2 that the aër "ought to be measured as well as the ground," he held it to be evident that the "aer is his who is owner of a plot of ground." (This is the same passage from the Digest cited by Grotius in his *De jure belli ac pacis*.)[83]

His conclusion was that "therefore, surely wee are owners of the ground, hous, and space, which wee possess in several as owners, that every one, for his best advantage, may freely and fully use and enjoy his bordering Aër (which is the element of mankind) how flitting soever it bee, together with the space thereof in such a manner, and restrain others thence at pleasure, that hee may bee both reputed and settled owner thereof in Particular."[84] Selden had no difficulty in thus stating the law of his day, without reference to the glosses or the maxim relied on by Coke, and based on his contemporary construction of the Roman texts as applicable to existing conditions. Airspace and air were different things at law. In airspace, private rights existed protected by law.

Blackstone, writing in 1765–1768 and relying upon Coke, (as Hazeltine and many other commentators have noted)[85] stated the maxim and its application as follows: "Land hath also, in its legal signification, an indefinite extent upwards as well as downwards. *Cujus est solum, ejus est usque ad coelum*, is the maxim of the law, upwards; therefore no man may erect any building, or the like, to overhang another's land . . . So that the word "land" is not only the face of the earth, but everything under it, or over it."[86]

XII

It is now generally conceded that the language of the maxim "Cujus est solum, ejus est usque ad coelum" was not part of Roman written law. It is not in the Corpus Juris Civilis. Literally translated the maxim leads to the obvious absurdity of claiming for the landowner private exclusive "dominium" (ownership) of space above his lands up to

---

[82] *Ibid.* Bk I, Chap. 21 (p. 132 of translation).
[83] See section IX *supra.*
[84] Selden, *op. cit.* Bk I, Chap. 21 (p. 133 of translation).
[85] Hazeltine, *op. cit.* p. 62.
[86] *Commentaries*, 4th ed., 1770, Bk II, Chap. 2, p. 18.

infinity. When the maxim is carefully analyzed, however, and reasonably construed, it is apparent that it must have sprung originally from principles of Roman law—though stated in a non-Roman manner.

Roman law was never guilty of extravagant statements of private property rights. It was always able to reconcile a certain amount of equitable discretion with fixed rules.[87] As will be seen from an examination of the texts of the Corpus Juris Civilis cited and discussed in Sections IV and VIII *supra*, Roman law protected the needed rights of the landowner to the use and enjoyment of space above his lands, whether occupied by buildings or used as cultivated fields, implying, though not stating, that these space rights constituted "dominium" (ownership), but without fixing definitely the height in space to which these rights extended. Similarly, Roman law protected from encroachment, for the benefit of the public, space above such land as highways, sacred places and tombs.

But nowhere in the original Roman texts has been found any statement that the owner of the surface also owned space above "up to the skies" or "to infinity" (as the maxim is capable of being translated and interpreted). It is at this point that the maxim may be charged with having a non-Roman origin. The closest approach to anything that would resemble this literal interpretation is found in a passage from Paul in the Digest (see Note 35 *supra* as to Digest VIII.2.24). In this passage the landowner is authorized to extend his building upward without limit. The Latin phrase used, "in infinito," is however an idiomatic expression properly translated as "without limit" or "as high as he pleases" or "as far as he wishes." Even this passage did not state that the landowner had "dominium" in space before he occupied it by the construction of a building or beyond the point where it was to his interest that such space be free of obstructions.

The maxim probably had, as indicated above, its indirect origin in the work of the glossators. But it is evident that between the date of the original glosses and the appearance of the maxim over three hundred years later in *Bury* v. *Pope* a significant change had been made. The words "debet esse" ("ought to be") of the more important glosses had become "est" ("is"). By this change the statement in the glosses that the landowner ought to have the use or enjoyment of the airspace over his property to an indefinite height had become, in the maxim (particularly as cited by Coke), a statement of the existence of present ownership of space to infinity. The principle received into the English common law that a landowner has legal rights in space was of Roman

---

[87] Sohm, *op. cit.* p. 130.

origin though the exaggerated form of the statement is probably not of Roman origin.

But to Roman law can certainly be attributed the source to which we must look for the more important principle that state law has, since time immemorial, been made effective to an undetermined height in space to protect the rights of landowners in such space. This principle the English law accepted certainly as early as the sixteenth century. No English lawmaker from then onwards would have questioned English sovereignty in space over its lands and water.

XIII

In France these principles of Roman law were similarly translated into rules of property. In the Coutume de Paris, effective by the end of the seventeenth century, Article 187 (which itself took the place of Articles 81 and 83 of an even earlier law), provided in substance that whoever has the land is able and ought to have all above and below his land and can build above and below. ("Quiconque a le sol, . . . il peut & doit avoir le dessus & le dessous de son sol, & peut édifier pardessus & pardessous . . ."[88]

Ferriers, in his authoritative 1714 commentaries on this article, summarizes certain of the Roman texts and says "cujus est solum ejus est coelum" ("whose is the land his is the airspace"). He adds that this article of the Coutume de Paris conforms to the common law in that it is permissible for the owner of a property to build on it as high as he pleases, founded on the principle "cujus est solum, ipsius coelum est." He remarks that no general ordinance in France had ever specifically limited buildings to a certain height. However, he makes it clear that private rights in space can be regulated by the sovereign power. He cites judicial decrees of 1558 and 1559 in which it had been held that a wall raised by a neighbor so high that the adjoining house was entirely obscured should be reduced in proportions fixed by the decrees. Certain local building ordinances are quoted, including a royal ordinance of August 1, 1609 providing building regulations in Paris.

As elsewhere in Europe it is apparent that French law prior to the discovery of the art of human flight had recognized rights in space in connection with the ownership of lands and that the state exercised sovereign powers in space either to protect these rights or to regulate the same if the public interest so required. This is the exercise of rights of territorial sovereignty.

---

[88] Claude de Ferriere, *Corps et compilation de tous les commentateurs anciens et modernes sur la Coutume de Paris*, 2d ed., Paris, C. Osmont, 1714, Vol. 2, column 1543.

XIV

The discovery of the art of flight in 1783 and the use of space thereafter as a medium of transport could not change prior existing authority of the state in space. When states assert and exercise exclusive territorial sovereignty in fixed areas for one purpose, they assert and exercise it for all other purposes in the same area. Sovereignty required and asserted to protect recognized private rights for building, for light and air, and other means of enjoyment in space connected with interests in lands below, would necessarily carry with it sovereign rights of the state to regulate all other human activity in the same space areas as part of its territory, including such activity as flight.

The civil codes adopted in the nineteenth century in many states, including France, Austria, Germany and Italy, and in the Province of Quebec (Canada), together with judicial decisions in Great Britain and the United States, defining landowners' space rights, are clear evidence of the continued assertion of territorial sovereignty in space above national lands and waters.

The French Civil Code (Code Napoléon) took effect in 1804. In later years it was used as the model for other civil codes in many parts of the world.

Article 552 of the French Civil Code categorically declares that ownership of the land includes ownership of what is over and under it.[89]

---

[89] The full French text of Article 552 is as follows:

"La propriété du sol emporte la propriété du dessus et du dessous.

"Le propriétaire peut faire au-dessus toutes les plantations et constructions qu'il juge à propos, sauf les exceptions établies au titre des Servitudes ou Services fonciers.

"Il peut faire au-dessous toutes les constructions et fouilles qu'il jugera à propos, et tirer de ces fouilles tous les produits qu'elles peuvent fournir, sauf les modifications résultant des lois et règlements relatifs aux mines, et des lois et règlements de police."

The French text of Article 552 was incorporated without change in the bilingual Civil Code of the Province of Quebec (Canada), effective August 1, 1866, as Article 414. The official English text of this Article of the Quebec Civil Code may, therefore, be taken as an authoritative translation of Article 552 of the French Code. It is as follows:

"414. Ownership of the soil carries with it ownership of what is above and what is below it.

"The proprietor may make upon the soil any plantations or buildings he thinks proper, saving the exceptions in the title 'Of Real Servitudes.'

"He may make below it any buildings or excavations he thinks proper, and draw from such excavations any products they may yield, saving the modifications resulting from the laws and regulations relating to mines, and the laws and regulations of police."

Such was still the Civil Law of both France and the Province of Quebec when the Paris Convention of 1919 was signed.

It is admittedly based on Article 187 of the Coutume de Paris, which, as stated above, provided that whoever has the land is able and ought to have all above and below and can build above and below. Portalis, one of the compilers of the French Civil Code, wrote that one would understand that ownership would not be perfect if the landowner were not master of the whole space his domain encloses.[90]

Much learning has been devoted to the legal construction and interpretation to be given to Article 552 so as to state exactly the landowner's rights.[91] Comments of various authors are at times contradictory. Decisions of the French courts have not been entirely consistent. The construction assigned to Article 552 has ranged from an analysis based on the restatement of the maxim "Cujus est solum," with its arbitrary construction of ownership of space to infinity, to the theory that the article creates no ownership rights except in buildings or other physical additions to the land, but does give the landowner the right to occupy such space over his land as may be used by buildings, trees, crops, and other physical improvements, together with the right to be protected from interference by third parties in the use and enjoyment of his lands and any improvements thereto. The range of meanings which have been given to this article are very reminiscent of the disputes as to the effect of the Roman law itself.

International law is not concerned with the technical construction of Article 552, except in the net result that every sound analysis of the article admits that it creates rights in space in connection with interests in the lands below and protects these rights to an undefined height, whether or not such rights are or are not "ownership." In this sense the adoption of the French Civil Code was a continued assertion as in

---

[90] "On comprend que la propriété serait imparfaite si le propriétaire n'était libre de mettre à profit pour son usage toutes les parties extérieures et intérieures du sol ou du fonds qui lui appartient, et s'il n'était le maître de tout l'espace que son domaine renferme." (Jean E. M. Portalis, *Code civil suivi de l'exposé des motifs*, 1820, Vol. IV, p. 38, as cited in Lycklama, *op. cit.* p. 75.)

[91] For general discussion of the effect of Article 552 and an analysis of adjudicated cases and various doctrinal theories, see the following:

Charles M. B. Aubry and Charles F. Rau, *Cours de droit civil français d'après la Méthode de Zachariae*, 5th ed., Paris, Marchalet Billard, 1897–1922, Vol. 2, Sec. 192; André Blachère, *L'Air, voie de Droit*, Paris, Larose & Tenin, 1911, pp. 29–67; Henri Guibé, *op. cit.* pp. 35–51; André Henry-Couannier, *Eléments créateurs du droit aérien*, Paris, P. Orbem, 1929, pp. 101–127; Raymond Jammes, *Des actions civiles et pénales qui peuvent naître du fait de la navigation aérienne*, Tulle, L. Mazeyrie, 1912; Charles Louis Julliot, *De l'abus du droit dans ses applications à la locomotion aérienne*, Paris, Larose & Tenin, 1910; and *De la propriété du domaine aérien*, Paris, Larose & Tenin, 1909, pp. 15–19; Marcel Le Goff, *Traité théorique et pratique de droit aérien*, Paris, Dalloz, 1934, Secs. 30–68, pp. 20–39; Maurice Lemoine, *Traité de droit aérien*, Paris, Sirey, 1947, Secs. 171–172, pp. 113–116.

Roman law by the state of its sovereignty in space over subjacent surface territory to such height as might at any time be necessary to create, protect and regulate the rights defined by Article 552. The later adaption of the French Code to the use of other states had a similar legal effect in those states.

Section 297 of the Austrian Civil Code produced legal results similar to those created by the French Code but in a somewhat more direct manner. The Austrian Code included in the definition of real property such permanent construction on the ground as houses and other buildings, and also the airspace in a vertical line above.[92] It thereby recognized that land and space above constitute a single legal unit in which the landowner has definite rights. This section has been construed on eminent authority as a grant of "private rights in airspace" and is one of the bases for a statement that such codes evidence a claim on the part of the state of "sovereignty over the airspace."[93]

The Italian Civil Code adopted in 1865 and effective January 1, 1866 was influenced by the French Civil Code. Article 440 of the Italian Code, dealing with property in space, provided that he who has ownership of the land has also ownership of the space above the land and of everything which is found above and below the surface.[94] This article carried into Italian law the older and stricter interpretations of Article 552 of the French Civil Code, for the Italian statute carefully says that the landowner has ownership ("la proprietà") of space above the land.

---

[92] Section 297 of the Austrian Civil Code adopted in 1811 (Allgemeine Bürgerliches Gesetzbuch für das Kaiserthum Österreich) reads:

"Ebenso gehoren zu den unbeweglichen Sachen diejenigen, welche auf Grund und Boden in der Absicht aufgeführt werden, dass sie stets darauf blieben sollen, als: Häuser und andero Gebäude mit dem in senkrechter Linie darüber befindlichen Luftraume."

Which may be translated as follows:

"Likewise is considered to be real proprty that which is permanently erected on the land and soil with the intention that it should remain thereon, such as houses and other buildings, together with the airspace vertically above them."

Comparing this Austrian Code with the much later German Code, Perich said:

"As to the Austrian Civil Code, which went into operation at a time (1811) when Roman law alone met all the needs of private legal relations, it is even more than the German Code saturated with Roman Law." *Progress of Continental Law in the 19th Century* (Vol. II Continental Legal History Series) Little Brown & Co., Boston (1918) p. 266.

[93] Ernst Zitelmann, "Luftschiffahrtrecht," *Zeitschrift für internationales privat — und offentliches Recht*, Vol. 19, 1909, p. 477.

[94] The Italian text of Article 440 reads:

"Chi ha la proprietà del suolo ha pur quella dello spazio sovrastante e di tutto ciò che si trova sopra e sotto la superficie."

It does not state the height to which such ownership extends. But Pampaloni in 1892, analyzing the entire question in a much quoted and authoritative article, concluded that the ownership rights of the landowner in space were not unlimited under Italian law and that the true rule was as follows: "The ownership of the space extends to where it is required by the interest of the owner in regard to the use which it is possible to make of the property in question in the present conditions of human art and industry (interest through any use of the property whatsoever, provided it is actually possible)."[95]

Bonfante, insisting that the Italian law did not grant private rights of ownership *in infinitum* as indicated in the maxim *cujus est solum*, re-examined the positions taken by von Jhering and by Pampaloni (as well as the writings of Hesse, Dernberg and others). He pointed out that there was a legislative lack in the failure of the law to fix the actual limit of ownership in space. This ownership Bonfante believed should be determined by an economic rule. He held that the state, for political reasons of defense and the enforcement of its power, had sovereign rights upwards *in infinitum* within such limits in which human dominion may be exercised, but that the right of private property ceased where economic interests ended. Thus the individual landowner had no right to exclude the entry of aircraft over his land at a height where his economic interest did not induce him to exercise such control. But the state for political reasons could prohibit foreign air navigation up to any height where airships might be found.[96] Clearly the adoption of Article 440 of the Italian Civil Code was a declaration by Italy of its sovereignty in space at least up to the undefined height where the landowner might have economic interests.

Section 905 of the German Civil Code of 1900 provided that the right of the owner of the land extended to space which is above and the earth which is below the surface of the land, but that the owner cannot prevent the use of such space above or below ground where he has no interest in excluding anyone therefrom.[97] The German Code was

---

[95] Pampaloni, *op. cit.* p. 51. As to further analysis of Pampaloni's views, see: Silvio Trentin, "Il diritto dello stato sullo spazio aereo," *Congresso giuridico internazionale per il regolamento dalla locomozione aerea, 31 maggio —1–2 giugno 1910, Atti e relazioni,* Verona, Società tipografica cooperativa, 9110, p. 83.

[96] Bonfante, *op. cit.* Vol. 2, Pts. 1–2, p. 219, note 2, 226–227.

[97] The German text of Section 905 (Bürgerliches Gesetzbuch für das Deutsche Reich) reads:

"Das Recht des Eigenthümers eines Grundstücks erstreckt sich auf den Raum über der Oberfläche und auf den Erdkörper unter der Oberfläche.

"Der Eigenthümer kann jedoch Einwirkungen nicht verbieten, die in solcher Höhe oder Tiefe vorgenommen werden, dass er an der Ausschliessung kein Interesse hat."

enacted in 1896 after more than twenty years of laborious codification, although it was not made effective until January 1, 1900. It is a legislative determination of the rights of the landowner in space effective long after the use of balloons (and even crude dirigibles) was well-known. It may be said to state a more modern point of view than the early French and Austrian Codes.

Before this Code was adopted, the rights of the landowner in space under Roman law, as generally accepted in Germany, had been the subject of serious and important doctrinal consideration by leading German scholars. In 1830 Gesterding had said that space was not a "thing" or "res" in a legal sense; that it was a pure abstraction and therefore not subject to become private property. To Gesterding this did not mean that the airspace was completely open to the use of all. He admitted that it was subject to the authority or occupation of the owner of the subjacent land as a normal consequence of the right of land ownership.[98]

In 1863 Werenberg denied that the landowner had rights of property in the air or airspace above, and sought to limit the landowner's actual rights in space to such use as the need of the particular subjacent lands require.[99]

Von Jhering, writing the same year, used his disagreement with Werenberg's thesis as the basis for a discussion of his own views. His resulting analysis perhaps did more to influence subsequent legal thinking on the subject of the rights of the landowner in space than anything published before or since. Re-examining in some detail the Roman sources, von Jhering concluded that the landowner had rights of ownership in airspace above, but that such rights were limited in height above the surface and did not extend to infinity. He felt that such rights did not in fact extend beyond the practical requirements and interests of the landowner.[100] Bonfante pointed out that von Jhering thus gave an economic basis and limitation to a landowner's rights in space.[101]

The thesis of von Jhering seems to have been carried forward in Section 905 of the German Civil Code discussed above. This section

---

[98] Franz Christian Gesterding, "Das Märchen von der Luftsäule," *Ausbeute von Nachforschungen über verschiedene rechts materien, Greifswald*, Vol. 3, 1830, p. 447; Bonfante, *op. cit.* p. 221; Pampaloni, *op. cit.* pp. 37–39; Trentin, *op. cit.* p. 83.

[99] Wilhelm Werenberg, "Ueber die Collision der Rechte verschiedener Grundstückseigentümer," *Jherings Jahrbücher für die Dogmatik des bürger-ichen Rechts*, Vol. 6, 1863, pp. 20–21; Bonfante, *op. cit.* p. 221; Pampaloni, *op. cit.* pp. 39–41; Trentin, *op. cit.* p. 83.

[100] Von Jhering, *op. cit.* p. 85. Pampaloni, *op. cit.* pp. 41–43; Trentin, *op. cit.* p. 83.

[101] Bonfante, *op. cit.* p. 225.

stated in substance that the landowner's rights extend indefinitely into space, without fixing any limit. But in actual practice the section does limit such rights by saying that the owner cannot interfere with others using his space if the owner has no interest to prevent such user. When Germany adopted this section of the Code, it thereby declared itself sovereign in space to an indefinite height so as to protect and regulate the conflicting recognized interests of the landowners and others in usable space.[102]

XV

The principle of Roman law as to exclusive private rights in space continued to influence the growth of the common law of Great Britain, notwithstanding the development of the art of human flight. The views of Coke and Blackstone, with their emphasis on the rights of the landowner in usable space above, repeatedly reappeared. The maxim "cujus est solum" was used as evidence of a well understood legal presumption. Decisions of the courts and writings of able jurists during the 19th century made it increasingly evident that British law recognized, regulated, and, if necessary, protected certain exclusive rights of the landowner in superjacent space. Thus British sovereignty was continuously asserted in the usable space above its national surface territories. Whether these private rights were those of ownership, or merely rights of protection in the full use of the lands in question, is not material. The space where these rights were held to exist was treated as part of the national sphere of sovereign action just as it had been since Roman times.

---

[102] Section 905 of the German Code should be considered in connection with Article 667 of the Swiss Civil Code adopted in 1907 in the following language:

"Das Eigentum an Grund und Boden erstreckt sich nach oben und unten auf den Luftraum und das Erdreich, soweit für die Ausübung des Eigentums ein Interesse besteht."

Which may be translated:

"Ownership of land extends upwards into the airspace and downwards into the earth, provided there is an interest in the utilization of the property."

As early as 1862 the law of the Canton of Grisons had provided that the ownership of land extends above and below the land up to a height and to a depth where such ownership can be exercised usefully. This principle was adopted by Article 667 of the Swiss Code of 1907.

Both the German Code and the Swiss Code necessarily raised in practice the difficulty of determining the height at which the owner of lands below has that character of interest in the space above which authorizes him to prevent or interfere with the use of such space by others.

See on this subject: Armando Koch, "Le Droit de l'air d'après le nouveau code civil Suisse," *Revue juridique internationale de la locomotion aérienne*, Vol. 2, 1911, pp. 233–235; André Henry-Coüannier. *op. cit.* Sec. 41, pp. 117–118.

While Lord Ellenborough is quoted as having held in 1815 in *Pickering* v. *Rudd*[103] that he did not "think it is a trespass to interfere with the column of air superincumbent on the close," it is evident from an examination of both reports of the case that he was holding nothing more than that the technical action of trespass would not lie— not that the owner of the land had no rights in the airspace affected by defendant's overhanging board. In fact both Campbell's and Starkie's reports make it clear that the learned judge would have given damages to the plaintiff in an "action on the case" if, as Starkie's report says "you could prove any inconvenience to have been sustained."

In *Fay* v. *Prentice*[104] decided in 1845, plaintiff recovered in an "action on the case" for nuisance resulting from a cornice of defendant's building overhanging plaintiff's garden, even though actual harm was not shown. Coltman, J., held "the mere fact of defendant's cornice overhanging the plaintiff's land may be considered as a nuisance, importing a damage which the law can estimate." In that case the maxim "cujus est solum" is referred to as a presumption of law, though not applicable in all cases.

In *Electric Telegraph Co.* v. *Overseers of Salford*,[105] decided in 1855, dealing with the question as to whether a company owning wires was taxable as occupying land, all four judges concurred in deciding that such occupation existed. Baron Martin, for example, cited Coke and the maxim, then held that the wires occupied "that which the law calls land."

In *Ellis* v. *Loftus Iron Co.*[106] it was held that trespass existed when defendant's horse kicked and bit plaintiff's mare through a wire fence, the mare being in plaintiff's field. The fact that some portion of the horse's body was over the boundary was held a trespass without proof of negligence even though plaintiff's land was not touched. Denman, J., referred to the maxim "cujus est solum" as a "technical rule," but held that on the authorities there was no escape from holding that a trespass existed.

In *Wandsworth Board of Works* v. *United Telephone Co.*,[107] decided in 1884, Bowen, L. J., said that "I should be extremely loath myself to suggest, or to acquiesce in any suggestion, that an owner of land had not the right to object to anybody putting anything over his land at any height in the sky." Fry, L. J., indicated that he entertained "no doubt that an ordinary proprietor of land can cut and remove a wire

---

[103] *Pickering* v. *Rudd* (1815), 4 Camp. 219, 1 Stark, 46.
[104] *Fay* v. *Prentice* (1845), 1 C.B. 828, 36 Digest 162.
[105] *Electric Telegraph Co.* v. *Overseers of Salford* (1885), 11 Exch. 181, 156 Eng. Rep. 795.
[106] *Ellis* v. *Loftus Iron Company*, 10 C.P. 10 (1874).
[107] *Wandsworth Bd. of Works* v. *Unitel Co.* (1884), 13 I.B.D., 104.

placed at any height above his freehold," though as he added "the point is not necessary for decision."

To the same effect are the leading text writers. Pollock, in the first (1886) edition of his now classic work on "The Law of Torts", quoted with approval the statement that "every invasion of private property, be it ever so minute, is a trespass."[108] In a note he added that "property" here "as constantly in our books, really means possession or right of possession." After recalling the fact that Lord Ellenborough in *Pickering* v. *Rudd*, supra, had thought it not a trespass "to interfere with the column of air superincumbent on the close," Pollock noted that fifty years later Lord Blackburn had inclined to think differently,[109] commenting "and his opinion seems the better." For, said Pollock, "it does not seem possible on the principles of the common law to assign any reason why an entry at any height above the surface should not also be a trespass." In later editions, Pollock somewhat qualified this position by adding, "unless indeed it can be said that the scope of possible trespass is limited by that of possible effective possession, which might be the most reasonable rule."[110]

Salmond in the first (1907) edition of his work on "The Law of Torts", discussing trespass, says: "It is commonly said that the owner-ship and possession of land bring with them the ownership and posses-sion of the column of space above the surface *ad infinitum. Cujus est solum ejus est usque ad coelum.* This is doubtless true to this extent, that the owner of land has the right to use for his own purposes, to the exclusion of all other persons, the space above it *ad infinitum.*" In the following paragraph he added that ". . . a mere entry into the airspace above the land is not an actionable wrong unless it causes some harm, danger, or inconvenience to the occupier of the surface," in which case "there is a cause of action in the nature of a nuisance."[111]

Pollock and Salmond concurred in the existence of exclusive private rights held by the landowner in superjacent space. They differed only as to the kind of action to be brought for unauthorized entry into such space and as to whether "harm, danger, or inconvenience" must be proved.

Such are some of the representative British cases and authorities from 1783, when the art of human flight was discovered, to 1919 when the Paris Convention was signed. They indicate with striking con-sistence the existence of a general rule as to the rights of the landowner

---

[108] Pollock *The Law of Torts*, p. 280, citing *Entick* v. *Carrington*, 19 St. Tr. 1066.

[109] *Kenyon* v. *Hart* (1865), 6 B & S 249; 34 L. J. M. C. 87.

[110] Pollock *The Law of Torts* (8th Ed), p. 348.

[111] Salmond *The Law of Torts*, Stevens and Haynes, London, 1907, pp. 163–164.

in superjacent space. Whether these exclusive rights are technically ownership, or a mere right to enjoy the surface to the fullest extent, is not material. Nor is it important by what type of court action such rights could be enforced. Similar questions might have been raised before the Roman praetor. The important thing is that the common law of Great Britain, by acknowledging these private rights, continuously asserted full national sovereignty over usable space above surface territories. Whether or not it be correct to say that the maxim "Cujus est solum" has in itself "no authority in English law,"[112] the fact remains that the sturdy principles of the Roman law continued to dictate the basic tenets of private property rights in space, and evidenced, as they had from the days of the Twelve Tables, the fact that the State held and exercised sovereign rights in such space to create, regulate and protect exclusive private rights. It was this same sovereign power which Great Britain later exercised in adopting the Air Navigation Act 1920 (10 and 11 Geo. 5, c. 80) for the purpose, among other things, of legislatively adjusting rights in usable space between the owner of lands below and the operator of an aircraft.[113]

---

[112] McNair, *op. cit.* p. 33. In summarizing his own considered views as to private rights in space under the common law, McNair stated two theories: "(i) that *prima facie* a surface-owner has ownership of the fixed contents of the airspace and the exclusive right of filling the airspace with contents, and alternatively, (ii) the same as (i) with the addition of ownership of the airspace within the limits of an 'area of ordinary user' surrounding and attendant upon the surface and any erections upon it." As to (ii) McNair added that "it is agreeable that a surface owner automatically owns that limited portion of the airspace which is necessary for the enjoyment of the ownership of the surface . . ." He personally preferred the first solution as he doubted whether ownership of space could be possible. It is suggested by the present author that both theories evidence the existence of exclusive private legal rights in space, and that either might have been accepted by the compilers of the Justinian Corpus Juris Civilis.

[113] Sec. 9 (1) of The Air Navigation Act 1920 (10 & 11 Geo. 5, c. 80) includes the following opening paragraph:

"No action shall lie in respect of trespass or in respect of nuisance, by reason only of the flight of aircraft over any property at a height above the ground, which, having regard to wind, weather, and all the cirucmstances of the case is reasonable, or the ordinary incidents of such flight, so long as the provisions of this Act and any Order made thereunder and of the Convention are duly complied with; but where material damage or loss is caused by an aircraft in flight, taking off, or landing or by any person in any such aircraft, or by any article falling from any such aircraft, to any person or property on land or water, damages shall be recoverable from the owner of the aircraft in respect of such damage or loss, without proof of negligence or intention or other cause of action, as though the same had been caused by his wilful act, neglect or default, except where the damage or loss was caused by or contributed to by the negligence of the person by whom the same was suffered . . ."

XVI

When English settlers moved into North America, they carried with them the accepted principles of the common law. These included the juridical concept that ownership of land included rights in superjacent space.

This is evidenced in the United States by a continuous chain of authoritative comments and court decisions. The right of the land-owner to build upward was not challenged, nor his right to be protected against fixed occupancy by another of any part of the space above his soil. The existence of these sound tenets of Roman law, inherited through the British common law, was not challenged. It was only after aviation became an important transport activity, thus creating new social problems, that the extent and character, though not the existence, of the surface-owner's rights were carefully examined and clarified.

Chancellor Kent of New York, in his much cited "Commentaries on American Law", first published in 1826 and 1830, accepted as valid the statements of Coke and Blackstone as to the ownership of land carrying with it certain rights of the surface owner in space above.[114]

This general position was affirmed in numerous cases in state courts of last resort, including the following often cited:

a) Lyman v. *Hall*[115]—Overhanging branches constitute a legal nuisance for "land comprehends everything in a direct line above it."

b) Smith v. *Smith*[116]—Eaves of defendant's barn overhanging plaintiff's property is trespass.

c) Hannabalson v. *Sessions*[117]—Reaching an arm across a boundary is trespass, for "it is one of the oldest rules of property that the title of the owner of the soil extends, not only downward to the center of the earth, but upward 'usque ad coelum . . .'."

d) Butler v. *Frontier Telephone Co.*[118]—Stringing electric wires above plaintiff's property thirty feet above ground authorizes an action of ejectment; "The law regards the empty space as if it were a solid,

---

[114] Kent, *Commentaries on American Law*, Vol. III, 1892, p. 402:

"Corporeal hereditaments are confined to *land*, which, according to Lord Coke, includes not only the ground or soil, but everything which is attached to the earth, whether by the course of nature, as trees, herbage, and water, or by the hand of man, as houses and other buildings; and which has an indefinite extent, upwards as well as downwards, so as to include everything terrestrial under or over it . . ."

[115] *Lyman* v. *Hall*, 11 Conn. 177 (1836).

[116] *Smith* v. *Smith*, 110 Mass. 302 (1872).

[117] *Hannabalson* v. *Sessions*, 116 Iowa 457; 90 N.W. 93 (1902).

[118] *Butler* v. *Frontier Telephone Co.*, 186 N.Y. 486, 79 N.E. 716 (1906).

inseparable from the soil, and protects it from hostile occupation accordingly," for ". . . within reasonable limitations land includes also the space above and the part beneath . . . 'usque ad coelum' is the upper boundary, and, while this may not be taken too literally, there is no limitation within the bounds of any structure yet erected by man."

United States official delegates took part in drafting, and later signed, the Paris Convention of 1919. They insisted on the rule that each nation is sovereign in the airspace over its surface territories.[119] The fact that the United States did not ratify the Convention was not caused by the adoption of this rule. The several states of the Union, as evidenced by the cases just cited, and many others, had continuously asserted their internal sovereignty over the airspace by the regulation and protection of exclusive rights of the surface owner in space above, thus declaring such airspace to be part of the territory of the state in question. As all the territory of each state is part also of the territory of the United States as a member of the family of nations, it necessarily followed that the airspace over each state was part of the national territory of the United States for purposes of external sovereignty in international law.

Decisions of both state and federal courts in the United States after 1919 reaffirmed the basic rights of the surface owner in space, while at the same time clarifying the extent of these rights and adjusting them against the public requirements for the development of aviation.

In *Portsmouth Harbor Land and Hotel Company* v. *United States*,[120] the Supreme Court of the United States, speaking through the great authority of Mr. Justice Holmes, held that the United States was guilty of "taking" the property of the plaintiff by firing large guns in such manner that the projectiles passed through the airspace over plaintiff's lands—a clear acceptance of the existence of property rights in space protected by the law of the territorial sovereign.

Twenty-four years later the Supreme Court in the presently controlling case of *U.S.* v. *Causby*[121] affirmed, clarified, and limited

---

[119] See the author's article "United States Participation in drafting Pari- Convention, 1919," *Journal of Air Law and Commerce*, Vol. 18, p. 266.

[120] *Portsmouth Harbor Land and Hotel Co.* v. *United States*, 260 U.S. 327 (1922).

[121] *United States* v. *Causby*, 328 U.S. 256 (1946).

Between the decisions of the U.S. Supreme Court in the Portsmouth Co. and Causby cases, a number of other cases were decided by State Supreme Courts and U.S. Circuit Courts of Appeal illustrating previously developed common law rights of the surface owner. The most important are the following:

Smith v. *New England Aircraft Co.* 270 Mass. 511 (1930); 170 N.E. 385; 1930 U.S. Av. R. 1; 1 Avi. 197. Low altitude flights held technically a trespass though injunction denied under facts in case. As to airspace rights, court

horizontally the surface-owner's space rights. In 1926 by the adoption of the Air Commerce Act, the United States had legislatively declared its national airspace sovereignty, and had reasserted the same position in the Civil Aeronautics Act of 1938. These acts, as the court pointed out in the Causby case, granted citizens of the United States "a public right of freedom of transit in air commerce through the navigable airspace of the United States," defined as "airspace above the minimum safe altitudes of flight prescribed by the Civil Aeronautics Authority", and definitely provided that "such navigable airspace shall be subject to a public right of freedom of interstate and foreign air navigation." The court found that passage of United States military aircraft at levels below the administratively fixed safe altitudes of flight across

---

said: "The bald question in the case at bar is whether aircraft, in order to reach or leave an airport, may of right fly so low as 100 feet over brush and woodland not otherwise utilized, against the protest of the owner, . . . There are numerous cases holding that invasion of the airspace above the land without contact with its surface constitutes trespass . . ." And later: "The combination of all these factors [low flights, noise, etc.] seems to us, under settled principles of law . . . to constitute trespass to the land of the plaintiff" so far as concerned flights as low as 100 feet.

Swetland v. *Curtis Airports Corp.* 55 Fed. (2d) 201 (1932); 1932 U.S. Av. R. 1; 1 Avi. 315. Held that surface owner "has a dominant right of occupancy [in airspace above his land] for purposes incident to his use and enjoyment of the surface, and there may be such a continuous and permanent use of the lower stratum which he may reasonably expect to occupy himself as to impose a servitude upon his use and enjoyment of the surface." (citing the Portsmouth Co. case, supra.). And again: "As to the upperstratum which he may not reasonably expect to occupy, he has no right . . . except to prevent the use of it by others to the extent of an unreasonable interference with his complete enjoyment of the surface."

Thrasher v. *City of Atlanta* 178 Ga. 514 (1934); 173 S.E. 817; 1934 U.S. Av. R. 166; 1 Avi. 518. Held that "the legal title [to airspace], can hardly extend above an altitude representing the reasonable possibility of man's occupation and dominion, although as respects the realm beyond this the owner of the land may complain of any use tending to diminish the free enjoyment of the soil beneath;" and again that "the occupant of the soil is entitled to be free from danger or annoyance by any use of the superincumbent space, and for any infringement of this right he may apply to the law for appropriate redress or relief."

Hinman v. *Pacific Air Transport Corp.* 84 Fed (2d) 755 (1936); 1936 U.S. Av. R. 1; I Avi. 640. Held that the *cujus est solum* maxim literally construed was not and had never been the law; that the formula "from the center of the earth to the sky" was "never taken literally but was a figurative phrase to express the full and complete ownership of land and the right to whatever superjacent airspace was necessary or convenient to the enjoyment of the land;" and later that "when it is said that man owns, or may own to the heavens, that merely means that no one can acquire a right to the space above him that will limit him in whatever use he can make of it as a part of his enjoyment of the land."

the Causby lands were equivalent to a taking of his property under the facts of the case. In doing so, the court reaffirmed the continued existence of common law airspace rights to the surface owner in the areas up to the minimum safe altitudes of flight. The opinion of Mr. Justice Douglas says in part:

> We have said that the airspace is a public highway. Yet it is obvious that if the landowner is to have full enjoyment of the land, he must have exclusive control of the immediate reaches of the enveloping atmosphere. Otherwise buildings could not be erected, trees could not be planted, and even fences could not be run. The principle is recognized when the law gives a remedy in case over-hanging structures are erected on adjoining land. The landowner owns at least as much of the space above the ground as he can occupy or use in connection with the land. The fact that he does not occupy it in a physical sense—by the erection of buildings and the like—is not material. As we have said, the flight of airplanes, which skim the surface but do not touch it, is as much an appropriation of the use of the land as a more conventional entry upon it. We would not doubt that if the United States erected an elevated railway over respondents' land at the precise altitude where its planes now fly, there would be a partial taking, even though none of the supports of the structure rested on the land. The reason is that there would be an intrusion so immediate and direct as to subtract from the owner's full enjoyment of the property and to limit his exploitation of it. While the owner does not in any physical manner occupy that stratum of airspace or make use of it in the conventional sense, he does use it in somewhat the same sense that space left between buildings for the purpose of light and air is used. The superadjacent airspace at this low altitude is so close to the land that continuous invasions of it affect the use of the surface of the land itself. We think that the landowner, as an incident to his ownership, has a claim to it and that invasions of it are in the same category as invasions of the surface.

> In this case, as in Portsmouth Co. v. United States, supra, the damages were not merely consequential. They were the produce of a direct invasion of respondents' domain.

In an earlier portion of the opinion the court had said: "It is ancient doctrine that at common law ownership of the land extended to the periphery of the universe—*Cujus est solum ejus est usque ad coelum* (citing Coke, Blackstone and Kent). But that doctrine has no place in the modern world."

Whether this arbitrary construction of the maxim can be accepted as a correct statement of the common law is more than open to question. But this is not material here. The primary importance of the whole decision is its reaffirmance that certain exclusive rights of the surface owner in usable superjacent space are protected by the territorial sovereign power of the State, even though these rights are held to have been horizontally limited by the legislative acts discussed. The decision clearly establishes the fact that the airspace over the surface territories of the United States was considered as territory in which the law of the sovereign could be and was enforced long before the signature of the Paris Convention by the United States, or its declaration of national sovereignty in the Air Commerce Act of 1926. The complex question of whether the airspace is both state and federal territory under United States constitutional provisions, or solely federal, is not in point.

XVII

In Canada the position is generally similar. In 1930 the Supreme Court of Canada was asked certain questions by the Governor General in Council as to the respective legislative powers of the Parliament and of the legislatures of the provinces in relation to the regulation of control of Aeronautics.[122] In the separate opinion of Newcombe, J. the following statement appears as part of his justification for finding that the provinces, not the Dominion Parliament, controlled the right of flight:

I would reject the argument urged on behalf of the Dominion that the subject of either of these questions is "navigation and shipping," within the 10th enumeration of s. 91 of the British North America Act, 1867, I see no evidence of any Parliamentary intention that this was ever intended.

"The earth hath in law a great extent upwards, not only of water, as hath been said, but of ayre and all other things even up to heaven; for *cujus est solum ejus est usque ad coelum*, as in holden 14 H.8. fo. 12, 22 Hen. 6. 59. 10 E. 4. 14. *Registrum origin.* and in other bookes."

These are the words of Coke's venerable Commentary upon Littleton (4 a.), and they express, as I have been taught to believe, the common law of England, which applies in the English provinces of Canada. In the province of Quebec, the law is not materially different, for, by art. 414 of the Civil Code, it is declared that

"ownership of the soil carries with it ownership of what is above and what is below it."

---

[122] Reference re Legislative Powers as to Regulation and Control of Aeronautics in Canada (1930) S.C.R. 663.

The principle is thus established, and the courts have no authority, so far as I can perceive, to explain and qualify it so as to admit of the introduction of a public right of way for the use of flying machines consequent upon the demonstrations in recent times of the practicability of artificial flight. The appropriate legislature may, of course, provide for airways as it has habitually done for roads and highways, notwithstanding the rights of the proprietors; but the project is legislative, not judicial.

He added later that "the right of way exercised within a province by a flying machine must, in some manner, be derived from or against the owners of the property traversed . . ."; and that if it were desired to confer immunity in the provinces of Canada in respect of trespass or nuisance by reason of flight at reasonable height as had been done in Great Britain by the Air Navigation Act 1920 (discussed above), resort would lie *prima facie* to the legislature of the provinces.[123] The existence of private rights in space held subject to legislative territorial regulation was not questioned—the only problem being whether the Dominion or the provinces could exercise this control.

The judgment of the Supreme Court of Canada was reversed in 1932 on appeal to the Privy Council.[124] In the arguments for the Attorney-General of Canada it was urged that the "maxim *Cujus est solum ejus est usque ad coelum* does not apply so as to prevent aerial navigation from being a public right; flying over land is not a trespass to any proprietary right: Pickering v. Rudd (1815, 4 Camp. 219); Clifton v. Bury (1887, 4 Times L.R. 8); Foy v. Prentice (1845, I C.B. 828)."[125]

Pickering v. Rudd and Foy v. Prentice are discussed in Section XV supra of this paper. In Clifton v. Bury the plaintiff asked an injunction and damages for shooting across his lands. Both were granted. Hawkins, J., held that plaintiff had "a legal grievance sufficient to enable him to maintain an action", though the shooting was not considered the basis for a technical action of trespass. These cases all admit the existence of exclusive rights of the surface-owner in superjacent space, even though such rights are not that full ownership of the airspace which would warrant the plaintiff to sue in trespass for entry above his lands. In reversing the Supreme Court of Canada, the Privy Council did not discuss this very technical point. The decision of the Privy Council holding that the Dominion had full control of aeronautics was based on the broad grounds that Canada must have national control of aeronautics in order to implement its obligations under the Paris Convention

---

[123] *Ibid* at p. 701–702.
[124] In re the Regulation and Control of Aeronautics in Canada (1932) A.C. 54.
[125] *Ibid* at p. 57.

of 1919 "Relating to the Regulation of Aerial Navigation", as well as on the ground that "aerial navigation is a class of subject which has attained such dimensions as to affect the body politic of the Dominion." So far as preexisting surface-owners' rights were affected, this meant nothing more than that the Dominion, not the provinces, had legislative power to regulate these airspace rights so as to authorize and regulate air navigation. The existence of private rights in space recognized and protected by law was not questioned.

XVIII

This somewhat brief and general historic survey would appear to demonstrate the correctness of the statement that sovereign states have since Roman times created, recognized, regulated and protected certain exclusive private rights of the surface-owner in usable space above his lands. Accepting as true the doctrine that such acts of the State can be exercised only by virtue of its rights of sovereignty within its national territory, it follows that States claimed, held, and in fact exercised sovereignty in the airspace above their national territories long prior to the age of flight, and that the recognition of an existing territorial airspace status by the Paris Convention of 1919 was well founded in law and history.

PART THREE

The Evolution of the Modern Principle of State Sovereignty in Airspace

6

The International Air
Navigation Conference
Paris 1910

Reprinted by permission of the
Journal of Air Law and Commerce
from 19 Journal of Air Law and
Commerce *127 (1952).*
© Journal of Air Law and
Commerce *1952.*

Author's Note. This article and the next, on "State Sovereignty in Space: Developments 1910 to 1914," were separately published. However, they were integral parts of continued research at the Institute for Advanced Study in Princeton on the historical development of State sovereignty in usable space, and were later used as lecture material while the author was Director of the Institute of International Air Law at McGill University.

T HE FIRST DIPLOMATIC CONFERENCE to consider flight regulation met in Paris May 10, 1910, and adjourned June 29, 1910, without having signed a convention. It did not reconvene later as planned, and was technically a diplomatic failure.

But the influence of this conference on subsequent developments mark it as second in historical importance only to the 1919 conference after World War I when the celebrated Paris Convention was drafted and signed. When the 1910 conference met, no acceptable plan existed for international flight regulation. When the conference adjourned, it had completed all but a few clauses of a draft convention, including such subjects as aircraft nationality, registration, aircraft certificates, crew licenses, logbooks, rules of the road, transport of explosives, photographic and radio equipment in aircraft, and special provisions dealing with public aircraft. The conference also agreed that subjacent States might set up prohibited zones above which no international flight was lawful, recognized that cabotage could be reserved for national aircraft, and provided that the establishment of international air lines will depend upon the assent of interested States. These principles were to reappear in the Paris Convention of 1919 and certainly influenced the Chicago Convention of 1944.

Of even more importance is the now demonstrable fact that this 1910 conference, not the 1919 conference as usually supposed, first evidenced general international agreement that usable space above the lands and waters of a State is part of the territory of that State. The debates of the conference and the draft provisions of the proposed convention, which were accepted in principle though not signed, show that States had concluded that they were entitled to regulate flight over their territories as fully as they had historically regulated other forms of human activity in national territory, and that no general freedom of international transit (innocent passage) for aircraft of all States existed as a matter of international law in the usable space over sovereign States.

BACKGROUND OF THE CONFERENCE

When the conference met in 1910, international flight was practically unregulated. Free balloons took off from one State and landed in another, or wherever they might drift. The early zeppelins started on test and training flights from their base in Germany and directed their flight over Switzerland without consideration of the need for a permit. The French aviator Bleriot took off on his famous 1909 airplane flight and crossed the English Channel from France to Great Britain without thought of creating an international incident.

Between April and November of 1908 at least ten German balloons crossed the frontier and landed in France carrying over twenty-five aviators at least half of whom were German officers.[1] In November 1908 debates in the French Senate indicated that aviation should be considered both for its effect on national defense and on international commercial relations, and that regulation of the aerial frontiers must therefore be studied.[2] German balloons and their pilots had been well received by local French police and the people where they landed. However, fearing a disagreeable incident, the French Ambassador in Berlin called the situation to the attention of the German Government in 1908, and German military authorities were said to have promised immediate measures to prevent the further landing of German balloons outside German frontiers.[3]

But the French Government, still concerned, decided in December 1908 to invite the European powers to hold a diplomatic conference on the regulation of air navigation. The representations made at that time by France to Great Britain are most interesting. They referred to the difficulties that had been occasioned by the number of German balloons landing on French soil. The United States was not invited as it was deemed to be out of the reach of such incidents, and the conference was therefore limited to Europe.[4] In addition to calling the conference, the French Government took certain regulatory measures to limit the number of balloon landings which had apparently con-

---

[1] Gaston Bonnefoy, *Le Code de l'air*, Paris, M. Rivière, 1909, pp. 186–190. See also: Giulio Castelli, "Il dominio dell'aria," *Rivista internazionale di scienze sociali e discipline ausiliarie*, Vol. 47, 1908, pp. 315–323.

[2] Speech by General Mercier in French Senate, November 5, 1908 in: *Journal officiel*, November 6, 1908, quoted by Georges Montenot, *La Circulation aérienne envisagée au point de vue juridique* (thesis—Dijon), Dijon, 1911, p. 5.

[3] *Journal du droit international privé*, Vol. 36, 1909, pp. 596–597.

[4] See Official Minute dated May 1, 1910, quoted by Peter G. Maesfield in "Some Aspects of Anglo-American Civil Aviation," *United Empire*, Vol. 38, 1947, pp. 26–33.

tinued in 1909 despite the earlier protests. The most important measure taken was an order issued March 12, 1909 by Clémenceau, then Minister of the Interior, addressed to the prefects of the French provinces. It stated that the frequency of landings of foreign balloons in France had led the government to give the matter serious consideration. It directed local authorities to hold such balloons for the collection of import duties, to obtain the details as to the purpose of the flight, and to advise the government in Paris by telegraph.[5] Such was the general background of the 1910 conference.

PROGRAM FOR THE CONFERENCE

The invitation of the French Government was accepted by the following European States: Austria-Hungary, Belgium, Bulgaria, Denmark, France, Germany, Great Britain, Italy, Luxembourg, Monaco, Netherlands, Portugal, Roumania, Russia, Spain, Sweden, Switzerland, Turkey. In August 1909 a questionnaire was sent by the French Government to each State asking for preliminary official views on certain questions to be presented to the conference. The program was surprisingly narrow and technical in scope. It would appear that between December 1908 and August 1909 France had decided to avoid discussion of the fundamental question as to whether or not space used by international flight was part of the territory of the subjacent State or whether such space was free to the use of all States. The program therefore omitted any reference to the character of right or privilege by which the aircraft of one State might enter flight-space over the lands or waters of another State. The questions submitted included such matters as the distinction to be made between public and private aircraft, nationality, navigability certificates, registration, crew competence, technical rules applicable to departure of aircraft, and papers to be carried.[6] However, the program did include certain questions as to whether international rules should be imposed on aircraft landings. These questions approached closest to the problem as to whether German aircraft did or did not have a right to fly over French territory and land without French permission, the basic problem which in 1908 had led to the conference.

The replies received from certain governments forced a widening of the scope of the conference. Belgium, for example, stated that the question as to freedom of landing ought to be preceded by a question

---

[5] *Journal du droit international privé*, Vol. 36, 1909, pp. 1281–1283; *Revue juridique internationale de la locomotion aérienne*, Vol. 1, 1910, p. 24.

[6] Conférence internationale de navigation aérienne, Paris 18 mai-28 juin 1910, *Procès-verbaux des séances et annexes*, Paris, Imp. Nationale, 1910, pp. 9–10.

relative to the extent of the freedom of navigation,[7] and as a State whose neutrality had been guaranteed urged international agreement to determine the nature and extent of the rights of each State in space above its lands and waters.[8] The Italian Minister of Public Works insisted that landings should be prohibited in military zones,[9] and recommended that the conference discuss whether or not a "territorial zone" ought to be established in which a State would exercise its sovereignty as in the case of territorial waters.[10] Russia appeared to support the view that, in principle, landing should be free except in prohibited zones,[11] but at the same time recommended that a further international conference should discuss the question of the rights of a sovereign State in the airspace above its territory.[12]

The German Government presented in advance as part of its reply to the questionnaire an entire draft convention. So far as present research will indicate this is the first multilateral air navigation convention ever prepared. It contained an entire chapter on "Admission of Air Navigation within the Limits of or above Foreign Territory."[13]

When the conference actually met, a supplemental question was added to the program entitled "Examination of the Principle of Admission of Air Navigation within the Limits of or above Foreign Territory; that is to say, Belonging to a State Other Than That from Which the Aircraft Comes." This supplementary question necessarily involved the fundamental problem of the legal status of flight-space and the extent of the authority of the subjacent State to regulate flight over its lands and internal waters. The positions taken by the various States and the decisions of the conference on this question were of paramount importance in the subsequent development of international air law.

FRENCH POSITION AT THE CONFERENCE

The chief of the French Delegation and president of the conference was the distinguished international lawyer, Louis Renault, for many years chief of the legal section of the French Foreign Office and a member of the Institute of International Law. At the first session Renault stated the apparent desire of the French Government to avoid a decision on the question of freedom of flight-space or State sovereignty.

---

[7] Conférence internationale de navigation aérienne, Paris 18 mai-28 juin 1910, *Exposé des vues des puissances d'apres les memorandums adressés au gouvernement français*, Paris, Imp. Nationale, 1909, p. 59.

[8] *Ibid.*, pp. 111–112.   [9] *Ibid.*, p. 65.   [10] *Ibid.*, p. 88.

[11] *Ibid.*, p. 65.   [12] *Ibid.*, p. 90.

[13] For original French text of this draft convention as presented by the German Government see *ibid.*, pp. 93–104.

He recommended that the conference seek to reconcile freedom of air navigation with legitimate State interests, without being too much concerned with the abstract principles as to the nature of the rights of States over the atmosphere.[14] The French Government thus adopted in principle the position which had been taken by Paul Fauchille (also a member of the delegation) in his 1910 report to the Institute of International Law wherein he had said: "Air navigation is free. Nevertheless subjacent States reserve rights necessary to their self-preservation; that is, to their own security and that of the persons and goods of their inhabitants."[15]

The question of the admission of foreign aircraft was put on the program and referred to the First Commission of the conference. Kriege, chief of the German Delegation and legal adviser to the Foreign Office in Berlin, was chairman of this commission, and Fauchille was named as its reporter. The first formal statement of French views on the entry of foreign aircraft appeared in a memorandum submitted to the commission which bears every evidence of Fauchille's authorship. The formula there presented and recommended for conference adoption was: Air navigation is free. No restrictions may be adopted by States other than those necessary to guarantee their own security and that of the persons and goods of their inhabitants.[16]

The French memorandum also recommended inclusion in the convention of the definite restrictions to which States would be limited. These were: (1) prohibition of flight of aircraft in a zone below a certain height fixed by the convention; (2) prohibition of flight in the interest of national security above such places as fortresses; (3) prohibition of carriage by aircraft, without authority, of explosives, munitions, photographic and telegraphic equipment, and merchandise particularly dangerous from a customs point of view; (4) right of the subjacent State to exercise over aircraft in the airspace above its territory police and customs supervision; (5) right of the subjacent State to deny passage of foreign military and police aircraft through such airspaces; (6) right of the subjacent State to submit to its jurisdiction

---

[14] *Procès-verbaux . . ., op. cit.*, p. 26.
[15] *Annuaire de l'Institut de droit international*, Vol. 23, 1910, pp. 297–311. Fauchille since 1901 had been the leading advocate of freedom of flight-space, opposing the principle of State sovereignty. See: Paul Fauchille, *Le Domaine aérien et le régime juridique des aérostats*, Paris, A. Pedone, 1901; his reports in *Annuaire de l'Institut de droit international*, Vol. 19, 1902, pp. 19–86, Vol. 21, 1906, pp. 76–87; and his article, "La Circulation aérienne et les droits des états en temps de paix," *Revue juridique internationale de la locomotion aérienne*, Vol. 1, 1910, pp. 9–16. In 1910 he began to seek general acceptance of the formula "air navigation is free" as a compromise. However, he personally never receded from his original 1902 position that "the air is free."
[16] *Procès-verbaux, op. cit.*, p. 244.

and laws those acts occurring on board aircraft affecting the right of self-preservation of such subjacent State.

The French position avoided any direct reference to freedom or sovereignty of flight-space. However, it seemed to assume the existence of a general international legal right of transit (innocent passage) and entry and landing for every State through flight-space over and into all other States.

At the opening of the conference the French Government had thus adopted Fauchille's position, including his failure or refusal (as evidenced in his earlier writings) to realize that a right of innocent passage did not necessarily exist in flight-space when recognized as part of the territory of the subjacent State. Certain of the fallacies in this position were made even more evident by the far-reaching proposed limitations on freedom of flight over subjacent States. These limitations were consistent with no legal theory except flight-space sovereignty of such subjacent State. Limitations of this character could have been made effective only in flight-space which was part of national territory, particularly as applied to aircraft of States which had not agreed to the proposed convention. Nor were these restrictions consistent with the normal right of innocent passage as recognized in maritime international law. They were far more drastic than those which an adjacent maritime State may exercise over foreign surface shipping passing through its territorial marginal sea.

It now appears in the light of history that what France really proposed at the opening of the conference was that sovereign States would by convention agree to the admission of foreign aircraft of all States, whether or not parties to the convention, but would restrict such international flight through territorial flight-space to no greater extent than directly authorized in the convention. The convention was thus to become a self-denying ordinance by which each contracting State would limit its rights of sovereign control over transport through its territory in aid of international air navigation.

GERMAN POSITION AT THE CONFERENCE

The German position was evidenced by the draft convention prepared and filed as the German reply to the French questionnaire, and referred to above. This is a document of great historical significance. It was the first concrete statement by a sovereign State of its position on the legal status of flight-space, and became the real basis for discussion at the 1910 conference. Its general plan and many of its articles found their way into the almost complete draft convention prepared by the conference itself.

Certain articles of the German draft disclosed that the government had accepted the theory of full and absolute territorial sovereignty in usable space over its lands and waters. This position had been previously stated by such German experts as Meurer, Zitelmann, and others. Article 11, for example, provided that aircraft of a *contracting* State should be *authorized* to take off, land, and fly over the territory of other contracting States—the key to the entire draft convention. By providing for authorization of foreign flight and limiting it to aircraft of contracting States, the convention thus in effect denied any general international law right of innocent passage or of entry of all foreign aircraft. Article 12 permitted the contracting States to regulate flight of other contracting States over its territory in the interests of security or protection of persons or property, provided that the same restrictions were applied to national aircraft. Article 14 provided for control of public air transport when not extending beyond the territory of the State—a reservation of cabotage; and also provided that the establishment of international air lines would be subject to the assent of interested States—a recognition that national economy as well as security was affected by international flight. Article 20 is particularly noteworthy in that it provided an undertaking by each contracting State to require observance by *all* aircraft within or above its territory of the air navigation rules set out in the annex to the convention—a commitment as to the exercise of police power which no State could assume unless the flight-space above its lands and waters were a part of its territory.

It is evident that the German draft convention did not admit the existence of any right of entry of aircraft of non-contracting States, and evidenced a clear insistence on complete right of sovereign territorial control of flight over German surface territory. Superjacent usable space was treated as legally part of such territory.

During the conference the German Delegation filed an additional statement of its position.[17] This is a careful, shrewd, and not altogether frank, document. Standing alone it appeared in part to favor general freedom of air navigation subject to restrictions. However, the statement concludes with recommendations based directly on the theory of the German draft convention: (1) that aircraft should be authorized in principle to take off or land in or pass over foreign territory; (2) that the subjacent State should have power to limit such freedom of navigation on the condition that such restrictions must be determined by the interests of the security of the State or the protection of persons or goods of its inhabitants, and that foreign aircraft ought not to be treated less favorably than national aircraft; (3) that States should have rights of retorsion and of cabotage, outlined in the statement exactly

---

[17] *Ibid.*, pp. 239–242.

as they had been in the draft convention. The only ambiguity arises from the use of the term "foreign territory" without limiting it to the territory of contracting States. To support the principles of national treatment for foreign aircraft and reservation of cabotage, the German statement cited the precedents of maritime treaties of commerce and navigation covering conditions of foreign entry into national ports and harbors. Such treaties grant privileges of entry and commerce only as between contracting States. The use of the reference to such treaties as precedents coupled with subsequent discussions in the commission makes it evident that the German statement had not changed the original position as evidenced by the draft convention. Germany still favored only those rights of entry into the airspace over foreign territory which would be authorized by a convention in the nature of the well-known reciprocal treaties of commerce and navigation.

BRITISH POSITION AT THE CONFERENCE

The British position at the opening of the conference was unequivocal. It recognized the existence in flight-space of private property rights of the landowner and of full sovereignty rights of the subjacent State. These principles were stated in a British interministerial memorandum dated October 11, 1909 filed with the French Government before the conference as part of the British reply to the questionnaire.[18] The memorandum said that:

> it is desirable that no regulation be instituted which implies in any manner whatsoever the right of an aircraft to fly over or land on private property, or which excludes or limits the right of every State to prescribe the conditions under which one may navigate in the air above its territory.

The British Government thus affirmed its full sovereignty in usable space over its surface territories. But it did not accept the dictum which had been put forward in 1906 by Westlake, the celebrated British professor of international law, who had supported the theory of sovereignty coupled with a right of innocent passage for foreign aircraft such as international law recognized for surface vessels through the marginal seas.[19] If the British Government had considered such international right of transit for foreign aircraft existed irrespective of convention, it could not have insisted on the reservation of the full right to prescribe conditions under which air navigation could take place above its surface territory. In maritime international law the adjacent State

---

[18] *Exposé des vues, op. cit.*, pp. 133–140.

[19] See statement of Westlake at Institute of International Law 1906 session, *Annuaire de l'Institut de droit international*, Vol. 21, 1906, p. 297.

may exert some jurisdiction over foreign shipping passing through the marginal sea, but certainly not that character of complete control which Great Britain felt that it had a right to assert as to foreign aircraft over its surface territories.

During the sessions of the First Commission the British Delegation presented an additional statement of its position in reply to the German statement.[20] It objected to the establishment of general principles covering the right of aircraft to navigate above foreign territory or to land there. It stated that while wishing as far as possible to encourage the development of air navigation, it was necessary to safeguard the interests and sovereignty of the States. It further objected to the German proposals that foreign aircraft should not be treated less favourably than national aircraft. Concretely, it recommended that each State should have the right to take those measures it desired to restrain air navigation above its territory when indispensable to national defense, and that such power should permit the State to determine special locations for landing of foreign aircraft and to prescribe zones where flight would be prohibited. It recommended that each State, as a matter of international courtesy, ought to agree to arrange all reasonable facilities for foreign aircraft to fly above its territory or to land there, subject to such restrictions as it believed indispensable to assure the security of its nationals.

DISCUSSIONS IN THE FIRST COMMISSION

The discussions in the First Commission of the conference on the question of the admission of foreign aircraft resulted in a decision that each contracting State would admit the flight of aircraft of other contracting States within and above its territory subject to certain restrictions to be discussed hereafter. This was in substance the original positions stated in the German draft convention.

When Kriege, chairman of the German Delegation, as president of the First Commission opened the discussion, the British statement had not been filed. He called the attention of the commission to the French and German statements, saying that they were in agreement on essential points, that both favored in principle freedom of air navigation subject to restriction, that subjacent States had a right to take measures necessary to guarantee their own security and that of the persons and goods of their inhabitants. Kriege was careful not to define freedom of air navigation. He noted that the German statement proposed to limit the right of restriction by a provision that no restriction could be applicable to foreign aircraft if it were not equally applicable to private

---

[20] *Procès-verbaux, op. cit.,* pp. 269–272.

aircraft. Discussing certain of the detailed restrictions supported by the French statement, he concurred in the advisability of providing that each State have a right to exercise police and customs supervision in the atmosphere above it and also a right to prevent unauthorized passage of foreign military and police aircraft.

Fauchille replying, pointed out the difference between the German and French proposals as he understood them. The French desired to have the restrictions which a State could adopt set out in the convention, while the German proposal would leave to each State the power to determine for itself those restrictions which it desired to impose. Fauchille considered that this would open the way to arbitrary action.

The British Delegation then presented its statement objecting to the German proposal. The Dutch chief delegate expressed his agreement with the British in opposing any general statement of freedom of air navigation, being particularly concerned as to the manner in which it would limit the right of each State to adopt local penal and regulatory statutes. The Swiss chief delegate also supported the objection to any general statement of freedom of navigation, stating that if any principle must be accepted, Switzerland would "reserve the principle of sovereignty."

During the discussion of the British statement the divergent French and German views as to freedom of navigation became apparent. Renault seemed to support a rather vague general right of international passage based on the fact that aircraft were actually flying from one State to another.[21] Kriege's statement was extremely guarded but certainly implied that obligation of a State to admit foreign aircraft would depend on an international convention.

The Austrian delegate added his objection to the formula that air navigation was free. He was not prepared to admit that freedom of navigation should be restrained only in the interest of security of the State, nor would he accept the formula that foreign aircraft should always be treated in the same manner as national aircraft. He supported in full the British position.

In the face of continued opposition to the formula that air navigation was free, Kriege clarified the German position in replying to the Dutch delegate, stating that he believed that the expression "freedom of air navigation" was the thing most displeasing to the Dutch delegate, and adding:

---

[21] *Ibid.*, p. 266. A careful examination of all the debates does not disclose any reference by Renault or the French Government to the concern that that government had felt in 1908 and 1909 resulting from the continued flight of German balloons into and over French territory.

but that expression does not figure in the German proposals—it is only a question of the admission of aircraft within the limits of and above foreign territory. It is not a matter of complete freedom but only the obligation of admission. Everything concerning the penal laws and jurisdiction remains outside the German proposal.[22]

Certainly Kriege was supporting the adoption of a convention which, by its terms, would obligate contracting States to admit aircraft of other contracting States, and was not going further in supporting any theory of a general international law right of innocent passage.

The main question was then referred to the examining committee of the commission. At the same time the commission adopted without debate the three original German proposals as to cabotage, as to the establishment of international air lines depending on the assent of interested States, and as to the right of retorsion.[23]

At a later session of the Commission, Kriege reported the decisions of the examining committee as to the admission of air navigation within the limits of or above foreign territory,[24] and presented the following rules recommended by the committee:

Rule 1: Each contracting State shall permit the navigation of aircraft of other contracting States within the limits of and above its territory subject to restrictions necessary to guarantee its own security and that of the persons and goods of its inhabitants.

The contracting States undertake to conform the private law of their countries to the preceding paragraph.

Sojourn required by necessity can not be refused in any case to aircraft of a contracting State.

Rule 2: The restrictions imposed by a contracting State, pursuant to Rule 1, paragraph 1, will be applied without any inequality to national aircraft and to aircraft of every other contracting State.

This obligation does not cover measures which a State should take in extraordinary circumstances to assure its national defense.

Rule 3: Each contracting State has the power to reserve the professional transport of persons and goods between two points on its territory to national aircraft alone, or to aircraft of certain contracting States, or to submit such navigation to special restrictions.

---

[22] *Ibid.*, pp. 280–281.

[23] *Ibid.*, p. 281. The provisions as to cabotage and establishment of "international lines" are of great importance. The German proposals generally would have admitted private aircraft of all contracting States for any purpose, commercial or otherwise. These provisions severely restricted general rights of transit and commerce granted between contracting States.

[24] *Ibid.*, pp. 315–318.

The establishment of international air lines depends upon the assent of interested States.

Rule 4: With regard to a contracting State which imposes restrictions of the kind foreseen in Rule 1, paragraph 1, analogous measures may be applied by every other contracting State.

Rule 5: The restrictions and reservations contemplated by rules 1 to 4 shall immediately be published and notified to the interested governments.[25]

Discussing these rules, Kriege stated that the committee did not wish to give a theoretical definition of the idea of free admission, that it had limited itself to establishing practical rules to reconcile different interests, and that accordingly the committee proposed as a rule that each contracting State should permit the navigation of aircraft of other contracting States within the limits of and above its territory subject to restrictions necessary to guarantee its own security and that of the persons and goods of its inhabitants. "It is in this sense" said Kriege "that the admission of aircraft to air navigation has been fully recognized."[26] He further reported the committee's decision that each State should accord the same treatment to foreign aircraft as to national. Thus Kriege succeeded in obtaining the adoption of rules as to admission of aircraft consistent with the theory of the original German draft convention.

Complete agreement existed on the important first paragraph of Rule 1 which limited the obligation of contracting States to permitting flight of aircraft of other contracting States, thereby implying that no obligation existed to admit aircraft of other States. But as to equal treatment of national and foreign aircraft, Admiral Gamble, chief British delegate, immediately stated his objection. He said that the application to national aircraft of the same restrictions as to foreign was not acceptable to the British Delegation, that the British Government would find itself in the impossible position of granting special navigation facilities to its nationals and being obliged to grant the same to the whole world. The Austrian and Russian delegates made similar reservations.

Subject to these reservations the proposed rules were adopted by the First Commission and ordered reported in its behalf to the conference.

DISCUSSION IN THE CONFERENCE

The report of Fauchille, including the proposed rules as recommended by the First Commission, was duly presented to the conference.[27]

---

[25] *Ibid.*, pp. 322–323.   [26] *Ibid.*, p. 315.   [27] *Ibid.*, pp. 97–104.

This report, together with reports of the other conference commissions, was referred to a drafting committee including Renault (France), Kriege (Germany), and Gamble (Great Britain). On June 24th Renault presented a proposed draft convention complete except as to Article 19 and 20.[28] The missing articles, as Renault explained, concerned the principle of the admission of air navigation within the limits of or above the territory of a foreign State which had raised "delicate questions." He proposed to the conference that it adjourn discussion on this matter.

The missing articles covered the substance of Rules 1 and 2 as recommended by the First Commission. With these omissions the proposed convention as recommended to the conference by the drafting committee, was adopted.[29]

At the conclusion of the conference session of June 24th, where the draft had been adopted, the chief Swiss delegate proposed an indefinite delay so that governments might have an opportunity to examine the convention before signature. This proposal was withdrawn so that the conference could adjourn for five days to give the drafting committee further opportunity to complete Articles 19 and 20.

The conference reconvened on June 29th. The British delegation presented an amendment[30] covering Rules 1 and 2 as to the admission of aircraft (the missing Articles 19 and 20 of the draft convention), thus disclosing the only points on which disagreement appeared to remain. The British proposal would have amended the second paragraph of Rule 1 to read: "The contracting States undertake to *take every practical measure* to conform the private law of their countries to the provisions of the preceding paragraph." The words in italics were the only material change. Paragraph 2 of Rule 2 would have been amended to read: "This obligation does not cover measures which a State should take to assure its security." This differs from the original rule adopted by the commission principally in substituting the word "security" for the words "national defense," and omits the words "in extraordinary circumstances" which appeared in the commission rule. The British proposed amendment also included a suggested Rule 2A which would read:

Notwithstanding the provisions contemplated in Rules 1 and 2, each contracting State reserves the right to forbid air navigation or regulate it as seems fit to such State in certain zones of reasonable extent.

The British added a note citing the report of the Second Commission

---

[28] *Ibid.*, p. 39.   [29] *Ibid.*, pp. 188–225.   [30] *Ibid.*, p. 65.

of the conference,[31] which had recommended a rule that "each State remains free to regulate at its will the prohibition of flight and landing in certain zones and to determine to whom such prohibition will be applied."

The British position on the last day of the conference may be summarized as follows: (1) It would not accept an absolute commitment to amend British law to cover the right of flight of foreign aircraft over private property, but proposed to take every practical measure to that end; (2) it was prepared to modify its prior objection to the application of national treatment to foreign aircraft provided that this obligation did not apply to any measure which the State took to ensure its security; (3) it insisted on a clear statement of the right of each State to set up prohibited zones, apparently not being satisfied with the indirect reference to prohibited zones in Articles 23 and 24 of the draft convention as adopted. Neither the original Rules 1 and 2 of the First Commission nor the British amendments were submitted to the final vote of the conference. The British chief delegate moved adjournment of the conference because "the British Government feels that the great importance of the questions which had been treated by the commissions makes necessary a profound examination by the Government itself before the draft convention may be approved.[32] A tentative date of November 29, 1910 was set for the conference to reconvene, but efforts to reconcile the existing differences of opinion were unavailing and the conference was never called back into session.

CONFERENCE DISAGREEMENTS WERE POLITICAL, NOT LEGAL

The failure to reach a final draft convention at Paris in 1910 on regulation of air navigation was almost entirely political. When the conference adjourned, only one legal point stood between Great Britain on one side and Germany and France on the other. This involved the legal status of private property rights in flight-space. The continental powers did not deny the existence of rights of the landowner in space over his surface properties, but they felt that each State must undertake to make such changes in its local laws as were required to permit foreign aircraft to enjoy the flight privileges granted by such State without interference from local landowners. As stated in the previous section, Great Britain finally suggested that it would "take all practical measures" to conform its local laws to the proposed convention. No one can suppose that compromise on this question would have been impossible if other non-legal questions could have been solved.

---

[31] *Ibid.*, p. 142.   [32] *Ibid.*, p. 62.

The real causes of the breakdown of the conference were political. Must restrictions on freedom of flight imposed by each State be applied equally to national aircraft and to aircraft of all other contracting States? Such "national treatment" for foreign aircraft was first proposed in the original German draft convention, was repeated in the German statement to the First Commission, and was urged in debate. It was opposed by Great Britain, Austria-Hungary, and Russia.[33] It was, however, included in the rules reported to the First Commission by the examining committee with the evident concurrence of France, and was adopted by that commission. Great Britain finally went so far as to suggest a compromise amendment offering to accept such national treatment of aircraft of other contracting States except as to "measures which a State takes to assure its security." This would have left contracting States a free hand as to national security measures, but would have required them to apply the same treatment to national and foreign aircraft insofar as safety regulations for the protection of persons and property were concerned. This was apparently not acceptable to Germany and France and the conference adjourned.

Neither the German nor French positions have ever been adequately explained. As to Germany it has been assumed, and perhaps rightly, that its great technical progress in the design and construction of the zeppelins and other dirigibles for both military and civil use had put it so far ahead of other European powers that it would have much to gain and little to lose by an exchange of the widest possible flight privileges.[34] As to France the 1910 position is even more difficult

---

[33] *Ibid.*, p. 102. See also Russian declaration [*Ibid.*, p. 179] as to Articles 19 and 20, stating that the principle of equality of treatment of nationals and foreigners in matters of air navigation could not be accepted by the Russian Delegation for various reasons, including the fact that this principle would affect the integrity of the sovereign rights of a State in matters of internal legislation.

[34] Catellani, writing about a year later, said that "in consequence of the more considerable progress made by Germany in the control of aircraft and in the formation of an air fleet more complete liberty for international navigation of aircraft would be more advantageous to the empire and to the expansion of its military power." [Enrico Catellani, *Il diritto aereo*, Turin, Bocca, 1911, pp. 100–101. Also translated into French by Maurice Bouteloup, *Le Droit aérien*, Paris, A. Rousseau, 1912.]

It is known that the German Government consulted von Zeppelin before accepting the French invitation to participate in the 1910 conference. Decision to accept the invitation was made at a meeting in the German Foreign Office at which he was present. [*Zeitschrift für Völkerrecht und Bundesstaatsrecht*, Vol. 4, 1910, p. 292.] This would appear to strengthen the view that the German position was based on its existing technical superiority and the desire for a convention which would give great latitude to the operation of German dirigibles.

to understand. It had invited the European States in 1908 to attend this conference largely because of its concern arising from the uncontrolled flight of German balloons into French territory. But at the conference France first supported Fauchille's formula for general freedom of air navigation subject only to restrictions required by national security—these restrictions to be stated in the convention. Defeated on that proposal, France apparently then accepted the German thesis under which it could have imposed no restrictions on German aircraft entering France without imposing similar restrictions on its own aircraft—the only exception being as to measures which it might take "in extraordinary circumstances to assure its national defense."

The conference came to final disagreement on this purely political question as to what restrictions could be applied by the subjacent State to aircraft of other contracting States. The breakdown was not, as popularly supposed, due to opposed theories of freedom of the air and State sovereignty.

GENERAL UNDERSTANDING ON STATE SOVEREIGNTY OF USABLE SPACE

Contrary to general understanding, the Paris 1910 conference did not break down because of a fundamental difference between Great Britain on one side and Germany on the other as to sovereignty or freedom of usable space. As a matter of fact at the close of the conference no State denied its legal *right* to restrict foreign flight over its surface territories. Agreement, though tacit, existed as to the legal status of flight-space. The only open problem was the political extent to which States should exercise their existing powers of control without unnecessarily impeding future development of international flight.

At Paris in 1910 the European States, for the first time since the Franco-Prussian War, were brought face to face with decisions involving the legal status of flight-space. The efforts of the French Government to keep this question out of the conference could never have been successful if a convention was to be drafted and signed. No conference could agree on the regulation of any phase of international transport in the absence of understanding as to whether the transport medium dealt with was or was not part of national territory. Thus treaties of commerce and navigation on the entry of surface shipping would be quite meaningless unless a stated or tacit understanding existed between the parties that the ports of entry concerned were within the national territory of the State authorizing foreign entry.

An examination of three articles of the draft convention approved at the plenary session of the conference shows that the government delegations then understood and acted upon the legal assumption that

120

flight-space over the national lands and waters was part of the territory of the subjacent State in which such State had complete and exclusive power to control all human activity including foreign flight. To the same effect are those parts of Rules 1 and 2 adopted by the First Commission on which no dispute existed.

Article 2 of the draft convention would alone determine the correctness of this assertion. Its first paragraph provided that an aircraft "is only governed by the present convention if it possesses the nationality of a contracting State." The second paragraph adds: "None of the contracting States shall permit free balloons or airships to fly over its territory unless they comply with the above conditions, though special and temporary authorization may be granted." This is an undertaking by each contracting State to prohibit the entry of all free balloons or airships except those possessing the nationality of contracting States or those specially authorized by such State. It is equivalent to the assertion of full and absolute sovereignty of the superjacent State with exclusive power to control all flight over its surface territories.

Article 30 is equally conclusive. Taken almost directly from the German draft convention, it provided that each State undertakes to require the observance by all aircraft "within the limits of or above its territory" of the rules relating to air traffic contained in an annex to the convention and "to punish those which fail to do so." This annex included aircraft lights and signals and rules of the road. No State could sign a convention containing a commitment of this character unless flight-space over its surface territories was also a part of its national territory in which its regulatory and penal statutes were exclusively effective.

Article 34 provided that the carriage of goods by air could take place only by virtue of special agreements between States concerned or pursuant to their legislation—a provision difficult to enforce if the flight-space involved was not part of national territory.

Interesting though not so conclusive, are Articles 23 and 24 as to prohibited zones, Article 29 as to the exercise of police jurisdiction and customs supervision above national surface territory, and Articles 35, 36 and 38 governing the carriage of explosives, munitions, photographic and wireless apparatus.[35]

---

[35] The paragraphs mentioned above are as follows:

Article 2: An aircraft is only governed by the present Convention if it possesses the nationality of a contracting State.

None of the contracting States shall permit a free balloon or airship to fly over its territory unless it complies with the above condition, though special and temporary authorization may be granted.

While the rules as to admission of foreign aircraft adopted by the First Commission did not come before the conference for formal approval, such parts of those rules as were not disputed certainly represent the conference position of the delegations of the principal Euro-

---

Article 23: The restrictions and reservations contemplated in Articles 19, 20, 21, and 22 shall immediately be published and notified to the Governments concerned.

The forbidden zones shall be defined with sufficient precision to enable them to be shown on aeronautical maps of a scale of at least 1/500000. The contracting states shall be obliged to communicate these maps to one another.

Article 24: As soon as the pilot of any aircraft perceives that he has entered the air space above a forbidden zone he must give the signal of distress specified in Article 16 of Annex (c) and land as soon as possible; he must also land if requested to do so by warning given from the ground. Each State shall give notice of the warning signals which it has adopted.

Article 29: The authorities of the country will always have the right to visit the aircraft on its departure and landing, and to exercise in the atmosphere above their territory police jurisdiction and customs supervision.

Each State can enact that if an aircraft of another contracting State lands on its territory the nearest police or customs authorities must immediately be notified.

The personnel on board the aircraft must conform strictly to the police regulations and provisions of the customs laws of the country.

Article 30: Each State undertakes to enact that all aircraft within the limits of, or above, its territory, and all its own aircraft within the limits of, or above, the territory of another contracting State shall comply with the "Rules relating to Aerial Traffic" annexed to the present Convention (Annex (6)) and to punish those which fail to do so.

Article 34: The carriage of goods by air can only take place in virtue of special conventions between the States concerned or of the provisions of their own legislation.

Article 35: The carriage by aircraft of explosives, arms, and munitions of war, and of traveler and other carrier pigeons, is forbidden in international traffic.

Article 36: Each State can forbid or regulate the carriage or use of photographic apparatus above its territory. It can cause the negatives found on board a foreign aircraft landing on its territory to be developed, and can, if necessary, seize the apparatus and negatives.

Article 38: Each State has the right to authorize aircraft within the limits of and above its territory to carry on board a radio-telegraphic apparatus. Such apparatus cannot, without special permission, be used except when the safety of the aircraft is concerned.

Procès-verbaux, op. cit., pp. 188–189. English translation from *Reports of the Civil Aerial Transport Committee . . . ,* London, H. M. Stationery Office, 1918, Cd. 9218 (Appendix A to Report of Special Committee No. 1).

pean States. No objection was made by any State to the first paragraph of Rule 1. In legal effect it created an obligation requiring that each State should permit navigation of other contracting States in superjacent flight-space. If the aircraft of foreign contracting States already had the right to fly over the subjacent contracting State, the permission of the latter would not have been required. The adoption of this rule evidenced understanding that flight-space over each contracting State was part of the territory of that State and that no right of innocent passage or right of entry then existed through such space.

In the French statement on the entry of foreign aircraft a recommendation was made that the convention should include a restriction prohibiting aircraft navigating below a height to be stated in the convention, so as to protect the population against the indiscretions of aircraft and the noise of their motors. The German delegation opposed this proposal and it had no support. The draft convention as approved by the conference and the rules adopted by the First Commission all dealt with flight-space as being subject to uniform regulation at whatever height used. The conference clearly rejected any division of usable space into horizontal zones.

As stated in previous sections, the French position at the opening of the conference recommended the inclusion in the draft convention of the proposal that air navigation is free. If any result of the conference is clear, it is the formal rejection of this theory. The first paragraph of Rule 1 as adopted by the First Commission is a negation of the principle of general freedom of air navigation. From the time the formula was first suggested in doctrinal discussions it had been supported on the theory that it was legally based on either freedom of the air (no State sovereignty in flight-space) or a right of innocent passage through such flight-space as was subject to State sovereignty. The direct refusal of the Paris 1910 conference to accept this formula was a denial both of freedom of the air and of the existence of a right of innocent passage. The articles of the draft convention and the undisputed rules of the First Commission also indicate the refusal of the governments represented at the conference to accept the Westlake dictum as to a right of innocent passage, and are consistent only with full and absolute State sovereignty in superjacent space, including the right of each State to regulate as it deemed fit the entry of foreign aircraft.

In summary, the Paris 1910 conference evidenced tacit but actual agreement of the delegations of the States there represented: (1) that each State had full sovereignty in flight-space over its national lands and waters as part of its territory; (2) that any division of such territorial flight-space into zones is impractical and unnecessary; (3) that no general right of international transit or commerce exists for aircraft of other States through such territorial flight-space. The conference demonstrated that the only practical legal method of regulating international flight was by international agreement providing for the grant of privileges of entry under terms and conditions there stated.[36]

---

[36] In *The Right to Fly*, published in 1947, I discussed certain of the legal and political questions [pp. 19–20] and stated an opinion as to the general views of the conference in the controversy between freedom and sovereignty of the airspace. On the latter question I said [p. 33]: "Although no one was willing to admit it, the fact is that had a majority rule been in effect at the Paris conference in 1910 and had a vote been taken, a convention might then have been adopted on this majority vote solemnly recognizing as the long-established Law of Nations that 'the air is free.' " Several years of intense research since *The Right to Fly* was written convince me that the conclusions which I reached in the statement above are unsound. Factually, the vote at the 1910 conference, adopting the draft articles of the proposed convention, was a vote in favor of sovereignty and against freedom of the air. Politically, as I am now convinced a majority of States present at Paris in 1910 would have gone further and voted against freedom of the air and in favor of a definite statement of State sovereignty had a vote on the direct issue been taken.

7

State Sovereignty in Space:
Developments 1910 to 1914

Reprinted from
Beiträge zum internationalen
Luftrecht: Festschrift für
Alex Meyer (Düsseldorf 1954)
Ministerium für Wirtschaft
Mittelstand und Verkher, Nordrhein-Westfalen.

Author's Note. This article was published as part of a group of essays prepared in honor of Dr. Alex Meyer of the University of Cologne in Germany on the occasion of his seventy-fifth birthday. The author is pleased to have had the opportunity thus to express his appreciation of the life-long work which Dr. Meyer has done in the varied fields of the law which affect human flight. It has been a great privilege to be his friend.

Oₙₑ OF THE LEAST UNDERSTOOD and at the same time one of the most important historical periods in the development of international air law lies between the breakdown of the Paris Conference of 1910 and the outbreak of World War I in 1914. It has sometimes been said that the period of World War I between 1914 and 1918, followed by the Paris Convention of 1919, first evidenced the acceptance by states of the principle of sovereignty in usable space over national lands and waters. Any careful historical analysis will demonstrate the fallacy of this position.

The International Air Navigation Conference held in Paris in 1910 was itself a major step in the development of international air law[1]. The most important document introduced at that conference was the draft convention prepared by the German Government. It is of great historical significance. It was the first concrete statement by any state of its position on the legal status of usable space. Certain articles of that draft evidenced the acceptance by the German Government of the principle of full and absolute territorial sovereignty in usable space over its lands and waters. This position had been previously stated by such German experts as Meurer, Zitelmann, and others.

Contrary to general understanding, the Paris Conference did not break down because of a difference between Germany and Great Britain as to the sovereignty or freedom of usable space. At the close of the conference, no state denied its legal right to restrict foreign flight above its surface territories.

Following this 1910 conference, international developments were rapid.

BRITISH POSITION

Following the adjournment of the Paris 1910 conference, the British Government asserted its unlimited sovereignty in usable space over its

---

[1] For full discussion, see THE INTERNATIONAL AIR NAVIGATION CONFERENCE, PARIS 1910, Chapter 6, *supra.*

lands and waters and its absolute unilateral right to control flight.

On July 29, 1910, a month after the conference adjourned, the British Foreign Office dispatched to its representatives in various European capitals a statement that "no regulations shall be framed which in any way exclude or limit the right of a State to prescribe the conditions under which the air above its territory should be navigated."[2] This is a textual restatement of part of the British answer to the French questionnaire preparatory to the 1910 conference. This position was doubtless brought quickly to the attention of the principal European governments. Although the conference was not called back into session, it is known that diplomatic negotiations continued for several years. The British 1910 position had become its fixed policy.

In 1911 the British Government apparently received an opinion from its Law Officers, presumably on the subject of its rights in space. While the contents of this opinion have not been released, it can reasonably be inferred from other known documents that the opinion sustained complete sovereignty.

On June 2, 1911 the Aerial Navigation Act, 1911 (1 & 2 Geo. V, ch. 4) was adopted. This authorized the Home Secretary from time to time by order to "prohibit the navigation of aircraft over such areas as may be prescribed in the order," and to apply any such order generally to those classes of aircraft which might be specified. This was a statutory declaration of a right of sovereign control and also a right to deal separately with foreign and national aircraft. A more detailed bill was drafted, but not introduced in Parliament. Later it became the model for postwar legislation. This draft bill declared in its preamble that "the sovereignty and rightful jurisdiction of His Majesty extends, and has always extended, over the air superincumbent on all parts of His Majesty's dominions and the territorial waters adjacent thereto."[3] This would now be accepted as an accurate statement of international law applicable to the status of usable space.

In 1913, the 1911 Act was amended by adoption of the Aerial Navigation Act, 1913 (2 & 3 Geo. V, ch. 22), extending the powers of the Home Secretary. By this amendment prohibited areas could include "the whole or any part of the coastline of the United Kingdom and the territorial waters adjacent to"—a declaration of British power to close its air boundaries. Pursuant to these statutes, the Home Secretary issued orders and regulations dated March 1, 1913 (S. R. & O. Nos. 228 and 243), fixing prohibited areas, landing places, and entry condi-

---

[2] See Part 1, paragraph 5 of the Report of Special Committee No. 1 in: *Reports of the Civil Aerial Transport Committee* . . ., London, H.M. Stationery Office, 1918 (Cd. 9218).

[3] *Ibid.*, p. 36.

tions for aircraft coming from abroad, and also prohibiting any entry of foreign military aircraft except with prior British permission. Different conditions were prescribed for entry of British and foreign civil aircraft. A further order was issued September 22, 1913 (S. R. & O. 1913, No. 1090) prohibiting flight over London. These orders and regulations in substance restated the Paris 1910 British position as to state sovereignty and as to the right to prescribe different flight regulations for foreign and national aircraft.

The entire course of conduct of the government of Great Britain up to the outbreak of World War I constituted an unequivocal assertion of the fact that usable space over British lands, interior waters, and the marginal sea was part of its national territory, and that no international rights of innocent passage existed through such territory.

FRENCH POSITION

The French Government also took active control of flight over its lands and waters. A presidential decree of November 21, 1911[4] provided, among other things: (a) that no aircraft could be put in service "in France" without a navigation permit, unless it satisfied the conditions contemplated by international conventions; (b) that such permits would be issued only under stated conditions; (c) that aircraft could not be navigated unless they had on board a pilot holding a certificate of competency; (d) that aircraft could not fly above certain designated and prohibited areas and could not, without permission, carry explosives and munitions, photographic or wireless equipment; (e) that the navigation "in France" of foreign military aircraft was prohibited. Such extensive police regulations could be justified and enforced, particularly against foreign aircraft, on no legal basis other than complete French sovereignty in the usable space over its lands and waters.[5] Pursuant to this decree, an ordinance was issued in 1912 prohibiting airplane landings in Paris and fixing the height of flight.[6]

On May 7, 1913, the President placed before the French Parliament a proposed law for the regulation of air navigation.[7] Many of its articles repeated the provisions of the decree of 1911. But Article 17 was new.

---

[4] *Journal officiel*, November 25, 1911. See also: *Revue juridique internationale de la locomotion aérienne*, Vol. 2, 1911, pp. 304–312.

[5] "The very words of the French Presidential Decret of 21 November, 1911—'La circulation *en France* des aéronefs militaires étrangers est interdite'—are a claim that the French clouds are France, England is England and France is France: that is the doctrine of sovereignty and it is the only sound one." James Molony Spaight, *Aircraft in Peace and the Law*, London, Macmillan, 1919, p. 8.

[6] *Revue juridique internationale de la locomotion aérienne*, Vol. 3, 1912, pp. 288–289.

[7] *Ibid.*, Vol. 4, 1913, pp. 175–186.

It provided for future public administrative regulation to determine the conditions and formalities to be satisfied by aircraft to authorize them to enter France and depart by air after landing. The proposal of this statute by the President and cabinet indicated administrative denial of freedom of the air and of any general international law right of entry for foreign aircraft. The entire draft statute tacitly asserted sovereignty in usable space.

On October 24, 1913, pursuant to the 1911 decree, important prohibited zones were prescribed particularly along the German border, leaving very narrow entry corridors.[8] On December 17, 1913 a new presidential decree replaced the 1911 decree, but with little change in the important provisions and no change in legal effect,[9] and detailed instructions were issued for its enforcement in the regulation of air navigation.[10]

GERMAN POSITION

The German Empire, and certain of its self-governing units, also asserted full sovereignty in superjacent space. The principal orders and decrees were: Brandenburg, 1910, prohibiting airplane flights unless pilots were furnished with certificates as approved by the International Aeronautic Federation;[11] Prussia, October 22, 1910, regulating flight, prohibiting passage over fortresses, requiring local pilots licences to be issued by German Aeronautic Union and foreign licences also to be approved by the Union;[12] Bavaria, October 11, 1911, requiring pilots to be licenced;[13] Prussia, January 17, 1913, effective February 1, 1913, prohibiting all foreign flights across Russo-German frontier;[14] Prussia, August 5, 1913, extending prohibited zones and regulating transport of photographic equipment.[15] Flight over other zones was limited by additional local orders.[16]

---

[8] *Journal officiel*, October 25, 1913. See also: *Revue juridique internationale de la locomotion aérienne*, Vol. 4, 1913, pp. 299–304; *Journal du droit international privé*, Vol. 41, 1914, p. 686.

[9] *Revue juridique internationale de la locomotion aérienne*, Vol. 5, 1914, pp. 9–20; *Journal du droit international privé*, Vol. 41, 1914, p. 688.

[10] *Ibid.*, pp. 20–23, 40–64, 81–85.

[11] *Revue juridique international de la locomotion aérienne*, Vol. 1, 1910, p. 221.

[12] *Gesetze betr. die Luftfahrt*, (Aero-Clubs von Deutschland), 1910, pp. 9–13. See also: *Revue juridique internationale de la locomotion aérienne*, Vol. 1, 1910, pp. 345–350.

[13] *Gesetze und Entwürfe von Gesetzen betr. die Luftfahrt*, (Aero-Clubs von Deutschland), Vol. 1, 1919, pp. 14–17.

[14] *Ibid.*, p. 163.

[15] *Ibid.*, p. 18. Also in: *Revue générale de droit international public*, Vol. 20, 1913, p. 76.

[16] *Revue juridique internationale de la locomotion aérienne*, Vol. 4, 1913, pp. 246–247.

In January 1914, an Air Navigation Bill, to be applicable throughout the Empire was introduced in the Reichstag,[17] indicating the government's understanding of its full right to regulate flight, This bill (passage of which was apparently put aside by outbreak of war) provided, among other things, that a licence would be required for commercial transport by aircraft for passengers and goods, and that if the flight covered the territories of several of the German states, licences should be granted jointly by the authorities of those states in which the aircraft landed or took off. In case of flights beginning or ending abroad, the consent of the Imperial Government would be required.

FRANCO-GERMAN AGREEMENT, JULY 1913

By the celebrated agreement of July 26, 1913 both France and Germany affirmed the right of each state to control all flight above its surface territories.[18] From 1911 to 1913 many instances had been claimed of German flights into and over France, Belgium, the Netherlands, and Switzerland. Two of these landings created serious international difficulties; one was that of a zeppelin at Luneville April 3, 1913 and the other that of a German military airplane at Arracourt April 22, 1913.[19] As a result the French ambassador made official representations to the Foreign Office in Berlin. Conferences followed, ending in the preparation of a draft agreement by the chief legal advisers of the two Foreign Offices, Renault and Kriege.[20] These two jurists had headed the French and German delegations respectively at the Paris 1910 conference and certainly understood the exact legal problems presented. The agreement was concluded as an exchange of letters between the French ambassador in Berlin (Cambon) and the German foreign minister (von Jagow).

The letters referred to aircraft "coming from Germany" and "coming from France". Nationality of aircraft was not specifically mentioned in the agreement. Aircraft were divided into two classes: those belonging to a military administration or carrying a crew composed in whole or in part of military men in uniform; and those not

---

[17] *Gesetze und Entwürfe von Gesetzen betr. die Luftfahrt*, Vol. 1, 1919, pp. 36–62.

[18] For text of the agreement, see: *Journal officiel*, August 12, 1913; *Reichsgesetzblatt*, 1913, p. 601, no. 48; *Revue générale de droit international public*, Vol. 20, 1913, pp. 697–701; *International Law Association*, Report of the 28th *Conference*, Madrid, 1913, pp. 542–548; Albert Roper, *La Convention internationale du 13 octobre* 1919 . . ., Paris, Recueil Sirey, 1930, pp. 246–251; *American Journal of International Law*, Vol. 8, Supplement, 1914, pp. 214–217.

[19] *Revue générale de droit international public*, Vol. 20, 1913, pp. 395–408.

[20] *Journal du droit international privé*, Vol. 40, 1913, pp. 540, 1142.

included in the first class. For convenience the terms of the agreement regarding aircraft entering France are specified below. Identical reciprocal regulations were contained in the agreement for aircraft entering Germany.

As to military aircraft, the agreement provided that those coming from Germany and into France could not navigate above French territory or land there except *on invitation* of the French Government. But special provisions were made for involuntary landings, including arrangements for military investigation as to whether such landings were really involuntary and requiring in certain cases that the German officer in charge of the aircraft should give his word of honor that neither he nor any member of the crew had committed any act affecting French national security. If the inquiry proved that the landing of the aircraft had not been caused by necessity, judicial authorities might take charge and the French Government be notified.

Navigation of non-military aircraft outside prohibited zones "fixed by French legislation" above French territory, also landings on such territory, were *authorized* under certain conditions: (1) the aircraft must have a navigation permit issued by competent German authorities and must carry distinctive marks permitting it to be identified during flight; (2) the pilot must have a certificate of competency delivered by German authorities; (3) the pilot must carry papers establishing his nationality, identity and military status, and each passenger must have similar papers; (4) the pilot must have a departure certificate ("certificat de sortie") issued by a diplomatic or consular representative of France on presentation before the voyage of the identification papers concerning the equipment and members of the crew together with a declaration of the purpose of the trip. Aircraft of this class and their crews would be subject to all general and customs legislation and aeronautic regulations in force in France. Permits and licences delivered to the aircraft and its pilot coming from German territory would have the same force as corresponding papers delivered in France. In case of involuntary landings, sojourn on French territory would not be refused to aircraft of this class coming from Germany even if the above conditions were not complied with. But such aircraft ought to land as soon as possible and advise the nearest civil authorities.

As to both classes of aircraft coming from German territory and landing on French territory, the French authorities would take steps necessary to ensure, so far as possible, the protection of the equipment and the security of the crew. The French Government further agreed to communicate with the German Government, on the basis of reciprocity, all regulations relative to air navigation. The agreement could be discontinued on notice from one government to the other.

The two governments concerned, France and Germany, put the agreement into force without delay. They prescribed the prohibited zones along the Franco-German border. Any semblance of free air navigation or right of innocent passage over that border disappeared. These and other prohibited zones took their authority from French and German unilateral sovereign powers respectively, not from the Franco-German agreement. Aircraft of all nations were equally prohibited from flight over the areas in question.

POSITIONS OF OTHER EUROPEAN GOVERNMENTS

Other European governments formally affirmed their legal right to control all flight above their surface territories, thereby asserting sovereignty in such usable space.

Austria-Hungary, by decree of October 22, 1912, required licences for certain types of air navigation;[21] by decree of December 20, 1912 authorized police measures against dangers to the public and private security created by flight of aircraft;[22] by proclamation of the Ministry of the Interior of January 20, 1913, established certain prohibited zones.[23]

Russia in December 1912 ordered the Russo-German border closed.[24] This decree was extended at various times so that it was still in force at the outbreak of World War I. In exceptional cases permission might be granted to fly across Russia's western frontier for purposes of sport, but requests were to be communicated through diplomatic channels, giving full information. Prohibited zones were also prescribed.

The Netherlands in 1912 provided by law for pilots licences, which could be issued by aviation societies, that landing fields must be approved, forbade flight without licence, forbade all flight of a nature to endanger public order or safety, allowed recognition of foreign pilots licences.[25]

Serbia in February 1913 issued a comprehensive regulation covering air navigation,[26] including requirements for flight permits, pilot certi-

---

[21] *Gesetze und Entwürfe von Gesetzen betr. die Luftfahrt*, Vol. 1, 1919, p. 66.

[22] *Revue générale de droit international public*, Vol. 20, 1913, Documents, p. 73; Kenneth W. Colegrove, *International Control of Aviation*, Boston, World Peace Foundation, 1930, p. 42.

[23] *Gesetze und Entwürfe von Gesetzen betr. die Luftfahrt*, Vol. 1, 1919, pp. 69–70.   [24] *Ibid.*, p. 155.

[25] For text of the law (translated into German), see: Albrecht Wolters, *Luftverkehrsrecht. Eine staatsrechtliche und völkerrechtliche Würdigung der Rechtsfragen der Luftfahrt*, Rostock, H. Warkentien, 1918, pp. 163–170.

[26] For text of Serbian decree (translated into German), see: *ibid.*, pp. 170–175. See also: *Revue juridique internationale de la locomotion aérienne*, Vol. 5, 1914, pp. 158–160.

ficates of competency, prohibition of the carriage of arms, photographic and wireless equipment, prohibition of flight near fortresses except with special permission, provision of fixing of flight routes by police authorities, requiring aircraft coming from abroad to pass over Serbian territory only at the places and times fixed by the Minister of the Interior, and prohibiting all foreign flight in time of mobilization or of war.

By 1914 every European state which had dealt with the subject of air navigation appeared to base its laws and police regulations on the understanding that superjacent and then usable space was part of national trritory in which it had the same regulatory rights as it had on the surface.[27] No European or other state protested these unilateral acts. Before the outbreak of World War I complete acceptance appeared to exist of the right of each sovereign state to regulate flight over its lands and waters without admitting any right of innocent passage.

OUTBREAK OF WORLD WAR I

Even before the actual outbreak of hostilities. France by decree of July 31, 1914 prohibited flight over national territory.[28] Perhaps a formal decree would not have been necessary. Under Article 10 of the presidential decree of October 24, 1913, creating prohibited zones, provision had been made that in case of total or partial mobilization, air navigation would be prohibited in the entire extent of the national territory, and such prohibition would enter into force upon the publication of the order of mobilization. Such publication in 1914 would have been sufficient to prohibit all flight over French national territory, but the French Government did not rely on this provision alone. On July 31, 1914, as stated above, while still technically at peace, the government by presidential decree, based on the prior presidential decree of November 21, 1911, ordered that "beginning from July 31, 1914 and until otherwise ordered, air navigation is prohibited in the entire extent of the national territory, in Algeria, in Tunis, and in the colonies," and that "the provisions of the present decree do not apply to State aircraft."

Great Britain, like France, prohibited flight over national territory prior to becoming involved in the hostilities. On August 2, 1914

---

[27] For another survey of national legislations, see: George G. Bogert, "Problems in Aviation Law," *Cornell Law Quarterly*, Vol. 6, 1921, pp. 271–309. Also in: *Civil Aeronatucs. Legislative History of the Air Commerce Act of 1926* . . ., Washington, U.S. Govt. Print. Office, 1943, pp. 66–97.

[28] *Journal officiel*, August 1, 1914, p. 7028. See also: *Revue générale de droit international public*, Vol. 22, 1915. Document, pp. 6–7.

pursuant to the Aerial Navigation Acts of 1911 and 1913, the Home Secretary issued an order in the following terms:

> I prohibit the navigation of aircraft of every class and description over the whole area of the United Kingdom, and over the whole of the coastline thereof and territorial waters adjacent thereto.
>
> This Order shall not apply to naval or military aircraft or to aircraft flying under naval or military orders; nor shall it apply to any aircraft flying within three miles of a recognized aerodrome.[29]

This order was a complete closing of British space boundaries. Foreign military aircraft, under the Aerial Navigation Acts, and prior orders, were not permitted to enter Great Britain without having obtained previous permission. The new order closed the boundaries to all civil aircraft. As no foreign civil aircraft could take advantage of the three miles provision in the new order due to the interposition of the marginal sea belt along the shore, the British coasts were closed to the approach of all foreign aircraft. As in the case of France no new legislation was necessary. The order of August 2, 1914 was a control measure based on existing statutes. But it forceably affirmed again the British position that usable space above its lands and waters was part of its national territory.

The little known and seldom read German Declaration of War on France was based in large part on claimed acts of French military aviators in flying over German and Belgian areas. On August 3, 1914 the German ambassador at Paris handed a letter to the French Minister for Foreign Affairs. The opening paragraph of this Declaration of War may be translated as follows:

> The German administrative and military authorities have established a certain number of flagrantly hostile acts committed on German territory by French military aviators. Several of these have openly violated the neutrality of Belgium by flying over the territory of that country; one has attempted to destroy buildings near Wesel; others have been seen in the district of the Eifel, one has thrown bombs on the railway near Carlsruhe and Nuremberg.[30]

The German Government thus assigned the same importance to French flights over Belgian and German territory as to attacks on part of the German surface areas. The neutrality of Belgium had been internationally guaranteed. According to the German point of view,

---

[29] S.R. & O. 1914, No. 1117, August 2, 1914.

[30] No. 147, The French Yellow Book, as reprinted in: *Collected Diplomatic Documents relating to the Outbreak of the European War*, London, H. M. Stationery Office, 1915, pp. 240-241. Also in: *American Journal of International Law*, Vol. 9, Supplement, 1915, pp. 277–278.

entry of French military aircraft into the space over Belgium constituted a violation by France of this Belgian territorial neutrality. Likewise, entry of French military aircraft into space over Germany was considered equivalent to entry of French forces into German land territories. Either was considered an act of war. Belgian space was part of Belgium, and German space was part of Germany.[31]

No new rule is stated in the German Declaration of War. An existing and fully understood rule of international law is assumed.

Of no less importance than the acts of belligerents were the acts of neutral states in closing their space boundaries.

The Netherlands on August 3, 1914, immediately upon the outbreak of European hostilities, by a decree provided that the crossing of its land frontiers by airships, not belonging to the Netherlands' land or sea forces, was prohibited.[32]

Switzerland, by ordinance of the Federal Council of August 4, 1914 on the maintenance of neutrality, provided in Article 17, among other things, that balloons and aircraft not belonging to the Swiss army "cannot rise and navigate in the aerial space situated above our territory unless the persons ascending in the apparatus are furnished with a special authorization," and that "the passage of all balloons and aircraft coming from abroad into our aerial space is forbidden" and "will be opposed if necessary by all available means, and these aircraft will be controlled whenever that appears advantageous."[33] Following this formal declaration of neutrality, the Swiss Government notified governments of adjoining states that the flight of foreign aviators in Switzerland had been prohibited and that every means would be used to oppose their passage.[34]

Sweden on September 7, 1914, adopted a law which provided that the King should order, when found necessary, that aircraft over Swedish territory would not be allowed without royal permission,

---

[31] The French Foreign Minister, in his address to the Chamber of Deputies on August 4, 1914, denied the charges stated in the German Declaration of War.

[32] *Staatsbladt*, 1914, No. 354. See also for translation: Francis Deak and Philip C. Jessup, eds., *A Collection of Neutrality Laws, Regulations and Treaties of Various Countries*, Washington, Carnegie Endowment for International Peace, 1939, Vol. 2, p. 807.

[33] *Recueil officiel* (N. S.), Vol. 30, p. 353; *British and Foreign State Papers*, Vol. 108, pp. 842–845; *Revue générale de droit international public*, Vol. 22, 1915, Document, pp. 183–185. See also translation in: Deak and Jessup, *op. cit.* Vol. 2, pp. 1008–1011.

[34] Louis Rolland, "Les Pratiques de la guerre aérienne . . .," *Revue générale de droit international public*, Vol. 23, 1916, pp. 497–604, text at p. 566. For text of the note of August 8, 1914 to the French Government, see: *Journal officiel*, August 10, 1914, p. 7301. Summary of text appears in *Revue générale de droit international public*, Vol. 22, 1915, Document, p. 187.

except airships belonging to the Swedish service or engaged in its service, and that the police and military authorities were empowered to prevent by all necessary means the navigation of airships in violation of this prohibition.[35] On the same day, September 7, 1914, the King of Sweden issued a proclamation ordering that air traffic, including passenger planes, over the territory of Sweden should be prohibited until further notice.[36]

The United States, by proclamation signed by President Woodrow Wilson on November 13, 1914, put into effect certain rules regarding the maintenance of neutrality by the United States in the Canal Zone. Rule 15 was as follows:

> Air craft of a belligerent Power, public or private, are forbidden to descend or arise within the jurisdiction of the United States at the Canal Zone, or to pass through the air spaces above the lands and waters within said jurisdiction.[37]

This was the first formal recognition by the government of the United States that the control of surface territory by a sovereign state carries with it the right to control superjacent space.

CONCLUSION

Thus it is apparent that by the outbreak of World War I the principle of sovereignty in usable space over national lands and waters had been accepted by the international community as a customary rule. None questioned the right of each state to control at its discretion all flight over its surface territories and to prohibit the entry into its usable space of any foreign aircraft. Events during World War I and the preparation and signature of the Paris Convention of 1919 merely acknowledged and restated this already existing rule of customary international air law—namely, the absolute sovereignty of the subjacent state over usable space above its national lands and waters. This rule lies at the base of almost all subsequent developments in the field of public international air law.

---

[35] *Svensk Författningssamling*, 1914, No. 182, p. 633. German text in: Martens, *Nouveau recueil général de traités* (3d ser.), Vol. 10, p. 687. For English translation, see: Deak and Jessup, *A Collection of Neutrality Laws . . ., op. cit.* Vol. 2, p. 964.

[36] *Svensk Författningssamling*, 1914, No. 183, p. 634. For English translation, see: Deak and Jessup, *op. cit.*, Vol. 2, p. 975.

[37] *38 U. S. Statutes at Large*, p. 2039; Deak and Jessup, *op. cit.* Vol. 2, pp. 1205–1207; *Revue générale de droit international public*, Vol. 22, 1915, Document, pp. 165–168; *American Journal of International Law*, Vol. 9, Supplement, 1915, pp. 126–130.

8

United States Participation
in Drafting Paris Convention
1919

Reprinted by permission of the
Journal of Air Law and Commerce
from 18 Journal of Air Law and
Commerce *266 (1951).*
© Journal of Air Law and
Commerce *1951.*

Author's Note. This publication had two major original purposes; first, to illustrate the very active part which the United States exercised in determining the principles and language of the Paris Convention of 1919; and second, to verify the fact that the United States delegation prepared a draft convention which, with other drafts, was actually used and influenced the final text. Attention was directed to this American draft by Ray Stannard Baker's *Woodrow Wilson and World Settlement* (1922). The British and French drafts, prepared before the Paris Peace Conference, are referred to in the original minutes of the Paris Aeronautical Commission but not the American draft. It is believed, however, that this study demonstrates the historic validity and influence of the American draft as part of the proceedings which resulted in the Paris Convention of 1919.

T HE EXTENT OF United States participation in the preparation and drafting of the Convention relating to the Regulation of Aerial Navigation (Paris 1919) has been little appreciated. The fact that the United States signed this convention but did not ratify it is well known. But the more important fact that its delegates took a leading part in urging the adoption of certain of the basic principles of the convention, and that its representative on the Legal Subcommission cast a crucial deciding vote which may have changed much of the subsequent development of the international law of commercial entry of the aircraft of one contracting State into the territory of another, is practically unknown.

The Paris Convention (as it will be referred to hereafter) was drafted by the Aeronautical Commission of the Peace Conference in Paris in 1919. The delegates of the United States on the Commission were Rear-Admiral H. S. Knapp, U.S. Navy, and Major-General M. M. Patrick, U.S. Army. Their report submitted to the Secretary of State of the United States, dated from Paris 10 July 1919,[1] together with the official minutes of the Aeronautical Commission,[2] and the verbatim stenographic report of the meetings of the Legal Subcommission

---

[1] Report of the United States Delegates to the Aeronautical Commission of the Peace Conference (transmitted to the Secretary of State July 10, 1919). [Ms. in National Archives, Washington.]

[2] Conférence de la paix, 1919–1920, *Recueil des actes de la conférence,* Partie VII, Préparation et signature des traités et conventions divers, Procès-verbaux et textes, A—Conventions générales entre alliés, 1) Commission de l'aéronautique. Paris, Imprimerie nationale, 1933.

of the Aeronautical Commission[3] constitute original source material which no student of the period should overlook. As stated by the United States delegates, the background of the organization of the Aeronautical Commission was as follows:

> The Aeronautical Commission of the Peace Conference was formed as the result of an invitation made by M. Clemenceau, President of the Preliminary Peace Conference, in his letter of 25 January, 1919, to the principal Allied and Associated Powers, in which he proposed that such a body be created. Considerable correspondence took place between Heads of Governments, and finally the President of the United States authorized participation by the United States on the new Aviation Committee, and the American Delegates received appointments as the representatives of the United States on the Inter-Allied Aviation Committee. The first meeting of this Committee took place on the 6th March, 1919. . . .
>
> The Aeronautical Commission was formally recognized by the Supreme Council of the Peace Conference by communications dated the 12th and 15th March, 1919 . . .[4]

The formal action of the Supreme Council of the Peace Conference referred to by the United States delegates was contained in the resolution prepared and introduced by Balfour of Great Britain, to which Clemenceau (France) and Lansing (United States) consented, as follows:

> It is agreed—
>
> 1. That the existing aviation Commission, consisting of two representatives each of the United States of America, the British Empire, France, Italy and Japan, with five representatives of other States at the Conference shall be recognised and invited to consider:—
>
> *a*) Aerial matters arising out of the work of the Preliminary Peace Conference or referred by the Commissions set up by the Conference.
>
> *b*) A Convention in regard to International Aerial Navigation in time of peace.

---

[3] *La Paix de Versailles-Aéronautique*, Paris, Editions internationales, 1934, p. 217s.

[4] Report of the United States Delegates to the Aeronautical Commission, *op. cit.* p. 1. For additional facts as to the background of the formation of the Aeronautical Commission, see: Albert Roper, *La Convention internationale du 13 octobre* 1919 . . ., Paris, Recueil Sirey, 1930, Chap. 2; Kenneth W. Colegrove, *International Control of Aviation*, Boston, World Peace Foundation, 1930, Chap. 4: John C. Cooper, *The Right to Fly*, New York, Henry Holt, 1947, pp. 57–58.

2. That the question of the commercial aviation to be allowed to Germany be referred to this Commission.[5]

When the Commission was finally set up, it actually consisted of two delegates from each of the following States: United States of America, Great Britain, France, Italy and Japan; and one delegate from each of the following seven States: Belgium, Brazil, Cuba, Greece, Portugal, Rumania and Serbia. A very considerable part of the work of this Commission was devoted to military problems, particularly the effort to prevent or limit German rearmament after the conclusion of peace. The historic failure of this effort must be charged to the Supreme War Council and not the Aeronautical Commission, whose views were overridden.[6] These current military problems did have some effect on the drafting of the Paris Convention, but not nearly so much so as has been sometimes charged. The men who actually wrote the convention were civilians and international lawyers familiar with much of the historic development of international transport law, although the basic principles on which the convention was founded were adopted by the Aeronautical Commission itself which consisted largely of military and naval officers. The Legal Subcommission, which actually prepared the convention, did not meet until after these principles had been agreed upon.

On March 17, 1919 the Aeronautical Commission met to examine "the fundamental principles which should be adopted for air navigation in such manner as to permit the Subcommissions to take up their work following the directives fixed by the Commission." Present among others were Admiral Knapp and General Patrick for the United States, assisted by Col. E. S. Gorrell, who in later life became president of the Air Transport Association of America. The United States delegates took an immediate and decisive part in directing the course of the discussion. On the motion of Admiral Knapp the Commission adopted as its first principle the acceptance of the rule that each State is sovereign in the airspace above its territory, as follows:

1. Recognition: (1) of the principle of the full and absolute sovereignty of each State over the air above its territories and territorial waters, carrying with it the right of exclusion of foreign aircraft;

---

[5] U. S. Department of State, *Papers relating to the Foreign Relations of the United States-The Paris Peace Conference* 1919, Washington, U.S. Govt. Print. Off., 1942-Vol. 4, p. 342.

[6] For discussion of these problems, see: Cooper, *The Right to Fly*, *op. cit.* Chaps. 4 and 5.

(2) of the right of each State to impose its jurisdiction over the air above its territory and territorial waters.

As its second principle, the Commission adopted the following:

2. Subject to the principle of sovereignty, recognition of the desirability of the greatest freedom of international air navigation in so far as this freedom is consistent with the security of the State, with the enforcement of reasonable regulations relative to the admission of aircraft of the contracting States and with the domestic legislation of the State.

On motion of General Patrick, it was decided that this principle would apply only to contracting States and not to all foreign States. This was clarified by the third principle adopted by the Commission as follows:

3. With regard to domestic regulations relative to the admission and treatment of the aircraft of the contracting States, recognition of the principle of the absence of all discrimination on the ground of nationality.

While no dissenting voice was heard on the acceptance of the principle of national airspace sovereignty, sharp differences later developed as to the extent to which aircraft of contracting States should be authorized by the convention itself to have commercial privileges into and through the territory (including the airspace) of other contracting States. It is interesting to note that the delegates of the United States took so positive a position on the subject, when the United States had taken practically no part in official discussions prior to World War I as to the extent of the right of a State to control the use of its airspace by foreign States.[7]

The United States had made no preparations prior to the Peace Conference to assist in drafting a post-war convention for the regulation of international peacetime air navigation. On the contrary, both Great Britain and France had given careful and extensive thought to the subject and had prepared drafts of proposed conventions and

---

[7] My own extensive research on the historical development of the law as to the right of a State in the airspace above its surface territories indicates that without question the rule of national airspace sovereignty was an accepted and generally understood part of international law prior to the outbreak of World War I, that the acts of States during the war were consistent with the existence of this rule, and that the attacks on the rule prior to World War I were purely doctrinal and never accepted or supported by any formal position of any State in the international community. The Paris Convention did nothing more than restate the existing international law on the subject.

international regulations. The official minutes of the Aeronautical Commission contain both British and French proposals for an international convention. But the evidence is incontrovertible that draft conventions were also prepared by the delegates of the United States (apparently while the Aeronautical Commission was in session) and were circulated to other delegations and were actually considered and used in the final draft of the convention. The report of the United States delegates to the Secretary of State says: "Draft Conventions relating to International Air Navigation, as drawn up by the Delegates of Great Britain, France, Italy and the United States were exchanged among the various Delegations and served as a basis for discussion and solution of the questions presented to the Sub-Commissions in their work of drawing up an international Convention. (Copies of these drafts appended, marked C-1 to C-6 enclosed herewith)."

The exhibits to the United States delegates' report are actually as follows: C-1, the British draft convention just as it appears in the minutes of the Aeronautical Commission, with added notes and comments by the United States delegation; C-2, a provisional draft of regulations for adoption in Great Britain to cover civil aviation "pending the settlement of an international convention;" C-3, an English translation of the draft convention proposed by France, together with added notes and comments by the United States delegation; C-4, an American draft international convention; C-5, a second American draft; C-6, a document entitled "Italian Proposed Draft Convention for Air Navigation," but correctly described in its sub-title as "Italian Air Ministry Proposal for Aerial Navigation Laws."

The evidence in the report is not clear as to which of the two United States drafts stated the final position of the delegation. However, comparison of the texts (to be discussed hereafter) and other evidence clearly indicates that the second draft stated the official United States position. The first draft (C-4) comprised thirty articles and seemed to be nothing more than a redraft of the British proposal. The second American draft (C-5) comprised twenty-six articles, was more condensed, and varied in important details from the British proposal. A copy of this draft was furnished after the Peace Conference by General Patrick to Mr. Ray Stannard Baker and appears as one of the documents in his semi-official work *Woodrow Wilson and World Settlement*. Referring to this draft, Baker states that "their draft furnished many of the articles finally incorporated in the convention."[8] The text of this second, and apparently official, American draft is printed with this article as an appendix.

---

[8] Ray Stannard Baker, *Woodrow Wilson and World Settlement . . .*, Garden City, N.Y., Doubleday Page, 1922, Vol. 2, p. 460, Vol. 3, p. 419.

The noteworthy feature of the British draft, so far as international air law is concerned, was its statement in favor of sovereignty in the air coupled with extremely broad privileges of flight—practically what we would now call the "Five Freedoms." Great Britain had long favored official acceptance of the right of each State to control flight over its territory as the basic principle of international air law. As early as 1911 a proposed "Aerial Navigation Bill" had been drafted in Great Britain (although never introduced in Parliament) which opened with the following recitals:

WHEREAS the sovereignty and rightful jurisdiction of His Majesty extends, and has always extended, over the air superincumbent on all parts of His Majesty's dominions and the territorial waters adjacent thereto:

And whereas it is expedient to regulate the navigation of aircraft, whether British or foreign, within the limits of such jurisdiction, and in the case of British aircraft to regulate the navigation thereof both within the limits of such jurisdiction and elsewhere:[9]

It was therefore not surprising that the British 1919 draft was based on sovereignty, but nothing in published discussions prior to World War I indicated that the British Government did favor the widely extended commercial air navigation privileges suggested in the draft presented at Paris. The critical articles of the British draft are as follows:

Article 1:—The High Contracting Parties recognise the full and absolute sovereignty and jurisdiction of every State over the air above its territories and territorial waters, but subject thereto the aircraft of a contracting State may fly freely into and over the territories of the other contracting States provided they comply with the regulations laid down by the latter. Such regulations will permit the free navigation of foreign aircraft except in so far as restrictions appear to the State to be necessary in order to guarantee its own security or that of the lives and property of its inhabitants and to exercise such jurisdiction and supervision as will secure observance of its municipal legislation. The regulations shall be imposed on foreign aircraft without discrimination except in times of great emergency when a State may deem it necessary to safeguard its own security. It is, however, agreed that any one contracting State may refuse to accord to the aircraft of any other

---

[9] *Reports of the Civil Aerial Transport Committee . . .*, London, H. M. Stationery Office, 1918 (Cd. 9218), Appendix B to Report of Special Committee No. 1.

contracting State any facilities which the latter does not itself accord under its regulations.

Article 2:—Each contracting State shall have the right to impose special restrictions by way of reservation or otherwise with respect to the public conveyance of persons and goods between two points on its territory, but such restrictions may not be imposed on a foreign aircraft where such aircraft is proceeding from one point to another within the territory of the contracting State either for the purpose (1) of landing the whole or part of its passengers or goods brought from abroad or (2) of taking on board the whole or part of its passengers or goods for a foreign destination, or (3) of carrying between the two points passengers holding through tickets or goods consigned for through transit to or from some place outside the territory of the contracting State.

The privileges contemplated by these two articles were limited to aircraft of contracting States. This was emphasized further by the provisions of Article 3 of the British draft which stipulated that "no contracting State shall, except by special and temporary authorization, permit any foreign aircraft to fly over its territory" unless it possessed the nationality of a contracting State.

The French draft presented at Paris was much shorter and simpler than the British draft. It contained no definitive statement as to national sovereignty in the airspace, but was based on that legal theory. This necessarily follows from Article 1 of the French draft which stated that "Only aircraft belonging entirely to owners belonging to one of the contracting States . . . shall be allowed to fly over the territories of the contracting States."

The notes included in the exhibits to the United States delegates' report referred to above are most illuminating. The form in which they are presented indicates that they were among the papers circulated to other delegations. Commenting on the French draft, the United States delegation suggested the inclusion of a preliminary article as follows:

The contracting States declare that the sovereignty of States extends throughout the atmosphere above their own territories, including their territorial waters; but that no State may claim sovereignty of any part of the atmosphere over the High Seas or over waste portions of the land that are subject to no particular jurisdiction.

Commenting on the necessity of an article of this kind, the United States delegates said:

The sovereignty of the atmosphere is nowhere the subject of any formal international agreement. It is fundamental to any consideration of international aerial intercourse, as it is also to aerial questions connected with a state of war. Even if it be held that there is a common consent to the effect of this proposed Article, it will be declaratory—a formal conventional statement removing the subject from the realms of speculation in so far as the attitude of the assenting contracting parties is concerned.

Commenting further on the French draft, they added:

The Draft nowhere expressly stipulates that a contracting State shall permit foreign aircraft, even of other contracting States, to enter its jurisdiction. It may be presumed that this has been intentional in a draft prepared with so much care. In the light of their peculiar qualities—in peace in connection with Customs, Health, Immigration and Espionage laws, and in war because of their ready conversion into powerful military instrumentalities, and the difficulties of effective control at all times—the day does not seem to have arrived when any obligation to permit foreign aircraft to enter a State's jurisdiction should be adopted by international agreement. The most that should be attempted is to arrive at a set of general rules governing aircraft if they are permitted to enter foreign jurisdiction. Intentionally or unintentionally the Draft does no more than this.

Commenting on the British draft, the United States delegates indicated that the first clause of the first paragraph (as to sovereignty) "should be made a separate and independent article," adding:

The remainder of Article I definitely permits the free navigation, with certain restrictions, over the territories of contracting States, in which it differs from the French Draft.

Apparently the United States delegation was at first inclined to accept the British position. The first American draft (Exhibit C-4 to the delegates' report) opens with definitions of "aircraft" and of "territory", then follows with an article to the effect that "The High Contracting Parties recognize the full and absolute sovereignty and jurisdiction of every State over the air above its territories," followed by new articles 3 and 4 as to the extent of the privileges of flight of contracting States:

Article 3:—Subject to the provisions of Article 2 and to the municipal regulations laid down by any contracting States, the aircraft of each contracting State may fly freely into and across the jurisdiction of the others. Such municipal regulations, except

145

in so far as restrictions appear to the State to be necessary in order to safeguard its own security or the lives and property of its inhabitants, will permit the free navigation of aircraft of the contracting States, and will not require foreign aircraft to land in an intervening State when on a through flight whose points of departure and arrival lie on opposite sides of that State. The regulations shall be imposed on aircraft of contracting States without discrimination except in times of great emergency when a State may deem it necessary to safeguard its own security. It is, however, agreed that any one contracting State may refuse to accord to the aircraft of any other contracting State any facilities which the latter does not itself accord under its regulations.

Nothing in this convention, however, shall be held to abridge the right of any contracting State to forbid the entrance of foreign aircraft within its jurisdiction upon due notification to the other contracting States.

Article 4:—Each contracting State shall have the right to impose special restrictions by way of reservation or otherwise with respect to the public conveyance of persons and goods between two points on its territory, but such restrictions may not be imposed on an aircraft of another contracting State where such aircraft is proceeding from one point to another within the territory of the former contracting State either for the purpose (1) of landing the whole or part of its passengers or goods brought from abroad or (2) of taking on board the whole or part of its passengers or goods for a foreign destination, or (3) of carrying between the two points passengers holding through tickets or goods consigned for through transit, to or from some place outside the territory of the contracting State.

The development and change in the position taken by the United States delegates can best be noted by comparing these paragraphs with Articles 1 to 4 inclusive and Article 7 of the later American draft (attached as an appendix hereto).

In Article 1 of the latter, State sovereignty is recognized "in the airspace" above the territory of a State. So far as extensive research discloses, this is the first occasion on which a draft convention used the more exact term "airspace" rather than the term "air".[10] The United States delegation is entitled to this credit.

_____

[10] Of course eminent legal authorities had for years insisted that State sovereignty existed over the airspace and not over the gaseous air. See, for example, what is perhaps the earliest statement of this distinction when Westlake in 1906 at the meeting of the Institute of International Law challenged Fauchille's doctrinal insistence on "freedom of the air," saying: "I accept battle on the basis of the report; that is to say, on the principle of the freedom of the air, or, more exactly, the airspace. The air is itself something that cannot

Article 2 recognized the right of every State to exercise "such jurisdiction and supervision as will secure observance of its municipal legislation." The only limitation is that regulations shall be imposed on foreign aircraft without discrimination. It is clear from Article 7 that the term "foreign aircraft" in Article 2 means aircraft of contracting States, so that in substance Article 2 would have permitted States to impose such regulation on the entry of foreign aircraft (aircraft of other contracting States) as any State might desire provided regulations were applied without discrimination. This is a far and radical departure from the position in the British draft which would have prevented a State from restricting landings of aircraft of contracting States for the purpose of discharging or taking on board passengers or goods from abroad or destined for a foreign point. Article 4 is a statement of the undertaking of each State in time of peace to accord the liberty of innocent passage above its territory to the aircraft of other contracting States. This appears to be the first statement of this principle in approximately the form in which it finally appeared in Article 2 of the Paris Convention.

The comparison of other articles of this American draft will indicate the extent to which it influenced textually the Paris Convention, although the other passages are not of equal importance.

The actual draft of what eventually became the Paris Convention was first discussed in the Legal Subcommission. The most active members of this subcommission were civilians, although two were holding temporary military rank. Professor Buzzati, the chief Italian spokesman in the Legal Subcommission, had long been known as an expert in international law. With other Italian jurists he had participated in the organization of the Verona conference in 1910, one of the earliest held on the subject of international air law. To Buzzati fell the task of taking the various drafts available at Paris and producing an actual text for the consideration of the Legal Subcommission. It is known that he had available the text of the almost completed draft convention which resulted from the abortive international conference in Paris in 1910, as well as the texts of the new drafts submitted at Paris in 1919. While the minutes do not show his actual use of the second American draft, the internal evidence, as indicated earlier, appears to be conclusive on the point.

Professor de La Pradelle of France was the chief spokesman for that State in the Legal Subcommission. He was already recognized as one

---

be possessed, which is carried at the will of the winds—today in Belgium, tomorrow in France or in Holland. What we have about us is not the air. It is the airspace." [*Annuaire de l'Institut de droit international*, Vol. 21, 1906, p. 297.]

of Europe's outstanding authorities on international law, had participated in pre-war air law discussions, and had assisted in drafting the French proposals for a post-war convention.

Captain H. S. Bacon was the chief spokesman for the United States on the Legal Subcommission. He had practiced law in New York prior to World War I, had been on duty with the United States Air Force in Paris in a legal capacity during the war. After the war he returned to civilian life and practiced law in Paris until World War II.

Captain Tindal-Atkinson and Mr. White-Smith were the chief British spokesmen. Both were members of the British bar. The former held a commission in the R.A.F. during the war, but returned to civil life and a distinguished career in England after the war.

Anyone who desires to understand the real legal background of some of the critical clauses of the Paris Convention should study with care the stenographic reports of the sessions of the Legal Subcommission and particularly the arguments presented by these thoroughly trained jurists and legal experts. Of special importance were the discussions that arose from the effort of the British delegates to have incorporated in the final convention the broad privileges of commercial flight between contracting States contemplated in Articles 1 and 2 of the British draft.

Though it is little known, the almost complete draft convention prepared at Paris in 1910 included a provision as to the establishment of international airlines, and as to cabotage. Article 21 of that draft, somewhat freely translated into English, read as follows:

> Each contracting State has the power to reserve the professional transport of persons and goods between two points on its territory to national aircraft alone, or to aircraft of certain contracting States, or to submit such navigation to special restrictions.
>
> The establishment of international airlines depends upon the assent of interested States.[11]

At one of the first meetings of the Legal Subcommission (March 20, 1919) Atkinson (Great Britain) had stated that the British point of view was that air navigation ought to be as free as possible, each

---

[11] The French text read:

"Chaque Etat contractant aura la faculté de réserver le transport professionnel de personnes et de marchandises, ayant lieu entre deux points de son territoire, aux aéronefs nationaux seuls ou aux aéronefs de certains Etats contractants ou de soumettre cette navigation à des restrictions spéciales.

"L'établissement de lignes internationales de communication aérienne dépendra de l'assentiment des Etats intéressés." [Conférence internationale de navigation aérienne, Paris 18 mai-28 juin 1910, *Procès-verbaux des séances et annexes*. Paris, Imprimerie nationale, 1910, pp. 188–199.]

State reserving the right to take measures which concerned its security and to lay out corridors over which air navigation would pass. At the meeting of March 22nd the early clauses of the convention were adopted almost in final form covering the questions of national airspace sovereignty, innocent passage, restricted zones, as well as the provision in original Article 5 that no contracting State would admit flight over its territory to the aircraft of non-contracting States except by special and temporary authorization. At the session of March 26th Buzzati brought forward his draft Article 15 as to the right of each State to reserve professional (commercial) air traffic between two points in its territory, suggesting language almost identical to that contained in Article 21 of the draft 1910 convention quoted above. He also suggested an Article 16, as to the establishment of international airlines depending on the consent of interested States, quite similar to that in the draft 1910 convention. At this point Atkinson (Great Britain) pressed the British point of view under which national restrictions could not be imposed on aircraft of contracting States seeking to disembark or to take on all or part of its passengers or goods coming from or destined abroad. He argued that if commercial aircraft provided passenger service from London to Constantinople and passed through Paris, it ought to be allowed to take on passengers at Paris for Constantinople, but that this could be prevented under the proposed Article 15. In other words, using more modern terminology, the British delegate insisted that the convention ought to give full Fifth Freedom rights to the commercial aircraft of every contracting State operating on through routes.

De La Pradelle (France) contested the British point of view. He was prepared to accept the position that an international line ought to have the right to fly over national territory without stopping or landing, but that concessions must stop there. He insisted that each State ought to remain absolute sovereign of what occurred on its territory—that no one had sufficient experience as to the conditions under which international lines would be established to fix definite regulations, and that France could not accept the commitments (suggested by the British proposal). Buzzati (Italy) stated that the Italian delegation supported the French position. In the case of an international line from London to Constantinople, he questioned whether passengers or goods should be picked up at Paris for Turkey if a French line existed between Paris and Constantinople. (A very modern statement of present day commercial Fourth and Fifth Freedom problems.) Buzzati added that these were new questions and that no one knew how international lines would be set up in future.

The question was further discussed at the meeting of March 26th. Atkinson and de La Pradelle restated the British and French positions.

The British proposal was formally put to a vote. It was supported by the delegations of Great Britain and of Japan (the latter having taken no active part in the discussion), and was opposed by the delegations of France, Italy and the United States.

Thus, the vote of the United States was controlling on this critical question. Had the United States representative in the legal Subcommission supported the British position, an entirely different draft convention might have been reported to the full Aeronautical Commission and might have been there adopted. Instead of a convention which authorized interested States to regulate the establishment of international airlines over their territories, such a convention would have denied the right of any State to restrict the disembarkation of passengers or goods from abroad brought in by airlines of other contracting States, or the embarkation of passengers or goods destined for points abroad. Such a convention would in substance have meant that what we now consider as Third, Fourth and Fifth Freedoms commercial privileges would have been written into the Paris Convention from the beginning.

The United States delegates took an active part in the discussions in other subcommissions and participated in the final discussions in the full Commission before the convention was opened for signature. The United States was also represented on the final drafting committee. But at no point was its influence as controlling or decisive as on the occasions mentioned in detail above.

In summary it may be said that the contributions of the United States to the drafting of the Paris Convention included the suggestion of the use of the technical term "airspace" and not "air" in stating the principle of sovereignty; in using the term "innocent passage" as it appeared in the final draft of the convention; in insisting on the principle of sovereignty in the airspace to the extent that it refused to support the British position which sought to write into the convention wide privileges for the future development of international airlines.

APPENDIX

DRAFT CONVENTION SUBMITTED TO THE AERONAUTICAL COMMISSION OF THE PEACE CONFERENCE HELD AT PARIS IN 1919 BY THE AMERICAN MEMBERS, REAR-ADMIRAL H. S. KNAPP AND MAJOR GENERAL MASON M. PATRICK

[Attached as Exhibit C-5 to Report of the U.S. Delegates to the Aeronautical Commission of the Peace Conference to the Secretary of State, July 10, 1919. Also in: Ray Stannard Baker, *Woodrow Wilson and World Settlement*, New York, Doubleday Page, 1922, Vol. 3, pp. 419–424.]

ARTICLE 1

The contracting states recognize the full and absolute sovereignty and jurisdiction of every state in the air space above its territory and territorial waters.

ARTICLE 2

The contracting states recognise the right of every state to establish such regulations and restrictions as appear to the state to be necessary in order to guarantee its own security or that of the lives and property of its inhabitants, and its right to exercise such jurisdiction and supervision as will secure observance of its municipal legislation. These regulations shall be imposed on foreign aircraft without discrimination, but it is agreed that any one contracting state may refuse to accord to the aircraft of any other contracting state any facilities which the latter does not itself accord under its regulations.

ARTICLE 3

Each contracting state shall have the right to impose special restrictions by way of reservation or otherwise with respect to the public conveyance of persons and goods between two points on its territory.

ARTICLE 4

Each contracting state undertakes in time of peace to accord the liberty of innocent passage above its territories to the aircraft of the other contracting states, subject to the conditions established by this convention.

ARTICLE 5

Each contracting state has the right to prohibit the aircraft of other contracting states from flying over certain zones of its territory.

If a state exercises this right, it must publish and notify beforehand to the other contracting states the location and extent of the forbidden zones. All of the aircraft of a state except those belonging to its military establishment and other state-owned aircraft engaged in public business, shall be excluded from any zones which are forbidden to foreign aircraft.

ARTICLE 6

Every aircraft which finds itself over a forbidden zone shall at once give the signal of distress provided for in Article —— of the regulations annexed hereto, and as soon as possible shall land at a station outside the prohibited zone but as near as possible thereto and within the territory of the state within which the prohibited zone is located.

Any aircraft when called upon to land by signal or otherwise must do so at once. Each state shall publish and notify to the other contracting states the landing signals adopted by it.

ARTICLE 7

The present convention applies solely to aircraft possessing the nationality of a contracting state. No contracting state shall, except by special and temporary authorization, permit any aircraft to fly over its territory unless such aircraft does possess the nationality of a contracting state.

ARTICLE 8

An aircraft shall possess the nationality of the state upon whose official register it is borne. Every aircraft of a contracting state which leaves its jurisdiction and enters the jurisdiction of another contracting state shall be borne upon the official register of the states whose nationality it possesses. No aircraft of a contracting state shall be permitted to enter the jurisdiction of another contracting state unless it belongs wholly to nationals of a single contracting state.

Joint stock companies, limited liability companies, and all other incorporated or associated bodies shall be considered nationals of the state under the laws of which they are created. At least two-thirds of the stock of all such companies which operate aircraft in interstate traffic shall be owned by nationals of the state under the laws of which they are created, and all of their directors shall be nationals of such state.

ARTICLE 9

So long as an aircraft possesses the nationality of one of the contracting states in accordance with Article ——, no other state shall confer its nationality upon it. In cases where the home station of an aircraft is in the territory of a contracting state whose nationality it does not possess, the latter shall be immediately notified of its registration by the state in which it is registered.

ARTICLE 10

The contracting states will exchange and will forward to the Permanent International Aerial Commission every month lists of new entries on their registers and of the annulment of entries made on their registers during the preceding month.

ARTICLE 11

The aircraft of a contracting state when within the jurisdiction of another contracting state must bear their nationality and registration marks and the name and address of their owners.

ARTICLE 12

Every aircraft which passes from the jurisdiction of the state whose nationality it possesses into the jurisdiction of another contracting state shall be provided with a certificate of air worthiness issued or authorized by the state whose nationality it possesses.

ARTICLE 13

All commanding officers, pilots, engineers, and other members of the operating crew of an aircraft of a contracting state which passes into the jurisdiction of another contracting state must be provided with certificates of their competency and licenses issued or authorized by the state whose nationality the aircraft possesses.

ARTICLE 14

Certificates of air worthiness and certificates of competency and licenses issued or authorized by the state conferring nationality upon an aircraft will be recognised as valid by the other contracting states, provided they are issued in accordance with the conditions of this convention and the regulations appended hereto.

Each contracting state shall have the right to refuse to recognise certificates of air worthiness or certificates of competency or licenses issued to any of its own nationals by another contracting state.

Such non-recognition shall immediately be notified to the state which had issued the certificates and to the state where the aircraft has its home station.

ARTICLE 15

Every aircraft engaged in interstate navigation must carry:

a) A certificate of nationality.
b) A certificate of air worthiness.
c) Certificates of competency and licences for its operating crew.
d) If merchandise is carried, a bill of lading and a manifest.
e) A log book.

ARTICLE 16

All aircraft log books shall be kept for two years after the last entry and shall be presented when demanded by the public officials of any contracting state within whose jurisdiction the aircraft may be.

ARTICLE 17

The proper authorities of a contracting state shall verify the documents which its aircraft must carry and it is their duty to verify the quantity, quality, weight and measure of any merchandise carried and to furnish the manifest.

ARTICLE 18

Each contracting state agrees to take all necessary measures to assist aircraft in distress.

ARTICLE 19

Each contracting state agrees to allow aircraft belonging to other contracting states to land on all landing fields in its territory which are available for general use by its own nationals. The landing charges and charges for sojourn will apply equally to all aircraft of the other contracting states without distinction on account of nationality.

ARTICLE 20

Transportation by aircraft of explosives, arms and ammunition, and of any other dangerous material is prohibited in international traffic.

ARTICLE 21

Each contracting state has the right to prohibit the use of photographic apparatus above its territory and also the right to develop any films or plates found on board an aircraft, and the right to take possession of any apparatus and plates which have been used above its territory.

ARTICLE 22

The following will be considered as state-owned aircraft:

a) Military aircraft.

b) Aircraft used for state service other than military, such as customs and postal service, police, etc.

c) All other aircraft which are the property of the state.

All other aircraft are considered as private aircraft.

ARTICLE 23

Without special authorisation which may be granted by any contracting state, military aircraft belonging to one contracting state will not enter the jurisdiction of another contracting state. Any military aircraft which finds itself or which without such authorisation is found within the jurisdiction of a contracting state shall be subject to all of the conditions contained in this convention.

ARTICLE 24

There shall be created under the name of ————— a central office at ——————————. The expenses connected therewith shall be borne by the contracting states in such proportions as shall be fixed by the permanent commission provided for in Article ——.

ARTICLE 25

This bureau shall be under the control of a permanent commission consisting of two representatives each of the United States, France, the British Empire, Italy and Japan, with five other representatives nominated by the remainder of the contracting states.

This commission is empowered to collect, collate, publish and distribute information of every kind concerning aerial navigation; to render opinions upon questions in dispute at the request of the contracting states concerned; to examine proposals for any modification of the provisions of this convention; to recommend such modifications as may seem necessary; in general, to conduct such investigations or carry on such other work as may be for the benefit of the international aerial traffic of the contracting states.

ARTICLE 26

To this convention there are attached regulations which have the same force and effect as the convention itself and which will be put in force at the same time. The provisions of this convention and of the attached regulations may be modified at any time after agreement between the contracting states.

9
State Sovereignty Versus Federal Sovereignty of Navigable Airspace

Reprinted by permission of the
Journal of Air Law and Commerce
from 15 Journal of Air Law and
Commerce *27 (1948).*
ⓒ Journal of Air Law and
Commerce *1948.*

Author's Note. This title may confuse non-American readers. The subject covers possible conflicts between the sovereignty and jurisdiction of the individual states which comprise the U.S.A. as against the federal government so far as usable space is concerned. Certain phases of such conflicts could have wide significance if they should involve or affect the flight of foreign aircraft. In 1951, three years after the original study, the author again reviewed the effect of the *Causby* case (328 U.S. 256) and the *California Tidelands* case (332 U.S. 19) and suggested that "the only logical conclusion which can be drawn from the entire opinion in the *Causby* case is that the Court believed the navigable airspace to be Federal territory not part of the states below." ("Crimes Aboard American Aircraft: Under What Jurisdiction Are They Punishable?" 37 *A.B.A. Journal* 257 (1951)). This possible construction was apparently not confirmed when the U.S. Supreme Court in 1954 said, in the *Braniff Airways* case (347 U.S. 590), that the Air Commerce Act of 1926 "was an assertion of exclusive national sovereignty" but later added that "the Act did not expressly exclude the sovereign powers of the states," leaving the situation still confused. The trend toward federal control has, however, later reappeared in the 1961 amendments to Sec. 902 of the U.S. Federal Aviation Act expanding greatly the federal jurisdiction over crimes "aboard an aircraft in flight in air commerce." Such statutory air commerce is defined in Sec. 101(4) of the same act, as including "interstate, overseas, or foreign air commerce" or "operation or navigation of aircraft which directly affects, or which may endanger safety in interstate, overseas, or foreign air commerce," thus giving wide federal jurisdiction.

TWO COMPARATIVELY RECENT decisions of the Supreme Court of the United States require an immediate and urgent reconsideration of the respective sovereign rights of the State Governments and the Federal Government in the airspace over the United States.

By its decision in *United States* v. *Causby*,[1] construing the Air Commerce Act of 1926 and the Civil Aeronautics Act of 1938, the Court has divided the airspace over the United States into two zones. In the lower zone next to the earth's surface, private property in the airspace

---

[1] 328 U.S. 256 (1946).

is permitted and we must assume that in that zone normal relationships exist between State and Federal sovereignty as elsewhere in State territory. But in the upper zone (the navigable airspace) the rights of the Federal Government seem to have been considered so paramount that Congress was able to place the navigable airspace, as stated in the Court's opinion, "within the public domain." The opinion does not indicate what rights, if any, the subjacent State has in that part of the navigable airspace public domain lying over its surface territory.

By its later decision in *United States* v. *State of California*,[2] the Court found that the State of California is not the owner of the three-mile marginal ocean belt along its coasts or the lands underlying that belt. The opinion in that case indicates that the Court felt that paramount rights in and power over this ocean belt had been acquired directly by the Federal Government since the adoption of the United States Constitution. It must be noted that the *Causby* case is there cited, apparently to sustain the need for the Federal Government having a paramount position as against State sovereignty when national rights are involved.

If these two cases are read together, surprising conclusions result. Either the several States may be held under these rulings to be entirely without sovereignty or right of control in the navigable airspace over their surface territories, or the power and rights of the Federal Government may be found so paramount in the navigable airspace as to produce the same legal results.

If the Federal Government alone has sovereign rights in the navigable airspace, and if such airspace is not part of the territory of the several subjacent States, then the statutes of such States do not govern crimes committed or other wrongful acts occurring in the navigable airspace, and the State courts are without jurisdiction to hear such cases. In addition, the entire problem of the respective rights of the Federal Government and the several States to regulate commerce in the navigable airspace must be fully re-examined. Admittedly these are serious questions—the answers to which should not be delayed.

ARGUMENTS FAVORING EXCLUSIVE FEDERAL SOVEREIGNTY

These are not new questions. In 1926 they were raised carefully and forcefully by Mr. Frederic P. Lee (then legislative counsel of the United States Senate), in an article entitled "The Air Domain of the

---

[2] 332 U.S. 19 (1947).

United States."[3] The same questions were later raised by Mr. Clement L. Bouvé in 1936.[4] Lee thus stated the problem:

If it is found that the airspace above the United States is part of the domain of the United States as against all foreign nations, there then remains the further question as to whether that portion of such airspace above the lands and waters of any one of the United States is a part of the domain of that State. Is the airspace above Massachusetts a part of the domain of Massachusetts, or is it exclusive Federal domain? From the conclusion that such airspace is part of the State's domain, it would follow that the territorial sovereignty of the State or the Federal Government, including its legislative powers, extends to such airspace in the same measure as it extends to the lands and waters of the State; that is, along the ordinary lines of demarcation which the Constitution sets forth as to State and Federal powers. For example, under the commerce power the Federal Government will be able to regulate broadcasting and commercial radio communication or air navigation only if such regulation constitutes "the regulation of commerce with foreign nations and among the several States."

On the other hand, if it is found that the airspace above the lands and waters of any State is not a part of the domain of that State, but only of the Federal Government, then the Federal Government will have, to the exclusion of the States, sole legislative powers as to radio communication and air navigation in such airspace. The various Territories and possessions, the District of Columbia, and the Canal Zone, together with places purchased with the consent of State legislatures for the erection of forts, magazines, arsenals, dockyards, and other needful public buildings, afford examples of land domain over which the Federal Government has exclusive territorial sovereignty as against the States.[5]

No one any longer questions the fact that the United States as a single nation exercises complete and exclusive sovereignty in the airspace over the lands and waters of the United States to the exclusion of all foreign governments. This exclusive national sovereignty has been asserted by the United States in the Air Commerce Act of 1926. the Havana Convention of 1928, the Civil Aeronautics Act of 1938, and the Chicago Convention of 1944.

But the fact that we have accepted the doctrine of exclusive national

---

[3] *Civil Aeronautics Legislative History of the Air Commerce Act of 1926, Corrected to August 1, 1928,* U.S. Gov't Printing Office (1943).

[4] Bouvé, *State Sovereignty or International Sovereignty Over Navigable Airspace?* 3 J.D.C. Bar Ass'n 5 (1936).

[5] *Legislative History, op. cit. supra* note 3, at 105.

sovereignty as against foreign governments does not necessarily mean that the several States are without sovereign rights in the airspace over their territories so far as the exercise of internal regulatory and police powers is concerned. For, as pointed out by Lee in the memorandum quoted above, if the airspace is not part of the exclusive domain of the Federal Government, such airspace must be considered as part of the domain of the several States in which the Federal Government exercises only those sovereign rights which it holds under the Constitution and as a single nation in the family of nations. This would put the airspace over a State in the same legal and constitutional status as the lands and waters of that State.

Lee concluded, however, in the article cited above, that the navigable airspace is the exclusive territory of the Federal Government, which thus, according to him, has exclusive sovereignty (both external and internal) except as to an airspace strata close to the surface. This strata may be considered, he said, as that part of the airspace which since earliest times has been used by mankind in the construction of buildings and other such similar uses as are required by human dwellers on the earth's surface. As to this "surface strata" he concluded that it was part of the territory of the several States, subject to the same Constitutional control by the Federal government as exists over the lands and waters of State territory. But all other airspace he considered as Federal territory. He reached this conclusion in the following way.

No nation, so he said, acquired any domain in what we now know as navigable airspace until such domain was needed to protect subjacent national territory. "It is necessary," said Lee, "that the domain over the airspace above the lands and waters of the United States be held by the United States so that it may lawfully exercise its sovereignty throughout its airspace in order adequately to protect the occupants of the lands and interior from attack, and regulate air commerce and radio communication to and from land and water ports." But as neither air navigation nor radio communication made substantial and continual use of the airspace until the present century, Lee insisted that no nation anywhere in the world had either by occupation or by need of protection acquired any domain in the upper airspace prior thereto. Accordingly, in his view, the United States did not acquire sovereignty in the upper airspace until long after the adoption of the Federal Constitution. From this it would follow that the original colonies had no domain in the upper airspace and it was not part of their territory when the Constitution was adopted. After the adoption of the Constitution, no State could acquire territory in the airspace as this would amount, in his judgment, to the acquirement of new or additional domain, a function vested solely in the Federal Government. Airspace domain, therefore, according to Lee, was acquired by the United States long after the adoption of the Constitution, as exclusive Federal territory and as an addition of the previously existing national public domain. The airspace thus acquired came under the exclusive sovereignty of the Federal Government as would other new territory thus acquired.

"If the conclusion is correct that the Federal government has exclusive sovereignty in the airspace above the surface of the several States," continued Lee, "it would seem to be beyond the power of the State to legislate as to the activities in the upper strata of airspace. So to legislate would be analogous to an attempt by the State to legislate as to activities in the District of Columbia, in the Territory of Hawaii or Alaska, in the possessions of the United States, or in any other area, such as forts, arsenals, magazines, and dockyards, over which the Federal government has exclusive sovereignty."

Mr. Bouvé reached similar conclusions. Writing in 1930[6] he had insisted that the airspace was, in international law, new territory added, as the result of the capacity of man to fly, to the territory previously subject to national sovereignty. Later, Bouvé asserted that "national sovereignty over navigable airspace could not exist in fact until the discovery of the art of human flight over a century following the adoption of the Constitution, during which the capacity to control—a *sine qua non* of national sovereignty—was lacking."[7] Accordingly, Bouvé concluded, as had Lee, that "national sovereignty" in the navigable airspace included sovereignty for all purposes external or internal. He summarizes his conclusions as follows:

> What are the facts of the case of State Sovereignty vs. Federal Sovereignty of Navigable Airspace? First: An attempt on the part of a political subdivision of a national power to extend its territorial domain into an expanse which constitutes a natural channel of international aerial navigation as truly as the high seas constitute a national channel of international water navigation. The considerations which led to the adoption of the doctrine of national air sovereignty with respect to these regions in no way applies to political subdivisions of national States. Second: An attempt on the part of a political subdivision of a national power to project its jurisdiction into regions no portion of which is physically susceptible of occupancy by its citizens in their private capacity or by any instrumentality of the subjacent State, and hence physically insusceptible of private or public ownership. Third: An attempt on the part of a State of the Union to establish sovereignty over a region consisting

---

[6] Bouvé, *The Development of International Rules of Conduct in Air Navigation*, 1 Air L. Rev. 1 (1930).

[7] Bouvé, *supra* note 4 at 11.

entirely of a navigable medium which, by nature, like the sea, can serve one purpose only—that of navigation; a region, sovereignty over which has been established by the law of nations for one purpose only, to wit, *national* control in the interests of the subjacent nation. Such control cannot be exercised by a State of the Union under the Constitution. Sovereignty involves the opportunity to exercise political power, and its exercise is the expression of that power; and where, as here, the only form in which that power is capable of being exerted is by the domestic as well as international law entrusted to the National Government the conception of its exercise by a political subdivision of the National State presents an anomaly from the standpoint of both legal systems. Fourth: An attempt on the part of a State of the Union to acquire territory beyond its borders—an attempt to exercise a power prohibited to the States under the Constitution. Fifth: An attempt to create a situation which, until the fallacy of the premise on which it rests is demonstrated and the demonstration accepted will constitute a barrier to the establishment of uniform rules of aerial traffic. These rules come within the exclusive field of Congressional authorization not only by virtue of the Commerce Clause of the Constitution, but because of the natural character of the territory which constitutes the navigable airspace of the United States.[8]

OPINIONS OF STATE COURTS BASED ON STATE SOVEREIGNTY

The views put forth by Lee and Bouvé do not express, very naturally, the authoritative opinion of State courts and legislatures. In the best analysis of the State's Rights position, Chief Justice Rugg of the Supreme Judicial Court of Massachusetts, has said:

It is essential to the safety of sovereign States that they possess jurisdiction to control the airspace above their territories. It seems to us to rest on the obvious practical necessity of self-protection. Every government completely sovereign in character must possess power to prevent from entering its confines those whom it determines to be undesirable. That power extends to the exclusion from the air of all hostile persons or demonstrations, and to the regulation of passage through the air of all persons in the interests of the public welfare and the safety of those on the face of the earth. This jurisdiction was vested in this Commonwealth when it became a sovereign State on its separation from Great Britain. So far as concerns interstate commerce, postal service and some other matters,

---

[8] *Id.* at 28.

jurisdiction over passage through the air in large part was surrendered to the United States by the adoption of the Federal Constitution. Constitution of the United States, Art. 1, §8.[9]

This language was cited with approval by the Supreme Court of Minnesota in 1944, *Erickson* v. *King, State Auditor, et al.*[10] In these and other cases affecting internal sovereignty over the airspace, it has been assumed that the airspace over a State is part of the territory of the State and that Federal sovereignty flows from the Constitution and can be exercised only to the extent needed to protect and assist Federal jurisdiction over interstate and foreign commerce. To sustain this point of view, it is interesting to note that Chief Justice Rugg felt it necessary to hold that sovereignty in the airspace had existed in the Government of Great Britain prior to the Revolution and had passed to the several colonies, and thence to the Federal Government "so far as concerns interstate commerce, postal service and some other matters." Both Lee and Bouvé contended that sovereignty in the airspace was not accepted in international law until the early part of the present century and after man had attained sufficient capacity to fly to indicate a practical ability to use and control the airspace.

In many of the States, as in North Carolina, whose statute is quoted and discussed in the *Causby* case, very definite statutory claim to State airspace sovereignty over navigable airspace has been put forward. In over twenty States there is still in effect the so-called "Uniform State Law of Aeronautics" which contains provisions to the effect that "sovereignty in the space above the land and waters of this State is declared to rest in the State, except where granted to and assumed by the United States pursuant to a Constitutional grant from the people of this State"—that "the ownership of the space above the land and waters of this State is declared to be vested in the several owners of the surface beneath," subject to a right of flight—that crimes, torts, or wrongs committed and all contractual and other legal relations entered into by persons "while in flight over this State" shall be governed by the laws of, or have the same effect as if entered into on the land or water of the subjacent State.

It must be admitted, however, that these or other similar State laws will be invalid in so much of the navigable airspace as may be found not to be within the territory of the several States. It must also be admitted that the declaration of a State that it has sovereignty in the airspace can be based on only one or the other of two theories:

---

[9] *Smith* v. *New England Aircraft Co.*, 270 Mass. 511, 521, 170 N.E. 385, 389, 1930 USAvR 1, 9 (1930).
[10] 218 Minn. 98, 15 N.W. (2d) 201 (1944).

either, first, that the several original American colonies became vested with sovereignty over and title to the airspace as part of their original territory and had such territory at the time of the adoption of the Constitution of the United States even though the art of flight did not then exist; or, second, that the States have acquired the airspace as additional territory since the adoption of the Constitution and the development of the art of flight.

Both Lee and Bouvé argue with great force, and it seems to me almost conclusively, that no State has a right to acquire new territory or to extend its boundaries, and that the acquisition of new territory is a function solely of the Federal Government. This would appear to leave the problem dependent on the historic status of airspace sovereignty—*when* did the nations of the world acquire such sovereignty? In other words, has the airspace always been within the sovereign control of the nations of the world, or, as Bouvé contended, is the airspace new territory that was acquired by the several sovereign nations after man demonstrated his capacity to fly?

AIR COMMERCE ACT AND CIVIL AERONAUTICS ACT

In the adoption of the Air Commerce Act of 1926, Congress did not attempt to fix the extent of State sovereignty in the airspace. The report of the Interstate and Foreign Commerce Committee of the House of Representatives, contained in Legislative History of the Air Commerce Act of 1926,[11] includes certain interesting comments. Section 4 of the Act authorized airspace reservations to be established by Executive Order of the President. It also authorized the several States to establish necessary airspace reservations, provided that they were "not in conflict either with airspace reservations established by the President under this Section or with any civil or military airway designated under provisions of the Act." Commenting on this Section, the House Committee said:

Airspace reservations must necessarily be established in order that domestic and foreign aircraft may not be able to fly over forts and certain other governmental structures, and in order to protect aircraft from dangers of flying over Weather Bureau stations where pilot balloons are used, or over experimental or training fields of the military or naval forces. The power of the President to establish Federal Government airspace reservations in the States in nowise diminishes the power of the States to establish airspace reservations for such other purposes as they deem advisable *so long as such*

[11] Note 3 *supra*.

reservations are within the airspace over which the States have acquired or retained sovereignty under the Constitution and so long as the establishment of the reservation is an exercise of a constitutional power reserved to the States and does not interfere with the Federal airspace reservations or with the Federal airways. (Italics supplied.)[12]

In Section 6 of the Act, Congress declared that the Government of the United States "has, to the exclusion of all foreign nations, complete sovereignty of the airspace over the lands and waters of the United States . . ."[13] Commenting on this Section, the House Committee said:

Article 1 of the International Air Navigation Convention provides that "the high contracting parties recognize that every power has complete and exclusive sovereignty of the airspace above its territory." In this Section the Congress declares that the United States adheres to the same principle and not to the principle urged by some international jurists that there is a free right of flight in the airspace above a nation regardless of the consent or the restrictions by law of that nation.

The Section in nowise affects the apportionment of sovereignty as between the several States and the United States, but only as between the United States and the rest of the world. *Insofar as the States had sovereignty in the airspace at the time of the adoption of the Constitution* and such sovereignty was not by that instrument delegated to the Federal Government, and *insofar as the States may have subsequently acquired sovereignty* in airspace in accordance with the Constitution, such sovereignty remains unchanged. (Italics supplied.)[14]

In Section 10 of the Act,[15] the term "navigable airspace" was defined to mean airspace above the minimum safe altitudes of flight as prescribed in the Act. The Section also provided that "such navigable airspace shall be subject to a public right of freedom of interstate and foreign air navigation in conformity with the requirements of this Act."[16] In discussing this definition of navigable airspace, the Committee pointed out that it was the intent of the applicable section ". . . to assert a public right of freedom of navigation by aircraft in the airspace above described within the safe altitudes of flight, which is superior to the right of the owner of the subjacent land to use

---

[12] *Legislative History, op. cit. supra* note 3, at 36.
[13] Air Commerce Act of 1926 §6, 44 Stat. 572, 49 USCA §176 (Supp. 1947).
[14] *Legislative History, op. cit. supra* note 3, at 38.
[15] *Id.* §10, 44 Stat. 574, 49 USCA §181 (Supp. 1947).
[16] *Ibid.*

such airspace for conflicting purpose," and that "this public right of freedom of navigation is analogous to the easement of public right of navigation over the navigable waters of the United States."[17] The Committee also said that it was of the opinion ". . . that the Federal Government may assert under the commerce clause *and other constitutional powers* a public right of navigation in the navigable airspace, regardless of the ownership of the land below and regardless of any question as to the ownership of the air or airspace itself." (Italics supplied.)[18]

It will be noted from the foregoing comments that the House Committee did not state what, if any, airspace sovereignty was held by the States at the time of the adoption of the Constitution, nor whether the States had actually acquired such sovereignty since that time, nor did it base the validity of the Air Commerce Act solely on the commerce clause of the Constitution. The most that can be said is that the Air Commerce Act was not apparently intended by Congress to take from the States such airspace sovereignty, *if any*, which they then had.

In the light of the decision in the *Causby* case, certain changes in the statutes made by the adoption of the Civil Aeronautics Act of 1938 are perhaps of importance.

Section 1 of the Civil Aeronautics Act broadened the term "air commerce" to include (in addition to interstate, overseas, or foreign air commerce) the transportation of mail by aircraft, operation or navigation of aircraft within the limits of any civil airway, or "any operation or navigation of aircraft which directly affects, or which may endanger safety in, interstate, overseas, or foreign air commerce."[19]

The declaration of national sovereignty was changed by amending Section 6 of the Air Commerce Act and striking out reference to "foreign nations" so as to read as follows:

> The United States of America is hereby declared to possess and exercise complete and exclusive national sovereignty in the airspace above the United States, including the airspace above all inland waters and the airspace above those portions of the adjacent marginal high seas, bays, and lakes, over which by international law or treaty or convention the United States exercises national jurisdiction.[20]

By Section 3 of the Civil Aeronautics Act, the public right of transit was restated to read as follows:

---

[17] *Legislative History, op. cit. supra* note 3, at 42.

[18] *Lesgislative History, op. cit. supra* note 3, at 45.

[19] Civil Aeronautics Act of 1938 §1, 52 Stat. 977, 49 USCA §401(3) (Supp. 1947).

[20] Note 13 *supra*.

There is hereby recognized and declared to exist in behalf of any citizen of the United States a public right of freedom of transit in air commerce through the navigable airspace of the United States.[21]

DISCUSSION OF RECENT U.S.
SUPREME COURT CASES

In 1936, prior to the adoption of the Civil Aeronautics Act, the Supreme Court of the United States, speaking through Mr. Justice Sutherland, in *United States* v. *Curtiss-Wright Export Corp., et al.*,[22] said:

> As a result of the separation from Great Britain by the colonies acting as a unit the powers of external sovereignty passed from the Crown not to the colonies severally, but to the colonies in their collective and corporate capacity as the United States of America. . . . It results that the investment of the Federal Government with the powers of external sovereignty did not depend on the affirmative grants of the Constitution. . . . The power to acquire territory by discovery and occupation, the power to expel undesirable aliens, the power to make such international agreements as do not constitute treaties in the constitutional sense, none of which is expressly affirmed by the Constitution, nevertheless exist as inherently inseparable from the conception of nationality.[23]

This opinion has affected many subsequent opinions of the Court where national sovereignty is involved.

Such was the situation when the Supreme Court of the United States in 1946 handed down its decision in the *Causby* case. In the first sentence of the majority opinion the case is stated to be "one of first impression." In discussing the Air Commerce Act and the Civil Aeronautics Act, the Court noted that under those statutes the United States has "complete and exclusive national sovereignty in the airspace" over this country; that these Acts grant any citizen of the United States "a public right of freedom of transit in air commerce through the navigable airspace of the United States"; that "the navigable airspace" is defined as "airspace above the minimum safe altitudes of flight prescribed by the Civil Aeronautics Authority." In deciding the case, the Court refused to accept the ancient doctrine that at common law ownership of the land extended to the periphery of the universe—stating that this "doctrine has no place in the modern world"—that "the air is a public highway, *as Congress has declared*."

---

[21] Civil Aeronautics Act of 1938 §3, 52 Stat. 980, 49 USCA §403 (Supp. 1947).

[22] 299 U.S. 304 (1936).   [23] *Id.* at 316.

(Italics supplied.) Continuing its opinion and discussing the low flights which were charged by the landowner as resulting in the "taking" of his property, the Court found that "the flights in question were not within the navigable airspace *which Congress placed within the public domain.*" (Italics supplied.)

Continuing the opinion and stating again that the airspace is a public highway, the Court found nevertheless that if the landowner is to have full enjoyment of the land he must have exclusive control of the immediate reaches of the enveloping atmosphere; that therefore "the landowner owns at least as much of the space above the ground as he can occupy or use in connection with the land." The Court further noted that, under the statute of the State of North Carolina in which the land was situated, sovereignty of the airspace rests in the State "except where granted to and assumed by the United States," and that, subject to a right of flight held lawful unless at such a low altitude as to interfere with the then existing use to which the land is put, "ownership of the space above the lands and waters of this State is declared to be vested in the several owners of the surface beneath." The Court then stated:

> Our holding that there was an invasion of respondents' property is thus not inconsistent with the local law *governing a landowner's claim to the immediate reaches of the superjacent airspace.* (Italics supplied.)[24]

The opinion does not disclose what rights, if any, the State retained in the navigable airspace in which the right of private property contemplated by the State statute was held in substance to be contrary to the action of Congress in declaring the upper strata or navigable airspace to be a public highway and part of the public domain. Nor does the opinion indicate how or when the State of North Carolina had granted to the United States such complete sovereignty in the upper strata of the airspace that the Congress was empowered to take the action just noted, or whether the Court's finding is based on the theory (as outlined by Lee in the article discussed above) that State sovereignty exists only in the lower airspace strata near the earth's surface in which private property can also exist.

Considering the references in the opinion to the claim of the United States that it has complete and exclusive national sovereignty in the airspace, and in the absence of any finding that national sovereignty in the navigable airspace arises solely from the commerce clause of the Constitution and is limited by that clause, we are almost forced to the assumption that the Court was actually of the opinion that no

---

[24] *Supra* note 1, at 266.

State sovereignty exists in the navigable airspace, or that the Federal Government has such paramount power therein as to make State sovereignty of no practical importance.

This conclusion is supported by the decision and opinion of the Court in *United States* v. *State of California*. In that case, as has been stated earlier, the Court denied the right of the State of California to the oil and other resources under the three-mile marginal ocean belt. The opinion includes the following findings: that the thirteen original colonies did not acquire from the Crown of England title to the three-mile marginal ocean belt nor the land underlying it; that after the United States became a nation our statesmen became interested in establishing national dominion over a definite marginal zone to protect our neutrality; that protection and control of this marginal belt is a function of national external sovereignty; that the State of California was not the owner of the marginal belt along its coast; that the Federal Government rather than the State, has paramount rights in and power over that belt.

No one reading this opinion can fail to note the striking similarity between the line of reasoning adopted by the Court and the position taken by both Lee and Bouvé in asserting that sovereignty in the navigable airspace never was vested in the original colonies nor in the States, but that it was acquired long after the adoption of the Constitution by the Federal Government as exclusive Federal territory needed for national purposes. The importance of the *Causby* case in this line of reasoning, and the force of the decision in the *United States* v. *Curtiss-Wright Export Corp., et al.*, is evidenced by the fact that the California case opinion cites both of these cases as authority in the finding that "national rights are paramount in waters lying to the seaward in the three-mile belt."

CONCLUSIONS

My own personal view has never been in accord with that expressed by Lee and Bouvé. I have always felt that the airspace over a nation was an integral part of the nation's territory. I have never been impressed with the argument that such airspace did not become part of national territory until nations had the physical ability to fly in that territory and thus to control and occupy it. It has always seemed to me that the airspace in the early days was in exactly the same status as those mountain peaks which mankind could not scale or the dense jungles which he could not penetrate. The lack of physical ability to reach and control such parts of a nation's territory can hardly be urged as a reason for denying that such mountains and jungles are under the sovereign domain of a nation if found within its recognized boundaries.

169

The obvious need of a nation to control its own airspace existed from the earliest days when mankind first envisaged the possibility of flight.

Strong legal arguments have, however, been put forward to sustain the view that the airspace did not become part of the territory of any nation until after the art of flight was fully developed in the early twentieth century. We cannot overlook the very obvious fact that the opinions of the Supreme Court in the *Causby* case and in the *California* case show a definite trend, if not a final decision, challenging the validity of State sovereignty in the navigable airspace. This trend seems to be based both on the argument that the States did not have sovereignty in the airspace at the time of adoption of the Constitution and could not acquire such sovereignty thereafter, and also on the argument that complete and exclusive national control of the navigable airspace is necessary to the nation as a single member of the family of nations.

It is obvious that this matter deserves the serious and early consideration of the Congress of the United States. If there be any doubt as to the existence of State sovereignty in the navigable airspace, Federal legislation should be passed without delay so that State statutes applicable in the territory of a subjacent State would also be applicable in the navigable airspace over that State, except when in direct conflict with other Federal legislation. Perhaps additional legislation should be adopted ceding to each State all Federal territorial claim to the airspace over such State, but reserving to the Federal Government exclusive national sovereignty as against foreign nations. This would eliminate possible sovereignty differences in the upper and lower airspace strata, would include the entire airspace over a state within the territory of that State for local administration, and would leave the constitutional sovereignty relations of State and Federal Governments in the same status throughout the territory within the boundaries of any State, whether on the surface or in the airspace.

10
Airspace Rights Over the Arctic

This article was written for
Encyclopedia Arctica
*a work projected by the late
Vilhjalmur Stefansson, the
manuscript of which is in the
Stefansson Collection of the
Dartmouth College Libraries.
Printed with the permission of the
Dartmouth College Libraries.*

Author's Note. The late Dr. Vilhjalmur Stefansson, a great scholar and writer, as well as explorer, many times noted the fact that potential air routes across the Arctic were the shortest distance between important parts of the Northern Hemisphere. Today, as Dr. Stefansson predicted, these routes are in daily use for intercontinental air transport. At his suggestion, this author undertook the research which resulted in this 1949 essay. The air transport operators who now fly across the Arctic must necessarily rely upon the legal assumption stated at the end of this study that "the ice covered areas of the Arctic Ocean must be treated as high seas, and the airspace over such areas as free to the use of all."

THE DETERMINATION of national airspace rights over the Arctic presents a challenging and vital problem. It is a problem that must be settled. It concerns directly the diplomatic, commercial, and military relations of those States which face the Arctic—Canada, Denmark (through its ownership of Greenland), Iceland, Norway, the USSR, and the United States (through its ownership of Alaska). Indirectly it affects every State with any pretense to long-range flying. Potential air routes across the Arctic are the shortest distance between important parts of the Northern hemisphere. In no other area of the world is there still such lack of certainty as to the rights of nations to fly.

The basic rule of international air law, fixing the legal status of airspace over the earth's surface may be stated as follows:

> If any area on the surface of the earth, whether land or water, is recognized as part of the territory of a State, then the airspace over such surface area is also part of the territory of the same State. Conversely, if an area on the earth's surface is not part of the territory of any State, such as the water areas included in the high seas, then the airspace over such surface areas are not subject to the sovereign control of any State and are free for the use of all States.

This is another way of saying that the old concept of national territory as a two-dimensional area on the earth's surface can no longer be accepted. National territory is three-dimensional. The surface of the earth and the airspace above cannot be separately treated. Together they must be considered as a single political unit. Entry into the surface areas under the control of a State or into the airspace over such surface areas constitute equally entry into the territory of the State. The background of this presently accepted rule must be stated in order to understand the problem of airspace rights over the Arctic.

In the latter part of the nineteenth century and the first decade of the twentieth century, doctrinal discussions developed in western Europe as to the legal status of the airspace. These were centered around the question as to whether the airspace was part of the territory of the State below or whether it was free to the navigation of all States as the high seas are free for all vessels. Various solutions were proposed, including those which would have held that a limited zone immediately over the earth's surface was subject to the sovereignty of the State below, but that the upper airspace was free. These discussions, it must be understood, were purely doctrinal. There is no evidence that any important sovereign State ever disclaimed control of any part of the airspace over its surface territories. In fact there is ample evidence that State sovereignty in the airspace has existed since Roman times.

The first international attempt to settle diplomatically the extent of national airspace rights ended with failure at the Paris Conference of 1910. Differences developed as to the extent to which foreign aircraft might have privileges of flight in the airspace over national territory. But not one of the European governments there represented was ready to accept the theory that the airspace over its territory was not part of its domain and thereby not subject to its control.

Concrete acts of the great powers soon thereafter affirmed the existence of airspace sovereignty. Great Britain, in the Air Navigation Acts of 1911 and 1913, stated its right to set up prohibited areas in its territory over which no foreign aircraft might fly and to control the terms under which such foreign aircraft might enter the airspace over its lands and waters. By an exchange of notes in 1913 between France and Germany, provisions were agreed upon under which no military aircraft of one nation could enter the airspace over the other except on *invitation,* and the civil aircraft of one nation were required to obtain a special permit from a consul of the other before starting on a flight to the latter's territory. These British Air Navigation Acts and the French–German air traffic agreement demonstrate that each of these powers claimed full right to control the airspace over its land and water territories as against all other nations. This is the exercise of external or national sovereignty in international law.

The outbreak of World War I in Europe further affirmed the existence of airspace sovereignty over national surface territories. In a letter handed by the German Ambassador to the French Foreign Minister on August 3, 1914 it was stated that the German Empire considered itself at war with France. Among the reasons given by Germany as a direct cause of the war was the allegation that French military aviators had been guilty of hostile acts on German territory

173

and that they had "openly violated the neutrality of Belgium by flying over the territory of that country." In other words, Germany insisted that the airspace over Germany was part of German territory and that the airspace over Belgium was part of Belgian territory, and that the flight of French aircraft into Belgian airspace constituted an invasion of Belgian territory and its internationally guaranteed neutrality.

Immediately after the outbreak of the war, various European nations closed their air boundaries. During the course of the war neutral states required belligerent aircraft flying into the airspace over their surface territories to land and be interned just as they required foot soldiers to be interned when crossing land boundaries into neutral territory.

During the meeting of the Peace Conference following the war, an aeronautical commission was organized and charged with preparing a convention for the regulation of air navigation. Its legal sub-commission (on which the United States was represented), in reporting a draft of the proposed convention, said:

> The first question placed before the Sub-commission was that of the *principle of freedom* or of *sovereignty of the air*.
>
> . . . the opinion expressed in the Legal Sub-commission is favorable to the full and exclusive submission of the airspace to the sovereignty of the subjacent territory. It is only when the column of air hangs over a *res nullius* or *communis*, the sea, that freedom becomes the law of the air.
>
> Therefore, the airspace is part of the legal regime of the subjacent territory. Is this territory that of a particular State? Then the airspace is subject to the sovereignty of that State. Does it escape all sovereignty as the free sea? Then the airspace is also free above the sea, as the sea itself.
>
> It results then that, by virtue of its sovereignty, the subjacent State, within its borders, can forbid flight and, with greater reason, landing.[1]

The convention came into effect as the Paris Convention of 1919 "relating to the Regulation of Aerial Navigation." It stated in Article 1 the basic problem of airspace sovereignty:

> The High Contracting Parties recognize that every Power has complete and exclusive sovereignty over the air space above its territory.

---

[1] Translated from the official French text in Conférence de la paix, 1919–1920, *Recueil des actes de la conférence*, Partie VII, Préparation et signature des traités et conventions divers, A—Conventions générales entre alliés, (1) Commission de l'aéronautique, Paris, Imprimerie nationale, 1933, pp. 428–429.

For the purpose of the present Convention the territory of a State shall be understood as including the national territory, both that of the mother country and of the colonies, and the territorial waters adjacent thereto.[2]

This Convention was later either ratified or adhered to by all of the European powers except Russia and Germany, and also by the British Dominions, including Canada. Its statement of airspace sovereignty became an accepted part of international law. The Convention does not purport to grant rights of sovereignty reciprocally between the States which are parties to the Convention. Instead it states the existence of an admitted rule that every State, whether a party to the Convention or not, "has complete and exclusive sovereignty over the airspace above its territory."

The United States signed, but did not ratify, the Paris Convention of 1919. This refusal to ratify had nothing to do with the fact that the convention acknowledged the existence of airspace sovereignty as the fundamental principle of international air law. The United States has in fact always been one of the chief proponents of the doctrine of airspace sovereignty. As early as 1912 in the unofficial but authoritative *International Law Situations* prepared by The United States Naval War College and published by the Government Printing Office, it was stated that "physical safety, military necessity, the enforcement of police, revenue, and sanitary regulations justify the claim that a State has jurisdiction in aerial space above its territory," and that "it would seem wise, therefore, to start from the premise that air over the high seas and territory that is res nullius is free, while other air is within the jurisdiction of the subjacent state . . ."[3]

This position was affirmed by the conduct of the United States during World War I. By proclamation of November 13, 1914, relating to neutrality of the Panama Canal Zone, "aircraft of a belligerent power, public or private, were forbidden to pass through the airspace above the lands and waters within the jurisdiction of the United States at the Zone.[4] By another proclamation of February 28, 1918, all flying

---

[2] Full text in: *International Convention Relating to the Regulation of Aerial Navigation*, dated October 13, 1919, . . . Department of State Publication 2143, Washington, U.S. Government Printing Office, 1944; Manley O. Hudson, ed., *International Legislation*, Washington, Carnegie Endowment for International Peace, 1931, Vol. 1, pp. 359–376.

[3] U.S. Naval War College, *International Law Situations 1912*, Washington, U.S. Government Printing Office, 1912, p. 71.

[4] *U.S. Statutes at Large*, Vol. 38, p. 2039. Also in: Francis Deák and Philip C. Jessup, eds. *A Collection of Neutrality Laws, Regulations and Treaties of Various Countries*, Washington, Carnegie Endowment for International Peace, 1939, Vol. 2, p. 807.

was prohibited unless specially licensed if the flight was to pass over "any place or region within the jurisdiction or occupation of the United States which may be designated by the President as a zone of war-like operations or of war-like preparations."[5] The whole of the United States and its territorial waters and possessions were designated as such a zone, thus assuming complete national control in the airspace over all the lands and waters of the United States.

The rule of airspace sovereignty became part of the peacetime law of the United States with the passage of the Air Commerce Act of 1926, asserting that "the Government of the United States has to the exclusion of all foreign nations complete sovereignty of the airspace over the lands and waters of the United States including the Canal Zone."[6] In 1928 the United States assisted in drafting and later signed and ratified the Havana Convention which in Article 1 recognizes that "every State has complete and exclusive sovereignty over the airspace above its territory and territorial waters."[7] Again in 1938, the United States affirmed the same principle in the present Civil Aeronautics Act.[8]

As parties to the Paris Convention of 1919, all of the States then directly interested in the Arctic (except the United States and the USSR) affirmed the existence of airspace sovereignty. The United States took the same position in its statutes and as a party to the Havana Convention. The Chicago Convention of 1944 has now taken the place of both the Paris Convention and the Havana Convention. It states the basic existing principles of air law for most of the world except the USSR. Among the parties to the Chicago Convention are Canada, Denmark, Iceland, Norway, and the United States—directly interested in the Arctic. The provisions of this convention directly applicable to the status of the airspace are the following:

> *Article 1:* The contracting States recognize that every State has complete and exclusive sovereignty over the airspace above its territory.
>
> *Article 2:* For the purposes of this Convention the territory of a State shall be deemed to be the land areas and territorial waters

---

[5] Henry Woodhouse, *Textbook of Aerial Laws and Regulations* for Aerial Navigation . . ., New York, F. A. Stokes, 1920, p. 141.

[6] *U.S. Statutes at Large*, Vol. 44, 1926, p. 568. 49 U.S.C. 176.

[7] *Commercial Aviation. Convention between the United States of America and other American Republics*, signed at Havana, February 20, 1928. Treaty Series No. 840, Washington, U.S. Government Printing Office, 1931; Hudson, *International Legislation, op. cit.*, Vol. 4, pp. 2356–2369.

[8] *U.S. Statutes at Large*, Vol. 52, 1938, p. 1028.

adjacent thereto under the sovereignty, suzerainty, protection or mandate of such State.[9]

The convention also recognizes that airspace over the high seas is not part of the territory of any State. In Article 12 it provides that each contracting State undertakes to adopt measures to insure that aircraft flying over its territory and that every aircraft carrying its nationality mark, wherever such aircraft may be, shall comply "with the rules and regulations relating to the flight and maneuver of aircraft there in force," and that "over the high seas, the rules in force shall be those established under this Convention." In other words, over the high seas no single State has sovereign power to make rules applicable to the flight of aircraft of other States. Such flight can be regulated only by agreement between several States and the rules thus agreed will apply only to the States which have adopted such rules.

The fact that the USSR did not become a party to the Paris Convention nor the Chicago Convention must not be taken to mean that the USSR refused to accept the principle of airspace sovereignty. The facts are quite the contrary. As early as the Decree of the Council of Peoples' Commissaries adopted January 17, 1921[10] this principle was tacitly recognized. Foreign aircraft were permitted to cross Soviet boundaries only by special permit and subject to special regulations. Other later decrees clarified the reservation by the Soviet Government of the right to regulate air navigation over Soviet surface territories. With the promulgation on April 27, 1932 of the Air Code, the Soviet position finally was made very clear. The directly applicable provisions are as follows:

1. The air code is in force throughout the land and fluvial territory of the Union of S.S.R. and the territorial waters established by the laws of the Union of S.S.R., and within the air space of the Union of S.S.R.

By the air space of the Union of S.S.R. is understood the air space above the land and fluvial territory of the Union of S.S.R., and above the territorial waters established by the laws of the Union of S.S.R.

2. To the Union of S.S.R. belongs the complete and exclusive sovereignty over the air space of the Union of S.S.R.[11]

---

[9] International Civil Aviation Conference, Chicago, Illinois, November 1 to December 7, 1944, *Final Act and Related Documents*, Washington, U.S. Government Printing Office, 1945, p. 59; John C. Cooper, *The Right to Fly*, New York, Henry Holt, 1947, pp. 331–359.

[10] Timothy Andrew Taracouzio, *The Soviet Union and International Law*, New York, Macmillan, 1935, p. 73.

[11] As reprinted and translated in Taracouzio, *ibid.*, p. 401.

It is apparent from the provisions of this Air Code that no difference exists between the USSR and the other States facing the Arctic as to airspace sovereignty, *except* in a possibly important difference in the definition of what constitutes surface territory. It will be noted from the citations above that in the Chicago Convention the territories of a State are defined to include "the land areas and territorial waters adjacent thereto," while in the USSR Air Code the airspace of the USSR includes the airspace "above the territorial waters established by the laws" of the USSR. This would appear to constitute a reservation by the USSR of the unilateral right to declare as "territorial waters" those waters which it may by its law determine to have such character, while in the Chicago Convention territorial waters are only those "adjacent" to land territories.

In summary, it may be said that international air law applicable to the question of the extent of national airspace sovereignty now includes the following rules:

a) Each State has complete and exclusive sovereignty over the airspace above its surface territory and such airspace is in fact an integral part of national territory.

b) Surface territory for the purpose of airspace sovereignty includes territorial waters. Airspace over such territorial waters is in exactly the same legal status as airspace over land territory.

c) Every sovereign State has complete control of the airspace included in its territory, has the exclusive right to fly in that airspace, and may exclude all foreign aircraft or admit them on such terms as it sees fit. The aircraft of one State do not have in the airspace of another State any right of entry or innocent passage and will only be admitted to such airspace with the consent of the State having sovereign control. No right of innocent passage in the airspace over territorial waters exists in favor of foreign aircraft although such right of innocent passage does exist in the territorial waters themselves for foreign seagoing vessels in time of peace. To this extent the law of the air and the law of the sea are not in accord.

d) Airspace over the high seas and over surface territory which is not part of the territory of any State is free for the use of the aircraft of all States.

From the foregoing rules the extent and character of national airspace rights over the Arctic can be determined. But such determination requires a decision as to what constitutes the Arctic surface territory, both land and territorial waters, of the interested States. On this depends the extent of the right of such States to control the flight of other States and the future of Arctic international flight.

The scope of this article will not permit an extended discussion of all of the questions entering into any definitive statement of national surface sovereignty rights in the Arctic.[12] Enough must be said, however, to lay the basis for a statement of at least presumptive airspace rights.

The normal rules of international law require that a State, to acquire sovereignty over lands not previously part of the territory of any other State, must show discovery and later effective possession with notice to other States. Also no State may claim sovereignty in those water areas known as the high seas where every State has equal rights. The primary difficulty in stating the extent of national sovereignty in the Arctic rests on the decision as to whether the normal rules of international law apply, and if not, how land territory may be acquired and what areas shall be treated as part of the high seas. It is necessary to decide:

1. Whether to accept the so-called "sector" theory under which a State facing toward the North Pole is supposed to have sovereign rights in the triangular area between its recognized territory and the North Pole itself irrespective of the normal rules of international law; or

2. If the "sector" theory is not accepted, whether (a) the rules of international law have been so modified as to permit the existence in the Arctic of sovereignty in land territories which have never been

---

[12] For a general discussion of some of the principal questions, see: Thomas Willing Balch, "Les Regions arctiques et antarctiques et le droit international," *Revue de droit international et de législation comparée*, Vol. 42, 1910, (2d series—Vol. 12), pp. 434–442; "The Arctic and Antarctic Regions and the Law of Nations," *American Journal of International Law*, Vol. 4, 1910, pp. 265–275; Paul Fauchille, *Traité de droit international public*, 8th ed., Paris, A. Rousseau, 1921–26, Vol. 1, Part 2, (1925), Sec. 531 (36–40), pp. 651–663; Green Haywood Hackworth, *Digest of International Law*, Washington, U.S. Government Printing Office, 1940, Vol. 1, Secs. 67–71, pp. 449–476; W. L. G. Joerg, *Brief History of Polar Exploration since the Introduction of Flying*, 2d rev. ed., New York, American Geographical Society (Special Publication No. 11), 1930; V. Kenneth Johnston, "Canada's Title to the Arctic Islands," *Canadian Historical Review*, Vol. 14, 1933, pp. 24–41; David Hunter Miller, "Political Rights in the Arctic," *Foreign Affairs*, Vol. 4, 1925, pp. 47–60; Lassa F. L. Oppenheim, *International Law: A Treatise*, 7th ed., London/New York/Toronto, Longmans Green, 1948, Vol. 1, Sec. 221, note 6, p. 508; Elmer Plischke, "Trans-Polar Aviation and Jurisdiction over Arctic Airspace," *American Political Science Review*, Vol. 37, 1943, pp. 999–1013; Walther Schoenborn, "La Nature juridique du territoire," Hague, Académie de droit international, *Recueil des cours*, Vol. 30, 1929–V, pp. 87, 162–166; James Brown Scott, "Arctic Exploration and International Law," *American Journal of International Law*, Vol. 3, 1909, pp. 928–941; Gustav Smodal, *Acquisition of Sovereignty over Polar Areas*, Oslo, Dybwad, 1931; U.S. Naval War College, *International Law Situations 1937*, Washington, D.C., U.S. Government Printing Office, 1939, pp. 69–131; René Waultrin, "Le Problème de la souveraineté des pôles," *Revue générale de droit international public*, Vol. 16, 1909, pp. 649–660; "La Question de la souveraineté des terres arctiques," *Revue générale de droit international public*, Vol. 15, 1908, pp. 78–125, 185–209, 401–423.

"effectively occupied" by the State claiming such sovereignty, and (*b*) whether any part of the vast ice-covered water areas in the Arctic beyond the limit of normal territorial waters may be treated as subject to the sovereignty of a particular State, or whether such areas should be considered as part of the high seas and not, therefore, subject to the sovereignty of any State.

The sector theory of Arctic sovereignty is a development of the twentieth century. It was first definitively stated in a debate in the Canadian Senate. On February 20, 1907, Senator Poirier proposed the following resolution:

> That it be resolved that the Senate is of opinion that the time has come for Canada to make a formal declaration of possession of the lands and islands situated in the north of the Dominion, and extending to the north pole.

He stated, in the debate, that:

> . . . in future partition of northern lands, a country whose possession today goes up to the Arctic regions, will have a right, or should have a right, or has a right to all the lands that are to be found in the waters between a line extending from its eastern extremity north, and another line extending from the western extremity north. All the lands between the two lines up to the North Pole should belong and do belong to the country whose territory abuts up there.[13]

The resolution was not adopted. But it evidenced a growing feeling that Canada had special rights in areas north of its then occupied territories. During the previous year, 1906, the first edition of the Canadian Atlas had been officially published under the title "Department of the Interior, Canada, Honourable Frank Oliver, Minister, 1906, Atlas of Canada, Prepared under the Direction of James White, F.R.G.S., Geographer." In this Atlas, Map 1 and some of the other maps show dotted lines running towards the North Pole—one on the 141st meridian, the other roughly on the meridian of 60°. In the same year the Canadian Parliament had amended the Fisheries Act of 1904 so as to require that a license fee be payable for hunting whales in Hudson Bay "inasmuch as Hudson Bay is wholly territorial water of Canada."[14] In 1909 a government expedition erected a tablet on

---

[13] *Debates of the Senate of the Dominion of Canada*, 1906–07, 10th Parliament, 3d Session, (1907), pp. 266–271. See also: Green Haywood Hackworth, *Digest of International Law*, Washington, U. S. Government Printing Office, 1940, Vol. 1, Sec. 67, p. 463; Timothy Andrew Taracouzio, *Soviets in the Arctic*, New York, Macmillan, 1938, p. 320; Leonid Breitfuss, "Territorial Division of the Arctic," *Dalhousie Review*, Vol. 8, 1928, p. 464.

[14] Hackworth, *Digest of International Law*, op. cit., Vol. 1, Sec. 102, p. 700.

Melville Island "to commemorate the taking possession for the Dominion of Canada of the whole Arctic Archipelago lying to the north of America from longitude 60 degrees west to 141 degrees west up to latitude 90 degrees north,"[15]—apparently a notice of claim to territorial rights within the sector described, certainly covering all islands and also perhaps the waters in the area of the archipelago. The Atlas of 1906, the statement of Poirier in the Canadian Senate in 1907, the tablet erected on Melville Island in 1909, together evidence Canadian support of the sector theory. This was further emphasized in 1921 by a note addressed to the Government of Denmark holding that any discoveries which the Danish explorer, Rasmussen, might make north of Canada would be considered as not affecting the rights of Canada in such territories.[16]

In 1924 the United States semi-officially took cognizance of the sector theory. Denby, then Secretary of the Navy, testifying in January 1924 before the House Committee on Naval Affairs as to a proposed flight of the U.S. Navy dirigible "Shenandoah" to the Arctic, and discussing possible lands north of Alaska, said:

> And furthermore, in my opinion it is highly desirable that if there is in that region land, either habitable or not, it should be the property of the United States. . . . And, for myself, I cannot view with equanimity any territory of that kind being in the hands of another Power.[17]

The proposed voyage did not take place. But Denby's remarks may have had international repercussions for it must be noted that later in the same year the USSR clarified its Arctic territorial claims.

In a note of November 4, 1924 to all other States[18] the USSR affirmed a prior notification given in 1916 by the Russian Imperial Government announcing the incorporation into the Russian Empire of various Arctic islands north of the Russian and Siberian mainland.[19]

---

[15] V. Kenneth Johnston, "Canada's Title to the Arctic Islands," *Canadian Historical Review*, Vol. 14, 1933, p. 33.

[16] Taracouzio, *Soviets in the Arctic, op. cit.*, pp. 327–328; David Hunter Miller, "Political Rights in the Arctic," *Foreign Affairs*, Vol. 4, 1925, p. 50.

[17] U.S. Congress, House of Representatives, Committee on Naval Affairs, *Hearing on House Resolution 149, concerning Contemplated Flight of the Shenandoah to the North Polar Regions*, 1924, pp. 452–453. See also: Charles Cheney Hyde, *International Law . . .*, 2d rev. ed., Boston, Little Brown, 1945, Vol. 1, Sec. 104D, p. 353; Taracouzio, *Soviets in the Arctic, op. cit.*, p. 326.

[18] Hackworth, *Digest of International Law, op. cit.*, Vol. 1, Sec. 67, p. 461; W. Lakhtine, "Rights over the Arctic," *American Journal of International Law*, Vol. 24, 1930, p. 708.

[19] *Ibid.* See also: Miller, "Political Rights in the Arctic," *op. cit.*, p. 53.

181

The note of 1924 evidenced a general claim to unoccupied islands in the Soviet sector, and perhaps to undiscovered lands.

The Canadian position was restated more formally in 1925. The Minister of the Interior, Mr. Stewart, said in the Canadian House of Commons:

> Mr. Speaker, this Government has been very much alive to what we claim to be the possessions of Canada in the northern territory adjacent to the Dominion. Indeed, I made the statement in the House the other evening that we claimed all the territory lying between meridians 60 and 141. This afternoon, when dealing with the estimates of the Department of the Interior, I propose to bring down a map to make it clear what precautions we are taking to establish ourselves in that territory, and to notify the nationals of foreign countries passing over it that we think Canada should be advised of their plans and that they should ask for permits from the Canadian Government.[20]

In the same debate he stated that Canada claimed jurisdiction to the North Pole. By an Order in Council issued the following year (1926) it was provided that all persons thereafter entering the territories of the Canadian Arctic should secure permits.[21]

Also in 1926, perhaps as a result of the definitive statement of the Canadian position, the USSR adopted a formal decree covering its territorial claims in the Arctic. This decree is more specific than the 1924 diplomatic note. The decree states:

> The Presidium of the Central Executive Committee of the Union of Soviet Socialist Republics decrees:
>
> All discovered lands and islands, as well as all those that may in the future be discovered, which are not at the date of the publication of this decree recognised by the Government of the U.S.S.R. as the territory of a foreign Power, are declared to be territories belonging to the U.S.S.R. within the following limits:
>
> In the Northern Arctic Ocean, from the northern coast of the U.S.S.R. up to the North Pole, between the meridian 32° 4' 35" east longitude from Greenwich, passing along the eastern side of Vaida

---

[20] *Debates of the House of Commons of the Dominion of Canada*, 14th Parliament, 4th Session (1925), p. 4238; Hackworth, *Digest of International Law, op. cit.*, Vol. 1, Sec. 67, p. 463; Miller, "Political Rights in the Arctic," *op. cit.*, p. 50; Taracouzio, *Soviets in the Arctic, op. cit.*, p. 328; Breitfuss, "Territorial Division of the Arctic," *op. cit.*, p. 464; U.S. Naval War College, *International Law Situations 1937*, Washington, U.S. Government Printing Office, 1939, p. 110.

[21] Hackworth, *Digest of International Law, op. cit.*, Vol. 1, Sec. 67, p. 463.

Bay through the triangulation mark on Kokursk Cape, and meridian 168° 49′ 30″ west longitude from Greenwich, passing through the middle of the strait which separates Ratmanov and Krusenstern Islands of the Diomede group of islands in the Behring Straits.[22]

This is the most formal action taken by any State affirming the sector principle. It is a distinct claim of sovereignty as against all the world over occupied, unoccupied, and even undiscovered land territories in the Soviet sector. The decree has never been repealed.

Construed strictly, the decree of 1926 applies only to lands in the Soviet sector. But authoritative Soviet writers have given it a much wider application. Korovin, writing soon after the decree was issued, stated that "this Decree must be understood to include in the conception of 'lands and islands,' as expressed by Soviet legislators, also ice formations and the seas surrounding them, for otherwise the polar sector adjacent to the U.S.S.R. would have to be considered as an open sea with all the consequences resulting from such an interpretation."[23] Sigrist (1928) insisted that "in the spirit of the Decree we must maintain that the whole region from the Soviet mainland to the Pole is Soviet possession . . ."[24] He included water areas.

Without question the most authoritative statement was made by Lakhtine. He was Secretary-Member of the Committee of Direction of the Section of Aerial Law of the Union of Societies "Ossoaviachim" of the U.S.S.R. and, as the U.S. Naval War College commentator said, he "would be expected to represent the Soviet point of view at the time when he was writing in 1930."[25] Lahktine's discussion of rights over the Arctic regions was originally published in 1928 in Moscow in Russian by the Soviet Commissariat of Foreign Affairs.[26] His views were republished in French in 1929[27] and in English in

[22] *British & Foreign State Papers*, Vol. 124, p. 1064. See also: U.S. Naval War College, *International Law Situations 1937, op. cit.*, p. 103; Taracouzio, *Soviets in the Arctic, op. cit.*, p. 381; Lakhtine, "Rights over the Arctic," *op. cit.*, p. 709.

[23] E. A. Korovin, "Problema Vozduchnoi Okkupatsii," *Voprosy Vozd. Prava*, Vol. 1, pp. 109–110, as cited in Taracouzio, *Soviets in the Arctic, op. cit.*, p. 348.

[24] S. V. Sigrist, "Sovetskoe Pravo v. Poliarnykh Prostranstvakh," *Rabochii Sud*, 1928, p. 984, as cited in Taracouzio, *Soviets in the Arctic, op. cit.*, p. 349.

[25] U.S. Naval War College, *International Law Situations 1937, op. cit.*, p. 101.

[26] V. L. Lakhtine, *Prava na Severnye Poliarnye Prostranstva*, Moscow, 1928. See also: W. L. G. Joerg, *Brief History of Polar Exploration since the Introduction of Flying*, 2d rev. ed., New York, American Geographical Society (Special Publication No. 11), 1930, p. 61, note 1.

[27] "La Voie aérienne arctique et l'état juridique des territoires polaires septentrionaux," *Droit aérien*, Vol. 13, 1929, pp. 532–556.

1930.[28] His position may be summarized as follows: that in polar regions the sector principle must be accepted; that "regardless of discovery and regardless of effective occupation, the discovered lands and islands belong as a matter of fact to States in the region of attraction in which they are situated;"[29] that the "lands and islands being still undiscovered are already presumed to belong to the national territory of the adjacent Polar State in the sector of the region of attraction in which they are to be found;"[30] that "floating ice should be assimilated legally to open polar seas, whilst ice formations that are more or less immovable should enjoy a legal status equivalent to polar territory;"[31] that the "legal status for the high seas of the Arctic, is, in its essential part, nearly identical with that of 'territorial waters;'"[32] that as "Polar States exercise sovereignty over known and unknown territory lying in their sectorial regions of attraction, and over more or less immovable permanent ice formations covering the north part of the Arctic Ocean, as well as over national and territorial waters, . . . the Polar States exercise sovereignty also over the atmosphere above these territories, ice and waters" and hence "each Polar State exercises sovereignty over the aerial space above the whole region of attraction of its sector."[33]

In arguing that polar States should have sovereignty even in the airspace over water areas of the Arctic Ocean free from ice, Lakhtine said:

Inasmuch as the legal status of these water areas is closely assimilated to that of territorial waters over which a State does exercise a limited sovereignty; and since, according to the international law of today, a littoral State exercises unlimited jurisdiction over the atmosphere above its territorial waters, there is no reason for treating the question of the legal status of these Arctic air regions in a different manner.

This argument is strengthened when we realize the impossibility of using airships for economic purposes exclusively in this part of Arctic aerial space. If an airship should be used for operations connected with fishing and hunting in these open waters, it would be as necessary to obtain the permission of the littoral State as it would be to obtain permission for fishing and hunting from vessels. Moreover, it is impossible to use the air for aerial communication without crossing ice regions, territorial waters and territories belonging to a State which exercises sovereignty over the atmosphere above.[34]

---

[28] "Rights over the Arctic," *American Journal of International Law*, Vol. 24, 1930, pp. 703–717. For extended discussions of Lakhtine's position, see: U.S. Naval War College, *International Law Situations 1937, op. cit.*, pp. 101–106; Taracouzio, *Soviets in the Arctic, op. cit.*, pp. 321–366.

[29] "Rights over the Arctic," *op. cit.*, p. 710.   [30] *Ibid.*, p. 711.

[31] *Ibid.*, p. 712.   [32] *Ibid.*, p. 713.   [33] *Ibid.*, pp. 714–715.   [34] *Ibid.*

Also in further support of his conclusion that polar States exercise sovereignty over the airspace above the whole region of the sector, Lakhtine quotes the 1928 statement of Breitfuss as follows:

Within each of these sectors, an adjacent State exercises its sovereignty over discovered as well as over undiscovered lands and islands, this sovereignty being exercised not only over land, but also to a certain extent (yet to be precisely fixed internationally) over seas covered with ice, surrounding these lands and islands and as well over air regions above this sector.[35]

The Government of the USSR has not in terms repudiated the position taken by Korovin, Sigrist and Lakhtine in support of the theory that the USSR and other polar States are sovereign over the entire land and water areas and airspace over their respective sectors. But the actual course of subsequent events creates doubts as to whether the USSR supports the sector principle beyond the strict terms of the decree of 1926.[36] In the first place the international agreement which Breitfuss assumed necessary in order to fix the status of sovereignty over the polar seas has not been accomplished or even sought. Instead the Soviet Government has, by its legislation, stated its claim to territorial waters. By a decree of May 24, 1921, the pre-revolutionary three-mile limit for territorial waters along the coast was changed to a twelve-mile limit in the White Sea and the Arctic Ocean.[37] By the statute of June 15, 1927, on "Protection of the Boundaries of the U.S.S.R." this twelve-mile limit was made applicable to all the coastal waters of the Soviet Union except where expressly provided otherwise by international agreement.[38] It must be assumed that this twelve-mile limit for territorial waters became thereby applicable to territorial waters around the land areas claimed by the USSR in the sector decree of 1926. In 1932, by the adoption of the Air Code, as previously cited in this article, the USSR declared that "by the air space of the Union of S.S.R. is understood the air space above the land and fluvial territory of the Union of S.S.R., and above the *territorial waters established by the laws of the Union of S.S.R.*" [Italics supplied]. From this it would appear that the USSR has limited its airspace claims with great care and that the claims do not extend beyond the airspace over

---

[35] *Ibid.*, p. 715. For another translation of this statement of Breitfuss, see: Breitfuss, "Territorial Division of the Arctic," *op. cit.*, p. 467.

[36] At least one careful student of the situation feels that the Soviet Government "has elected to forego the application of sectorism to airspace in the Arctic, adhering rather to the older, established principles of aerial jurisdiction." [Elmer Plischke, "Trans-Polar Aviation and Jurisdiction over Arctic Airspace," *American Political Science Review*, Vol. 37, 1943, p. 1010.]

[37] Taracouzio, *The Soviet Union and International Law. op. cit.*, p. 63.

[38] *Ibid.*

lands and waters within the Soviet twelve-mile limit. At least other States are certainly entitled to rely upon this construction, notwithstanding the broad claims sought to be established by Lakhtine.

Further doubt as to whether the Soviet Government supports the sector theory as a basis of airspace sovereignty beyond the terms of the decree of 1926 is furnished by its action in 1937 in seeking to take physical possession of a north polar area. Lakhtine had called attention to the fact that the North Pole is an intersection of the meridian lines of the sectors into which he divided the Arctic, stating:

> Neither legally, nor in fact does it belong to anyone. It might be represented as an hexahedral frontier post on the sides of which might be painted the national colors of the State of the corresponding sector.[39]

If Lakhtine expressed the Soviet views as to the polar seas (and as to airspace above), then no occupation of any part of the polar seas was needed to establish Soviet title within its sector, and no Soviet entry into sectors of other States would be legally justified. Nevertheless, in preparation for the trans-polar flights which later took place, the Soviet Government dispatched an expedition by air to the north polar area. This expedition landed on May 21, 1937, near the Pole, seeking to establish a permanent base for radio and meteorological purposes. According to press dispatches from Moscow, the Soviet Government immediately claimed sovereignty over the polar area on the basis that it was the first to establish a permanent settlement in the vicinity.[40] No reference to the sector theory to support such claim seems to have been made. In fact it has been stated that the settlement was originally located on pack ice which, under the sector theory, was in Canadian territory.[41] But by August 8, 1937, this "permanent" base had drifted 138 miles toward Greenland.[42] By August 29 the camp had drifted 330 miles.[43] By February 6, 1938 it had apparently drifted about 1100 miles.[44] When the party was rescued on February 19, 1938, the total drift in 274 days had been approximately 1500 miles.[45] The settlement originally established under the Soviet flag in the "Canadian sector" was rescued from the floating pack ice near the coast of Greenland in the "Danish sector." Nothing could demonstrate more clearly that not even the Soviet Government relies upon the sector theory as a

---

[39] Lakhtine, "Rights over the Arctic," *op. cit.*, p. 717.
[40] *New York Times*, May 23, 1937, p. 1, col. 8.
[41] Taracouzio, *Soviets in the Arctic, op. cit.*, p. 359.
[42] *New York Times*, August 8, 1937, p. 27, col. 2.
[43] *Ibid.*, August 29, 1937.
[44] *Ibid.*, February 6, 1938, p. 32, col. 2.
[45] *Ibid.*, February 20, 1938, p. 1, col. 6.

basis for international determination of surface or airspace rights over the Arctic Ocean. In fact the attempted settlement on the polar ice appears to be an abandonment of the sector theory and a reliance upon the principles of "effective occupation" as the basis of territorial sovereignty.

The States other than the USSR which face the Arctic (Canada, Denmark, Iceland, Norway and the United States) are parties to the Chicago Convention on International Civil Aviation of 1944 (cited previously in this article). By this convention each contracting State recognizes that every State has complete and exclusive sovereignty over the airspace above its land areas and the territorial waters adjacent thereto. Inherent in the convention is the accepted doctrine that airspace over lands which are under the sovereignty of no State and airspace over the high seas is not under the sovereignty of any State and is free to the use of all States. Unless by unwritten and customary international law the parties to the Chicago convention are in agreement that a special regime (such as the sector theory) exists in the Arctic and that this special regime shall determine what areas constitute national lands and territorial waters in the Arctic area, the only basis which can be used to determine territorial surface rights in the Arctic (and therefore airspace rights) are the normal and generally accepted rules of international law as to what constitutes land territory, territorial waters, and the high seas.

But it is quite apparent that neither the sector theory nor any other special regime as to Arctic surface sovereignty has been accepted into international law by the parties to the Chicago Convention. While the sector principle has been semi-officially supported in Canada as to discovered and undiscovered lands in the so-called "Canadian sector," the extent of the Canadian claims to control water areas in the sector beyond the accepted three-mile limit of territorial waters has never been stated. The sector principle has been authoritatively denied by both the United States and Norway, directly interested in the Arctic, and does not appear to have been accepted by any other State.

As to the United States, a suggestion was made in 1929 to President Hoover that the Government should initiate an international arrangement to partition the Arctic between the United States, Canada, Denmark, Norway and Russia. The proposal was referred to the U.S. Navy Department. The Secretary of the Navy officially replied to the Secretary of State on September 23, 1929 to the effect that the action proposed:

a) Is an effort arbitrarily to divide up a large part of the world's area amongst several countries;

b) Contains no justification for claiming sovereignty over large areas of the world's surface;

187

c) Violates the long recognized custom of establishing sovereignty over territory by right of discovery;

d) Is in effect a claim of sovereignty over high seas, which are universally recognized as free to all nations, and is a novel attempt to create artificially a closed sea and thereby infringe the rights of all nations to the free use of this area.

I, therefore, consider that this government should not enter into any such agreement as proposed.[46]

This authoritative statement refutes any implications which might be drawn from the 1924 testimony of Secretary of the Navy Denby,[47] which seemed to give some support to the sector theory. It must also be recalled that Secretary of State Hull on November 13, 1934, advised the British Ambassador (in a discussion as to discoveries in the Antarctic) that "in the light of long established principles of international law . . . I can not admit that sovereignty accrues from mere discovery unaccompanied by occupancy and use."[48] As further indication of the United States position, the U.S. Naval War College in 1937, when considering problems as to polar areas, discussed the possibility of a State with land bordering on the polar area seeking to prohibit the entrance of aircraft polarward from its coast. It held that no such right existed—thus in substance denying the validity of the sector principle as applicable to polar water areas beyond the normal three-mile limit from the coast line of the State facing the Arctic and the airspace over such areas, saying:

c) The right of a state to prevent or to regulate the movement of foreign aircraft is limited to the air within its jurisdiction which extends to the air above its land and maritime boundaries. Generally accepted maritime boundaries now extend at least to three miles from the low-water mark along the coast and three miles outside the limits of its bays. Whether the direction is toward the equator or toward the pole makes no difference—the jurisdiction extends seaward for three miles."[49]

Clearly the United States has never agreed to a special rule applicable to the Arctic for a determination of what constitutes land and territorial waters.

In 1930 the Government of Norway expressly disapproved the sector theory. In recognizing the sovereignty of Canada over the

---

[46] Hackworth, *Digest of International Law, op. cit.*, Vol. 1, Sec. 67, p. 464.
[47] See note 17 *supra*.
[48] Hackworth, *Digest of International Law, op. cit.*, Vol. 1, Sec. 67, p. 457; Hyde, *International Law, op. cit.*, Vol. 1, Sec. 104D, pp. 343–354.
[49] U.S. Naval War College, *International Law Situations 1937, op. cit.*, p. 127.

Sverdrup Islands, a Norwegian note stated that the recognition of such sovereignty "over these islands is in no way based on any sanction whatever of what is named the 'sector principle.'"[50]

The Permanent Court of International Justice in stating that international law "governs relations between independent States" held "The rules of law binding upon States therefore emanate from their own free will as expressed in conventions or by usages generally accepted as expressing principles of law and established in order to regulate the relations between these coexisting independent communities or with a view to the achievement of common aims."[51]

The sector principle has obviously not been accepted as part of international law as thus authoritatively stated. No general international convention has affirmed the sector principle, nor has it been recognized by international usage. Rather the normal rules of international law as to what may be considered as land and territorial waters must be the source for fixing the recognized extent of national airspace Arctic rights.

The first question to be answered is whether the rules of international law have been so modified as to permit the existence in the Arctic of sovereignty in land territories which have never been "effectively occupied." The answer to this question would seem to depend on a statement of what is meant by effective occupation. The denial of the sector theory carries with it the denial of sovereignty to undiscovered lands and the superjacent airspace. As to lands already discovered, von de Heydte has thus stated the rule:

> Effectiveness means actual displaying of sovereign rights; it means maintenance of a certain order corresponding to the international standard, which, of course, is different in territories sparsely inhabited and scarcely frequented by foreigners from what it is in densely peopled trading places.[52]

Lindley, speaking of the north polar regions, states the applicable international law rule to be:

> In such cases, it would seem that an occupation would be rendered effective by the establishment of any organization (however rudi-

---

[50] Hackworth, *Digest of International Law, op. cit.*, Vol. 1, Sec. 67, p. 463; U.S. Naval War College, *International Law Situations 1937, op. cit.*, p. 111.
[51] *The S.S. Lotus* (France v. Turkey), Permanent Court of International Justice, Judgment 9, Sept. 7, 1927, Ser. A, No. 10, p. 18; Manley O. Hudson, ed., *World Court Reports*, Washington, Carnegie Endowment for International Peace 1934–43, Vol. 2 (1935), p. 35.
[52] Friedrich August Freiherr von der Heydte, "Discovery, Symbolic Annexation and Virtual Effectiveness in International Law," *American Journal of International Law*, Vol. 29, 1935, p. 463.

mentary) or of any system of control, which, having regard to the conditions under which the area appropriated was being used or was likely to be used, was reasonably sufficient to maintain order among such persons as might resort there.[53]

The rules of effective occupation, as thus stated, may be applied in the Arctic without any departure from the accepted principles of international law in view of the character of the terrain. A State which there claims territorial rights and reasonably exercises jurisdiction and control over the land areas concerned may be admitted to have sovereignty. This sovereignty extends to the airspace over the lands in question and to normal adjacent territorial waters. It does not extend further.

The remaining question—as to whether any part of the vast ice-covered water areas of the Arctic Ocean beyond the limit of normal territorial waters may be treated as possibly coming under the sovereignty of a single State—presents much greater difficulty. It has been suggested that claims of sovereignty might be considered if a particular area "is possessed of a surface sufficiently solid to enable a man to pursue his occupations thereon and which also in consequence of its solidity and permanence constitutes in itself a barrier to navigation as it is normally enjoyed in the open seas."[54]

As to most of the Arctic Ocean area the answer to the problem seems fairly clear. From Alaska across the North Pole to Spitzbergen is about 1900 statute miles. From the north coast of Ellesmere Island (in Canada) also across the Pole to the nearest known Soviet island is about 1100 miles. This great ocean area contains no known land. It is admittedly almost continuously ice-covered. Only near the coasts is it ever navigable, and that for only a limited period each year. But the ice which covers by far the greatest part of the Arctic Ocean is constantly, though slowly, in motion. Established habitation and occupation is clearly impracticable. This was demonstrated by the fruitless effort of the 1937–38 Soviet expedition to place a "permanent" settlement near the North Pole (as described earlier in this article). As Balch said in 1910:

> But the ice at the North Pole is never at rest. It is in continual motion. It moves slowly in a direction from Bering's Strait towards the Atlantic Ocean. Consequently any habitation fixed upon it would be continually moving. And such possible occupation would be too precarious and shifting to and fro to give any one a good title. And so the rules of the Law of Nations that recognize the freedom

---

[53] M. F. Lindley, *The Acquisition and Government of Backward Territory in International Law*, New York *et al.*, Longmans Green, 1926, p. 158.

[54] Hyde, *International Law, op. cit.*, Vol. 1, Sec. 104A, p. 348.

of the high seas would seem to apply naturally to a moving and shifting substance like the North Polar Sea ice at all points beyond the customary three-mile limit from the shore.[55]

While it may be contended that under modern aviation conditions such ice-covered seas can be controlled from the air and thus occupied, the same thing can be said of the open seas. But without question an attempt by a single State in time of peace to seize any part of the high seas or the airspace above and to maintain exclusive control in such areas would be an act of aggression against all other States. No more reason or excuse exists to admit that ice-covered seas and the airspace above them may be seized by a single State and all other States thereby excluded, than to admit that the open seas and the airspace above them may legally be similarly seized and held.

A century and a quarter ago a great and wise jurist, Justice Story, stated the basic rule of the freedom of the seas:

> Upon the ocean, then, in time of peace, all possess an entire equality. It is the common highway of all, appropriated to the use of all; and no one can vindicate to himself a superior or exclusive prerogative there. Every ship sails there with the unquestionable right of pursuing her own lawful business without interruption; but, whatever may be that business, she is bound to pursue it in such a manner as not to violate the rights of others.[56]

Justice Story's statement is as true today of the airspace over the open sea and the sea itself as it was in his time as to the sea alone. The airspace over the sea is today a "highway common to all, appropriated to the use of all." No adequate reason could be stated why this highway should be blocked by the act of any single State because ice and not open water lies below. The airspace over the Arctic Ocean is and should be as free for the aircraft of all States, whether having land territories in the Arctic or not, as is the airspace over the other great water areas of the world.

Two corollary problems must be considered: (1) What is the status of the airspace over fixed ice along occupied coasts in the Arctic? and (2) What is the status of the airspace over straits bounded on each side by the land territory of the same State and connecting sea areas which are wholly or at times navigable?

As stated earlier, the subjacent State has exclusive sovereignty in the airspace over such territorial waters adjacent to its coasts as are recognized by international law as properly coming within its jurisdic-

---

[55] Thomas Willing Balch, "The Arctic and Antarctic Regions and the Law of Nations," *American Journal of International Law*, Vol. 4, 1910, p. 266.

[56] *The Marianna Flora*, (1826), 11 Wheaton (24 U.S.) 1, p. 42.

tion. This rule should be normally applied in the Arctic. Territorial waters, except in extraordinary cases, should be considered as beginning at the shore of the land and extending outward over the water to the width recognized for territorial waters by international law, even though the water is permanently ice-covered to that distance and beyond. The only exception to this rule which, in the judgment of the present author, can be considered as valid would be a case where the permanent ice adjacent to the shore is actually occupied and permanently used throughout the entire year as fully as the adjoining land and as a definite part of the State's occupied territory. If any State can demonstrate the existence of such permanently used and occupied fixed ice as part of its land territory, then the true coastline might be considered as being on the fixed ice at the edge of the occupied area. From such a line territorial waters would then be considered as extending out to the normal width, and the subjacent State might reasonably claim airspace sovereignty over such permanently occupied and used areas and a normal width of territorial waters adjacent thereto. But this case should not be considered as a normal rule, but only as an exception to be claimed and validly demonstrated by the State seeking surface and airspace sovereignty by actual occupation of the fixed ice beyond the real coastline. This suggested exception is analogous to the right of a State bordering on the sea to extend its land territories by filling in and physically occupying areas which had formerly been part of its navigable territorial waters.

As to the straits, the normal rule of international law is that straits dividing the land of one and the same State are part of the territory of that State when not more than six miles wide.[57] As to straits more than six miles wide, but sufficiently narrow to be controlled by coastal batteries placed on each side, the rule is not so clear. It is believed that the rule suggested at The Hague Conference on the Codification of International Law in 1930 is reasonably sound. According to this rule, "when the width of the straits exceeds the breadth of the two belts of territorial sea, the waters between those two belts form part of the high sea. If the result of the delimitation is to leave an area of high sea not exceeding two miles in breadth surrounded by territorial sea, this area may be assimilated to territorial sea."[58] If such straits are thereby territorial waters, the airspace above is under the sovereignty of the adjacent State. If, on the other hand, an area through the center of the strait should be considered under the rule as part of the high seas, such airspace is usable for international flight even though the area below be frozen.

---

[57] Lassa F. L. Oppenheim, *International Law: A Treatise*, 7th ed., London/New York/Toronto, Longmans Green, 1948, Vol. 1, Sec. 194, p. 463.

[58] Hackworth, *Digest of International Law, op. cit.*, Vol. 1, Sec. 90, p. 611.

SUMMARY

The following rules of international air law applicable to airspace sovereignty in the Arctic may therefore be stated:

1. The "sector theory is not part of international law and cannot be accepted or used as the basis for determining Arctic airspace rights.

2. In the Arctic as elsewhere each State has complete and exclusive sovereignty in the airspace over its territory and such space is in fact an integral part of national territory.

3. Surface territory in the Arctic, as elsewhere for the purpose of airspace sovereignty, includes lands and adjacent territorial waters. Airspace over recognized and admitted territorial waters is in the same legal status as airspace over land territory.

4. Every State has complete control of the airspace included within its territory, has the exclusive right to fly in that airspace, and may exclude all foreign aircraft or admit them on such terms as it sees fit.

5. In the determination of what areas in the Arctic constitute the lands and territorial waters of any State the normal rules of international law will apply subject to the following observations:

a) In determining whether or not a State has "effectively occupied" lands in the Arctic the nature of the terrain must be considered and such occupation will be deemed effective if the State maintains adequate jurisdiction and control in the area so as to protect such inhabitants as may be there and to maintain order.

b) In determining the extent of territorial waters, the normal rules will apply unless water areas adjoining occupied lands are permanently covered with ice and continuously used and occupied by the adjacent State as if they were land, in which case and on proof of such occupation, the coast line may be considered as beginning at the edge of the permanently occupied ice.

6. Airspace over the high seas is free to the use of all States and cannot be subject to the sovereignty of any single State. The ice-covered areas of the Arctic Ocean must be treated as high seas, and the airspace over such areas as free to the use of all.

11
Space Above the Seas

Author's Note. The Office of the U.S. Judge Advocate General of the Navy originally suggested and later published this study in its "JAG Journal." This author has always felt that too little consideration has been given to the legal control of flight above the high seas which cover a large percentage of the earth's surface. Intercontinental overseas air traffic is increasing daily. Article 12 of the Chicago Convention provides that "over the high seas the rules in force shall be those established under this Convention," thus delegating full authority to the International Civil Aviation Organization to adopt rules which apply so far as its member States are concerned to civil aircraft in the airspace. A major unsettled question involves the control of spacecraft and rockets over the high seas, which is made even more complicated by the present lack of certainty as to what flight instrumentalities are or should be included in the term "aircraft."

T̲HE PURPOSE OF this Article is to state certain of the major problems of the legal status of flight space above the seas. Flight space means so much of universal space above the surface of the earth as is now used, or may hereafter be used, as the area in which flight takes place. Flight space includes both the "airspace" and "outer-space." Flight includes any movement through space of man operated or man controlled devices or instrumentalities such as balloons, dirigibles, airplanes, rockets, guided missiles, artificial satellites or space ships. The term "seas" includes both the "high seas" and the "territorial waters," or marginal seas.

HIGH SEAS

The legal status of usable space above the high seas has always been of particular interest to the Navy. One of the earliest and most authoritative American discussions of the problem of the extent of national sovereignty in space is found in the remarks of Professor George Grafton Wilson in the Naval War College "International Law Situations" for 1912, pages 71–72. Repeating what he had said in a paper published the prior year in the American Political Science Review, and basing his remarks on a quotation from a decision by Mr. Justice Story in *Santissima Trinidad* (7 Wheaton 354), Professor Wilson asserted:

It would seem wise . . . to start from the premise that air above the high seas and territory that is res nullius is free, while other air is

195

within the jurisdiction of the subjacent State "and that the exceptions to this rule are such only as by common usage and public policy have been allowed, in order to preserve the peace and harmony of nations and to regulate their intercourse in a manner best suited to their dignity and rights," and for these exceptions to the exclusive right of aerial jurisdiction of the subjacent State, international conferences should by agreement immediately provide.

Professor Wilson thus assimilated the freedom of flight above the high seas to the freedom of navigation by ships on the high seas. Many years earlier Story had said in *The Marianna Flora* (1826) 11 Wheaton 1:

> Upon the ocean then, in time of peace, all possess an entire equality. It is the common highway of all, appropriated to the use of all; and no one can vindicate to himself a superior or exclusive prerogative there. Every ship sails there with the unquestionable right of pursuing her own lawful business without interruption; but, whatever may be that business, she is bound to pursue it in such a manner as not to violate the rights of others.

When the aeronautical Commission of the 1919 Paris Peace Conference was organized, President Wilson appointed Rear Admiral H. S. Knapp, United States Navy, as one of the Chief Delegates. That Commission had before it the task of drafting an international convention for the regulation of future international flight. At one of the earliest meetings of the Commission, on motion of Admiral Knapp, the following principle was adopted:

> 1. Recognition: (1) of the principle of the full and absolute sovereignty of each State over the air above its territories and territorial waters, carrying with it the right of exclusion of foreign aircraft;
> 2. of the right of each State to impose its jurisdiction over the air above its territory and territorial waters.

The United States delegation fully understood, however, that the principle thus stated did not apply over the high seas. In a note circulated to other delegations (still preserved in the National Archives in Washington) appears the following proposed convention article:

> The contracting States declare that the sovereignty of States extends throughout the atmosphere above their own territories, including their territorial waters; but that no State may claim sovereignty of any part of the atmosphere over the High Seas or over waste portions of the land that are subject to no particular jurisdiction.

When the legal Subcommission submitted to the full Aeronautical Commission the draft of what is now known as the Paris Convention of 1919, the basic legal conclusions on which the draft depended were thus stated:

> The first question placed before the Subcommission was that of the *principle of freedom or of sovereignty of the air.*
>
> ... the opinion expressed in the Legal Subcommission is favorable to the full and exclusive submission of the airspace to the sovereignty of the subjacent territory. It is only when the column of air hangs over a *res nullius* or *communis*, the sea, that freedom becomes the law of the air.
>
> Therefore, the airspace is part of the legal regime of the subjacent territory. Is this territory that of a particular State? Then the airspace is subject to the sovereignty of that State. Does it escape all sovereignty as the free sea? Then the airspace is also free above the sea, as the sea itself.

The Paris Convention of 1919 was signed but not ratified by the United States. It included in Article I a provision that "Every Power has complete and exclusive sovereignty over the airspace above its territory." No mention was made of the status of the airspace over the high seas. However, the part of the report of the Legal Subcommission quoted above clearly shows that the drafters of the convention, including the United States delegation, fully intended that airspace over the high seas would have the same legal status as the high seas themselves.

This principle was fully accepted in public international law prior to the outbreak of World War II, subject to one open question, namely, the status of the airspace over the Arctic ice. An interesting comment on the position of the U. S. S. R. in this connection will be found in the United States Naval War College "International Law Situations" for 1937. On page 101[1] is a reference to the published views of Lakhtine, who, in support of the "Sector Theory of Arctic Sovereignty" had insisted that States bounding on the Arctic had sovereignty over discovered and undiscovered lands between their shores and the North Pole as well as "over seas covered with ice, surrounding these lands and islands and as well over air regions above this sector."

Clearly the United States has not accepted this thesis. A suggestion was made in 1929 to President Hoover that the Government should initiate an international arrangement to partition the Arctic between the United States, Canada, Denmark, Norway and Russia. The

---

[1] Cited in AIRSPACE RIGHTS OVER THE ARCTIC, see *supra* at 185.

proposal was referred to the United States Navy Department. The Secretary of the Navy officially replied to the Secretary of State on September 23, 1929 to the effect that the action proposed:

a) Is an effort arbitrarily to divide up a large part of the world's area amongst several countries;

b) Contains no justification for claiming sovereignty over large areas of the world's surface;

c) Violates the long recognized custom of establishing sovereignty over territory by right of discovery:

d) Is in effect a claim of sovereignty over high seas, which are universally recognized as free to all nations, and is a novel attempt to create artificially a closed sea and thereby infringe the rights of all nations to the free use of this area.[2]

Such was the situation when the Chicago Conference met in 1944 to draft what is now the widely accepted "Convention on International Civil Aviation." In that convention, which the United States has signed and ratified, Article I states that "the contracting States recognize that every State has complete and exclusive sovereignty over the airspace above its territory." Again, as in the Paris Convention of 1919, no direct statement is made as to the legal status of the space above the high seas. However, so well understood was the principle of free air navigation in such areas that the United States delegation, acting through the late Dr. Edward P. Warner (and myself as Chairman of the Drafting Committee) had no difficulty in urging the adoption of the provision which now appears in Article XII of the Convention dealing with "Rules of the Air" to the effect that "over the high seas, the rules in force shall be those established under the convention." The meaning of this sentence has not been questioned. The drafters of the convention fully understood that each State could unilaterally adopt rules of the air in its territorial airspace. Complementing that right, the States who were parties to the convention have, under Article 12, delegated to the authority set up under the convention (International Civil Aviation Organization) the power to adopt flight rules applicable to their aircraft in the area where no national sovereignty exists, namely over the high seas.

The comparatively simple rule which is historically apparent, that international law accepts the fact that space over the high seas is not subject to the sovereignty of any single State, would appear to be subject, however, to the principle that every soverign State may, under certain circumstances, act beyond the limits of its territory to assure itself from injury. In 1950 the United States and Canada

---

[2] Hackworth, *Digest of International Law*, Vol. 1, Sec. 67, p. 464.

established air defense identification zones around parts of their respective shores. Admittedly the airspace over the high seas is not territorial space and enjoys the same international status as the high seas themselves. Yet the United States and Canada did not hesitate to establish regulations to prevent unidentified aircraft approaching their shores from the seas. The United States regulation, for example, requires that foreign aircraft must report their presence and identification when not less than one hour nor more than two hours average cruising distance via the most direct route to the shore. This is a clear application of the right of self-preservation and self-defense applicable outside national territory and within international flightspace. Squadron Leader Murchison, R. C. A. F., in "The Contiguous Air Space Zone in International Law" (published 1956 by Canadian Dept. of National Defence) has argued vigorously that the United States and Canadian regulations do not violate international law nor the Chicago Convention and are entirely valid on the basis of the right of each State to self-protection. The ultimate relationship between the doctrine of freedom of air navigation over the high seas for all States and this unilateral right of self-defense for single States bordering the seas may not yet, however, be finally determined.

One thing is, however, certain, that States such as the United States are entitled to launch satellites and other high altitude instrumentalities from their coasts over the seas, provided, of course, that such flights do not create arbitrary interference with other flight instrumentalities.

A most difficult problem is, however, posed by future possible construction of Article 12 of the Chicago Convention, referred to above, insofar as a high altitude flight is concerned. At the present time the annexes to the Convention provide for the registration and regulation of normal civil aircraft types which require atmospheric aerodynamic lift to maintain flight. If, however, the International Civil Aviation Organization should seek to amend these annexes in such manner that they apply to civil artificial satellites, or space ships, the question will then arise as to whether the "rules of the air" adopted by the International Civil Aviation Organization apply to high altitude flight in areas of flight space above and beyond the areas used by normal types of aircraft. The article of the convention does not in terms limit its application to "airspace." In other words, has the International Civil Aviation Organization already been given full authority to regulate flight over the high seas at whatever height, or are its powers limited to the areas used by aircraft of the general type in existence when the Chicago Convention became effective? This may create international questions if hereafter a new agency is set up to regulate outer space flight throughout the world. It will be most difficult to have one

199

agency regulating flight over the high seas in areas immediately adjacent to the sea itself, and another regulating such flight at higher altitudes. This problem may be met as soon as the United Nations, or other international body, seeks to draft a new convention, or to amend the Chicago Convention, so as to regulate flight in outerspace.

In summary, space over the high seas is free from national sovereignty claims at any height. But this may not preclude national action in such space when required for self-preservation by an adjacent State. Nor is it clear whether the power of the International Civil Aviation Organization to regulate flight "over the high seas" is limited to normal types of aircraft in the airspace, or may be expanded without amending the Convention to cover flight of any type of civil flight instrumentality in outer space, as well as in the airspace.

TERRITORIAL WATERS

The legal status of flight space over the territorial waters (marginal seas) adjacent to a State is diametrically opposed to that over the high seas. The territorial waters are part of the territory of the sovereign State. In the development of the law of flight, States have made exactly the same claim to the airspace over their territorial waters as to the airspace over their lands. They have never conceded the right of innocent passage for aircraft through airspace over territorial waters that exists for merchant vessels in time of peace through the territorial waters below.

Historically the position is clear. For example, in the British proposal for a convention submitted at Paris in 1919, the first article opened with the statement that "the High Contracting Parties recognize that the full and absolute sovereignty and jurisdiction of every State over the air above its territories and territorial waters etc." The accepted proposal of Admiral Knapp, quoted above, adopted the same principle of sovereignty over the air above its land and above territorial waters, adding that this carried with it "the right of exclusion of foreign aircraft." The Paris Convention as signed included territorial waters in the "territory of a State."

To the same effect is the present Chicago Convention. Article 1 asserts that every State has complete and exclusive sovereignty over the airspace above its territory. Article 2 provides that "for the purposes of the Convention the territory of a State shall be deemed to be the land areas and territorial waters adjacent thereto under the sovereignty, suzerainty, protection or mandate of such State.

Such being the present legal position, two major problems are immediately apparent:

1. The outward sea boundary of national airspace is a perpendicular line extending upward from the outer boundary of the territorial waters, but the width of these is nowhere stated. Does the convention mean "territorial waters" as generally accepted in international law, or does it mean such as may be claimed by the State in question?

2. The upper boundary of the airspace is not fixed, and every question now posed as to the upper boundary of airspace over national lands applies equally to the airspace over territorial waters.

As to the first of these questions, my own view has always been that both the Paris and Chicago Convention dealt with the term "territorial waters" as meaning the area accepted as such by customary international law. Had some other effect been intended, I believe evidence could be found in the Conventions themselves, or in the proceedings at the respective conferences. I have found no such evidence.

National statutes, however, are not uniform. The United States Air Commerce Act of 1926, as amended by the Civil Aeronautics Act of 1938, asserts national sovereignty in the airspace "above those portions of the adjacent marginal high seas, bays, and lakes over which by international law or treaty or convention the United States exercises national jurisdiction." This has recently been repeated in the "Federal Aviation Act of 1958," Section 1108.

On the other hand, the Soviet Air Code promulgated in 1932, and affirmed in 1935, states:

> The airspace of the USSR shall be understood to be the airspace above the land and water territory of the USSR, and above the zone of sea coastal waters as determined *by the laws of the USSR.* (Emphasis supplied.)

This appears to be a firm declaration claiming sovereignty in the airspace to whatever distance from the shore the national statutes may fix for the territorial waters. The USSR is not a party to the Chicago Convention.

It must therefore be admitted that there is no settled rule applicable world wide as to the basis for determining the boundary between national airspace over territorial waters and free airspace over the high seas. All that can be said is that if the width of the particular territorial sea is fixed and generally accepted, such is the width of national airspace beyond the shoreline.

As to the second question, one answer alone can be given—when international agreement is reached as to the upper boundary of national airspace over the lands of a State, that will also be the boundary applicable over territorial waters.

The limits of this paper will not permit a re-examination in detail of

201

the suggestions that have been made, particularly since the launching of Sputnik I brought forward the pressing legal and diplomatic question as to whether the satellites, or any of them, had flown through national airspace of any State. These suggestions vary widely. Those with some historical and logical support include:

a) Height up to which "aircraft" (instrumentalities requiring aerodynamic lift) can ascend (approximately 25 miles).

b) Height at which aerodynamic lift ceases entirely, and Kepler force takes over (approximately 52 miles).

c) Height at which an artificial satellite may be put in orbit (estimated at 70 to 75 miles).

d) Height at which no molecules of gaseous air are found (variously estimated at 1,000 to 10,000 miles).

e) Height without limit, on the theory that "airspace" as used in the Paris and Chicago Conventions, means "usable space."

f) Height to which the subjacent State may exercise effective control in space above it.

It is apparent that the two questions just discussed leave the dimensions of the national airspace over the territorial sea in a dangerously vague status. Vital air power problems are involved. The wider the band of airspace from the shore, the greater protection may exist for the adjacent State, but, at the same time, the less will be its freedom of flight inbound from the high seas toward foreign shores. The higher the upper boundary of the airspace, the greater will be the ability of the subjacent State to determine what high altitude flight may be permitted above its territorial waters. At the same time the high altitude flight of its own space ships, or missiles, will be similarly limited above foreign territorial waters. These questions require early and urgent policy consideration. The international law is certainly not now fixed, except to the extent that wide and logical support exists for the traditional three mile width of territorial waters.

If it is hereafter determined that there is a finite upper boundary to the national airspace of the subjacent State, that boundary will apply equally above the territorial waters of such State. If the "outerspace" beyond national airspace is determined to be an area of free flight, not controlled by the State below, the rule will apply equally above the territorial waters as well as the lands of the State. If an international agency should be vested with outer space control, its functions will be applicable in outer space over territorial waters. In other words, any final decision as to the legal status of space above the lands of a State will determine the status of space over territorial waters, including the rights of defense and self-preservation of the subjacent State in outer space.

PART FOUR
The Legal Status of
Flight Vehicles

12
A Study on the Legal
Status of Aircraft

Author's Note. When the Air Law Committee of the
International Law Association was reconstructed in 1948
with the late Major K. M. Beaumont as Chairman, the
author was asked to act as rapporteur on the subject "International Juridical Status of Aircraft." This study was submitted in 1949 for the use of the Committee. Due to its
length, it could not be included in the Committee's report,
but a summary of some of the points raised appear on pages
227–230 of the I.L.A. *Report of the Forty-Fourth Conference, Copenhagen 1950.*

INTERNATIONAL AIR law is concerned with two major problems:
first, the legal status of those areas of space above the earth's surface
usable as a medium for the flight of self-propelled and man-controlled
or man-operated instrumentalities, including aircraft; and, second, the
legal status of such flight instrumentalities themselves.

The first problem (the legal status of usable space) involves a determination of the relation of the several States to such usable space—here
called flight-space—particularly the right of each State to use or control flight-space over its land and water territories and over the high
seas or other areas not subject to the territorial sovereignty of any
State. The second problem (the legal status of flight instrumentalities)
involves the determination (*a*) in public law, of the relationship
between the State and such flight instrumentalities, and (*b*) in private
law, the relationship between such flight instrumentalities themselves
and those persons who furnish supplies or services for their operation
or maintenance or suffer damage or other wrong by reason of such
operation.

This study assumes that the problem of the legal status of flight-
space has been settled insofar as those areas ordinarily called "airspace"
are concerned, areas in which "aircraft" normally operate. In the
language of Article 1 of the Chicago Convention of 1944, each State
has "complete and exclusive sovereignty over the airspace above its
territory," such territory including both land areas and territorial
waters adjacent thereto. This study also assumes that no State has
sovereignty in any part of space over the high seas or over other areas
on the surface of the earth not part of the territory of any State.

The present discussion does not deal with or make any assumptions
as to the legal status of those areas of space above the "airspace," even
though such areas are today usable for such flight instrumentalities
as guided missiles. Nor does this study deal with the legal status of any
type of flight instrumentality except "aircraft" capable of being used

for the carriage of men or cargo. In particular it does not deal with such flight instrumentalities as guided missiles or rockets, even though they be self-propelled and continuously man-operated. Nor does it seek to state the legal status of such flight instrumentalities as space ships or satellites now considered scientifically possible of operation in areas beyond and above the "airspace."

Aircraft are instrumentalities of transport. Transport, in its broadest sense, is the movement of men or cargo from a determined point of departure to or toward a desired destination. It involves: first, motion; second, a medium on or through which such motion takes place; and, third, instrumentalities or means used through such medium to effectuate the transport. The four principal instrumentalities of transport, in the order of their historic development, are (1) vessels, (2) railway trains, (3) automotive vehicles such as buses, trucks and automobiles, and (4) aircraft. The first three use areas on the earth's surface as mediums of transport. With the discovery of the art of human flight, space above the earth took its place as an entirely new transport medium. New legal problems immediately arose. To understand the resulting difficulties in the determination of the legal status of aircraft, an historic analysis of the development of the legal status of the older forms of transport instrumentalities is useful and perhaps necessary.

I. VESSELS

Centuries of international custom have invested vessels with a status of legal quasi-personality. In public law a vessel may be said to have the quality of *nationality*, indicating a relationship to a given State somewhat similar to the relationship of an individual to the State to which he owes allegiance. In private law, a vessel may be said to have the quality of *responsibility*, indicating that the vessel itself, irrespective of the responsibility of the owner or operator, is accountable as an individual would be for services and supplies furnished it, as well as for damages and injuries resulting from its use in maritime transport. These two attributes of a vessel are quite distinct, although they have at times been unnecessarily confused.

A. NATIONALITY OF VESSELS

Nationality has been stated to be "the status of a natural person who is attached to a state by the tie of allegiance."[1] A vessel is an inanimate object, a movable thing, but it is "a thing of a very particular kind and

---

[1] Harvard Research in International Law—Nationality, in: *American Journal of International Law*, Vol. 23, 1929, Supplement, pp. 13, 22.

which from several points of view may be compared to a person."[2] Like persons, vessels are said to possess a nationality. "Such a statement" says Hyde, "implies the existence of a relationship between a vessel and a State of such distinctive closeness and intimacy that the latter may fairly regard the vessel as belonging to itself rather than to any other country."[3]

The possession by a vessel of nationality is "the basis for the intervention and protection by a State" and "it is also a protection for other States for the redress of wrongs committed by those on board against their nationals."[4] On the concept that vessels belong each to a determined State, they are submitted to its control, are exposed to its sanctions in case of disobedience, and have at the same time a guarantor (from the international point of view) of the manner in which they will use the seas, and a protector against the abuse which they might be compelled to suffer on the part of vessels of other States. This quality of guarantor and protector given to the State whose flag the vessel carries has in modern times led to the valid conclusion that the nationality of a vessel "is the primary condition for the peaceful utilization of the high seas."[5] In the absence of sovereignty over the high seas chaos might result if the fact of the nationality of vessels had not been accepted into maritime law. But with this concept international order may be maintained. As Westlake said, "Action on the open sea by a ship belonging to one State or covered by its sovereignty, on or against a ship belonging to another state or covered by its sovereignty, is of the nature of intervention and is normally unlawful."[6]

The identification of a vessel with a particular people, country, or State (the ultimate basis of "nationality") appears actually to be far older than the general acceptance of the doctrine of the freedom of the high seas. It is involved in the earliest historic development of the rights and privileges of belligerency and neutrality in naval warfare and in the rights of one people to navigate or trade in the open waters or harbors claimed or controlled by another. In the first treaty between Rome and Carthage, concluded about 509–508 B.C., "neither the Romans nor their allies" were to sail in the eastern Mediterranean

---

[2] Gilbert Charles Gidel, *Le Droit international public de la mer*, Chateauroux, Les éstablissements Mellottée, 1932–34, Vol. 1 (1932), p. 72.

[3] Charles Cheney Hyde, *International Law . . .*, 2d rev. ed., Boston, Little Brown, 1945, Vol. 1, Sec. 243A, p. 809.

[4] Alexander Pearce Higgins and C. John Colombos, *The International Law of the Sea*, London/New York/Toronto, Longmans Green, 1943, p. 189.

[5] Gidel, *op. cit.*, Vol. 1, pp. 73–74.

[6] John Westlake, *International Law—Part I, Peace*, Cambridge, Cambridge Univ. Press, 1910, p. 168.

beyond a fixed point "unless driven by stress of weather or the fear of enemies," and if any Roman be driven ashore, he was not to "buy or take aught for himself save what is needful for the repair of his ship."[7] In wars between the Greek City-States it was customary upon a declaration of war for an embargo to be laid on "enemy vessels" in the harbors of the other belligerent, and enemy merchant vessels and their cargoes were liable to capture and confiscation.[8]

Both Grotius[9] and Bynkershoek[10] cite the case described by Livy of the seven Carthaginian ships of war which refrained from attacking three Roman ships in the neutral port of the Numidian king, then at peace with both Carthage and Rome. As Bynkershoek said, "he who commits hostilities on the territory of a neutral makes war upon the sovereign who governs there." An attack by the Carthaginian ships on the Roman ships would have been an attack by Carthage itself on the Numidian king in whose territory the ships then were.

The earliest records of maritime law and custom in the Middle Ages show the continued identification of vessels with particular peoples. The whole history of the development of the law of prize, of neutral goods on enemy vessels and of enemy goods on neutral vessels, illustrates the recognition in the Middle Ages of the national status of the vessel seized.[11] In *The Blacke Booke of the Admiralty* (usually assigned to the early fifteenth century) vessels of the fleet are authorized to visit and search "any forreigne vessells upon the sea or in the enemies ports." Twiss, the learned editor, in a note to this passage states that "the right of confiscating enemy's goods on board *neutral vessels* seems to have been recognized both by Christian and Mohammedan powers, in the early part of the twelfth century."[12] [Italics supplied.]

The earliest commercial treaties show that the national status of a

---

[7] Coleman Phillipson, *The International Law and Custom of Ancient Greece and Rome*, London, Macmillan, 1911, Vol. 2, pp. 74–75.

[8] *Ibid.*, pp. 380–381.

[9] Hugo Grotius, *De jure belli ac pacis libri tres*, translation of 1646 edition by Francis W. Kelsey, Oxford, Clarendon Press, London, H. Milford, 1925 (*Classics of International Law* No. 3—publications of the Carnegie Endowment for International Peace, Division of International Law, Washington, D.C.), Bk III, Chap. 4, Sec. 8, para. 2 (pp. 647–648 of translation).

[10] Cornelius van Bynkershoek, *Quaestionum juris publici libri duo*, translation of 1737 edition by Tenney Frank, Oxford, Clarendon Press, London, H. Milford, 1930, (*Classics of International Law* No. 14—publications of the Carnegie Endowment for International Peace, Division of International Law, Washington, D.C.), Bk I, Chap. 8, (p. 54 of translation).

[11] Westlake, *op. cit.*, *Part II, War*, pp. 123–125.

[12] *The Black Book of the Admiralty with an Appendix*, edited by Sir Travers Twiss, London, Longman etc., 1871–76, Vol. 1, p. 29.

particular vessel was often determinative of its right to enter a foreign harbor. In the 1353 treaty between King Edward III of England and the maritime communities of Lisbon and Oporto, for example, it was agreed that the vessels of both parties should be free to enter into any port of either country.[13] To the same effect was the 1407 treaty between the English king and the Duke of Burgundy,[14] while in the 1417 treaty between the same powers it was provided that vessels belonging to either party, taken by corsairs, and carried into the ports of the other party, should be restored to their owners or the value be made good to them, that provisions might be imported in neutral vessels into either country.[15] In a 1490 treaty between England and Denmark the passage of "English vessels" into the Baltic Sea was authorized.[16] In the celebrated 1496 treaty between England and the Netherlands (long called the *intercursus magnus*) reciprocal rights of trade and navigation were provided for the ships of either party.[17]

The nationality of a vessel is that of the flag rightfully carried by her. The State concerned accepts the authority and responsibility resulting from the vessel's nationality.[18] But once a merchant vessel is registered and documented, an owner who has permitted such vessel to take a flag of a country not his own may not thereafter challenge the vessel's nationality. The primary rule is that "the ship is bound by the character impressed upon her by the authority of the government from which all her documents issue."[19]

Public vessels are not ordinarily registered. Merchant vessels, according to the laws of most States, must however be registered. Each State determines for itself the political conditions as to ownership, where the vessel was built, or otherwise, which will authorize registration. With the basis to be applied by any State as a condition of nationality and subsequent registration, international law is not concerned. Historically the practice of registering merchant vessels developed

---

[13] David Macpherson, *Annals of Commerce, Manufactures, Fisheries, and Navigation* . . ., London, Nichols, 1805, Vol. 1, p. 551; Boris Nolde, "Droit et technique des traités de commerce," Hague, Académie de droit international, *Recueil des cours*, Vol. 3, 1924–II, p. 301; Thomas Rymer, *Foedera*, Vol. 5, p. 763.

[14] Macpherson, *op. cit.*, Vol. 1, p. 617; Rymer, *op. cit.*, Vol. 8, pp. 469–477, 530–548.

[15] Macpherson, *op. cit.*, Vol. 1, p. 631; Rymer, *op. cit.*, Vol. 9, pp. 476, 483.

[16] Macpherson, *op. cit.*, Vol. 1, p. 713; Rymer, *op. cit.*, Vol. 12, pp. 374, 381.

[17] Thomas Wemyss Fulton, *The Sovereignty of the Sea*, Edinburgh/London, Wm. Blackwood, 1911, p. 386; Macpherson, *op. cit.*, Vol. 2, p. 8; Rymer, *op. cit.*, Vol. 12, p. 578.

[18] Westlake, *op. cit.*, *Part I, Peace*, p. 169.

[19] *The William Bagaley*, (1866), 5 Wallace (72 U.S.) 377, p. 410; *The Industrie*, 33 Eng. Law & Eq. 572.

after the concept of nationality of vessels had been recognized in maritime law, registration being first required in English law in 1660 and in French law in 1681.[20] In the Act of 1646, designed to exclude Dutch vessels from participating in the trade with the English colonies, such trade was limited to "English bottoms" but no provision was made for registration.[21] In the more stringent Navigation Act of 1660 (12 Car. II c. 18) an even greater part of the trade with England was required to be carried in English-built vessels, but still no provision was made requiring such vessels to be "registered." However, in Section IX of that Act it was provided that a foreign-built vessel might "enjoy the privileges of one belonging to England" if the owners proved that no foreigners owned any share therein, "of all which a certificate shall be produced and a register kept."[22] This seems to be the beginning of the practice of registering merchant vessels. It was not until later that registration statutes were extended to English-built vessels.

The fact that vessels have the nationality of the State of the flag has led to complicated problems affecting the jurisdiction of such State and other States over such vessels, over those on board, and over crimes or other occurrences there. These problems are concerned, among other things, with the legal distinction between public and private vessels, also with the difference existing between the competence of the flag State and other States dependent on whether the vessel is in its home waters, on the high seas, or in foreign waters. Any adequate statement of these questions is quite beyond the scope of this study, except to the extent that any necessary analogies to be drawn between the situation of vessels and of aircraft will be covered hereafter when discussing the nationality of aircraft.[23]

---

[20] Charles Abbott, *A Treatise on the Law Relative to Merchant Ships and Seamen*, 3d Amer. ed., Exeter, New Hampshire, G. Lamson, 1822, p. 35.

[21] Macpherson, *op. cit.*, Vol. 2, p. 430.

[22] *Ibid.*, pp. 485–486.

[23] For some of the basic problems, see: Harvard Research in International Law—Jurisdiction with Respect to Crime, in: *American Journal of International Law*, Vol. 29, 1935, Supplement, pp. 508–519; Higgins and Colombos, *op. cit.*, Chaps. 7 & 8, pp. 164–222; Lassa F. L. Oppenheim, *International Law: A Treatise*, 7th ed., London/New York/Toronto, Longmans Green, 1948, Vol. 1, Secs. 260–264, pp. 545–549, Secs. 450–451, pp. 764–767; *The S.S. Lotus* (France v. Turkey), Permanent Court of International Justice, Judgment 9, Sept. 7, 1927, Ser. A, No. 10—also in: Manley O. Hudson, *World Court Reports*, Washington, Carnegie Endowment for International Peace, 1934–43, Vol. 2, 1927–1932, pp. 20–92; Philip C. Jessup, *The Law of Territorial Waters and Maritime Jurisdiction*, New York, Jennings, 1927, p. 191.

B. RESPONSIBILITY OF VESSELS

A natural person is responsible for goods sold to him and services performed for his benefit with his authority. He is also responsible to compensate for damages negligently or wrongfully caused an injured person.

In customary maritime law a vessel has been considered to have such legal quasi-personality as to make it similarly responsible under circumstances well known to the maritime law. The responsibility of the vessel is enforceable in the admiralty courts by proceedings in rem against the vessel itself. Salient features of the "maritime lien" thus enforced are that such lien is not dependent upon the possession by the lienor of the vessel; that the lien is not cut off by a sale even to a bona-fide purchaser except by proceedings in an admiralty court; and that the vessel may be responsible in rem even if the owner is not responsible in personam.

The responsibility of the vessel for certain supplies and services is as old as the Roman law. As said by Abbott almost a century and a half ago: "Every man, who had repaired, or fitted out a ship, or lent money to be employed in those services, had by the law of Rome, and still possesses in those nations which have adopted the Civil Law as the basis of their jurisprudence, a privilege or right of payment in preference to other creditors, upon the value of the ship itself, without any instrument of hypothecation, or any express contract, or agreement, subjecting the ship to such a claim."[24]

Maritime liens are generally now recognized on a contractual or

---

[24] Abbott, *op. cit.*, pp. 151–153. See also the following quotations from the *Corpus juris civilis* (Krueger-Mommsen edition, Berlin, Weidmannos, 1915–1928):

Digest XLII.5.26: PAULUS *libro sexto decimo brevis edicti* Qui in navem exstruendam vel instruendam credidit vel etiam emendam, privilegium habet.

Digest XLII.5.34: MARCIANUS *libro quinto regularum* Quod quis navis fabricandae vel emendae vel armandae vel instruendae causa vel quoquo modo crediderit vel ob navem venditam petat, habet privilegium post fiscum.

Digest XX.4.5: ULPIANUS *libro tertio disputationum* Interdum posterior potior est priori, ut puta si in rem istam conservandam impensum est quod sequens credidit: veluti si navis fuit obligata et ad armandam eam vel reficiendam ego credidero.

Digest XX.4.6: IDEM *libro septuagesimo tertio ad edictum* huius enim pecunia salvam fecit totius pignoris causam. quod poterit quis admittere et si in cibaria nautarum fuerit creditum, sine quibus navis salva pervenire non poterat. 1. Item si quis in merces sibi obligatas crediderit, vel ut salvae fiant vel ut naulum exsolvatur, potentior erit, licet posterior sit: nam et ipsum naulum potentius est. 2. Tantundem dicetur, et si merces horreorum vel areae vel vecturae iumentorum debetur: nam et hic potentior erit.

quasi-contractual basis for such services as master's and seamen's wages, towage, wharfage, necessary repairs and supplies furnished to the vessel on its credit outside its home port, claims arising from a bottomry bond, claims arising from salvage, and perhaps certain others.

Even more striking is the responsibility of the vessel for the tort damages which it causes. As was said by Justice Story in a leading case: "It is not an uncommon course in the admiralty, acting under the law of nations, to treat the vessel in which or by which, or by the master or crew thereof, a wrong or offence has been done as the offender, without any regard whatsoever to the personal misconduct or the responsibility of the owner thereof. . . . The ship is . . . by the general maritime law held responsible for the torts and misconduct of the master and crew thereof, whether arising from negligence or a wilful disregard of duty; as for example, in cases of collision and other wrongs done upon the high seas or elsewhere within the admiralty and maritime jurisdiction, upon the general policy of that law, which looks to the instrument itself, used as the means of the mischief, as the best and surest pledge for the compensation and indemnity to the injured party."[25]

In the case just cited Justice Story quoted a statement of Chief Justice Marshall to the following effect: "This is not a proceeding against the owner; it is a proceeding against the vessel for an offence committed by the vessel; which is not the less an offence, and does not the less subject her to forfeiture because it was committed without the authority and against the will of the owner. It is true that inanimate matter can commit no offence. But this body is animated and put in action by the crew, who are guided by the master. The vessel acts and speaks by the master. She reports herself by the master. It is therefore not unreasonable that the vessel should be affected by this report."[26] Another outstanding jurist, commenting on these statements of Story and Marshall, said that ". . . those great judges, although of course aware that a ship is no more alive than a mill-wheel, thought that not only the law did in fact deal with it as if it were alive, but that it was reasonable that the law should do so."[27] This is ancient doctrine in the admiralty. Responsibility of the vessel itself for damages caused when entering a harbor and colliding with another vessel at anchor was stated in *The Blacke Booke of the Admiralty*,[28] in *The Customs of*

---

[25] *The United States* v. *The Cargo of the Brig Malek Adhel*, (1844), 2 Howard (43 U.S.) 210, pp. 233–234.

[26] *Ibid.*, p. 234.

[27] Oliver Wendell Holmes, Jr., *The Common Law*, Boston, Little Brown, 1946, p. 29.

[28] *Black Book of the Admiralty*, *op. cit.*, Vol. 1, p. 109.

Oleron and of the Judgments of the Sea,[29] in the *Rolle of Olayron,*[30] and in *The Customs of the Sea.*[31]

It is still the law in the admiralty. As stated in a leading case: "According to the admiralty law, the collision impresses upon the wrongdoing vessel a maritime lien. This the vessel carries with it into whosesoever hands it may come."[32]

The responsibility of the vessel for both contractual or tort claims is subject to a well-known exception. Ordinarily public vessels are considered immune. As Justice Holmes said: "The personality of a public vessel is merged in that of the sovereign."[33] Unless the sovereign consents to be sued, war vessels and other public vessels in the service of a State appear to be immune from the direct responsibility which other vessels in like circumstances would incur.

From the foregoing it is apparent that vessels have both nationality in public international law and responsibility in private law within the admiralty jurisdiction. As instrumentalities of international transport they are under the protection of the State whose flag they carry and that State is the guarantor to other States of their international conduct. For the supplies, services, and wrong-doings recognized as the bases of maritime liens they are responsible as if they were legal persons.

II. RAILWAY TRAINS AND AUTOMOTIVE VEHICLES

Neither railway trains nor automotive vehicles have the nationality in public international law nor the responsibility in private law so characteristic of the legal status of seagoing vessels.

A. NATIONALITY OF RAILWAY TRAINS AND AUTOMOTIVE VEHICLES

There has never been any suggestion in international law that railway trains should have "national character."

In the case of automotive vehicles it is true that a convention was entered into in 1909 to cover the international circulation of motor vehicles.[34] This convention provided that for a motor car to be al-

---

[29] *Ibid.*, Vol. 2, p. 229.   [30] *Ibid.*, Vol. 2, p. 449.
[31] *Ibid.*, Vol. 3, p. 283.
[32] *The China*, (1868), 7 Wallace (74 U.S.) 53, p. 68. See also: *The Bold Buccleugh*, 7 Moore, P.C.C. 267.
[33] *The Western Maid* (1922), 257 U.S. 419, p. 433.
[34] Convention with Respect to the International Circulation of Motor Vehicles, Paris, October 11, 1909, in: U.S. Dept. of State, *Treaty Information Bulletin*, No. 13, October 31, 1930, pp. 25–36; *Br. and For. State Papers*, Vol. 102, p. 64.

lowed to be driven on a highway in a foreign country it must have been recognized as suitable for use on the highway after an examination by competent authority. It is also true that Article 4 of that convention provided that "No motor-car shall be allowed to pass from one country into another unless it carries, fixed in a visible position on the back of the car, in addition to the number plate of its own nationality, a distinctive plate displaying letters indicating that nationality." But when this convention was modified by the amendatory convention of 1926[35] Article 4 was replaced by a new Article 5 which provided that "Every motor vehicle, to receive international authorization to travel on a road to which the public have access, must carry, in a visible position in the rear, a distinguishing mark consisting of from one to three letters written on a plate or on the vehicle itself." It was further provided that ". . . the distinguishing mark corresponds either to a State or to a territory which constitutes a distinct unit from the point of view of registration of motor vehicles." The reference to "nationality" was carefully omitted from the amendatory convention. Nor does it appear in the Pan American Convention for the Regulation of Automotive Traffic signed in Washington, October 6, 1930.[36] These conventions seem to provide nothing more than a means of identifying the motor vehicle as having been registered and licensed in a particular State, without investing the motor vehicle with the true international law characteristic of nationality.

The convention of 1926 provides in Article 4 for the issuance of an international certificate by the authority of one contracting State giving the right for the motor vehicle to travel freely in all other contracting States. This certificate seems to be nothing more than a certification that the automotive vehicle in question has been examined and found to fulfill the technical qualifications of the convention. It does not appear to carry with it that degree of responsibility of one contracting State for the conduct abroad of the registered vehicle which is characteristic of the nationality of vessels. Nor is there anything in the convention of 1909 as originally signed or as amended in 1926 or in the Pan American Convention of 1930 indicating that the contracting State which has issued the international certificate to a particular motor vehicle would consider itself responsible to protect that vehicle while in foreign territory as a legal entity, apart from its owner or operator, as the same State would protect its national vessels.

---

[35] International Convention Relative to Motor Traffic, Paris, April 24, 1926, in: *Treaty Information Bulletin, op. cit.*, pp. 36–55; Manley O. Hudson, *International Legislation*, Washington, Carnegie Endowment for International Peace, 1931, Vol. 3, pp. 1859–1872.

[36] *Treaty Information Bulletin, op. cit.*, pp. 20–24; Hudson, *International Legislation, op. cit.*, Vol. 5, pp. 786–792.

B. RESPONSIBILITY OF RAILWAY TRAINS AND AUTOMOTIVE VEHICLES

Similarly, neither railway trains nor automotive vehicles have been recognized as having individual international responsibility for services, supplies, and damages caused. It is true that before deodands were abolished by statute, inanimate objects in motion which caused damage could be forfeited, and that a case seems to exist in England where this doctrine was applied as late as 1842 in the case of a locomotive engine.[37] Nevertheless the true rule of responsibility applicable to vessels in maritime law has never been applied to railway trains or automotive vehicles. If by local law a lien exists for supplies or services, it is ordinarily lost by surrender of possession of the thing to which the lien attaches. Nor does separate responsibility of the thing exist beyond the responsibility of the owner. In short, nothing resembling the rule of responsibility of vessels has ever appeared in private international law as applicable to either railway trains or automotive vehicles as instrumentalities of international transport. Even though the railway train or the automotive vehicle may, under some systems of law, be classified as dangerous instrumentalities so that the owner is responsible for damages caused by them irrespective of negligence, nevertheless the responsibility is that of the owner or operator and not that of the thing itself, as distinguished from the rule of responsibility applicable to vessels.

III. AIRCRAFT

Aircraft, like vessels, and unlike railway trains and automotive vehicles, now have that quality of legal quasi-personality in public international law discussed above as *nationality*. But unlike vessels, and like railway trains and automotive vehicles, aircraft are not yet considered as having the quality of *responsibility* in private law. The legal status of aircraft thus places them in a class apart from other instrumentalities of transport and requires separate consideration. Analogies to the status of either vessels or railway trains and automotive vehicles may lead to inaccurate results.

A. NATIONALITY OF AIRCRAFT

Included in the term "aircraft," as here considered, are balloons, both free and dirigible, as well as airplanes, helicopters, and other forms of man- and cargo-carrying flight instrumentalities. As stated

---

[37] *Queen v. Eastern Counties R. Co.*, 10 M. & W. 58, cited in: John Chipman Gray, *The Nature and Sources of the Law*, New York, Macmillan, 1921, p. 47.

earlier, guided missiles and rockets are not to be included in the term.

The first balloon flights were in 1783, but it was not until the beginning of the twentieth century that international law began to assign the quality of nationality to flight instrumentalities. In the first important international flight—that of Blanchard and Jeffries in 1785 from Dover across the Channel to a point near Calais—the pilot, Blanchard, was French and the passenger, Jeffries, was an American-born physician who had served with the English forces and was then living in London. When the flight started, Blanchard carried a French flag and Jeffries an English flag. But there is nothing in the accounts of this flight to indicate that the balloon itself was considered as having national character.[38]

Balloons were later used as part of the armed forces in several countries; for example, by the French army beginning in the latter part of the eighteenth century, and by both armies in the Civil War in the United States (1861–65). But there is no intimation in the records that such balloons were considered as other than ordinary military equipment, or that they had a legal status differing from that of the wagons, guns or other movables used by the army. Balloons were normally inflated immediately prior to a flight and deflated afterwards. They had no continuing separate existence.

Although many balloons carried individual names when used in military or private flights and often carried flags, legal national character was lacking. This was true even of the earliest experimental dirigibles, such as that of Giffard (France) in 1852, Haenlein (Germany) in 1872, Tissandier (France) in 1883, Renard and Krebs (France) in 1884, Wölfert (Germany) in 1896, and Schwarz (Hungary) in 1897. None of these dirigibles were ever used internationally. The problem of their status when moving from the airspace over one country into that over another did not arise.

The international problems raised by the use of balloons as a means of communication from besieged Paris over the German lines in the Franco-Prussian War of 1870–71 do not seem to have included that of the legal status of the balloons themselves. Bismarck had threatened to punish those persons who crossed above the German lines. After the war, when the great German publicist, Bluntschli, stated his views of the legal background for Bismarck's position and, for that purpose, added a new section (632a) to his *Codification of International Law*, he held that the occupying army had a right to control airspace up to the range of cannon, but that if the aviator passed above such range he would escape the sovereign power of the foreign State and the laws of

---

[38] John Jeffries, *A Narrative of the Two Aerial Voyages of Doctor Jeffries with Mons. Blanchard . . .*, London, J. Robson, 1783, [New York, 1941].

the occupying army.[39] Bluntschli was concerned with the unauthorized entry into German de jure occupied airspace by those on board the balloon, and not with the entry of the balloon itself as a separate legal entity.

At the first International Aeronautical Congress, held in Paris in 1889, the question of the status and licensing of aviators was discussed, but not the status of the balloons used.[40] So with the second Congress held at Paris in 1900.[41]

In what has been termed the first international air navigation agreement—that entered into in 1898 between Germany and Austria-Hungary—authority was given for military aviation officers to cross the frontiers in military balloons while in training. This agreement provided directly for the entry of the officers themselves into foreign airspace and landing in foreign territory. But the balloons involved appear to have been considered merely as incidental vehicles.[42]

The Hague Declaration of 1899 prohibited for a term of five years the launching of projectiles and explosives from balloons. This assumed the control by each of the belligerent powers of the conduct of personnel on board the balloons to be used, but the resulting analogy between the status of the balloons themselves and naval vessels does not appear to have been stressed or specifically set out.[43]

The first definite statement that aircraft should have nationality like that of vessels seems to have been made by Fauchille in 1901[44] as part of his statement of a legal system applicable to the status of usable space. Fauchille's views have often been misunderstood. While he denied that any State had technical rights of sovereignty or property in airspace above its surface territories, he conceded to the State broad powers to control flight in such airspace based on what he termed the State's "right of self-preservation" ("droit de conservation"). These

---

[39] Johann Kaspar Bluntschli, *Das moderne Völkerrecht der civilisirten staten als Rechtsbuch dargestellt*, Nördlingen, C. H. Beck, 1878, pp. 355–356—translated into French by C. Lardy, *Le Droit international codifié*, 5th ed., Paris, Guillaumin, 1895, pp. 356–357.

[40] Congrès international d'aéronautique de 1889. Séance générale de cloture (avec les colombophiles), du 3 août 1889, in: *L'Aéronaute*, 23 année, No. 3, 1890.

[41] Congrès international d'aéronautique, 2d, Paris, 1900, *Procès-verbaux sommaires*, Paris, Imprimerie, Wellhoff & Roche, 1906.

[42] Text of this agreement is given in Erwin Riesch, "Das erste Luftfahrtabkommen der Welt," *Archiv für Luftrecht*, Vol. 10, 1940, p. 41.

[43] James Brown Scott, ed., *The Hague Conventions and Declarations of 1899 and 1907* New York, Oxford Univ. Press, London/Toronto et al., H. Milford, 1915, (Carnegie Endowment for International Peace, Division of International Law, Washington, D.C.).

[44] Paul Fauchille, *Le Domaine aérien et le régime juridique des aérostats*, Paris, A. Pedone, 1901. Also in: *Revue générale de droit international public*, Vol. 8, 1901, pp. 414–485. Text at p. 471.

ideas were clarified in his report to the *Institut de droit international* in 1902.[45] His proposals then included, among others, the following: Aircraft are of two categories—public and private;[46] aircraft may carry only the flag of the State to which they belong—private aircraft belong to the State where they have been inscribed on an official register kept for that purpose, such registration being based on the nationality of the owner, the commander, and three-quarters of the crew;[47] the air is free—States having only rights necessary for their self-preservation, such rights relating to the prevention of spying, to the customs, to the sanitary police, and to the necessities of defense;[48] subject to certain exceptions, air navigation is prohibited in a "security" zone extending 1500 meters up from the surface territory of a State;[49] only public aircraft of a State are permitted to fly freely in the security zone of that State;[50] the subjacent State may also regulate landing and departure through the security zone above its territory;[51] nationality of infants born on board aircraft is to be determined by the laws of the State to which the aircraft belonged;[52] belligerent States are prohibited from engaging in hostilities above territories of neutrals at whatever height;[53] neutral States are prohibited from engaging in flight above the territories of belligerents;[54] public belligerent aircraft entering neutral territory should remain until the end of hostilities.[55]

Fauchille's system logically required that all aircraft must have nationality. No question should exist as to the State responsible for the conduct of any given aircraft. Whether or not any valid distinction exists between "airspace sovereignty" and the broad rights to control flight flowing from Fauchille's "droit de conservation," necessity exists in either case that aircraft may be internationally identified to determine which may enter airspace above any given State, also to provide a national protector and guarantor in international law for the conduct of each such aircraft, both over national territory and over the high seas.

Fauchille's proposals to the Institute in 1902 were never acted upon. But the concept of applying the doctrine of nationality to aircraft as it had long been applied to vessels soon began to receive wide acceptance. Mérignhac in 1903, holding that the extent of "territorial atmosphere" above each State should be fixed by international convention, pointed out that if this were done the State could deny access as it judged necessary "to foreign aircraft and even to national private aircraft."[56]

---

[45] *Annuaire de l'Institut de droit international*, Vol. 19, 1902, pp. 19–86.
[46] *Ibid.*, p. 25.   [47] *Ibid.*, p. 27.   [48] *Ibid.*, p. 32.   [49] *Ibid.*, p. 34.
[50] *Ibid.*, p. 45.   [51] *Ibid.*, p. 45.   [52] *Ibid.*, p. 56.   [53] *Ibid.*, p. 58.
[54] *Ibid.*, p. 64.   [55] *Ibid.*, p. 75.
[56] Alexandre G. J. A. Mérignhac, *Les Lois et coutumes de la guerre sur terre* . . ., Paris, A. Chevalier-Marescq, 1903, p. 196.

Hilty, in 1905, discussed the control of the entry of foreign State balloons into the airspace over another State.[57] Von Grote, in 1907, likening territorial airspace to territorial waters, held that the State should allow aircraft of all nations to fly through its airspace, that in time of war hostilities should be forbidden over a neutral State, that airships should have nationality like vessels and be regarded as portions of their home territory, public aircraft being entitled to rights of "extraterritoriality."[58] Meyer, in 1908, held that each airship must have nationality, that the State can reserve for its own nationals the establishment of regular airlines between two places within its own territory, that State airships are entitled to extraterritoriality, and that private airships should be regarded as flying portions of the home State even when flying in the airspace above foreign territory in which they are to some extent subject to the jurisdiction of a foreign State.[59]

Meili, impressed with the flight of the Zeppelin dirigible in July 1908 over part of his native Switzerland, and writing of the airship in internal law and international law, held that the airworthiness of an airship must be established by its State, under a procedure granting the airship the right to carry the national flag and entering the airship on a register, provided such airship belonged to nationals of the State granting the license.[60] Daus, also writing of the July 1908 Zeppelin flight, held that airships flying above the open sea should be regarded as portions of the territory of the home State, that private airships flying in the territorial zone of a foreign State were subject to its jurisdiction but that public airships everywhere were subject to the jurisdiction of their own States.[61] Grünwald (1908) was of the opinion that State airships, like State vessels, were to be regarded as portions of their respective States, but that to treat private airships like private vessels would be possible only when special provisions were laid down determining their nationality.[62] In a paper read at the 1908 meeting of the American Political Science Association (perhaps the first publica-

---

[57] Karl Hilty, "Die völkerrechtlichen Gebräuche in der atmosphärischen Zone," *Archiv für öffentliches Recht*, Vol. 19, 1905, pp. 87–94.

[58] Friedrich von Grote, *Beiträge zum Recht der Luftschiffahrt*, Borna-Leipzig, R. Noske, 1907, pp. 22–23.

[59] Alex Meyer, *Die Erschliessung des Luftraumes in Ihren rechtlichen Folgen*, Frankfurt a. M., Gebrüder Knauer, 1908, pp. 26–33.

[60] Friedrich Meili, *Das Luftschiff im internen Recht und Völkerrecht*, Zurich, O. Füssli, 1908, pp. 10–52.

[61] Edgar Daus, *Die Luftschiffahrt in staats- und völkerrechtlicher Hinsicht*, Erlangen, E. J. Jacob, 1908, p. 16.

[62] Friedrich Grünwald, *Das Luftschiff in völkerrechtlicher und strafrechtlicher Beziehung*, Hannover, Helwing, 1908, pp. 37–45. See also his: "Standesamliche Beurkundung von Todesfällen und Geburten auf Luftschiffen," *Archiv für öffentliches Recht*, Vol. 24, 1909, pp. 478–483.

tion in English on international air law) Kuhn suggested a system of governmental inspection for aircraft "like that now prevailing over ships of the sea," together with registration of all aircraft in a particular locality and "a nationality symbolized in the carrying of the flag."[63]

Zitelmann in 1909 held that airships flying above the open sea should be treated as portions of their respective States when provision was made for them legally to have nationality and carry the national flag.[64] In the same year Meurer stated, as had Meili, that the airworthiness of airships must be officially established, that each airship should have a name and number and be entered upon a public register, that a certificate of registration should be issued and thereafter the airship should carry the flag of its State.[65]

Although no formal international action had yet been taken, official and semi-official documents indicate that by the end of the year 1909 governments had informally recognized that balloons and other aircraft had something resembling national status. On March 12, 1909 Clemenceau, as Minister of the Interior of France, issued a circular on the subject of foreign balloons ("ballons étrangers") landing in France.[66] This circular stated that the frequency of the landing of foreign balloons in France had led the government to concern itself with that question. He directed that such balloons be held for the payment of import duty and the officials should notify him by telegraph of each landing. At the International Aeronautical Congress held the same year in Nancy,[67] in which certain governments were officially represented, one of the speakers noted that customs duties on foreign balloons had been introduced in France in 1909 to prevent spying over French territory.[68] Another speaker recommended that aircraft be given a civil status and be registered.[69] The Congress closed by stating, among other things, that registration of aircraft would perhaps be the only manner of assuring liberal regulation of air navigation.[70]

During the year 1909 the French Government had also decided to invoke a formal diplomatic conference of European powers to settle pressing questions involving air navigation. A preliminary program

---

[63] Arthur K. Kuhn, "Aerial Navigation in its Relation to International Law," *Proceedings of American Political Science Association*, 5th annual meeting, 1908, p. 85.

[64] Ernst Zitelmann, "Luftschiffahrtrecht," *Zeitschrift für internationales privat- und öffentliches Recht*, Vol. 19, 1909, pp. 458–496.

[65] Christian Meurer, *Luftschiffahrtsrecht*, Munich/Berlin, J. Schweitzer, 1909, pp. 21–27.

[66] *Revue juridique internationale de la locomotion aérienne*, Vol. 1, 1910, p. 24.

[67] Congrès international d'aéronautique, 4th, Nancy, 1909, *Procès-verbaux, rapports & mémoires . . .*, Paris, H. Dunod & E. Pinat, 1909.

[68] *Ibid.*, p. 428.   [69] *Ibid.*, p. 436.   [70] *Ibid.*, p. 470.

was submitted to the invited powers. The first and second questions on this program were whether public and private aircraft should be distinguished and whether aircraft should have nationality.[71] Replies were received from twelve of the twenty-two invited powers. The answers to both questions were generally in the affirmative. The conference itself, although originally scheduled to be held in 1909, was postponed until May of 1910.

Before this conference finally met, other non-official meetings had recognized the need for aircraft nationality. The *Comité juridique international de l'aviation*, organized at the end of 1909, announced in January 1910 its first plan for "Le Code de l'air."[72] In this plan Chapter 2(b) was to cover home ports and nationality of aircraft. Later in the year the German[73] and French[74] subcommittees recommended that aircraft have nationality and be registered.

At the meeting of the *Institut de droit international* held in Paris in March 1910, Fauchille submitted a new report covering the legal régime of aircraft in time of peace, to be considered in lieu of his 1902 report which had never been acted on. With the new report he presented a draft international convention.[75] This convention included the following provisions: Art. 1—aircraft are public and private—public aircraft are military or civil; Art. 2—every aircraft ought to have a nationality, the nationality of public aircraft being that of the State to whose service they are attached, and that of private aircraft being determined by the nationality of its owner; Art. 3—every aircraft ought to be entered on a list kept by the public authority of the State to which it belongs or of the country where the owner resides; Art. 4—aircraft ought to carry names and other insignia of identification; Art. 5—to be permitted to fly, every private aircraft should have a flight permit indicating its nationality and other details. Other provisions held that the circulation of aircraft would be free but that the subjacent States could protect those rights needed for their self-preservation, such as their own security and that of the persons and goods of their inhabitants; that to safeguard their right of self-preservation, States might close to navigation certain parts of the atmosphere (the text of the 1910 report suggesting a zone of 500 meters in height in place of the 1500 meters security zone of the 1902 report); that military and police aircraft could not cross the frontier of their own

---

[71] Conférence internationale de navigation aérienne, Paris, 1910, *Exposé des vues des puissances d'après les memorandums adressés au gouvernement français*, Paris, Imprimerie nationale, 1909, p. 9.

[72] *Revue juridique internationale de la locomotion aérienne*, Vol. 1, 1910, p. 45.

[73] *Ibid.*, p. 171.   [74] *Ibid.*, p. 174.

[75] *Annuaire de l'Institut de droit international*, Vol. 23, 1910, p. 305.

country except with the authority of the State above which they wished to fly or in which they proposed to land; that acts occurring on board public and private aircraft fell under the competence of the tribunals of the State to which the aircraft belonged, and would be judged according to the laws of that State; that acts affecting the right of self-preservation of the subjacent State or causing damage in its territory, should be judged by the tribunals of and in accordance with the laws of the territorial State; that public aircraft in a foreign country ought to have the privilege of extraterritoriality. All of these provisions assumed the national status of the aircraft concerned.

At the same session of the Institute von Bar proposed a somewhat simpler regulation for the registration and nationality of aircraft.[76] He provided among other things that aircraft should be considered as part of the territory of the State on the register of which they were entered so long as they were in the air. The Institute determined to submit these proposals to the diplomatic conference already arranged for by the French Government.[77]

On May 31, 1910 an international congress of legal experts was held at Verona to consider questions concerning the regulation of air navigation. One of the topics on the agenda was that of the ownership of aircraft.[78] After discussing the question of nationality, the Congress adopted formal "views" that an aircraft ought to have a nationality (of which it would carry evidence), that the basis for the determination of nationality ought to be identical for all States, that it ought to be that of the nationality of the owner, that nationality should follow the entry of the aircraft on an official register.[79]

The first formal diplomatic conference on air navigation (originally scheduled for 1909, as discussed above) met in Paris on May 18, 1910 and adjourned on June 29, 1910. Its importance in the development of international air law has been consistently underestimated. Emphasis has been given to the failure of the conference to agree on the final terms of an international convention. Too little has been said of what the conference accomplished. In the matter of determining

---

[76] *Ibid.*, p. 317.

[77] *Revue juridique internationale de la locomotion aérienne*, Vol. 1, 1910, p. 106.

[78] Antonio Brunetti, "Lineamenti d'una legislazione sulla proprietà dei veicoli aerei," Congresso giuridico internazionale per il regolamento dalla locomozione aerea, 31 maggio—1–2 giugno, 1910, *Atti e relazioni*, Verona, Società tipografica cooperativa, 1910, pp. 48–55.

[79] Congresso giuridico internationale . . ., *Atti e relazioni, op. cit.*, p. 142; *Revue juridique internationale de la locomotion aérienne*, Vol. 1, 1910, pp. 181, 185.

whether aircraft should be classified as public and private and whether all aircraft should have nationality, the discussions and decisions at the 1910 conference were determinative of many subsequent developments. The views there expressed soon appeared in national legislation, in international agreements, and in the actual conduct of States under the pressure of war conditions between 1914 and 1918. The tentative decisions at Paris in 1910 also reappeared in the international legislation included in the Convention Relating to the Regulation of Aerial Navigation signed at Paris in 1919, which served as the basis for much of the public international air law of today.

The scope of this study will not permit a detailed examination of the discussions at Paris in 1910. The results of these discussions appear in the proposed international convention (complete except for Articles 19 and 20 regarding the freedom or control of the circulation of aircraft) as agreed upon when the conference adjourned.[80] Chapter I, which may be briefly examined, was entitled "Nationality and Registration of Aircraft." Article 2 of this chapter provided that only those aircraft which possessed the "nationality" of a contracting State were governed by the convention, and that none of the contracting States should permit a free balloon or airship to fly over its territory unless it complied with the above conditions, although special authorization might be granted. Article 3 stated that nationality of aircraft should be based, by the legislation of each contracting State, on the nationality or domicile of the owner in the State's territory. Article 4 required that when the aircraft possessed the nationality of one contracting State, no other State could confer nationality upon it. Other articles provided that aircraft be entered on the register of the State conferring nationality, such entry containing a description and identification mark of the aircraft; also that each aircraft should bear its nationality mark and registration number and should carry a certificate of navigability issued by the national State.

In a later chapter public aircraft were defined (Article 40) as "the aircraft employed in the service of a contracting State, and placed under the orders of a duly commissioned official of that State." The provisions applicable to determination of nationality and registration were not to apply to such public aircraft. The distinctive national mark to be borne by military aircraft (Article 42) would be "the Sovereign

---

[80] Conférence internationale de navigation aérienne, Paris, 1910, *Procès-verbaux des séances et annexes*, Paris, Imprimerie nationale, 1910, pp. 188–205. Fro French text of the proposed convention, see also: Albert Roper, *La Convention internationale du 13 octobre 1919 . . .*, Paris, Sirey, 1930, pp. 212–225. For an English translation, see: *Reports of the Civil Aerial Transport Committee . . .*, Presented to Parliament by Command of His Majesty, London, H.M. Stationery Office, 1918 [Cd. 9218], pp. 25–35.

emblem of their State;" the departure or landing of military aircraft of a contracting State in the territory of another State would be allowed (Article 44) only with the latter's authorization, and each contracting State might forbid or regulate the passage of military aircraft of other contracting States over its territory. But military aircraft (Article 46), when legitimately within or above the territory of a foreign State, should "enjoy the privilege of extraterritoriality," as also the members of the crew wearing uniform while forming a distinct unit or carrying out their duties.

The principle of nationality of aircraft as thus accepted by the 1910 conference was carefully explained in the proceedings. In the report filed on behalf of the First Commission of the conference by Fauchille (serving as reporter and one of the French delegates), it was pointed out that the delegations of Switzerland and of the Netherlands had considered that aircraft should be treated in a manner similar to automobiles and needed only identification,[81] but that the other States had adopted the view that an aircraft was more like a vessel than an automobile—that it constituted a kind of legal entity—that it should have its own nationality. The majority of the States present felt that aircraft should be thus under the control of a particular State, responsible for it to other States, and that the aircraft itself should be entitled to the protection of such State. It was recognized that this responsibility and right of protection constituted, between that State and the aircraft, a relationship analogous to that existing between a vessel and the State whose flag it carries, called (as stated in the report) "the nationality of the vessel." It was made clear, however, that the State of the flag of the aircraft would not thereby be responsible in private law for damages caused by force majeure or resulting from fault or negligence of the aviators, nor would the national character of aircraft prejudge the solution of questions of conflict of laws and jurisdiction which air navigation might raise in civil and penal matters.[82]

---

[81] *Procès-verbaux des séances et annexes*, p. 73.

[82] *Ibid.*, p. 74. The language contained in Fauchille's report was originally offered by Dr. Kriege, Chief of the German Delegation and Legal Adviser of the German Foreign Office. [p. 299] It is still one of the most accurate definitions of the status of nationality. As stated by Dr. Kriege and accepted by the conference, it is as follows:

En proposant qu'un aéronef, pour tomber sous le régime de la Convention, doit avoir une nationalité, le Comité s'est laissé guider par les considérations suivantes:

1. La nature même de la navigation aérienne exclut pour les Etats la possibilité de vérifier, au moment où un aéronef pénètre dans l'espace au-dessus de son territoire, que cet aéronef réponde aux conditions indispensables dans l'intérêt de la sécurité générale. Il semble donc que, pour être admis à la circulation internationale, l'aéronef doit être placé sous le

As further indication that the use of the term "nationality" in connection with aircraft followed the analogy of the nationality of seagoing vessels in public international law, it is necessary to note the proposed status of military aircraft when over or in foreign surface territory. As stated above, Article 46 of the proposed convention gave "the privilege of extraterritoriality" to such military aircraft and crew when legitimately in foreign territory. It also provided that the foreign State was not precluded from applying to the military aircraft of another contracting State and to their crews "the measures required either to assure the safety of the State, or the observance of sanitary regulations, or to protect lives and property from imminent danger." The term "extraterritoriality" was explained in the proceedings as resulting in the exemption of the aircraft and its crew on duty from civil and penal tribunals of the foreign State and of restraining action of these authorities in police and customs matters, but that the authorities of such foreign State would have the right to reserve measures needed by their security and other interests stated above.[83] This "privilege of extraterritoriality" was admittedly drawn from the international law practice as to war vessels.[84] The position taken at Paris in 1910 is quite consistent with the resolutions of the Institute in 1898 and in 1928 regarding the rights and duties of war vessels in foreign ports.[85]

Nothing that has occurred since 1910 detracts from the soundness

contrôle d'un Etat qui sera responsable envers les autres États de l'exercice consciencieux de ce contrôle. Il va sans dire que la responsabilité de l'État ne s'étend pas aux dommages causés par la force majeure ou résultant de la faute ou de la négligence des aéronautes seuls.

2. La contrepartie des obligations imposées à l'aéronef dans la circulation internationale est les droits qu'on lui reconnaîtra. Pour faire valoir ces droits, l'aéronef peut avoir besoin de la protection d'un État qui, dans les limites tracées par le droit des gens, ait qualité pour intervenir dans son intérêt auprès d'un autre Gouvernement. Ce rôle reviendra, tout naturellement, à celui des Etats qui sera chargé du contrôle de l'aéronef.

3. La responsabilité et le droit de protection, réunis dans les mains d'un seul et même Etat, constituent entre cet Etat et l'aéronef un lien analogue à celui qui existe entre le navire et l'Etat dont il porte le pavillon, et qu'on appelle la nationalité du navire. On pourra, sans inconvénient, se servir du même terme en parlant de la situation de l'aéronef vis-à-vis de l'Etat qui le contrôle et qui en est responsable.

4. La portée de la disposition qui reconnaît à l'aéronef un caractère national se borne à ces deux points: responsabilité et protection. On n'entend pas y rattacher d'autres conséquences. Notamment, la disposition ne préjuge en rien la solution des conflits de lois et de juridictions auxquels la navigation aérienne pourrait donner lieu en matière civile et pénale.

[83] *Ibid.*, p. 113.   [84] *Ibid.*, p. 289.

[85] *Annuaire de l'Institut de droit international*, Vol. 17, 1898, p. 275; Vol. 34, 1928, p. 739.

of the explanation of nationality of aircraft as then accepted. In public international law the nationality of vessels and the nationality of aircraft indicate the responsibility of the flag State to other States for the conduct of the vessel or aircraft in question and the right of such vessel or aircraft to international protection by such State. As pointed out hereafter, nationality of vessels and of aircraft have not always, particularly in time of war, resulted in exactly similar international treatment of such vessels and aircraft, but this does not mean that the legal concept of nationality is materially different in the two cases.

Following the 1910 conference the application of the concept of such nationality to aircraft was rapidly accepted both in doctrine and in practice. At the meeting of the Institute in April 1911 at Madrid Fauchille submitted additional reports on the legal regime of aircraft, with a draft convention comprising sixty-three articles.[86] Due to the complexity of these proposals, certain principal bases of discussion were stated, including the distinction between public and private aircraft and the question of nationality and registration.[87] By a vote at the close of the session it was decided that aircraft should be classified as public and private; that each aircraft should have nationality and one only; that this nationality should be that of the country where the aircraft was registered; that the aircraft ought to carry special marks of identification; that the State in which registration is asked should determine to what persons and under what conditions it would accord the right of registration, but that a State registering an aircraft of which the owner is a foreigner could not always seek to protect that aircraft in the territory of the State of the owner contrary to the application of laws by which that State would have prevented its nationals from having their aircraft registered abroad.[88]

At the first legal congress organized by the *Comité juridique international de l'aviation,* held in Paris on May 31, 1911, among the principles adopted were that every aircraft should have a nationality and one only; that the nationality of the aircraft was that of its owner; that it should carry a distinctive mark of its nationality; that every owner, before putting the aircraft in flight outside of a private airport, should obtain public authority, namely, the entry of the aircraft on the register kept by competent authorities; that the registration lists should be published.[89]

In 1911 the first British Aerial Navigation Act (1 & 2 Geo. 5) was adopted, granting to a Secretary of State wide powers to prohibit by

---

[86] *Ibid.,* Vol. 24, 1911, pp. 105–122.

[87] *Ibid.,* p. 123.   [88] *Ibid.,* p. 346.

[89] *Revue juridique internationale de la locomotion aérienne,* **Vol. 2,** 1911, pp. 201–202.

order the navigation of aircraft over such areas as might be prescribed in the order. While it did not specifically differentiate between national and foreign aircraft, and simply stated that any such order might "apply generally to all aircraft or to such aircraft of classes and descriptions as may be specified in the order," the power to classify and differentiate between national and foreign aircraft was certainly implicit in the act.

French action later in 1911 was much more pointed. By a decree signed by the President of France on November 21, 1911,[90] it was provided that no aircraft could be put in service in France without a navigation permit, unless it satisfied the conditions foreseen by international conventions. As no international convention had been entered into, this meant that no aircraft could be flown in France unless a French permit were issued. The decree set out the particulars to be furnished when a permit was requested, including the name, domicile, and nationality of the owner. It also provided for registration, the issuance of certificates of navigability, and the navigation permit; also that no aircraft could fly without carrying insignia on the aircraft itself, including the letter "F" if the aircraft belonged to a French national, or to a foreigner domiciled in France, or to a company with its principal place of business in France. This procedure for a nationality mark was an adaptation of Annex A of the draft convention of 1910.[91] The decree further provided that public aircraft should be those attached to the service of the State and under command of a State official, and that military aircraft are those public aircraft under the orders of a commanding officer in uniform and carrying a certificate establishing their military character. The provisions as to permits of navigability and registration were not to apply to public aircraft. By specific provision of the decree (Article 32) flight in France of foreign military aircraft was prohibited.

This decree was a clear adaptation into national practice of the principles accepted at the 1910 Paris conference differentiating between public and private aircraft, and providing for registration of the latter and separate flight regulations and nationality provisions applicable to the two classes. It also recognized the difference between national and foreign aircraft, thus putting into effect as to aircraft the basic principle of the nationality of seagoing vessels.

The concept of nationality was further clarified in practice in 1913. Great Britain, on February 14, 1913, passed the "Aerial Navigation Act, 1913" (2 & 3 Geo. 5, c. 22) amending the Act of 1911 and specifically providing for the issuance of orders prescribing "the areas within which aircraft coming from any place outside the United Kingdom

---

[90] *Ibid.*, pp. 304–312.
[91] Conférence internationale de navigation aérienne, *op. cit.*, p. 199.

are to land and the other conditions to be complied with by such aircraft . . ." Pursuant to this Act, the Home Secretary on March 1, 1913 issued Order No. 228 setting out prohibited areas, portions of the coastline "prohibited to aircraft from abroad," conditions imposed on aircraft from abroad including a requirement that such aircraft before commencing a voyage to the United Kingdom must obtain a clearance from a duly authorized British consular officer in the country from which the voyage is to be commenced, exempting British aircraft returning to the United Kingdom, under certain conditions, from obtaining such consular clearance, prohibiting "foreign naval or military aircraft" from passing over or landing in the United Kingdom "except on the express invitation or with the express permission previously obtained of His Majesty's Government," and exempting British naval and military aircraft from the order. The principle of nationality was clearly recognized in this 1913 British procedure, both for public and private aircraft.

In the same year an international arrangement was made between France and Germany by an Exchange of Notes dated July 16, 1913, under which French aircraft might fly into and over Germany and German aircraft might fly into and over France subject to very strict conditions. Military aircraft of one nation were authorized to enter the airspace over the other only upon invitation. Civil aircraft could enter only on compliance with certain detailed conditions. A French aircraft was required to obtain a departure certificate from a German diplomatic or consular representative in France before starting a flight to Germany, and reciprocally German aircraft were required to obtain a similar certificate from French representatives in Germany before departing for France.[92] If such clearance was obtained, the two nations would reciprocally recognize navigation permits and pilot licenses issued by the other.

On December 13, 1913 a new presidential decree was issued in France replacing the 1911 decree regulating air navigation.[93] The new decree continued in effect and amplified most of the old provisions. In the ministerial order of December 19, 1913, implementing this decree, attention was directed to the fact that no aircraft could fly in France without a permit except in accordance with international conventions, and calling attention to the arrangement between Germany and

---

[92] For text of this agreement, see: Roper, *op. cit.*, pp. 246–251; *Revue juridique internationale de la locomotion aérienne*, Vol. 4, 1913, pp. 240–242; See also: John C. Cooper, *The Right to Fly*, New York, Henry Holt, 1947, pp. 20–22.

[93] *Revue juridique internationale de la locomotion aérienne*, Vol. 5, 1914, pp. 9–20.

France concluded earlier in the year.[94] Again the principle of nationality was fully accepted and recognized.

At the third congress of the *Comité juridique international de l'aviation* held in Frankfurt in September 1913, the earlier decisions and text of the proposed "Code de l'air" as to nationality of aircraft were affirmed.[95]

With the outbreak of World War I the actions of both neutral and belligerent powers recognized that aircraft had acquired national character and should be dealt with as legal entities. For example, the Netherlands, by decree of August 3, 1914, prohibited airships not belonging to the Netherlands' forces from crossing its land frontiers.[96] Sweden, in the law of September 7, 1914, authorized the king by order to prohibit air traffic over Swedish territory except to aircraft of the Swedish State or engaged in its service;[97] and by proclamation of the same date the king prohibited such air traffic,[98] and on July 14, 1916 amended the prohibitory order to apply to "airplanes other than those belonging to Sweden."[99] Switzerland, by ordinance of the Federal Council of August 4, 1914, provided that balloons and aircraft not belonging to the Swiss army could not rise and navigate in airspace over Swiss territory except with special permission, and that passage of all balloons and aircraft coming from abroad was forbidden.[100] The United States, by the proclamation of November 13, 1914, relating to the neutrality of the Panama Canal Zone, forbade by Rule 15 "aircraft of a belligerent power, public or private" from descending or rising within the jurisdiction of the United States at the Canal Zone or to pass through the airspace above the lands and waters within such jurisdiction.[101]

Aircraft, during World War I, were thus treated as having national character and neutral States recognized their duty to treat belligerent

---

[94] *Ibid.*, pp. 20–23.

[95] *Ibid.*, Vol. 4, 1913, pp. 328–329; Roper, *op. cit.*, pp. 252–253.

[96] *Staatsblad*, 1914, No. 354. Also in: Francis Deák and Philip C. Jessup, eds., *A Collection of Neutrality Laws, Regulations and Treaties of Various Countries*, Washington, Carnegie Endowment for International Peace, 1939, Vol. 2, p. 807.

[97] *Svensk Författningssamling*, 1914, No. 182, p. 633. Also in: *British & Foreign State Papers*, Vol. 110, p. 560; Deák and Jessup, *op. cit.*, p. 964.

[98] *Svensk Författningssamling*, 1914, No. 183, p. 634. Also in: Deák and Jessup, *op. cit.*, p. 975.

[99] *Svensk Författningssamling*, 1916, No. 278, p. 708. Also in: Deák and Jessup, *op. cit.*, p. 975.

[100] *Recueil officiel* (N.S.), Vol. 30, p. 353. Also in: *British & Foreign State Papers*, Vol. 108, p. 842; Deák and Jessup, *op. cit.*, p. 1008.

[101] *Statutes at Large*, Vol. 38, p. 2039. Also in: Deák and Jessup, *op. cit.*, p. 1205.

military aircraft as legal entities requiring special treatment apart from the crew.[102] But the privilege of asylum and temporary sojourn for repairs, usually accorded to war vessels in international law, was not accorded to belligerent aircraft.[103] In Fauchille's proposed international convention, submitted to the Institute in 1911, provisions had been inserted permitting belligerent military aircraft to leave any neutral territory within twenty-four hours after entry, and that in general The Hague Convention of October 18, 1907, applicable to rights of neutrals in naval warfare, should be applied to air warfare.[104] In practice the principle of twenty-four hour asylum was not accepted. When, on August 29, 1914, the German Government protested to the Dutch Government against the seizure of a German naval airplane in a Dutch port, the Dutch Government replied that aircraft could not be treated as warships due to their liberty of action and the facility with which they could carry out reconnaissance and escape from all control, and that aircraft must therefore require special treatment.[105] The nationality of aircraft was thus recognized, but certain privileges in time of war accorded to war vessels were denied. It may be said here that this rule of international air law, pursuant to which belligerent aircraft are treated as being sui generis and, upon entering neutral territory, must be interned by the neutral State together with the crew, has by custom of World War I and World War II become a recognized and generally accepted principle.[106]

While World War I was being fought in Europe, the concept of nationality of aircraft began to receive general recognition in the western hemisphere. For example, at the unofficial Pan American Aeronautic Conference held at Santiago, Chile, in March 1916 recommendations were adopted which included rules that all aircraft should have nationality—public aircraft to be that of the State to which they belonged, and private to be that of the owner—and that all aircraft should carry a distinctive national emblem.[107] Also in the project for the regulation of maritime neutrality adopted by the American Institute of International Law in 1917 the nationality of

---

[102] Harvard Research in International Law—Rights and Duties of Neutral States in Naval and Aerial War, in: *American Journal of International Law*, Vol. 33, 1939, Supplement, pp. 766–767.

[103] James Molony Spaight, *Aircraft in Peace and the Law*, London, Macmillan, 1919, p. 9.

[104] *Annuaire de l'Institut de droit international*, Vol. 24, 1911, p. 117.

[105] Spaight, *op. cit.*, p. 203.

[106] James Molony Spaight, *Air Power and War Rights*, 3d ed., London/New York/Toronto, Longmans Green, 1947, pp. 42–428.

[107] Henry Woodhouse, *Textbook of Aerial Laws . . .*, New York, Stokes, 1920, p. 12; Brower V. York, "International Air Law in the American Republics," *Journal of Air Law and Commerce*, Vol. 3, 1932, p. 415.

aircraft was tacitly recognized by the provisions of Article 20 stating that airplanes, dirigibles, or aircraft of belligerent countries were not permitted to fly over the territory or the jurisdictional sea of neutral powers.[108]

The principle of nationality, accepted by State legislation and decrees, by the international agreement between France and Germany, in doctrinal discussions prior to World War I, and confirmed by the conduct of States during the war itself was formally incorporated into the body of international air law by the adoption of the Paris Convention of 1919.

When the Aeronautical Commission of the Peace Conference was established in March of 1919 and directed to prepare a convention on international air navigation in time of peace, two draft conventions had already been prepared—one by Great Britain and the other by France. The Commission also had available the work of the 1910 Paris conference. At one of its first sessions the Commission adopted certain principles to govern its work, including the following: "4. The recognition that every aircraft must possess the nationality of one contracting State only, and that every aircraft must be entered upon the register of a contracting State, the nationality of which it possesses."[109] The British draft convention contained a chapter on "Nationality and Registration" providing that the convention should apply only to aircraft possessing the nationality of a contracting State and that the nationality should be determined by the nationality of the owner, as well as provisions for registration.[110] The French draft convention also provided that only those aircraft would be permitted to fly over territories of contracting States which belonged entirely to owners of one of the contracting States and satisfied certain conditions including registration.[111]

When the Legal Subcommission reported to the Aeronautical Commission, it discussed the question of nationality.[112] Having first

---

[108] Institut Américain de droit international, *Acte final de la session de la Havane*, 22–27 *janvier* 1917, *Résolutions et projets*, New York *et al.*, Oxford Univ. Press, 1917, p. 92.

[109] Conférence de la paix, 1919–1920, *Recueil des actes de la conférence*, Partie VII, Préparation et signature des traités et conventions divers, A— Conventions générales entre alliés, (1) Commission de l'aéronautique, Paris, Imprimerie nationale, 1933, pp. 14, 143; *La Paix de Versailles: aéronautique*, Paris, Les Editions internationales, 1934, pp. 20, 129.

[110] Conférence de la paix, *op. cit.*, p. 446; *La Paix de Versailles*, *op. cit.*, p. 219 (3); Roper, *op. cit.*, p. 257.

[111] Conférence de la paix, *op. cit.*, p. 445; *La Paix de Versailles*, *op. cit.*, p. 219 (18); Roper, *op. cit.*, p. 274.

[112] Conférence de la paix, *op. cit.*, p. 429; *La Paix de Versailles*, *op. cit.*, p. 499.

decided that the proposed convention should be based on the principle that each State has sovereignty in the airspace over its territory and having then discussed the question of innocent passage for aircraft of contracting States in the airspace over other contracting States, the Subcommission said, in substance, that access into airspace being open to aircraft of contracting States, the first question logically presenting itself was that of "nationality." Reasons were then stated as to why the Subcommission recommended that aircraft could be registered only in the State of which its owner was a national. The general effect of nationality does not seem to have been fully discussed, at least so far as available records of the actual proceedings indicate. But the text reported to the Commission, and adopted by the Commission, and ultimately incorporated into the final convention of 1919, leaves no doubt that nationality was considered as having the characteristics in international law contemplated in the 1910 conference. The analogy to the nationality of seagoing vessels and the similarity of the language of the 1919 convention and the 1910 draft convention leave little doubt of the correctness of this assumption.

The articles of the convention of 1919, as actually signed, which are directly applicable to the question of nationality are as follows:

Article 5. No contracting State shall, except by a special and temporary authorisation, permit the flight above its territory of an aircraft which does not possess the nationality of a contracting State.[113]

---

[113] Article 5 was amended by Protocol of October 27, 1922 to read as follows:

No contracting State shall, except by a special and temporary authorisation, permit the flight above its territory of an aircraft which does not possess the nationality of a contracting State, unless it has concluded a special convention with the State in which the aircraft is registered. The stipulations of such special convention must not infringe the rights of the contracting parties to the present Convention and must conform to the rules laid down by the said Convention and its annexes. Such special convention shall be communicated to the International Commission for Air Navigation, which will bring it to the knowledge of the other contracting States.

Article 5 was further amended by Protocol of June 15, 1929 and inserted as the last article of Chapter I:

Each contracting State is entitled to conclude special conventions with non-contracting States.

The stipulations of such special conventions shall not infringe the rights of the contracting Parties to the present Convention.

Such special conventions in so far as may be consistent with their objects shall not be contradictory to the general principles of the present Convention.

They shall be communicated to the International Commission for Air Navigation which will notify them to the other contracting States.

Article 6. Aircraft possess the nationality of the State on the register of which they are entered, in accordance with the provisions of Section I (c) of Annex A.

Article 7. No aircraft shall be entered on the register of one of the contracting States unless it belongs wholly to nationals of such State.

No incorporated company can be registered as the owner of an aircraft unless it possess the nationality of the State in which the aircraft is registered, unless the President or chairman of the company and at least two-thirds of the directors possess such nationality, and unless the company fulfils all other conditions which may be prescribed by the laws of the said State.[114]

Article 8. An aircraft cannot be validly registered in more than one State.

Article 9. The contracting States shall exchange every month among themselves and transmit to the International Commission for Air Navigation referred to in Article 34 copies of registrations and of cancellations of registrations which shall have been entered on their official registers during the preceding month.

Article 10. All aircraft engaged in international navigation shall bear their nationality and registration marks as well as the name and residence of the owner in accordance with Annex A.

Article 30. The following shall be deemed to be State aircraft:

a) Military aircraft.
b) Aircraft exclusively employed in State service, such as posts, customs, police.
c) Every other aircraft shall be deemed to be a private aircraft.

All state aircraft other than military, customs and police aircraft shall be treated as private aircraft and as such shall be subject to all the provisions of the present Convention.

Article 31. Every aircraft commanded by a person in military service detailed for the purpose shall be deemed to be a military aircraft.

Article 32. No military aircraft of a contracting State shall fly over the territory of another contracting State nor land thereon without special authorisation. In case of such authorisation the military aircraft shall enjoy, in principle, in the absence of special

---

[114] Article 7 was amended by Protocol of June 15, 1929 to read as follows:
The registration of aircraft referred to in the last preceding Article shall be made in accordance with the laws and special provisions of each contracting State.

stipulation the privileges which are customarily accorded to foreign ships of war.

A military aircraft which is forced to land or which is requested or summoned to land shall by reason thereof acquire no right to the privileges referred to in the above paragraph.

Article 33. Special arrangements between the States concerned will determine in what cases police and customs aircraft may be authorised to cross the frontier. They shall in no case be entitled to the privileges referred to in Article 32.

In addition, the important Article 15, providing that "every aircraft of a contracting State has the right to cross the air space of another State without landing" shows without question that the convention is based on the theory that States consider aircraft as legal entities representing the State of the flag. Also, Article 25 shows the assumption by States of the responsibility for the conduct of aircraft having its nationality. According to that article of the 1919 convention "each contracting State undertakes to adopt measures to ensure that every aircraft flying above the limits of its territory and that every aircraft *wherever it may be, carrying its nationality mark,* shall comply with the regulations contained in Annex D," being the annex applicable to conduct of air traffic. [Italics supplied].

The Paris Convention was discussed at the meeting of the International Law Association at Portsmouth in 1920 before the convention had been ratified. Professor Hazeltine, certainly one of the greatest experts on international air law then living, pointed out the analogy in the convention between the nationality and registration of aircraft and existing international law as to the nationality and registration of seagoing vessels.[115] Another outstanding expert, Dr. Lycklama à Nijeholt, also analyzed the nationality provisions of the convention.[116] The entire discussion at Portsmouth indicates that those present accepted the view that the convention would give to aircraft national character similar to that of seagoing vessels under existing international law.

The principle of nationality was so clear throughout the entire convention that it prevented its immediate acceptance by those European powers which had been neutral in World War I. Under Article 5 it was apparent that such ex-neutrals would not be able to have air navigation relations with Germany and become a contracting State at the same time. It was this recognition of the basic force of the principle

---

[115] International Law Association, *Report of the 29th Conference*, Portsmouth, 1920, London, Sweet & Maxwell, 1920, p. 396.
[116] *Ibid.*, p. 417.

of nationality which brought about the subsequent amendments of Article 5 as shown in Note 113 above.[117]

The principle that each aircraft shall have nationality and be registered was also incorporated into the Ibero-American Convention Relating to Air Navigation[118] signed at Madrid in 1926 and in the Pan American Convention on Commercial Aviation[119] signed at Havana in 1928. However, Article 8 of the Pan American Convention abandoned the requirement that contracting States must be governed by the nationality of the owner of the aircraft when authorizing registration and adopted the generally understood international rule as to vessels by which each State determines for itself the basis on which it will allow its flag to be carried. Accordingly the Pan American Convention provided that "the registration of aircraft . . . shall be made in accordance with the laws and the special provisions of each contracting State."

This principle was also accepted when amendments to the Paris Convention were discussed at the Extraordinary Session of the ICAN in 1929 and is the basis for the amendment to Article 7 of the Paris Convention shown above in Note 114. With this amendment the general body of international air law was brought into even closer analogy with international maritime law and the principle became generally accepted that each State was the sole judge of the basis on which aircraft might be registered and thereby assume the nationality of the State in question.

Several important doctrinal discussions between World War I and World War II further clarified the principle of nationality. The "Proposed Rules for the Regulation of Aerial Warfare" drafted by the Commission of Jurists at The Hague in 1923, although never adopted as an actual international convention, have always had great weight as a sound statement of the rules of international air law applicable in time of war.[120] These rules provided for a distinction between public and private aircraft, and also between military aircraft and others employed in public service. They further provided that aircraft should carry external marks to show nationality and that "no aircraft

---

[117] See note of February 14, 1929 by Roper as Secretary-General of the ICAN on "the origin of the Air Convention of 13 October 1919" in: International Commission for Air Navigation, *Minutes*, 16th Session (Extraordinary Session), June 1929, Annex A, pp. 1–4.

[118] *Ibid.*, Annex C; Hudson, *International Legislation, op. cit.*, Vol. 3, pp. 2019–2032.

[119] Hudson, *International Legislation   op. cit.*, Vol. 4, pp. 2354–2369.

[120] For text of The Hague air rules of 1923, see: Kenneth W. Colegrove, *International Control of Aviation*, Boston, World Peace Foundation, 1930, Appendix VI, pp. 211–223; Spaight, *Air Power and War Rights, op. cit.*, pp. 498–508.

may possess more than one nationality." The rules themselves have a striking resemblance to certain of the accepted practices of naval warfare, except that Rule 40 stated that "belligerent military aircraft are forbidden to enter the jurisdiction of a neutral State," and Rule 42 stated that "a neutral government shall use the means at its disposal to intern any belligerent military aircraft which is within its jurisdiction after having alighted for any reason whatsoever, together with its crew and the passengers, if any." Similarly, in the exhaustive study on "Rights and Duties of Neutral States in Naval and Aerial War" made by the Harvard Research in International Law,[121] and in the draft convention prepared as the result of its study, the nationality of aircraft was accepted as the basis for the proposed rules so far as "aerial war" was concerned. In an earlier study made by the Harvard Research in International Law, dealing with "Jurisdiction with Respect to Crime," the conclusion reached was that "a State has jurisdiction with respect to any crime committed in whole or in part upon a public or private ship or aircraft which has its national character."[122] As to the status of aircraft, the comment on this provision says that "ships and aircraft are not territory"—that "it is recognized, nevertheless, that a State has with respect to such ships or aircraft a jurisdiction which is similar to its jurisdiction over its territory."[123] The commentary further notes that "it is of course true that most aircraft are much less self-contained than seagoing vessels at the present time"—that "it seems, however, that in their legal relations to their own State and to foreign States they have many points of resemblance and that they may well be regarded, for present purposes, in substantially the same way."[124]

The Institute of International Law reviewed its position on international air navigation at its meeting at Lausanne in 1927, again holding that every aircraft should have one nationality and one only, and that this nationality should be that of the country where the aircraft is registered.[125] Again, in 1937, when considering the question of conflict of laws on board "private aircraft," the Institute accepted nationality of aircraft as an existing status, using such language as "the State of the nationality of the aircraft."[126]

Such was the general legal situation at the outbreak of World War II. In actual use the status of aircraft was radically changed between 1919 and 1929. International, and in fact intercontinental, air trans-

---

[121] *American Journal of International Law*, Vol. 33, 1939, Supplement, pp. 167–817.

[122] *Ibid.*, Vol. 29, 1935, Supplement, p. 508.

[123] *Ibid.*, p. 509.   [124] *Ibid.*, pp. 516–517.

[125] *Annuaire de l'Institut de droit international*, Vol. 33 (3), 1927, p. 338.

[126] *Ibid.*, Vol. 40, 1937, p. 276.

port had become a fact. Aircraft had become, even in time of peace, instruments of national policy. States had become accustomed to entering into complicated bilateral agreements to ensure the entry of the commercial aircraft bearing their nationality into the territory of other States and there to enjoy the benefits of commercial intercourse. With the outbreak of World War II aircraft became immediately primary international carriers. During the war years the normal method of crossing both the Atlantic and Pacific Oceans for most of those who traveled, except for mass troop movements, was by air. The nationality of aircraft was accepted into customary international law as fully as the nationality of merchant vessels had been in the past, and the rights and duties of nationality were recognized and universally accorded to aircraft when over the high seas, over the territories of their own State and of other States, and in airports anywhere in the world. The protective jurisdiction of the State of the flag and the responsibility of that State were fully recognized, This principle of international law existed whether the State of the flag of the aircraft was or was not a party to the Paris Convention or the Havana Convention (the Madrid Convention never having had actual international importance).

On September 11, 1944 the Government of the United States issued to members of the United Nations, to the nations associated with the United Nations in World War II, and to European and Asiatic neutral nations an invitation to participate in "an international civil aviation conference." This conference met in Chicago, Illinois, from November 1 to December 7, 1944. In analyzing the results of the conference, and in particular the emphasis given to the status of civil aircraft and the little that was said as to military aircraft, it must be recalled that the sole purpose of the conference, as originally convened, was to provide international regulation for civil aviation in the post-war period.

When the conference met, two draft conventions were presented—one having been prepared by Canada,[127] and one by the United States.[128] The Canadian draft convention, in Articles XVI through XIX as to nationality of aircraft, followed almost exactly the language of the Paris Convention. Similarly, Articles XXXVII through XL as to state aircraft, also followed the Paris Convention. Thus the Canadian draft followed the Paris distinction between military aircraft and other

---

[127] See: *Canadian Revised Preliminary Draft of an International Air Convention* [Chicago Conference Document 50], reprinted in: U.S. Dept. of State, *Proceedings of the International Civil Aviation Conference*, Chicago, Illinois, November 1–December 7, 1944 [Dept. of State Pub. No. 2820],Vol. 1, pp. 570–591.

[128] See: *United States Proposal of a Convention on Air Navigation* [Chicago Conference Document 16], reprinted: *ibid.*, Vol. 1, pp. 554–566.

aircraft exclusively employed in State service, such as posts, customs, and police, with the provision that military aircraft could fly over the territory of other States only when specially authorized, but that in case of such authorization military aircraft should enjoy in principle, in the absence of special stipulation, the privileges accorded to foreign ships of war.

The draft convention presented by the United States, on the other hand, stated in Article 4 that it would "be applicable only to civil aircraft." The term "civil aircraft" was defined in Article 1 as meaning "any aircraft other than military, naval, customs and police aircraft of any State or any political subdivision thereof." Article 19 of the United States draft provided: (a) that aircraft shall possess the nationality of the State on the register of which they are entered; (b) that no aircraft may be validly registered in more than one State; (c) that aircraft engaged in international navigation shall bear their own nationality and registration marks; and (d) that the registration of aircraft shall be in accordance with the laws and regulations of each contracting State.

The Canadian and United States drafts therefore differed principally in the extent to which they dealt with the status of military and other State aircraft. The Canadian draft presented the technical difficulty which had sometimes been noted in connection with the Paris Convention: namely, that the provisions as to registration of aircraft, as well as certain other provisions of the convention, possibly applied to all aircraft and not simply to "private aircraft."

The Chicago Convention, as finally signed and now in force, represents a compromise between the Canadian and United States draft provisions as to classification, nationality and registration of aircraft. Article 3 is as follows:

a) This Convention shall be applicable only to civil aircraft, and shall not be applicable to state aircraft.

b) Aircraft used in military, customs and police services shall be deemed to be state aircraft.

c) No state aircraft of a contracting State shall fly over the territory of another State or land thereon without authorization by special agreement or otherwise, and in accordance with the terms thereof.

d) The contracting States undertake, when issuing regulations for their state aircraft, that they will have due regard for the safety of navigation of civil aircraft.

While there may be some seeming ambiguity between the provisions of subparagraph (a) of Article 3 and the subparagraphs (c) and (d) of this article, it was certainly intended to mean that the convention as a whole, with the exception of subparagraphs (c) and (d), should be applicable only to "civil aircraft."[129] The terms "public" and "private" are not used in the convention in the classification of aircraft. The convention is therefore applicable to all aircraft, whether owned and operated by a State, unless such aircraft are actually "used in military, customs and police services" by a contracting State. Due to the fact that the convention is primarily concerned with international civil air transport, no provision is made in it (as it was in the Paris Convention) to define the privileges to be accorded in foreign territory to military aircraft as distinguished from other state aircraft. The effect of the omission of the Paris Convention provision, giving military aircraft the privileges customarily accorded in foreign territory to ships of war, will be discussed hereafter.

The articles applicable directly to "Nationality of Aircraft" constitute Chapter III of the Chicago Convention and are as follows:

Article 17. Aircraft have the nationality of the State in which they are registered.

Article 18. An aircraft cannot be validly registered in more than one State, but its registration may be changed from one State to another.

Article 19. The registration or transfer of registration of aircraft in any contracting State shall be made in accordance with its laws and regulations.

Article 20. Every aircraft engaged in international air navigation shall bear its appropriate nationality and registration marks.

Article 21. Each contracting State undertakes to supply to any other contracting State or to the International Civil Aviation Organization, on demand, information concerning the registration and ownership of any particular aircraft registered in that State. In addition, each contracting State shall furnish reports to the International Civil Aviation Organization, under such regulations as the latter may prescribe, giving such pertinent data as can be made available concerning the ownership and control of aircraft registered in that State and habitually engaged in international air navigation. The data thus obtained by the International Civil Aviation Organization shall be made available by it on request to the other contracting States.

It will be noted that the Chicago Convention adopts the principle that each State will decide for itself the basis on which it will permit

---

[129] The writer of this study was chairman of the drafting committee which reported out parts of the convention, including Article 3, and therefore has no hesitation in criticizing and taking some responsibility for the draft.

aircraft to be registered, but also commits itself to give such information as it has as to the ownership of any aircraft thus registered. Article 17, providing that aircraft have the nationality of the State in which they are registered, accepts the principle of Article 6 of the Paris Convention that "aircraft possess the nationality of the State of the register on which they are entered." This is a rule as between contracting States, but it certainly does not mean that "state aircraft" of all States and civil aircraft of non-contracting States are without nationality. By the time the Chicago Convention was drafted, customary international air law, as stated above, had so completely accepted the concept of nationality of aircraft that no question could possibly exist as to the fact of nationality of any aircraft lawfully carrying national insignia of a particular State. Registration does not create nationality. It is simply an evidence of nationality, and nothing in the Chicago Convention should be read to the contrary.

The Chicago Convention directly recognizes the State as the guarantor of the conduct of aircraft possessing its nationality, as well as the protector of such aircraft. For example, Article 12 provides that each contracting State "undertakes to adopt measures to ensure . . . that every aircraft carrying its nationality mark, wherever such aircraft may be, shall comply with the rules and regulations relating to the flight and maneuver of aircraft there in force." The same article contains an entirely new principle in international air law to the effect that over the high seas the rules in force shall be those established under the convention. Each State therefore guarantees that aircraft having its nationality will comply, while over the high seas, with the rules set up under the convention, and, when in national territory of another State, will comply with the rules there applicable.

The status of an aircraft as a legal entity is emphasized by such provisions as Article 11, providing that the laws and regulations of a contracting State relating to the admission to or departure from its territory of aircraft engaged in international air navigation, or to the operation or navigation of such aircraft while within its territory "shall be applied to the aircraft of all contracting States without distinction as to nationality and *shall be complied with by such aircraft* upon entering or departing from or while within the territory of that State." [Italics supplied] Under this article the State of the nationality of the aircraft will be entitled to protect its aircraft in case of discrimination, but will also be responsible to guarantee the conduct of its aircraft as to compliance with the local rules.

The most important and direct recognition of aircraft as being legal entities is found in Article 5 of the Chicago Convention. This article is a direct commitment of each contracting State to accord to "all aircraft of the other contracting States" certain transit and non-scheduled traffic privileges. If an aircraft has the nationality of a contracting State, it has the privileges contemplated under this article, and the State of its flag may proceed against any other State to enforce these privileges in international law for the benefit of its aircraft. Such aircraft are dealt with in the article directly as objects of international law. The resulting general position is quite analogous to that created since the fourteenth century by those international maritime law commercial treaties which accorded to merchant vessels of one contracting State the privilege of entering the ports and harbors of another contracting State.

It is submitted that the foregoing general historic analysis is conclusive of the correctness of the premise stated earlier in this study; namely, that aircraft, like seagoing vessels, and unlike railway trains and automotive vehicles, now have that quality of legal quasi-personality in public international law known as "nationality." The development of air law, both by custom and international legislation, has demonstrated the soundnesss of the statement made by Kriege and repeated and used in the report of the First Commission of the 1910 conference.[130] No one today can question Kriege's basic theses: (1) that an aircraft to engage in international flights should be placed under the control of a State which would be responsible to other States for the conscientious exercise of such control; (2) that setting off the obligations imposed on the aircraft in such international flight are the rights accorded to it, and that to enforce these rights the aircraft may need the protection of a State which, within the limits of international law, may intervene in its interest; (3) that this role belongs naturally to the State charged with the control of the aircraft; (4) that the responsibility and right of protection joined in the hands of one and the same State constitute between that State and the aircraft a tie analogous to that existing between a vessel and the State whose flag it carries and which is called "the nationality of the vessel;" (5) that it is possible without inconvenience to use the same term when speaking of the status of the aircraft in relation to the State which controls it and which is responsible for it.

The acceptance into international air law of the principle that every aircraft must have nationality and that this nationality is at least similar to that of vessels has created cognate problems some of which still require settlement. These problems are of two general classes: (a) the rights of State aircraft, and (b) the respective jurisdiction and competence of the State of the flag of the aircraft and of other States, in whose territory the aircraft may be, to deal with matters occurring on board the aircraft. These questions must be resolved before it

---

[130] See Note 82 *supra*.

can be said that the legal status of aircraft has been finally determined for all places and for all conditions arising in international flight.

The Chicago Convention, as stated earlier in this paper, divides aircraft into two classes: state aircraft and civil aircraft, abandoning the older use of the terms "public" and "private." According to Article 3(b) "Aircraft used in military, customs and police services shall be deemed to be state aircraft." All other aircraft are civil aircraft. In general, the treatment to be accorded to civil aircraft is covered by the convention, but nothing is said as to the treatment to be accorded state aircraft except the provision of Article 3(c) that no state aircraft of a contracting State "shall fly over the territory of another State or land thereon without authorization by special agreement or otherwise, and in accordance with the terms thereof."

These provisions as to state aircraft raise two questions. First, *is the definition of state aircraft adequate?* Second, *in the absence of special terms in the authorization contemplated by Article 3(c), are military, customs and police aircraft to be treated alike when in foreign territory?*

As to the first of these questions it must be said that the Chicago Convention is purposely less definite than some of its predecessors. The language used was understood to be vague but was considered a more practical solution than any of the several attempts which had been made in the past to define such classes as, for example, military aircraft. The determining factor under the Chicago definition is whether a particular aircraft is, at a particular time, actually used in one of the three special types of services. If so, it is a "state aircraft." Otherwise, it is a "civil aircraft." This solution leaves for settlement, under the facts of a particular case, such difficult problems as those arising when aircraft operated by the armed services carry non-military passengers and cargo. These questions the governments affected must settle from time to time.

The second question is more difficult. The Paris Convention, as appears from Articles 32 and 33 quoted earlier in this study, provided that in the absence of special stipulation military aircraft, when authorized to fly over the territory of another contracting State or to land therein, should enjoy "the privileges which are customarily accorded to foreign ships of war," but that these privileges should in no case be enjoyed by police and customs aircraft. In the report presented to the Aeronautical Commission at Paris in 1919 by the Legal Subcommission the status of state aircraft is discussed at some length.[131] The position taken at that time was that military aircraft personified in a higher degree than police and customs aircraft the

---

[131] Conférence de la paix, *op. cit.*, pp. 433–434; *La Paix de Versailles, op. cit.*, pp. 503–504.

public power of the State, and that military aircraft had the same character of a political organ removed from every intervention by another sovereign power as had a foreign warship in a national port.

The Chicago Convention does not make the distinction made at Paris between military aircraft on the one hand and police and customs aircraft on the other. It is in fact entirely silent on the subject. Strong arguments can be made that the distinction made in the Paris Convention between the different types of state aircraft is not sound and that all state aircraft ought to enjoy the same exemptions when in foreign territory.[132] But it is submitted here that no such principle has as yet been accepted into either conventional or customary international air law. It is felt that the rule stated in the Paris Convention—that aircraft engaged in military services should, in the absence of stipulation to the contrary, be given the privileges of foreign warships when in a national port—is sound and may be considered as still part of international air law even though not restated in the Chicago Convention. But if it is felt that police and customs aircraft should enjoy similar exemption in the absence of stipulation to the contrary in the authorization given them to proceed to a foreign country, such exemption must be covered by an amendment to the Chicago Convention or by other international legislation.

The second question still unsettled which flows from the acceptance of the principle of nationality of aircraft involves the respective competence and jurisdiction of the State of the flag of the aircraft and other States to deal with the matters occurring on board the aircraft. In the draft of the Paris Convention, as prepared by the Aeronautical Commission, this matter was proposed to be dealt with by the following article:

Article 23. All persons on board an aircraft shall conform to the laws and regulations of the State visited.

In case of flight made without landing from frontier to frontier, all persons on board shall conform to the laws and regulations of the country flown over, the purpose of which is to ensure that the passage is innocent.

Legal relations between persons on board an aircraft in flight are governed by the law of the nationality of the aircraft.

In case of crime or misdemeanour committed by one person against

---

[132] Alex Meyer, "Crimes et délits a bord des aéronefs," *Revue générale de l'air*, IX année (nouvelle série), 1946, p. 553. As to treatment of military aircraft, see also: Amedeo Giannini, "Gli aeromobili militari," *Revue aéronautique internationale*, Vol. 1, 1931, pp. 226–231 [Italian text with French translation].

another on board an aircraft in flight the jurisdiction of the State flown over applies only in case the crime or misdemeanour is committed against a national of such State and is followed by a landing during the same journey upon its territory.

The State flown over has jurisdiction:

1. With regard to every breach of its laws for the public safety and its military and fiscal laws;
2. In case of a breach of its regulations concerning air navigation.[133]

But before the convention was actually signed this article was omitted nor does any article in the Chicago Convention cover the same subject matter except to the very limited extent of Article 13 which is as follows:

Article 13. The laws and regulations of a contracting State as to the admission to or departure from its territory of passengers, crew or cargo of aircraft, such as regulations relating to entry, clearance, immigration, passports, customs, and quarantine shall be complied with by or on behalf of such passengers, crew or cargo upon entrance into or departure from, or while within the territory of that State.

The International Law Association, realizing the necessity of settling the possible conflict in competence of the State of the flag and the State of the territory where the aircraft might be, in case they were not the same, considered this matter at its 31st Conference in Buenos Aires in 1922, and again at its 33rd Conference in Stockholm in 1924. The resolutions finally affirmed at Stockholm, and drafted for the purpose of inclusion in an international convention, are as follows:

a) *Civil Jurisdiction*:

Art. 1

The airship which is above the open sea or such territory as is not under the sovereignty of any State is subject to the laws and civil jurisdiction of the country of which it has the nationality.

Art. 2

A public airship which is above territory of a foreign State remains under the exclusive jurisdiction of the State of which it has the nationality.

---

[133] Conférence de la paix, *op. cit.*, p. 155.

A private airship which is above the territory of a foreign State is subject to the laws and jurisdiction of such State only in the following cases:

1. With regard to every breach of its laws for the public safety and its military and fiscal laws.
2. In case of a breach of its regulations concerning air navigation.
3. For all acts committed on board the airship and having effect on the territory of the said State.

In all other respects a private airship follows the laws and jurisdiction of the State of the flag.

b) *Criminal Jurisdiction*:

Art. 3

If at the commencement or during the progress of any flight of any aircraft passing over any State or States or their territorial waters or over the high seas without landing, any person on board such aircraft commits any crime or misdemeanour, the person charged shall forthwith be arrested if necessary. Such felony or misdemeanour may be enquired into and the accused tried and punished in accordance with the Rules given under Art. 2. The State of the place where such aircraft lands shall be bound to arrest the accused if necessary and to extradite him to the State which has jurisdiction over him.

Art. 4

Acts committed on board a private aircraft not in flight in a foreign State shall be subject to the jurisdiction of such State, and any person or persons charged with the commission of such act shall be tried and, if found guilty, punished according to the laws of such State.[134]

These resolutions, prepared twenty-five years ago, still stand as the position of the International Law Association. The subject matter which they cover has not been included in any international convention, nor have sufficient cases arisen to assume that the questions covered are settled as part of customary international law. The problem is still open.

B. RESPONSIBILITY OF AIRCRAFT

As stated earlier in this study, aircraft unlike vessels and like railway trains and automotive vehicles are not yet considered as having the

---

[134] International Law Association, *Report of the 33rd Conference*, Stockholm, 1924, London, Sweet & Maxwell, 1925, pp. 117–118.

quality of responsibility in private law. As instrumentalities of international transport, aircraft are not directly responsible as are vessels for supplies, services and wrong-doings recognized as the bases for what are ordinarily known as maritime liens. Aircraft, like other chattels generally, may be held for the debts of the owner or, under certain local statutes, may be held for the satisfaction of specific liens. But such claims against an aircraft do not have the characteristics of a maritime lien for which a vessel is responsible, in many cases irrespective of the responsibility of the owner, nor does international law recognize (in the absence of statute or convention) the validity of claims against an aircraft, when the aircraft has passed into the hands of a bonafide purchaser without notice of the prior claim.

It has been held, for example, that a lien for repairs performed on a seaplane in a shop on land is not a maritime lien and does not have precedence over a penalty government lien which accrued later in time. Without deciding what would have been the case if the repairs had been performed on the seaplane while it was in the water, the court held that the claim for repairs "is no better than a lien against an ordinary airplane," thereby holding that there is no claim generally recognized in international air law for a lien for repairs against an airplane as there would be in maritime law against a vessel.[135]

As to supplies furnished on aircraft, it may be noted that Article 25 of the Pan American Convention provided that "the commander of an aircraft shall have rights and duties analogous to those of a captain of a merchant steamer," but this provision was not repeated in the Chicago Convention. While it might have been argued that under the Pan American Convention the aircraft commander could obligate the aircraft in a foreign port for repairs and supplies as the captain of a merchant vessel may do, this provision is no longer in force even as between those States which were parties to the Pan American Convention. In fact, the draft convention "on the Legal Status of the

---

[135] *United States of America, Libellant of one Fairchild Seaplane, etc.*, appellant, vs. *Northwest Air Service, Inc.*, appellee, U.S. Circuit Court of Appeals, 9th Circuit, December 20, 1935, 80 F. (2d) 804, cited in: *U.S. Aviation Reports*, 1936, pp. 148–149.

See also: *Andrew Foss* vs. *Airplane Crawford Bros. No. 2*, U.S. District Court, Western District of Washington, June 27, 1914, 215 Fed. 269, cited in: *U.S. Aviation Reports*, 1928, pp. 1–3; Arnold D. McNair, *The Law of the Air*, London, Butterworth, 1932, Chap. 8, pp. 144–151.

The decision in 1921 by Judge Cardozo in *Reinhardt* vs. *Newport Flying Service Corporation, et al.*, [232 N.Y. 115, cited in: *U.S. Aviation Reports*, 1928, pp. 4–7] to the effect that a hydroplane moored in navigable waters is a vessel was, in the judgment of the present writer, dicta and not necessary to the determination of the issues presented.

Aircraft Commander" (originally drafted by CITEJA and now before the Legal Committee of the International Civil Aviation Organization)[136] does authorize the aircraft commander to buy items necessary for the completion of the trip and to have repairs made which are necessary to enable the aircraft to proceed promptly. But the terms of the draft convention make it clear that this power given the aircraft commander is a power to obligate the owner and not to bind the aircraft itself. Further, Article 4 states definitely that "the Commander may not, without special authority, sell the aircraft, or, by any contractual act, mortgage or subject it to any similar claim." This draft convention appears to be a repudiation of any suggestion that the aircraft, irrespective of special authority from the owner, is responsible as a vessel would be for supplies and repairs in a foreign port.

The characteristic responsibility of vessels for salvage services has been held not to apply to aircraft in the absence of special statute. This was held in a leading case in which it was determined that even a seaplane does not satisfy the definition or description of a ship or a vessel, and that the British Air Navigation Act of 1920 (10 & 11 Geo. 5, c. 80) was restricted to British and foreign aircraft within the limits of British territorial jurisdiction and to British aircraft all over the world, but did not apply to salvage claims against a foreign aircraft or its cargo.[137] Section 11 of this Act had provided that the law relating direct to salvage of life or property should apply to aircraft on or over the sea or tidal waters as it applies to vessels. But this was held to be insufficient to cover salvage by British vessels of the cargo of an American seaplane wrecked on the coast of Greenland. After the *Watson* case was decided, the British Air Navigation Act of 1936 (25 Geo. 5, & 1 Edw. 8, c. 44) sought to extend the provisions of British law to cover salvage claims against foreign aircraft and claims for salvage services generally outside the limits of British territorial waters. But irrespective of how these new provisions may be construed, obviously they are statutory provisions and not statements of existing international law. This is further borne out by the fact that the convention signed at Brussels entitled "The Salvage of Aircraft at Sea Convention, 1938" provides for an indemnity payable by the operator of the aircraft assisted, and for remuneration in case of salvage also payable by the operator of the aircraft, but no provision is included giving a lien

---

[136] International Civil Aviation Organization, Document No. 5190, LC/88, March 2, 1948, p. 3.

[137] *Thomas Watson* vs. *R.C.A. Victor Company, Inc.*, Great Britain, Aberdeen Sheriff Court, October 31, 1934, 50 Ll.L.R. 77, cited in: *U.S. Aviation Reports*, 1935, pp. 147–156.

against the aircraft such as would exist in maritime law against a vessel for which salvage services had been rendered.[138]

As further indication that international air law has developed in the general direction of denying that aircraft are responsible in private law as are vessels, it should be noted that Article 23 of the Paris Convention provided that with regard to the salvage of aircraft wrecked at sea "the principles of maritime law will apply, in the absence of any agreement to the contrary," and in the Pan American Convention it was provided that "the salvage of aircraft lost at sea shall be regulated, in the absence of any agreement to the contrary, by the principles of maritime law."[139] But the Chicago Convention omits any reference to salvage. If it be said that Article 23 of the Paris Convention and Article 26 of the Pan American Convention indicated an intent to adopt the general principles of salvage, including a lien against the aircraft or cargo which had been saved, the omission of these provisions from the Chicago Convention and the signature at Brussels in 1938 of a specific convention applicable to salvage omitting any claim for lien against the aircraft is adequate evidence that no such lien now exists in international air law.

The characteristic lien against a vessel for damages caused by it when in collision with another vessel also does not apply to aircraft. As authoritatively stated by McNair, collisions between aircraft are governed by principles applicable to torts generally.[140] Even in the case of damage to a ship caused by an aircraft, though the admiralty court might have jurisdiction, no maritime lien would attach to the aircraft. The action "on behalf of the ship against the person responsible for the aircraft would be *in personam* and could not lie in rem."[141] In the draft convention "for the Unification of Certain Rules Relating to Aerial Collisions"[142] now pending before the Legal Committee of the International Civil Aviation Organization provision is made for the payment of an indemnity by the operator of the aircraft responsible in case of collision between aircraft. No provision is made for a lien against the aircraft itself irrespective of the indemnity due by the operator. The principle of responsibility of the aircraft as a legal

---

[138] For text of the Brussels aircraft salvage convention, see: Hudson, *International Legislation, op. cit.,* Vol. 8, pp. 135–147; Christopher N. Shawcross and Kenneth M. Beaumont, *Air Law,* London, Butterworth, 1945, Sec. 794–810, pp. 405–409; *U.S. Aviation Reports,* 1938, pp. 253–273.

[139] For the possible effect of these two conventions, had they remained in force, see: Arnold W. Knauth, "Aviation and Salvage: The Application of Salvage Principles to Aircraft," *Columbia Law Review,* Vol. 36, 1936, p. 234.

[140] McNair, *op. cit.,* p. 99.

[141] *Ibid.,* p. 102.

[142] International Civil Aviation Organization, Legal Committee, Subcommittee "Rome," Working Draft No. 27, May 27, 1949, p. 17.

quasi-personality is entirely absent in the draft convention on collision just as it is also absent in the salvage at sea convention applicable to aircraft signed at Brussels in 1938 and discussed above.

The Convention on "the International Recognition of Rights in Aircraft" signed at Geneva in 1948 provides the first recent (and very limited) international legislation for what might be called responsibility of aircraft. In Article 4 of that convention it is provided that in the event that any claims in respect of compensation for salvage or extraordinary expenses give rise "under the law of the Contracting State where the operations of salvage or preservation were terminated, to a right conferring a charge against the aircraft, such right shall be recognised by Contracting States and shall take priority over all other rights in the aircraft." Such rights may be noted on the record within three months and shall not be recognized by other contracting States after expiration of the three month period unless the right has been noted on the record and the amount has been agreed upon or judicial action on the right has been commended.[143] It would appear that this convention will give international force to compensation due for salvage or preservation services if the State in which such operations are completed creates a lien against the aircraft for such charges, and provided the claimant carries out the technical requirements of recording the claim in the State of the registry of the aircraft and proceeds to enforce it as required by the convention. The inclusion of these provisions seems conclusive proof that international air law generally does not recognize responsibility of the aircraft for such claims.

IV. CONCLUSIONS AND RECOMMENDATIONS

From the foregoing it is submitted that aircraft, like vessels, and unlike railway trains and automative vehicles, now have that quality of legal quasi-personality in public international law discussed above as *nationality*, but that unlike vessels, and like railway trains and automotive vehicles, aircraft are not yet considered as having the quality of personal *responsibility* in private law. The legal status of aircraft is therefore sui generis and places them in a class apart from other instrumentalities of commerce.

Resulting from the acceptance into international air law of the nationality of aircraft, certain cognate problems require solution. As

---

[143] For text of the convention and an excellent analysis of the difficult problems created by these provisions, see: Richard O. Wilberforce, "The International Recognition of Rights in Aircraft," *International Law Quarterly*, Vol. 2, 1948, pp. 421–458.

to the first of these—whether the distinction between state and civil aircraft in the Chicago Convention is sufficient—it is submitted that the solution there presented should be allowed to stand unless and until international practice indicates that confusion has resulted. No such evidence is at this time available. As to the treatment to be accorded state aircraft when in foreign territory, it is likewise submitted that no additional international legislation is at this time needed. The Chicago Convention provides that no state aircraft, whether military, customs or police, may enter foreign territory except under special authorization. No good reason seems to exist as to why such authorizations cannot from time to time determine the extent to which such state aircraft may be exempt from local jurisdiction when entering such foreign territory.

But it is further submitted that the question as to conflicts in the competence and jurisdiction of the State of the flag of the aircraft and of other States does require solution by international legislation. Conflicts already exist between the statute laws of certain States.[144] As Lemoine has well said: "The determination of the law applicable to events occurring and acts performed on board an aircraft is a complex and difficult problem. It is only fragmentarily settled by positive law and the different national systems do not furnish altogether consistent solutions."[145]

It is therefore submitted that the Air Law Committee of the International Law Association should determine (a) whether to urge the Association to reaffirm the position taken at Stockholm in 1924, or (b) to amend that position.

In any event it is recommended that the International Law Association should propose to the International Civil Aviation Organization a short draft convention seeking to fix and determine the respective competence and jurisdiction of the State of the flag of the aircraft when such aircraft is over its own territory, over the high seas, or in the territories of other States, as against the competence and jurisdiction of other States.

---

[144] Harvard Research in International Law—Jurisdiction with Respect to Crime, op. cit., p. 515; Meyer, op. cit., p. 619.

[145] Maurice Lemoine, Traité de droit aérien, Paris, Recueil Sirey, 1947, p. 201. For a general discussion of conflicts of law affecting aircraft, see: Fernand de Visscher, "Les Conflits de lois en matière de droit aérien," Hague, Académie de droit international, Recueil des cours, Vol. 48, 1934–II, pp. 279–385.

(Author's Supplemental Note, 1966)

BASIC PROBLEMS OF SPACECRAFT NATIONALITY

As evidenced by the above article, international law has assigned to ships and to aircraft the attribute of "nationality". The question now is: Should objects launched into outer space have the same or a similar characteristic so that a particular State is responsible for each such object and entitled to protect its rights. As early as 1952, five years before Sputnik, the distinguished scholar, Mr. Oscar Schachter, answered this question in the affirmative, saying:

> A more immediate problem is presented by the rocket ship itself. When we consider the possible uses of such ships, all sorts of questions arise. Will they be permitted to move about, free from the authority of any particular country and free of any other restraints? One might, for instance, envisage a space station high above the earth equipped to send radio or television signals to the earth. Would that satellite, therefore, be free of all the regulations, both international and national, which safeguard the public interest in this field? And if control is to be exercised, how should it be made compatible with the principle of freedom in outer space which we have urged?
>
> The best way to meet this problem, it seems to me, is to begin with the idea that each space craft must bear the flag of a particular country; that is, it must have a nationality. (Perhaps, as an exception, some space craft could belong to an international organization.) If a ship tried to evade this rule, it would be in the same position as a pirate of old and subject to seizure by any government able to lay hands on it.
>
> By requiring that each space craft have a nationality and a flag, it becomes possible to supervise them and control them. They then become subject to the discipline and the laws of the flag-state. If they fail to comply with those rules, they would become subject to penalties. At the same time, the government whose flag they fly would have to guarantee the proper use of the craft. The flag would also protect them against any abuses from other governments.[1]

This argument is difficult to answer. It states the position accurately as of today when spacecraft have been manned, are becoming manoeuverable, carry sophisticated scientific and communication payloads,

---

[1] Special Senate Comm. on Space and Astronautics, *Space Law: A Symposium.* 85th Cong., 2nd Sess. (Comm. Print 1958), p. 12.

and when rockets landed on the moon have transmitted pictures back to earth. Nationality has become a necessary, not merely an advisable spacecraft characteristic. Others had reached conclusions similar to that of Mr. Schachter even before Sputnik. Mr. C. E. S. Hosford, writing in England in 1955, said that: "Every space vehicle shall carry the flag of a particular nation as with sea-going vessels."[2] In 1956, the present author, addressing the American Society of International Law, said:

> While the application of the rule of nationality to rockets and satellites may be difficult, nevertheless, if upper space is to be free like the high seas, then certainly a State must be prepared to be responsible for the international good conduct of its rockets and satellites; otherwise chaos might result.[3]

Dr. Alex Meyer of Germany, for many years one of the world's leading authorities on the legal problem of flight, who was present, concurred in this view, saying that either nationality or something akin thereto must be considered when rockets are brought within the sphere of international regulation.[4]

The next major problem will involve a decision as to which flight instrumentalities capable of being launched into outer space should have nationality. This author has always felt that much difficulty can be put aside if there is a definite international decision to the effect that it is useless to include such rockets, guided missiles, or other projectile-like instrumentalities, carrying no cargo except a warhead. However, all other instrumentalities used or designed for use outside the atmosphere should have nationality as spacecraft even though they be also classified as aircraft. Particularly, this should include all spacecraft, whether manned or unmanned, which carry or can carry any type of load whether it be human, scientific instruments, communication equipment or otherwise.

One of the confusing present difficulties is the vagueness of accepted definitions of "aircraft". The ICAO Annexes to the Chicago Convention include the following definition: "*Aircraft*. Any machine that can derive support in the atmosphere from the reactions of the air." While these Annexes are not part of the Convention and the definition is therefore not binding on States who are parties to the Convention, this definition has been widely accepted in national statutes and regulations. It has not been amended by ICAO since Sputnik and it is

---

[2] Senate Comm. On Aeronautical and Space Sciences, *Legal Problems of Space Exploration: A Symposium*. S. Doc. No. 26, 87th Cong., 1st Sess. (1961), p. 24.

[3] LEGAL PROBLEMS OF UPPER SPACE, see *infra* at 277.

[4] *Legal Problems of Space Exploration: A Symposium*, p. 77.

necessary to assume its continued approval. Such flight instrumentalities as the American X-15, which has wings for use in the airspace and rocket motors for use beyond, are aircraft under this definition. But certainly they should also be classified as spacecraft. Even more confusing is the definition of aircraft in United States' statutes:

"Aircraft" means any contrivance now known or hereafter invented, used, or designed for navigation of or flight in the air.

Under this definition every spacecraft which uses United States' airspace while ascending toward or descending from outer space is subject to regulation as an aircraft.

It is the author's view that the only way to obviate these difficulties is to require that every spacecraft, or other flight instrumentality used or designed for flight beyond the atmosphere (except missiles and other projectiles) shall have nationality as spacecraft even though they may also be subject to regulation as aircraft while passing through the airspace.

The third major problem involves the question of how nationality shall become a required characteristic applicable to spacecraft. Obviously this can only be done by international agreement and will require the preliminary answer as to how the use of outer space shall be controlled.

The classic evidence of nationality has always been registration. As to vessels, this early became customary law. As to aircraft, the Paris, Havana, and Chicago Conventions each provided that aircraft should have the nationality of the State in which they are registered. Thus, each aircraft is identified with one State responsible for the aircraft's international good conduct.

But as to spacecraft, the situation will not be so simple. The Chicago Convention, for example, applies only to civil aircraft and not to state aircraft used for military purposes. The mandatory registration provision of the Convention does not apply to military aircraft although in practice each State usually assigns identification marks to its military aircraft and carries them on a special register. In the case of spacecraft, it seems obvious that a large proportion of those launched in the next several years will be State owned and operated. Also, certain spacecraft may be owned and operated by international organizations or, jointly, by several States.

The need for national registration of spacecraft for identification and other purposes was foreseen in Paragraph 7 of Resolution 1962 (XVIII), adopted by the U.N. General Assembly in 1963. This provides that "the State on whose registry an object launched into outerspace is carried shall retain jurisdiction and control over such object, and any personnel thereon, while in outerspace."

253

On the other hand, in the case of spacecraft, national registration may not be all that is required. If any international organization is to have supervision in any manner of outer space activities, such organization should provide an international registry. Under such a system each State would carry on its own registry those spacecraft for which it is directly responsible and would also register such spacecraft with the international body concerned. If spacecraft are to be operated jointly by several States, the spacecraft would be registered with each State and also with the international body. Spacecraft operated by an international organization would be carried only on the international register. It seems quite necessary for practical purposes that all spacecraft, whether civil or state, should be uniformly registered, and that provision be made by international convention that no object be launched into outer space unless or until the provisions of national and international registration have been carried out. In no other way does it seem possible to prevent confusion, or even chaos, in the use of outerspace and celestial bodies, and in no other way can national responsibility be insured in case of damage caused on the earth's surface or collision in the airspace or in outer space. Such registration is also a necessity for the proper working of any convention dealing with the return of astronauts or spacecraft in case of accidental landing.

PART FIVE

The Emerging Principles of
Law for Outer Space

13

High Altitude Flight
and National Sovereignty

*The first section of this study is the
author's Address delivered at the
Escuela Libre de Derecho, Mexico
City, 5 January 1951.
The last section, reproduced here by
permission of the Naval War
College, Newport, Rhode Island, is
from the author's Address,
"International Air Law,"
delivered at the College, 20
December 1948.*

Author's Note. This Address was delivered in January, 1951. It was the first or one of the first analyses in the English language of the still basic problem: "How far upward in space does the territory of a State extend?" It was also, apparently, the earliest effort to discuss from a legal point of view the launching and orbiting about the earth of "an artificial satellite".

It was the author's misfortune that he had not then heard of the German language pamphlet by Vladimir Mandl, published in 1932, entitled "Das Weltraumrecht: ein Problem der Raumfahrt," *i.e.,* "The Law of Outer Space, a Problem of Space Flight." In 1951, this author said, "In the first place it is obvious that we must agree that there is an upper boundary in space to the territory of the subjacent State." In 1932, as I found long after, Mandl had said, speaking of air space sovereignty: "But this sovereignty must have a territorial boundary somewhere and it cannot extend endlessly. The question is, at what distance from the ground this boundary should be set." Had Mandl's work been known to the author during his years of research at the Institute for Advanced Study in Princeton, he would have discussed it in this paper and given due credit to the thinking of a real pioneer, but no reference to Mandl's essay had then appeared in English.

HIGH ALTITUDE ROCKET flights have reopened an old question: How far upward in space does the territory of the State extend? This is a simple question to state, but a very difficult question to analyze, and perhaps even now an impossible question to answer. Nevertheless it must be considered.

If international relations are to be conducted in the future in anything approaching a normal manner, both the statesman and the jurist ought to know the extent to which a State has the acknowledged right to control all activity in the areas of space above its surface territory.

The territory of a State, geographically considered, is a three-dimensional region. It includes an area on the surface of the earth, a sector of the earth below, and a sector of space above. Legally considered, the territory of a State may be defined as those regions in which the State is recognized by international law as having the right to exercise national sovereignty to the exclusion of all other States. As the distinguished jurist Max Huber said in his opinion in the Island of

257

Palmas arbitration between the United States of America and the Netherlands: "Sovereignty in the relations between States signifies independence. Independence in regard to a portion of the globe is the right to exercise therein to the exclusion of any other State the functions of a State . . . Territorial sovereignty . . . involves the exclusive right to display the activities of a State." Among these territorial functions are included the right of a State to determine the extent to which it will control and police human activity within its territory.

The legal concept that a State has territorial rights above the surface of the earth is far older than the discovery of the art of human flight. Rome did not hesitate to control the use of space whenever deemed necessary to protect public or private rights on the surface of the earth. The airspace over public highways and over sacred ground was kept open by law. The Roman emperors limited the height to which buildings could be erected. Private rights in space above the landowner's property on the surface were carefully protected. The Roman State made its laws as effective above the surface of the earth as it did on the surface. The great jurists of a much later era fully recognized the existence of State sovereignty in space. Pufendorf, for example, in the latter part of the seventeenth century remarked that "since man has been denied the ability to be in the air to the extent that he rest in it alone, and be separated from the earth, he has been unable to exercise sovereignty over the air except insofar as men standing upon the earth can reach it." To Pufendorf sovereignty in space was thus limited by the ability for effective control, and not otherwise.

With the discovery of the balloon in 1783 and the gradual development of the art of man-controlled flight culminating with the Wright brothers in 1903, man found a way "to be in the air to the extent that he rest in it alone," and the problem of the extent of State sovereignty upward became acute. In analyzing this period it must always be remembered that neither statesmen nor lawyers conceived of the possibility of man-made flight through space beyond a region where there would be sufficient gaseous air to support a flight instrumentality of the general nature of a balloon or an airplane. So in 1906 when Professor Westlake, at a meeting of the Institute of International Law, first put into concrete legal statement the doctrine of State airspace sovereignty, he added that there was no limit upward of such sovereignty. Discussing the necessity for State control in the air over its territory, he said: "In the air the higher one ascends, the more damage the fall of objects will cause on the earth. If there exists a limit as to the sovereignty of the State over the oceanic space, none exists for the sovereignty of the State over the air space. The right of the subjacent State remains the same whatever may be the distance."

It is perfectly obvious that Westlake assumed that the State had territorial rights in space as high as flight could exist, but at the same time he assumed that such flight must take place in what he termed "air space."

In 1911 the British Government prepared a draft statute to be entitled "Aerial Navigation Bill" which, in its preamble, recited that "the sovereignty and rightful jurisdiction of His Majesty extends, and has always extended, over the air superincumbent on all parts of His Majesty's dominions and the territorial waters adjacent thereto." Again it was assumed that if the State had sovereignty "over the air," it had the right to regulate all flight over its lands and waters.

Whether the term "air" or the term "airspace" was used, the basic idea was the same. In the first great international legislative enactment of the fundamental principles of air law, the Paris Convention of 1919, Article 1 stated that "The High Contracting Parties recognize that every Power has complete and exclusive sovereignty over the air space above its territory." The convention then proceeded to the regulation of the use of "aircraft." In the Annex to the convention, adopted shortly after it came into effect, aircraft were defined as comprising "all machines which can derive support in the atmosphere from reactions of the air."

The Paris Convention was a statement of long existing and fully recognized State sovereignty over a region called "airspace," but otherwise undefined, in which "aircraft" might operate. But the Paris Convention is not to be construed as meaning that in international law States have territorial rights only in this airspace. The airspace was accepted as part of State territory but no international determination was made as to the regions of space above. The same argument can probably be made with reference to the statutes of various States not parties to the Paris Convention which asserted sovereignty over the "airspace."

It might be argued that the Paris Convention, and certain other conventions, asserted State sovereignty in the earth's "atmosphere" beyond the regions where sufficient air exists to support the flight of aircraft as defined in the Paris Convention. Both the French and Italian versions of the Paris Convention use language in Article 1 which literally translated into English means "atmospheric space" (French: espace atmosphérique, Italian: spazio atmosferico). My own view has always been that these terms were intended to mean exactly what the English version meant, namely, the region of space where the "air" was present in, it must be assumed, sufficient quantities to support flight in the balloons or airplanes which were regulated by the convention. This argument is supported by the fact that the Madrid Convention of 1926, signed by Spain and various Latin American countries, referred in Article 1 to sovereignty over "atmospheric space" (espacio atmosférico); while in the Havana Convention of 1928, signed by many of the same States, State sovereignty is recognized over the "airspace" (official Spanish text: "espacio aéreo"). Although, as will be indicated hereafter, the earth's atmosphere from the purely scientific point of view extends much further above the surface of the earth than does the region in which "air" is present in sufficient quantities to maintain aircraft flight, it would seem that in the Paris, Madrid, and Havana Conventions the terms "airspace" and "atmospheric space" must be considered as synonymous, constituting legally a recognition that every State has territorial rights at least through these regions where sufficient gaseous air is found to support such flight.

This view is further borne out by the fact that the Chicago Convention of 1944, now in force, states in Article 1 that "The contracting States recognize that every State has complete and exclusive sovereignty over the airspace above its territory." While the convention recites that French and Spanish texts were to be drawn up and opened for signature, this was apparently never done and the English text is still the only text which was officially signed. In the French translation of the convention which is ordinarily used, so I am advised, the English word "airspace" has been translated as "espace atmosphérique," while in the Spanish translation distributed by the International Civil Aviation Organization it has been translated as "espacio aéreo."

It may, therefore, be said that international law now answers the question "How far upward in space does the territory of the State extend?" as follows: The territory of the State extends upward *at least* as far above the surface as to include a region which can be roughly defined as "airspace." And international law contains no presently accepted rule covering the question as to whether usable space above and beyond the "airspace" is or is not part of the territory of the State below.

It is at this point that high altitude rocket flights open unsolved legal and political problems. Just how high such flights have been made I do not know. But as long ago as the spring of 1949 it was disclosed in the public press that a two-stage rocket had reached a height of at least 250 miles (400 kilometers) above the surface of the earth.[1] This rocket passed far above the region which can, under any theory, be described as "airspace." The question is: Did it pass out of the territory of the State below when it left the airspace, and re-enter that territory

---

[1] For much of the data as to the scientific characteristics of the upper atmosphere, the author is greatly indebted to the article and chart entitled "The Earth's Atmosphere," by Howard E. Roberts, *Aeronautical Engineering Review*, Vol. 8 (October 1949), pp. 18–31.

on returning; or was it at all times within the territory of the State below?

Before even suggesting an answer it is necessary to consider very briefly certain of the scientific views now generally held as to what constitutes the earth's atmosphere. This atmosphere is usually described as constituting four gaseous layers known as the troposphere, stratosphere, ionosphere, and exosphere. The troposphere is next the earth and the exosphere is the far distant region which gradually merges into outer space. The "airspace" is part of the lower atmospheric region. The troposphere extends upward about 54,000 feet (16,200 meters) at the equator, and 28,000 feet (8,400 meters) at the poles. It contains about three-quarters in weight of the gases composing the earth's atmosphere, and is characterized by continually decreasing temperatures with increase of altitude. The stratosphere extends from the upper level of the troposphere to about 60 or 70 miles (100 or 115 kilometers) above the earth's surface. It contains slightly less than one-fourth in weight of the earth's atmosphere, is characterized by constant temperature of about minus 67 degrees Fahrenheit (20 degrees Centigrade) for part of its area, then a rapidly increasing temperature up to about 170 degrees Fahrenheit (75 degrees Centigrade), then decreasing again to about minus 28 degrees Fahrenheit (minus 33 degrees Centigrade).

The ionosphere extends from the upper levels of the stratosphere to approximately 400 miles (640 kilometers) above the surface of the earth. It is said to be characterized by the existence of what have been termed by some authors as "free electrical discharges." The temperature is estimated to increase steadily up to approximately 4000 degrees Fahrenheit (2200 degrees Centigrade).

The exosphere is the fringe area beyond the ionosphere in which the density of the gaseous atmosphere is even less, and is supposedly characterized by a uniform temperature of approximately 4000 degrees Fahrenheit (2200 degrees Centigrade).

It will be seen from the foregoing that the rocket which reached 250 miles (400 kilometers) above the surface of the earth was high up in the ionosphere. It was far past any region that could be termed "airspace." It is generally believed that above 60 miles beyond the earth's surface (approximately 100 kilometers) what we would term as a vacuum exists and that all of the aerodynamic features of flight which result in the "lift" of a normal type of aircraft have disappeared. It may be recalled in this connection that no airplane has ever been flown more than approximately 60,000 feet above the surface, sounding balloons have probably reached an altitude of 120,000 feet—both of these distances being far below the theoretical absolute outside limit of what might be termed "airspace."

Scientific investigation and progress in known rocket flights have therefore demonstrated that none of the international legislative procedure set up in the Paris and Chicago Conventions applies in a very large percentage of the region to which these rockets have already reached. Future scientific progress makes the problem even more difficult. Rockets now in use are leaving the earth's surface at speeds of at least 5000 miles per hour (8000 kilometers). It has been estimated that if this speed can be increased to approximately 25,000 miles per hour (40,000 kilometers) at the top of the atmosphere, the power can then be shut off and the rocket would continue moving upward indefinitely. Certain scientists believe that these speeds can be attained with fuels now available, although at very great costs; others believe that new methods of propulsion may be required. One of my friends, a well-known astronomer, has indicated to me that the point at which such a rocket would leave the earth's area of attraction and pass under the predominance of the sun would be approximately 161,000 miles (256,000 kilometers) above the earth's surface. It is well to bear that figure in mind because if we hold to the old classic legal theory, as stated by Westlake, that a State must have sovereignty as high up into space as necessary to protect itself from "falling" bodies, then perhaps the State's territory is 161,000 miles in height.

But the problem is even more complicated than as just indicated. If a rocket or other man-controlled missile can take off from the earth with a speed of approximately 17,500 miles an hour (26,400 kilometers), it will be able to proceed upward for several hundred miles and could then be deflected off of its course so as to be aimed somewhat parallel to the surface of the earth, the power could be turned off, and the rocket would continue on a course around the earth as its momentum would approximately balance the earth's attraction. It would become an artificial satellite. From the international lawyer's point of view the question then arises: Does such an artificial satellite, flying several times per day around the earth and passing far above the surface territories of many States, enter and leave the territory of each of such States when immediately above their surface boundaries? If we accept the theory that the territory of the State extends as far upward into space, even though that space be a vacuum, as required to prevent the entry of man-made activity which may result in injury to persons and property on the surface of the State, then we must assume that such a satellite is violating the sovereignty of every State below which has not consented in advance to its passage. There are scientists who believe that such a satellite can and will be constructed before many years have passed.

It is obvious that it is the duty of the trained jurist to suggest an answer to these problems. It may be that a new international convention is required which will include some sort of agreed international limitation on the extent to which States will engage in high altitude flight somewhat similar to Article 8 of the Chicago Convention which provides that no *aircraft* capable of being flown without a pilot shall be flown without a pilot over the territory of a contracting State without special authorization by that State.

In the absence of such new convention, basic legal theories must be re-examined and the practical questions at issue must be understood.

In the first place it is obvious that we must agree that there is an upper boundary in space to the territory of the subjacent State. Under no possible theory can it be said that a State can exercise sovereign rights in outer space beyond the region of the earth's attraction. The arguments for State sovereignty in space have always gone back to the proposition that it is both the right and the duty of the State to protect itself and that on no other basis can such protection be considered adequate except that it have the right to control, as part of its territory, those regions above it which, if used by other States, may bring damage and loss to persons and property on the State below. Carrying this old rule to its extreme, the outer boundary of the State cannot be further than the point where the earth's attraction will govern the movement of an object in space so that such object will "fall" onto the earth.

On the other hand, this boundary cannot be lower than the upper limit of the airspace. The rule of international law—that the territory of the subjacent State includes at least the region above it known as airspace—need not be challenged. In other words, it would appear that the upper boundary of the State's territory lies at a point between the upper limit of the "airspace" and the upper limit of the earth's attraction. Somewhere in this vast intervening region the rights of the State below cease to exist as against other States.

Certain jurists have insisted that the territory of a State is limited by the ability of that State to make its law effective. This is a harsh rule when applied to sovereignty in space. The richest and most powerful States now have means through high altitude rockets to control more or less effectively the "airspace" over their surface territories. But the weaker States have no such power. Can we be said to live in such a world where the physical power at any one time of any particular State determines its *international right* to consider the region above its surface territories as part of its national territory? I may say here that my own belief is and has always been that if the rule of effectiveness is to be applied to determine the limit of State territory in space, then the rule should be that every State, no matter how small or how weak, as a State of equal sovereignty with every other State, has and should be admitted to have territorial rights upwards above its surface territories as high as the rights of every other State no matter how powerful.

Perhaps the rule should be, in the absence of international agreement, that the territory of every State extends upward as far into space as it is physically and scientifically possible for any one State to control the regions of space directly above it. In considering the possibility of adopting such a rule as this as part of international law, its limitations must be understood. The enormous distances involved must not be forgotten. Assuming that a State has acquired the use of a rocket that will leave the earth at the suggested speed of 25,000 miles per hour, it must be remembered that as it moves upward it will be continually slowed by the earth's pull. Therefore it would take a rocket traveling at even this tremendous velocity well over six hours to reach the theoretical distance of 161,000 miles beyond the earth's surface, at which point it enters into the area where the sun's attraction begins to predominate.

By the time that the rocket reached this far distant region, for the purpose of policing or controlling its use by other States, the rocket may have itself passed through the theoretical territory of several States. It must be recalled that the earth itself is rotating. If this rocket is driven directly upward, it may not be directly over the territory of the State which fired it for a very long period. Any theoretical possibility of a State controlling far distant regions in space is absolutely out of the question. I am convinced that we must abandon the theory that the State has the right to claim territory out into space as far as the earth's attraction extends, and that we must admit some such reasonable rules as I have suggested above—namely, that at any particular time the territory of each State extends upward into space as far as then scientific progress of any State in the international community permits such State to control space above it.

Frankly, this is not put forward as a final solution. It is realized that it leaves open such vital questions as to what extent of control is contemplated. It also leaves open the question of by what means an international determination will be made of the ability of the most powerful State to extend its control into outer space. I could argue at forceful and great length against the solution suggested. In its favor I can only say that it is worthy of consideration; that it provides the basis for a fairly livable world in which the weak State is not at the mercy of the strong. The mere suggestion of the rule, above all else, shows the gravity of the problem and the need for an answer.

EDITOR'S NOTE. *An indication of the problems which would confront International Law as a result of developments in space technology had been given by Professor Cooper as early as 1948 in a lecture delivered*

at the U.S. Naval War College, Newport, Rhode Island. The follow-
ing are excerpts from that lecture, International Air Law.

Air law has been defined as "the whole of the rules which govern the
air space and its utilization for the purpose of aviation."[2] The difficulty with this definition today is that technical progress now requires
that we consider both airspace and certain parts of space beyond as
scientifically practical mediums of flight. Nor can we limit the means
of flight, with which Air Law must deal to such instrumentalities as
the normal types of aircraft usually operated in the "airspace."
Rockets are now being propelled seventy miles and more into space
above the surface of the earth, far outside of what we ordinarily refer
to as "airspace" and its "atmosphere." It is suggested that the term
"flight-space" might better be used in place of airspace to indicate all
that space above the earth's surface used or usable as a medium of man-
made or controlled flight. Perhaps the definition of Air Law might
then be restated as "comprising the whole of the rules governing
flight-space and its utilization as a medium of flight for aircraft or
other self-propelled and man-controlled devices."

Such a definition has the advantage of directing attention to the
two basic problems of Air Law—its concern with the legal status of
space and the legal regulation of flight. It is obvious that until we
know whether flight-space is part of the national territory of the state
lying below it, or free of all control and usable by all States, it is quite
impossible to determine the rules applicable to the regulation of flight
in such space. Hence Air Law must first determine the legal status of
flight-space over the various parts of the earth's surface, such as the
national territory of sovereign States below and the high seas, and,
having determined such status, it must then provide the rules for the
regulation of flight.

As to the first of these problems, it is the function of International
Air Law, as law governing the relations between States, to determine
what parts of flight-space can become or are parts of the territory of
sovereign States and what parts of such space must be free for the use
of all peoples. Exactly the same problem developed in the law of the
seas. Complete confusion and strife existed between nations as to the
right to control the high seas until customary international law was
tacitly accepted under which it is now agreed that the high seas are
not and can not become part of the sovereign territory of any State
and must be open and free to the navigation of all States. As pointed
out by Kelsen[3] "each State can claim as its 'territory' only a part of

[2] Goedhuis, *Air Law in the Making*, The Hague, Nijhoff, 1938.
[3] Kelsen, *General Theory of Law and State*, Cambridge, Mass., **Harv.**
Univ. Press, 1945, p. 349.

space and as its people only a part of mankind." Any interference by one State with these spheres of another State is a violation of the rights of the other State. Hence no single State can determine what part of space is of the character which it has the right to include within its territory, and only international law, which governs the relations between States, can provide the applicable rules.

International Air Law has recognized these problems. It has sought first to determine rules acceptable to the community of States as to the legal status of flight-space and then provide international regulation of flight through such space as is not part of the territory of individual States, and also, by such international legislation, to provide certain rules to be applied by all States even as to flight within their territorial flight-space. Agreement exists as to the principles covering the legal status of the "airspace." The problem is new as to the legal status of space beyond the airspace. Agreement also exists among most States as to rules regulating flight in time of peace. No substantial agreement exists as to such regulation in time of war.

FUTURE USE OF GUIDED MISSILES ABOVE THE AIRSPACE

In closing this discussion I wish to present a problem to the Naval War College and request the assistance of the officers on duty here. Thus far I have not been able to produce a solution which satisfies me. Suppose that Country A and C are at war. Their land territories do not touch at any point. A neutral Country B occupies the surface territory between A and C. Let us then assume that Country A starts bombarding Country C with guided missiles passing through flight-space over Country B at an altitude which may be considered beyond the airspace and at a height where Country B may find it impossible, with any devices in its possession or even in existence, to intercept such guided missiles or otherwise prevent their passage over its territory. Had the neutral rights of Country B been affected?

Inherent in the answer to this problem is the basic difficulty of future International Air Law—to what height above the surface of the earth can the sovereignty of a State be extended. Able experts will contend that territory never exists beyond the ability of the State claiming such territory to make its laws effective and that sovereignty is the power to control. Other experts will contend that sovereignty is the right to control territory and that every State may be assumed to have sovereignty in space up to any height which any other State can reach with devices or missiles in its possession. In view of the fact that some of my scientific friends are convinced that rockets or other guided missiles may be propelled from the earth to the moon within a comparatively few years, the problem presents curious political and geographic difficulties.

14
Legal Problems of
Upper Space

Reprinted by permission of The American Society of International Law from Proceedings of the Fiftieth Annual Meeting of the American Society of International Law, *p. 85 (1956).*

Author's Note. The following paper was presented a year before Sputnik, but after the United States had announced in 1955 its intention of putting artificial satellites into orbit as part of the 1957–1958 International Geophysical Year program. As Director of the Institute of International Air Law at McGill University since 1951, the author had kept in close touch with both scientific and legal thinking. This paper was the result of certain conclusions then reached: (*a*) The author's still unshaken belief that the upper limit of national airspace must be fixed, preferably by a new convention; (*b*) that through at least part of space in which sovereignty is exercised, provision must be made for a "right of transit" for non-military spacecraft ascending or descending; (*c*) that all space above areas in which national sovereignty is recognized, now called "outer space," should be free; (*d*) that the question of nationality for rockets and satellites must be considered.

It is hoped that the reader will also examine the relevant portions of the 1956 Proceedings of the American Society of International Law so as to have the benefit of the valuable comments made by Professor Oliver Lissitzyn, Mr. P. K. Roy, Dr. Alex Meyer, Miss H. Alberta Colclaser, the late Mr. Arnold W. Knauth, Professor Myres S. McDougal, and others who were present when the paper was first read. Dr. Meyer then mentioned the Mandl essay published in 1932 but did not discuss its contents.

T ODAY NEITHER lawyers nor governments are prepared to state the legal flight rules applicable to presently operating rockets and planned satellites. For the second time in the present century science and engineers have far outstripped the law. Such delay may be normal where legal rules must depend on known and accepted factual situations, but the gap between technological and legal progress must never be permitted to become too wide.

The present problem confronting us is this: Flight *instrumentalities*, such as rockets, satellites and other spacecraft do not fall within existing national or international regulatory provisions. Nor is there any agreement as to what, if any, national or international regulation is applicable to *space* above the atmosphere where such rockets and satellites will normally be used. This existing legal hiatus can lead to grave international misunderstanding if permitted to continue too long.

Flight technology first outdistanced the law in the early years of the present century when it became necessary to determine whether air-

269

craft and balloons were vehicles like automobiles or whether they had nationality like ships; also, whether the atmospheric space in which they operated was or was not part of the territory of the subjacent state. The manner in which these questions were settled reveals the extent of the dangerous legal hiatus which now confronts us.

Flight became a factor in international affairs when it could be controlled by man. The airship flights of von Zeppelin between 1900 and 1902, and the airplane flight of the Wright brothers in 1903, were the real beginning. But governments were slow to fix the legal rules, and jurists were not in agreement. In 1906, in the much-discussed debates in the Institute of International Law, Fauchille urged freedom of flight and Westlake insisted upon national airspace sovereignty. But the importance of this discussion has, in my judgment, been exaggerated. It had little, if any, influence on the subsequent activities of states. Fauchille ignored the fact that distinguished jurists had long insisted that territory must be three dimensional. Westlake, while supporting sovereignty, appeared to believe that such sovereignty should be subject to an international right of innocent passage through the airspace, although no state ever accepted this dictum in practice.

Governments did not become really concerned until France, in 1908 and 1909, took alarm at the number of German balloons which were drifting into France, many apparently manned by military personnel, and called the celebrated 1910 International Air Navigation Conference. This met in Paris to consider the possible regulations of international flight. The United States was not invited, as it was considered too far away to be affected. On more than one occasion I have stated my view that the proceedings of this 1910 Paris Conference, with its almost completed draft convention, indicated general agreement that each state had full sovereignty in then usable space over its national lands and waters, that no general right of international transit existed for aircraft of other states in the absence of international convention, and that the only practical legal method of regulating international flight was by agreement which would provide for the grant of privileges of flight through such national space.

By legislative acts and diplomatic conduct in the intervening years between the 1910 Conference and the outbreak of World War I, Europe indicated acceptance of these principles. Events at the outbreak of World War I and during that war, as well as the preparation and signature of the Paris Convention of 1919, gave further evidence of the validity of the principle of absolute sovereignty of the subjacent state over the "air space," and also of the fact that aircraft have nationality.

The Paris 1919 Convention was signed and ratified in French and Italian as well as in English. The words "air space" appear in the French version as *"espace atmosphérique"* and in the Italian as

270

"*spazio atmosferico*." It seems apparent from this that the words "air space" in the English version meant, without question, "atmospheric space."

In many articles of the convention, the flight instrumentalities to be regulated are described as "aircraft," and their nationality is recognized. Under the system of the Paris Convention, its subsequently adopted annexes became part of the convention itself. In these annexes an "aircraft" is defined as follows: "The word 'aircraft' shall comprise all machines which can derive support in the atmosphere from reactions of the air." In Annex A various classes of "aircraft" included balloons, airships, land planes, sea planes and helicopters.

Taking together the assertion of state sovereignty in Article I, with this definition of "aircraft," it may be said that the Paris Convention declared that each state was sovereign in those areas of space where sufficient gaseous atmosphere existed to lift and support balloons, airships, and airplanes, as well as other types of flight instrumentalities which could "derive support in the atmosphere from reactions of the air." Man had not yet conceived the possibility of any other type of flight instrumentality, nor had he had occasion to regulate areas of space other than those used by "aircraft."

In 1926, by the adoption of the Air Commerce Act, the United States (which signed but did not ratify the Paris Convention) declared itself to possess complete and exclusive national sovereignty in the airspace over the United States, and defined aircraft to mean "any contrivance now known or hereafter invented, used or designed for navigation or flight in the air." These rules were carried forward in the Civil Aeronautics Act of 1938, and are still part of our law. It is conceivable that this definition of aircraft is broader than the Paris definition, as it seems to include flight instrumentalities used for flight in the air even though not supported thereby.

The Chicago Convention of 1944, to which most of the states engaged in international aviation are parties, except the U.S.S.R., restated in Article I the provisions of the Paris Convention as to airspace sovereignty in this manner: "The contracting States recognize that every State has complete and exclusive sovereignty of the airspace above its territory." Again, as in the Paris Convention, this is a statement of customary international law and not an exchange of privileges between the states concerned. Also, the Chicago Convention deals with the regulation of "aircraft" which are given the attribute of nationality. But neither "airspace" nor "aircraft" is defined.

Under the Chicago Convention the technical standards, called annexes, do not become parts of the convention. They are prepared by the International Civil Aviation Organization, and are then submitted to the member states for acceptance. Any state finding it impractical to

271

comply in all respects with such standards must so advise the International Civil Aviation Organization.

During the Chicago Conference, the United States submitted suggestions for future annexes, including the definition of aircraft similar to that in the Air Commerce Act of 1926 as stated above. But the Chicago Conference inserted in the tentative annexes the definition of aircraft as it had already existed in its narrower form in the Paris Convention annex. Subsequently, the International Civil Aviation Organization, when formally adopting the present Annex 7 dealing with Aircraft Nationality and Registration Marks, defined aircraft as "any machine that can derive support in the atmosphere from the reactions of the air." This is almost exactly the Paris definition adopted many years earlier. In the same annex, the term "aircraft" is stated to include balloons, airships, airplanes, and helicopters, and other similar instrumentalities requiring support in the atmosphere from reactions of the air in order to maintain flight.

When this annex was submitted to the member states of the International Civil Aviation Organization, no objection was apparently raised by the United States or any other member state, and it may therefore be that this is the definition which the United States must apply in international use rather than its own definition. This, however, is a problem which has not yet arisen, but which may become acute if a type of flight instrumentality is launched by the United States, which is covered by our own definition of "aircraft," but is not included in the international definition adopted pursuant to the Chicago Convention.

From the foregoing the following appears to be the present *legal* situation:

a) Both the Paris and Chicago conventions have dealt only with those flight instrumentalities which derive support in the atmosphere from reactions of the air, such as the balloon or airplane, and have not dealt with such instrumentalities as rockets, satellites, and other spacecraft which are designed to move through space without atmospheric support.

b) The Chicago Convention contains no definition of "airspace" but it may well be argued that, as it was adapted from the Paris Convention, it deals with no areas of space other than those parts of the atmosphere where the gaseous air is sufficiently dense to support balloons and airplanes. The highest flight by any unmanned balloon up to the present time is 140,000 feet, by a manned balloon 72,395 feet, and the highest airplane flight is 90,000 feet.

c) Nothing in the Chicago Convention precludes the possibility of state sovereignty being extended by international agreement, or by unilateral force, above the areas in which the airplane and balloon can be used, but there is certainly no basis on which any customary international law can as yet be considered applicable to such higher areas.

d) Airspace over the high seas is now free for use by all.

The present *technical* situation is also of major importance. Basing my information solely upon public disclosures in the press and the current literature, I would invite your attention to the following:

a) Rockets of the so-called V-2 type, as used in the German attacks on London, are understood to have been driven to a height of about 114 miles. An American rocket, which consisted of a V-2 plus an additional rocket stage, has been publicly stated to have reached an altitude of about 250 miles.

b) It now appears that there is an area between the highest possible balloon flight—let us say, 50 miles above the surface of the earth—and 200 to 300 miles above the surface of the earth, in which continuous or extended satellite flights may be extremely difficult due to the presence of sufficient atmosphere to create serious "drag" or heating.

c) In other words, it is now suggested that the future satellite flight will be most practical for long distances only if conducted not less than 200 or 300 miles above the surface of the earth.

In July, 1955, the United States announced that it would support a series of satellite flights as part of the wide scientific investigation of the 1957–1958 International Geophysical Year. Some of the details of the proposed flights have now been disclosed. It is planned to drive a three-stage rocket at least 200 miles above the surface of the earth, carrying in its nose the "satellite," which will be a round object about the size of a basketball. The directions of the various stages of the rocket will be so changed that when the satellite is discharged and starts on its free orbit it should be approximately parallel to the surface of the earth. Based on the much-discussed principle that if the speed of the rocket at that point is sufficient to counterbalance the attraction of the earth, the satellite shonld continue on an orbit around the earth for several days or even for several weeks, the time being dependent, among other things, on the amount of atmospheric "drag." The satellite will carry in its small bulk an amazing collection of instruments for obtaining information deemed by the scientists to be of the greatest possible future value. The International Geophysical Year, of which this satellite program is part, is directed by committees made up of scientists of many different nations. But the satellite itself will be launched by the United States Government.

Two authorities have already dealt with the legal problems of this flight. Mr. Andrew G. Haley, General Counsel of the American Rocket Society, presented a paper at the annual meeting of that Society in

November 1955, in which he seemed to suggest that the areas of space above the atmosphere to be used by the satellite might be subject to some sovereign control of the subjacent states, but that failure of any state to object to the International Geophysical Year satellite program at the time of its announcement was all that was required in order to make the completion of the program possible. He added that "The Scientists have benefited mankind as a whole in a field where the lawyers might well have failed."

Quite a different thesis has been put forward by Mr. C. Wilfred Jenks, an Associate of the Institute of International Law.[1] In his article Mr. Jenks noted the announcement by the White House of a satellite program "to circle the earth in 90 minutes at a height of 300 miles." His legal position is, apparently, that space beyond the atmosphere of the earth is and must always be incapable of appropriation by the projection into such space of any particular sovereignty based on a fraction of the earth's surface. He argues that the acceptance of such complete international freedom in these areas of space is required by astronomical and physical facts, and he contends that only activities "within the atmosphere of the earth would appear to be susceptible of the degree of control similar in general nature to that which can be exercised in territorial waters or over a wider maritime frontier belt." It would therefore appear that Mr. Jenks denies the existence or possibility of national sovereignty in areas of space beyond the atmosphere—say from 300 miles above the earth's surface upward. He continues:

> It would seem important to accept this principle fully from the earliest stages of the exploitation and exploration of space, and it is of interest that the United States plan for launching space satellites appears to be based upon it. There is no indication in the United States plan that it is proposed to negotiate passage agreements with the subjacent sovereignties. Moreover, such rights cannot be claimed under the International Civil Aviation Convention, since, even assuming the Convention to be applicable beyond the atmosphere and disregarding the fact that certain States, including the U.S.S.R., are not parties to it, the Convention provides that pilotless aircraft will not be flown over the territory of contracting States without special authorization.

The statements by Mr. Haley and Mr. Jenks point up the importance of the problem to be considered—namely, What is the legal status of the space beyond the atmosphere where rockets and satellites can be operated without undue atmospheric interference?

---

[1] "International Law and Activities in Space," 5 International and Comparative Law Quarterly 99–114 (January, 1956).

A subsidiary question involves the status of the intermediate area between the upper level of the atmosphere used by aircraft and the lowest height at which a rocket or satellite may freely be operated. I am not sure that we yet have the scientific data necessary to determine the extent to which rockets or satellites may safely use this intermediate area. At least I do not feel that sufficient data is publicly available.

Five years ago, in what may have been the earliest present-day discussion of the question of the legal status of space at high altitudes, I suggested that the time had come when "we must agree that there is an upper boundary in space to the territory of the subjacent State," and I said:

> Certain jurists have insisted that the territory of a State is limited by the ability of that State to make its law effective. This is a harsh rule when applied to sovereignty in space. The richest and most powerful States now have means through high altitude rockets to control more or less effectively the "airspace" over their surface territories. But the weaker States have no such power. Can we be said to live in such a world where the physical power at any one time of any particular State determines its international right to consider the region above its surface territories as part of its national territory? I may say here that my own belief is and has always been that if the rule of effectiveness is to be applied to determine the limit of State territory in space, then the rule should be that every State, no matter how small or how weak, as a State of equal sovereignty with every other State, has and should be admitted to have territorial rights upwards above its surface territories as high as the rights of every other State no matter how powerful.[2]

At the same time I indicated that this left open such questions as the extent of contemplated control, and the means by which an international determination could be made of the ability of the most powerful state to extend its control into outer space. Long and careful consideration during the past five years has convinced me of the existence of almost insuperable difficulties in applying the rule which I then suggested. The only practical way to solve the questions as to the legal status of areas above those covered by a strict construction of Article I of the Chicago Convention will be the adoption of some form of international agreement.

Such a new convention might include these solutions:

---

[2] See HIGH ALTITUDE FLIGHT AND NATIONAL SOVEREIGNTY, *supra* at 263–64.

a) Reaffirm Article I of the Chicago Convention, giving the subjacent state full sovereignty in the areas of atmospheric space above it, up to the height where "aircraft" as now defined, may be operated, such areas to be designated "territorial space."

b) Extend the sovereignty of the subjacent state upward to 300 miles above the earth's surface, designating this second area as "contiguous space," and provide for a right of transit through this zone for all non-military flight instrumentalities when ascending or descending.

c) Accept the principle that all space above "contiguous space" is free for the passage of all instrumentalities.

These solutions would aid future peaceful use of rockets and satellites and would seem to provide reasonable security for the subjacent state. At the same time, the territory of the state would be extended upward even beyond the areas in which it might make its normal laws effective. For I venture to suggest that, due in part to the physical problems involved, in part to the enormous speeds of the flight instrumentalities concerned, as well as many other difficulties, it will be most unlikely that any state can make its normal day-by-day laws effective very high in space. I do not deny the possibility that with modern weapons, such as guided missiles, a state may exercise *military command* quite high into space, provided it is certain that its activities are within the areas which are really above its own territory. But I must differentiate between such military control as may be involved in shooting down an intruder, and the normal civil control that a state must have day by day to enforce in its territory the peacetime laws under which men live together.

These ideas are put forward only as suggestions. The main problem is that an agreement would be most useful regarding the status of space above the "territorial space" covered by the Chicago Convention. As a word of caution, I would again suggest that we may not yet have the physical and scientific information needed to reach immediately the soundest decisions. The data being collected by the International Geophysical Year program will help tremendously. But it would be unfortunate if international rules of future high altitude flight control were adopted, and if it were then found that they were based on incorrect theories as to the physical characteristics and usefulness of various areas in the upper atmosphere and beyond.

At this point I wish to express my appreciation to my one-time colleague at the Institute of International Air Law, Mr. R. S. S. Allen of London, who under my direction has done a great deal of research in certain of the problems here discussed. It was Mr. Allen who first suggested to me the advisability of three zones, although the zones which are now indicated are not exactly those he had in mind.

Certain additional questions require consideration. If a new convention is not adopted, should the International Civil Aviation Organization amend its annexes so as to expand its definition of "aircraft" to include instrumentalities which, like rockets and satellites, were not contemplated at Chicago? It must be recalled that Article XII of the Chicago Convention already gives to the International Civil Aviation Organization the power to adopt flight rules as to the operation of aircraft when over the high seas. This article would have greater significance if "aircraft" included rockets and satellites when flying above the high seas.

Another problem to be dealt with is the difficult question of nationality. The whole theory of nationality, as derived from the law of the sea, is based on the concept that when a state gives to a ship the right to use its flag, such state assumes certain international responsibilities for the good conduct of that ship on the high seas and in foreign ports and at the same time acts as the protector of the ship to enforce its international rights. Under the Chicago Convention, aircraft are given the same characteristics of nationality. In addition, Article VIII deals with aircraft "capable of being flown without a pilot," and it would seem that such pilotless aircraft also have nationality. While the application of the rule of nationality to rockets and satellites may be difficult, nevertheless if upper space is to be free like the high seas, then certainly a state must be prepared to be responsible for the international good conduct of its rockets and satellites; otherwise chaos might result. Nationality must be considered when these new types of flight instrumentalities are brought within the sphere of international regulation.

Assuming that decisions are made as to the legal status of the various usable zones in space and as to the legal status of flight instrumentalities not now included in the international definition of "aircraft," a further problem must be solved: Some jurists appear to doubt if the International Civil Aviation Organization, set up under the Chicago Convention, should be designated as the international body to regulate and control the use of all areas of space for non-military purposes, and indicate that the problems of future rocket and satellite flight in upper space are so interlinked with other international problems that some new world organization must be created to deal with the new questions involved. I am not yet convinced of the need for a new organization.

In summary, the purpose of this paper is to place before you certain basic problems. The solutions which I have tentatively suggested may not be accepted, but I do urge that as soon as the physical characteristics of the upper atmosphere and space beyond are sufficiently known to warrant the adoption of acceptable rules, then an international conference be held to amend the Chicago Convention, or to adopt a new convention, so that all areas of space now usable, or which may become usable within a reasonable time, may be considered, and agreement reached as to the status of each. Agreement must also be reached as to how, and by whom, and under what circumstances, new instrumentalities of flight, such as rockets and satellites, will be regulated. It is certainly the duty of international lawyers to give these matters their earnest attention so as to be in position, when the time comes, to aid in reaching an international accord.

15
The Russian Satellite— Legal and Political Problems

Reprinted by permission of the Journal of Air Law and Commerce *from 24* Journal of Air Law and Commerce 379 *(1957).* © Journal of Air Law and Commerce *1957.*

Author's Note. This essay was read at the annual meeting of the American Rocket Society on December 2, 1957. It was written in Europe two weeks after the U.S.S.R. launched Sputnik I on October 4, 1957. It is very difficult to recreate the excitement of those days, nine years ago. The author was in southern France when Sputnik was launched. A week later he was at Cambridge University talking to one of the scientists who first measured Sputnik's orbit and learned that earlier scientific belief that a satellite could not be put in orbit much below 300 miles above the earth's surface was erroneous and that Sputnik, in fact, on its regular orbit, was approaching within 150 miles. This modified the author's thinking, as expressed in 1956 in the preceding paper. However, the launching of Sputnik and the fact that the U.S.S.R. is not a member of the International Civil Aviation Organization forced the conclusion that "only the United Nations itself can now serve as a forum for further discussion" of outer space. This has proved correct.

O N OCTOBER 4th, 1957, the U.S.S.R. launched the first man-made satellite. This memorandum is written in Europe only two weeks later. The satellite and the shell of the last rocket stage from which it was launched have already circled the earth over two hundred times. Before the launching only a small group of jurists were concerned by the lack of any international agreement as to the extent of national sovereignty in space above the surface of the earth and by the legal status of possible space flight instrumentalities. Today worldwide recognition of the gravity of these questions is more than apparent.

As the *New York Times* said in a leading article on October 13th:

> Is the earth satellite trespassing on the air-space of all nations? If the sky is the limit of national sovereignty, how high is it? Who pays if a United States satellite falls on Westminster Abbey?
>
> These are some of the questions that, until a week ago, were hypothetical. They are so no longer, for since then a 184-pound sphere has been circling the earth at 18,000 miles an hour.

Behind most of the present difficulties lie certain basic, but at times forgotten, legal principles:

a) The territory of a sovereign State is the area within which it has the right to make its law effective, to the exclusion of all other States.

b) As part of that right, the State has full control of transport in its territory, including the determination of what foreign transport instrumentalities may be permitted to enter.

c) Territory of a State is three dimensional, including the lands and territorial waters within its recognized surface boundaries, and the "airspace" above.

The prime difficulty is that no international agreement exists as to how far above the surface lies the upper boundary of this three-dimensional national territory. In other words, how far upwards is the "roof on sovereignty," and what is meant by "air-space."

Many nations, including the United States, but not the U.S.S.R., participated in drafting the Paris "International Convention for the Regulation of Aerial Navigation, 1919," which recognized that "every Power has complete and exclusive sovereignty over the air-space above its territory." For reasons not connected with air-space sovereignty, this convention was not ratified by the United States. However, in 1926, by the passage of the Air Commerce Act, the United States unilaterally asserted its exclusive sovereignty in the air-space over its surface territories. The U.S.S.R., in various statutes, going back to just after the Second World War, also declared superjacent air-space to be part of its territory.

The present Chicago Convention of 1944, to which the United States is a party, recognizes the existence of State sovereignty in superjacent air-space just as did the Paris Convention. This is not limited to member States of the Convention. It is a recognition of an existing principle of international law, binding and benefiting all States, under which the "air-space" is accepted as part of the territory of the State below. Under this principle, no State may use the air-space over another State without the consent of the latter. On this principle rests the ever-widening group of bilateral agreements through which international air transport now operates.

The U.S.S.R. is not a party to the Chicago Convention. But no State has asserted more forcefully its right to deny the entry of foreign aircraft into its "air-space."

Such was the situation when scientists of many nations, including the United States and the U.S.S.R., planned the present Geophysical Year to learn more about the earth and its surroundings. As part of this plan, the United States more than two years ago announced that it would launch one or more satellites designed to collect scientific data in upper space. No statement has ever been made, at least none has come to my attention, indicating that the United States Government asked formal permission of any other State to project the proposed satellites over such States. Shortly after the American announcement, the U.S.S.R. disclosed a similar program, again, so far as I am aware, without any formal inter-governmental exchange of flight permits.

On October fourth of this year, the U.S.S.R. program resulted in startling success. The world still awaits, at this writing, for the first American satellite. In addition press reports indicate that the Russian satellite is many times heavier than the carefully planned American "Vanguard." The U.S.S.R. has gained world-wide technical acclaim.

But what of the legal and political problems? Has international conduct already, as some appear to feel, begun to create new customary rules as to the extent upward of national sovereignty?

As I pointed out at the 1956 meeting of the American Society of International Law,[1] jurists had taken two different positions. It was insisted on the one hand that the United States by its satellite announcement, had in effect declared that space above the atmosphere was not part of the territory of any State, and could be used by any State, just as in the case of the high seas. It had been argued by others that the failure of any State to object to the proposed Geophysical Year Satellite program evidenced consent. Under this latter agreement, no position need be asserted as to the extent upwards of sovereignty, as a special case existed which would not mature into a general rule of customary law.

In this summer of 1957, prior to the satellite launching, the question of guided, or other intercontinental missiles, appears to have been brought before the United Nations disarmament subcommittee meeting in London. The minutes are not yet available. However, it is stated in a paper prepared by Mr. A. G. Haley, for delivery at the recent Barcelona meeting of the International Astronautical Federation, that in press briefings between certain delegates and reporters, statements were made as to a proposed technical committee to study design of an inspection system which would make it possible to assure that sending of objects through "outer space" should be exclusively for peaceful and scientific purposes. In the same briefing, it appears that the term "outer space" was used to refer to space at a distance beyond the earth at which "you no longer have friction of air to delay and retard the speed."

On October eleventh, one week after the satellite had been launched, twenty-one nations (including Canada, France, Britain and the United States according to the *London Times*) introduced into the General Assembly of the United Nations in New York a draft disarmament resolution which urged a disarmament agreement to include the study "of an inspection system designed to ensure that the sending of objects

---

[1] See LEGAL PROBLEMS OF UPPER SPACE, *supra* at 273–74.

through outer space will be exclusively for peaceful and scientific purposes." No definition of "outer space" seems to have been included, although it may have been mentioned in debate. It may, however, be assumed that it was used in the sense mentioned in the London press conference, namely areas where the gaseous air no longer interferes with free satellite flight.

The introduction of this most important resolution must support strongly the argument that its sponsors feel that national sovereignty does not exist in "outer space." If it did, the subjacent states could unilaterally prohibit foreign activity in areas above their territory, and would not be compelled to rely upon a multilateral inspection agreement as to the type of space flight instrumentalities to be permitted in "outer space." This resolution is today still pending, so far as I am advised, in the political committees of the United Nations. Whatever happens to it, however, cannot lessen its far-reaching importance as an admission by an imposing group of States that national sovereignty does not exist in those areas where a satellite, or, unfortunately, a war-like missile may be used free of atmospheric drag.

If this be the case, then we face nothing but accurate scientific data to fix the rules of Space Sovereignty, unless, and this is of paramount importance, the international community to protect its future may determine to extend national sovereignty by agreement into "outer space." At the 1956 meeting of the American Society of International Law, I suggested the need of a treaty to resolve then existing doubts, and as a purely tentative basis the following:

"Reaffirm Article I of the Chicago Convention, giving the subjacent state full sovereignty in the areas of atmospheric space above it, up to the height where aircraft as now defined, may be operated; such areas to be designated 'territorial space';

"Extend the sovereignty of the subjacent State upward to 300 miles above the Earth's surface, designating this second area as 'contiguous space' and provide for a right of transit through this zone for all non-military flight instrumentalities, when ascending or descending;

"Accept the principle that all space above 'Contiguous Space' is free for passage of all instrumentalities."

The suggestion of a "Contiguous zone" between the upper level of true "air-space" where "aircraft" may operate, and free space has been criticized, at times, I think, without considering the context. This zone depends for its depth on scientific data not yet available. When I suggested 300 miles, I was relying on what was then generally accepted scientific opinion to the effect that somewhere not far below 300 miles the atmosphere had sufficient density to prevent real satellite flight. It seemed to me in 1956, and still does, that the subjacent State properly has sovereignty in the atmospheric area where airplanes and balloons can operate. These depend for their lift on the existence of fairly dense gaseous air in the true air-space. It also seemed then, and still does, that the area in which sufficient gaseous air exists to prevent free satellite flight, might very well, by agreement, be deemed part of the "air-space."

The only difficulty is that the Russian satellite, "Sputnik," seems to refuse to follow the pre-suggested rules, at least as to usable altitude. When it was first launched it was stated, apparently from Soviet sources, that its altitude was about 585 miles above the Earth's surface —clearly in "outer space." Soon, however, the press began to report Moscow items to the effect that the area in which flight was progressing was much colder and much less dense than expected—in other words that heating and drag were less. Soon very careful observations in England indicated that the orbit of the satellite was an ellipse, and that at its nearest point it was less than 150 miles above the Earth's surface, and was still not losing altitude nor disintegrating. As I indicated in 1956, we must wait for accurate data from the Geophysical Year final calculations before deciding how far up the suggested "contiguous zone" should extend.

As to the need of a widely accepted treaty, recent events have made this more urgent than ever before. An international decision must be made as to what is meant by "outer space," if that now apparently official term must be used. The status of the atmosphere between the true "air-space" where "aircraft" may be used, and this "outer space" must be fixed. International misunderstanding must not be allowed to develop. For example, the *London Times* of October 18th refers to a very recent article by a Russian jurist proposing complete freedom in the region beyond 12 or 18 miles above the Earth's surface. This would certainly include areas where free satellite flight still seems impossible and may well include areas in which future improved types of aircraft might navigate if powered by rocket engines.

Such a treaty is also needed for an entirely different reason. When the great French jurist Fauchille drafted his first proposed code of the air in 1902, he insisted on "freedom of the air," contending that the air, or air-space, could not be part of national territory. He followed with the logical assertion that "aerostats," as he termed flight instrumentalities, must have nationality, otherwise chaos would result. This "nationality" to which he referred is the characteristic which centuries of international usage has attributed to a vessel carrying a national flag on the high seas. The State of the flag is responsible for the international good conduct of such vessels, though not for their private torts. Similarly, if "outer space" is to be free for the use of all, rules will certainly develop by custom or agreement to be followed by flight instrumentalities such as satellites or other space craft, and the State responsible for their launching must be answerable for their good conduct in following the rules. Such satellites and other space craft must, by treaty, have nationality. Even now we speak of the "Russian Satellite" as we would of a "Russian Vessel." Particularly is such "nationality" required when radio transmitters are carried, as in the case of "Sputnik." If frequencies and transmission methods are not the international responsibility of the launching State, radio interference amounting to telecommunications chaos will soon follow.

Space in this short memorandum does not permit any adequate discussion of methods of international control. Until the Russian Satellite was launched, I had hoped that such control could be lodged in the International Civil Aviation Organization, created under the Chicago Convention. That is no longer practical. The U.S.S.R. has taken the lead. ICAO had an opportunity in 1956 to express its views about upper space when it was on the agenda at the Caracas Assembly. It failed to do so. The U.S.S.R. is not a member of ICAO. Only the United Nations itself can now serve as a forum for further discussion. Recent press discussion indicates some possibility of an "outer space" United Nations trusteeship to enforce future agreed rules on space-craft good conduct. This might succeed. But whatever the ultimate answer, every day that passes with no attempt at real international discussion of the legal status of space beyond the air space and the legal status of the flight instrumentalities using such space only adds to the chances for fatal international confusion and perhaps conflict.

16
Fundamental Questions
of Outer Space Law

*An Address delivered at the
University of Leiden, 10 October
1960.*

Author's Note. In this lecture given at Leiden University, the author suggested, among other things, that in a convention fixing the lower boundary of free outer space, consideration be given to the lowest altitude above the earth's surface at which an artificial satellite may be put in orbit. He made the same suggestion at the Stockholm Colloquium on the law of outer space. This, however, was not intended to alter the earlier proposal that such a convention should also reaffirm absolute sovereignty of the subjacent State in air space where normal aircraft were operating, and extend such sovereignty, subject to a "right of transit," through contiguous space up to the lower boundary of free outer space as finally fixed.

INTRODUCTION

International peace and the future welfare of mankind demand that the Rule of Law shall be applicable with certainty in outer space. My friend and colleague Professor Dr. Goedhuis, in his 1960 report as Chairman of the International Law Association Sub-Committee on "Air Sovereignty and the Legal Status of Outer Space," directed attention to the statement made by the Netherlands Representative at the United Nations to the effect that in our dealing with outer space we certainly should not jettison all our ideas of law and of right and justice. With this I fully concur. In fact I am prepared to go further.

President Eisenhower a few weeks ago (September 22, 1960) made a notable address before the United Nations. He said:

> Another problem confronting us involves outer space. The emergence of this new world poses a vital issue: Will outer space be preserved for peaceful use and developed for the benefit of all mankind? Or will it become another focus for the arms race—and thus an area of dangerous and sterile competition? The choice is urgent. It is ours to make.
>
> The nations of the world have recently united in declaring the Continent of Antarctica "off limits" to military preparations. We could extend this principle to an even more important sphere. National vested interests have not yet been developed in space or in celestial bodies. Barriers to agreement are now lower than they will ever be again.
>
> The opportunity may be fleeting. Before many years have passed, the point of no return may be behind us . . . .
>
> We must not lose the chance we still have to control the future of outer space.

I propose that:

1. We agree that celestial bodies are not subject to national appropriation by any claims of sovereignty.

2. We agree that the nations of the world shall not engage in warlike activities on these bodies.

3. We agree, subject to appropriate verification, that no nation will put into orbit or station in outer space weapons of mass destruction. All launchings of space craft should be verified in advance by the United Nations.

4. We press forward with a programme of international co-operation for constructive peaceful uses of outer space under the United Nations. Better weather forecasting, improved world-wide communications, and more effective exploration not only of outer space but of our own earth—these are but a few of the benefits of such co-operation.

Agreement on these proposals would enable future generations to find peaceful and scientific progress, not another fearful dimension to the arms race, as they explore the universe.

In the background of this statement was the unanimous resolution of the General Assembly of the United Nations adopted December 12, 1959, entitled "International Co-operation in the Peaceful Uses of Outer Space." It declared that the General Assembly recognized the common interests of mankind as a whole in furthering the peaceful use of outer space and the belief "that the exploration and use of outer space should be only for the betterment of mankind and to the benefit of States irrespective of the stage of their economic or scientific development."

These stirring words of President Eisenhower and of the United Nations General Assembly emphasize the necessity of applying the Rule of Law in outer space. But if this is to be done, certain fundamental questions must be solved. Law, as a rule of human conduct, and international law, as a rule of the conduct of States, require clarity and certainty. If the Rule of Law is to be applied in outer space, then I submit, as I have on other occasions, that the area of outer space must be determined, that its legal status be agreed upon, that the rights of States in the area be universally acknowledged and that the legal status of flight instrumentalities to be used in outer space be also fixed. It is unfortunate, and may well be disastrous, that no international agreement now exists on any of these fundamental questions. Until this does exist the objectives stated by President Eisenhower and by the General Assembly of the United Nations cannot, in my view, be successfully reached.

1. WHAT IS MEANT BY THE TERM
"OUTER SPACE"

The United Nations, heads of States, diplomats, and jurists continue to use the term "Outer Space" as meaning a geographic area, but as yet without any agreed definition. The original United Nations Ad Hoc Committee on the Peaceful Uses of Outer Space, established under the resolution of December, 1958, in its report of 14 July, 1959, expressed the view that the question of determining where airspace ends and where outer space begins was not a question requiring priority of treatment and that any present international agreement on the subject would be premature. With this view I have always vigorously disagreed. I do not believe that the Rule of Law can be established with certainty as to outer space, a finite geographic area, unless the boundaries of that area are known and understood. The same United Nations report noted, however, that the upper boundary of the airspace and the lower boundary of outer space do not necessarily coincide. With this view I have long been in agreement.

The legal status of the airspace is well known and is now undisputed. The airspace over a State is subject to the exclusive sovereignty of that State, and, in my judgment, is part of its territory. Certainly that State has sole right to control all flight in the airspace above its lands and waters. However flight over stateless lands and over the high seas is, with certain exceptions, subject to no ulterior control. Admittedly no present agreement exists as to the upper boundary of the airspace. But few would dispute the view that the airspace extends upward from the surface of the earth through those areas where "aircraft" may be operated which depend solely on the gaseous air for aerodynamic lift to maintain flight. Possibly airspace may extend further upward to include all areas where the atmosphere is sufficiently dense to contribute in any degree to aerodynamic lift, or even higher to include all areas where the atmosphere is sufficiently dense to prevent a satellite's orbit around the earth. Of these questions time does not permit further discussion here. Certainly, however, the airspace and outer space do not overlap if the airspace is subject to the sovereignty of the State below while outer space is free for use by all.

It was with great pleasure that I learned of the recent action of the International Law Association 1960 Hamburg Conference in adopting a resolution on "Air Sovereignty and the Legal Status of Outer Space" which included a request to the Air Law Committee of the Association to continue its study of "the question of defining the lower limits of Outer Space."

May I state my personal views? Before Sputnik I was launched, I

289

suggested to the American Society of International Law, a new convention: first, reaffirming absolute sovereignty of the subjacent State up to the height at which "aircraft" could be operated; then further extending limited sovereignty upward to 300 miles above the earth's surface; then accepting the principle that all space above should be free for passage.

In 1957, a few weeks after Sputnik I was launched, I published a memorandum in which I pointed out that my 1956 suggestion was based on earlier and then widely accepted scientific opinion to the effect that somewhere not far below 300 miles the atmosphere had sufficient density to prevent free satellite flight, but that Sputnik I had proved this premise to be unsound. My primary view has always been that the airspace does not include any area in which a satellite may be put in orbit around the earth.

The most recent data generally available indicates that at least one or two satellites have been as close to the earth as 100 miles (160 kilometers), or a little less, at the perigee (lower limit) of orbit. A well known astronomer has stated that studies of meteors entering the earth's atmosphere show that the atmosphere below 70 miles approximately (112 kilometers) is too dense for a satellite to pursue an orbit. It would therefore appear that it may be possible for a satellite to be put in orbit at least once round the earth at some minimum altitude between 70 and 100 miles (112 and 160 kilometers) above us.

In this area of possible satellite flight the gases present bear little resemblance to the "air" which we breathe and in which normal types of aircraft may be flown. Distinguished scientists have expressed views which you may find of interest;

a) At the surface of the earth the "air" consists of about 78 percent molecular nitrogen, 20 percent molecular oxygen, and small quantities of argon, carbon dioxide, and water vapor.

b) At 50 miles (80 kilometers) altitude the temperature has dropped sharply, the atmospheric density is only about one-millionth (1/1,000,000) of the surface density, and not sufficient to contribute in any degree to the aerodynamic lift of flight instrumentalities.

c) At 100 miles (160 kilometers) or less, the temperature has increased up to 2,000° Fahrenheit or more, the atmospheric density has further decreased to one-billionth (1/1,000,000,000) of the surface density, the oxygen molecules have already broken down into separate oxygen atoms. This extremely thin gaseous combination of a few nitrogen molecules, oxygen atoms, and perhaps particles of other gases, has little if any resemblance to the substance, ordinarily called "air," which we breathe and which is needed to support the flight of "aircraft" as envisaged when the Paris and Chicago Conventions accepted the principle of "airspace" sovereignty.

If the lower boundary of outer space is fixed, by international agreement, as the lowest altitude above the earth's surface at which an artificial satellite may be put in orbit around the earth, we would then have more than a theoretical boundary. Below this boundary most objects moving from outer space towards the earth would be destroyed by heat from atmospheric friction. Above the boundary satellite flight would be practical. Also it might be added that biologists hold that at about 100 miles above the earth's surface human blood will boil.

Considering the entire physical situation as now known I would, therefoe, suggest, as I did in substance at the recent Third Colloquium On the Law of Outer Space held in Stockholm during the meeting of the XIth International Astronautical Congress, that, in any international convention dealing with flight into outer space, the following statement might be included: "Outer space, for the purposes of this convention, is defined as the area whose lower or inner boundary is the lowest altitude above the earth's surface at which an artificial satellite may be put in orbit at least once around the earth, and whose upper or outer boundary is the outer limit of our solar system." Flight beyond our solar system, if ever practical, will present new problems.

The wide acceptance of such an agreement would enable the Rule of Law to be applied without difficulty and with certainty in a reasonably definite geographic area. It should be noted that in fixing the suggested lower limit for outer space, no decision is required as to whether the absolute sovereignty of a subjacent state extends upward to this lower limit of outer space or whether, as I have previously urged, it would be well to admit the existence of an intervening area in which national rights of transit might be accepted, particularly for the purpose of launching artificial satellites over the lands and waters of adjacent states without violating the territory and sovereignty of the latter, and similarly of bringing back national space craft to national territory above the airspace of the adjacent state but below the limit of outer space. I submit the foregoing as worthy of practical consideration.

2. WHAT IS OR SHOULD BE THE LEGAL STATUS OF OUTER SPACE?

To me it is quite impossible to apply international legal principles in a satisfactory manner in any geographic area whose legal status is unknown. Today the legal status of outer space is as vague and uncertain as was the legal status of the high seas in the centuries before Grotius, in the Mare Liberum, focused attention on the need of the world to accept the doctrine of the freedom of the seas. Years after that historic event, a great American jurist, Mr. Justice Story, said in the case of *The Marianna Flora* (1826):

Upon the ocean, then, in time of peace, all possess an entire equality. It is the common highway of all, appropriated to the use of all; and no one can vindicate to himself a superior prerogative there. Every ship sails there with the unquestionable right of pursuing her own lawful business without interruption; but whatever may be that business, she is bound to pursue it in such a manner as not to violate the rights of others.

This statement I would urge as a sound solution of the legal status of outer space. But I fear that it can be made certain only by international agreement. I fully realize the arguments that have been made to the effect that the failure of States to protest present satellite flights indicates an acceptance of this status for outer space without further agreement. I also appreciate the force of the arguments which have been made that it is not possible logically to conceive of the extension of sovereignty into outer space. I have also studied with the greatest care and interest the 1959 report of the United Nations Committee on this subject, particularly the following:

9. During the International Geophysical Year 1957–1958 and subsequently, countries throughout the world proceeded on the premise of the permissibility of the launching and flight of the space vehicles which were launched, regardless of what territory they passed "over" during the course of their flight through outer space. The Committee, bearing in mind that its terms of reference refer exclusively to the peaceful uses of outer space, believes that with this practice, there may have been initiated the recognition or establishment of a generally accepted rule to the effect that, in principle, outer space is, on conditions of equality, freely available for exploration and use by all in accordance with existing or future international law or agreements.

But we must deal with hard facts. A well known American lawyer and air law lecturer Mr. Arnold W. Knauth, pointed out in an address in Beunos Aires on August 24, 1960, that only about 35 months had then passed since Sputnik I was launched, that since that time there had been, perhaps, less than 50 launchings of other satellites and perhaps 100 attempts, but that these launchings and attempts at launchings "are not adequate to formulate and create any customary law in space."

In a memorandum which I filed with the International Law Association for the Hamburg Conference I suggested: "No general rule of customary international law exists as to the subjacent State's rights to control all flight in areas above the air-space, nor whether on the contrary such areas should be treated as free for international flight as the high seas are for shipping, although strong arguments can be made that this should be future law."

It must never be forgotten that the Chicago Convention goes no further than declaring that each State has sovereignty in the airspace over its land and waters. Nowhere does that Convention, nor any other international agreement of which I am aware, state that claims of sovereignty of a State must be limited to its airspace. Jurists may urge doubts as to the right of States to claim sovereignty in areas beyond the airspace, but there is no international agreement to that effect nor am I aware of any formal and binding declaration of any State waiving any rights to claim sovereignty beyond the airspace, even to the far reaches of outer space.

This situation can be rectified only by a new international agreement. As I suggested in Stockholm, such a Convention might include a statement to the following effect, in addition to the statement as to boundaries: "The contracting States hereby declare that no State has or can have sovereignty over such area, namely outer space, or any part thereof, or any celestial bodies therein."

If the lower limit of outer space is fixed, as suggested, at the lower limit of the area in which a satellite may be put in orbit around the earth, and if States agree, as also suggested, that no State can have sovereignty over such areas or a part thereof or any celestial bodies therein, the Rule of Law may be made applicable in a reasonably definite area, whose legal status has been fixed. Two of the fundamental questions now undetermined will then no longer pose threats to world peace.

3. WHAT ARE THE INDEPENDENT RIGHTS OF SOVEREIGN STATES IN OUTER SPACE?

To me only one part of this question asserts a fundamental problem. Whether the legal status of outer space be left undetermined as at present or whether, as I hope, its legal status will be fixed as an area in which no State may claim sovereignty, the right of every State in the international community to act for its individual self-protection and self-defense must be acknowledged and preserved. Time will not permit me to discuss here more than a bare outline of how United States thinking, with which I am reasonably familiar, has historically dealt with this question, applicable in areas on the surface of the earth and in the airspace.

As early as 1804 Chief Justice Marshall of the United States Supreme Court, one of our greatest jurists, said (*Church* v. *Hubbart,* 2 Cranch 187): "The authority of a nation within its own territory is absolute and exclusive ... But its power to secure itself from injury may certainly be exercised beyond the limits of its territory." This statement still stands in our jurisprudence. It would be directly applicable to the right of a subjacent State to "secure itself from injury" in outer space beyond its territorial airspace.

In 1837, Daniel Webster, as Secretary of State of the United States, said during consideration of the celebrated *Caroline* case, that the necessity which justifies acts of self-defense outside national territory is "confined to cases in which the necessity of that self-defence is instant, overwhelming, and leaving no choice of means, and no moment for deliberation." This statement was cited with approval in the Nuremberg cases after World War II. However, I would point out that no emergency could leave less chance for deliberation than a threat from outer space.

Perhaps the most important analysis of the problem made in the United States is found in an address delivered in 1914 by the late Elihu Root speaking as President of the American Society of International Law. Mr. Root served as Secretary of State and also as United States Senator from New York. In discussing the "right of self-protection" as "a right recognized by international law" he said (8 AJIL-6): "The right is a necessary corollary of independent sovereignty. It is well understood that the exercise of the right of self-protection may and frequently does extend in its effect beyond the limits of the territorial jurisdiction of the State exercising it." Later, in the same address, in a much quoted phrase he insisted upon "the right of every sovereign State to protect itself by preventing a condition of affairs in which it will be too late to protect itself."

May I point out that this principle of the right of a State to act for its self-protection outside its national territory has already been applied in connection with aircraft flight. In 1950 the United States and Canada established air defence identification zones around parts of their respective shores. Admittedly the airspace over the high seas is not territorial space and enjoys the same international status as the high seas themselves. Yet the United States and Canada did not hesitate to establish regulations to prevent unidentified aircraft approaching their shores from the seas. The United States regulation, for example, requires that foreign aircraft must report their presence and identification when not less than one hour or more than two hours average cruising distance via the most direct route to the shore. This is a clear application of the right of self-preservation and self-defence applicable outside national territory and within international flight space. It would seem that the same right exists for subjacent States to act in outer space above national territorial airspace to the extent deemed necessary for the protection and defense of the lands below.

Certainly any future agreement for international regulation of outer space flight, or control of outer space, must preserve such national rights of self-protection and self-defence. It is submitted that nothing in the United Nations charter is opposed to this view. While Article 51 deals solely with the right of individual or collective self-defence "if an armed attack occurs against a member of the United Nations," it is my firm belief that this does not take away already existing international law rights of self-protection which have long been supported as part of the international law applicable to all States.

4. WHAT IS THE LEGAL STATUS OF SATELLITES AND FUTURE SPACE CRAFT?

In the law of the sea the legal status of the waters used and the vessels employed has long been settled. The high seas are free for the use of all. Territorial waters, bays, harbours, and rivers have certain varying national characteristics. Vessels employed are said to have the "nationality" of the State of the flag. Under the law of the air, as exemplified in the Chicago convention, the legal status of the airspace has been fixed, and it was agreed, as in the predecessor Paris convention of 1919, that aircraft should have nationality.

The meaning of this term "nationality," as applied to ships and to aircraft, is quite well known. It symbolizes the acceptance of a rule of international law which states that a special relationship exists between a particular State and the transport instrumentality which has the "nationality" of that State. The effect of this special relationship is that the State of the flag is responsible for the international good conduct of its vessels and its aircraft when in use beyond national territory. And reciprocally, that State has the right, as against other States, to see to it that its national vessels and aircraft are accorded the privileges and rights to which they are legally entitled when away from home. This is a rule of public law and not of private law. It does not make the State of the flag responsible for such things as debts incurred in the operation of the vessel or the aircraft, but it does make the State of the flag responsible if such vessel or aircraft violates a rule of international law affecting the rights of other States.

International law writers have often pointed out that on the high seas, uncontrolled by any national sovereignty, chaos would be the rule but for the fact that the principle of nationality of vessels has for centuries been accepted into maritime law, and that with this concept international order may be maintained. The State of the flag of each vessel is responsible for the latter's good conduct while passing over the high seas where no national territorial sovereignty exists.

It is interesting historically to note that the necessity of balloons having this quality of "nationality" was suggested in one of the earliest air law discussions. Fauchille's major thesis in 1902 and 1903 was that the air was free. But as a very able international lawyer, he accepted the fact that chaos might result if the instrumentalities in flight did not have the nationality of some particular State.

A few years later the problem was discussed at length at the 1910 Conference called by the French Government. While the Conference did not, for very different reasons, conclude a Convention to regulate flight no serious contention was ever made later against the application to aircraft of the maritime principle of "nationality." In fact this principle was widely recognized in the conduct of States between 1910 and the signature of the Paris Convention of 1919. For example, neutral States, such as very notably the Netherlands, enacted and enforced rules during World War I which outlawed the flight of foreign aircraft over Netherlands territory. At the close of the war, the nationality of aircraft was recognized in the Paris Convention, as it has been in every subsequent convention regulating air navigation, including the presently effective Chicago Convention of 1944. But the gravest doubt exists as to whether satellites and other flight instrumentalities, which can operate freely only in outer space, are "aircraft" within the present rules of international law dealing with required "nationality." If outer space is to be free for the use of all, the logic of Fauchille must again be applied. Every type of flight instrumentality usable in outer space must have the nationality of a State of the international community. Normally, this would be the launching State, which would thereby become responsible for the behaviour of the satellite, or other space craft, so far as rules of international law are concerned.

The complicated functions which satellites are already performing illustrates this need. If the Rule of Law is to be effective in outer space, international regulations must be recognized and enforced dealing, for example, with frequencies permitted to be used by radio equipment on a satellite. If it is admitted that a satellite has the "nationality" of the launching State, then such State can be held responsible without question if the satellite uses unauthorized frequencies and thereby creates jamming or other types of international radio interference. This is but one example. Also reciprocally, when future control of outer space flight internationally has become effective, as it must, each State will have the right to protest against the interference with the flight of its satellites or other space craft, provided they are following authorized and internationally agreed patterns.

In the absence of the application of the requirement of flight instrumentality nationality, chaos and conflict will be inevitable in outer space.

CONCLUSION

Four fundamental problems have been stated, and tentative answers suggested. First, that the boundaries of outer space must be fixed and that the important lower boundary should be at a point above the surface of the earth where it is possible to put a satellite in orbit at least once round the earth.

Second, that the legal status of outer space must be fixed and that this could best be done by accepting a status similar to that of the high seas, thus permitting its equal use by all and denying to any State the right to assert sovereignty over outer space or any celestial bodies therein.

Third, that the international law right of a State to take action for its self-protection and self-defence must be preserved and acknowledged so far as outer space is concerned, even though no state has a right to claim sovereignty therein.

Fourth, that the legal status of satellites and of other space craft used in outer space must be determined, and that this status should be that of "nationality" of the launching State, or other agreed State, otherwise chaos will result.

It is respectfully suggested that these four fundamental questions of outer space law stated demand urgent international settlement. It is also suggested that the solutions here put forward, when taken together, would provide a reasonable and practical foundation for the future application of the Rule of Law in outer space.

17

The Boundary Between Territorial Airspace and International Outer Space

An Address delivered at the International Symposium on Space Law, Federal Bar Association National Convention, Washington, D.C., 11 September 1964.

Author's Note. The thoughts expressed in this paper were motivated largely by the unanimous adoption of the 1963 United Nation's resolution asserting, among other things, that outer space is not subject to national claims of sovereignty. The resolution further strengthened the author's belief that an international convention is needed to fix the lower boundary of free outer space. However, this objective does not minimize the urgency for the United States to establish the upper statutory limit of its territorial air space. Below this boundary it would have the right to control all flight instrumentalities whether rockets, missiles, aircraft, spacecraft, or any combinations until an international convention finally fixes widely agreed limits.

T HE UNITED STATES should not delay longer in stating a definitive position as to the upper boundary of its territorial airspace. The unanimous adoption by the United Nations on December 13, 1963 of Resolution 1962 (XVIII) has created a new and urgent situation. It is understood that the United States assisted in drafting the resolution and the United Nations records clearly show vigorous American support. One of the major purposes of that resolution was to fix the legal status of the areas generally called "outer space" in which satellites and other spacecraft may operate with minimum interference from the earth's atmosphere. The effect of the resolution was to declare that such outer space is a highway which is and must remain open for the use of all nations, free of any claim or rights of sovereign control by any nation. The Declaration of Principles set out in the United Nations resolution contains the following statements:

> Outer space and celestial bodies are free for exploration and use by all States on a basis of equality and in accordance with international law.
> Outer space and celestial bodies are not subject to national appropriation by claim of sovereignty, by means of use or occupation, or by any other means.

The legal status of outer space as thus stated is in direct conflict with the accepted legal principles applicable to our national airspace.

The legal status of national airspace as part of our territory is not subject to question. The United States assisted in drafting the Paris Convention of 1919 with its much quoted statement in Article I that the parties to the convention "recognize that every Power has complete and exclusive sovereignty over the airspace above its territory." For

299

other reasons we did not ratify the Paris Convention, but in adopting the Air Commerce Act of 1926 a provision was carefully inserted in Section 6 to the effect "that the government of the United States has to the exclusion of all foreign nations, complete sovereignty of the airspace over the lands and waters above the United States."

This was the declaration to the effect that such airspace is part of our territory. The same principle was even more forcefully stated in Section 9 of the same act defining the term "United States":

> The term "United States", when used in a geographical sense, means the territory comprising the several States, Territories, possessions, and the District of Columbia (including the territorial waters thereof) and the overlying airspace; but shall not include the Canal Zone.

Substantially the same definition was carried forward into Section 1 (31) of the Civil Aeronautics Act of 1938 (omitting the reference to the Canal Zone) and has since been repeated in subsequent statutes. The United States has thus firmly declared that the airspace over its lands and waters is part of its national territory.

As a result the United States has the same right to complete unilateral control of all foreign movement within its airspace as it has in other parts of its territory. The only recognized exception to this right of absolute control is that which is enjoyed by foreign merchant ships in time of peace passing through the territorial waters of the United States. But even this limited right has never been accorded to foreign aircraft flying in the airspace over our territorial waters.

While it is true that the 1963 United Nations resolution quoted above has not yet been incorporated into our statutes nor into a duly ratified treaty, nevertheless it would be most difficult for the United States hereafter to claim any rights of territorial control in "outer space."

Admittedly there is as yet no general agreement as to the lower boundary of outer space but this does not obviate the necessity for the United States to fix its own upper boundary of its national airspace territory.

It has been said that there is no general agreement as to the outer boundary of territorial waters and this fact has been used as an argument to support delay in reaching agreement as to the boundary between the airspace and outer space. The argument is unsound so far as it applies to our national action. It overlooks the fact that every State which has maritime boundaries has formally asserted a fixed outer boundary for its territorial waters so that no other State can question its position. The high seas are an international highway open to all. A ship leaving a United States port passes through part of our territory which we call territorial waters and thence into the high seas which is not part of our territory. Since the early years of our history, we have repeatedly asserted that there is a definitive boundary out to which the United States has territorial control of all foreign movement. In these territorial waters we are sovereign. In the high seas we are not. Similarly in national airspace over our lands and waters we are sovereign, but with the passage of the United Nations 1963 resolution we have joined other States in asserting that there can be no claim of sovereignty in outer space.

To prevent international misunderstanding we have always asserted the right to fix an outer boundary for our territorial waters. Exactly the same situation now exists as to flight. We have the right to control all flight in our territorial airspace. We have in substance surrendered that right, if it ever existed, in the area termed "outer space." But where lies the boundary between these areas? Can any logical reason be brought forward as to why the United States must not promptly assert its upper airspace boundary so as to give notice to the world of the area above its lands and waters in which it reserves the right to control all flight?

The time is not far distant, and in fact may be with us today, when the right of foreign spacecraft to pass through our territorial airspace will require an immediate and vigorous answer. Are foreign spacecraft, military or civil, to be permitted to fly within twenty-five miles above our lands and waters, or fifty miles, or one hundred miles? A decision must be made.

This decision is necessarily political. It involves consideration of matters of great importance both civil and military. The accepted boundary should have reasonable scientific background. For example, twenty-five miles above sea level is perhaps the maximum height for the practical use of aircraft requiring aerodynamic support to sustain flight and using air-breathing motive power. Fifty miles above sea level is perhaps the maximum height at which the atmosphere is sufficiently dense to provide any appreciable aerodynamic lift. A point somewhere between seventy-five miles and ninety miles is perhaps the lowest point of practical orbital unpowered flight around the earth.

The most urgent reason for an early decision is the problem of the flight of spacecraft through the airspace when ascending or descending. Careful examination of the known records of past successful flights into or from outer space indicate that no such flights have ever been recorded at an altitude below seventy-five miles above a foreign State. Perhaps ninety-miles might be an even more correct figure. But this will not continue. Problems of launching and landing are becoming more complex.

Until now flights have passed only through the airspace of the State of launching or the airspace over the high seas when ascending toward or descending from outer space. The airspace over the high seas is as free for flight use as are the high seas themselves for shipping. The spacecraft launched into orbit from Cape Kennedy (formerly Cape Canaveral) have ascended through airspace over the United States lands and territorial waters and thence over the high seas into outer space. When descending, our manned orbital flights have started the descent in outer space over the Pacific Ocean and have thence proceeded downward through the airspace over the United States and finally through the airspace over the Atlantic Ocean to a landing at sea. No foreign airspace has been used. It is understood that Russian spacecraft when being put into orbit or brought back for landing have passed solely through Russian airspace before entering the outer space and before landing at the end of orbital flight. The enormous Russian national landmass permits this procedure.

But, as orbital flights become more frequent and diverse, it is certain that we will face the very practical question of whether or not foreign spacecraft should be permitted to use our territorial airspace for ascent and descent, and we will certainly wish to know whether we have similar privileges in the airspace of other States.

The adoption of the United Nations resolution discussed earlier did not directly or indirectly grant any privileges of passage to foreign spacecraft through the national airspace of any State. In the case of the United States, national airspace has by statute been made a part of the territory of the United States, carrying with it our right to determine unilaterally what flight instrumentalities may enter or otherwise use such airspace. No resolution of the United Nations could alter our law so as to grant rights of passage. Historically the United States has permitted foreign aircraft to enter and use United States airspace only when and to the extent that such use has been authorized by treaty or other international agreement to which the United States is a party, or at times by special permission or authority. No general rights of passage for foreign aircraft exist in the United States airspace even though we accept the rule of international law that the airspace over the high seas is free. In other words, an aircraft approaching our shores and intending to land here cannot proceed past the outer boundary of the airspace above our territorial waters unless it has specific authority so to do. Obviously the same rule is applicable legally to the use of United States airspace by any foreign spacecraft.

But it must be noted that academic suggestions have been made that the United Nations resolutions as to the freedom of use of outer space have carried with them a consequential privilege of passage by spacecraft through foreign airspace in order to enjoy the rights of use of outer space. To some this theory may be politically attractive, but it is certainly legally unsound. The United States, for its part, should without delay fix a definite statutory upper boundary of its national airspace. When this is done, existing law will without question require the operator of any foreign spacecraft to seek authority to use our airspace if such use is found necessary in connection with the free international use of outer space.

When the upper limit of our national airspace has been fixed and our unconditional sovereignty thus reasserted, the United States will be in a position to deal reciprocally either by general convention, or through bilateral arrangements, so that the United States will enjoy for its spacecraft the same privileges extended to the spacecraft of other States who are parties to such arrangement.

Ultimately a broad international convention will certainly be arrived at fixing the height of national airspace and determining what rights of passage, if any, will be permitted. In a convention of this kind the United States might alter its own upper national airspace boundary if then deemed useful, and could also determine what rights of passage, if any, foreign spacecraft would reciprocally enjoy.

Certainly the unilateral right of each State to control all flight in its national airspace can be modified only by direct national act, or international agreement, and not by inference or interpretation based on any theoretical effect of any agreement for the use of outer space. The legal status of territorial airspace and international outer space is diametrically opposed. May I say that I have long recognized the need to determine by international agreement any rights of airspace passage for spacecraft. In the convention which I proposed in 1956 to the American Society of International Law, this problem was considered. I suggested that a new convention might include the following as then stated:

a) Reaffirm Article I of the Chicago Convention, giving the subjacent State full sovereignty in the areas of atmospheric space above it, up to the height where "aircraft" as now defined, may be operated, such areas to be designated "territorial space."

b) Extend the sovereignty of the subjacent State upward to 300 miles above the earth's surface, designating this second area as "contiguous space," and provide for a right of transit through this zone for all non-military flight instrumentalities when ascending or descending.

c) Accept the principle that all space above "contiguous space" is free for the passage of all instrumentalities.

As I have often explained, my 1956 suggestion of 300 miles in paragraph (*b*) above was based on erroneous scientific views existing before Sputnik that atmospheric conditions below a 300 mile altitude would make free satellite orbital flights difficult, if not impossible.

Subsequent developments have indicated that this scientific position was not correct and that satellite flight is practical at much lower altitudes. It will be noted, however, that I carefully recommended rights of transit through the extended sovereignty zone for non-military flight instrumentalities when ascending or descending. So far as I recall, this is the first time that the problem was considered.

Considering present conditions, scientific, political and legal, the type of international convention which I proposed in 1956 might be very practical if the upper boundary of "territorial space" were now fixed at twenty-five miles above sealevel and the upper limit of "contiguous space" were fixed at seventy-five miles, or in the alternative, at such other figure as might be scientifically determined to be the lowest limit of practical free orbital flight. The principle that all space above what I called "contiguous space" should be free for the passage of all flight instrumentalities has now been accepted by the United Nations resolutions with the strong support of the United States. The principle that the United States has full and absolute sovereignty in its "airspace" is still part of our law.

A convention of this kind is desirable as an early goal. But this objective does not minimize the urgency of present definitive action by the United States fixing the upper limit of its territorial airspace, thus notifying the world of its assertion of unilateral sovereign control of the usable areas below this national boundary. This control is applicable to all flight instrumentalities, whether they be rockets, missiles, aircraft, spacecraft, or any combination of these basic types.

18
Legal Problems of Spacecraft in Airspace

Reprinted by permission of Verlag
C. F. Müller, Karlsruhe, Germany,
from Festschrift für Otto Riese,
Karlsruhe, 1964, p. 465.
© *Verlag C. F. Müller.*

Author's Note. This article was included in a volume of essays by various authors, compiled in honor of Dr. Otto Riese. The author had the pleasure of first meeting Dr. Riese when the latter was a member of the German delegation and this author was Chairman of the United States delegation at the Diplomatic Conference in Rome in 1933 when the "Rome Convention" was drafted and signed. It can only be regretted that so much of Dr. Riese's distinguished career in many legal and political fields has precluded his wider contributions to the recent expanding legal problems of flight. His air-law writings will always be consulted by thoughtful students.

THE PASSAGE OF spacecraft through the airspace, when ascending toward or descending from outer space, has created new legal problems. The most urgent are: (1) what rights of passage has a spacecraft through the airspace, and (2) what liability flows from a collision between such spacecraft and an aircraft. A corollary to each of these problems is the still unanswered question of the altitude above the earth's surface of the upper airspace boundary.

I. LEGAL STATUS OF THE AIRSPACE

Spacecraft must normally pass through the airspace to reach outer space, and return the same way. The airspace used may be above the national lands and waters of the launching State, or above its territorial waters, or above the lands and waters of another State, or stateless territory or the high seas. To determine the rights of passage of a spacecraft it is necessary to re-examine briefly the legal status of each of these airspace areas.

1. AIRSPACE ABOVE THE NATIONAL LANDS

No one now challenges the rule that the territory of a State is three dimensional, and that the airspace above the lands and internal waters of every sovereign State is part of the territory of that State. In such airspace it has had, by long standing international law, customary and conventional, the sole right to control all flight. It may use such airspace as it deems best and may permit or deny the entry of any foreign flight instrumentality. Even before World War I. the principle of sovereignty in then usable space over national lands and waters had been accepted as a customary rule. Events during World War I and the preparation and signature of the Paris Convention of 1919 merely acknowledged and restated this rule.[1]

The rule was restated in such national statutes as the United States Air Commerce Act of 1926, and the Air Code of the U.S.S.R. of 1935, also in Article 1 of the Chicago Convention of 1944. As indicated to the 47th Meeting of the International Law Association held in 1956, my recollection as a former chairman of one of the drafting committees at the Chicago Conference is very clear that no other principle was then proposed and that no general right of innocent passage for foreign aircraft through national airspace was even suggested. The limited freedom of passage found in Article 5 of the Chicago Convention is nothing more than a privilege accorded to the aircraft of Contracting States and not to others.

The belt of the sea adjacent to the coast of a State, usually referred to as territorial waters or territorial sea or marginal sea, and the airspace above, also are parts of the territory of the adjacent State. It has long been accepted international law that the State has the same power to control flight in the airspace above its territorial waters as it has in the airspace above its national lands. The right of innocent passage through territorial waters, accorded by international law to surface shipping, has never been accepted as a rule applicable to flight through the airspace above such waters. Both the Paris and Chicago Conventions, in recognizing the complete and exclusive sovereignty of a State in the airspace above its territory, have defined such territory as including territorial waters. The recent "Convention on the Territorial Sea," signed at Geneva in 1958, provides in Article 1 that the sovereignty of a State extends beyond its land territory and its internal waters to a belt of sea adjacent to its coast, described as the "territorial sea." Article 2 states that "the sovereignty of a coastal State extends to the airspace over the territorial sea. . . ."

2. AIRSPACE OVER THE HIGH SEAS

The legal status of the airspace over the high seas is in all respects similar to that of the seas below. Neither the Paris nor Chicago Conventions specifically state this customary rule of freedom of flight over the high seas. But its existence has never been challenged. In fact, the report of the sub-committee which drafted the Paris Convention of 1919, in discussing the acceptance of the principle of full and exclusive airspace sovereignty over national territory, said: "It is only when the column of air rests upon a *res nullius* or *communis*, the sea, that free-

---

[1] For discussion of the development of the rule of state sovereignty, see STATE SOVEREIGNTY IN SPACE: DEVELOPMENTS 1910–1914, Chapter 7, *supra.*

dom becomes the rule of the air. Thus the air space shares the jurisdiction of the underlying territory. Is this territory that of an individual State? If so, the airspace is subject to the sovereignty of this State. Is it, like the high sea, free of sovereignty? Then the airspace is as free as the sea itself. It follows that in consequence of its sovereignty the underlying State within the limits of its frontiers may forbid flight over and, *a fortiori*, landing upon its territory."

When the Chicago Convention was being drafted, the principle that no single State had a right to control flight through the airspace over the high seas was fully understood and accepted. As a result, the Chicago Convention provides in substance in article 12 that the rules and regulations relating to the flight and maneuver of aircraft over the high seas shall be those established under the convention. In other words, the parties to the convention as sovereign States, having each the right to regulate the flight of its own aircraft over the high seas, have together delegated that right to the International Civil Aviation Organization created by the Convention. While technically this delegation applies only to the flight of "aircraft" and not to the flight of other instrumentalities, nevertheless the fact of such delegation is clear proof that no part of the airspace over the high seas is subject to the sovereignty of any single State.

This position was further confirmed in the 1958 Geneva "Convention on the High Seas." The preamble to the Convention states that its provisions were adopted "as generally declaratory of established principles of international law." Article 1 then defines the high seas as "all parts of the sea that are not included in the territorial sea or in the internal waters of a State." Article 2 provides that "the High Seas being open to all nations, no State may validly purport to subject any part of them to a sovereignty." The freedom of the high seas is stated to comprise, *inter alia*, freedom to fly over the high seas. It is interesting to note that this freedom to fly over the high seas is nowhere limited in the Convention to flight through the airspace over the high seas or to the flight of "aircraft." This Convention is now in force between many States.

All available evidence therefore now supports the existence of an accepted rule of international law to the effect that flight above the high seas and other stateless territory is not subject to the sovereign permanent control of any single State.

It is thus apparent that any State may launch its spacecraft through its own airspace, or over the high seas and stateless lands, without seeking the consent of any other State. It may follow a similar pattern in bringing the spacecraft back to the surface of the earth. But it is equally clear that no State may use the territorial airspace over another State for passage of its spacecraft without the consent of the latter unless the accepted rule of absolute national airspace sovereignty has been modified for the specific benefit of the passage of spacecraft. It has been suggested that the adoption by the General Assembly of the United Nations of Resolution 1721A of December 1961 may have created such an exception. But, in my judgment, this is not correct.

3. UNITED NATIONS RESOLUTION 1721A OF DECEMBER 1961

The operative parts of the Resolution 1721A are as follows:

1. Commends to States for their guidance in the exploration and use of outer space the following principles:

a) International law, including the United Nations Charter, applies to outer space and celestial bodies;

b) Outer space and celestial bodies are free for exploration and use by all States in conformity with international law, and are not subject to national appropriation.

2. Invites the Committee on the Peaceful Uses of Outer Space to study and report on the legal problems which may arise from the exploration and use of outer space.

Certainly this resolution has not changed any customary or conventional or national law as to the use of the airspace. In practice, all flight through the airspace of one State by another State has always required the specific consent of the State whose airspace is being used. To imply that the United Nations Resolution, even though unanimously adopted, indirectly evidences such consent for the benefit of spacecraft ascending toward or descending from outer space would mean that the resolution had the legislative effect of modifying the statute laws of many states, the specific provisions of Article 1 of the Chicago Convention, and many bi-lateral international agreements.

But the United Nations Resolution cannot logically be construed to have this force. The United Nations is not a legislative body. Its resolutions, even when unanimously adopted, do not thereby automatically modify the statutes of an individual State which is a member of the United Nations, nor set aside the formal provisions of treaties and other international agreements to which member States may be parties.

In addition, an examination of the resolution, and the debates which preceded its adoption, indicates that no modification of existing law as to the airspace was ever recommended. It should be noted that the resolution says nothing except that member States are commended to accept certain principles in the exploration and use of outer space,

309

particularly that outer space is free for exploration and use by all states and is not subject to national appropriation. The resolution goes no further.

II. RIGHT OF EACH STATE TO DENY PASSAGE THROUGH ITS AIRSPACE

International law has never accepted the view that the right of passage through one part of a transport medium automatically carries with it the right of passage through other parts of the same medium. For example, even though the right of all States to use the airspace over the high seas is universally accepted, the right of each State to deny entry into its airspace of foreign aircraft approaching its shores has been equally accepted and enforced. It might have been advantageous in the development of world air transport if there had been an acceptance of the doctrinaire theory of free right of passage for all aircraft through the national airspace of every State. But this is not and never has been the law. Similarly it cannot be said that the United Nations resolution urging free use of outer space carries with it by inference a legal right for any State to propel its spacecraft through the national airspace of every other State merely to ascend into or descend from free outer space even though such passage might be deemed desirable. But no State has thus far surrendered its right to insist on prior consent for the passage of spacecraft just as it may insist on prior consent for the passage of any other flight instrumentality.

1. THE HEIGHT OF THE UPPER BOUNDARY OF NATIONAL AIRSPACE

The present and future importance of this right of each State to deny passage through its airspace for spacecraft launched by other States is best illustrated by a factual analysis of how and when the airspace has been used in the actual launching and descent of the manned space capsules in the United States program known as "Project Mercury." These capsules were launched by rockets rising from United States lands near the Atlantic Ocean coastline, then passing through United States airspace over its lands and territorial waters, and then sent into outer space above the high seas. After orbiting the earth, the descent began over the Pacific Ocean, then continued over the United States, finally ended on the Atlantic Ocean. The airspace used was only that over United States territory and over the high seas. No flight over foreign territory occurred below orbital altitudes.

At a meeting of the Section of International and Comparative Law of the American Bar Association held in San Francisco on 4 August 1962, Mr. *John A. Johnson,* then General Counsel of the National Aeronautics & Space Administration, gave some interesting figures as to the launching, orbit and subsequent re-entry of the manned spacecraft used in "Project Mercury." He said:

> When the astronaut reaches an altitude of 10 miles after launching, he is also about 10 miles, horizontally measured, from the launching site. At an altitude of 25 miles, the horizontal distance is about 25 miles; at an altitude of 50 miles, it is still only 70 miles; and when the astronaut goes into orbit at an altitude of approximately 100 miles, he is about 575 miles from the launching site."

At the time of firing the retro-rockets which initiate re-entry, the astronaut is at an altitude of about 100 miles, approximately 2,600 miles from the intended point of landing. In the first 2,000 miles after retro-fire, the astronaut comes down to an altitude of about 50 miles. While descending to an altitude of 25 miles, he moves another 550 miles horizontally, bringing him only 50 miles from his destination. Thereafter he descends very rapidly; and by the time he comes down to an altitude of 10 miles, he is over the landing site and making a vertical descent.

These figures demonstrate very clearly that the height of the upper boundary of national airspace is a limiting factor in the future development of orbital flight. Unless this boundary is fairly close to the earth's surface, few States will be able to put a satellite into orbit from national territory, and later return it, without passing through the national airspace of other States. In other words, few States will be free of a political veto by other States in planning orbital flights.

The future may aggravate the problem. In order to bring larger spacecraft back to the earth a glide may be necessary of 7,000 to 10,000 miles at altitudes of 60 to 25 miles.[2]

2. AN INTERNATIONAL CONVENTION AS A SOLUTION
TO THE PROBLEMS

It has long been my considered judgment that the only sound solution of these legal-political problems must be found in a new international convention fixing the height of the upper boundary of national territorial airspace. 40 kms. (25 miles) is probably the maximum height to which normal types of aircraft may be flown. 80 kms. (50 miles) is approximately the upper limit of any aerodynamic lift. 120

---

[2] See also: John A. Johnson, "The Developing Law of Space Activities," *Virginia Journal of International Law,* Vol. III, No. 2, p. 75.

kms. (75 miles) is approximately the lowest practical altitude of free orbital flight. If future international agreement fixes the upper airspace boundary at 40 kms. (25 miles) above the earth's surface, most States will be able to put a satellite into orbit and return it later with little, if any, need to use the territorial airspace of other States. But if a higher figure is accepted, the international convention should include provisions setting out the conditions under which spacecraft of one State might pass through the territorial airspace of another State when ascending toward or descending from outer space beyond.

The "Declaration of Legal Principles Governing the Activities of States in the Exploration and Use of Outer Space" unanimously approved Resolution 1962 (XVIII) on 13 December 1963 by the General Assembly of the United Nations, has not, in my judgment, altered the situation in any manner. The Declaration, in its operative parts solemnly declares that in the exploration and use of outer space States should be guided by the following principles:

1. The exploration and use of outer space shall be carried on for the benefit and in the interests of all mankind.

2. Outer space and celestial bodies are free for exploration and use by all States on a basis of equality and in accordance with international law.

3. Outer space and celestial bodies are not subject to national appropriation by claim of sovereignty, by means of use or occupation, or by any other means.

4. The activities of States in the exploration and use of outer space shall be carried on in accordance with international law including the Charter of the United Nations, in the interest of maintaining international peace and security and promoting international co-operation and understanding.

During the discussions which preceded the unanimous adoption of this Declaration in the General Assembly of the United Nations, representatives of the United States, the Soviet Union, the United Kingdom, and others, stated that their respective nations would comply with the Declaration. Its effect is therefore to indicate that in practice freedom of navigation in outer space is accepted as a rule of customary international law. But nowhere was any indication given that the rule of national and exclusive airspace sovereignty had been waived or modified.

III. LIABILITY IN CASE OF COLLISION

The second major problem arising from the flight of spacecraft through the airspace, as indicated at the opening of this paper, concerns the rule of liability which should be applied in case of a collision between a spacecraft and an aircraft when both are using the airspace. This question was raised in the legal section of the 1959 report of the United Nations Ad Hoc Committee on the Peaceful Uses of Outer Space. It was discussed at the Third Colloquium On the Law of Outer Space, held at Stockholm in August 1960, during the XIth International Astronautical Congress. During that discussion I suggested that the principles in the Rome Convention on damage caused by aircraft to third parties on the surface might well be applied to damage caused by spacecraft to aircraft. Several years of additional study have only strengthened this view and I wish therefore to repeat now what I said in Stockholm:[3]

> The Rome Convention provides for compensation without proof other than that the damage was caused by an aircraft in flight or persons or things falling therefrom. In other words, no proof of fault is required. While the Rome Convention applies solely to surface damage, it is suggested that the same rule should apply as to damage caused by a space vehicle to aircraft, and to persons or goods thereon, engaged in flight in the airspace. Such aircraft will have no better opportunity to avoid a space vehicle falling or passing through airspace, or something falling therefrom, than would a person on the surface be able to avoid a falling aircraft. The practical difference in speeds between the space vehicle and the aircraft must be controlling as to the rule of liability.

This problem as to the rule of liability for damage caused by spacecraft was one of the subjects considered by the Legal Sub-Committee of the United Nations Committee on Peaceful Uses of Outer Space. The United States introduced a "Draft Proposal on Liability for Space Vehicle Accidents".[4] In this draft proposal the following principles were urged for adoption:

> a) States or international organizations responsible for the launching of space vehicles should be liable internationally for personal injury, loss of life or property damage caused thereby, whether such injury, loss or damage occurs on land, on the sea or in the air;
> b) A claim based on personal injury, loss of life or property damage caused by a space vehicle should not require proof of fault on the

---

[3] See Cooper, "Memorandum of Suggestions for an International Convention on Third Party Damage Caused by Space Vehicles," *Proceedings Third Colloquium on The Law of Outer Space* (Stockholm, 1960), pp. 141–144. See also discussion, *ibid.*, pp. 133–136.

[4] See "Report of the Legal Sub-Committee on the Work of its Second Session (16 April–3 May 1963) to the Committee on the Peaceful Uses of Outer Space," United Nations document A/AC. 105/12, 6 May 1963, p. 5.

part of the State or States or international organization responsible for launching the space vehicle in question, although the degree of care which ought reasonably to have been exercised by the person or entity on whose behalf claim is made might properly be taken into account;

c) A claim may be presented internationally to the State or States or international organization responsible for the launching of a space vehicle causing injury, loss or damage without regard to the prior exhaustion of any local remedies that may be available.

It should be noted that this United States proposal follows the general trend of the discussions at the Stockholm Space Law Colloquium referred to above, that is to say, the United States proposal urged a rule of absolute liability for damage caused by spacecraft on land and on the sea and in the air. But the United States proposal said nothing as to the rule of liability for collisions between two spacecraft in outer space, nor was it clear as to the rule which should be applicable in case of a spacecraft collision in the airspace. It seems obvious that in those cases some rule of comparative negligence should apply as absolute liability would be impractical in the relations between two colliding spacecraft.

When the United Nations adopted the 1963 Declaration referred to earlier in this paper, the United States proposal was followed only in part. Agreement was reached on a much more general provision. In paragraph 8, the Declaration now states:

8. Each State which launches or procures the launching of an object into outer space, and each State from whose territory or facility an object is launched, is internationally liable for damage to a foreign State or to its natural or juridical persons by such object or its component parts on the earth, in air space, or in outer space.

It will be seen that the Declaration provides for liability resulting from damage caused by spacecraft while in the airspace, but does not determine whether the rule of fault liability or of absolute liability should be applied. This must be worked out in the convention still to be drafted. Resolution 1963 (XVIII) unanimously adopted by the Assembly after the acceptance of the Declaration requested the Committee on the Peaceful Uses of Outer Space to continue to study and report on legal problems which may arise in the exploration and use of outer space, "and in particular to arrange for the prompt preparation of draft international agreements on liability for damage caused by objects launched into outer space and on assistance to and return of astronauts and space vehicles." The Committee was also requested to report on these proposed agreements at the 1964 General Assembly.

It will be noted that the Declaration does not state the rule of liability to be adopted.

In summary, it may be said that the spacecraft of one State may not pass through the airspace of another State except with the consent of the latter; that such national airspace includes the airspace over territorial seas; that flight in the airspace over the high seas is free to the spacecraft of all States; that an international agreement should be reached fixing the upper limit of the territorial airspace of any State; that the Committee of the United Nations on the Peaceful Uses of Outer Space has been charged by the General Assembly with the task of drafting an international convention to cover the liability of spacecraft for damage caused in the airspace, as well as in outer space and on the surface of the earth, and that this draft convention will probably be submitted to the General Assembly of the United Nations at its next meeting to be held in 1964. No decision has been made as to what the rule of liability should be for damage caused by spacecraft while passing through the airspace.

19

Contiguous Zones in Aerospace—Preventive and Protective Jurisdiction

Reprinted by permission of Air Force JAG Law Review *from 7* Air Force JAG Law Review *15 (September–October 1965).* Views and opinions expressed in this article are those of the author, and they are not necessarily concurred in by The Judge Advocate General of the Air Force.
© Air Force JAG Law Review 1965.

Author's Note .This paper, prepared at the suggestion of the Office of the Judge Advocate General of the U.S. Air Force, expresses the author's personal opinion as a jurist. The paper reviews certain earlier expressed opinions. It also seeks to emphasize again the difficulties which exist because of the absence of any United States' decision, statutory, conventional, or otherwise, as to "the exact extent upward of the area in which our complete, preventive and protective jurisdiction is applicable."

THE TERM *aerospace* has been thus defined: The earth's envelope of air and the space above it, the two considered as a single realm for activity in the flight of air vehicles and in the launching, guidance, and control of ballistic missiles, earth satellites, dirigible space vehicles, and the like.[1]

But the difficulty with this definition is that it has led to an assumption that all aerospace has a single uniform legal status. Nothing could be further from the facts. Present international understanding now accepts the existence of at least two entirely different zones in the aerospace above a sovereign State, namely *airspace* and *outer space*. Perhaps there is a third zone lying between these two which has some of the characteristics of both.

The airspace zone, next to the earth, is characterized by the presence of *atmosphere*. In fact the original French text of the Paris Convention of 1919 Relating to the Regulation of Aerial Navigation uses the term *l'espace atmospherique*, while the corresponding English language text uses the term *airspace*.

The legal status of the airspace zone is simple. It is as much a part of the territory of the State below as are the national lands and waters of such State. This territorial status was widely accepted before World War I, was confirmed by the acts of neutrals and belligerents during that war, and was restated as an already existing rule of international law in article I of the Paris Convention of 1919 referred to above. There the parties recognize "that every Power has complete and exclusive sovereignty over the airspace above its territory." It should be particularly noted that this declaration asserted the territorial status of the airspace zone above every sovereign State and did not refer to contracting States alone. In saying that each State has "complete and exclusive sovereignty" the Convention in substance said that the

---

[1] Aerospace Glossary—Research Studies Institute, Air University, Maxwell Air Force Base, September, 1959.

airspace zone was part of national territory. The existence of exclusive sovereignty as to any geographic area is the basis for and the equivalent of territoriality.

The United States assisted in drafting the Paris Convention, and signed it but did not ratify. However, in Section 6 of the Air Commerce Act of 1926, we asserted that the United States has to the exclusion of all foreign nations complete sovereignty of the airspace over the lands and waters above the United States. The same statute in Section 9 defined the term *United States* and included *the overlying airspace.* Also Article 1 of the Chicago Convention of 1944, to which the United States is a party, again asserted the principle of Article 1 of the Paris Convention. Articles 3 (*c*), 5 and 6 of the Chicago Convention emphasize the territoriality of national airspace by providing the terms under which state and civil *aircraft* of other contracting states may use such airspace.

The fact that the Paris and Chicago Conventions deal primarily with *aircraft* has led to the suggestion that the preventive and protective jurisdiction of a subjacent State applies only to the flight of such aircraft in its territorial airspace zone and not to other flight instrumentalities. This is an unsound position, particularly so far as the statutory position of the United States is concerned. The same Air Commerce Act of 1926 which asserted our airspace sovereignty defined *aircraft* so as to include all flight instrumentalities used for flight in the air. The full definition as then adopted is as follows:

Aircraft means any contrivance now known or hereafter invented, used or designed for navigation of or flight in the air.

This definition was re-enacted in Section 1, paragraph (4) of the Civil Aeronautics Act of 1938. Later, at the Chicago Conference of 1944, the United States submitted a *United States Draft of Annex on Aircraft Registration and Identification Marks.* This draft included a proposed definition of aircraft exactly as it appeared in the United States statutes quoted above.

However, the subcommittee which was considering the matter at Chicago prepared a tentative draft of an annex to the convention to cover registration *etc.*, and there defined aircraft as follows:

Aircraft shall comprise all apparatus or contrivances which can derive support in the atmosphere from reactions of the air.[2]

The Chicago Conference did not formulate the final texts of the several annexes to the Convention. These were later adopted by the

---

[2] "Proceedings of International Civil Aviation Conference, Chicago, Illinois, November 1–December 7, 1944, Vol. II," published by the Department of State; pages 1128 and 1134.

International Civil Aviation Organization, including Annex 7, in which the definition of aircraft is thus stated:

Aircraft—Any machine that can derive support in the atmosphere from the reactions of the air.

This follows in substance the definition which appeared in Annex A to the Paris Convention of 1919:

The word "Aircraft" shall comprise all machines which can derive support in the atmosphere from reactions of the air.[3]

Article 37 of the Chicago Convention provides that each contracting State undertakes to collaborate in securing the highest practicable degree of uniformity in regulations, standards, *etc.* It then authorizes ICAO to adopt standards including those applicable to registration and identification of aircraft. On this authority ICAO adopted Annex 7 referred to above. Article 38 of the Chicago Convention also requires any State finding it impracticable to comply with the ICAO standards to give immediate notice to ICAO. I have found no evidence that the United States officially advised ICAO of the differences between the United States definition of "aircraft" and the definition in the Annex. This might have indicated a United States acceptance of the ICAO definition.

However, the passage of the *Federal Aviation Act of 1958* has clarified the situation. Section 101 of that act repeats the definition of aircraft as it had appeared in the Civil Aeronautics Act of 1938 and disregards the intervening ICAO annex definition. Clearly the letter is narrower and includes only those flight instrumentalities which derive support in the atmosphere from reactions of the air. This would not apply to an earth satellite or rocket while passing through the airspace. On the other hand, these flight instrumentalities are *used* for flight in the air while ascending toward and descending from outer space beyond.

The resulting position may be thus stated. Customary international law, affirmed in Article I of the Paris and Chicago Conventions, asserts the complete and exclusive sovereignty of a subjacent State in its airspace zone, carrying with it unqualified preventive and protective jurisdiction. The United States has clarified this general position through its statutes by insisting that this jurisdiction applies to all types of flight instrumentalities used for *flight in the air*.

In summary, the United States has complete, absolute and exclusive

---

[3] "International Convention Relating to the Regulation of Aerial Navigation dated October 13, 1919"—publication number 2143, Department of State, 1944; page 15.

jurisdiction to control all types of flight in its territorial airspace zone, and thereby prevent danger to itself and protect against violation of national laws and regulations.

But what is the upward extent of this jurisdiction? If the territory of the subjacent State extended upward through the aerospace as high as flight might occur, then it could be said that a State had the same power to assert its jurisdiction in those areas as it has on its national lands and waters. But this is not the case. As early as 1951, several years before Sputnik, I suggested that "it is obvious that we must agree that there is an upper boundary in space to the territory of the subjacent State."[4]

This point of view is now considered sound. But the difficulty is that the United States has thus far failed to reach a decision, by statute, international agreement or otherwise, as to the upper boundary of its national airspace zone. We have not yet asserted the exact extent upward of the area in which our complete preventive and protective jurisdiction is applicable. Suggestions have been made that the upper boundary should be the upper limit of the flight of instrumentalities, such as normal airplanes, which rely on aerodynamic lift and air-breathing engines to maintain flight. Such a boundary might be 20 to 25 miles above the surface of the earth. Other suggestions have been made that the upper limit should be at the point where the atmosphere ceases to provide any lift, say for example 45 to 50 miles upward. Again, it has been suggested that complete preventive jurisdiction should extend upward to the lowest point where unpowered orbital flight is practical. But until the United States decides the upward extent of its territorial airspace zone, the present confused and difficult legal situation will continue.

What has been said above as to the unqualified preventive and protective jurisdiction of the United States in the airspace zone above its national lands and waters applies equally to the airspace over territorial waters. The maritime rule which permits the passage of foreign merchant vessels, in time of peace, through the territorial waters of a State, has no application as to flight. The outward airspace boundaries of a State facing the sea is at the outward boundary of its territorial waters. In such airspace the adjacent State has the same absolute and unilateral jurisdiction to control all flight as it has in other parts of its national airspace. But some difficulties have arisen due to the lack of full international understanding regarding the width of territorial

---

[4] *High Altitude Flight and National Sovereignty*—an address delivered in Mexico City, January 5, 1951—republished in *Legal Problems of Space Exploration: A Symposium*, pages 1–7—S. Doc. No. 26, 87th Cong., 1st Sess. (1961), U.S. Govt. Printing Office. [See *supra* at 263.]

waters. In my judgment, the present situation is reasonably clear, though not satisfactory. The adjacent State has complete and absolute sovereignty in the airspace zone beyond its shores up to the outer boundary of its asserted and generally accepted territorial waters. Eventually it may be hoped that this situation will be clarified. But, at the moment, it would seem, for example, that the complete jurisdiction of the United States extends three miles beyond its shores, and the U.S.S.R. claims twelve miles.

The legal status of usable space above the high seas is directly opposed to that of the airspace zone above the surface territories of a State. The high seas are not subject to the sovereignty of any State, and this rule applies equally to space above. Article 2 of the *Convention on the High Seas* signed at Geneva, April 29, 1958, restated existing rules. It provides that the high seas are open to all nations and that "no State may validly purport to subject any part of them to its sovereignty."[5] Freedom of the high seas is there stated as including *freedom to fly over the high seas.* This freedom, as well as others, "shall be exercised by all states with reasonable regard to the interests of other states in their exercise of the freedom of the high seas." It would thus appear that present international law has completely assimilated rights of navigation on the high seas and over the high seas. It is most noteworthy that the Geneva Convention referred to flight over the high seas, and not in the airspace over the high seas. This in my judgment was a statement that all usable space above the high seas at whatever height can be used by all States subject only to the limitation that such use shall be "with reasonable regard to the interests of other states" in the exercise of such freedom.

A State bordering the high seas thus has, in my view, much the same preventive and protective jurisdiction against foreign flight instrumentalities in aerospace above the high seas as it has against foreign ships on the high seas. While it has been fashionable to assert that the law of the air is something quite different from the law of the sea, nevertheless, it would appear that in this case such assertion is not valid. Whatever action an adjacent State may take on the high seas to prevent injury to itself and its national interests, it has legal authority to take in the aerospace over such high seas. This applies to threatened smuggling, entry of undesirable aliens, violation of health regulations, as well as to precautionary military measures designed to ward off attack from abroad. Of course there are practical differences. Where reasons exist to fear violations of our statutes, ships approaching our shores may be stopped and inspected. But a foreign aircraft cannot be

---

[5] *See* 52 Am. J. Int'l. L. 842–843.

inspected in flight. However, other measures can be taken with the same legal and political background.

The most notable example of the practical application of such protective jurisdiction, applied to foreign aircraft over the high seas, was the adoption by the United States in 1950 of regulations creating certain Air Defense Identification Zones adjacent to our coasts. The regulations provide in substance that foreign aircraft shall not operate into the United States without reporting in advance when the aircraft is not less than one hour and not more than two hours average cruising distance, via the most direct route, to the United States shore. This is a clear assertion of control for preventive and protective purposes exercised in usable space over the high seas. It has been in effect for fifteen years and its validity is no longer internationally challenged.[6]

Toward the end of World War II high altitude self-propelled bombs and rockets came into use, passing above the airspace zone. Similar rocket experiments were carried out after the war. But it was not until after Sputnik I that much attention was directed toward the legal status of the zone which is now termed "outer space." Only recently has there been substantial agreement resulting in sharp contrast with the lower airspace zone. As a result entirely new and unsolved problems of preventive and protective jurisdiction demand solution.

It is now generally agreed that the outer space zone is a continuous international highway—open to all, with equal freedom above the lands and waters of sovereign States and above the high seas. Its status was affirmed by resolution 1962 (XVIII), unanimously adopted by the General Assembly of the United Nations on December 13, 1963. The Declaration of Principles set out in that resolution includes the following statements:

> Outer Space and celestial bodies are free for exploration and use by all States on a basis of equality and in accordance with international law. Outer Space and celestial bodies are not subject to national appropriation by claim of sovereignty, by means of use or occupation, or by any other means.

It is true that the United Nations General Assembly is not an international legislative body. Its resolutions cannot set aside or amend the national statutes of any member State. However, its resolutions certainly may be accepted as evidence of existing customary international law, when not in conflict with national statutes. The United States

---

[6] For a complete examination of the American and Canadian air defense zones and the basis for their legal and political justification *see The Contiguous Air Space Zone in International Law* by Squadron Leader John Taylor Murchison, R.C.A.F., published by Dept. of Nat'l. Defense, Ottawa, Canada, 1956.

has not incorporated the substance of the 1963 resolution into its statutes nor has it become part of a formal ratified international agreement. Nevertheless, the unanimous adoption of the resolution may, in my judgment, be considered evidence that a customary rule now exists which denies to any subjacent state the right to exercise arbitrary preventive jurisdiction in such outer space zone.

In certain fundamental aspects outer space now seems to assimilate many of the characteristics of the high seas in international law. If that persuasive position is accepted, the international rules as to the extent of the preventive and protective jurisdiction of adjacent states in and over the high seas, beyond their territorial waters and shores would warrant careful consideration.

But two major difficulties exist. No decision has been reached, first, as to the lower geographic limit of this continuous zone called *outer space*, and, second, as to the nationality status of flight instrumentalities launched into outer space. The high seas are bounded by the territorial waters of adjacent maritime states and it is reasonably easy to determine whether a ship is or is not navigating the high seas. Also maritime practice has adopted the principle of nationality as to ships, pursuant to which the State of the flag of the ship is responsible for its international good conduct and has a right to insist that the ship enjoys its privileges under international law. Customary rules as to exercise of preventive and protective jurisdiction by an adjacent State against foreign ships are bound up with the defined geographic limits of the high seas and the national status of the ships which use it. A ship which has no national status is assumed to be piratical in character, taking it outside the limits normally applied to the exercise of jurisdiction by States acting beyond their territorial borders.

Up to the present only two States, namely the United States of America and the U.S.S.R., have launched objects into outer space. But this will not long continue. Certainly agreement must be reached as to the means of determining the State responsible for the presence and good conduct of every object traversing outer space before final rules as to preventive and protective jurisdiction of other States can be finally fixed. In this connection it must be noted that the 1963 United Nations Assembly resolution referred to above apparently contemplated some form of registration of all objects launched into outer space. Paragraph 7 of that resolution stated in substance that "the State on whose registry an object launched into outer space is carried shall retain jurisdiction and control over such object, and any personnel thereon, while in outer space". This is a restatement of the essence of the principle of registration and nationality applicable to ships on the high seas.

Present tentative arrangements under which States are expected to advise the United Nations of the launching of objects to be used in outer space are not sufficiently certain nor effective. Further understanding is needed and better registry provisions are required, perhaps including an obligation of the launching State to effect the removal from outer space of objects placed in orbit which have become useless and create danger similar to that of a derelict on the high seas.

But even now some rules can be foreseen as to the extent of the preventive and protective jurisdiction of States applicable to the use by other States of the outer space zone. In the first place, every State retains its inherent rights of self-defense notwithstanding the otherwise free use of outer space. The same international rule would justify preventive and protective acts of self-defense in outer space as on or over the high seas or on the lands and waters of other States or in their sovereign airspace. The character of acts which warrant preventive self-defense in any other transport medium will also justify preventive measures in outer space.[7]

In the second place, it is suggested that the States must apply to navigation in outer space the same qualification that applies to freedom of maritime navigation, namely, that such freedom should be exercised with regard to the interests of other States in their free use of outer space. This rule has the effect that if any State launches into outer space such objects as would endanger its use by others, then any State would have the right to exercise preventive and protective jurisdiction to remove the dangerous object, if the launching State did not. Such an object has an essentially piratical or derelict character. As indicated, this rule should apply only when the object concerned is a danger to flight in outer space.[8]

It is yet impossible to state other definitive rules as to preventive and protective jurisdiction in the outer space zone. When the time comes that high altitude flight is so practical that landing and take-off in foreign territory is planned, provisions for advance notice similar to those now applicable in our air defense identification zones may be instituted. Other fully justified protective measures may also be put into effect as against foreign spacecraft navigating the outer space zone but planning to enter the territory of another State.

It is apparent from what has been said that the major present

---

[7] See SELF-DEFENSE IN OUTER SPACE AND THE UNITED NATIONS, Chapter 25, *infra*; see also 108 Congressional Record, A2723 (daily ed. April 9, 1962).

[8] This statement indicates the author's personal views notwithstanding the provisions of par. 6 of the 1963 U.N. Resolution which provides in vague terms for *prior consultation*, before launching, if a state "has reason to believe that an outer space activity or experiment planned by another State would cause potentially harmful interference with activities in the peaceful exploration and use of outer space. . . ."

difficulty involves a clear understanding as to the geographic areas in which the unilateral preventive jurisdiction of a subjacent State may apply. If it is determined that outer space, free for the use of all, extends downward to a point just below the area in which unpowered orbital flight is practical, or if it extends downward to a point even fifty miles above the surface of the earth, the question must still be answered as to whether the preventive jurisdiction of the subjacent State extends upward without exception to such lower boundary of outer space. The problem is very practical and very urgent.

If the complete preventive jurisdiction of a State above its lands and waters extends upward even fifty miles, future intercontinental and orbital outer space flight will be seriously handicapped. Until the time arrives when flight instrumentalities are available with almost vertical take-off into and subsequent descent from outer space it will continue necessary to plan outer space flight with gradual ascent and even more gradual descent. Few States are geographically located so that they can, without difficulty, plan outerspace flight without assuming descent from outer space at altitudes less than fifty miles above the surface territories of other States.

If the lower limit of the free outer space zone is brought down to a lower boundary only twenty or twenty-five miles above the earth's surface, so as to assist free outer space flight, new political difficulties will arise. Spacecraft which are capable of flight in the airspace as well as outer space will subject to the right of self-defense, be able to approach foreign surface territories at that altitude without the consent of the State below.

Perhaps most of these difficulties could be solved by international agreement as to the existence of a contiguous zone between the territorial airspace zone of a sovereign State and the free outer space zone above. The lower boundary of this contiguous zone might be the point where normal airplane flight is practical and the upper boundary just below the point where unpowered orbital flight can be made effective. In such contiguous zone a subjacent State could exercise the same preventive and protective jurisdiction as against foreign flight instrumentalities as it has in its airspace zone except that rights of passage would be permitted for nonmilitary flight instrumentalities when ascending toward or descending from outer space above. Detailed protective measures would certainly be developed.

If such an international arrangement were eventually agreed upon the result would be that the complete preventive and protective jurisdiction of a State would extend upward to areas where free orbital flight was practical, but innocent passage for nonmilitary flight instrumentalities would be excepted in the area between the airspace zone and the outer space zone.

325

V. EMERGING PRINCIPLES OF LAW FOR OUTER SPACE

The problem is largely political but must be answered. The legal status of the territorial airspace zone has long been settled but its upper boundary not yet determined. The legal status of the outer space zone as a highway open to all has now been widely accepted but if confusion is to be eliminated a decision must be taken as to whether these two zones have a common boundary or whether a contiguous zone lies between in which spacial limitations will be agreed upon so as to assist future high altitude flight while preserving complete preventive jurisdiction in areas used for normal flight near the lands and waters of a State.

20
Aerospace Law:
Progress in the UN

Reprinted by permission of the
American Institute of Aeronautics
and Astronautics from
Astronautics and Aerospace
Engineering 42 (March 1964).
© American Institute of
Aeronautics and Astronautics 1964.

Author's Note. This article, published in 1964, must be read in conjunction with the one that follows, "Who Will Own the Moon? The Need for an Answer," published eighteen months later. In the 1964 article, the author, encouraged by the unanimous adoption of the UN General Assembly resolution 1962 (XVIII), said: "If a landing is made on the moon, no territorial rights will follow. Freedom of exploration and use of celestial bodies now seem assured." Subsequent events shook the author's confidence in these conclusions, and led him to believe that nothing short of an international treaty would provide permanent acceptance of the principle that celestial bodies cannot be subject to territorial claims. As to outer space, it is believed that rules of customary law are now sufficiently settled to warrant the conclusion that "outer space", though not yet fully defined, is "free for use by all States on a basis of equality and in accordance with international law," as stated in the UN resolution. Though just what the phrase "in accordance with international law" means is not yet clear.

THE GENERAL ASSEMBLY of the United Nations in December 1963 by Resolution 1962 (XVIII) unanimously approved a "Declaration of Legal Principles Governing the Activities of States in the Exploration and Use of Outer Space," prepared by the Committee on the Peaceful Uses of Outer Space, thus ending in large measure its two-year stalemate in the development of aerospace law.

"Aerospace Law" is the aggregate of the accepted legal rules applicable directly or indirectly to man-made or man-controlled flight. It combines the law of aeronautics and the law of astronautics, or "air law" and "space law." "Aerospace" was defined in the glossary published in 1959 by the Research Studies Institute at Maxwell Air Force Base as follows: "The earth's envelope of air and the space above it, the two considered as a single realm for activity in the flight of air vehicles and in the launching, guidance and control of ballistic missiles, earth satellites, dirigible space vehicles, and the like." The terms "aerospace engineering" and "aerospace sciences" are now widely used to indicate the indivisible and inclusive character of engineering and scientific functions related to flight at any altitude.

In December 1961, the UN General Assembly had adopted the now celebrated resolution 1721A (XVI):

The General Assembly,
Recognizing the common interest of mankind in furthering the

peaceful uses of outer space and the urgent need to strengthen international cooperation in this important field,

Believing that the exploration and use of outer space should be only for the betterment of mankind and to the benefit of States irrespective of the stage of their economic or scientific development,

1. Commends to States for their guidance in the exploration and use of outer space the following principles:

a) International law, including the United Nations Charter, applies to outer space and celestial bodies;

b) Outer space and celestial bodies are free for exploration and use by all States in conformity with international law, and are not subject to national appropriation;

2. Invites the Committee on the Peaceful Uses of Outer Space to study and report on the legal problems which may arise from the exploration and use of outer space.

Following the adoption of this 1961 resolution by the Assembly, the UN Outer Space Committee created a Legal Subcommittee. This Subcommittee met in Geneva in May and June 1962, followed later by a further meeting of the full Committee, and finally by the First (Political) Committee of the 1962 Assembly. No agreement was reached on any of the proposals which had been submitted.

On December 19, 1962 the UN Assembly adopted Resolution 1802 (XVII). It (1) noted with regret that the Committee on the Peaceful Uses of Outer Space had not yet made recommendations on legal questions; (2) called upon all Member States to cooperate in the further development of law for outer space; (3) requested the Committee to continue urgently its work on the further elaboration "of basic legal principles governing the activities of States in the exploration or use of outer space," on liability for space vehicle accidents, and on assistance to and return of astronauts and space vehicles, as well as on other legal problems; (4) referred to the Committee, as a basis for its work, all proposals thus far brought forward, including the draft proposals as to basic principles submitted by the USSR, the United Arab Republic, the United Kingdom, and the United States, as well as the U.S. proposal as to liability, and the USSR and U.S. proposals on assistance to and return of astronauts and space vehicles.

The primary problem as to the "basic legal principles governing States in the exploration and use of outer space" was thus returned to the Committee on the Peaceful Uses of Outer Space, together with the subsidiary questions of assistance and liability. The Legal Subcommittee met again in New York on April 16, 1963. In addition to the earlier proposals, the Subcommittee had before it a new USSR "Draft Declaration of the basic Principles governing the Activities of States in the Exploration and Use of Outer Space" (A/AC.105/C.2/L.6), discussed later in this paper. The Subcommittee adjourned without final agreement.

LEGAL STATUS OF AIRSPACE AND OUTER SPACE

All of the proposals before the UN Committee tacitly, though not specifically, recognized the territorial sovereignty of the subjacent State in the airspace above its lands and waters. Similarly, if they had been accepted as part of an international obligation, any of these proposals would have recognized the non-territorial status of "outer space." The new Soviet Draft Declaration of basic principles stated: "Outer space and celestial bodies are free for exploration and use by all States; sovereignty over outer space or celestial bodies cannot be acquired by use or occupation or in any other way." The U.K. draft declaration included the statements that "outer space and celestial bodies are free for exploration and use by all States in conformity with international law," and that "outer space and celestial bodies are not capable of appropriation or exclusive use by any State." The U.S. draft declaration of principles asserted that "outer space and celestial bodies are free for exploration and use by all States, on the basis of equal rights, in conformity with international law," and that "outer space and celestial bodies are not subject to national appropriation."

But the Legal Subcommittee adjourned without formal agreement on any of the proposed statements of general principles. One of the areas of disagreement dealt with the form under which action should be taken. A group of States, headed by the USSR, insisted upon UN action in a form which would be "legally binding" on participating States, holding apparently that General Assembly resolutions were mere recommendations. This position necessarily created the gravest doubt as to whether any UN action, including the 1961 resolution, quoted earlier in this paper, could be considered as a binding commitment on member States, even though the resolution was unanimously adopted. It will be noted, in fact, that the resolution was actually limited to *commending* "to States for their guidance in the exploration and use of outer space" certain principles, including the principles that "outer space and celestial bodies are free for exploration and use by all States in conformity with international law, and are not subject to national appropriation."

The Committee on the Peaceful Uses of Outer Space met in September 1963. It noted that, as a result of the work of the Legal Sub-committee and subsequent exchanges of views, differences had narrowed. The Committee expressed the hope that a wider consensus might be achieved by the time the subject was to be considered by the

General Assembly. The Committee met again in November 1963. As a result of consultations which had occurred between members of the Committee, a working paper had been prepared. This paper presented the draft declaration which was eventually submitted to the General Assembly for consideration, and was unanimously approved without change on December 13, 1963. This declaration marks a historic advance toward international agreement on rules of conduct to be followed by States in the exploration and use of outer space.

The four major principles thus approved by the General Assembly directly reflect its 1961 resolution, as well as the major provisions of the various drafts, referred to above, prepared by the Soviet Union, UK, UAR, and U.S. The Declaration, after noting the fact that the 1961 and 1962 resolutions had been approved unanimously, then states that the General Assembly "solemnly declares that in the exploration and use of outer space States should be guided by the following principles:

1. The exploration and use of outer space shall be carried on for the benefit and in the interests of all mankind.

2. Outer space and celestial bodies are free for exploration and use by all States on a basis of equality and in accordance with international law.

3. Outer space and celestial bodies are not subject to national appropriation by claim of sovereignty, by means of use or occupation, or by any other means.

4. The activities of States in the exploration and use of outer space shall be carried on in accordance with international law including the Charter of the United Nations, in the interest of maintaining international peace and security and promoting international co-operation and understanding."

Additional paragraphs of the Declaration contain provisions which deal with responsibility of States for national activities in outer space, also provisions that such activities should be conducted with due regard for the interests of other States, that the State on whose registry an object launched into outer space is carried shall retain jurisdiction and control, that each State that launches or procures the launching of an object into outer space and each State from whose territory the object is launched is internationally liable for damages caused, and that astronauts making a landing on the territory of a foreign State or on the high seas shall be safely and promptly returned to the State of registry of their space vehicle.

Academic questions may still exist as to whether this "Declaration," not being in Treaty form, is of itself legally binding on the UN member States who voted in its favor. However, its practical effect is clear. As between those member States now exploring outer space, and those others which may soon be added, the non-territorial status of outer space and of celestial bodies has been accepted, together with an effective denial of any right to claim outer space sovereignty. This far-reaching result of the UN actions arises both from the fact that the Declaration was drafted following conferences between the Soviet Union and the U.S. and other UN members, and, even more important, from the manner in which the Declaration was received.

During the General Assembly debates, the U.S. representative said: "We believe these legal principles reflect international law as it is accepted by the Members of the United Nations. The United States, for its part, intends to respect these principles. We hope that the conduct which the resolution commends to nations in the exploration of outer space will become the practice of all nations." The representative of the Soviet Union, after noting the statement of the United States, said: "The Soviet Union, for its part, will also respect the principles contained in this declaration if it is unanimously adopted." The representative of the United Kingdom said: "My government intends to respect these principles and believes that the conduct they enjoin will become the practice of every State and thus serve to ensure the exploration and use of outer space for peaceful purposes."

These are international commitments of deep significance. No State indicated that it would refuse to regulate its international conduct in the manner provided by the Declaration.

Admittedly, unanimity did not exist in the views expressed as to the technical legal effect of the Declaration standing alone. For example, the representative of France said: "I will add, however, that, while supporting and subscribing to the principles contained in the Declaration to which I have just referred, my delegation could not for the moment give this Declaration more value than that of a declaration of intention. We do not, in fact, consider that a resolution of the General Assembly, even though adopted unanimously, can in this case create, stricto sensu, juridical obligations incumbent upon Member States. Such obligations can flow only from international agreements." But the fact remains that the Declaration was thereafter unanimously adopted.

For practical purposes, it can now be stated with great assurance that no member of the United Nations will hereafter seek to project its territorial sovereign claims into outer space. If a landing is made on the moon, no territorial rights will follow. Freedom of exploration and use of outer space and celestial bodies now seem assured.

REMAINING AREAS OF UNCERTAINTY OR DISAGREEMENT

Notwithstanding the acceptance of the principle of the freedom of outer space, certain areas of uncertainty or disagreement may still exist as to future limitations of national use of outer space. In a paper presented by the present author at the summer meeting of the AIAA in June 1963 before the Declaration had been drafted, it was suggested that certain questions were then unresolved. These included the problem as to whether the "peaceful use" of outer space means non-aggressive use or strictly non-military use; whether observation satellites should be restricted in photographing or otherwise recording conditions or objects on the earth's surface; the extent to which communication satellites may be used for propaganda; the question as to what uses of outer space by one State require prior agreement by other States; and the question whether States alone as such may use outer space. The present status of each of these questions must be re-examined in the light of the new Declaration.

MILITARY USE OF OUTER SPACE

None of the early draft declarations considered by the Committee contained a definition of the term "peaceful uses." However, the UAR proposed that "the activities of Member States in outer space should be confined solely to the peaceful uses." This was construed in the Subcommittee discussions to mean non-military uses.

The problem is far-reaching. Freedom of navigation on the high seas has always permitted passage and maneuver of naval vessels in time of peace, also transit in the airspace over the high seas of military aircraft. If a different rule is to be applied in outer space, and all forms of military use are to be prohibited by international agreement, then the freedom of use of outer space and the freedom of use of the high seas and the airspace above it will mean very different things.

Strong views were expressed in the legal subcommittee, at both its 1962 and 1963 meetings, that this was a question which could be resolved only as part of a general agreement on disarmament. The same position was maintained by certain States before the Declaration was approved. Its terms do not directly limit the military use of outer space. If there is to be any such limitation, this must now await ultimate decisions on disarmament. The Declaration does not contain even a reference to resolution 1884 (XVIII), adopted by the General Assembly on October 17, 1963. This resolution had welcomed expressions by the Soviet Union and the US of their intention not to station in outer space any objects carrying nuclear weapons, or other kinds of weapons of mass destruction, and had called on all States to refrain from placing any such weapons in orbit around the earth.

OBSERVATION SATELLITES

The draft declaration proposed earlier by the Soviet Union stated: "The use of artificial satellites for the collection of intelligence information in the territory of a foreign State is incompatible with the objectives of mankind in its conquest of outer space." The discussions in the Legal Subcommittee demonstrated that the Soviet Union and its supporters were still as insistent on this position as they had been in the 1962 meetings. They refused to accept the contention that satellite observation from outer space was permissible under international law just as observation from ships on the high seas. The 1963 UN Declaration makes no mention of artificial satellites, nor were they directly referred to in the public discussions which immediately preceded its approval. But it must be noted that paragraph 4 of the Declaration specifically states that "the activities of States in the exploration and use of outer space shall be carried on in accordance with international law . . . in the interest of maintaining international peace and security and promoting international cooperation and understanding."

The possibility certainly exists that the Soviet Union may hereafter repeat its assertion that the use of artificial satellites for the collection of intelligence information in the territory of a foreign State is not permissible under international law.

USE OF COMMUNICATION SATELLITES FOR PROPAGANDA

Another condition of free use of outer space was thus stated in the Soviet Union draft declaration of basic principles: "The use of outer space for propagating war, national or racial hatred or enmity between nations is inadmissible." The far-reaching possible effect of this vague declaration was difficult to state. It would apply apparently to the use of satellites even for relay purposes. The 1963 Declaration does not directly contain this proposed Soviet Union provision. However, one of the preambles to the Declaration recalled General Assembly resolutions 110 (II) of November 3, 1947 "which condemned propaganda designed or likely to provoke or encourage any threat to the peace, breach of the peace, or active aggression," and considered "that the aforementioned resolution is applicable to outer space." It would therefore appear that the adoption of the 1963 Declaration has made the 1947 resolution as to propaganda fully effective in outer space. The future effect is far from clear.

PRIOR CONSULTATION AND AGREEMENT AS TO USES OF OUTER SPACE

The draft declaration proposed by the United Kingdom provided that freedom in the use of outer space "shall be exercised by all States with due regard to the interests of other States in the exploration and use of outer space, and to the need for consultation and cooperation between States in relation to such exploration and use." The Soviet Union draft stated that "any measures that might in any way hinder the exploration or use of outer space for peaceful purposes by other countries may be implemented only after prior discussion of and agreement upon such measures between the countries concerned." In the discussions in the Legal Subcommittee it appeared that the Soviet Union insisted upon an actual prior intergovernmental agreement and was not then prepared to accept reference to any international consultative body, such as a committee of COSPAR, to determine what uses of outer space were harmful to other States.

The 1963 Declaration contains a compromise provision, drafted in very broad terms, and certainly leaving the possibility of future discussions. The provision is as follows:

6. In the exploration and use of outer space, States shall be guided by the principle of co-operation and mutual assistance and shall conduct all their activities in outer space with due regard for the corresponding interests of other States. If a State has reason to believe that an outer space activity or experiment planned by it or its nationals would cause potentially harmful interference with activities of other States in the peaceful exploration and use of outer space, it shall undertake appropriate international consultations before proceeding with any such activity or experiment. A State which has reason to believe that an outer space activity or experiment planned by another State would cause potentially harmful interference with activities in the peaceful exploration and use of outer space may request consultation concerning the activity or experiment.

FREE ENTERPRISE IN OUTER SPACE

The Soviet Union, in its last draft, did not change its earlier position that 'all activities of any kind pertaining to the exploration and use of outer space shall be carried out solely by States." It apparently was not willing to accept suggested compromises which would permit activity in outer space by organizations other than a "State," when such activity was licensed by a State assuming responsibility for any result-ing damage or misconduct.

The 1963 Declaration, however, clearly indicates that, under stated conditions, non-governmental entities may now act in outer space. The provision reads as follows:

> 5. States bear international responsibility for national activities in outer space, whether carried on by governmental agencies or by non-governmental entities, and for assuring that national activities are carried on in conformity with the principles set forth in this Declaration. The activities of non-governmental entities in outer space shall require authorization and continuing supervision by the State concerned. When activities are carried on in outer space by an international organization, responsibility for compliance with the principles set forth in this Declaration shall be borne by the international organization and by the States participating in it.

CONCLUSION

Notwithstanding these remaining areas of uncertainty, it is fortu-nate that five years of discussion in the United Nations has been climaxed in a unanimous Declaration that States, in the exploration and use of outer space, should be guided by the principle that outer space and celestial bodies are free for exploration and use by all States and are not subject to national appropriation by claim of sovereignty, by means of use or occupation, or by any other means. While this Declaration was not a legislative enactment, its unanimous acceptance goes far towards proving the existence of an agreed rule of customary international law. It will, in my judgment, eventually become part of a new convention. But even before that occurs, world public opinion would hardly now countenance any national claim of sovereignty in outer space or on celestial bodies.

The discussions in the United Nations must continue. Outer space, as an area of freedom from sovereignty, has not been defined. Every State has the right to control all flight in the "airspace" above its lands and waters. According to the UN Declaration, it has no such right in "outer space." Where do the sovereign rights of States end and where does international freedom of use begin? Is the boundary be-tween territorial airspace and free outer space to be fixed or are the rules agreed by the United Nations to be applied solely to "spacecraft" wherever they are and not to "aircraft"? If so, a definition of spacecraft must be found and the difficult problem created by the X-15 must be answered—that is, how does one classify the X-15 and other flight instrumentalities which will operate both in the airspace and in outer space?

In the able "Draft Code of Rules on the Exploration and Uses of Outer Space" prepared by a group of legal and aviation experts working under the auspices of The David Davies Memorial Institute of International Studies, London, an effort was made to meet some of these difficulties. This unofficial code might well be given further consideration by intergovernmental organizations. The Code recognized the necessity of defining airspace and outer space, fixing the boundary between them and differentiating between aircraft and space craft. The major definitions included in the Draft Code are the following:

"Aircraft" means any craft which depends, as means of flight upon the consumption of air, or upon aerodynamic lift, or both;

"spacecraft" means any craft capable of orbital movement or manoeuvre in outer space and includes any craft which is being operated as a space station;

"airspace" means the volume of space between the surface of the earth at sea level and an altitude of 80,000 meters above it; (and)

"outer space" means space outside the airspace.

In discussing the question of sovereignty and defending the suggestion of 80,000 meters (50 mi.) "as the limit of sovereignty and the beginning of outer space," the commentary to the Draft Code points out that the principle that each State has sovereignty over the airspace above its territory is now an established rule; that, although the Soviet Union is not a party to the Chicago Convention, it has adopted the rule in substance in its own legislation; that neither the Paris Convention in 1919 nor the Chicago Convention define the altitude of the airspace for the purpose of sovereignty, nor has it been authoritatively defined elsewhere; that 25 mi. is probably the outside limit of effective aerodynamic lift.

The commentary then continues:

There are, however, three considerations which favor a definition of airspace yielding a more extended sovereignty than 25 miles: The fact that airspace begins to lose its character of a continuous medium only when a height of 50–55 miles is reached; the likely range of effective control of objects from the ground; and the logic of treating the frontier between airspace or outer space as being at or near orbiting altitude.

The commentary also notes that 70 mi. is about the present low limit of effective orbiting, and that the rocket-driven winged X-15 which can be operated as an aircraft or as if it were a spacecraft "has already obtained an altitude of 47 mi. and its descendants will certainly go higher."

It will be recalled that calculations made by the late Dr. Von Kármán indicated an upper range of any aerodynamic lift as being in the neighborhood of 45–55 mi. above the surface of the earth. The view has been ably argued by Andrew G. Haley that this should be accepted as the upper altitude of sovereignty airspace. In considering the validity of the suggestion that an altitude of 50 mi. be definitely accepted as the boundary between airspace and outer space, the views expressed to the writer of this paper by Maj. Robert M. White are of interest.

Several months before the David Davies Memorial Institute Draft Code was published in England, he had flown the X-15 to altitudes of over 46 mi. and again over 59 mi. Under date of July 27, 1962, Maj. White wrote:

> To conclude, I felt it would be practical to consider 50 mi. as a boundary even though it may be arbitrary in some respects. I feel this because:
>
> a) It is well above the altitude where we can generate aerodynamic lift to control a vehicle.
>
> b) Even at speeds approaching satellite velocities, much of a vehicle's capabilities are received from dynamic lift compared to aerodynamic lift; and
>
> c) At 50 miles altitude the density is such a small fraction of 1% of the atmosphere that it should be acceptable to consider that all useful qualities of the atmosphere are below this level.

The question as to the upper boundary of national sovereignty cannot be overlooked if future grave international problems are to be avoided.

Fortunately, the aerospace legal work of the United Nations is not at an end. On December 13, 1963, the same day that the Declaration was approved, a further resolution 1963 (XVIII) was adopted recommending that consideration be given "to incorporating in international agreement form, in the future as appropriate, legal principles governing the activities of States in the exploration and use of outer space." It also requested the Committee on the Peaceful Uses of Outer Space to continue to study and report "on legal problems which may arise in the exploration and use of outer space, and in particular to arrange for the prompt preparation of draft international agreements on liability for damage caused by objects launched into outer space and on assistance to and return of astronauts and space vehicles."

Aerospace engineering and aerospace science are progressing daily. It now appears that the United Nations is determined that the development of aerospace law shall not lag behind.

21
Who Will Own the Moon?
The Need for an Answer

The body of this article is reprinted by permission of University, A Princeton Quarterly, *from* University (*winter 1965–66*) *No. 27, p. 3. The footnotes and Addendum are reprinted by permission of the* Journal of Air Law and Commerce *from 32* Journal of Air Law and Commerce *155 (1966).*

Author's Note. As stated earlier, this article, published at the end of 1965, must be read in conjunction with the preceding article. Here the author reached the reluctant conclusion that only an international treaty could create binding obligations on States not to make territorial claims to any part of the moon or other celestial bodies. [*See editor's note at the end of this chapter.*]

C AN THE FIRST NATION to land men on the moon claim rights of possession and exclusive sovereignty over occupied areas which would give that nation political and perhaps military advantages?

Both the Soviet Union and the United States have disavowed any such intention. But the legal picture is not nearly as clear as it might be.

Long before any sane man thought seriously of the question of territorial rights on celestial bodies it was an accepted worldwide principle that the nation which effectively occupies an area of stateless lands may acquire rights of territorial sovereignty; indeed, this principle has been accepted as law by the community of nations.

Is there any rule of unwritten customary international law which would exempt the moon from this long established rule, or is there any special and effective political understanding to the same effect? In other words, have the Soviet Union, the United States, and other nations reached any formal, binding agreements by which they are obligated, one to another, to waive claims to national appropriation of areas on the moon following a manned landing and subsequent effective occupation? It should be said at once that the answer can be found, if at all, in the resolutions unanimously adopted in the 1961 and 1963 General Assemblies of the United Nations.

On 20 December 1961, the General Assembly unanimously adopted Resolution No. 1721 (XVI) entitled "International Cooperation in the Peaceful Uses of Outer Space." It stated:

The General Assembly
Recognizing the common interest of mankind in furthering the peaceful uses of outer space and the urgent need to strengthen international cooperation in this important field,
Believing that the exploration and use of outer space should be only for the betterment of mankind and to the benefit of States irrespective of the stage of their economic or scientific development,

1. *Commends* to States for their guidance in the exploration and use of outer space the following principles:

a) International law, including the Charter of the United Nations, applies to outer space and celestial bodies;

b) Outer space and celestial bodies are free for exploration and use by all States in conformity with international law and are not subject to national appropriation;

2. *Invites* the Committee on the Peaceful Uses of Outer Space to study and report on the legal problems which may arise from the exploration and use of outer space.

Two years later, on 13 December 1963, the General Assembly adopted Resolution No. 1962 (XVIII) entitled "Declaration of Legal Principles Governing the Activities of States in the Exploration and Use of Outer Space." It stated in part:

The General Assembly . . .
Solemnly declares that in the exploration and use of outer space States should be guided by the following principles:

1. The exploration and use of outer space shall be carried on for the benefit and in the interests of all mankind.

2. Outer space and celestial bodies are free for exploration and use by all States on a basis of equality and in accordance with international law.

3. Outer space and celestial bodies are not subject to national appropriation by claim of sovereignty, by means of use or occupation, or by any other means.

4. The activities of States in the exploration and use of outer space shall be carried on in accordance with international law, including the Charter of the United Nations, in the interest of maintaining international peace and security and promoting cooperation and understanding.

If there is any formal agreement between the Member States of the United Nations obligating them not to seek national appropriation of areas on the moon, it must be found in these resolutions. No other public documents appear pertinent. There are no known agreements with non-member governments, such as Peking, though their future rocket possibility should not be overlooked.

Public statements made prior to the adoption of these two resolutions make it quite clear that there had been no agreement up to that time.

Three years before the 1961 resolution quoted above had been adopted, Senator Lyndon Johnson addressed the First Committee of the United Nations General Assembly on the need to ban national claims in space. While Chairman of the United States Senate Special Committee on Space and Astronautics he had been actively concerned with the drafting and final passage of the statute which created the present National Aeronautics and Space Administration. One of the objectives of that statute was to further "cooperation by the United States with other nations and groups of nations" in the work done pursuant to the act and in the peaceful application of its results. Later Congress requested the President to submit to the United Nations the question of international cooperation in dedicating outer space to peaceful purposes. In 1958 a resolution was introduced in the United Nations General Assembly to provide for the creation of an Ad Hoc Committee on the Peaceful Uses of Outer Space and Senator Johnson was invited to state the United States position. Speaking on 17 November 1958, before the First Committee of the General Assembly, he said in part:

> At this moment the nations of the Earth are explorers in space, not colonizers. . . . We of the United States have recognized and do recognize, as must all men, that the penetration into outer space is the concern of all mankind. All nations and all men, without regard to their roles on Earth, are affected alike by what is accomplished over their heads in outer space.
> If nations proceed unilaterally, then their penetrations into space become only extensions of their national policies on Earth. . . .
> Today outer space is free. It is unscarred by conflict. No nation holds a concession there. It must remain this way.
> We of the United States do not acknowledge that there are landlords of outer space who can presume to bargain with the nations of the Earth on the price of access to this new domain. We must not —and need not—corrupt this great opportunity by bringing to it the very antagonisms which we may, by courage, overcome and leave behind forever through a joint adventure into this new realm.[1]

The proposed Ad Hoc Committee was later created by resolution of the General Assembly. But the Soviet Union and certain other States which had been named to membership refused to cooperate in its work, asserting that the membership was unbalanced. However, a majority of that committee met and prepared a final report, dealing

---

[1] SPECIAL SENATE COMM. ON SPACE AND ASTRONAUTICS, 85TH CONG., 2D SESS., SPACE LAW—A SYMPOSIUM 558–61 (Comm. Print 1959). See also S. REP. No. 100, 86th Cong., 1st Sess. 58–62 (1959).

with many aspects of the use of outer space. In discussing the legal problems the report indicated that orbital flights already made may have "initiated the recognition or establishment of a generally accepted rule to the effect that in principle" outer space was on conditions of equality freely available for exploration and use by all. But the committee, apparently feeling the questions relating to exploration of celestial bodies created separate problems not covered by freedom of orbital flight, said:

> The Committee was of the view that serious problems could arise if States claimed, on one ground or another, exclusive rights over all or part of a celestial body. One suggestion was that celestial bodies are incapable of appropriation to national sovereignty. Another suggestion was that the exploration and exploitation of celestial bodies should be carried out exclusively for the benefit of all mankind. It was also suggested that some form of international administration over celestial bodies might be adopted.
>
> The Committee noted that, while scientific programmes envisaged relatively early exploration of celestial bodies, human settlement and extensive exploitation of resources were not likely in the near future. For this reason the Committee believed that problems relating to the settlement and exploitation of celestial bodies did not require priority treatment.[2]

This report was dated 14 July 1959. If there had at that time been any accepted rule of international law holding that celestial bodies were not subject to occupation and territorial claims, the Committee would certainly have so stated.

In September 1959 the Soviet Union launched a rocket (Lunik II) which made impact with the moon. This followed by only two months the report of the Ad Hoc Committee. Fortunately, however, no international difficulties followed the landing of the Soviet rocket. Chairman Khrushchev is quoted as having denied any resulting claims to territorial rights.

The report of the Ad Hoc Committee was not acted upon by the General Assembly. Instead a new "Committee on the Peaceful Uses of Outer Space" was named. The problem of the effect of moon landings could no longer be set aside. President Eisenhower addressing the General Assembly in September 1960 urged adoption of an agreement

---

[2] Ad Hoc Comm. on the Peaceful Uses of Outer Space, *Report*, U.N. GEN. ASS., U. N. DOC. No. A/4141, paras. 30, 31 (1959). See also SENATE COMM. ON AERONAUTICAL AND SPACE SCIENCES, 87th CONG., 1st SESS., *Legal Problems of Space Exploration* 1246–75 (Comm. Print 1961).

that would declare celestial bodies not subject to national appropriation. He said:

> Another problem confronting us involves outer space. The emergence of this new world poses a vital issue: Will outer space be preserved for peaceful use and developed for the benefit of all mankind? Or will it become another focus for the arms race—and thus an area of dangerous and sterile competition? The choice is urgent. It is ours to make.
>
> The nations of the world have recently united in declaring the Continent of Antarctica "off limits" to military preparations. We could extend this principle to an even more important sphere. National vested interests have not yet been developed in space or in celestial bodies. Barriers to agreement are now lower than they will ever be again.
>
> The opportunity may be fleeting. Before many years have passed, the point of no return may be behind us.
>
> We must not lose the chance we still have to control the future of outer space. I propose that—
>
> 1. We agree that celestial bodies are not subject to national appropriation by any claims of sovereignty.
>
> 2. We agree that the nations of the world shall not engage in warlike activities on these bodies. . . .
>
> Agreements on these proposals would enable future generations to find peaceful and scientific progress, not another fearful dimension to the arms race, as they explore the universe.[3]

Again it is obvious that no rule of law or international agreement then existed which would have forbidden national appropriation of celestial bodies, including the moon, or President Eisenhower would not have cited the need for such an agreement.

The following year the General Assembly adopted Resolution 1721, quoted above, which *commended* to states for their guidance the principle, among others, that celestial bodies are not subject to national appropriation. This appears to be the first positive reference in any United Nations resolution to possible national appropriation of celestial bodies. But whether this resolution, even though unanimously adopted, can be accepted as legally binding on United Nations Member States will be discussed later.

In September 1963, only a few weeks before his death, President Kennedy delivered a stirring address before the General Assembly in

---

[3] *Legal Problems of Space Exploration, supra* note 2, at 1009. See also *International Cooperation and Organization for Outer Space*, S. Doc. No. 66, 89th Cong., 1st Sess. 195–96 (1965); 42 *Dep't State Bull.* 554–55 (1960).

which he sought to end the competitive race to the moon and substitute international cooperation. Politically he based his appeal on the assumption that problems of sovereignty no longer existed. He was patently referring to Resolution 1721. He said:

> Space offers no problems of sovereignty; by resolution of this Assembly, the Members of the United Nations have forsworn any claim to territorial rights in outer space or on celestial bodies, and declared that international law and the United Nations Charter will apply. Why, therefore, should man's first flight to the moon be a matter of national competition? Why should the United States and the Soviet Union, in preparation for such expeditions, become involved in immense duplications of research, construction and expenditure? Surely we should explore whether the scientists and astronauts of our two countries—indeed of all the world—cannot work together in the conquest of space, sending some day in this decade to the moon, not the representatives of a single nation, but the representatives of all of our countries.[4]

Was President Kennedy justified in taking the position that the 1961 resolution of the General Assembly was in substance an international agreement between Member States by which they bound themselves not to claim rights of territorial sovereignty following any manned landing on the moon? No sound answer to this question can be made without careful consideration of views expressed in the United Nations in connection with its later action on the 1963 resolution.

Following the adoption of the 1961 resolution referred to by President Kennedy, the United Nations Committee on the Peaceful Uses of Outer Space met to consider, as directed by the resolution, "the legal problems which may arise from the exploration and use of outer space." Proposals of basic principles were submitted by the Soviet Union, the United Arab Republic, the United Kingdom, and the United States. Agreement could not be reached. In December 1962 the General Assembly adopted Resolution 1802 (XVII) in which it noted with regret that the committee had not made recommendations on legal questions and it referred back to the committee the proposals which had been made. These proposals followed the spirit of the 1961 resolution but other areas of disagreement were so serious as to delay action. The legal sub-committee being unable to agree on positive recommendations, all of the proposals were brought before the First Committee of the General Assembly late in 1963. Various compromises were apparently reached before a draft resolution was finally

---

[4] *International Cooperation and Organization for Outer Space, supra* note 3, at 158. See also 48 *Dep't State Bull.* 532–33 (1963).

prepared for consideration. This text was eventually incorporated in Resolution 1962 (XVIII) adopted 13 December 1963 and quoted above.

An examination of the 1961 and 1963 resolutions points up the fact that little change was made in the original provisions as to celestial bodies. Both resolutions seek to establish the principle that such bodies are not subject to "national appropriation." The 1963 resolution clarifies the meaning of the latter phrase by adding the words "by claim of sovereignty, by means of use or occupation, or by any other means."

Both resolutions assert the principle that celestial bodies are free for exploration and use by all states in accordance with international law. But the 1961 resolution merely commended these principles to states while the 1963 resolution "solemnly declares" that states should be guided by the principles set out in the resolution. Whether the use of the words "solemnly declares" and the designation of the resolution as a "declaration" in its title gives more force to the 1963 resolution than to the 1961 resolution is debatable in the judgment of the present author. The "declaration" was not formally signed by members of the United Nations in their capacity as sovereign states and can hardly be considered to be classed with those historic "declarations" under which parties have formally entered into undertakings as in a treaty between them.

The discussions which took place in the First Committee when the draft resolution was under consideration throw light on its international legal effect as well as on how it should be construed. The position of the United States was explained by the late Ambassador Adlai E. Stevenson in part as follows on 2 December 1963:

> In the view of the United States, the operative paragraphs of the draft resolution contained legal principles which the General Assembly, in adopting the resolution, would declare should guide States in the exploration and use of outer space. We believe these legal principles reflect international law as it is accepted by the Members of the United Nations. The United States, for its part, intends to respect these principles. We hope that the conduct which the resolution commends to nations in the exploration of outer space will become the practice of all nations.[5]

Earlier in the same statement Ambassador Stevenson had referred to the fact that the growth "of custom and usage must be present to provide the basis of sound law." Nowhere did he intimate that the proposed resolution created new and binding obligations which had not already been supported by international custom and conduct.

---

[5] U. N. Doc. No. A/C.1/PV.1342, at 12 (1963).

During the same session the Soviet representative stated:

> We still consider that the declaration of the principles governing the activities of States in the exploration and use of outer space must be an international document similar to a treaty, which would contain firm legal obligations on the part of States. This problem must, of course, be solved.[6]

This appears to be tantamount to a statement that the proposed resolution would create no legal obligations not already existing. He did add, however, later in his statement:

> Let it be said in passing that one should note the statement of the delegation of the United States of America to the effect that the United States considers that these legal principles reflect international law as it is accepted by the Members of the United Nations and that, on its part, the United States intends to respect the principles. The Soviet Union, for its part, will also respect the principles contained in this declaration if it is unanimously adopted.

The United Kingdom representative at the same meeting expressed his approval of the principles stated in the draft resolution as constituting "a significant contribution to the development of the law of outer space." He added: "My government intends to respect these principles and believes that the conduct they enjoin will become the practice of every State and thus serve to ensure the exploration and use of outer space for peaceful purposes."[7]

It should be noted that the Soviet representative specifically stated that a treaty or "similar document" was required. The United Kingdom representative believed that the principles would "become the practice of every State." This is quite different from a statement that the principles in the resolution were already part of international law or that the adoption of the resolution would create binding obligations.

The representative of France was more specific in denying that the proposed resolution would create of itself new and binding international legal obligations. He said:

> I will add, however, that, while supporting and subscribing to the principles contained in the declaration to which I have just referred, my delegation could not for the moment give this declaration more value than that of a declaration of intention. We do not, in fact, consider that a resolution of the General Assembly, even though adopted unanimously, can in this case create, *stricto sensu*, juridical

---

[6] *Id.* at 41.   [7] *Id.* at 77.

obligations incumbent upon Member States. Such obligations can flow only from international agreements.[8]

The resolution was approved in the First Committee and later unanimously adopted in the General Assembly.

The United Nations is certainly not a world government. Its General Assembly does not have legislative powers which would permit it to amend national constitutions or statutes of Member States, or to create new and binding legal obligations on such States. The United Nations may, however, in the judgment of the present author, restate and clarify, by unanimously adopted resolutions, general international understanding as to what constitutes existing customary international law. When the late Ambassador Stevenson discussed the 1963 resolution which sought to ban national appropriation of celestial bodies, his major position was that the operative paragraphs of the draft resolution "reflect international law as it is accepted by the Member States of the United Nations." This was a factual statement. Nothing in the debates directly challenged the facts. Certainly his statement was well supported so far as flights in outer space were involved. But there had been no manned landings on celestial bodies. The only fact supporting his statement as to celestial bodies was the landing of the Soviet Lunik II on the moon in 1959 followed by Soviet statements that territorial rights were not claimed. A distinguished Soviet expert on international law, the late Professor Y. Korovin, had written in 1962 as follows:

> The head of the Soviet Government, N. S. Khrushchev, replying to questions put by American correspondents on whether the landing of a Soviet pennant on the moon gave the Soviet Union grounds for making any property claims on this planet, said: "We regard the launching of a space rocket and the delivery of our pennant to the moon as our achievement. And when we say 'our' we imply all the countries of the world, that is, we imply that it is also your achievement and the achievement of all people living on earth."
>
> In another statement Khrushchev said he had no doubt that U.S. engineers, scientists and workers engaged in space exploration would also send their pennant to the moon and "the Soviet pennant, as an old resident of the moon, will welcome your pennant, and they will live in peace and friendship."[9]

Whether this single landing on the moon of an unmanned rocket, not followed by occupation, could be considered as evidence of customary

---

[8] U. N. Doc. No. A/C.1/PV.1545, at 21 (1963).

[9] Korovin, "Peaceful Cooperation in Space," *International Affairs*, June 1962, p. 61.

international law banning territorial claims, may well be open to question. But it seems to have been the sole factual background for Ambassador Stevenson's statement as it related to celestial bodies.

At least two able European experts have asserted that the 1961 and 1963 United Nations resolutions, and the manner of their unanimous acceptance, constitute a legal ban on seizures of areas on the moon. In a 1963 lecture, Professor Dr. Goedhuis of the Netherlands (Chairman of the Space Law Committee of the International Law Association), said in discussing the 1961 resolution:

On the basis of statements of governments [and others] . . . the conclusion can be drawn that before the acceptance of the resolution a general conviction had been formed according to which, through the recognition of the principle of freedom of exploration and use both of outer space and celestial bodies, the interests of mankind were best served. The resolution did, therefore, do no more than confirm a common consent of mankind which had already been created before its adoption.[10]

In a note to his lecture, written after the 1963 resolution had been adopted, he referred to the claim that the resolution "would only represent a declaration of intent." Dr. Goedhuis asserted that the 1963 resolution reinforced the thesis that the principles of the 1961 resolution "formed part of general international law and as such are binding on all States. No States have made legal claims or taken legal positions inconsistent with those laid down in the resolution."

Dr. C. Wilfred Jenks of Great Britain, who had served as Reporter on Space Law for the Institute of International Law, wrote, following the adoption of the 1963 resolution, that theoretical controversy as to the status of celestial bodies:

has been superseded by unanimous endorsement by the General Assembly of the United Nations on two successive occasions of the principle that celestial bodies are free for exploration and use by all states in accordance with international law and are not subject to national appropriation. . . . No claims to sovereignty or any lesser national appropriation of any celestial body were asserted or recognized before the General Assembly acted in the matter. No one was or is constrained to recognize any such claim asserted unilaterally. The General Assembly by unanimous decision has recorded the collective refusal of the Members of the United Nations to recognize any such claim, and has thereby placed the celestial bodies beyond

---

[10] Goedhuis, "Regimes of Air Space and Outer Space," 2 *Recueil Des Cours* 295–97 (1963).

the possibility of national appropriation. In these circumstances the theoretical controversy now belongs to history.[11]

In the United States, the present author, among others, indicated his hope that the matter was indeed settled. Writing, just after the adoption of the 1963 resolution, he said:

Academic questions may still exist as to whether this declaration [in the 1963 resolution] not being in treaty form is of itself legally binding on the U.N. Member States who voted in its favor. However its practical effect is clear. As between those Member States now exploring outer space and those others, which may soon be added, the non-territorial status of outer space and of celestial bodies has been accepted together with an effective denial of any right to claim outer space sovereignty.

After referring to statements made by various delegations before the resolution was adopted, which have been quoted here earlier, he noted the fact that no State indicated that it would refuse to regulate its international conduct in the manner provided by the declaration, and concluded:

For practical purposes, it can now be stated with great assurance that no member of the United Nations will hereafter seek to project its territorial sovereign claims into outer space. If a landing is made on the moon, no territorial rights will follow. Freedom of exploration and use of outer space and celestial bodies now seem assured.[12]

Unfortunately the situation has changed and freedom of use of celestial bodies seems no longer positively "assured." Statements made in the United Nations since the adjournment of the 1963 General Assembly have raised grave doubts as to the force to be given to the 1961 and 1963 resolutions.

The present difficulties have arisen from a later and little discussed resolution of the 1963 General Assembly. This *recommended* "that considerations should be given to incorporating in international agreement form, in the future as appropriate, legal principles governing the activities of States in the exploration and use of outer space," then *requested* the Committee on the Peaceful Uses of Outer Space to continue to study and report on legal problems governing the activities of states in the exploration and use of outer space, and in particular to arrange for the prompt preparation of draft international agreements on liability for damage caused by objects launched into outer

---

[11] JENKS, *Space Law* 171 (1965).
[12] AEROSPACE LAW—PROGRESS IN THE U.N., *supra* at 332.

space and on assistance to, and return of, astronauts and space vehicles, and to report to the next General Assembly as to the two latter agreements.[13]

This resolution was referred to the Legal Sub-Committee. As a result, statements were made by various national representatives which can neither be overlooked nor minimized. For example, the representative of Hungary said "the preparation of an international agreement embodying the principles set out in the Declaration was of primary importance, for the Declaration in the General Assembly Resolution No. 1962 (XVIII) was only a recommendation and therefore not binding."[14] The representative of the Soviet Union stated that the adoption of the Declaration was only a beginning and the next step "was to incorporate the principles of the Declaration in an international agreement or treaty whose provisions would be binding on all parties."[15] The representative of Italy, himself a distinguished expert on air and space law, said: "The Declaration was not, however, entirely satisfactory. It lacked the legal force of an international instrument and was weaker than the resolution adopted by the Sub-Committee in 1961 which had affirmed that all international law should apply to outer space."[16]

The representative of France restated the position of that government as indicated before the 1963 resolution was adopted. He said that the French position with regard to the law of outer space was that no such law yet existed. He continued:

> Existing international law did not necessarily apply to outer space without certain adaptations. In addition, the legal principles governing the use of outer space and celestial bodies had yet to be defined. It was for the Sub-Committee to give them precise formulation in draft agreements, for the principles would never become binding on States until they were embodied in international agreements accepted by States. The resolutions which had been adopted could not give rise to legal obligations for Member States; they had no binding force and were no more than declarations of intention. It was now for the Sub-Committee to prepare the legal instruments which would later become the law of outer space.[17]

When the Legal Sub-Committee met again, in November 1964, the representative of the Soviet Union restated his position that the 1963 resolution did not create legal obligations. He said:

---

[13] U. N. Resolution 1963 (XVIII), 13 Dec. 1963, U.N. Doc. No. A/5441, Supp. 1.
[14] U. N. Doc. No. A/C.105/C.2/SR.29–37, at 3 (1963).
[15] *Id.* at 10.   [16] *Id.* at 44.   [17] *Id.* at 46.

[T]he Declaration adopted by the General Assembly represented an important step forward, for it constituted the first legal text governing the activities of States in the utilization of outer space. The Soviet delegation regretted, however, that that Declaration was in the form of a General Assembly resolution which laid no legal obligation on the Governments of States Members of the United Nations. It also deplored the fact that, in spite of the efforts which the Soviet delegation, supported by certain other delegations, had made in that direction, it had not proved possible to work out a draft international agreement on legal principles. It was worth noting that one of the main tasks of the Sub-Committee was in fact to draft such an agreement. The Soviet delegation therefore hoped that the Governments represented on the Sub-Committee would make increased efforts to bring their points of view on that question into agreement, particularly as the Declaration of Legal Principles had enjoyed the unanimous support of the States Members of the United Nations.[18]

These responsible expressions of opinion by representatives of Member States of the United Nations must be given great weight in any determination as to whether the winner in the race to the moon is, in fact, now bound by existing law or international agreement to refrain from claiming territorial rights over any occupied areas. Admittedly, no draft agreement or treaty as to celestial bodies has yet been prepared.

For practical purposes these 1964 national statements seem to have reopened the old controversy. The Soviet Union has said that the General Assembly resolution as to outer space and celestial bodies "laid no legal obligation on the governments of States Members of the United Nations." If that be true, no obligation exists to acknowledge as true Ambassador Stevenson's position that the 1963 resolution reflected "international law as it is accepted by the members of the United Nations" even though the Soviet Union voted for the resolution. Nor does any obligation exist to recognize the resolution as creating binding rules of conduct.

Perhaps even more disturbing is the statement of France (a member of NATO) that the resolution has no binding force and is no more than a "declaration of intention." Certainly a declaration of intention, valid when made, could be repudiated on later occasion if political conditions changed.

As difficult as it may be at this time, still it would appear that a formal treaty may be the only final answer. This is what was done

---

[18] U.N. Doc. No. A/AC.105/C.2/SR.38, at 4 (1963).

when the dangerous status of Antarctica demanded settlement. This is what was done to ban certain nuclear tests. True, treaties can be and have been broken. But at least a formal treaty would state unequivocally the rights and obligations of the parties. The world would not be left in the difficult position of looking to the correct legal interpretation of a somewhat vague resolution, particularly when important States which have voted for its adoption in the United Nations thereafter assert that it has not created any binding obligations.

Until such a treaty is signed, it cannot be stated with certainty whether or not the victor in the race to the moon may claim territorial sovereignty over occupied areas.

ADDENDUM

Since the above article was written for *University: A Princeton Quarterly*, several things have occurred which warrant serious consideration.

On 23 September 1965 Ambassador Arthur J. Goldberg, addressing the United Nations, referred to the resolution sponsored seven years earlier by President (then Senator) Johnson on the use of outer space for peaceful purposes, and said:

> Since then the General Assembly has laid down valuable ground rules for activities in space and on celestial bodies. In accordance with these rules, our space activities have been, and will continue to be, nonaggressive, peaceful and beneficial in character.
>
> But these rules are not enough. Instruments from earth have already reached the moon and photographed Mars. And man will soon follow. Accordingly we suggest that the United Nations begin work on a comprehensive treaty on the exploration of the celestial bodies.[19]

On 31 January 1966 President Johnson submitted a Report to the Congress on "United States Aeronautics and Space Activities—1965." A chapter of the report dealing with the Department of State refers to an address by Ambassador Goldberg in the United Nations on 18 December and says: "Recalling his suggestion of September 23 that the United Nations begin work on a comprehensive treaty on the exploration of celestial bodies, he said that the United States plans to present a definite proposal as to the contents of such a treaty."[20]

On 3 February 1966 the Soviets soft-landed on the moon rocket Luna-9 which transmitted back radio and television signals. At a press

---

[19] U.S. Delegation to the U.N., Press Release No. 4649, 23 Sept. 1965.

[20] "Report to the Congress from the President," *United States Aeronautics and Space Activities* 1965, chap. VI, pp. 75–76 (31 Jan. 1966).

conference held 10 February 1966, according to a Tass Moscow news release, the President of the Soviet Academy of Sciences is quoted as having said "that the Soviet Union does not claim ownership of that part of the territory of the moon where the automatic station soft-landed." Other news reports indicated that Luna-9 carried a Soviet pennant.

As stated in a Moscow dispatch of 1 March 1966 (quoted in The New York Times on 2 March 1966): "An unmanned spacecraft bearing an emblem with the Soviet hammer and sickle crashed onto the surface of the planet Venus today, the Soviet Union announced."[21]

These incidents indicate that the exploration of celestial bodies is no longer a "science-fiction" theory, but has become in fact a subject requiring present international decision.

On 7 May 1966 President Johnson issued a formal statement proposing a treaty on the peaceful exploration of the moon and other heavenly bodies, saying among other things:

> In my view we need a treaty laying down rules and procedures for the exploration of celestial bodies.

---

[21] N.Y. Times, 2 Mar. 1966, p. 1, col. 4 (city ed.).

[*Since the* Author's Note *to this chapter was written, the United Nations General Assembly on* 19 *December* 1966 *adopted a Resolution approving and recommending for signature and ratification a* "*Treaty of Principles Governing the Activities of States in the Exploration and Use of Outer Space, including the Moon and Other Celestial Bodies.*" *Article II of this Treaty prescribes that outer space, including the moon and other celestial bodies, is not subject to national appropriation by claim of sovereignty, by means of use or occupation, or by any other means. The Treaty will take effect when ratified by the USSR, the United States of America, the United Kingdom, and two other governments.*]

PART SIX
Selected Problems in
International Regulation
of Aerospace Activities

22
Air Transport and World Organization

Reprinted by permission of the
Yale Law Journal *from 55* Yale
Law Journal *119 (August 1946)*.
© Yale Law Journal *1946*.

Author's Note. This article was published in 1946. It should be read in conjunction with the next article on the "Bermuda Plan," published only a few months later. World organization has changed little in the past twenty years. The problems discussed here seem to be still present. Both the United Nations and the International Civil Aviation Organization still have their separate and perhaps unco-ordinated powers and functions. It must be recalled that the Chicago Conference of 1944, which drafted the present convention on "International Civil Aviation" took place before the United Nations Charter was drafted. Unfortunately, the Soviet Union is not a member of the International Civil Aviation Organization, though an active and powerful member of the United Nations. However, an agreement between the two organizations was negotiated in 1946. It contains an article under which ICAO agrees to cooperate with the economic and social council of the U.N. in furnishing such information and rendering such assistance to the Security Council as that Council may request, including assistance in carrying out decisions for the maintenance or restoration of international peace and security. But just what this means or how it will apply is not clear, particularly if sanctions are sought by the Security Council involving air transport. Such assistance should never become the victim of ideological rivalries or other misunderstandings.

I

AIR TRANSPORT, because of certain interrelated legal, economic, and political fundamentals, is itself essentially international, and must be so considered in any realistic plan for world organization. The conflicts between national and international interests inherent in these fundamentals, as shown below, have not been resolved.

LEGAL

Every State has complete and exclusive sovereignty over the airspace above its territory. It has, therefore, full right to exclude or admit such foreign aircraft as it may determine, and to that extent can unilaterally control international air trade routes.

ECONOMIC

Every State, by such exclusion or admission into its territory of foreign aircraft engaged in international commerce, directly affects world trade and the economic position of itself and of others.

357

POLITICAL

Every State in the exercise of its sovereignty, has the moral right to develop its air transport to the extent needed by its domestic and foreign commerce and other legitimate objectives. However, world organization may well require sufficient international control so that air transport does not become an instrument of unfair nationalistic competition or aggression and, thus, the source of serious international misunderstanding and dangerous ill-feeling.

II

These three fundamentals are closely related. It is impossible to give sound consideration to the economic and political questions of international air transport without a clear understanding of what is included in the legal concept of "sovereignty over the airspace." From this concept spring most of the practical problems of air transport as an element of international relations.

Prior to World War I, no agreement existed either between jurists or between statesmen as to the extent of national sovereignty in the airspace. Between 1901 and the outbreak of World War I in 1914 the question was actively discussed. Various theories were brought forward. These included: complete sovereignty through the whole airspace over national territory, with resulting political control of flight in national airspace; no sovereignty, with consequent complete freedom of flight; differing zone systems, generally with the upper airspace free and a lower stratum next the earth's surface under national control; variants of these. Questions of national security rather than economic problems, were the basis of most of these early discussions.[1]

An ambitious international conference held in Paris in 1910, after careful diplomatic preparation, adjourned without reaching any deci-

---

[1] HAZELTINE, THE LAW OF THE AIR (1911) 1–53; GARNER, RECENT DEVELOPMENTS IN INTERNATIONAL LAW (1925) 141–188; LYCKLAMA A NIJEHOLT, AIR SOVEREIGNTY (1910) 1–21; HENRY-COÜANNIER, ÉLÉMENTS CRÉATEURS DU DROIT AÉRIEN (1929) 1–25; COLEGROVE, INTERNATIONAL CONTROL OF AVIATION (1930) 42; 1 HYDE, INTERNATIONAL LAW (2d rev. ed. 1945) 585; Fauchille, Le Domaine Aérien et le Régime Juridique des Aérostats (1901) 8 REVUE GÉNÉRALE DE DROIT INTERNATIONAL PUBLIC 414; Fauchille, La Circulation Aérienne et les Droits des Etats en Temps de Paix (1910) 17 REVUE GÉNÉRALE DE DROIT INTERNATIONAL PUBLIC 55; Baldwin, Law of the Airship (1910) 4 AM. J. INT. L. 95–108; Kuhn, The Beginnings of an Aerial Law, id. at 109–132; McNair, The Beginnings and the Growth of Aeronautical Law (1930) 1 J. AIR L., 383; Bogert Problems in Aviation Law (1921) 6 CORN. L. Q. 271.

sion on the primary problem—to what extent should international air navigation be free of political control by the State flown over.[2]

With the outbreak of World War I, military considerations immediately forced general acceptance of the sovereignty of each nation over its airspace. Air boundaries, as well as land boundaries, were promptly closed for security reasons. Belligerent aircraft flying over neutral territory were forced to land and their crews interned exactly as if surface boundaries had been crossed.[3]

At the close of World War I, the Aeronautical Commission of the Peace Conference was directed to prepare an air navigation convention. The purpose of this convention was to provide, for the first time, international rules to govern air navigation in time of peace. The United States took an active part in the preparation of this Convention but did not ratify it. The Convention was accepted by the other Allied and Associated Powers, and was adhered to by many neutrals. As the now celebrated "Air Navigation Convention of 1919," usually called the Paris Convention, it became the basis for much of the modern international law of the air.[4]

Article I states:

The High Contracting Parties recognize that every power has complete and exclusive sovereignty over the airspace above its territory. For the purpose of the present Convention the territory of a State shall be understood as including the national territory, both that of the mother country and of the colonies, and the territorial waters adjacent thereto.[5]

With the passage of the Air Commerce Act of 1926,[6] later amplified by the Civil Aeronautics Act of 1938,[7] the United States definitely asserted, by federal statute, its sovereignty in the airspace over its territory. A similar position was taken by treaty. In the Pan American

[2] COLEGROVE, op. cit. supra note 1, at 48; BLACHERE, L'AIR, VOIE DE COMMUNICATION ET LE DROIT (1911) 129–211; SPAIGHT, AIRCRAFT IN PEACE AND THE LAW (1919) 5; SLOTEMAKER, FREEDOM OF PASSAGE FOR INTERNATIONAL AIR SERVICES (1932) 12.

[3] SPAIGHT, op. cit. supra note 2, at 8.

[4] For the best account of the origins of the Paris Convention see ROPER, LA CONVENTION INTERNATIONALE DU 13 OCTOBRE 1919 (1930). Dr. Roper, now Secretary-General of the Provisional International Civil Aviation Organization, Montreal, took part in drafting the Paris Convention. See also COLEGROVE, op. cit. supra note 1, at 53–65; TOMBS, INTERNATIONAL ORGANIZATION IN EUROPEAN AIR TRANSPORT (1936) 42.

[5] International Convention Relating to the Regulation of Aerial Navigation, October 13, 1919, reproduced from Official Bulletin No. 26, Dep't of State Publication 2143 (1944); COLEGROVE, op. cit. supra note 1, at 149.

[6] 44 STAT. 568 (1926), §6, 49 U.S.C. §176 (1939).

[7] 52 STAT. 973 (1938), 49 U.S.C. §§ 401–682 (1938).

Convention on Commercial Aviation, signed at Havana in 1928 by the United States and various American republics, and later ratified by the United States and others, it is provided in Article I that:

> The high contracting parties recognize that every state has complete and exclusive sovereignty over the airspace above its territory and territorial waters.[8]

Flowing from national sovereignty of the airspace, each State has complete control, for political purposes, of the airspace over its territory and territorial waters. In practice it has been universally admitted since World War I that the aircraft of one State can enter the airspace over the territory and territorial waters of another State, in time of peace, only when authorized. This authorization may be by multilateral convention among several States concerned, by bilateral convention between two States only, or by permit issued by one State to a particular airline or a particular aircraft of another State. In every case, however, the authority to operate into the national airspace, or to land, either for refueling or to discharge or pick up cargo, must be granted by direct license of the State concerned.

The Paris Convention, in Article 2, provided that each contracting State should undertake in time of peace to accord "freedom of innocent passage" above its territory to the aircraft of other contracting States. In Article 15 it also provided that every aircraft of a contracting State should have the right to cross the airspace of another State without landing, following the route fixed by the State flown over, with an additional proviso that the State flown over might require the aircraft to land for security reasons.

To that extent the Paris Convention provided by multilateral agreement among its member States for certain transit privileges. These privileges were, however, of no importance to international air transport as they applied only to private and other occasional flights. The last clause of Article 15, as finally amended and clarified, limited the rights of air transport, stating:

> Every contracting State may make conditional on its prior authorization the establishment of international airways and the creation and operation of regular international air navigation lines, with or without landing, on its territory.[9]

---

[8] DEP'T OF STATE TREATY SER. 840 (1931); COLEGROVE, *op. cit. supra* note 1, at 173.

[9] TOMBS, *op. cit. supra* note 4, at 60; Roper, *Recent Developments in International Aeronautical Law* (1930) 1 J. AIR L. 395; SLOTEMAKER, *op. cit. supra* note 2, at 37, 105; 4 HACKWORTH, DIGEST INT. LAW, 359–362; INTERNATIONAL CONVENTION RELATING TO THE REGULATION OF AERIAL NAVIGATION, OCTOBER 13, 1919, Dep't of State Publication 2143 (1944).

This provision gave to each State flown over unilateral power to determine whether world air trade routes might cross its territory with or without landing.

The Havana Convention of 1928 also contained provisions for the innocent passage of aircraft of member States. This was again of no particular importance in solving the transit problem. Few world routes were involved, as the only ratifying States, in addition to the United States, were Mexico, the Dominican Republic, and certain of the Central and South American States. Also, the rights of innocent passage, so far as scheduled air transport operations are concerned, have been construed as if the Convention contained a requirement for special license for such operations.[10]

As a result of the rights of route control flowing from the doctrine of sovereignty of the airspace, many bilateral agreements for the establishment of air trade routes were entered into before World War II, and franchises and licenses were issued directly to international air line operators.[11] Certain States, however, did not hesitate to withhold or severely limit the issuance of transit privileges. Neither Turkey nor China granted such permits to foreign air transport. The United States maintained exclusive control of trans-Pacific aviation. It granted no permits for scheduled foreign flights through Alaska, Hawaii, Midway, Wake, or Guam, nor through the Philippines during the period of its political control. Security reasons undoubtedly entered into some, if not all, of these decisions.

Across the North Atlantic were two practical air routes. One of these was controlled by Great Britain through its sovereignty over Newfoundland, an almost necessary stopping-place when safe range of aircraft was considered. The other route was via British-controlled Bermuda and via the Portuguese-controlled Azores to Lisbon. Portugal had authorized the use of the Azores for one British and one American operating company, but required that Lisbon be the first and last port of call in Europe when the Azores were used in trans-Atlantic service. Great Britain had permitted only American operations through Newfoundland and Bermuda (in addition to its own proposed operation), and such American operations were limited by the permit to two round trips per week. The United States reciprocally granted to a British company a permit for two trans-Atlantic weekly landings in United States territory. Other examples could be cited.

---

[10] 4 HACKWORTH, *op. cit. supra* note 9, at 366; 1 HYDE, *op. cit. supra* note 1, at 600; Latchford, *The Right of Innocent Passage in International Civil Air Navigations Agreements*, 11 DEP'T OF STATE BULL. (1944) 19.

[11] TOMBS, *op. cit. supra* note 4, at 100–121; LISSITZYN, INTERNATIONAL AIR TRANSPORT AND NATIONAL POLICY (1942) 373–402.

The International Civil Aviation Conference held at Chicago in 1944 again considered the entire question. Present were members of the United Nations (except Russia) and certain neutrals. The Conference adopted a new Convention on International Civil Aviation which, it is hoped, will soon come into force in substitution for both the Paris and the Havana Conventions. In Article 1 of the Chicago Convention, it is again asserted that:

> The contracting States recognize that every State has complete sovereignty over the airspace above its territory.

Territory, as defined in this Convention, includes territorial waters, following the earlier precedents.[12]

On many points the Chicago Conference failed to agree. But no one challenged the doctrine of sovereignty of the airspace. It may certainly now be accepted as the primary rule of the international law of the air, and must be so considered by any world organization. Any change in this doctrine can come into effect only if the States concerned agree to surrender part of their recognized sovereignty.

The Chicago Convention, in Article 5, gives certain limited rights of transit to the aircraft not engaged in scheduled international air services and to that extent is a multilateral transit agreement. The same Convention, however, restates, in Article 6, in the strongest possible terms, the rights of each State as to scheduled services:

> No scheduled international air service may be operated over or into the territory of a contracting State, except with the special permission or other authorization of that State, and in accordance with the terms of such permission or authorization.

The Chicago Conference also prepared and opened for signature two agreements known respectively as the "International Air Services Transit Agreement"[13] and the "International Air Transport Agreement"[14], to be discussed later. They are legally multilateral permits under Article 6 of the Chicago Convention, authorizing, in the Transit Agreement, certain privileges, not rights, of flight over and landing for refueling in the territory of accepting States and, in the Transport

---

[12] *International Civil Aviation Conference*, Chicago, 1944, *Final Act and Related Documents*, DEP'T OF STATE CONFERENCE SER. 64 (1945) 59; Convention transmitted by President Roosevelt to U.S. Senate, Message from the President of the United States—Convention on International Civil Aviation, 79th Cong., 1st Sess., Senate, Executive A, March 12, 1945; Convention favorably reported by Committee on Foreign Relations, U.S. Senate, 79th Cong., 2d Sess., SEN. EXEC. REP. No. 8, June 19, 1946; ratification by U.S. Senate approved July 25, 1946.

[13] *International Civil Aviation Conference, op. cit. supra* note 12, at 87.

[14] *Id.* at 91.

Agreement, certain added commercial privileges. Any State accepting either agreement may renounce it on one year's notice. Fundamentally, therefore, the legal position since the Chicago Conference and World War II continues as before.

Any State, except during the time that it is committed otherwise by the Transit or Transport or other special Agreements, is still fully authorized to take advantage of its own political position and bargaining power, as well as the fortunate geographical position of its homeland and outlying possessions, and unilaterally determine (for economic or security reasons) what foreign aircraft will be permitted to enter or be excluded from its airspace, as well as the extent to which such airspace may be used as part of world air trade routes.

III

The legal position of air transport as thus developed poses serious economic problems to any world organization. The decision of a State to admit or exclude foreign aircraft engaged in international commerce, either in transit elsewhere or for the purpose of discharging and picking up cargo, directly affects world trade and the internal economy of the State taking such action and that of other States.

Air transport has become an inseparable part of the complicated fabric of world transport. It is fast taking its place today beside ocean shipping as one of the great economic factors in the development of international commerce. Both serve the public—both are instruments of national transport and communication policy—both enter foreign territory to compete with local services for international trade. But the right of a State to control the use of these two world economic forces has in certain respects developed very differently.[15] Any State may refuse to allow the entry of aircraft of a second State, but it would be guilty of an almost unfriendly act if it refused the entry of merchant vessels of that State. In other respects the international rights and privileges of air transport and ocean shipping, as they affect world economy, are very similar—much more so than is indicated by popular discussion of "freedom of the air" and "freedom of the seas." A brief statement of some of the historic background of the development of world transport may be useful.

The name of Hugo Grotius, the great Dutch lawyer and scholar, will always be linked with the rights now enjoyed by ocean shipping on the high seas. His arguments must today be reconsidered as applicable to world transport. It will be recalled that in the early years of the 17th Century claim was made in the name of the Portuguese

---

[15] LISSITZYN, *op. cit. supra* note 11, at 403–405.

(although really on behalf of Spain) that the Portuguese had exclusive control of parts of the high seas and the Indian Ocean on the trade route between Europe and the East Indies, that the Portuguese had sole right to navigate these seas and to trade with the Indies, that the Dutch must withdraw from this trade. On behalf of his countrymen, Grotius prepared his celebrated dissertation: "The Freedom of the Seas or the Right which belongs to the Dutch to take part in the East Indian Trade."[16] He denied the right of the Portuguese, or anyone else, to claim sovereignty of the high seas or exclusive right to their navigation, and asserted the right of the Dutch to proceed to and trade with the Indies. He based his argument, as he states, on "the following most specific and unimpeachable axiom of the Law of Nations, called a primary rule or first principle, the spirit of which is self-evident and immutable, to wit: Every nation is free to travel to every other nation, and to trade with it."[17]

To sustain his first proposition, *the right to travel,* Grotius insisted in unanswerable terms on the inequity if not impossibility of national sovereignty over any part of the high seas and the consequent freedom of navigation open to all. In support of his second proposition, *the right to trade,* he claimed: first, that the Portuguese had no sovereignty over the Indies and that, as third parties, they had no right to interfere with the desire of the Dutch and the people of the Indies to trade with each other; and, second, that under the Law of Nations, no State or ruler "can debar foreigners from having access to their subjects and trading with them."[18] In concluding Chapter I of his dissertation, he summarizes his position as follows:

> It follows, therefore, that the Portuguese, even if they had been sovereigns in those parts to which the Dutch make voyages, would nevertheless be doing them an injury if they should forbid them access to those places and from trading there.
>
> Is it not then an incalculably greater injury for nations which desire reciprocal commercial relations to be debarred therefrom by the acts of those who are sovereigns neither of the nations interested, nor of the element over which their connecting high road runs? Is not that the very cause which for the most part prompts us to execrate robbers and pirates, namely, that they beset and infest our trade routes?[19]

To apply his argument more easily to present day conditions, it may be restated as follows:

---

[16] GROTIUS, FREEDOM OF THE SEAS (Magoffin's Trans. 1916) Introductory Note.

[17] *Id.* at 7.　　　[18] *Id.* at 8.　　　[19] *Id.* at 10.

1. No State has sovereignty over the high seas, and its navigation is free to all.

2. No State, whose sovereignty is not affected, has the right to interfere with reciprocal trading arrangements between two other States.

3. No State has the right to limit or control the entry into its territory for trading purposes of the transport of another State.

On his first contention the verdict of history is with Grotius. It is no longer disputed that the high seas are free to the commerce and navigation of all nations. No State would now be allowed to claim or to exercise rights of sovereignty over the high seas. In the language of Oppenheim: "The term 'Freedom of the Open Sea' indicates the rule of the Law of Nations that the open sea is not, and never can be, under the sovereignty of any State whatever."[20] This is the true doctrine of "Freedom of the Seas."

International air transport enjoys exactly the same "freedom of the air." As no State has or can exercise sovereignty over the high seas, similarly it can exercise no sovereignty in the airspace above the high seas. Every State has equal right to navigate in the airspace over the high seas without obtaining the consent of any other State.[21] This common right was formally acknowledged for the first time in Article 12 of the Chicago Convention. Under this provision States bound thereby agree that "over the high seas, the rules in force shall be those established under this Convention,"[22] In other words, no single State can adopt such rules binding on the others, but the parties to the Convention as among themselves may properly agree to the rules which they will accept in the airspace over which none of them can claim sovereignty.

On his second contention, namely, that the Portuguese were not in fact sovereigns of the East Indies and could not, therefore, interfere with Dutch trading arrangements with the peoples of those islands, Grotius was fully sustained in his own time by the facts, and is now by the law. What he then asked is fully enjoyed today by both shipping and air transport. Arrangements between States under which they agree to the conditions and terms governing the entry into their territories of their respective aircraft are fully recognized under the doctrine of national sovereignty of the airspace. No State would be heard to claim a right to interfere in the trade route between the other States, unless the airspace sovereignty of this third State became involved. If only the high seas are between two States, they may agree as they

---

[20] 2 HACKWORTH, *op. cit. supra* note 9, at 654.
[21] 1 GIDEL, LE DROIT INTERNATIONAL PUBLIC DE LA MER (1932) 517; LISSITZYN, *op. cit. supra* note 11, at 403.
[22] *International Civil Aviation Conference, op. cit. supra* note 12, at 62.

alone wish as to the trade between them, whether it be by ocean shipping or air transport.

Grotius' third position, is, however, not so clear, either as a legal or economic proposition—that the Dutch should be entitled to trade with the people of the Indies even though the Portuguese held rights of sovereignty over the islands and objected to the entry of the Dutch ships. This assumes that there is a recognized right under international law for ocean shipping to pass through such territorial waters as it sees fit and to enter and trade in such national ports as may be desired, irrespective of the will of the State holding sovereignty over the territorial waters and ports thus entered. It also assumes that world economics and world trade will benefit if a State may unilaterally and against the will of the second State control the amount of trade between the two States so far as entry of the transport of the first State into the territory of the second is concerned.

No such technical legal right seems to exist. To the extent that a similar practice now exists as to ocean shipping, it would appear to result from various conditions quite apart from the doctrine of "freedom of the seas." National sovereignty over seaports is still fully recognized. In theory a State may open or close its ports as it desires. But the international right to exert this sovereignty by keeping all the ports of any country closed became, during the 19th Century, a very open question. Under international custom, developed in the first half of the 19th Century, merchant ships do enter foreign ports without special license, provided such ports have been opened to international commerce. This privilege has been variously ascribed to the existence of some type of implied license—also to the existence and indirect effect of various treaties of navigation and commerce, which reciprocally authorized the commercial entry of merchant ships into the ports of the States concerned. These treaties (together with the most-favored nation clauses in other treaties) created a situation which made it most difficult for any State, without good reason, to regulate the terms of entry, including freights to be charged, or to bar entirely foreign merchant vessels of another State from entering one of its ports open to the foreign commerce of others.[23]

---

[23] This generalization is that of the author of this article, not based on any single authority. For consideration of this difficult subject, see: 2 GIDEL, *op. cit. supra* note 21, at 9–58; 2 MOORE, INT. L. DIGEST (1906) 269–272; 5 *id.* 736–742; 2 HACKWORTH, *op. cit. supra* note 9, at 206–208. As to very limited indirect extent (except in time of war) of government control of ocean freight rates in foreign trade, see: Sanderson, *Wartime Control of Ocean Freight Rates in Foreign Trade, A World Survey*, BUREAU OF FOREIGN AND DOMESTIC COMMERCE TRADE PROMOTION SER. 212 (1940); Sanderson, *Control of Ocean Freight Rates in Foreign Trade, A World Survey*, BUREAU OF FOREIGN AND DOMESTIC COMMERCE TRADE PROMOTION SER. 185 (1938).

This historic process seems to have been initiated largely by a change in British shipping policy. Mance[24] quotes as follows from a British Board of Trade Departmental Committee of 1918:

The commercial treaties which govern our maritime relations cover a period of more than 250 years, during which our policy has gradually changed from the mercantilism of the Navigation Laws to the freedom of more recent times. Most of these treaties are relatively modern, but some, especially those with the old maritime Powers such as Sweden, Denmark, Spain and even France, Holland and the United States, go far back and bear the impress of the policy underlying them. Since the middle of the last century the navigation policy of this country has been based on the great ascendancy of the British mercantile marine and the widespread character of our trades, which made protection both unnecessary and undesirable. Our object was to obtain free access to the ports and the trade of foreign countries. It was therefore inexpedient to give British shipping privileged treatment at home since such action could only have afforded foreign countries an excuse for similarly differentiating in favor of their own vessels. In view of its relative size the British mercantile marine stood to gain more from free access to foreign countries than foreign flags stood to gain from free access to British ports; and conversely a policy of mutual restriction would for the same reason have caused more harm to British than to foreign shipping.

The present legal position as to shipping seems, therefore, to be about as follows: a State retains sovereignty over its ports and may in theory close them to others. However, by treaty and custom, there now exists what amounts to a general license, under which maritime States accord to shipping a privilege of passage through territorial waters adjacent to the high seas and of entry into ports to refuel or to discharge and pick up cargo. So far as shipping is concerned, Grotius is, under present practice, winning his last point—but not on the basis of a recognized international law *right* of access and trade.

But such is not the situation in the air. When the Paris Convention was being drafted, aviation security questions, not commercial problems, were still uppermost in the minds of men. Aircraft flying over cities and into the interior posed problems quite different from those of the entry of merchant shipping into coastal ports. Today, with the emergence of new airborne weapons of mass destruction, these security questions seem even more important. When the law of the air became fixed and national sovereignty of the airspace was accepted, the license

[24] MANCE, INTERNATIONAL SEA TRANSPORT (1944) 73.

to enter national territory for trading purposes, claimed by Grotius and historically developed for merchant shipping, was denied to air transport. Control was retained by the State flown over. It follows that:

a) Any maritime State may (with its ocean ship operators) unilaterally determine the volume and cost to the public of ocean shipping under its flag engaged in international trade to and through the open ports of a second State, irrespective of the economic effect on the latter or on world trade.

b) The second State, at the same time, may unilaterally determine the volume of the air transport of the first State which it may allow to enter its territory and may fix any conditions or limitations on such entry, irrespective of the economic effect on the first State or on world trade.

The international conflicts resulting from this situation are clear. They must be faced by any world organization.

As to the economic advantages of the free right to trade claimed by Grotius under his view of the Law of Nations, the present writer is not at all certain that the economically uncontrolled right of entry of foreign merchant vessels into national ports has always been a source of ultimate advantage to world economy. It may approach treason to make such a suggestion, but the world is in a state of transition, and it might be advantageous to reconsider world transport, both ocean shipping and air transport, as a single economic unit.

When a merchant vessel, for example of British registry, enters a foreign port, for example American, and discharges its cargo and then offers for sale its available load capacity for the carriage of outbound American cargo, the British vessel is actually offering for sale in the American port a British product in direct competition with a similar American product (the load capacity of American vessels) and without the price protection of a protective or other tariff. The British vessel was probably constructed in British shipyards under British costs. It is certainly manned by British seamen paid under British wage scales. It is operated under British regulations. The freights which it will charge are based on these conditions and costs. The capacity which it has to take on cargo in the American port is as much a British export as would be an automobile transported from Great Britain and unloaded for local sale in an American port. Under international practice, the United States has no direct government control of the rate at which the British ship offers its available capacity in the American port, nor has it retained control of when or how often the British ship or others of British or other foreign registry enter the same port.

This is the unlimited "right to trade" for which Grotius contended.

In practice in our own times and because of national ship-operating cost differentials, it has contributed toward the necessity for mounting government ship subsidies.

These and other economic problems of world shipping must not be overlooked in any final determination of the position of air transport and its national and international control. The sale of aircraft capacity to the public in a foreign airport does not seem to differ in economic theory or effect from the sale of ocean shipping capacity. Both provide competition with local services.

At the same time the present arbitrary right of any State to control world trade and trade routes insofar as is possible by barring or admitting foreign aircraft, irrespective of the effect on other States, is difficult to defend except when local national security and economic conditions are directly and vitally affected. Unjustified control and regulation, whether it be by a single State or an international body, must be kept to a minimum and the needs of the public for adequate transportation must always be in the forefront of any discussion. At some point, by some process, and through some international procedure not yet determined, the right to trade by air must be fostered, but at the same time controlled, so that world trade and the internal national economy of the States concerned is not at the mercy of the unilateral action of any one State, whether it be the State dispatching its aircraft in world trade or the State through or to which they will fly. These are international questions and must be decided accordingly.

IV

International air transport involves political problems equally as difficult as the economic questions discussed above. In any State, civil as well as military aviation is an instrument of national air power and must be so recognized.

"Air power," as the present writer has stated elsewhere, "is the ability of a nation to act through the airspace, in other words, to use controlled flight—such for instance, as the flight of aircraft. It is part of national power, to be used at home or abroad, in peace or in war. Though its uses are various, both military and civil, it is basically indivisible. The armed air forces represent but one use of the nation's air power. Civil and commercial aviation are supported by and spring from the same basic national elements."[25]

To the extent that any State consents to control or limitation of its civil air transport by the act of any other State or any international body, it foregoes one development of its potential air power. Every

---

[25] COOPER, *Air Power and the Coming Peace Treaties* (1946) 24 FOREIGN AFFAIRS 442.

State has legitimate national objectives. Within the bounds of international comity it is entitled to bend its efforts to attain these objectives through such activities and instrumentalities as it may choose. In the exercise of its sovereignty, it has the right to develop its air transport to the extent needed by such legitimate objectives.

In the United States this has been recognized by federal statute. In the Civil Aeronautics Act of 1938, the public interest is held to include "the encouragement and development of an air-transportation system properly adapted to the present and future needs of the foreign and domestic commerce of the United States, of the Postal Service, and of the national defense."[26]

These are the objectives to which air transport, as part of the air power of the United States, has been dedicated. Its government and people are moved by the conscious and unconscious national desire for commerce, communications, and defense.

Such national incentives must always be included among the long range elements of national air power which contribute to its development.[27] They are the driving forces which spur the State and its people to action. National defense is such an incentive in every State. Air transport, though developed for civil purposes, is a vitally necessary part of the equipment for military operations, as the experience of World War II demonstrated far beyond further argument. Aircraft need not be armed or carry bombs to take part in war. Witness the parachute troops, the troop carrier commands, the air transport services of both army and navy. The aircraft used in war for such purposes are designed and used in time of peace for foreign and domestic commerce, as are civil air transport routes both national and international. When a State's freedom of action in time of peace in activities such as these is limited, its air power is directly affected.

Other national incentives in the development of air power are equally as important as that of military defense. The United States has recognized the development of its foreign and domestic commerce and communications as a national need. Other States have tacitly indicated similar incentives. The British, the Germans, the Dutch, the French, the Swedes, the Japanese—all of the great trading nations of our time, were driven to develop air transport by the need for foreign commerce and communications. In parts of Canada, China, Australia and Russia air transport was the only practical mode of reasonably rapid domestic transport—built up in those cases by the national desire and demand for internal economic and political unity and trade. In the great colonial powers—Great Britain, France, the

---

[26] 52 STAT. 973 (1938); 49 U.S.C. § 402 (1941).
[27] See NOTES ON AIR POWER IN TIME OF PEACE, Chapter 2, *supra.*

Netherlands, Italy, Belgium—an additional incentive appeared—the need to tie together through rapid air routes politically disintegrating empires.

Other incentives (toward objectives perhaps legitimate to the States concerned, though not in the eyes of the world) give much cause for concern. German foreign air transport, for example, was pushed far afield—particularly in South America—with the obvious desire of extending political and ideological infiltration. In the Pacific, supposedly civil air routes to Korea, Manchuria and the originally mandated islands were used by the Japanese to bind together an empire seized through violence and disregard of international commitments.

But it is not alone in such clearly improper cases that the development of international air transport may come into conflict with world interests. In the race for foreign commerce and national expansion, subsidy wars may develop; local air service of smaller and weaker nations may be forced to discontinue; national economy of other states may be seriously affected. Many things may occur that, in the meaning of the United Nations Charter, would create a "situation which might lead to international friction." While this possibility may be still debated by some, it is wise to recall that it was directly admitted by the Chicago Conference. The Preamble of the Convention on International Civil Aviation states that "the future development of international civil aviation can greatly help to create and preserve friendship and understanding among the nations and the peoples of the world, yet its abuse can become a threat to the general security."[28]

As stated earlier, any State in the exercise of its sovereignty has the right (as well as the duty to itself) to develop its air power, as represented in part by its air transport, to the extent needed by its domestic and foreign commerce and other legitimate objectives. But somewhere an impartial forum must exist in which the legitimacy of these objectives can be challenged by other States directly concerned. The development of national air transport of one State may injuriously affect another or cause a dangerous dispute. Again there must be a forum and machinery to remedy such a situation. World organization may well require sufficient international control so that air transport does not become an instrument of unfair nationalistic economic competition or political aggression and thus the source of serious international misunderstanding and dangerous ill-feeling.[29] But such regulation and interference with national action by any international body must, as stated earlier, be kept at a minimum. The needs of the public for ade-

---

[28] *International Civil Aviation Conference, op. cit. supra* note 12, at 59.
[29] MANCE, INTERNATIONAL AIR TRANSPORT (1944) 103.

quate transportation must be always in the forefront of any discussion or decision. World commerce must never be unduly retarded.

V

Such are the fundamental and difficult problems of international air transport. The machinery of inter-government world organization now available to meet these problems may perhaps be readjusted to become effective. It is ineffective today. The existing machinery includes: the United Nations Assembly, with the Security Council, the Economic and Social Council and its proposed Transport and Communications Commission; the Provisional International Civil Aviation Organization (PICAO), located in Montreal, with its Assembly and Council—to be succeeded by the permanent International Civil Aviation Organization (ICAO).

In August 1944 the United States issued invitations to member States of the United Nations and certain neutral States for an international civil aviation conference, referred to earlier in this article as the "Chicago Conference." It had before it two main objectives—first, to provide an organization to set up uniform technical and safety standards for world wide air navigation, as successor to the International Commission for Air Navigation organized under the Paris Convention of 1919; second, and at least of equal importance, to determine how and to what extent air transport could be subjected to international economic and political control. This conference succeeded in its first objective. It made progress towards its second objective but without final success.

The Conference drafted and opened for signature four international agreements: the Convention on International Civil Aviation;[30] an Interim Agreement[31] to continue in effect until the Convention becomes itself effective; the Transit[32] and the Transport Agreements,[33] previously mentioned in this article.

Under the Convention the permanent International Civil Aviation Organization (ICAO) includes an Assembly on which each member State is represented, and a Council elected by the Assembly. Under the Interim Agreement, a similar temporary organization (PICAO) is now actively functioning.

ICAO (and temporarily PICAO) is fully authorized to adopt any necessary international standards for world wide unification of the technical and safety procedure so vital to every phase of international air navigation. No further world organization is needed to meet these problems.

---

[30] *International Civil Aviation Conference, op. cit. supra* note 12, at 59.
[31] *Id.* at 44.   [32] *Id.* at 87.   [33] *Id.* at 91.

In the economic and political fields the need for international organization remains unsatisfied. The Convention has given ICAO very limited economic powers, and these are largely of an administrative and advisory character, such as: research; study of operation of international air transport, including ownership of international services on trunk routes; investigation of situations appearing to present avoidable obstacles to development of air navigation; collection and publication of information, including cost of international operations and subsidies from public funds. Under certain circumstances ICAO may provide and administer airports and facilities required by international air services. But ICAO has no power to fix or control rates, allocate routes, or control operating frequencies or capacity. Nor can it require any State to admit into its territory air transport operations of another State. The legal unilateral ability of any State to control world air trade routes, as discussed earlier in this article, and the ability of any State to affect world economy by excluding or admitting to its territory the scheduled air transport of other States, have not been affected by the Convention.

In approaching the economic regulatory problem at Chicago, three diverse plans, or theories, were urged. Australia and New Zealand, fearing the political effect of international competition, wished to have all main international air transport operations owned by a single world authority with local lines under national flags. Great Britain and Canada proposed separate but fundamentally similar plans for economic control through an international organization having definite powers to fix and allocate international routes, frequencies, capacity, and rates. The United States opposed economic or political control by an international organization and favored wide freedom of operation, No agreement was reached.[34]

At the end of the Conference, the Transit and Transport Agreements were separately brought forward to cover the economic control problems omitted from the permanent Convention. Had the provisions of either the Transit or the Transport Agreements been included in the main Convention, certain States would not have signed it.

These separate Agreements are based on the so-called "Five Freedoms of the Air," as originally defined by Canada. As stated by Assistant Secretary of Commerce for Air, William A. M. Burden, in an article appearing shortly after the Chicago Conference:

---

[34] For an account of the Chicago Conference and particularly the position taken by the United States delegation, see *Blueprint for World Civil Aviation —The Chicago International Civil Aviation Conference of 1944 as viewed by Four Members of the United States Delegation in Recent Magazine Articles*, DEP'T OF STATE CONFERENCE SER. 70 (1945).

These freedoms . . . are really privileges, since every country reserves the sovereignty of its air space.[35]

As stated in the Transport Agreement mentioned above:

Each contracting State grants to the other contracting States the following freedoms of the air in respect of scheduled international air services:

1. The privilege to fly across the territory of a contracting State without landing.
2. The privilege to land for non-traffic purposes.
3. The privilege to put down passengers, mail, and cargo taken on in the territory of the State whose nationality the aircraft possesses.
4. The privilege to take on passengers, mail, and cargo destined for the territory of the State whose nationality the aircraft possesses.
5. The privilege to take on passengers, mail, and cargo destined for the territory of any other contracting State and the privilege to put down passengers, mail, and cargo coming from any such territory.

The first two "freedoms" cover privileges of air navigation and the last three privileges of commercial trade. The Transit Agreement includes the first two and the Transport Agreement all five.

If the Transit Agreement were universally accepted in more permanent form, it would largely solve the difficulties caused by the legal right of any State to prevent the establishment of world air trade routes through its territory. In addition to the privilege of transit, the Agreement also authorizes any State flown over to require the international operator to land and offer reasonable commercial services; it meets the security problem by allowing each State to designate the route and airports to be used in its territory; it gives added powers to ICAO by authorizing any State, which deems that action by another State is causing injustice or hardship under the Agreement, to request ICAO to investigate; and authorizes ICAO to suspend the guilty State if corrective action is ordered and not taken.

The Transit Agreement, however, is not now an adequate part of world organization. It has been accepted by twenty-eight States, including the United States and Great Britain, but not yet by certain other important world route States such as Brazil, Egypt and Portugal. As it can be denounced on one year's notice by any one State, it is not a basis for permanent routes. Its acceptance by the United States, as

---

[35] *Id.* at 21.

well as that of the Transport Agreement, has been attacked as illegal, it being contended that they are not valid as Executive Agreements, and that their subject matter required execution and submission to the United States Senate for ratification as treaties.[36] The right of the United States to sign them as Executive Agreements has been as vigorously defended.[37]

For quite other reasons the Transport Agreement cannot now be considered as part of a permanent world organization. Vigorously sponsored by the United States at the Chicago Conference, it covers the so-called five "freedoms" listed above, including both navigation and commercial privileges. It contains no provisions for rate control, or limitation of capacity and frequencies, but does include other limitations. These are: the route and airports to be used in national territory may be designated by the State flown over, as in the Transit Agreement; in the operation of through services "due consideration shall be given to the interests of the other contracting States so as not to interfere unduly with their regional services or to hamper the development of their through services"; any State may refuse to accord the so-called Fifth Freedom privilege, that is to say, refuse the right of other States to take on and discharge traffic destined to or coming from the territory of a third contracting State;—the Fifth Freedom, traffic itself, is limited to traffic between contracting States; the Third, Fourth and Fifth Freedom privileges (the commercial privileges) are applicable only to "through services on a route constituting a reasonably direct line out from and back to the homeland of the State whose nationality the aircraft possesses"; and the agreement may be renounced on one year's notice.

The Transport Agreement is obviously provisional in character. It is less liberal in certain respects than present international ocean shipping practice. But many of the objections to its acceptance, so the present writer understands, have been based not on this, but because, on the contrary, it is said to go too far in relinquishing economic control by the State flown over. The Agreement has been ac-

---

[36] Wiprud, *Some Aspects of Public International Air Law* (1945) 13 GEO. WASH. L. REV. 264–275; *International Commercial Aviation*, Resolution of the Committee on Commerce, SEN. DOC. No. 173, 79th Cong., 2d. Sess. (1946), (Transport and Bermuda Agreements); N. Y. State Bar Ass'n, *Agreements on International Aviation*, LAWYER SERVICE LETTER No. 100 (1946) 408.

[37] *Concerning Acceptance of Aviation Agreements as Executive Agreements —Exchange of Letters between Senator Bilbo and Acting Secretary Grew*, 12 DEP'T OF STATE BULL. (1945) 1101; also, Article by Stephen Latchford, at 1104; Letter of June 18, 1946 to Secretary of State from Attorney-General Clark quoted p. 6 of U. S. Sen., 79th Cong., 2d Sess., EXECUTIVE REPORT No. 8 (1946) *Convention on International Civil Aviation.*

cepted by comparatively few States of great importance to world air transport. Those accepting include the United States, Sweden, and the Netherlands, but not Great Britain. For reasons discussed below, the Agreement has now been renounced by the United States.

At the end of the Chicago Conference, the various proposals for future economic control were referred to PICAO for study. In May, 1946, when the first Assembly met in Montreal, its agenda included the draft of a new permanent multilateral convention prepared by the PICAO Council to meet the economic problems unsolved at Chicago, and differing in many respects from the Transport Agreement. When this proposed new convention was presented for consideration at Montreal, the United States delegation, through its chairman, Mr. Burden, urged that it be not then acted upon, that no multilateral convention be then adopted, and that the whole problem of economic control be fully discussed and referred back for future study and action at a later Assembly. The United States did not, however, insist that the Transport Agreement be accepted as a permanent solution—quite the contrary. In presenting the United States proposal, which was adopted, Mr. Burden stated:

A year and a half ago the United States assumed the responsibility of initiating a multilateral agreement, known as the Air Transport Agreement. The passage of time and further study of the problem by many nations led them to reject it for a variety of reasons. In fact it has been accepted by such a small number of countries that it can no longer be considered as the basis of a world-wide scheme for international civil aviation.[38]

Prior to the Montreal meeting, certain bilateral agreements had come into force on the North Atlantic quite inconsistent with the basic theory of the Transport Agreement. These may point the way toward a possible compromise pattern for future general international control. The most important is that between the United States and Great Britain, concluded at Bermuda on February 11, 1946.[39] In this "Bermuda Agreement," the United States for the first time conceded a certain measure of control of economic questions, including interna-

---

[38] Statement on behalf of the United States by William A. M. Burden, Chairman of the United States Delegation, on the REPORT OF THE AIR TRANS- PORT COMMITTEE OF THE INTERIM ASSEMBLY on the matters on which it was not possible to reach agreement among the Nations represented at the Chicago Conference. Provisional International Civil Aviation Organization Doc. 1733, EC/21 (1946).

[39] Final Act of the Civil Aviation Conference held at Bermuda, January 15 to February 11, 1946, U. S. TREATY SER. 1507 (1946); also (1946) 14 DEP'T OF STATE BULL. 584.

tional rate regulation by the governments concerned (with a reference to PICAO or its successor for an advisory opinion in case of dispute), and Great Britain waived its prior insistence on direct international control of traffic and frequencies and capacities. Certain important principles were included in the Agreement by which each government is to be bound in providing service. The routes to be used were definitely agreed on. The Bermuda Agreement does not constitute a general "right to trade" by air as between the two countries. Similar agreements have since been concluded between the United States and France, and between the United States and Belgium. In view of the new diplomatic approach to international air transport evidenced by these agreements, few were surprised when the State Department on July 25, 1946 announced that the United States was giving notice of its withdrawal from the Transport Agreement. While the withdrawal cannot take effect for one year, it ends any possibility that the Transport Agreement will be the basis for worldwide economic understanding.

In the Bermuda Agreement reference is made (in connection with inter-government control of rates) to the rate-making conference procedure of the International Air Transport Association (IATA). This Association, organized after the Chicago Conference, now includes in its membership practically all of the important international air transport operators in the world.[40] Through regional rate traffic conferences, somewhat similar to steamship rate conferences, IATA is seeking to stabilize traffic conditions and prevent rate wars. Under the Civil Aeronautics Act of 1938 the Civil Aeronautics Board is authorized to approve rate and other intercarrier agreements when United States air carriers are involved. When approved, such agreements are free from the onus of the anti-trust acts. The Civil Aeronautics Board has approved for one year the rate conference machinery set up by IATA,[41] but has disapproved its first proposed North Atlantic rates.[42] New conference agreements have been submitted to the Board for approval. The existence and utility of the IATA rate conference machinery, thus recognized in the Bermuda Agreement, may prove to be a useful indirect asset in future world economic control.

Remaining for consideration is the status of international air transport under the Charter of the United Nations. In this respect it must be recalled that the preamble of the Chicago Convention admits that

[40] Hildred, *International Air Transport?* (June 1946) WORLD REVIEW 46; Cooper, *IATA—League of Airlines*, (1946) 4 AIR TRANSPORT No. 1, at 29.

[41] Civil Aeronautics Board Order Serial 4525, decided Feb. 19, 1946; *Agreement CAB No. 493, IATA Traffic Conference Resolution.*

[42] Civil Aeronautics Board Order Serial 4748, decided May 8, 1946; *Agreement CAB 586, Resolutions of North Atlantic Traffic Conference.*

through abuse international civil aviation "can become a threat to the general security."

Among the purposes of the United Nations are:[43] (Article 1) ". . . to take effective collective measures . . . for the suppression of acts of aggression . . . and to bring about by peaceful means . . . settlement of international disputes or situations which might lead to a breach of the peace;" also "to achieve international cooperation in solving international problems of an economic . . . character."

It follows that the United Nations must consider the status of international air transport whenever it presents a case of aggression threatening general security, or a problem in international economic cooperation.

The General Assembly (Article 13) is directed to initiate studies and make recommendations for the purpose of promoting international cooperation in the political field, and also international cooperation in the economic field. The Security Council (Article 34) may investigate any dispute or any situation which might lead to international friction; (Article 39) determine the existence of any threat to peace or act of aggression; and (Article 41) may decide what measures not involving the use of armed force are to be employed to give effect to decisions, including "complete or partial interruption of economic relations and of . . . air . . . and other means of communications."

The Economic and Social Council (Article 60) is responsible under the authority of the General Assembly for economic problems; (Article 62) may make or initiate studies and reports with respect to international economic matters and make recommendations on such matters to the General Assembly; (Article 63) may enter into agreements with specialized agencies established by inter-government agreement and having wide international responsibility in the economic field; (Article 64) may take appropriate steps to obtain reports from such specialized agencies and communicate its observations on these reports to the General Assembly; (Article 65) may furnish information to the Security Council and shall assist the Security Council upon its request.

The Economic and Social Council in recognition of its responsibilities (Article 68) set up a "Temporary Transport and Communications Commission." On May 25, 1946 this temporary Commission filed its first report with the Economic and Social Council.[44] This report states that the Commission has made a preliminary general survey of the inter-governmental organizations in the field of transport and communications; has noted among other things the existence of certain

---

[43] *Charter of the United Nations*, DEP'T OF STATE CONFERENCE SER. 74 (1945).

[44] UNICIO, Economic and Social Council, Doc. E/42, (May 25, 1946).

organizations, including "the recently created Provisional International Civil Aviation Organization (to be superseded by the definitive International Civil Aviation Organization);" has also noted that inter-governmental agreement and organization in the transport fields dealt with were concerned principally with cooperation in administration and technical matters concerning effectiveness or safety of service, but that inter-governmental agreement on commercial questions such as rates, routes, subsidies, etc., is a much more difficult question; that "these matters are regulated to some degree by unofficial international organizations of operators, such, for example, as IATA in the field of aviation." The Commission indicated that inter-governmental agencies in the field of transport and communications dealing with security matters had existed only in wartime and that "The question now arises of permanent arrangements to implement decisions which may be taken by the Security Council to impose sanctions."

In its recommendations, the Commission includes the suggestion that PICAO be brought into relation with the Economic and Social Council as one of the specialized agencies contemplated by Article 57 of the Charter; also that the Commission be authorized to enter into contact with certain unofficial bodies, for the purpose of exchanging documents, observers, etc., including IATA. At the Montreal meeting of the PICAO Assembly in May, 1946, its Council was authorized to enter into a working agreement with the United Nations. It is therefore assumed that some arrangement will be worked out between the Economic and Social Council of the United Nations and PICAO for future cooperation—the nature and extent of which have not yet been determined.[45]

It is hoped that this complicated machinery can be made effective so that many vital questions may be answered. If PICAO, or its successor ICAO, fails to adopt and have ratified a multilateral convention providing permanent and acceptable world economic control of international air transport, is the United Nations, through the Economic and Social Council or otherwise, authorized to do so, and if so, in what manner? If the United Nations should determine that international air transport is being used as a means of dangerous aggression which may threaten world security, or if it determines that world economic conditions otherwise require remedial action from some situation growing out of the use of international air transport by one or

---

[45] United Nations Economic and Social Council has now adopted Resolution of June 21, 1946 (UNCIO, Docs. E/58/Rev. 1 and E/84, par. 2, both as amended by the Council) to make permanent the Transport and Communications Commission and authorized negotiations with PICAO "for the purpose of bringing it into relationship with the United Nations." JOURNAL OF THE ECONOMIC AND SOCIAL COUNCIL (July 13, 1946), 515.

more States, what specific machinery will be put into effect to meet the situation? If rate wars and subsidies threaten international discord, who will stop them, and how? If the Security Council determines on the necessity of sanctions to be applied by stopping civil air communication with one or more States, how is this very difficult situation to be handled?

Admittedly serious difficulties are ahead in answering these and many other questions. Russia is a powerful member of the United Nations, but declined an invitation to attend the Chicago Conference and is not a member of PICAO, nor has Russia even been represented by observers. Certain neutral nations (including Spain, Portugal, Ireland, Switzerland and Sweden) are members of PICAO but are not members of the United Nations. No provision has been made for control of air transport in the Axis States or the extent to which they will be allowed to exercise airspace sovereignty in the future.

World air transport may be dealt with as a single problem through one cohesive international agency. The respective powers and functions of the United Nations, of its Security Council, of its Economic and Social Council, and also of PICAO and its successor ICAO, must be coordinated if world wide economic and security problems are to be met. Aviation is a dynamic force. World air transport is its most important instrumentality in time of peace. Such a dynamic force cannot long await the final decision of political discussions.

23
The Bermuda Plan: World Pattern for Air Transport

*Reprinted by special permission
from* Foreign Affairs, *October 1946.*
© *Council on Foreign Relations,
Inc. New York.*

Author's Note. The influence of the Bermuda Agreement, as suggested in this essay, has proved very important. Many other bilateral air transport agreements have followed its economic regulatory provisions. At Geneva in 1947, when an international commission organized by ICAO attempted to draft a multilateral convention on the same general topics, the Bermuda principles as to frequencies, capacity, and rates received wide support, leaving for bilateral negotiations only the determination of routes. However, the attempt failed. It should be added that the original Bermuda provisions relating to advisory opinions of PICAO, now ICAO, which seemed important in 1946, have apparently not been used. They are omitted from many of the subsequent bilateral agreements which otherwise generally follow the Bermuda plan.

T HE AGREEMENT signed at Bermuda on February 11, 1946, between the United States and Great Britain, and subsequent similar agreements with France and Belgium, indicate a major shift in United States policy for the operation and development of air transport. The announcement by the State Department on July 25, 1946, that the United States would withdraw from the Chicago Air Transport Agreement in a year's time was concrete evidence of the changed policy foreshadowed by the "Bermuda plan." The Air Transport Agreement —to which only the United States, Sweden, the Netherlands and a few other countries had subscribed—was the product of the sharp disagreement between Great Britain and the United States at the Chicago Air Conference in 1944.[1]

No one questions the importance of this "Bermuda plan." On February 26, 1946, President Truman followed the unusual course of giving out a special statement expressing his satisfaction with it. Official statements in the same tenor were made in both Houses of the British Parliament; and in the House of Lords, on February 28, Lord Swinton, the Conservative ex-Minister of Civil Aviation and Chairman of the British delegation at Chicago, called it "probably the most important civil aviation agreement that this country has entered into." The renunciation of the Air Transport Agreement was preceded by the action of the Assembly of the Provisional International Civil Aviation Organization (the body created by the Chicago Interim Agreement

---

[1] *Cf.* Edward Warner, "The Chicago Air Conference," FOREIGN AFFAIRS, April 1945.

and now functioning at Montreal) in May of this year, postponing consideration of a proposed multilateral international civil aviation agreement which had been prepared after long study by the Council of PICAO. That action also clears the path for the Bermuda Agreement.

The principles on which the Agreement stands are not those for which either Great Britain or the United States contended so bitterly at the Chicago Conference. Admittedly the plan represents a compromise. There are still important differences between the points of view of the two countries in regard to the principles which shall govern commercial air transport, and there seem already to be varying interpretations of the plan by British and American spokesmen. These require immediate clarification, and may, indeed, presage serious new difficulties. Nonetheless, the Bermuda plan holds out the possibility of world-wide acceptance of uniform rules of air commerce.

To sketch in the general background of the old differences and the new understanding (even at the risk of oversimplification), it may be said that every international air agreement now in force, and every plan proposed, involves one or more of the following factors: *routes, privileges* (accorded to an air carrier of one nation in the airspace of a second), *rates, frequency of operation, capacity of aircraft,* and *degree of economic control accorded to an international authority.* The full list of privileges is called the five freedoms. The first and second freedoms are transit privileges—to operate non-stop through the airspace of a second nation, and to stop for non-traffic purposes; the third, fourth and fifth are commercial privileges—to discharge cargo from a first nation in the territory of a second, to pick up cargo in the second destined to the first, and to pick up or discharge cargo in the second nation destined to or coming from territory of a third.

By international law, each nation has complete and exclusive sovereignty over the airspace above its territory, and no foreign aircraft may enter its airspace or land in its territory for refueling or other non-traffic purposes, or to pick up and discharge passengers or cargo, except as authorized. For example, in the late fall of 1945, before the Bermuda Agreement was signed, Great Britain advised the United States that it would permit United States commercial air services to discharge and pick up transatlantic traffic, but not in excess of 14 times a week, nor with total seat capacity of more than 500 per week, and with a passenger rate of not less than $375.[2]

The Bermuda plan is a result of the acceptance by Great Britain and the United States of the so-called Transit Agreement drafted at the Chicago Conference covering the first and second freedoms, plus the

---

[2] On two flights per week no rate control was in effect, as Pan American Airways still held a prewar British permit for that number.

principles incorporated in the Final Act of the Bermuda Conference, the bilateral agreement signed at Bermuda, and the detailed annex to this latter agreement.

The general effect of the plan may be summarized as follows. Each nation grants to the air carriers of the other nation transit privileges (freedoms one and two) to operate through the airspace of the other and to land for non-traffic purposes on routes anywhere in the world subject to the provisions of the Chicago Transit Agreement, including the right of the nation flown over to designate the transit route to be followed within its territory and the airports to be used. Each nation also grants to the other commercial privileges of entry and departure to discharge and pick up traffic (freedoms three, four and five); but these commercial privileges are valid, in contrast to the transit privileges, only at airports named in the agreement and on routes generally indicated, and in accord with certain general traffic principles and limitations. Rates to be charged between points in the territory of the two nations are to be subject to approval of the governments within their respective powers. As to frequencies and capacities, each nation, or its designated air carrier, is free at the outset to determine for itself the traffic offered to the public on the designated commercial routes, but the operations must be related to traffic demands and conducted according to the agreed principles affecting frequency and capacity.[3]

In case of a dispute not settled by consultation, each nation has the right to insist on an advisory opinion of the Provisional International Civil Aviation Organization and, in the case of rates, each nation will use its best efforts within its powers to make the rate recommended by PICAO effective. As the advisory opinion of PICAO can cover any dispute, it apparently follows that PICAO can be asked for an opinion as to whether either party to the agreement is violating the principles applicable to traffic frequency and capacity and the special limitations as to fifth freedom traffic. But nothing in the agreement provides for the enforcement of a decision.

In the absence of general agreement at Chicago as to economic control of international air transport, the United States supported the Air Transit Agreement and the Air Transport Agreement which the Conference offered for signature. The Transit Agreement covered the transit privileges of freedoms one and two; the Transport Agreement embraced these transit privileges plus the commercial privileges of freedoms three, four and five. Great Britain and many other states refused to accept the Transport Agreement, but together with certain

---

[3] The delegates to the Conference also initialed "Heads of Agreement" relating to the proposed future civil use of the air bases constructed by the United States on leased British territory. Since it is not a necessary part of the "Bermuda plan" it will not be discussed here.

others advised that it would accept the Air Transit Agreement. Under the latter agreement, Great Britain could have organized an air service through the United States or through Alaska and across the Pacific, using such United States airports as the latter might assign for that purpose; but the British planes could not have picked up and discharged passengers in the United States. Similarly, the United States could have authorized services to continental Europe through England, but with no right to pick up or discharge traffic in England (except under the special conditions mentioned earlier).

Between the close of the Chicago Conference and the meeting at Bermuda, the United States concluded bilateral agreements with Ireland, Sweden, Norway and Denmark, each providing for reciprocal transatlantic services with no limitation on rates, frequency or capacity of transatlantic service. In addition, Sweden, the Netherlands and the United States had signed the Air Transport Agreement. Under that agreement the parties accorded each other the five freedoms, but the commercial rights are to be available only on routes constituting "a reasonably direct line out from and back to the homeland." It contained no provision for the regulation of rates, and only a very vague provision for possible limitation of frequency or capacity.

ROUTES AND PRIVILEGES

The advantages and difficulties of the Bermuda plan can best be understood by comparing it with other agreements and plans for economic control. The general interchange of the transit privileges (freedoms one and two), with the right to specify the route and airports reserved for security purposes to the nation flown over, is gaining approval as time goes on. To that extent the Bermuda plan is already widely accepted. However, Ireland, France and Portugal (among other important gateway nations) have not yet accepted the Transit Agreement, and apparently intend to insist that the exchange of transit privileges be limited to special bilateral agreements.

The Bermuda plan contrasts sharply with the arrangements governing commercial privileges in force under the Transport Agreement. Under the Bermuda plan, as stated above, definite routes and airports for commercial traffic are named, and the traffic is to be governed (as will be discussed later under frequencies and capacities) in accord with agreed principles. Under the Transport Agreement, which controls transatlantic service between the United States and the Netherlands, the commercial privileges are available on generally direct routes out from the homeland and back, the nation flown over fixing only the airports and routes to be used in its territory. In fact, the Transport Agreement is so vague in this respect that serious questions had already

385

appeared as to how the agreement should be applied between the United States and certain Latin American countries which had accepted it, particularly as to the number of carriers to be received and the number of ports of entry to be named. The plan proposed at Montreal by PICAO was even more vague in that it authorized unnamed routes constituting "reasonably direct lines out from and back to the territory of the contracting state whose nationality the aircraft possesses."

For the first time in our history, foreign air carriers are granted fixed routes across the United States. This possibility was inherent in the Transport Agreement, but never became definite. Among the routes named for use by Great Britain are those under which British air carriers can fly from London to New York, then to San Francisco, and then via Honolulu, Midway, Wake, Guam or Manila to Singapore or Hong Kong. Routes are also specified along which a British carrier may fly from London or Scotland to New York, and then either to New Orleans and on to Mexico City, or to Cuba and thence via Jamaica or Panama to Colombia, Ecuador, Peru and Chile. Reciprocally, the United States carriers can fly transatlantic services to London or Scotland, and thence to Holland, Germany, Scandinavia and Russia, or to Belgium, central Europe, the Near East and on to India; also across the Pacific via Honolulu to Hong Kong, China and India, or to Singapore and then to the Netherlands East Indies. At each named point in United States territory, British air carriers can pick up or discharge traffic from or to its own territory or third countries; and reciprocally, at each named point in British territory, American carriers can discharge or pick up international traffic. A British carrier can pick up transpacific traffic in New York, and returning can pick up transatlantic traffic at San Francisco or New York. On other routes a British carrier at New York can pick up traffic for Cuba and South America or for Mexico via New Orleans. Foreign air carriers will compete indirectly with internal American transport operations; and so, of course, will American carriers compete with British carriers on British routes from England to and from Europe and other points. In other words, air transport is now a business in which a foreign commodity is sold in the local market in competition with domestic sellers and without the protection of a tariff. This may be the case under any multilateral convention. Under the proposed Montreal Agreement, as under the Chicago Transport Agreement, the competitive traffic points and the particular routes themselves are not fixed.

Certain further differences as to fifth freedom traffic between the Bermuda plan and the Transport Agreement must be noted. In the latter, any contracting state could, on six months' notice, withdraw itself from fifth freedom rights and obligations. Under the Bermuda Agreement, fifth freedom privileges cannot be separated from the rest of the plan. In the Transport Agreement, fifth freedom privileges extended only to traffic to or from other nations parties to the agreement. For example, the United States air carrier on the route from the United States to Sweden via Great Britain and the Netherlands could pick up international traffic in the Netherlands for Sweden, because both of those countries and the United States are parties to the Transport Agreement. On the return journey, however, traffic could not be picked up under the Transport Agreement in the Netherlands for Great Britain because the latter was not a party to the agreement. Under the Bermuda plan, the United States can pick up and discharge at London traffic to or from any country on the route. Under the Transport Agreement, the nation flown over fixed the port of entry, and it was not clear whether the same port of entry had to be made available for traffic from all nations parties to the agreement. Under the Bermuda plan, ports of entry are named and cannot be changed except by agreement. The route through third countries can be changed by the nation doing the flying, but the other nation may ask PICAO to determine by advisory opinion whether such changes are prejudicial.

RATES

Rates to be charged by the air carriers of each party operating between points in British and United States territory shall be subject to the approval of the Contracting Parties within their respective constitutional powers and obligations." In signing such an agreement the United States has passed a milestone in diplomatic and legal international transport history. It is the first time, so far as the writer is aware, that the United States has made an international agreement for the control of transport rates. At the present time the Civil Aeronautics Board has no legal authority to fix rates of American air carriers in foreign commerce, such as it has in interstate operation. The Board does have authority, however, to approve rate agreements in which American carriers participate. Accordingly, the Board announced that it would approve for a period of one year the traffic conference rate-making machinery of the International Air Transport Association (IATA), an operators' organization of which American international operators are members. Thus the Board would have an opportunity to approve or disapprove international rates when submitted by the operators. The United States Government has also applied to Congress for extension of the powers of the Civil Aeronautics Board so as to give that Board authority directly to fix international rates. If the two countries are unable through IATA or otherwise to agree on rates, the Bermuda Agreement makes provision for handling the rate problem.

Before the Civil Aeronautics Board has power to fix rates and compel its carriers to charge a rate agreed between the two governments, either government objecting to a rate "may take such steps as it may consider necessary to prevent the inauguration or continuation of the service in question at the rate complained of." After the Civil Aeronautics Board acquires rate-fixing powers, if the two countries cannot agree on a proposed rate, the dispute will be referred to PICAO for an advisory opinion. Each country agrees to use its best efforts to put into effect the rate recommended by PICAO. Obviously, this means that if the Civil Aeronautics Board receives power to fix international rates, the advisory opinion of PICAO will actually determine the question in case of disagreement between the two countries. At Bermuda the United States has gone further than it was apparently willing to go at the outset of the Chicago Conference, by granting that economic power may be given to an international authority to fix rates where the governments concerned could not agree.

In his White House statement referred to earlier, President Truman said: "In the Bermuda Agreement the Executive branch of the United States Government has concurred in the plan for the setting-up of machinery which should protect against the type of rate war feared by so many of the countries through whose air space we desire that our airlines have the right to fly. Part of the plan for future rate control will be dependent on the granting of additional powers by Congress to the Civil Aeronautics Board." It is obvious from this statement that the United States has accepted international rate regulation as part of its civil air policy. This brings into sharp relief the fact that in none of the bilateral agreements for transatlantic service in force prior to the Bermuda Agreement, nor in the Transport Agreement, is there any provision for rate regulation. The United States must now agree on rates with England, France and Belgium, but has no method of government control of rates that may be charged by Scandinavian or Dutch operators in the North Atlantic area. Unless the terms of the Bermuda compromise are generally adopted, a most confusing situation will arise.

FREQUENCY AND CAPACITY

The question of the control of the frequency and capacity of the services offered by international air lines, was, of course, the stumbling block for the Chicago Conference. If, under the Bermuda plan, the United States on the one side and Great Britain, France and Belgium on the other are now actually in agreement, great progress has been made.

In the Final Act of Bermuda the parties agreed on principles which are so important that they must be set out in full:

3. That the air transport facilities available to the travelling public should bear a close relationship to the requirements of the public for such transport.

4. That there shall be a fair and equal opportunity for the carriers of the two nations to operate on any route between their respective territories (as defined in the Agreement) covered by the Agreement and its Annex.

5. That in the operation by the air carriers of either Government of the trunk services described in the Annex to the Agreement, the interest of the air carriers of the other Government shall be taken into consideration so as not to affect unduly the services which the latter provides on all or part of the same routes.

6. That it is the understanding of both Governments that services provided by a designated air carrier under the Agreement and its Annex shall retain as their primary objective the provision of capacity adequate to the traffic demands between the country of which such air carrier is a national and the country of ultimate destination of the traffic. The right to embark or disembark on such services international traffic destined for and coming from third countries at a point or points on the routes specified in the Annex to the agreement shall be applied in accordance with the general principles of orderly development to which both Governments subscribe and shall be subject to the general principle that capacity should be related: (a) to traffic requirements between the country of origin and the countries of destination; (b) to the requirements of through airline operation, and (c) to the traffic requirements of the area through which the airline passes after taking account of local and regional services.

7. That insofar as the air carrier or carriers of one Government may be temporarily prevented through difficulties arising from the War from taking immediate advantage of the opportunity referred to in sub-paragraph (4) above, the situation shall be reviewed between the Governments with the object of facilitating the necessary development, as soon as the air carrier or carriers of the first Government is or are in a position increasingly to make their proper contribution to the service.

The Annex to the Bermuda Agreement provides that the rights accorded of commercial entry and departure to discharge and pick up international traffic shall be in full accord and compliance with the principles set out in the Final Act (including, of course, those just quoted). Also, under the agreement, any dispute between the parties not settled by consultation can be referred to PICAO for an advisory report, but nothing is said as to the enforcement of the report. It appears to follow, therefore, that the transport operations of either nation which the other considers inconsistent with the fundamental principles of the Final Act as quoted above may become the subject of an advisory opinion of PICAO. Thus PICAO is given jurisdiction to consider whether the principles applicable to traffic frequencies and capacities are complied with by both nations.

It is apparently the view of both parties, as evidenced by the statement jointly issued by the two delegations at the close of the Bermuda Conference,[4] that the plan contemplates "freedom by each country to determine the frequency of operations of its airlines," and "freedom to carry fifth freedom traffic in accordance with defined principles subject to adjustment in particular cases where such adjustment may be found necessary in the light of experience." The same joint statement referring to the principles for fair and equal opportunity for the air carriers of the two nations says that this "does not imply the allocation of frequencies by agreement but only the right of each nation to offer the services it believes justified under the principles agreed to." In a further comment the delegates state that "the Conference has placed no specific limitation on frequencies. Each nation operating under the principles agreed to is to be free to determine for itself the number of frequencies which are justified; services being related to traffic demands."

Apparently, therefore, under the Bermuda plan frequencies are not to be allocated in advance; but each nation has promised that its own air carriers do not offer frequencies or capacities or indulge in competitive practices not authorized under the quoted principles. The procedure for a review by an advisory opinion by PICAO is not an idle gesture and must be accepted as part of the agreed plan.

It is not entirely certain that the United States and British Governments are in full accord on this matter. In the House of Lords on February 12, 1946, the Minister of Civil Aviation, Lord Winster, stated:

> As regards the control of capacity operated on the routes, it has been recognized that pre-determination on the basis of estimated traffic potentials is beset with practical difficulties and instead, it has been agreed that the principle for which we stand, namely, the maintenance of a close relationship between capacity operated on the various routes of mutual interest and traffic offering, can best be put into practical effect by providing for an *ex post facto* review on

---

[4] "Joint Statement by the United Kingdom and United States Delegations," *Department of State Bulletin*, Vol. XIV, No. 347, February 24, 1946, p. 302–306.

the basis of this principle. Machinery for close and continuing collaboration between the two Governments will be established to this end.[5]

There can be no doubt that Lord Winster was referring to the general principles of traffic offering and not to the added special limitations of fifth freedom traffic which he quoted later.

CONCLUSION

In the general debate of February 28 on the Bermuda Agreement in the House of Lords, Lord Swinton asked very pointed questions as to how the principles of the Final Act would work in practice, and particularly as to what would happen under the equal opportunity principles when Great Britain was fully prepared to fly. He said:

> The Agreement, as I understand it, that there shall be a fair chance for both, means that each will be able, or ought to be in a position to put on enough planes, on this load factor principle, to carry half the traffic. That must mean, if it is to be carried out, that the United States, will reduce their number of aircraft as we increase our number of aircraft. If not, we can get our share of the traffic only by putting on a large number of planes, while the United States' number of planes remains unreduced. In that event, it means that there would be, in fact, more planes operating than the traffic would justify, and that completely knocks the bottom out of the earlier provision that the amount of capacity shall be related to the amount of traffic.[6]

In reply, the official British Government spokesman stated, referring to Lord Swinton's remarks:

> As he said, quite correctly, so far as that is concerned the United States have a great start over ourselves, but I think that Paragraphs (4) and (5) to which he referred quite fairly cover the point. It is perfectly evident that as things develop in the course of time, the tribunal which will be set up to consider disputes or questions will be able to adjudicate on the difficulties as they arise.[7]

Then, referring to Paragraph 7 of the principles, which describe the situation in which the air carriers of one government are temporarily prevented by war from proceeding immediately with develop-

---

[5] Parliamentary Debates (Hansard), House of Lords, v. 139, no. 53, p. 367–368.

[6] Parliamentary Debates (Hansard), House of Lords, v. 139, no. 62, p. 988.

[7] Ibid. p. 1007.

ment of traffic, he added: "That is clearly designed in order to meet the kind of development to which the noble Viscount has referred." Without question the view of the British Government appears to be that frequency and capacity questions, as well as others under the agreed principles, are subject to review by PICAO in case of disagreement. On the other hand, President Truman in his statement of February 26 made no mention of these principles of the Final Act nor of the provision for review, stating simply:

> Under the Bermuda Agreement there will be no control of frequencies, and no control of so-called Fifth Freedom rights on trunk routes operated primarily for through service. It gives to the airline operators the great opportunity of using their initiative and enterprise in developing air transportation over great areas of the world's surface.

If differences do exist in the interpretation of the Bermuda plan, they must be clarified. The plan cannot be used as the basis for a world wide scheme for economic control of international air transport unless those most directly concerned fully agree on its meaning. On the face of the documents, it seems very clear to this writer that PICAO can give an advisory opinion, in case of complaint, and can find that one or the other nation is operating more frequencies or capacities than it is entitled to under the principles of the Final Act. No machinery except the force of public opinion is provided to police such a finding. However, subsequent uncorrected operations after such a finding might create a most unpleasant diplomatic situation. It may well be, therefore, that in actual practice the Bermuda plan will result in a certain amount of control of frequencies and capacities, as Lord Winster stated, by "*ex post facto* review."

The proposed Montreal agreement favors local operators by requiring the foreign operator of fifth freedom traffic to charge higher fares than the local operator for the same service. For example, a United States air carrier's rate from London to Amsterdam on the through route from New York to Amsterdam would be higher by a fixed percentage than the rate for competitive local British or Dutch services. Such a formula appears exceedingly difficult to administer, and not fair to the traveling public. The Montreal agreement also proposes giving to the international authority definite power to determine whether a nation is operating general (or fifth freedom) traffic frequency or capacity in violation of principles similar to those outlined under the Bermuda plan, and to order corrective action. In other words, the Montreal plan would provide for control by review, as in the Bermuda plan, but would vest actual police power in the international organization. This raises a fundamental question. Should this problem of economic control be met by asking the nations of the world to yield part of their sovereign power over their own national transport—a thing never done in merchant shipping? Or is it better to reach a definite treaty agreement, as in the Bermuda plan, and leave to each nation the responsibility for carrying out its air transport obligations, exactly as every country is expected to abide by other international obligations and to control its own citizens accordingly? That is the question running through all the great decisions of our time.

The Bermuda Agreement is under certain legal clouds in the United States. Both it and the Chicago Transport Agreement were put into effect as executive agreements. Both have been vigorously attacked on the ground that their subject matter should have been included in treaties and submitted to the Senate for ratification. Much testimony has been taken. On April 19, 1946, the Committee on Commerce of the United States Senate filed with the Senate a report on "International Civil Aviation" with a copy of a Resolution from the Committee indicating its view that the agreements are ineffective and illegal unless and until they are ratified as treaties. The executive departments of the government have insisted on the propriety of the procedure followed. On June 18, 1946, the Attorney General in a letter to the Secretary of State expressed a very definite view that the President has the right to enter into executive agreements of this general character. The withdrawal of the Transport Agreement by the State Department now settles part of the practical problem. But the principle involved should be definitely determined. It involves complex legal questions which need not be discussed in an article intended only to consider whether the Bermuda plan is suitable for incorporation in a widely-accepted multilateral convention.

The reader will have seen that, in the author's opinion, the answer to this is yes. If there is accord as to the construction of the principles of the Bermuda Final Act and Agreement, the plan could easily become the basis of a general international air transport convention. Such a convention would provide for general exchange of transit privileges between the parties, giving the nation flown over the right of fixing airports and transit routes in its territory. The convention would not fix commercial routes or grant commercial privileges, but would include the commercial operations and traffic principles of the Bermuda plan and provide that when two or more nations, parties to the agreement, should determine to exchange commercial privileges and agree on commercial routes, the operations would always be conducted according to the principles of the plan. Such an agreement would bring about international commercial uniformity but would leave to the nations concerned the right to determine with what nations and over what routes they might wish to trade. A further provision might be included giving to any nation, when accepting the agreement, the right then and there to name ports of entry and airways open for international commercial traffic when operated in accord with the principles of the plan, thus obviating the need for subsequent special agreements as to ports of entry and routes. Some nations might prefer this means of inviting world traffic to their territories. If such a general and permanent convention were adopted it certainly would be submitted for ratification as a treaty, as were the Havana Convention of 1928 and the permanent International Civil Aviation Convention signed at Chicago.

24
Internationalization of Air Transport

Reprinted from 2 Air Affairs *546 (1949).*

Author's Note. This study records an important historical period, sometimes forgotten, when the national policies of Great Britain, Australia, and New Zealand all favored the international operation of world air transport. The developments subsequent to the period here described, as is well known, took a very different direction. But times and policies sometimes change. This study has been included in the present volume to record the author's firm view that no one can predict the long range future of so dynamic a world activity as air transport and that a knowledge of past events may be useful.

THE FUTURE of the Western World may depend on complete cooperation between the United States on one hand and the United Kingdom and the Dominion members of the British Commonwealth on the other. Therefore any international political question on which these great powers disagree is of sufficient significance to warrant careful consideration. Such a question is that involved in the decision as to the relevant advantages and disadvantages of international ownership and operation of air transport services connecting the nations of the world.

The United States, the United Kingdom, and each of the great British Dominions signed and have ratified the Convention on International Civil Aviation drawn up at Chicago in 1944, ordinarily called the Chicago Convention. By such signature and ratification each of these great nations has signified its approval of the primary objectives of the Convention as evidenced by its Preamble and certain of its articles.

The Preamble recites that "the future development of international civil aviation can greatly help to create and preserve friendship and understanding among the nations and peoples of the world, yet its abuse can become a threat to the general security," and that "it is desirable to avoid friction and to promote that cooperation between nations and peoples upon which the peace of the world depends." Article 44 of the Convention includes among the objectives of the International Civil Aviation Organization the development of international air transport so as to: "(a) insure the safe and orderly growth of international civil aviation throughout the world; . . . (d) meet the needs of the peoples of the world for safe, regular efficient and economical air transport; (e) prevent economic waste caused by unreasonable competition; (f) insure that the rights of contracting States are fully respected and that every contracting State has a fair opportunity to operate international airlines; (g) avoid discrimination between contracting States; . . ."

These are the agreed objectives. It would appear, however, that agreement does not exist as to the basic political method of international organization of air transport services so as to achieve such objectives. The policy of the United States favors continued operation of international air transport services under the flags of the several separate nations concerned, while the policies of the United Kingdom and those of at least two of the great Dominions, Australia and New Zealand, favor the international ownership and operation of trunk services.

International ownership and operation of world air transport services, or internationalization as it will be called hereafter, is not a new subject. It has been considered in the past from two points of view: (a) from that of security in making effective military and naval air disarmament; and (b) from that of economic gain and elimination of nationalism in the development of air transport as a means of international communication. It is not the purpose of this article to discuss internationalization as an aid to disarmament. Someday the United Nations, if it is to fulfill its ultimate objectives, must reach a decision and take a position on the reduction or elimination of competitive armaments, including the air military arm. When that time comes, a decision must also be reached as to how and in what manner civil aviation is to be limited or controlled so as to make air disarmament effective. The United Nations must ultimately face the same difficulties which appeared in the discussions during the 1933 meetings of the Conference for the Reduction and Limitation of Armaments of the League of Nations. Lord Londonderry, in behalf of the United Kingdom, at a meeting of the Air Committee held on February 20, 1933, stated the crux of the problem when he announced that "the United Kingdom Government are prepared to subscribe to universal acceptance of the abolition of naval and military aircraft and of air bombing, except for police purposes, provided only that there can be devised an effective scheme for the international control of civil aviation which will prevent all possibility of the misuse of civil aircraft for miltary purposes."[1] It was during the meetings of the same Air Committee that M. Pierre Cot, in behalf of the French Government, outlined in some detail the much discussed French proposal for the in-

---

[1] League of Nations. Conference for the Reduction and Limitation of Armaments. General Commission, Air Committee. *Provisional Minutes of the First Meeting, February 20, 1933.* Conf. D./C.G./C.A./P.V.1–10.

ternationalization of all civil air transport,[2] as necessary to make air disarmament effective. These questions, however, will not be discussed here.

The question on which the United States on the one side and the United Kingdom and Australia and New Zealand on the other disagree on policy involves a method of ownership and operation of international air transport services under present world conditions, irrespective of any scheme for air disarmament. Historically, the earliest discussions of internationalization of civil air transport for purely economic reasons arose as a result of the preparatory work for the 1932–34 League of Nations Conference for the Reduction and Limitation of Armaments. The first recorded discussions of internationalization as an economic problem appear to have taken place at a meeting held in Geneva in 1930 of the Air Transport Co-operation Committee under the auspices of the League of Nations Organization for Communications and Transit.[3] A Belgian delegate, supported by a French delegate, suggested the possibility of improving European air mail services by various means including the organization of a single company. The French delegate actually suggested that "the solution was to be found in an international company or an operation on an international scale in the interest of all the countries of western Europe." The German delegate strongly objected. The British delegate indicated that such a solution might some day in the future be found advisable, but did not otherwise commit himself. The United States was not represented on the Committee.

In 1932 the question of internationalization as a means of economic co-operation was discussed before the Air Transport Co-operation Committee of the League of Nations.[4] An observer from the United

---

[2] *Ibid.* See also: League of Nations. Conference for the Reduction and Limitation of Armaments. *Memorandum Relating to the French Delegation's Proposals on the Internationalisation of Civil Air Transport.* Official No. Conf. D.115, Series of League of Nations Publications: IX. Disarmament. 1932. IX. 42. Geneva, April 14, 1932. League of Nations, Conference for the Reduction and Limitation of Armaments, General Commission, Air Committee. *Brief Outline of the Internationalisation of Civil Transport Aircraft,* Submitted by the French Delegation. Conf. D./C.G./C.A./5. Geneva, February 23, 1933.

[3] League of Nations. Organisation for Communications and Transit. Air Transport Co-operation Committee. *Minutes of the First Session held at Geneva from July 8th to 12th, 1930.* League of Nations Publications: VIII. Transit. 1930. VIII. 14. Official No.: C.C.T./A.C./1st Session/P.V. (Revised). Geneva, October 20, 1930.

[4] League of Nations. Organisation for Communications and Transit. *Report of the Air Transport Co-operation Committee on its Second Session held at Geneva, May 9th to 12th, 1932.* Official No.: C.467.M.237.1932.VIII (Conf.D/C.A.15), Series of League of Nations Publications: VIII. Transit 1932. VIII. 3. Geneva, May 12th, 1932.

States served on this committee. He, like other members, appeared simply as an expert and not with power to bind his government. Among the points discussed by the Committee was one favoring the "creation of international companies operating over vast regions which have common interests." The Belgian, French and certain other delegates favored the proposal. It was opposed by the United States, British, German, Dutch and certain other delegates.

Nothing came of these early discussions. No official government positions were taken prior to World War II for or against internationalization, except that the adoption of the Civil Aeronautics Act of 1938 by the United States was a clear indication of its basic position in favour of national flag operations. No one can read the Civil Aeronautics Act without being impressed with the fact that its whole purpose is to develop operations, both interstate and foreign, under the American flag and to promote air commerce on a competitive basis. This has been held by the U. S. Civil Aeronautics Board to include competition not only between American and foreign air carriers but also between American carriers on a single route in foreign commerce. Section 2 of that Act, in declaring certain things to be "in the public interest," includes the following: "(a) The encouragement and development of an air-transportation system properly adapted to the present and future needs of the foreign and domestic commerce of the United States, of the Postal Service, and of the national defense; . . . (d) Competition to the extent necessary to assure the sound development of an air-transportation system properly adapted to the needs of the foreign and domestic commerce of the United States, of the Postal Service, and of the national defense; . . ." The policy thus announced is clearly inconsistent with any type of internationalization of air transport services. Internationalization assumes and would require the substitution over a particular international route of a single operation conducted by the nations jointly interested in the route in place of all or any operations on the route by one of such nations. National flag operations are inconsistent with internationalization. Air services are not built up in aid of the national defense of any particular State except by operations under the flag of that State. The spirit and the letter of the Civil Aeronautics Act of 1938 therefore commits the United States to a national policy directly opposed to the fundamental theories of internationalization.

The national policies of Great Britain, Australia and New Zealand have since 1944 developed in an entirely different direction.

On January 21, 1944 the Commonwealth of Australia and the Dominion of New Zealand, acting as sovereign States within the British Commonwealth of Nations, signed their now-celebrated "Cooperation Agreement."[5] Among the questions of great significance in this agreement was one on civil aviation. In this historic document the two governments agreed that "the air services using the international air trunk routes should be operated by an international air transport authority"—that "full control of international air trunk routes and the ownership of all aircraft and ancillary equipment should be vested in the international air transport authority"—that this international air transport authority should be set up by international agreement— and that each country should have the right to conduct all air transport services "within its own national jurisdiction including its own contiguous territories, subject only to agreed international requirements regarding safety facilities, landing and transport rights for international services, and exchange of mails."

No more concise nor powerful statement could be made in favor of internationalization of civil aviation on "trunk routes" than that contained in this Australia-New Zealand "Co-operation Agreement." It has had great influence in all subsequent international discussions. It still expresses the positive policy of both countries. Its one fault, from the point of view of accuracy, is that it has introduced into the field of discussion the term "trunk routes," without defining just what is meant. Australia and New Zealand are both at the end of long international lines. The Australia-New Zealand formula for the internationalization of trunk routes while retaining national control of local services may be very clear so far as Australia and New Zealand are concerned, but it has been found difficult to apply when countries, such as Egypt, which lie across many international routes, are considered.

This Australia-New Zealand agreement had immediate repercussions in England. A Labour Party was in power in each of these countries when the agreement was signed, but the British Labour Party was not then in power. However, as part of its active campaign looking toward the expected national elections, it published in April 1944 the now celebrated pamphlet *Wings for Peace—Labour's Post-War Policy for Civil Flying.* The conclusion of this pamphlet contains the following important statement:

> The Labour Party believes that all civil flying the world over, should be subject to certain controls, and be aided by certain services, provided by a World Air Authority.
>
> We believe that air transport should, so far as practicable, be internationalised. In particular, we urge that the trunk air lines round the world—"World Airways'—should be owned and operated

---

[5] *Agreement Between His Majesty's Government in the Commonwealth of Australia and His Majesty's Government in New Zealand,* signed at Canberra, January 21, 1944 Gt. Brit. Parliament Cmd. 6513.

as a public service by a body responsible to the World Air Authority and competent to act as trustee for all the peoples, whether they happen to be able to run an aircraft industry or not. Militant nationalism should have no part, as hitherto, in the opening up of the world's air routes.

Such was the situation when the Chicago Conference met in the Autumn of 1944. At the opening of that conference the principal nations of the world stated their several positions on the future of international air transport. The United Kingdom and Canada both urged international control of civil aviation by an authority which should have broad economic powers, but without authority actually to own and operate international air services. The United States desired a world organization to take care of technical and safety problems leaving each nation with wide and uncontrolled economic and competitive powers. Australia and New Zealand brought forward the internationalization of civil air trunk routes along the lines of their "Co-operation Agreement" entered into earlier the same year. This proposal was set out formally in the following resolution:[6]

RESOLVED THAT we, the nations and authorities represented at this international Civil Aviation Conference

being determined that the fullest measure of cooperation should be secured in the development of air transport services between the nations of the world

believing that the unregulated development of air transport can only lead to misunderstanding and rivalries between nations

being convinced that air transport can and should be utilized as a powerful instrument in the cause of international security and in the attainment of 'Freedom from Fear' as embodied in the Atlantic Charter

believing that the interests of all nations, both large and small, can best be advanced by the joint utilization and the material, technical and operational resources of all countries for the development of air transport

believing that the creation of an effective economic and nondiscriminatory instrument responsible for the ownership and operation of air transport services between nations of the world is in the best interests of orderly world progress

AGREE THAT these objectives can best be achieved by the establishment of an international air transport authority which would

---

[6] International Civil Aviation Conference. *Verbatim Minutes of Meeting of Committee I*, November 8, 1944. Document No. 117, I/9.

be responsible for the operation of air services on prescribed international trunk routes and which would own the aircraft and ancillary equipment employed on these routes; it being understood that each nation would retain the right to conduct all air transport services within its own national jurisdiction, including its own contiguous territories subject only to agreed international requirements regarding landing and transit rights, safety facilities, etc., to which end it is desirable that this Committee of the Conference should consider the organization and machinery necessary for the implementation of this resolution.

In opposing this resolution the Brazilian delegation introduced a motion to the effect that "while Brazil shares the determination of those delegations [Australia and New Zealand] that civil air transport should be a source of benefit and security to the world, Brazil is not in a position to accept such a proposal and therefore suggests that this Committee declare that there is no opportunity and necessary unanimity for the organization, at the present time, of an all-embracing international company."[7] The statement of the chief Brazilian delegate went further in opposition to the internationalization proposal than did the resolution itself. He said that "our times are not yet ripe for the internationalization of aviation and perhaps the time will never be ripe for it," that "the solution of human conflicts will not be internationalization but an organization of nationalities," that "we cannot accept internationalization of aviation or international ownership of aircraft—the ownership of aircraft must continue to be national."

In supporting the motion of Brazil, the chief of the United States delegation made the following statement (perhaps the first formal statement ever made in behalf of the United States on this subject of internationalization):[8]

> Mr. Chairman, in rising to support the amendment of the Delegate of Brazil, one cannot but be impressed with a sense of great tragedy. If the apple of the Hesperides had never been thrown among the attending goddesses, the world would have been a great deal happier.
>
> Yet, in fact, for centuries and for millenia, the world has built up its life through national effort. Slowly and painfully we are beginning to come to a method of handling national activities so that they may be in less conflict. Now we are fighting a huge war to make it clear that international collaboration shall not come through world domination, but rather through the cooperative handling of national effort. A beginning toward that end has already been made at the

---

[7] *Ibid.*   [8] *Ibid.*

Conference of Dumbarton Oaks and other difficult steps by which we hope to promote certain collective activities leading toward international world peace.

Everyone of us in this room knows that we should be glad if we could give effect to the kind of plan that Australia and New Zealand have thus bravely and appropriately offered but everyone of us knows that it will require years of work before we can bring about such a situation. Hoping for the ideal, as we do, recognizing the real situation as we must, are we not obligated to tread the slower and more painful path of working together in the simplest steps making for world peace before we undertake the faster and more complicated task of putting the interest of many peoples in the hands of an instrument still unfashioned and whose potentialities are still unknown?

Possibly the work that we do here, and I hope the work that has been done at the Dumbarton Oaks Conference and the contemplated subsequent conferences, will lead us in that direction. I trust that our friends from New Zealand and Australia will not believe that our inability to make their dream come true now reflects any lack of sympathy with the value of the dream itself.

This proposal could not come with better grace from any country than New Zealand, far away in the middle of a great and troubled sea. She has paid more than her measured price for the solution of world problems. But in New Zealand, as in Brazil, and in the United States and, if I may say so, even in France and Great Britain, we still have to create that order of the world which will make these things possible. Only then will we have these fixed relationships which will permit the people of these and other great countries to place themselves in the hands of organizations of this kind.

May we speed the day and express the hope that that time will come. As it stands, there is not that unanimity which would make the New Zealand proposal possible; and we must confine our actions today, it seems to me, to recognizing that there is not that general assent which would make it attainable. At the same time let us recognize the splendor of the intellectual bark which Prime Minister Frazier of New Zealand has set afloat and wish it Godspeed as the world moves on.

In the summer of 1945, the year following the Chicago Conference, as World War II was coming to an end, a general election was held in Great Britain resulting in a victory for the Labour Party. This in turn brought about a major change in British air policy. Prior to the election the British Labour Party had announced, as noted above, its support of the internationalization of civil air transport by the publication of its pamphlet *Wings for Peace.* After the elections the new government (still today in power in the United Kingdom), in a White Paper on *British Air Services*, stated its policy as follows:[9]

1. His Majesty's Government wish to secure the universal acceptance of conditions which would ensure the orderly expansion of air transport. The nations, however, are not yet prepared to place their air services under the control of a single international owning and operating body and there is insufficient support to make possible the formation of such bodies on a regional basis.

2. Attempts at the Chicago Conference to achieve a plan of orderly development in the air were not successful. Accordingly, the plan which His Majesty's Government now present to Parliament is necessarily a national plan, but it has been so framed that it can be readily fitted into any future scheme of international organization.

3. It is the policy of His Majesty's Government to endeavor to negotiate agreements with other countries in conformity with their ultimate objective of securing well-ordered development on a full international basis and so facilitate the later establishment of a multilateral Convention based on order in the air.

4. *Commonwealth Co-operation.* Arrangements have been made for the fullest co-operation with the Dominions and Colonies. By agreement with the Governments concerned, services on Commonwealth air routes will be operated in parallel by independent national air lines under partnership arrangements which will provide for pooling of traffic receipts, avoidance of duplication, and common user of facilities required by operators and for equitable division of receipts and expenditure. If and when Dominion Governments so desire, these arrangements lend themselves readily to transformation into joint organisations for particular routes or into a Commonwealth Corporation to operate all Commonwealth trunk services. His Majesty's Government are prepared to negotiate with foreign Governments similar arrangements for the formation of joint undertakings to operate services on routes of mutual interest.

The first time that the resulting opposing positions of the United Kingdom and the United States were brought directly into open debate was during the meeting of the Interim Assembly of the Provisional International Civil Aviation Organization [PICAO] held in Montreal in 1946. Commission No. 3 had become involved in a discussion of the development of a proposed multilateral agreement on commercial rights in international civil air transport. This discussion was used by

---

[9] Gt. Brit. Ministry of Civil Aviation. *British Air Services.* Presented by the Minister of Civil Aviation to Parliament by Cmd. December 1945. Cmd. 6712.

the representative of the United Kingdom to state the new policy of his government, foreseen in the terms of the White Paper mentioned above and the prior and pre-election statement of Labour Party policies in the pamphlet *Wings for Peace.*

The discussion included the following statements by the delegate of the United Kingdom and by the delegate of the United States:[10]

Delegate of the United Kingdom: It is incumbent on me, however, to record that His Majesty's Government in the United Kingdom, in pursuing such orderly development on international routes, regard the establishment of an international organization to own and operate trunk services as the most effective means of attaining this objective. Nevertheless, until the necessary degree of international support for such an organization is forthcoming, they favour a multilateral agreement, which, while providing for all the contracting parties a code of rules of universal application, would conserve the highest degree of Freedom for air transport for commercial purposes, and safeguard all States, mutually, against undue infringement of their legitimate rights.

Delegate of the United States: The remarks I refer to, are those which recommend an internationally owned and operated airline as the solution for the development of international air transportation. It is a very interesting idea. It is not new because there are many here who knew that it was proposed at Chicago at the end of 1944 by the Representatives of New Zealand and Australia and supported in an eloquent manner which warmed the heart of everyone who listened to the idea as presented by these gentlemen at the conference. You will remember it was not accepted at that conference, so, although the idea is interesting, it is not new; but it is new so far as the United Kingdom's position is concerned. I heard about that position here, for the first time, this afternoon.

We have found that the competitive system, reasonably regulated, is the best way to cause an industry to grow and develop, and give to the users the greatest possible benefits from the industry concerned. If we look at the alternative suggestion, we have not only a new experiment in international operations—so far as I am concerned, it is quite new, and perhaps the only thing of its kind that has been launched, and for that reason it deserves careful analysis—, but the common sense of mankind leads you to the conclusion that, in such a vast enterprise as this, it will take us years to get organized

---

[10] Provisional International Civil Aviation Organization. Commission No. 3. First Interim Assembly. *Discussion on the Development of a Multilateral Agreement on Commercial Rights in International Civil Air Transport.* May 22–24, 27,28, 30, 31, June 3–5, 1946. Document 2089. EC/57.

and years to get the problems solved (if they are solvable) and to get the experiment under way. In the meantime—for the next twenty-five years, or fifty years, or forever—, we would not have a vigorous development of air transportation over the world. It seems a pity to take a small infant industry, which has so much promise and on which a younger generation is beginning to depend, and put it in a position where there is not only a good deal of doubt, but, in our way of thinking, there is a very strong probability that this industry's growth will be arrested and delayed for years and, maybe, for generations.

I conclude my general remarks by stating clearly that the United States are in favor of the continuance of international competitive airline operations under reasonable rules which we are here endeavouring to work out, the comments of this Assembly being a second great step forward in working out that result.

Both New Zealand and Australia filed written statements[11] reaffirming their prior positions and stating, in the language of the delegation of Australia that "full control and operation of the international air trunk routes and the ownership of the requisite aircraft and ancillary equipment should be vested in an international air transport authority, and that international agreement should be reached as to the international air trunk routes which should be so operated."

In 1947 during the meeting of the First Assembly of the International Civil Aviation Organization [ICAO], further discussions of the internationalization problem arose in connection with the resolution offered by the United Kingdom delegation which, if adopted, would have directed the Air Transport Committee of ICAO to make certain studies and to submit to the Assembly during the following year plans for the organization and operation of international air transport under a single organization to operate the world's trunk air routes, or organizations to operate trunk services within a given area, or on individual routes. This resolution was debated in Commission No. 3 of the Assembly. The discussion at that time contains some of the most recent official statements made by the governments concerned on the subject of internationalization. The following excerpts from the discussion are noteworthy:[12]

The Delegate of the United Kingdom: A single organization, of an international character, to operate the world's trunk air services, would clearly dispose of many of the difficulties which now clearly

---

[11] *Ibid.*, pp. 159–161.

[12] International Civil Aviation Organization. *Discussions of Commission No. 3 of the First Assembly*: Volume II: *International Ownership and Operation of Trunk Air Routes*. Document No. 4521, A1–EC/73. May 1947.

confront us. All the arguments and counterarguments to which we have listened in this commission about capacity clauses, Fifth Freedom, arbitration and fixing of fares would disappear if the countries of the world could decide to submerge their national identities into one operating organization. This does not necessarily imply a vast incubus. Our conception of it is that the whole of its policy and general develop ment would be centralised on an international council. Its operations would be controlled by an executive board, and in order to avoid over-centralisation, operational regions would be set up under the control of regional boards responsible to the central board. This would serve the dual object of ensuring close attention to the problems of individual regions and would permit of the healthy rivalry between different regions and so provide the stimulus which would normally be provided by competition between national airlines.

Two other extremely important advantages would accrue from such an organization. First, it would be possible to dispose of the security fear which is inherent in air transport development and allow this important new activity to develop solely in relation to its commercial contribution to the world's economy. Second, and of equal importance, it would ensure that air transport could be developed in the interests of the general publics of the world. Under the present system of national operations, the natural tendency is for the remunerative routes to be exploited, leaving untouched the operation of routes which would be of advantage to the public and which could lead to the exploitation of the natural resources of areas of the world which have been hitherto untapped. It may be suggested that this conception envisages a permanent deficit on operations. I submit that this need not be so. The balance would always be maintained between the remunerative and the unremunerative routes, under which the profits of the former could be applied to the latter, without any need for deficits. Under such a system the maximum advantages and maximum pace of development of air transport in the interests of the general publics of the world could be achieved.

The Delegate of the United States: The nations of the world have different ways of running their airlines. The United Kingdom and other nations have chosen to run them as government owned monopolies. Other nations have also handled them as monopolies, but have handled them as private monopolies, and other nations, like us, chose to put the thing entirely on a basis of private, regulated competition. I see no reason why anybody should assume that one of those methods is the chosen answer to the difficulties of air transportation. We believe profoundly in ours. I assume other people believe profoundly in their methods of operation.

407

With reference to this suggested gargantuan instrumentality, I would like to make a few observations. The first is this: that there is not the slightest shred of evidence to indicate that largeness and economy go hand in hand. There is not the slightest shred of evidence to indicate that. They are only bold assertions made without any proof. In fact, I might turn to an observation of His Majesty's Government with reference to this type of operation. In 1945, in a White Paper issued by the Government of Great Britain in which they decided to bring an end to the single monopoly of BOAC, the Government made this statement. It said: 'The Government is convinced that the policy of a single chosen instrument, whatever may have been its merits in the past, is unsuited to deal with the great expansion of the future. There must, therefore, be several air transport undertakings. A single entity, even if it could effectively include and use all the varied experience of aviation and transportation which it is necessary to bring in, would be too large forbidding and too far-flung to fulfill the requirements of individual supervision of all the routes operated.' That, Gentlemen, has reference only to a limited route mileage of the United Kingdom. It did not conceive the world.

With reference to my other point on economy and efficiency, I think that one could challenge the assertion that any efficiency would be achieved by an operation of this type. Monopoly under our tradition is deemed to breed inefficiency. Other countries may think otherwise, but I see little reason for trying to impose upon the rest of the world certain ideas that a single nation may have, as to how to run an aviation enterprise. We have respect for the nationalization measures of Great Britain but at the moment we do not choose to follow them. Nor do we want to be asked or pressured into following them in any particular field. We are as proud as our own operation as they are of theirs.

A few other points I think might be made here. Those of us who have had experience with this Assembly and other international assemblies know the difficulties of producing a good efficient international civil service. It is not done overnight. The development of the civil service in our various States has taken us years to build up from the 'spoils' system to an effective institution. With that in mind, to take the whole field of this difficult and challenging field of aviation and to hope you can develop an international civil service which will have enough energy, enough insight, enough wisdom, to run that kind of a thing is certainly beyond the possibilities of realization.

Following this debate, in which many other nations also took part, a compromise resolution was adopted by the ICAO Assembly directing that contracting States be invited to submit for consideration by the Council the results of their studies of possible plans for the organization of international transport under a single organization to operate the world's trunk air routes, or organizations to operate trunk services in a given area or on a particular route. The Council of ICAO was directed to study such reports when received. The results of this resolution are stated in paragraphs 153 and 154 of the report of the ICAO Council to the Second Assembly held in Geneva in 1948.[13] From this it appears that only eight replies had been received from member States, six of which were from States "not identified with the active furtherance of schemes for international ownership and operation of international air services on trunk routes." The Argentine reply "indicated that it did not favor international ownership and operation." The Union of South Africa "considered that the world had not yet reached the stage at which concrete proposals on the matter could be put forward." The ICAO Council's report then continues: "the two States already embarked on international ownership and operation (Denmark and Sweden) felt that they had not had sufficient experience from which to draw useful conclusions in regard to the possibility and desirability of extensive internationalization."

Notwithstanding the meager results from the resolution of the previous year, the Second Assembly of ICAO (1948) adopted a further resolution requesting the States who were members of ICAO to submit the results of their studies of internationalization on or before July 31, 1949 for presentation to the Assembly in 1950.

Internationalization of civil air transport on world trunk routes is not, therefore, a dead issue. As just noted, the 1948 Assembly of ICAO has again formally requested its member States to study the problem and to submit possible plans for such international ownership or operation of world trunk air services. When these replies are received and can be studied, the position of the various States concerned, including the United States, the United Kingdom, Australia, New Zealand, and others, will be formally presented to the world. But nothing has transpired up to this time to indicate that there has been any change in the position of the United States in opposition to internationalization, and of the United Kingdom, Australia and New Zealand favoring such internationalization.

Two air transport operations now in existence have been pointed to as examples of internationalization or as steps in that direction. One

---

[13] International Civil Aviation Organization. *Report of the Council to the Assembly on the Activities of the Organization June 1, 1947–March 1, 1948.* Document No. 5221, A2–P/5. March 19, 1948.

of these is British Commonwealth Pacific Airlines which has been granted a foreign air carrier permit to enter the United States.[14] The records in the proceedings before the Civil Aeronautics Board indicate that this organization is a corporation organized under the laws of the Commonwealth of Australia, pursuant to a tripartite agreement between the governments of Australia, New Zealand and the United Kingdom, the stock to be held on the basis of 50% by Australia, 30% by New Zealand and 20% by the United Kingdom. As the company is incorporated under the laws of Australia, it lacks one of the salient features of true internationalization; namely, the disappearance of national flags from world air trunk routes. It is really an Australian operation owned jointly by Australia and two other governments. It is, however, evidence of a definite continued policy of the United Kingdom and the two Dominions concerned to eliminate competition between themselves on important world trunk routes and may to that extent be considered as a step toward implementing the policy of internationalization still apparently favored by each of these three governments.

The other organization which has been cited at times as an evidence of internationalization is Scandinavian Airlines System which has also been granted a foreign air carrier permit by the United States.[15] The record in the SAS case before the U. S. Civil Aeronautics Board disclosed that the organization is not a single corporation but is what is sometimes called a consortium. Management is vested in a six-member board of trustees, two of whom are appointed by each of the parties to the agreement; namely, the Swedish, Norwegian and Danish air transport concerns which are parties to the consortium agreement. It is understood that flight equipment and ground facilities used by SAS in the joint trans-atlantic and other services to be performed will be provided by the three member airlines, and that the net result of operations will be shared in the following ratio: Swedish Airlines 3/7ths, Norwegian Airlines 2/7ths, Danish Airlines 2/7ths. As to third parties, these three companies have agreed to be jointly and severally liable for any obligation that the consortium may undertake or incur in connection with its business. A description of this operation has recently been published by Mr. Per Norlin, President of SAS.[16]

---

[14] U. S. Civil Aeronautics Board. Docket No. 2688. British Commonwealth Pacific Airlines Limited. Decided January 24, 1947. E-284. Docket No. 2777. Decided March 21, 1947. E-438.

[15] U. S. Civil Aeronautics Board. Docket No. 2560. Scandinavian Airlines System. Decided November 24, 1947. E-1013.

[16] "Scandinavian Airlines System," INTERAVIA: REVIEW OF WORLD AVIATION, Volume 3, Number 9, September 1948. Pp. 511–513.

Whether the Scandinavian Airlines System operation does or does not constitute internationalization may be an open question. The participating companies keep title to the aircraft and charter them to the consortium. While the consortium has no national flag, each of the aircraft still has a national character. Nor are the routes over which SAS operates to be considered as internationalized routes. SAS, as a "Scandinavian air union", operates on such routes as the transatlantic in direct competition with American, British, Dutch, French, Canadian, Belgian, and perhaps other national air transport lines. On these particular routes competition between the Scandinavian operators has been eliminated, it is true, but with the result that seems to resemble financially and politically something nearer a pool operation than theoretical and true internationalization. However, no one can deny that SAS is a highly interesting experiment in the general direction of internationalization.

It has been the purpose of this article to state the existence and history of the disagreement between major powers as to whether internationalization should or should not be accepted as the basis for future organization and operation of world air trunk services. No attempt has been made to argue the merits of either side of the controversy. When the formal replies of the several governments concerned have been filed with ICAO, the entire problem can be re-examined and the political and economic advantages and disadvantages can be appraised. In the meantime it is of grave importance that there seems to be complete lack of accord in the national policies of the United States and of the United Kingdom on such a basic question as the future method of handling what may become, before many years have passed, the most important means of communication between the nations of the world.

25

Self-Defense in Outer Space and the United Nations

Reprinted by permission of Air
Force and Space Digest *from 5*
Air Force and Space Digest *51*
(*February 1962*).
ⓒ Air Force and Space Digest.

Author's Note. The position taken in this article may be deemed controversial. Since its publication, works other than those mentioned have been read with care. But the passage of time has served only to confirm the views here expressed. It is hoped that no emergency will provide a concrete testing ground.

T HE UNITED STATES, as a member of the United Nations, subscribes to its purposes, including the commitment "to maintain international peace and security." As a party to the North Atlantic Treaty, the US reaffirmed its faith "in the purposes and principles of the Charter of the United Nations, and their desire to live in peace with all peoples and all governments."[1] But as a sovereign State, the US did not surrender its individual right to defend its territorial integrity and political independence. As Secretary of State Kellogg properly said during the course of the negotiations for the 1928 Briand-Kellogg Pact renouncing war: "That right [of self-defense] is inherent in every sovereign State and is implicit in every treaty."[2]

The Briand-Kellogg Pact, the UN Charter, and the organization of NATO all antedate the present space age. Now new problems face the US and other members of the UN and of NATO:

What are the rights of self-defense in outer space?

If spacecraft threaten national survival of a member of the United Nations, must that nation stand by and await an actual physical attack, or may it take necessary preventive measures before receiving a crippling blow?

Concretely, when and where may a nation in self-defense attack a suspected spacecraft?

The limits of this paper will not permit detailed discussion, but some broad outlines of the questions now involved may be suggested.

Such questions have not been answered by the recent and already historic resolution adopted by the United Nations. On December 11, 1961, the First (Political) Committee of the UN General Assembly unanimously accepted a draft resolution on International Cooperation in the Peaceful Uses of Outer Space. This resolution was sponsored by the US, the USSR, Great Britain, France, and the other States which

---

[1] Preamble to North Atlantic Treaty, April 4, 1949: US Treaties and Other Int. Acts-Series 1949.

[2] Papers Relating to the Foreign Relations of the US (1928) I, 36; Briggs, *The Law of Nations*, 2d ed. p. 977.

had been members of the dormant Committee on the Peaceful Uses of Outer Space. The resolution extended the life of the Committee, added one Asiatic and three African States to membership, and requested the Committee to meet not later than March 31, 1962, to go forward with the program of study which had been adopted two years earlier. Part A of the resolution is of major significance. It said:

The General Assembly,

Recognizing the common interest of mankind in furthering the peaceful uses of outer space and the urgent need to strengthen international cooperation in this important field,

Believing that the exploration and use of outer space should be only for the betterment of mankind and to the benefit of States irrespective of the stage of their economic or scientific development,

1. *Commends* to States for their guidance in the exploration and use of outer space the following principles:

a) International law, including the United Nations Charter, applies to outer space and celestial bodies;

b) Outer space and celestial bodies are free for exploration and use by all States in conformity with international law, and are not subject to national appropriation;

2. *Invites* the Committee on the Peaceful Uses of Outer Space to study and report on the legal problems which may arise from the exploration and use of outer space.[3]

It must be noted that the resolution does not define the term "outer space" or the term "peaceful uses." However, the resolution clearly commits the UN to the basic principles that international law and the Charter are there applicable also that this area and celestial bodies are free for exploration and use by all States "in conformity with international law," and "are not subject to national appropriation." This can only mean that neither outer space nor celestial bodies are now subject to territorial claims of any single State nor can they be hereafter. The UN has thus determined that outer space has an international status analogous to that of the high seas where, as Mr. Justice Storey of the United States Supreme Court said in the case of the *Mariana Flora* in 1826: "It is the common highway of all, appropriated to the use of all, and no one can vindicate to himself a superior prerogative there."

Also it has been ably argued that peaceful uses of outer space include

---

[3] Report of UN First Committee Doc. A/5026 approved by General Assembly 20 December 1961.

defense uses. As Dr. Edward C. Welsh, Executive Secretary of the National Aeronautics and Space Council, speaking at the recent Air Force Association Symposium on "Space and National Security," said, in part:

> The National Aeronautics and Space Act of 1958 states that it is the policy of the United States that "activities in space should be devoted to peaceful purposes for the benefit of all mankind."
>
> That is a sound policy for any vigorous, peace-loving nation. Even though it is sound, however, I know also that it is sometimes misinterpreted. It does not mean that space has no military or defense uses. . . . Nothing is more essential for peace than the capability to discourage or deter attack.
>
> In my view, we do not have a division between peaceful and non-peaceful objectives for space. Rather, *we have space missions to help keep the peace, and space missions to help increase our ability to live well in peace.*[4]

With this view the present writer fully concurs. Nor is there anything in the resolution adopted by the United Nations which of itself precludes the bona fide use of outer space for self-defense against an aggressor, particularly in view of the fact that the resolution asserts in effect that outer space is not part of the territory of any State.

The major question, however, is whether or not any principle of international law or any provision of the UN Charter, now agreed to be applicable in outer space, prevents or limits acts of self-defense. For example, is it permissible for a State to intercept in outer space a foreign spacecraft known to be armed with a nuclear warhead and thereby constituting a source of potential attack on any State flown over?

States have traditionally claimed the right to act in self-defense and self-protection outside national territory. As Elihu Root said in a 1914 address as President of the American Society of International Law: "The right is a necessary corollary of independent sovereignty. It is well understood that the exercise of the right of self-protection may and frequently does extend in its effect beyond the limits of the territorial jurisdiction of the State exercising it." In the same address, discussing the background of the Monroe Doctrine, Mr. Root insisted upon "the right of every sovereign State to protect itself by preventing a condition of affairs in which it will be too late to protect itself."[5]

---

[4] *Air Force and Space Digest* (Nov. 1961) pp. 73–74.
[5] 8 *Am. Jour. Int. Law* (1914) p. 6.

The circumstances in which a State may use force in self-defense outside national territory were carefully stated by Daniel Webster, when he was Secretary of State, in an exchange of notes with the British government following the destruction of the American vessel *Caroline* and the loss of two American lives. Webster's dictum has become part of traditional international law.

The *Caroline* was a small American vessel used in 1837 to transport men and supplies from the American side of the Niagara River to two Canadian islands occupied by Canadian insurgents. On the night of December 29, 1837, a British force crossed from Canada and seized and burned the *Caroline*, which was moored on the American side of the river. The US protested the violation of its territory. The British government claimed justifiable self-defense, even though two Americans had been killed escaping from the vessel. In 1841, a British citizen named McLeod was arrested in New York and indicted for murder on the ground that he had participated in the attack on the *Caroline*. The British government protested the arrest, again claiming that the attack was justified as military preventive self-defense. Daniel Webster, who had become Secretary of State, insisted, in words now famous, that the British and Canadian authorities, to justify the attack in American territory, must show "*a necessity of self-defense, instant, overwhelming, leaving no choice of means and no moment of deliberation.*" [italics supplied]

He added that even supposing necessity authorized entry into American territory, it must also be shown that nothing unreasonable or excessive was done, "since the act, justified by the necessity of self-defense, must be limited by that necessity and kept clearly within it." These phrases have been repeatedly acknowledged as valid statements of customary international law.[6]

The Caroline Case dealt directly with violation of foreign territory while acting in self-defense. The same rule applies on the high seas. For example, a vessel sailing to a port of the capturing State for the purpose of invasion or bringing help to insurgents presents a case of necessity in that the danger is imminent and can be frustrated only by the capture of the vessel.[7]

Judge Jessup, writing in 1927 and referring to the Caroline Case, said: "It must be remembered that the great principle of the inviolability of national territory is qualified by the right of self-defense.

---

[6] Moore, *International Law Digest*, vol. II, sec. 217, pp. 409–414; R. Y. Jennings, *The Caroline and McLeod Cases*, 32 Am. Jour. Int. Law (1938) p. 82.

[7] Oppenheim, *International Law*, 8th ed. (Lauterpacht) (1955) vol. I, p. 301, n. 1; D. W. Bowett, *Self Defense in International Law* (1958) p. 72.

Why should it be denied that the freedom of the seas may also be subject to qualifications?"[8] Later he said that circumstances applicable when the act of self-defense involves the invasion of the territory of a neighbouring State apply "a fortiori . . . upon the ocean."[9]

There is no reason why the rule in the Caroline Case is not now also applicable in nonterritorial outer space.

The substance of Webster's now famous dictum as to justifiable acts of self-defense beyond national territory was directly approved in 1946 by the judgment of the International Military Tribunal at Nuremberg. It accepted the contention that preventive self-defense was justified to meet an imminent attack but held that the facts showed that the German invasions of Denmark and Norway could not be thus excused, saying: "It must be remembered that preventive action in foreign territory is justified only in case of an instant and overwhelming necessity for self-defense, leaving no choice of means, and no moment of deliberation. (The Caroline Case, Moore's *International Law Digest*, vol. II, p. 412)" Then after discussing the facts, the Tribunal held: "In the light of all the available evidence it is impossible to accept the contention that the invasions of Denmark and Norway were defensive, and in the opinion of the Tribunal they were acts of aggressive war."[10]

In 1947 the International Military Tribunal for the Far East, sitting at Tokyo, sustained the Netherlands declaration of war against Japan as justifiable preventive self-defense, the proof showing that the Netherlands had become aware of an imminent Japanese attack.[11]

It therefore appears that the rule in the Caroline Case states present international law as to the circumstances when a State may exercise its rights of self-defense in any area outside its national territory, unless some change in the law has become effective since World War II. It has, in fact, been contended that such change did take place and that the UN Charter now denies the use of force in self-defense except under much more limited circumstances. In particular some writers have urged that the imminence of attack is not sufficient, and that force may be used in self-defense *only after an actual attack.*

Article 2 (4) and Article 51 of the United Nations Charter require consideration.

Article 2 (4). All Members shall refrain in their international relations from the threat or use of force against the territorial

---

[8] Philip C. Jessup, *The International Law of Territorial Waters and Maritime Jurisdiction* (1927) p. 76.

[9] *Ibid.*, p. 97.

[10] Judgment International Military Tribunal (Nuremberg) Oct. 1, 1946, 41 Am. Jour. Int. Law (1947) p. 172, 205.

[11] Bowett, *op. cit.* p. 144.

integrity or political independence of any State, or in any other manner inconsistent with the Purposes of the United Nations.

Article 51. Nothing in the present Charter shall impair the inherent right of individual or collective self-defense if an armed attack occurs against a Member of the United Nations, until the Security Council has taken the measures necessary to maintain international peace and security. Measures taken by Members in the exercise of this right of self-defense shall be immediately reported to the Security Council and shall not in any way affect the authority and responsibility of the Security Council under the present Charter to take at any time such action as it deems necessary in order to maintain or restore international peace and security.

The views of certain well known authorities on international law construing these Articles must be noted. One said in 1947 that Article 51 limits the right of individual and collective self-defense to the one case of armed attack against a member of the United Nations—that the term "armed attack" means something that has taken place—that Article 51 prohibits preventive war—that the threat of aggression does not justify self-defense under Article 51 and that imminent armed attack does not suffice.[12]

Another legal expert wrote in 1950 that it is "of importance to note that Article 51 does not use the term aggression but the much narrower concept of armed attack which means that a merely imminent attack or any act of aggression which has not the character of an attack involving the use of armed force does not justify resort to force as an exercise of the right established by Article 51."[13] The same commentator had stated earlier that Article 51 applies only in the case of an armed attack, and that "the delinquent State which is in actual possession of the illegal advantage is protected by the Charter against any enforcement action other than that taken by the Security Council"— that "the Charter forbids any use of force on the part of the individual members except for the exercise of the right of self-defense against armed attack."[14]

Another commentator wrote in 1958 that Article 51 suggests a limitation on the right of self-defense, namely "it may be exercised only if an armed attack occurs"—that the restriction in Article 51 "very definitely narrows the freedom of action which States had under traditional law" —that a "case could be made out for self-defense under

---

[12] Joseph L. Kunz, *Individual and Collective Self-Defense in Article 51 of the Charter of the United Nations*, 41 *Am. Jour. Int. Law* (1947) p. 871.

[13] Hans Kelsen, *The Law of the United Nations* (1950) pp. 797–789.

[14] *Ibid.*, p. 269.

the traditional law where the injury was threatened but no attack had yet taken place," but that "under the Charter, alarming military preparations by a neighboring State would justify a resort to the Security Council, but would not justify a resort to anticipatory force by the State which believed itself threatened."[15]

At the 1958 meeting of the International Law Association, Judge Krylov, a distinguished jurist from the USSR, is reported to have said: "We have before us the text of the Charter and we must interpret this text exclusively. Article 51 speaks of self-defense, but the text of the Charter does not mention preventive self-defense. Self-defense is permissible only if an armed attack occurs. So, once more, I repeat that the interpretation of the Article must be a restrictive one. . . . It is surprising to listen to the citation of the Caroline Case which took place about 150 years ago. This citation and this opinion cannot be defended against the clear and unquestionable text of the Charter."[16]

It is impossible for this writer to accept the result of these interpretations. Neither Article 2 nor Article 51 nor the Charter as a whole has, in my considered judgment, limited or destroyed the fundamental right of a State to defend itself by force against imminent attack or danger threatening its existence. I have long held this view. If the restrictive interpretation were correct, and if the Charter had been in force during World War II, the judgment of the Tokyo Tribunal would not have been valid when it found that the Netherlands was justified in declaring war on learning that a Japanese attack was imminent. Certainly the Charter was not intended as an instrument to reverse world feeling against aggression.

The problem is to some extent based on the manner in which the Charter should be construed. Prof. Arthur L. Goodhart, now Master of University College at Oxford, states the correct rule, namely that "all powers which have not been expressly or by necessary implication transferred to the United Nations remain in the individual States. They hold these powers not by grant but by sovereign right."[17] Commenting on the contention that Article 51 establishes the right of self-defense and that this right has no other content than the one determined by Article 51, Professor Goodhart continues: "It is

---

[15] Philip C. Jessup, *A Modern Law of Nations* (1958) pp. 163–166.

[16] Int. Law Assn., Report of the 48th Conference (New York, 1958) p. 512.

[17] A. L. Goodhart, *The North Atlantic Treaty*, 79 Recueil des Cours, Academie de Droit International (1951-II) p. 188, 193; see also remarks of L. C. Green (United Kingdom) Int. Law Assn., Report *op. cit.* p. 517: "The right of self-defense was inherent before the Charter was written; it has remained inherent, and as such it covers preventive self-defense as well as self-defense resorted to after you have already been exterminated."

obvious that this interpretation of the Charter must narrow the rights of the individual States, because their rights can then be found only within the terms of the Charter itself. On the other hand, if the Charter is regarded as leaving all residual rights in the hands of the States, then the question will always be: To what extent has any particular provision of the Charter limited the existing liberty of the individual States? . . . As the Charter does not limit the right of self-defense in any way, it follows that a State or a group of States may defend themselves in any manner consonant with that end." Discussing Article 2 (4) Professor Goodhart points out that this Article does not establish a "universal obligation not to use force," but prohibits it only in three instances, namely, the following:

a) Use of force against the territorial integrity of any State. It is clear that defense against aggression cannot be regarded as an attack against the territorial integrity of the aggressor.

b) Use of force against the political independence of any State. Here again it is clear that the use of force against an aggressor is not an attack on its political independence.

c) Use of force in any other manner inconsistent with the purposes of the United Nations. It cannot be regarded as inconsistent with the purposes of the United Nations that States should defend themselves against a wanton attack. It follows that the right of self-defense is not "an essential restriction of the obligation established by Article 2, paragraph 4," but is an independent inherent right which is not within the purview of that Article and is in no way restricted by it.[18]

An authoritative statement as to the continued effect of the Caroline Case doctrine was made by the Lord Chancellor of Great Britain (Lord Kilmuir) in the British Parliament on November 1, 1956: "Article 51 must be read in the light that it is part of Chapter VII of the Charter and concerned with the defense against grave breaches of the peace. It would be an entire misreading of the whole intention of Article 51 to interpret it as forbidding forcible self-defense in resistance to an illegal use of force not constituting an armed attack. In my view, it is equally clear that Article 51 does not cut down the customary right by restricting forcible self-defense in cases where the attack provoking it has actually been launched. I think that every one of your Lordships will appreciate that if that were done it would be a travesty of the purpose of the Charter to compel a defending State to allow its opponent to deliver the first fatal blow. . . . The doctrine that I have put forward is an old and well established doctrine. It was established at

---

[18] Goodhart, *op. cit.*, p. 231.

least 100 years ago in the case of the *Caroline*, which was a matter discussed between the United States and ourselves. The foundation of the doctrine was accepted as 'imminent threat to your nationals.' The doctrine arises, and that form of self-defense becomes legal, when the imminent threat is made."[19]

Professor McDougal of Yale recently published an able, extensive, and persuasive analysis of these difficult questions. Limits of space here prevent my referring to more than a few passages of his excellent discussion. He points out in connection with the formulation at San Francisco of Article 2 (4) of the UN Charter, that in a committee report approved at the plenary conference it was made clear that the traditional position of self-defense was not intended to be abridged, but on the contrary, was intended to be reserved and maintained.[20] In forceful language dealing with Article 51, Professor McDougal states that "it is scarcely conceivable . . . that the major security purposes of the parties to the Charter could in contemporary conditions be adequately, if at all, served by an interpretation which would reduce self-defense to assumption of the posture of the sitting duck."[21] Later he quoted Professor Waldock of Oxford to the effect that "to cut down the customary right of self-defense beyond even the *Caroline* doctrine does not make sense."[22]

The views expressed by these recent authorities appear to me to present the soundest position on a difficult and most important question. I join them in the belief that the traditional right of preventive self-defense has not been limited by membership in the United Nations. Under present conditions this would be a fatal assumption. Consider the possibility of a satellite in flight around the earth in an orbit which brings it repeatedly over a great number of States. If it is equipped with a nuclear device which can be released and propelled downward by radio command, the satellite is an imminent threat to every State in its path. But it is not "an armed attack" on any single State until the warhead is released minutes before striking the eventual victim. Can it be argued that no State has a right to intercept the satellite even though such State is aware of its possible danger?

In my judgment, the Webster dictum in the Caroline Case is still sound international law and is applicable to self-defense in outer space. It is part of the international law referred to in the resolution of the

---

[19] *Int. and Comp. Law Quar.*, vol. 6 (1957) p. 330, quoting "House of Lords Debates," vol. 200, cols. 847 and 849, Dec. 11, 1956; see also Bowett, *op. cit.*, p. 186.

[20] Myres S. McDougal and Florentino P. Feliciano, *Legal Regulation of Resort to International Coercion: Aggression and Self-Defense in Policy Perspective*, Yale Law Journal, vol. 68, no. 6 (May 1959) p. 1057, 1146.

[21] *Ibid.*, p. 1147, n. 260.   [22] *Ibid.*, p. 1148.

General Assembly. As stated by the Nuremberg Tribunal, preventive action "is justified only in case of an instant and overwhelming necessity for self-defense, leaving no choice of means, and no moment of deliberation." If these conditions are deemed to be present, action is not denied by the Charter of the UN nor precluded by the recent UN resolution.

The real problem is therefore not legal. The question is rather one of scientific progress, military strategy, and national policy. If a State determines that the conditions are present justifying action, and if effective means are available, action can be taken in self-defense on land, at sea, in the air—or in outer space.

26

The Manned Orbiting Laboratory: A Major Legal and Political Decision

Reprinted by permission of the
American Bar Association from 51
American Bar Association Journal
1137 (1965).

Author's Note. It is believed that this article is completely consistent with certain of the basic conclusions
reached in the preceding article on self-defense in outer
space, published three years earlier.

O N AUGUST 25, 1965, President Johnson announced that he was
"today instructing the Department of Defense to immediately proceed with the development of a manned orbiting laboratory".

By this action the President formally notified the world that under
American law and policy the "peaceful use" of outer space includes
military defense, that such is the proper construction of the National
Aeronautics and Space Act of 1958, that our Government has not
withdrawn from this position by supporting various resolutions in the
United Nations and that outer space may in time of peace be used by
military spacecraft as the high seas are by naval vessels. Few legal and
political decisions of recent years are of equal international importance
and gravity.

President Johnson said:

> This program will bring us new knowledge about what man is
> able to do in space. It will enable us to relate that ability to the
> defense of America. It will develop technology and equipment which
> will help advance manned and unmanned space flight and it will
> make it possible to perform very new and rewarding experiments
> with that technology and equipment. . . . We believe the heavens
> belong to the people of every country. We are working and we will
> continue to work through the United Nations . . . to extend the rule
> of law into outer space.

President Johnson's statement was clearly consistent with prior
basic United States policy. While it may be true that the term "peaceful use of outer space" in some earlier public statements might have
led to the erroneous conclusion that the United States was committed
to a policy which banned all military use, it is quite certain that no
such policy ever existed.

In 1958 both houses of Congress adopted and President Eisenhower
signed the National Aeronautics and Space Act of 1958. This followed
long public hearings and the most serious consideration. Section 102
of that act contains a "declaration of policy and purpose", which reads,
in part, as follows:

> *a*) The Congress hereby declares that it is the policy of the United
> States that activities in space should be devoted to peaceful purposes
> for the benefit of all mankind.

424

b) The Congress declares that the general welfare and security of the United States require that adequate provision be made for aeronautical and space activities. The Congress further declares that such activities shall be the responsibility of, and shall be directed by, a civilian agency exercising control over aeronautical and space activities sponsored by the United States, except that activities peculiar to or primarily associated with the development of weapons systems, military operations, or the defense of the United States (including the research and development necessary to make effective provision for the defense of the United States) shall be the responsibility of, and shall be directed by, the Department of Defense; and that determination as to which such agency has responsibility for and direction of any such activity shall be made by the President. . . .[1]

The act had been drafted in a Senate committee of which President Johnson, as a United States Senator, was then chairman, and in a House Committee of which the present Speaker, John W. McCormick, was chairman. After the final text of the act had been settled in a conference committee composed of representatives of the Senate and the House committees, the managers on the part of the House who participated in the conference filed a statement clarifying the "declaration of policy and purpose" contained in the act. This said:

Subsection (*a*) declares it to be the policy of the United States that activities in space should be devoted to peaceful purposes. . . .

Subsection (*b*) delineates in the field of aeronautical and space activities the responsibility which will be exercised by the new civilian space agency and that which will be exercised by the Department of Defense. . . .

The Congress recognizes that the development of aeronautics and space capabilities is important both to peaceful purposes and to the defense of the United States and for the preservation of peace everywhere. It is the intent of the Congress that the necessary freedom to carry on research, development, and exploration be afforded both a civilian agency and the Defense Establishment to insure the full development of these peaceful and defense uses without unnecessary delay, to exclude the possibility that one agency would be able to preempt a field of activity so as to preclude the other agency from moving along related lines of development necessary to the full accomplishment of its duties assigned under this act. . . . It is clearly recognized that activities which are peculiar to or primarily associated with weapons systems or military operations or to the defense of the United States (including the research and development necessary

---

[1] 42 U.S.C. § 2451 (*a*) and (*b*).

to make effective provision for the defense of the United States) shall be under the jurisdiction of the Department of Defense. However, because there is a gray area between civilian and military interests, and unavoidable overlapping, it is necessary that machinery be provided at the highest level of Government to make determinations of responsibility and jurisdiction. . . .

This act makes such provision by providing that the President, assisted by an Advisory Council . . . shall make the actual determinations in the assignment of new programs or projects. . . .[2]

For the past several years the United Nations has considered what recommendations it should make to member states as to the use of outer space. This has given an opportunity for various states to explain basic policy positions. The United States has insisted firmly that its policy did not include any ban on military nonaggressive use. For example, on December 3, 1962, Senator Albert A. Gore, speaking in the First (Political) Committee of the General Assembly as one of the official representatives of the United States, said:

It is the view of the United States that outer space should be used only for peaceful—that is, nonaggressive and beneficial—purposes. The question of military activities in space cannot be divorced from the question of military activities on earth. To banish these activities in both environments we must continue our efforts for general and complete disarmament with adequate safeguards. Until this is achieved, the test of any space activity must not be whether it is military or nonmilitary, but whether or not it is consistent with the United Nations Charter and other obligations of international law.

There is, in any event, no workable dividing line between military uses of space. For instance, both American and Russian astronauts are members of the armed forces of their respective countries; but this is not reason to challenge their activities or to depreciate their accomplishments. A navigation satellite in outer space can guide a submarine as well as a merchant ship. The instruments which guide a space vehicle on a scientific mission can also guide a space vehicle on a military mission.

One of the consequences of these facts is that any nation may use space satellites for such purposes as observation and information gathering. Observation from space is consistent with international law, just as is observation from the high seas. Moreover, it serves many useful purposes. Observation satellites can measure solar and stellar radiation and observe the atmosphere and surfaces of other planets. They can observe cloud formations and weather conditions.

---

[2] 1598 U. S. Code Cong. & Ad. News 3191.

They can observe the earth and add to the science of geodesy. Observation satellites obviously have military as well as scientific and commercial applications. But this can provide no basis for objection to observation satellites.

Speaking in 1961 at an Air Force Association Symposium on Space and National Security, E. C. Welsh, Executive Secretary of the National Aeronautics and Space Council, which was created by the 1958 act, said:

> The National Aeronautics and Space Act of 1958 states that it is the policy of the United States that "activities in space should be devoted to peaceful purposes for the benefit of all mankind". That is a sound policy for any vigorous, peace-loving nation. Even though it is sound, however, I know also that it is sometimes misinterpreted. It does not mean that space has no military or defense uses. I believe that the Defense Department's space vehicles, such as ICBM's. Midas, Samos, and others, in the hands of the United States, are designed for peaceful purposes. Nothing is more essential for peace than the capability to discourage or deter attack. In my view, we do *not* have a division between peaceful and nonpeaceful objectives for space. Rather *we have space missions to help keep the peace and space missions to help increase our ability to live well in peace.* The Space Act itself goes on to recognize this dual approach to peaceful uses of space in its subsequent language.

In 1963 the United Nations General Assembly, after extended negotiations among the members of its Committee on the Peaceful Uses of Outer Space and the Political Committee of the General Assembly, adopted Resolution 1962 (XVIII) containing a declaration of legal principles "governing the activities of states in the exploration and use of outer space". The United States supported this resolution. The preamble recognizes the "common interest of all mankind in the progress of the exploration and use of outer space for peaceful purposes" The operative paragraphs state, among other things, that "the exploration and use of outer space shall be carried on for the benefit and in the interests of all mankind", that outer space and celestial bodies are free for exploration and use in accordance with international law and that they are not subject to national appropriation by claim of sovereignty or otherwise. Nothing in the resolution seeks to ban military use of outer space.

In the discussions both before and after the adoption of this resolution, certain states, particularly India, Japan, Lebanon and the United Arab Republic insisted that the United Nations take a position that would ban all military activity in outer space. The Soviet Union at

427

that time seems to have opposed this view, insisting that a ban of this kind could be considered only in connection with discussions of general and complete disarmament. While the draft resolution was under consideration, the representative of the U.S.S.R. stated:

> The draft declaration does not and could not, of course, deal with the matter of military uses of outer space. As the members of the committee all know, the Soviet Union has often stated that it is prepared within the framework of a programme of general and complete disarmament under strict international control, to destroy all types of weapons. That would also solve the problem of prohibiting the use of outer space for military purposes. However, we did not agree and still do not agree with attempts to divorce the matter of the military uses of outer space from other measures of disarmament which are intimately linked to it. As has been stated many times, the question of the prohibition of the use of outer space for military ends is organically linked with the question of the liquidation of foreign military bases on the territory of other countries. It is quite clear that the question of the prohibition of the military uses of outer space can be solved only in the context of disarmament, with parallel and simultaneous liquidation of foreign military bases on the territory of other countries.[3]

The draft resolution was unanimously adopted without change by the General Assembly of the United Nations on December 13, 1963.

Earlier, in connection with disarmament discussions, the United States and the U.S.S.R. had stated that they did not intend to station in outer space any objects carrying nuclear weapons or other kinds of weapons of mass destruction. The General Assembly on October 17, 1963, adopted Resolution 1884 welcoming these statements and calling upon all states to refrain from placing such objects in orbit around the earth or on celestial bodies. Even this resolution cannot be construed as a binding provision of international law. President Johnson in his statement announcing the manned orbiting laboratory program did, however say: "We intend to live up to our agreement not to orbit weapons of mass destruction . . .". To the extent that this might be deemed a legally binding obligation on the part of the United States, it represents the only existing ban on our military use of outer space for nonaggressive purposes.

It is thus apparent that the authorization by the President of the construction and subsequent operation of a manned orbiting laboratory by the Defense Department is entirely consistent with the established policy of the United States, as evidenced by the provisions of the

---

[3] U. N. Doc. No. A/C/1 P.V. 1342 (December 2, 1963).

National Aeronautics and Space Act of 1958 and by the discussions in the United Nations and elsewhere.

To this administrative construction of our existing national statute law must be added the important effect of President Johnson's announcement on our understanding of the growing international law of outer space. We have now asserted in substance that outer space, like the high seas, may be used for defense purposes.

Ships of the armed services of any nation may, in time of peace, navigate the high seas unmolested, making observations, perfecting weapons and otherwise preparing the defenses of their country. Mr. Justice Story of the United States Supreme Court in 1826 described in unmatched language the political and legal status of the high seas. He said:

> Upon the ocean, then, in time of peace, all possess an entire equality. It is the common highway of all, appropriated to the use of all; and no one can vindicate to himself a superior or exclusive prerogative there. Every ship sails there with the unquestionable right of pursuing her own lawful business without interruption; but, whatever may be that business, she is bound to pursue it in such a manner as not to violate the rights of others. . . .[4]

Now President Johnson has authorized the construction and operation by the Department of Defense of a spacecraft, the manned orbiting laboratory, to perform duties in outer space similar to those of a naval research vessel on the high seas. But at the same time, he has said: "We believe the heavens belong to the people of every country."

Slowly and inexorably we are coming to accept the fact that the legal status of outer space and the high seas differs very little, if at all. Historically, it should be noted that space above the high seas has long been accepted as having the status of the seas themselves. When a commission of the World War I Peace Conference met in Paris in 1919 to draft a treaty to regulate future aviation, the subcommittee which prepared the draft pointed out that it favored "the full and exclusive subjection of the air space to the territory underlying it. . . . It is only when the column of air rests upon a *res nullius* or *communis*, the sea, that freedom becomes the rule of the air." The United States was represented on that committee.

In a file in the National Archives in Washington, examined by this writer, is a memorandum showing that the United States delegation at Paris actually proposed a clause to be inserted in the convention that would have stated: "No state may claim sovereignty of the atmosphere

---

[4] *The Marianna Flora*, 11 Wheat. 1, 42.

over the high seas." While this clause was not actually included in the convention, no one has since sought to claim sovereignty in any area above the high seas. The United States, for example, has in its statutes since 1926 treated the airspace above its lands, internal and territorial waters as part of its territory, but has accepted the fact that airspace over the high seas is free. This has become a universal rule of international law.

In 1958 the diplomatic conference that met at Geneva and drafted the well-known Convention of the High Seas dealt even more fully with the problem. The preamble to that convention refers to its provisions "as generally declaratory of established principles of international law". The most important provision of the treaty is contained in Article 2:

> The high seas being open to all nations, no state may validly purport to subject any part of them to its sovereignty. Freedom of the high seas is exercised under the conditions laid down by these articles and by the other rules of international law. It comprises, inter alia, both for coastal and noncoastal states:
>
> 1) Freedom of navigation;
> 2) Freedom of fishing;
> 3) Freedom to lay submarine cables and pipelines;
> 4) Freedom to fly over the high seas.
>
> These freedoms, and others which are recognized by the general principles of international law, shall be exercised by all states with reasonable regard to the interests of other states in their exercise of the freedom of the high seas.

It will be noted that the freedom of flight, as stated in the high seas convention, is not limited to freedom to fly through the airspace. It is simply "freedom to fly over the high seas", available to both coastal and noncoastal states. No difference is made between flight through the airspace over the high seas and flight above the airspace.

From every point of view of international law, President Johnson's decision is sound. It is necessary to assign the same status to outer space areas above the high seas and above national lands and waters of sovereign states. It would be quite impossible to consider a situation in which a spacecraft orbiting at more than 17,000 miles an hour found itself theoretically subject to one rule over the high seas and a different one over a subjacent state. This practical point of view was fully understood in the discussions in the United Nations. The resolutions adopted in 1961 and 1963 dealt with outer space as a single undivided area "free for exploration and use by all states on the basis of equality and in accordance with international law."

President Johnson's statement has clarified the present position. Outer space is free for the use of all states just as is the airspace over the high seas. This freedom can be limited only by the consent of the state concerned or by accepted international law. As Mr. Justice Story said of navigation on the high seas, a ship (and now a spacecraft) is bound to pursue its lawful business in such a manner as not to violate the rights of others.

The United States has now formally asserted that no rule of international law bans such use of outer space for military defense purposes. This has always been the rule for naval ships on the high seas and for military aircraft in the airspace above the high seas. We have now reached the position where we assert the same rule whether it be on or above the high seas, or in all of usable outer space.

No rule of international law is violated by the provisions of the National Aeronautics and Space Act of 1958 providing for military defense action in outer space. This objective we are now carrying forward.

27

Liability for Space Damage—The United Nations—The Rome Convention

A Paper submitted to the Eighth Colloquium of Space Law, Athens, 14–15 September 1965.

Author's Note. This paper evidences the author's continued concern as to possible conflicts of jurisdiction under the present world organization between the United Nations and the International Civil Aviation Organization. The former is dealing with flight problems affecting instrumentalities capable of use in outer space and the latter with similar problems as to "aircraft." Confusion may well result.

T HE GENERAL ASSEMBLY of the United Nations on December 13, 1963, by resolution 1962 (XVIII), adopted the now well known "Declaration of Legal Principles Governing the Activities of States in the Exploration and Use of Outer Space." Paragraph 5 of that Declaration provides that "States bear international responsibility for national activities in outer space, whether carried on by governmental agencies or non-governmental entities . . .". Paragraph 8, fixing the rules of liability, provides:

Each State which launches or procures the launching of an object into outer space, and each State from whose territory or facility an object is launched, is internationally liable for damage to a foreign State or to its natural or juridical persons by such object or its component parts on the Earth, in air space, or in outer space.

The General Assembly on December 24, 1963, by resolution 1963 (XVIII), in order to implement the provisions in the Declaration as to liability, requested its Committee on the Peaceful Uses of Outer Space to arrange for the prompt preparation of an international agreement "on liability for damage caused by objects launched into outer space." Through a legal sub-committee, active work on this project was begun in 1964.

Professor Berezowski, in his excellent report presented at this Colloquium, has referred to some of the work of this subcommittee, and has presented certain important problems which require study. The purpose of this paper is to suggest that consideration also be given to what is meant by "objects launched into outer space" in the United Nations resolutions and as to whether damage caused on the earth's surface by some of these "objects" may now be covered by the "Convention on Damage Caused by Foreign Aircraft to Third Parties on the Surface" signed at Rome in 1952.

Article 1 paragraph 1 of that Convention states that "any person who suffers damage on the surface, shall, upon proof only that the damage was caused by an aircraft in flight or by any person or thing falling therefrom, be entitled to compensation as provided by this Convention." Article 23 paragraph 1 provides that the Convention applies to damage contemplated in Article 1 caused in the territory of a Contracting State by an aircraft registered in the territory of another Contracting State. The term "aircraft" is not, however, defined in the Convention, but the present writer feels that the historical background of the Convention leaves little doubt as to how the term "aircraft," as then used, should be construed.

The present Rome Convention of 1952 was drafted to take the place of the earlier Rome Convention of 1933 which dealt with the same subject matter. The coverage of the two Conventions is practically the same, each being applicable to damage caused by "aircraft" in flight to persons or property on the surface. What was meant by the term "aircraft" in the 1933 Convention is reasonably clear. The "International Convention Relating to the Regulation of Aerial Navigation," usually referred to as the Paris Convention of 1919, was then in force. Certain annexes had been adopted which thereby became parts of the Convention. Annex A included various definitions, the most important of which was the following: "The word 'aircraft' shall comprise all machines which can derive support in the atmosphere from reactions of the air."

A large majority of the States which signed the Rome Convention of 1933 were already parties to the Paris Convention of 1919 and thus bound by its definition of "aircraft." Considering that the coverage in the present 1952 Convention is the same as that of the 1933 Convention, and that Article 29 of the present Convention states specifically that it shall supersede the 1933 Convention, it would appear that the definition of "aircraft" quoted above should also apply to the 1952 Convention. This position is borne out by other important facts.

When the present Rome Convention of 1952 was signed, the Paris Convention of 1919 had been superseded by the "Convention on International Civil Aviation" signed at Chicago in 1944. Under the terms of the latter, certain Annexes were adopted by The International Civil Aviation Organization, including an Annex containing a definition of "aircraft" in practically the same words as the old Paris Convention. While it is true that the Annexes to the Chicago Convention are not legally parts of the Convention, nevertheless, States which are parties to the Chicago Convention are obligated to keep their own regulations uniform to the extent practicable with standards set up in the Annexes.

It may therefore be considered that the term "aircraft" in the Rome Convention of 1952 should be construed to include all those flight instrumentalities which can be brought within the old Paris definition, that is to say, those instrumentalities "which can derive support in the atmosphere from reactions of the air." The possibility of aerodynamic lift is the primary test.

It must be noted that the definition does not limit the term "aircraft" to those instrumentalities which rely solely on aerodynamic lift. The United States experimental aircraft X-15 is a case in point. It was so designed as to use aerodynamic lift while in flight through the atmosphere. But being equipped with rocket engines not requiring external oxygen, it could continue its flight into areas beyond the atmosphere, namely, outer space. In the judgment of the present writer, all aircraft of that general type are within the Paris 1919 definition of "aircraft." While it may be true that no such man-carrying aircraft was in existence when the Rome Convention of 1952 was signed, flight both within and beyond the atmosphere with certain types of flight instrumentalities had been found possible, as for example, self-propelled rockets which used both aerodynamic lift and rocket propulsion.

The probability must now be considered that unmanned cargo and mail carrying aircraft may soon be used, designed to take off through the atmosphere using aerodynamic lift, passing through outer space at tremendous speeds, then gliding through the atmosphere back to earth. They will be both "aircraft" and "objects launched into outer space."

If they cause damage on the earth, which Convention will apply, the Rome Convention of 1952 or the new United Nations Convention when drafted? Or will both apply? In any event, real legal confusion will result which should, if possible, be avoided. The basic structure of the Rome Convention has not been followed in the drafts for a new convention now before the United Nations Sub-Committee. In these, the launching State is primarily responsible. In the Rome Convention, only the "operator" of the aircraft may be sued. In the Rome Convention, liability limitation is based on the weight of the offending aircraft. No such provision has been suggested in the United Nations discussions. Many other differences are also evident. So much so, that there should be included in the new convention clear provisions which by definition or otherwise will prevent any overlap. The instructions from the United Nations General Assembly were to prepare a draft agreement dealing with liability for damage caused by objects launched into outer space. The Sub-Committee, very naturally, has given primary consideration to the fact that the instrumentalities to be covered by the new convention were so designed as to be capable of flight beyond the atmosphere. But direct consideration does not seem to have been given to the possibility that certain of the instrumentalities launched into outer space would also derive atmospheric support before entering or after leaving outer space and thereby possibly come within the legal ambit of the Rome Convention of 1952.

Certain provisions of the drafts before the United Nations Legal

Sub-Committee illustrate the difficulties. For example, the Hungarian proposal states in Article I that the agreement should apply to compensation for loss of life, personal injury, and damage to property caused by an object launched into outer space or caused in outer space, in the atmosphere, or on the ground by any manned or un-manned space vehicle, or any object after being launched or conveyed into outer space in any other way. Then follows this important definition: "For the purposes of this Agreement 'Space Object' means space ships, satellites, orbital laboratories, containers and any other devices designed for movement in outer space and sustained there otherwise than by the reaction of air, as well as the means of launching of such objects." Clearly, this definition does not exclude flight instrumentalities which are so designed as to be sustained by reaction of the air while passing through the atmosphere before or after passage through outer space.

The United States draft does not contain any specific definition of the instrumentalities to which it would be applied. The nearest approach to a definition is found in Article II-(1) as follows:

> The launching State shall be absolutely liable and undertakes to pay compensation to the Presenting State, in accordance with the provisions of this Convention, for damage on the earth, in air space, or in outer space, which is caused by the launching of an object into outer space, regardless of whether such damage occurs during launching, after the object has gone into orbit, or during the process of re-entry, including damage caused by apparatus or equipment used in such launching.

It must again be suggested that certain "aircraft" covered by the Rome Convention would also be covered by the above provision if damage were caused on the surface.

The definition in the Belgium proposal is quite distinct. Article 1 of that draft convention provides that it shall apply to compensation for damage caused by a "space device." The latter term is defined in Article 2 as follows: "'Space device' shall be understood to mean any device intended to move in space and sustained there by means other than the reaction of air, as well as the equipment used for the launching and propulsion of the device." The difficulty with this definition is the uncertainty as to what is intended to be meant by the term "space." If this includes all areas from the surface of the earth outward, then the definition would seem to exclude from the application of the proposed convention all flight instrumentalities which could derive support from reaction of the air while passing through the atmosphere. If the word "space" does not include atmospheric space, then the

Belgian and Hungarian definitions would appear to be generally consistent.

This paper does not include any adequate consideration of the effect of national statutes defining "aircraft" when such definitions are in effect in States which are parties to the Rome Convention or which, as members of the United Nations may hereafter become parties to the proposed United Nations Convention. However, a short analysis of the complicated situation which appears to exist in the United States may be useful. Since the adoption of the original "Air Commerce Act" of 1926, the United States has continuously included in its statutes a definition of "aircraft" to the effect that "aircraft" means any contrivance now known or hereafter used or designed for navigation of, or flight in the air. In 1958, when legislation was under consideration as to control of flight in the airspace, a congressional committee indicated that regulatory jurisdiction "should extend not only to vehicles commonly considered as aircraft, but also, during their flight through airspace, other vehicles such as rockets, missiles and other airborne objects." The congressional committee decided that no new definition was needed, saying: "After due deliberation, the committee concluded that no change in the definition of the term 'aircraft' was necessary in order to achieve this objective, since all vehicles, rockets, and missiles, as well as aircraft, are in fact used at least in part for navigation of the airspace."

The United States has not ratified the Rome Convention. But if it had done so, questions might have arisen as to whether or not the Convention would apply, so far as the United States is concerned, to its very broad definition of "aircraft" stated above. This certainly includes flight instrumentalities used in the air which are not included in the definition found in the Annexes to the Paris and Chicago Conventions. Similar situations may exist in the national legislation of other States.

It might be said that the application of the Rome Convention is so limited that conflict with the proposed United Nations Convention will not be a matter of importance. It is true that the Rome Convention, according to Article 26, does not apply to damage caused by military, customs, or police aircraft, but it is also true that the term "person" in the Convention applies according to Article 30 to "any natural or legal person, including a State." In other words, if a sovereign State operates a flight instrumentality for exploratory or scientific purposes and if such instrumentality is so designed as to enjoy aerodynamic lift while passing through the atmosphere, the State may be subject, under the Rome Convention, to liability for damage caused by the fall of the instrumentality to the earth's surface if the State in question and the State where damage is caused are both parties to the

Rome Convention. If the same damage is also to be covered by the proposed United Nations Convention difficulties must necessarily arise. It is hoped they can be avoided.

A further problem is involved in the power of ICAO to amend its Annexes. If the archaic Paris definition of "aircraft" should be modified so as to be broadened in line with the United States definition, for example, or if the ICAO definition should be narrowed so that it applies only to those instrumentalities which can be used solely for flight in the atmosphere, then questions must be answered as to the indirect effect on the application of the Rome Convention.

28

The Chicago Convention—After Twenty Years

Reprinted by permission of the
University of Miami Law Review
from 19 University of Miami Law
Review *333 (1965).*
© University of Miami Law
Review *1965.*

Author's Note. At the invitation of the State Department, the author served as one of the advisors to the United States Delegation at the 1944 Chicago Conference, and later as Chairman of one of the two drafting committees in the preparation of the Convention. Only those who were at Chicago can appreciate the strain of those wartime weeks. The delegates lived and worked in the same hotel. Only twice between the opening and closing of the Conference was the author fortunate enough to leave the hotel—once for dinner and again to take an Irish delegate, who had played "rugger" for his country, to see an American football game. It is still a source of amazement that a Convention emerged which has stood the test of the years in which world air transport has grown beyond all expectations. In this article the author expresses his deep concern as to whether the coming of the "space age" may require a very different international arrangement.

THE CHICAGO CONVENTION on International Civil Aviation signed December 7, 1944 came into force just eighteen years ago on April 4, 1947.[1] It is an international agreement "on certain principles and arrangements in order that international civil aviation may be developed in a safe and orderly manner and that international air transport services may be established on the basis of equality of opportunity and operated soundly and economically." It created the International Civil Aviation Organization, an inter-governmental agency later affiliated with the United Nations.

The success of the Chicago Convention as a major international regulatory arrangement can be measured by the fact that 108 states have ratified or adhered to it as a formal treaty and have thereby become members of the International Civil Aviation Organization (ICAO). All of these states except the Federal Republic of Germany, Indonesia, Republic of Korea, Switzerland and Viet Nam are also members of the United Nations. At the same time certain members of the United Nations are not members of ICAO, namely: Albania, Bulgaria, Burundi, Byelorussian SSR, Hungary, Mongolia, Romania, Togo, Uganda, Ukrainian SSR, Union of Soviet Socialist Republics.

Delegates from Moscow were actually en route to the Chicago Conference in 1944 when suddenly recalled without explanation. The Union of Soviet Socialist Republics has never since shown public in-

---

[1] Convention on International Civil Aviation, 61 Stat. 1180 (1947).

terest in adhering to the Convention. But nevertheless, the principles of the Chicago Convention and its regulations have been accepted by a large majority of the world powers actively engaged in international civil aviation.

The twenty years which have passed since the Chicago Convention was signed have witnessed giant strides and startling new developments in man made flight, both in the airspace and in space beyond. It seems useful therefore, to review briefly to what extent the Convention has stood the test of time and also to examine possible present and future weaknesses. Certain major fields are of particular importance. These are:

I. The Convention as a continuing vehicle for the restatement of principles of international law.

II. The general nature of the International Civil Aviation Organization (ICAO).

III. The relationship between the Convention and its Technical Annexes.

IV. Some major ambiguities in the Convention.

V. Can the Convention continue to function successfully in the light of present and future outer space developments?

I. PRINCIPLES OF INTERNATIONAL LAW IN THE CONVENTION

The Convention has served as a useful and powerful vehicle to restate certain principles of international law applicable world-wide, irrespective of ICAO membership. These are: (a) sovereignty of each state in its airspace; (b) freedom of flight over the high seas; (c) nationality of aircraft as transport instrumentalities; and (d) special limitations on flight of "state" aircraft.

A. AIRSPACE SOVEREIGNTY

Article 1 of the Convention states that "The contracting States recognize that every State has complete and exclusive sovereignty over the airspace above its territory."

This was a restatement of similar provisions in the Paris Convention of 1919 and the Havana Convention of 1928. My own views are, I believe, well known. It is true that between 1900 and 1914 there were certain over-emphasized doctrinal disputes as to whether the "air" was free. But I have long been convinced after years of careful historical research that interested states prior to the Paris Convention had factually assumed that national territory is three dimensional, including then usable space above its land and waters. The quoted article means that every member state of ICAO has formally acknowledged that airspace above national lands and waters is an integral part of the territory of a subjacent state whether the latter is or is not a member of ICAO. Article 1 thus states international law believed to have already had world-wide acceptance when the Chicago Convention was signed.

The decision to include this important provision at Chicago was not accidental. It had been recommended in substance in the British statement of position and had been included practically verbatim in the Canadian draft convention. The United States, on the other hand, had presented a draft convention which would have provided that the high contracting parties recognized that *each contracting state* has complete and exclusive sovereignty over its airspace. The conference did not accept the limited United States proposal but reasserted the broad provisions of the Paris and Havana Conventions, thereby accepting again the principle of airspace sovereignty as an existing part of international law applicable world-wide.

B. FREEDOM OF FLIGHT OVER THE HIGH SEAS

The principle that the seas are a highway open to all nations and subject to the sovereignty of none is one of the foundations of international transport law. Long before the Chicago Conference it had been asserted that the same freedom should be available to aircraft flying over the high seas as was enjoyed by vessels on the surface. For example, the report of the drafting committee at the Paris 1919 Conference said: "It is only when the column of air rests on a res nullius or communis, the sea, that freedom becomes the rule of the air," This principle was finally affirmed in article 12 of the Chicago Convention dealing with "rules of the air." This requires each contracting state to keep its own rules of the air uniform to the greatest possible extent with those established from time to time in the Convention. But it then adds that "over the high seas the rules in force shall be those established under this Convention." The legal effect is clear. Member states thus admit that they have no sovereignty in space above the high seas and thus no power to regulate the flight of any aircraft except their own. They have then delegated to ICAO the right to adopt rules of the air which shall be applicable to their aircraft in this non-sovereign area without exception or limitation. These rules must be complied with by the civil aircraft of all ICAO states. The legal status of usable space over the high seas has since been formally restated in the "Geneva 1958 Convention On the High Seas." This includes the "freedom to fly over the high seas" as one of the elements of the freedom of the seas. It should be noted that neither the Chicago nor Geneva Conventions limit this freedom to the "airspace."

C. NATIONALITY OF AIRCRAFT AS
TRANSPORT INSTRUMENTALITIES

Chapter 3 of the Convention is entitled "Nationality of Aircraft." Article 17 states that "aircraft have the nationality of the State in which they are registered," and article 18 provides that an aircraft cannot be validly registered in more than one state but that its registration may be changed from one state to another. The term "nationality" is nowhere defined but the term has long had a well known background in international maritime law. A ship flying the flag of a sovereign state is said to have the nationality of that state. The latter thereby accepts responsibility to other states for the public good conduct of the ship and is internationally authorized to see to it that the ship enjoys the rights and privileges to which it may be entitled as against other states.

At the first important international aviation conference held in Paris in 1910 it was agreed in substance that aircraft should have the maritime law characteristics of "nationality" and the principle has since been accepted. Article 6 of the Paris Convention of 1919 is practically identical with article 17 of the Chicago Convention. The provisions as to registration in the Chicago Convention are legislative and effective between member states of ICAO. They apply only to civil aircraft. On the other hand international air law applies the characteristic of nationality to all aircraft, state and civil, whether or not operated by a member state of ICAO. Registration does not confer nationality but is merely evidence thereof.

D. SPECIAL LIMITATIONS ON FLIGHT OF STATE AIRCRAFT

The Convention by its title and major provisions establishes legislative rules as to civil aircraft. Article 3(b) provides that aircraft used in military, customs and police service shall "be deemed State aircraft," but does not say that no other aircraft used by a state shall be so deemed. Article 3(c) then provides:

No state aircraft of a contracting State shall fly over the territory of another State or land thereon without authorization by special agreement or otherwise, and in accordance with the terms thereof.

It is submitted that the term "territory" as thus used refers to the technical definition of territory contained in article 2 of the Convention where it is described as "land areas and territorial waters adjacent thereto" and that the prohibition should be construed to apply to state "aircraft" flying in the "airspace" as the terms were then understood

International maritime law has traditionally permitted a sovereign state to regulate strictly the conditions under which foreign warships are permitted to enter its ports. Before World War II a similar customary rule was widely effective as to military aircraft. Article 3(c) merely restated the understanding that state aircraft may not use the airspace or surface territories of another state without the latter's specific permission. It is my understanding that the article was inserted in the Convention so as to assure continued acceptance of the general rule and to make it clear that rights of entry provided in the Convention would not apply to state aircraft.

II. THE GENERAL NATURE OF THE INTERNATIONAL CIVIL AVIATION ORGANIZATION (ICAO)

Among the most important provisions of the Convention are those creating the International Civil Aviation Organization (ICAO). The miracle is that an international conference working under continuous and sometimes controversial pressure between November 1 and December 5, 1944 could have produced an organization which has functioned so well. The final statement as to its powers and duties was of course a compromise. It is not an international "Civil Aeronautics Board" such as Great Britain proposed and Canada supported in modified form, with the objective that the Board would grant international route certificates and exercise control generally over capacity, frequency of flights and rates. I have often wondered what would now be the international transport situation if that type of organization had been created. Instead, ICAO was given strong technical powers together with economic functions applicable generally within the advisory and research fields. After twenty years I am convinced that the decisions made at Chicago were sound.

III. THE RELATIONSHIP BETWEEN THE CONVENTION AND ITS TECHNICAL ANNEXES

Many of the American republics, including the United States, have strict constitutional and legislative provisions applicable to the ratification of a treaty and of any amendment to it before the same can become effective. One of the major objectives of the Chicago Convention is, as stated in the preamble, to agree on "certain principles and arrangements in order that international civil aviation may be developed in a safe and orderly manner . . . ." To meet similar objectives the Paris Convention had contained technical annexes designed to assure uniform regulations wherever the Convention was in effect. These

444

annexes were parts of the Convention, but nevertheless could be modified by the internal machinery provided in the Convention without the amendments going back to states for formal ratification. A weakness of the Havana Convention was that it had no adequate machinery for the adoption of uniform regulations.

One of the major problems behind the scenes at Chicago was how to provide practical international uniformity of flight regulations without infringing on the constitutional procedures of those states which require formal ratification of treaty amendments. A compromise was finally adopted which I believe has worked well. Article 37 contains a statement that each contracting state undertakes to collaborate in securing the *highest practicable degree* of *uniformity* in regulations, standards, procedures and organization in relation to aircraft, personnel, airways and auxilliary services in all matters in which uniformity will facilitate and improve air navigation. ICAO is then directed to adopt and amend from time to time international standards and recommended practices and procedures dealing with such matters as communications systems and air navigation aids, characteristics of airports, rules of the air and traffic control practices, licensing of operating and mechanical personnel, air worthiness of aircraft, registration and identification of aircraft, meteorological information, maps, customs and immigration procedures, aircraft in distress and investigation of accidents and "such other matters concerned with the safety, regularity and efficiency of air navigation as may from time to time appear appropriate."

Article 38 requires member states of ICAO to notify it when any state finds it impracticable to comply with such standards or to bring its own regulations or practices into full accord therewith. Article 54 directs the Council of ICAO to adopt such international standards and recommended practices and "for convenience designate them as annexes to this Convention."

It was fully understood at Chicago, and is apparent from the text of the Convention, that the annexes when adopted do not thereby become parts of the Convention. But in practice, so I understand, wide uniformity of regulations has nevertheless resulted. At the same time the convention has been ratified by many states which would have had difficulty in accepting it with a delegation of power to ICAO which might have resulted in modifying the annexes as parts of the Convention without re-ratification. I believe that the compromise arrived at in Chicago was wise and has been successful.

In the Department of State Bulletin of March 11, 1945, published shortly after the Chicago Conference, Mr. Stephen Latchford, then air law adviser in the aviation division of the State Department and one of the advisers to the United States delegation at Chicago, wrote:

Although it is evident from the proceedings and Final Act of the Chicago Aviation Conference that it is expected and urged that all the countries becoming parties to the Convention shall cooperate with a view to attaining the highest degree of uniformity with reference to the application of international standards and practices, it was realized by the delegates at Chicago that there might be some exceptional cases where a particular country would find it highly desirable and necessary to adopt some departure from an international standard. This, it is believed, will not constitute any serious impediment to the general acceptance and application of uniform international standards and practices and it is thought that the various states will accept and apply them to the greatest extent possible.

After twenty years I am convinced that Mr. Latchford's statement was sound.

IV. SOME MAJOR AMBIGUITIES IN
THE CONVENTION

The passing of time has brought out certain ambiguities and difficulties in the language of parts of the Convention. But none have destroyed its usefulness. Perhaps the major difficulties have been encountered in articles 5 and 6 dealing with non-scheduled and scheduled flight, in article 15 dealing with airport and similar charges, and in article 77 dealing with joint air transport operating organizations.

Article 5 authorizes aircraft of other contracting states "not engaged in scheduled international air services" to make flights into or non-stop across the territory of a contracting state and to make stops for non-traffic purposes without the necessity of obtaining prior permission. It also authorizes such aircraft, if engaged in the carriage of passengers, cargo or mail for remuneration to have the privilege of taking on or discharging the same, subject to the right of any state where such embarkation or discharge takes place "to impose such regulations, conditions or limitations as it may consider desirable." Article 6 states flatly that no scheduled international air service may be operated over or into the territory of a contracting state except with the special permission of such state and in accordance therewith.

The term "scheduled" was not defined, though on such definition rests the decision as to whether a particular international air service is entitled to the privileges described in article 5 or is subject to the strict limitations of article 6. Questions also arose as to whether prior permission was needed for non-scheduled passenger and cargo flights and as to the nature of the "regulations, conditions or limitations" which might in that case be imposed.

Article 84 of the Convention authorizes the Council of ICAO to decide any disagreement between contracting states relating to the interpretation or application of the Convention. In the absence of such formal dispute the power of ICAO to construe is doubtful. In this situation the second and fourth assemblies of ICAO took cognizance of the difficulties created by articles 5 and 6 and requested the Council to provide a definition of the term "scheduled international air services" for the guidance of contracting states, and also to present an analysis of the rights conferred by article 5. The Council formally complied with these directions. A summary in part of its decisions can be found in ICAO document 7278-C/841 as follows:

Definition of a Scheduled International Air Service

A scheduled international air service is a series of flights that possesses all the following characteristics:

a) it passes through the air-space over the territory of more than one State;

b) it is performed by aircraft for the transport of passengers, mail or cargo for remuneration, in such a manner that each flight is open to use by members of the public;

c) it is operated, so as to serve traffic between the same two or more points, either

(i) according to a published time-table, or

(ii) with flights so regular or frequent that they constitute a recognizably systematic series.[2]

After defining what was meant by a scheduled air service the Council analyzed article 5. It found that no permit should normally be required of non-scheduled transport as this would render this form of air transport impossible or non-effective. But it also found that the right of each state included the right to require special permission for the operation of taking on or discharging such passengers, cargo or mail in its territory, or for any specified category of such operations.

While it is understood that certain states then advised ICAO that they had not accepted the definitions and recommendations referred to above, nevertheless during the thirteen years that have intervened no serious disputes appear to have developed, even though the ICAO decisions are not technically binding on member states.

Article 15 of the Convention deals with airport and similar charges. Its provisions, in my judgment, constitute definite limitations on the general power of a state to fix charges for the airports and navigation

---

[2] This definition was adopted by the Council on March 25, 1952 for the guidance of contracting states in the application of articles 5 and 6 of the Convention.

facilities constructed on its territory. It provides in substance that airports and air navigation facilities open to public use by national aircraft shall also be open under uniform conditions to the aircraft of all other contracting states; that charges imposed for the use of such airports and air navigation facilities shall not be higher than those paid by national aircraft for similar services; and that charges imposed shall be subject to review by the Council of ICAO which shall make recommendations thereon for the consideration of the state or states concerned. No authority is given to contracting states by the Convention to impose charges for other than the use of such airports or facilities. Also no provision is made in article 15 that a decision by the Council as to particular charges shall be binding on the states concerned. Of even more importance is the fact that the article ends with the following provision:

> No fees, dues or other charges shall be imposed by any contracting State in respect solely of the right of transit over or entry into or exit from its territory or any aircraft of a contracting State or persons or property thereon.

It is understood that ICAO now has under consideration certain applications of this article. Important questions are obvious. Can a state make any charges against foreign aircraft when its national aircraft used in similar service are not subject to charges? Can a state assess charges merely because it has provided airports, and such air navigation facilities as radio and weather information? Can a state levy charges against aircraft flying over the high seas when the aircraft concerned does not enter the territory of that state? Can a state levy charges for air traffic control services and require payment of such charges by aircraft beyond its territory even though such service is not required or desired by the aircraft concerned? In such case is the quoted provision in the article applicable which denies the right to levy charges based solely on the right of transit over or entry into or exit from the territory of the state concerned? These and other similar questions have not been as yet definitively settled. It is of interest that the only court decision of importance involving article 15 arose from operations of the Miami airport.[3]

Article 77 states that nothing in the Convention shall prevent two or more contracting states from constituting joint air transport operating

---

[3] Board of County Comm'rs v. Peruansa, 307 F.2d 802 (5th Cir. 1962), *cert. denied sub nom.*, 371 U.S. 961, *petition for rehearing denied*, 372 U.S. 932 (1963). This case is commented upon in Bayitch, *Florida and International Legal Developments 1962–1963*, 18 U. MIAMI L. REV. 321, 339–41 (1963); see also Note, 18 U. MIAMI L. REV. 482 (1963).

organizations or international operating agencies. It further provides that "the Council shall determine in what manner the provisions of this convention relating to nationality of aircraft shall apply to aircraft operated by international operating agencies." Questions have arisen as to whether some form of international registration might be provided under this article, notwithstanding the provisions of articles 17 and 18 which state that aircraft have the nationality of the state in which they are registered and that an aircraft cannot be validly registered in more than one state.

In 1960, ICAO assembled a panel of experts to advise the Council on various questions raised by article 77, and in particular on the application of the last sentence dealing with nationality of aircraft operated by international operating agencies. In this report to the Council this panel concluded among other things, that the power of the Council under the last sentence of article 77 must be limited to determining the manner in which the provisions of the Convention relating to nationality shall apply and that such power does not extend to authorizing operation under the Convention of an aircraft without nationality. The panel felt that only aircraft having nationality of a contracting state are entitled to the privileges of the Chicago Convention "since by the terms of that treaty such privileges are given only to States as distinguished from international organizations." This was apparently a majority decision of the panel. These questions have now been re-opened.

On December 11, 1964 the Council of ICAO asked the Chairman of the Legal Committee to appoint a subcommittee to make a study and report. The subcommittee will meet later this year and its decisions will thereafter be acted upon by the full Legal Committee of ICAO. It is obvious that the problem created by the organization of international operating transport units must be settled, with particular reference as to how the aircraft operated by such units shall be registered, and on what state or states shall rest the responsibility that the aircraft in question comply with the provisions of the Convention.

V. CAN THE CONVENTION CONTINUE TO FUNCTION SUCCESSFULLY IN THE LIGHT OF PRESENT AND FUTURE OUTER SPACE DEVELOPMENTS?

The convention, as signed at Chicago in 1944, with its annexes as later adopted, has limited application as to the areas in which its rules are in force, and as to what flight instrumentalities are governed by these rules. By its terms the Convention applies only to civil aircraft. As to other aircraft each state retains its individual power of regulation. Of even more importance the Convention does not define the term "aircraft." Nor does it define the term "airspace."

Today, man-carrying flight-instrumentalities are in use high above the areas deemed usable in 1944. The question is: Can the Chicago Convention as now framed survive these changes, or are we to be faced with two different international organizations, one regulating "civil aircraft" operating in the airspace with no power over state aircraft operating in the same areas, nor any power to regulate flight beyond the airspace, and another organization dealing with flight-instrumentalities which can operate through the airspace into areas beyond?

In this situation, a primary weakness of the Convention flows from the self-imposed limitations under which ICAO now operates in determining the flight-instrumentalities to which its rules apply. More than forty years ago the parties to the Paris Convention adopted, through one of its binding annexes, a definition to the effect that the word "aircraft" shall comprise all machines which derive support in the atmosphere from reactions of the air. Later the United States in the Air Commerce Act of 1926 adopted the following definition:

> Aircraft means any contrivance now known or hereafter invented, used or designed for navigation of or flight in the air.

It will be noted that the United States definition included instrumentalities *used* for flight in the air while the old Paris definition was limited to machines which can derive support in the atmosphere from reactions in the air.

At Chicago in 1944, when tentative annexes were under consideration, the United States suggested a definition similar to that in the Air Commerce Act quoted above. But this was not accepted and a definition was recommended substantially the same as the one in the Paris Convention. When the annexes to the Chicago Convention were finally adopted, annex 7 stated the following definition following the Paris Convention:

> *Aircraft*—Any machine that can derive support in the atmosphere from the reactions of the air.

No effort, so far as I am advised, has ever been made to widen this definition. As a result ICAO has imposed on itself the limitation that its rules do not apply to flight-instrumentalities used in the air unless such instrumentalities can derive support in the atmosphere from the reactions of the air. Obviously the ICAO definition will not apply to most spacecraft and satellites even while passing through the airspace en route toward outer space or when returning. As to those instrumentalities which may be operated through the airspace using partial atmospheric lift, an even more difficult question must be answered—are they aircraft or are they spacecraft and when does the Chicago Convention apply if at all?

Certainly the rules of the Chicago Convention are in force only in the "airspace." But again this area has not been defined. The sovereignty of the subjacent state, one of the primary and basic rules of the Convention, ceases to be effective beyond the airspace. The recent unanimous resolutions of the United Nations make it apparent that we now have general international agreement to the effect that outer space is like the high seas, namely not subject to the sovereignty of any state. But where is the line between the airspace in which ICAO regulations are effective and outer space beyond? It seems obvious that there must be international regulation of the registration, responsibility and general conduct of flight instrumentalities usable in outer space. If this results in a second international organization, grave confusion may well result, as ICAO has no effective jurisdiction beyond the use of "aircraft" in the "airspace."

While it is quite true that most instrumentalities usable in outer space are not civil in character but are launched and controlled by a particular state, nevertheless this will not always be true. It is my understanding that the communications satellites to be put in use by the Communications Satellite Corporation, a United States privately owned body, are in no sense "aircraft", are not subject to ICAO regulations, but might well be subject to rules adopted by a new organization set up to control outer space flight. In that event the ICAO rules could not apply to such satellites when being launched through the airspace, but they could well be subject to the rules of a new outer space organization even while passing through the airspace.

These remarks indicate very briefly my personal grave concern as to the future of the Chicago Convention if its powers continue to be limited solely to civil *aircraft* (as now defined) when in the *airspace*. As long as flight-instrumentalities, which required no support from reactions of the air, were not used, and as long as flight operations were limited to the use of the "airspace," then the Chicago Convention might have survived for many years to come. But under present conditions its future may be subject to international difficulties which may well be fatal. This problem must be faced. It seems obvious that a single set of future rules must govern all international flight, at whatever altitude. Whether the Chicago Convention can meet this test is most doubtful.

Appendices

JOHN COBB COOPER
Curriculum
Vitae

Born 18 September 1887 in Jacksonville, Florida. Died 22 July 1967 in Princeton, New Jersey. Son of John Cobb Cooper and Mary Coldwell Cooper; grandson of Charles P. Cooper, also of Jacksonville, Florida. Married Martha Helen Marvel, 1918 (died 1962). Children: Rachel (Mrs. R. W. Baker, Jr.), John C. III, Jane M.

Educated in Jacksonville Public Schools and graduated Lawrenceville School, Lawrenceville, New Jersey, 1905 (Editor: *Lawrenceville Literary Magazine*). Entered Princeton University, 1905; Editor-in-Chief, *Nassau Literary Magazine*; elected to Phi Beta Kappa; graduated 1909. Degree A.B.

Studied Law in office of Cooper & Cooper, Jacksonville, Florida. Admitted to practice after examination by Supreme Court of Florida, June, 1911. Practiced law Jacksonville, Florida 1911–17.

Chairman, Duval County (Florida) School Board, 1915–17. Delegate, Democratic National Convention, St. Louis, 1916.

Called to Active Duty as Ensign, U. S. Naval Reserve Force, Charleston, S.C. Navy Yard, July, 1917. Transferred to Office of Director of Naval Communications, Washington, D. C., September, 1917. Promoted to Lt. (jg) and then Lt. in 1918. Officer-in-Charge, U. S. Naval Transatlantic Distant Control Radio Station, Washington, D. C., October 1918–January, 1919. Released from Active Duty, March, 1919. Inactive Duty as Lt. Commander, U. S. Naval Reserve Force, 1919–34.

Resumed practice of law, Jacksonville, Florida, 1919–34 as member of firms of Cooper, Cooper & Osborne and later Knight, Adair, Cooper & Osborne.

Member, Board of Control, University of Florida and Florida State College for Women, 1921–25.

Vice-Chairman, Florida Delegation, Democratic National Convention, New York, 1924.

Founded and edited *Florida State Bar Association Law Journal*, 1927–34. President, Florida State Bar Association, 1931.

455

Admitted to practice, Supreme Court of the United States, 1932.

Chairman, American Bar Association, Committee on Aeronautical Law, 1932–35.

Appointed by the Department of State as one of the first United States members on International Technical Committee of Aerial Legal Experts (CITEJA), 1932.

Appointed by President Roosevelt as Chairman, United States Delegation to Third International Conference on Private Air Law, Rome, 1933, and signed for the United States the Convention on Liability for Damages Caused to Third Parties on Surface, and Convention on Precautionary Attachment of Aircraft.

Elected Vice President, Pan-American Airways, September 1, 1934, and moved residence from Jacksonville, Florida, to Princeton, New Jersey.

Observer, Inter-American Aviation Conference, Lima, Peru, 1937.

Appointed by State Department as one of the legal advisers, United States Delegation, International Civil Aviation Conference, Chicago, 1944, and served as Chairman of one of the Drafting Committees in preparation of the Convention on International Civil Aviation.

Chairman of Organizing Committee and Vice-President of International Air Transport Conference, Havana, 1945, when Articles were adopted for the International Air Transport Association (IATA).

Member, first Executive Committee IATA and Chairman, 1945.

Retired as Vice-President, Pan-American Airways, 1945, and as Director, 1946.

Appointed Legal Advisor, IATA, 1946. As observer for IATA, attended and participated in meetings of Legal Committee of International Civil Aviation Organization (ICAO) and in diplomatic conferences in Geneva, 1948, when Convention on Rights in Aircraft was drafted, and Rome, 1952, when the new Convention on Damage Caused to Third Persons on the Surface was drafted, and the Hague in 1955, when the Protocol for the Warsaw Convention was drafted.

Elected member of Institute for Advanced Study, Princeton, New Jersey, 1946, for a five-year term to engage in research in international air law and similar topics under a grant from the Rockefeller Foundation. Published *The Right to Fly*, 1947.

Served as Consultant, President Truman's Air Policy Commission 1947.

Appointed first Director, Institute of International Air Law, McGill University, Montreal, 1951 with rank of Professor. Awarded degree LL.M. by McGill University, 1952. Retired as Director, 1955 and continued as Lecturer until 1958. Appointed Professor Emeritus, 1958.

Served as Consultant, President Truman's Airport Commission, 1952.

Chairman, American Bar Association Committee on American Citizenship, 1949–53; Chairman, Research and Library Committee, American Bar Foundation, 1953–54; First Administrator, 1954–57. Supervised editing and publication of *Sources of our Liberties*, 1959. Received American Bar Foundation Annual Award for Research in Law and Government, 1959.

Awarded Honorary Degree, LL.D. by Princeton University, June 15, 1960.

Awarded first Gold Medal of the International Institute of Space Law of the International Astronautical Federation, 1961. President of the Institute, 1961–62.

Retired as Legal Advisor, International Air Transport Association (IATA), 1964.

Professional Societies:

American Academy of Arts & Sciences (Fellow)
American Bar Association
American Bar Foundation (Fellow)
Federal Bar Association
Florida State Bar
American Law Institute (Emeritus Member)
American Society of International Law
International Law Association (Member, Air & Space Law Committees)
International Academy of Astronautics (Founding Member)
International Institute of Space Law (Founding Member)
American Institute of Aeronautics and Astronautics
British Interplanetary Society (Fellow)
Instituto De Derecho Aeronautico E Interplanetario, Republica Argentina, (Honorary Member).

JOHN COBB COOPER
Bibliography of Aerospace Law Writings 1931–1967

1. "Aircraft Liability to Persons and Property on Ground" 17 AMERICAN BAR ASSOCIATION JOURNAL 435 (1931)
2. "Rules of Aircraft Liability in the Proposed Federal Merchant Airship Act" 2 AIR LAW REVIEW 327 (1931)
3. "Some Legal Aspects of Gasoline Taxation as Affecting Aviation" 4 JOURNAL OF AIR LAW AND COMMERCE 17 (1933)
4. "The Pan-American Convention on Commercial Aviation and the Treaty-Making Power" 19 AMERICAN BAR ASSOCIATION JOURNAL 22 (1933)
5. "IATA—League of Airlines" 4 AIR TRANSPORT 29 (January 1946)
6. "Aviation Law Comes Home to the Main Street Lawyer" 11 LAW AND CONTEMPORARY PROBLEMS 556 (1946)
7. "Air Power and the Coming Peace Treaties" 24 FOREIGN AFFAIRS 441 (1946)
8. "Air Transport and World Organization" 55 YALE LAW JOURNAL 1191 (1946)
9. "Notes on Air Power in Time of Peace" 1 AIR AFFAIRS 80 (September 1946)
10. "The Bermuda Plan: World Pattern for Air Transport" 25 FOREIGN AFFAIRS 59 (1946)
 ———— "Le Plan des Bermudes" 1 REVUE FRANÇAISE DE DROIT AÉRIEN 139 (1947)
11. "ICAO'S Big Problem at Rio" 4 AIR TRANSPORT 34 (September 1947)
12. "New Problems in International Civil Aviation Arbitral Procedure" 2 ARBITRATION JOURNAL 119 (1947)
13. "The Proposed Multilateral Agreement on Commercial Rights in International Civil Air Transport" 14 JOURNAL OF AIR LAW AND COMMERCE 125 (1947)
14. "United Nations Trusteeships" 2 AIR AFFAIRS 115 (April 1947)
15. "Some Historic Phases of British International Civil Aviation Policy" 23 INTERNATIONAL AFFAIRS 189 (1947)
16. *The Right to Fly*. Henry Holt and Company, New York, New York (1947)
 ———— *Le Droit de Voler*. Les Éditiones Internationales, Paris, France (1950)
 ———— *El Derecho de Volar*. Circulo de Aéronáutica, Buenos Aires, Argentina (1950)
17. "The Fundamentals of Air Power" Library of Congress, Washington, D.C. (1948)
 ———— "Les Principes Fondamentaux de la Puissance Aérienne" 11 REVUE GÉNÉRALE DE L'AIR 3 (1948)
 ———— reprinted in part IN Emme, *The Impact of Air Power*. D. Van Nostrand Company, Princeton, New Jersey, pp. 128–135 (1959)
18. "International Air Transport and Foreign Policy" IN *The United States in World Affairs* 1947–1948. New York, New York, pp. 276–304 (1948)

19. "The Impact of Air Power" 43 UNIVERSITY OF FLORIDA RECORD 3 (1948)
20. "State Sovereignty vs. Federal Sovereignty of Navigable Airspace" 15 JOURNAL OF AIR LAW AND COMMERCE 27 (1948)
21. "International Air Law" [Lecture delivered in 1948 at the U.S. Naval War College] Hearings on H.R. 11881 Before the U.S. House Select Committee on Astronautics and Space Exploration, *Astronautics and Space Exploration*, 85th Cong., 2d Sess. 1317–1327 (1958)
22. "Internationalization of Air Transport" 2 AIR AFFAIRS 546 (1949)
23. "Étude sur le Statut juridique des Aéronefs" 4 REVUE FRANÇAISE DE DROIT AÉRIEN 125, 205 (1950)
    ——— Condensed version "National Status of Aircraft" 17 JOURNAL OF AIR LAW AND COMMERCE 292 (1950)
    ——— Summary of conclusions, International Law Association, *Report of the Forty-Fourth Conference, Copenhagen 1950*, 227–230 (1950)
24. "Airspace Rights Over the Arctic" 3 AIR AFFAIRS 517 (1950)
25. "Governmental Financial Aid to Foreign Air Carriers" PUBLIC AFFAIRS BULLETIN NO. 87 (October 1950)
26. "Recognition of Foreign Judgments under Article 15 of Proposed Revision of Rome Convention" 17 JOURNAL OF AIR LAW AND COMMERCE 212 (1950)
27. "The Legal Status of Aircraft" 31 CHICAGO BAR RECORD 227 (1950)
28. "Highways on the Earth and in the Air" IN Labatut (ed.), *Highways In Our National Life*. Princeton University Press, Princeton, New Jersey, pp. 240–246 (1950)
29. "Crimes Aboard American Aircraft: Under What Jurisdiction Are They Punishable?" 37 AMERICAN BAR ASSOCIATION JOURNAL 257 (1951)
30. "High Altitude Flight and National Sovereignty" address delivered before the Escuela Libre de Derecho, Mexico City 4 INTERNATIONAL LAW QUARTERLY 411 (1951)
    ——— "High Altitude Flight and National Sovereignty" 13 INTERNATIONAL AIR TRANSPORT ASSOCIATION BULLETIN 46 (June 1951)
    ——— "Les Vols à haute altitude et la Souveraineté nationale" 5 REVUE FRANÇAISE DE DROIT AÉRIEN 123 (1951)
    ——— "Der Flug in Grosse Hohen und die Nationale Staatsgewalt" 1 ZEITSCHRIFT FÜR LUFTRECHT 237 (1952)
    ——— "High Altitude Flight and National Sovereignty" Hearings on H.R. 11881 Before the U.S. House Select Committee on Astronautics and Space Exploration, *Astronautics and Space Exploration*, 85th Cong., 2d Sess. 1327–1331 (1958)
    ——— "High Altitude Flight and National Sovereignty" Staff of U.S. Senate Special Committee on Space and Astronautics, 85th Cong., 2d Sess., *Space Law: A Symposium* 1 (Comm. Print 1959)
    ——— "High Altitude Flight and National Sovereignty" U.S. Senate Committee on Aeronautical and Space Sciences, *Legal Problems of Space Exploration: A Symposium* Senate Doc. No. 26, 87th Cong., 1st Sess. 1 (1961)
31. "United States Participation in Drafting Paris Convention 1919" 18 JOURNAL OF AIR LAW AND COMMERCE 266 (1951)
32. "Air Law—A Field for International Thinking" 4 [U.N.] TRANSPORT AND COMMUNICATIONS REVIEW 1 (October–December 1951)
33. "McGill's Institute of International Air Law" 29 CANADIAN BAR REVIEW 515 (1951)

———— [Revised] "McGill Institute of International Air Law" AIRLANES 12 (September 1951)

34. "International Air Law Research" 15 INTERNATIONAL AIR TRANSPORT ASSOCIATION BULLETIN 68 (June 1952)

35. "Aviation Cabotage and Territory" (1952) U.S. AND CANADIAN AVIATION REPORTS 256

36. "The International Air Navigation Conference, Paris 1910" 19 JOURNAL OF AIR LAW AND COMMERCE 127 (1952)

37. "Roman Law and the Maxim 'Cujus est Solum' in International Air Law" Institute of International Air Law, McGill University, Montreal, Quebec, Publication No. 1 (1952)

———— "Roman Law and the Maxim 'Cujus est Solum' in International Air Law" 1 MCGILL LAW JOURNAL 23 (1952)

———— "Roman Law and the Maxim 'Cujus est Solum' in International Air Law" (1952) U.S. AND CANADIAN AVIATION REPORTS 600

———— "Le Droit romain et la maxime 'Cujus est solum' dans le droit international aérien" 6 REVUE FRANÇAISE DE DROIT AÉRIEN 339 (1952)

38. "Canada and the Warsaw Convention" 13 REVUE DU BARREAU DE QUÉBEC 68 (1953)

39. "The Institute of International Air Law" 2 JOURNAL OF THE SOCIETY OF PUBLIC TEACHERS OF LAW 122 (1953)

———— "Il Diritto del Volo e dello Spazio" 7 RIVISTA AERONAUTICA 745 (1954)

40. "State Sovereignty in Space: Developments 1910–1914" IN *Beitrage zum internationalen Luftrecht: Festschrift für Alex Meyer.* Droste-Verlag, Düsseldorf, Germany, pp. 41–49 (1954)

41. "Comments" (On Limitation of Sovereignty) International Law Association, *Report of the Forty-Seventh Conference, Dubrovnik* 1956, 207–212 (1956)

42. "Legal Problems of Upper Space" 50 PROCEEDINGS OF THE AMERICAN SOCIETY OF INTERNATIONAL LAW 85 (1956)

———— "Legal Problems of Upper Space" 23 JOURNAL OF AIR LAW AND COMMERCE 308 (1956)

———— "Legal Problems of Upper Space" 15 JOURNAL OF THE BRITISH INTERPLANETARY SOCIETY 305 (1956)

———— "Rechtliche Probleme des Weltraums" 5 ZEITSCHRIFT FÜR LUFTRECHT 171 (1956)

———— "Problemas Juridicos del Espacio Superior" 5 REVISTA DEL INSTITUTO DE DERECHO AERONAUTICO 379 (1956)

———— "Legal Problems of Upper Space" Hearings on H.R. 11881 Before the U.S. House Select Committee on Astronautics and Space Exploration, *Astronautics and Space Exploration*, 85th Cong., 2d Sess. 1332–1336 (1958)

———— "Legal Problems of Upper Space" Staff of U.S. Senate Special Committee on Space and Astronautics, 85th Cong., 2d Sess., *Space Law: A Symposium* 123 (Comm. Print 1959)

———— "Legal Problems of Upper Space" U.S. Senate Committee on Aeronautical and Space Sciences, *Legal Problems of Space Exploration: A Symposium* Senate Doc. No. 26, 87th Cong., 1st Sess. 66 (1961)

43. "Who Owns the Upper Air?" Letter to the Editor, *The Times* (London), September 2, 1957, p. 9, col. 5

———— "Who Owns the Upper Air?" *The Times Weekly Review* (London), October 12, 1957

44. "The Russian Satellite—Legal and Political Problems" 24 JOURNAL OF AIR LAW AND COMMERCE 379 (1957)
———— "The Russian Satellite—Legal and Political Problems" Staff of U.S. Senate Special Committee on Space and Astronautics, 85th Cong., 2nd Sess., *Space Law: A Symposium* 238 (Comm. Print 1959)
45. "Flight-space and the Satellites" 17 FEDERAL BAR JOURNAL 460 (1957)
———— "Flight-space and the Satellites" 32 FLORIDA BAR JOURNAL 60 (March 1958)
———— "Flight-space and the Satellites" 7 INTERNATIONAL AND COMPARATIVE LAW QUARTERLY 82 (1958)
———— "Flight-space and the Satellites" Hearings on H.R. 11881 Before the U.S. House Select Committee on Astronautics and Space Exploration, *Astronautics and Space Exploration*, 85th Cong., 2d Sess. 1342–1347 (1958)
———— "Espace navigable et Satellites" 12 REVUE FRANÇAISE DE DROIT AÉRIEN 18 (1958)
———— "Espace navigable et Satellites" LA VIE JUDIÇIAIRE, No. 637, 1 (1958)
———— "Flugraum und Satelliten" 7 ZEITSCHRIFT FÜR LUFTRECHT 175 (1958)
———— Revised "Flight-space and the Satellites" 3 ASTRONAUTICS 32 (March 1958)
46. "Missiles and Satellites: The Law and Our National Policy" 44 AMERICAN BAR ASSOCIATION JOURNAL 317 (1958)
———— "Missiles and Satellites: The Law and Our National Policy" Hearings on H.R. 11881 Before the U.S. House Select Committee on Astronautics and Space Exploration, *Astronautics and Space Exploration*, 85th Cong., 2d Sess. 1337–1341 (1958)
———— "Raketen und Satelliten: Das Recht und unsere nationale Politik" 7 ZEITSCHRIFT FÜR LUFTRECHT 394 (1958)
47. (Statement and Answers) Hearings on H.R. 11881 Before the U.S. House Select Committee on Astronautics and Space Exploration, *Astronautics and Space Exploration*, 85th Cong., 2d Sess. 1262–1269, 1310–1311, 1313–1314 (1958)
48. "Memorandum on the National Aeronautics and Space Act of 1958" 25 JOURNAL OF AIR LAW AND COMMERCE 247 (1958)
49. "The Problem of a Definition of 'Air Space' " *Proceedings of the First Colloquium on the Law of Outer Space* 38–44 (1959)
———— "The Problem of a Definition of 'Airspace' " Staff of U.S. Senate Special Committee on Space and Astronautics, 85th Cong., 2d Sess., *Space Law: A Symposium* 403 (Comm. Print 1959)
50. "Sovereignty in Space" 64 FLYING 30 (January 1959)
51. "Space Above the Seas" JAG JOURNAL 8 (February 1959)
52. "Flight-Space Law" IN *Handbuch der Astronautik*. Akademische Verlagsgesellschaft Athenaion, Konstanz, Germany, pp. 55–64 (1960)
53. "Air Sovereignty and the Legal Status of Outer Space" International Law Association, *Report of the Forty-Ninth Conference, Hamburg 1960*, 288–289 (1960)
54. "International Control of Outer Space—Some Preliminary Problems" *Proceedings of the Third Colloquium on the Law of Outer Space* 21–25 (1960)
———— "International Control of Outer Space—Some Preliminary Problems" CONGRESSIONAL RECORD A6161 (daily ed. August 22, 1960)

———— "Die internationale Kontrolle des Weltraums—Einige Vorfragen" 9 ZEITSCHRIFT FÜR LUFTRECHT UND WELTRAUMRECHTSFRAGEN 288 (1960)

———— "Additional Remarks" 10 ZEITSCHRIFT FÜR LUFTRECHT UND WELTRAUMRECHTSFRAGEN 102 (1960)

———— "Ergänzende Bemerkungen" 10 ZEITSCHRIFT FÜR LUFTRECHT UND WELTRAUMRECHTSFRAGEN 103 (1960)

55. "Memorandum of Suggestions for an International Convention on Third Party Damage Caused by Space Vehicles" *Proceedings of the Third Colloquium on the Law of Outer Space* 141–144 (1960)

———— "Memorandum of Suggestions for an International Convention on Third Party Damage Caused by Space Vehicles" U.S. Senate Committee on Aeronautical and Space Sciences, *Legal Problems of Space Exploration: A Symposium*, Senate Doc. No. 26, 87th Cong., 1st Sess. 680 (1961)

56. "Fundamental Questions of Outer Space Law" U.S. Senate Committee on Aeronautical and Space Sciences, *Legal Problems of Space Exploration: A Symposium*, Senate Doc. No. 26, 87th Cong., 1st Sess. 764 (1961)

———— "Questions fondamentales du Droit interspacial" 15 REVUE FRANÇAISE DE DROIT AÉRIEN 219 (1961)

———— "Questiones Fundamentales De La Ley Sobre El Espacio Exterior" 7 CIENCIA AERONAUTICA Y ASTRONAUTICA 18 (Febrero 1961)

57. "New Developments in International Law: Proposal for a Convention on Outer Space" 15 *Columbia Law School News* 1 (December 7, 1960)

58. "The Rule of Law in Outer Space" 47 AMERICAN BAR ASSOCIATION JOURNAL 23 (1961)

———— "The Rule of Law in Outer Space" 107 CONGRESSIONAL RECORD A1936 (daily ed. March 21, 1961)

59. "Questions of Space Law" 3 SPACEFLIGHT 95 (1961)

60. "Outer Space and the Law: An Engineering Problem" ASTRONAUTICS 64 (October 1961)

61. "Self-Defense in Outer Space and the United Nations" 5 AIR FORCE AND SPACE DIGEST 51 (February 1962)

———— "Self-Defense in Outer Space and the United Nations" 108 CONGRESSIONAL RECORD A2723 (daily ed. April 9, 1962)

———— "Self-Defense in Outer Space and the United Nations" 11 ZEITSCHRIFT FÜR LUFTRECHT UND WELTRAUMRECHTSFRAGEN 186 (1962)

———— "Selbstverteidigung im Weltraum und die Vereinten Nationen" 11 ZEITSCHRIFT FÜR LUFTRECHT UND WELTRAUMRECHTSFRAGEN 187 (1962)

62. "Status of Orbit Law Still Up in the Air" *Los Angeles Times*, June 17, 1962, Sec. K, p. 10

63. "Current Developments in Space Law" 41 NORTH CAROLINA LAW REVIEW 339 (1963)

———— "Current Developments in Space Law" 5 SPACEFLIGHT 134 (1963)

———— "Current Developments in Space Law" 109 CONGRESSIONAL RECORD A1349 (daily ed. March 12, 1963)

———— "Gegenwärtige Entwicklungen im Weltraumrecht" 12 ZEITSCHRIFT FÜR LUFTRECHT UND WELTRAUMRECHTSFRAGEN 199 (1963)

———— "L'évolution actuelle du droit de l'espace" 17 REVUE FRANÇAISE DE DROIT AÉRIEN 275 (1963)

64. "Aerospace Law—Subject Matter and Terminology" 29 JOURNAL OF AIR LAW AND COMMERCE 89 (1963)

———— "Ley Del Espacio Aereo—Tema Expuesto y Terminologia" 10 CIENCIA AERONAUTICA Y ASTRONAUTICA 31 (Septiembre–Octubre 1963)

——— "Luft-Weltraumrecht—Gegenstand und Begriffsbestimmung" 13 ZEITSCHFRIT FÜR LUFTRECHT UND WELTRAUMRECHTSFRAGEN 1 (1964)

65. "The Air Carrier and Passenger: The Legal Position" TRANSPORT ANNUAL [Bombay] 53 (March 1963)

66. "Aerospace Law—Recent Developments" 10 AIRPOWER HISTORIAN 118 (October 1963)

67. "The Upper Airspace Boundary Question" *Proceedings of the Sixth Colloquium on the Law of Outer Space* (1963)

68. "Passage of Spacecraft Through the Airspace" *Proceedings of the Sixth Colloquium on the Law of Outer Space* (1963)
——— "El Pasaje de los Vehículos Espaciales a Través del Espacio Aéreo" 10 CIENCIA AERONAUTICA Y ASTRONAUTICA 14 (Noviembre–Deciembre 1963) and 10 CIENCIA AERONAUTICA Y ASTRONAUTICA 10 (Enero-Febrero 1964)

69. "Aerospace Law Over the High Seas" *Proceedings of the Fifth International Symposium on Space Technology and Science* [Tokyo 1963] 1147 (1964)

70. "Pollution and Contamination in Space" IN Cohen (ed.), *Law and Politics in Space*. McGill University Press, Montreal, Quebec, 51 (1964)

71. "Aerospace Law: Progress in the U.N." ASTRONAUTICS AND AERONAUTICS 42 (March 1964)
——— "Aerospace Law: Progress in the U.N." 110 CONGRESSIONAL RECORD A3129 (daily ed. June 10, 1964)
——— "Luft-Weltraumrecht: Fortschritt in der Vereinten Nationen" 13 ZEITSCHRIFT FÜR LUFTRECHT UND WELTRAUMRECHTSFRAGEN 153 (1964)
——— "Progreso De Las Naciones Unidas" 11 CIENCIA AERONAUTICA Y ASTRONAUTICA 18 (Julio–Agosto 1964) and 11 CIENCIA AERONAUTICA Y ASTRONAUTICA 10 (Septiembre–Octubre 1964)

72. "Must We Give Up Self-Defense Rights To Attain General Disarmament" AIR FORCE MAGAZINE 71 (July 1964)

73. "The Boundary Between Territorial Airspace and International Outer Space" 110 CONGRESSIONAL RECORD 23158 (daily ed. September 29, 1964)
——— "The Boundary Between Territorial Airspace and International Outer Space" 110 CONGRESSIONAL RECORD A5039 (daily ed. October 1, 1964)

74. "Legal Problems of Spacecraft in Airspace" IN *Festschrift Für Otto Riese* Verlag C. F. Müller, Karlsruhe, Germany, 465–473 (1964)

75. "Report of Chairman of Working Group I dealing with 'Legal Status of Outer Space'" *Proceedings of the Seventh Colloquium on the Law of Outer Space* 344–346 (1964)

76. "The Chicago Convention—After Twenty Years" 19 UNIVERSITY OF MIAMI LAW REVIEW 333 (1965)
——— "The Chicago Convention—After Twenty Years" 14 ZEITSCHRIFT FÜR LUFTRECHT UND WELTRAUMRECHTSFRAGEN 272 (1965)
——— "Zwanzig Jahre Abkommen von Chikago" 14 ZEITSCHRIFT FÜR LUFTRECHT UND WELTRAUMRECHTSFRAGEN 273 (1965)

77. "Contiguous Zones in Aerospace—Preventive and Protective Jurisdiction" 7 JAG LAW REVIEW 15 (September–October 1965)
——— "Zonen im Luft-Weltraum—Vorbeugungs und Schutzzwecken dienende Hoheitsbefugnisse" 15 ZEITSCHRIFT FÜR LUFTRECHT UND WELTRAUMRECHTSFRAGEN 101 (1966)

78. "Liability for Space Damage—The United Nations—The Rome Convention" *Proceedings of the Eighth Colloquium on the Law of Outer Space* (1965)

79. "The Manned Orbiting Laboratory: A Major Legal and Political Decision" 51 AMERICAN BAR ASSOCIATION JOURNAL 1137 (1965)
——— "Le Laboratoire habité sur orbite: Décision Juridique et Politique de première importance" 20 REVUE FRANÇAISE DE DROIT AÉRIEN 269 (1966)
——— "Bemannte Weltraumlaboratorien: Eine Entscheidung von grosser rechtlicher und politischer Bedeutung" 15 ZEITSCHRIFT FÜR LUFTRECHT UND WELTRAUMRECHTSFRAGEN 245 (1966)

80. "Who Will Own the Moon? The Need for an Answer" UNIVERSITY, A PRINCETON QUARTERLY 3 (Winter 1965–1966)
——— "Who Will Own the Moon? The Need for an Answer" 66 *Princeton Alumni Weekly* 15 (December 7, 1965)
——— "Who Will Own the Moon? The Need for an Answer" with footnotes and addendum 32 JOURNAL OF AIR LAW AND COMMERCE 155 (1966)
——— "Who Will Own the Moon? The Need for an Answer" 8 SPACEFLIGHT 230 (1966)
——— "A qui appartiendra la Lune" 20 REVUE FRANÇAISE DE DROIT AÉRIEN 169 (1966)

81. "Report on Nationality and Registration of Aircraft with Special Reference to Article 77 of the 1944 Chicago Convention on International Civil Aviation" International Law Association, Air Law Committee, *Helsinki Conference*, 7–23 (1966)

82. "Backgrounds of International Public Air Law" 1 YEARBOOK OF AIR AND SPACE LAW 3 (1967)

83. "Some Crucial Questions About the Space Treaty" 50 AIR FORCE AND SPACE DIGEST 104 (March 1967)

Table of Cases

Name Index

Abbot, Charles 211
Accursius, Franciscus 74–76, 82
Ader, Clement 5
Allen, Raymond S. S. 276
Anzilotti, Dionisio 62n
Arnold, H. H. 19, 21
Augustus, Antonius 68
Augustus, Severus 68

Bacon, H. S. 148
Baker, Ray Stannard 138, 142
Balch, Thomas Willing 190
Balfour, Arthur James 139
Berezowski, Cezary 433
Bismarck, Otto 216
Blackburn, Colin 94
Blackstone, William 84, 92, 96
Blanchard, Jean-Pierre 4, 216
Blunt, V. E. R. 20
Bluntschli, Johann Kaspar 216–17
Bonfante, Pietro 60–61, 90
Bouvé, Clement L. 159, 161–64, 169
Bowen, Charles Christopher 93
Branly, Edouard 10
Breitfuss, 185
Buckland, William Warwick 59
Burden, William A. M. 373, 376
Buzzati, 147, 149
Bynkershoek, Cornelius van 208

Cambon, Jules 130
Campbell, John 93
Catellani, Enrico 119n
Cayley, George 5
Celsus, 70
Cicero, Marcus Tullius 71
Cipollo, Bartolomeo 78n
Clemenceau, Georges 107, 139, 220
Cocceius, Henricus de 79n–80n
Coke, Thomas 83–84, 92, 96, 100

Coltman, 93
Cot, M. Pierre 397

Danck, Jean-Etienne 81
Daus, Edgar 219
da Vinci, Leonardo 5
de Lana, Francesco 4–5
de la Pradelle, Paul de Geouffre 147, 149
de Montmorency, James E. G. 60
de Visscher, Fernand 11
Denby, 181, 188
Denman, George 93
Dernberg, Heinrich 90
Diocletian, Gaius Aurelius Valerius 69
Douglas, William O. 99

Edward III (King of England) 209
Eisenhower, Dwight D. 42, 287–88, 343–44, 424
Ellenborough, Edward Law 93–94
Fauchille, Paul 9–11, 109, 114, 116, 120, 217–18, 221, 224, 226, 230, 270, 284, 296
Fawcett, J. E. S. 46
Ferriers, Claude de 86
Fiore, Pasquale 57n
Frazier, Peter 403
Fry, Edward 93

Gamble, Douglas A. 116–17
Garner, James W. 12
Gesterding, 91
Giffard, Henri 216
Goedhuis, Daniel 287, 349
Goldberg, Arthur J. 353
Goodhart, Arthur L. 38, 419–20
Gore, Albert A. 426
Gorrell, E. S. 140
Goudy, Henry 59, 62–63
Green, Leslie C. 419n

469

Subject Index

473